COUNTRY LIVING
MAGAZINE

GUIDE TO RURAL SCOTLAND

By James Gracie

© Travel Publishing Ltd.

Published by:
Travel Publishing Ltd
7a Apollo House, Calleva Park
Aldermaston, Berks, RG7 8TN
ISBN 1-904-43433-9
© Travel Publishing Ltd

Country Living is a registered trademark of The National
Magazine Company Limited.

First Published: *2003*   *Second Edition:*   *2005*

COUNTRY LIVING GUIDES:

East Anglia   Scotland
Heart of England   The South of England
Ireland   The South East of England
The North East of England   The West Country
The North West of England   Wales

PLEASE NOTE:

All advertisements in this publication have been accepted in good faith by Travel
Publishing and they have not necessarily been endorsed by *Country Living*
Magazine.

All information is included by the publishers in good faith and is believed to be
correct at the time of going to press. No responsibility can be accepted for errors.

Editor: James Gracie

Printing by: Scotprint, Haddington

Location Maps:© Maps in Minutes ™ (2005)   © Crown Copyright, Ordnance Survey 2005

Walks: Walks have been reproduced with kind permission of the internet
               walking site www.walkingworld.com

Walk Maps: Reproduced from Ordnance Survey mapping on behalf of the
               Controller of Her Majesty's Stationery Office, © Crown Copyright.
               Licence Number MC 100035812

Cover Design: Lines & Words, Aldermaston

Cover Photo: Eilean Donan castle fron across the loch, West Highlands
               © www.britainonview.com

Text Photos: Text photos have been kindly supplied by the Pictures of Britain photo
               library © www.picturesofbritain.co.uk

Contents

LOCATOR MAP

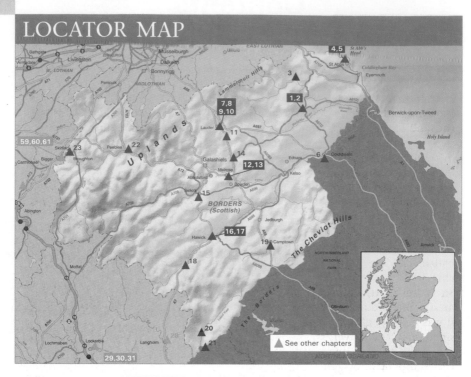

ADVERTISERS AND PLACES OF INTEREST

THE BORDERS 1

Of all the regions in Scotland, the Borders has the bloodiest history. It was here, in the 15th and 16th centuries, that the constant bickering between Scotland and England boiled over into bloodshed and outright war. This was the land of the reivers, or "moss troopers" - men from both countries who regularly crossed the border and raped, pillaged, burnt and rustled their way into the history books. People nowadays tend to romanticise them, but in fact most were merciless thugs, and no one was safe from their activities. They even gave the word "blackmail" to the English language. An old legend states that when a male born in the Borders was baptised, his right hand was excluded from the ceremony so that he could use it to kill and maim.

But it was also the land of romance, of Border ballads and tales of high chivalry. The literature of Sir Walter Scott, a Borders man, is steeped in them. It was he who, almost single-handedly, invented Scotland's modern image, which depends not on the softer scenery of the Borders, but on lofty mountains, clan chiefs, skirling bagpipes and kilts. This has not been lost on the hardy Borderers, who know there is more to Scotland than that. In fact, there are, strictly speaking, no clans in the Scottish Borders. Instead there are families, such as the Armstrongs, the Kerrs, the Maxwells and the Homes.

The Borders are sometimes dismissed by people who consider them to be 'not the real

Gate into England, Windy Gyle

Scotland'. And yet they have more historical associations than anywhere else in Scotland, and it was here, and not the Highlands, that the Scottish nation as we know it today was forged. The area stretches from the North Sea in the east to the borders of Dumfriesshire in the west, and contains four former counties – Peeblesshire, Selkirkshire, Roxburghshire and Berwickshire. The scenery is gentler than the Highlands, and the hills are rounded and green, with fertile valleys, quiet villages and cosy market towns to explore. That flat area of Berwickshire known as the Merse, roughly between the Lammermuir Hills and the English border, is one of the most intensely farmed areas in Britain.

There are castles and old houses aplenty, from Floors Castle just outside Kelso, home of the Duke of Roxburgh, to 10th century Traquair House in Peeblesshire, said to be the oldest continually inhabited house in Scotland. Mellerstain too, is worth visiting, as is Paxton, Manderston, Thirlestane and Abbotsford.

But perhaps the area's most beautiful and haunting buildings are its ruined abbeys. Again and again English soldiers attacked them, and again and again, as the Scots crossed the border bent on revenge, the monks quietly got on with rebuilding and repairing them. Now the ruins at Melrose, Kelso, Dryburgh and Jedburgh rest easy under the care of Historic Scotland, and they can be easily visited and appreciated.

The area's great icon is the River Tweed which, for part of its length, forms the boundary between Scotland and England. Just east of Kelso, the border turns south, and the river is wholly Scottish. Its fame rests on salmon, though not as many are caught nowadays as there used to be. But it is still a river that in some ways defines the region, and most of its larger towns and villages, from Peebles to Coldstream, are to be found on its banks.

The Borders is also an area of woodland and forests, with plenty of woodland walks. The newly created Tweed Valley Forest Park, between Peebles and Selkirk, is one of the best. At Glentress Forest, a few miles east of Peebles, you can hire mountain bikes at the Hub car park. This is one of the most visited woodland areas in Scotland, and attracts over 250,000 visitors a year. But for all their leisure facilities, these are 'working forests', managed by the Forestry Commission, and form an integral part of the area's economy.

DUNS

Berwickshire is an unusual county, in that the town which gave it its name has been part of England since 1482. Therefore Greenlaw, and then in 1853 Duns, was chosen as the county town. It is a quiet, restful place with a wide and gracious market square. Up until the 18th century, it was known as "Dunse". Its motto, *Duns Dings A*, means "Duns overcomes everything".

On its outskirts is the 713 feet high **Duns Law**, which from the top gives a magnificent view of the surrounding countryside. The Cheviot Hills to the south and the Lammermuir Hills to the north can be seen on a clear day, as can the North Sea, 12 miles away. In 1639 a Covenanting army of 12,000 men, which opposed the imposition of bishops on the Scottish church by Charles I, set up camp here under General Leslie, and a **Covenanter's Stone** commemorates this event. There are also the remains of an Iron Age fort, plus some defensive works built by the Covenanting army.

General Leslie was quartered in **Duns Castle**, built round the core of a 14th century pele tower owned by the Earl of Moray, who had been given the surrounding lands by Robert the Bruce. In 1696 it was bought by the Hay family, who enlarged it between 1818 and 1822, creating the Gothic Revival building we see today. The family has lived here ever since. Though not open to the public, it is a venue for weddings and corporate hospitality.

On the western edge of Duns Law is a cairn, which marks the original site of the town, now called The Bruntons, or "burnt towns". It was here that **John Duns Scotus**, known as "Doctor Subtilis", or the "subtle doctor", was supposed to have been born in about

1266 (though some people put his place of birth as Duns in Ireland). He was a Franciscan monk who became one of the greatest theologians and philosophers of his time. His followers were known as Scotists, and his influence is still felt within the Catholic Church to this day. However, his opponents had another, less flattering, name for them - "Dunses" - from which we get the word "dunce". He eventually died at Cologne on November 8th 1308, and on his tomb are the words "Scotland bore me, England adopted me, Cologne holds". In 1991 the Pope made him "Blessed", the first step on the ladder to sainthood (see also North Uist).

In Duns Public Park there is a bronze statue of him and in the grounds of Duns Castle the modern Franciscan Order erected a cairn to his memory in 1966.

Also in the grounds of Duns Castle is the quaintly named **Hen Poo**, a lake which is the centrepiece of the **Duns Castle Nature Reserve**, owned and run by the Scottish Wildlife Trust. There is a bird hide on the northern shore, and from here you can see mallard ducks, tufted ducks, swans, and coots. Close by, the **Mill Dam** is also home to many bird species.

Within the town there is a memorial to a famous man who lived in more recent times. Jim Clark, the racing driver, was born in Fife in 1936, but from the age of six lived on Eddington Mains, a farm near Duns. He was killed in Germany in 1968 and the **Jim Clark Memorial Trophy Room** in Newtown Street is dedicated to his memory. He won 25 of his 72 Grand Prix, and his win at the 1965 Indianapolis Grand Prix astonished the Americans, who considered that no one but an American could cross the finishing line first. He was world champion in 1963 and

KINGFISHER CRAFTS

18 Market Square, Duns, Berwickshire TD11 3BY
Tel: 01361 884800
e-mail: michael.dixon44@ntlworld.com

There's no finer shop in the Scottish Borders for all your gift and souvenir needs than **Kingfisher Crafts** in the picturesque old town of Duns. It is a family-run business stocking a superb range of oil paintings, glass paintings, jewellery, cards, silk paintings, watercolours, pencil sketches, coffee tables, needlework, frames, pottery and a whole lot more besides.

It is owned and managed by Gail and Michael Dixon, along with their daughter Gemma and son Paul. Each member of the family has his or her own speciality, which means that there is a wealth of

knowledge and experience that the customer can draw on when choosing a purchase. Mike specialises in oil landscapes, woodwork, picture framing and photography. Gail's speciality is glass painting, black and white drawings, original pictures and cards. Paul specialises in woodwork - cabinets, jewellery boxes, coffee tables, while Gemma does black and white sketches, jewellery, cards and silk paintings. About forty per cent of the items sold in the shop is made by the family, the rest being sourced throughout Scotland. Kingfisher Crafts also has a small café where you can enjoy a cup of coffee with organic baking.

1965, and motor racing enthusiasts from all over the world now make the pilgrimage to view the trophies (including the two world championship trophies he won) and mementoes on display. He was killed at Hockenheim in Germany in 1968 aged 32, when a rear tyre burst during a Formula 2 race, and is buried in Chirnside Parish Church cemetery, about five miles east of Duns (see also Chirnside).

On the west side of Market Square is the 19th century **Tolbooth House**, situated on the site of the town house of Sir James Cockburn, who owned most of the land surrounding Duns in the 17th century. The local council have recently laid out a town trail, taking you to places of interest. A leaflet is available, linked to plaques at many places within the town.

Manderston House lies a mile-and-a-half east of the town in 56 acres of formal gardens and is open to the public. It was built between 1903 and 1905, and was the last great stately home built in Britain. Designed by architect John Kinross, it incorporates a silver staircase that is said to be the only one in the world, and was built for Sir James Miller and his wife, the Hon. Eveline Curzon, A member of one of the oldest families in the country. Nowadays Manderston is the home of the Palmer family, of the famous Huntly and Palmer biscuit empire, which explains why it houses a large collection of biscuit tins.

East of Duns, at Broomhouse, is the grave of the **Seigneur de la Beaute**, a handsome Frenchman who was warden of the Merse and Teviotdale, murdered in the 16th century by the powerful David Home of Wedderburn, who considered that James V should have made him warden. The seigneur's head was hacked from his body and the rest of him was buried where he fell. The head was subsequently paraded round Duns by David Home.

AROUND DUNS

COCKBURNSPATH

13 miles N of Duns just off the A1

The **Parish Church of St Helens** is partly 15th century, and close by is ruined **Cockburnspath Tower**, dating from the 15th and 16th centuries. In its time it has been owned by the Dunbars, the Homes, the Sinclairs and the Douglases. The **Mercat Cross**, at the heart of the village, was erected in 1503 to celebrate the marriage of James V1 to the sister of Henry VIII of England. The village sits close to **Pease Dean**, a Scottish Wildlife Trust Reserve, where you can see butterflies, lichens and rare mosses. **Pease Bridge** was built in in 1783 and at the time was the highest stone bridge in Europe.

ABBEY ST BATHANS

7 miles N of Duns on a minor road off the B6355

The pretty village of Abbey St Bathans lies in the steep-sided valley of the Whiteadder Water, deep within the Lammermuir Hills, five miles north of Duns. It is truly a hidden gem, and sits on the **Southern Upland Way**, the coast-to-coast footpath that transverses Southern Scotland from Portpatrick in the west to Cockburnspath in the east. It's name is misleading, as there was never an abbey here. However, in 1170, Ada, Countess of Dunbar, founded the priory of St Mary in the village, and parts of the priory church have been incorporated into the present **Parish Church**. The village was chosen because, in about AD500, St Bathan, a follower of St Columba, established a Celtic monastery here.

The tombstone of a former prioress, which touchingly shows her pet dog, is preserved within the present church. To the south, at **Cockburn Law**, are the

ABBEY ARTIFACTS GALLERY & RIVERSIDE RESTAURANT

Abbey Saint Bathans, Near Duns, Berwickshire TD11 3TX
Tel: 01361 840312
e-mail: karen@abbeyartifacts.co.uk website: www.abbeyartifacts.co.uk

The **Riverside Restaurant** was established in 1991 by Richard Parkinson. Meals are served all day, with only private functions in the evening. The food is cooked to order using only the finest and freshest of local produce to give you a superb eating experience. This is slow food, not fast food, and yet the prices represent remarkable value for money. The place is spacious and light, with high walls and crisp linen on the tables. You can also dine in a spectacular garden, full of daturas (brugmansia), lilies, a banana plant, dahlias and gunnera which surround the tables in summer. In winter there is a wood burning stove to keep you cosy and warm as you eat with a small tropical jungle in the corner. The River Whiteadder runs past the Riverside, and fishing permits are available from the restaurant.

The high walls are the perfect showcase for the **Abbey Artifacts Gallery**, founded by Richard's wife Karen in 1997. Here she displays original paintings, prints and drawings by local and invited artists. The subject matter consists of landscapes, wildlife, botanical art, dogs and farm animals. The media

used ranges from oils, watercolour, acrylic to charcoal. Karen also sells creative woodturning, ceramics, printed textiles and stick dressing. A full framing service is available. Several times a year there are private exhibitions in the evening, with great food and a guest artist. Private viewings by appointment.

Abbey Artifacts Gallery and the Riverside Restaurant are open Tuesday to Friday from 11am to 4pm, Saturday and Sunday 11am to 5pm. Closed on Mondays. From November to April times may vary so please phone. Booking essential at weekends.

DUNLAVEROCK GUEST HOUSE

Coldingham Bay, Berwickshire TD14 5PH
Tel: 01890 771450 Fax: 01890 771103
e-mail: info@dunlaverock.com website: www.dunlaverock.com

With seven extremely spacious rooms, the **Dunlaverock Guest House** is the perfect place to stay when you are exploring Berwickshire and the Scottish Borders. A former Edwardian villa, it sits overlooking the blue waters of Coldingham Bay, and has spectacular views of the rugged coastline. Six of the rooms are en suite, while the seventh has private facilities. Some have wonderful sea views and all are traditionally decorated and furnished to an extremely high standard.

The guest house offers bed and breakfast or dinner, bed and breakfast. The food is beautifully cooked and presented, and only the finest and freshest of local produce is used wherever possible. A

sumptuous Scottish breakfast is offered with cereals, yogurts, grapefruit, fruit juices and a hearty cooked breakfast of bacon, sausage, eggs, mushrooms, black pudding and so on. Lighter options are also available, as well as kippers from Eyemouth, a few miles away. Local produce is also used in the preparation of the Dunlaverock dinners, which consist of three courses, a cheese board and coffee. A residents' licence means that diners can enjoy wine as they eat.

There are scenic walks along the cliff tops near the guest house, which has a private path through its gardens to the seashore.

ruins of the Iron Age **Edins Hall Broch**, one of the few brochs (a round, fortified stone tower) to be found in Southern Scotland. It is named after Etin, a legendary giant with three heads who is said to have terrorised the area in olden times.

COLDINGHAM

13 miles NE of Duns on the A1107

The village of Coldingham, a mile from the coast, is visited mainly for the remains of **Coldingham Priory**. It was founded in 1098 by King Edgar, son of Malcolm Canmore, and he gifted it to the monks of Durham. Originally it had

St Abb's

been the site of a monastery founded by St Ebba, sister of King Oswy of Northumbria, in the seventh century, and suffered badly during the Scottish Wars of Independence. it was finally blown up by Cromwell in 1648, with repairs being carried out in about 1670, though only the tower and a couple of walls were left standing. Between 1854 and 1855 the remains were restored, and

today they are incorporated into the village's parish church.

Four miles north west of the village, on the coast, are the ruins of **Fast Castle**, a former Hume stronghold. In 1410 it was held by the English, but was recovered again in 1548. The ruins are perched 70 feet above the sea on a cliff top and can be reached via a minor road, though the last few hundred yards must

ST ABBS HEAD NATIONAL NATURE RESERVE

Ranger's Cottage, Northfield, St Abbs, Eyemouth, Borders TD14 5QF
Tel: 018907 71443   Fax: 018907 71606.
website: www.nts.org.uk

Formed by an extinct volcano, The Head is the best known landmark along the magnificent Berwickshire coast. Home to thousands of nesting seabirds in summer, the Head also has a wealth of other wildlife and fine views along the coast. In recognition of its importance to both wildlife and people, the Head was declared a National Nature Reserve in 1983. The offshore waters lie within a Special Area of Conservation and form part of Scotland's only Voluntary Marine Nature Reserve. New remote camera links to the Nature Reserve Centre allows visitors to observe seabirds during nesting season (recorded footage out of season). Exhibition, toilets.

be done on foot. Great care must be taken when visiting, however.

St. Abb's
12 miles NE of Duns, on the B6438

The picturesque fishing village of St Abb's is named after St Ebba (see Coldingham), and has a small, picturesque harbour. The whole coastline here is rugged and spectacular, one of the most magnificent parts being **St Abb's Head** (National Trust for Scotland - see panel on page 9) to the north of the village. The cliffs are over 300 feet high, and are riddled with caves once haunted by smugglers. A monastery for monks and nuns was established on the cliff tops in the 7th century, and St Ebba eventually became a nun here. An old legend recounts that the nuns, instead of living a life of austerity and prayer, eventually spent all their time eating, drinking and gossiping. This was because St Ebba had become too old and infirm to have control over them. The whole area is now managed by the National Trust for Scotland and is a National Nature Reserve. Offshore there is one of the best diving sites in the country.

Chirnside
5 miles E of Duns on the B6355

Chirnside sits on the south side of a low hill with wonderful views over the surrounding countryside, and close to where the Blackadder Water and the Whiteadder Water meet. During World War I the peace of the village was shattered when a Zeppelin bombed it by accident. The **Parish Church** was founded by King Edgar of Scotland in the 12th century, and is partly Norman, with an impressive Norman doorway at its west end. The substantial church tower was built in memory of Lady Tweedsmuir. Within the cemetery is the

grave of Jim Clark the racing driver (see also Duns). The **Jim Clark Memorial Clock**, with a silhouette of a Lotus racing car on it, stands in the middle of the village.

David Hulme, the 18th century philosopher, though born in Edinburgh, was educated at Chirnside School until he was 12 years old.

Edrom
3 miles E of Duns on a minor road off the A6105

The small village of Edrom has a fine **Parish Church** originally dedicated to St Mary. It was built in 1732 on the site of a much earlier Norman church, and the present south aisle rests on foundations from this period. Attached to it is the Blackadder Aisle, built for Archbishop Blackadder of Glasgow in 1499. It contains a tomb and effigy dating from 1553. A burial vault in the graveyard incorporates a Norman arch which was originally attached to the original Norman church. The building was gifted to the monks of Coldingham in 1130, and was enlarged in 1499.

Hutton
10 miles E of Duns on a minor road off the B6460

Close to the village stands **Hutton Castle**, one time home of Sir William Burrell, shipping magnate and art collector, who donated the Burrell Collection to the city of Glasgow in 1944 (see also Largs). It sits overlooking the River Whiteadder. **Hutton Parish Church** dates from 1835 and has an old bell of 1661.

Ayton
10 miles E of Duns on the B6355

Ayton, a mile or so from the A1, is a pleasant village that sits on the River Eye. Close by is **Ayton Castle**, which was bought in 1834 by William Mitchell

Innes, the governor of the Bank of Scotland. He commissioned James Gillespie Graham, a leading Gothic Revival architect, to design the present day Ayton Castle, which was built between 1846 and 1841. It is reckoned to be one of the best examples in the country of that style of architecture called "Scottish Baronial", and is surrounded by a 6,000-acre estate. It is open from May - September by appointment, and houses fine paintings, furniture and porcelain.

The Parish Church was built in 1864, and beside it are the ruins of its medieval predecessor.

Eyemouth Harbour

EYEMOUTH

12 miles E of Duns on the A1107

Eyemouth is a picturesque little fishing town standing, as the name suggests, at the mouth of the River Eye, five miles north of the Scotland/England border. The monks of Coldingham Priory founded it as a small fishing port sometime in the 13th century.

At one time it was a smuggling centre, and some of the harbour-side houses still have old cellars and tunnels where contraband was stored. The centre of the trade was at **Gunsgreen House**, to the south of the harbour. It dates from the 1755, and was designed by James and John Adam. Though not a museum, the **World of Boats** is a collection of over 400 historic boats from all over the world, and the owner can show you around by appointment. Every year in July the **Herring Queen Festival** takes place, when the gaily be-decked fishing fleet escorts the "Herring Queen" into Eyemouth Harbour.

Eyemouth Museum, housed in the Auld Kirk built in 1812, records the history of the town and its fishing industry. Perhaps the most poignant exhibit is a 15-feet long by four feet wide tapestry sewn in 1981 that commemorates "Black Friday" - October 14, 1881. A great storm wrecked the whole of the town's fishing fleet, and 189 fishermen, 129 from Eyemouth alone, perished in sight of the shore.

FOULDEN

9 miles E of Duns on the A6105

Foulden Parish Church, at the far end of the village, dates from 1786, and was built on the foundations of a medieval church. In 1587 commissioners appointed by Elizabeth I of England and James VI of Scotland met here to discuss the execution of James VI's mother, Mary Queen of Scots. Near it is an old two-storey **Tithe Barn** (Historic Scotland), dating from medieval times, though it was restored in the 18th and 19th centuries. "Tithe" means a tenth, and each farmer in the parish was supposed to donate a tenth of his crops to the church. It was in the barn that it was stored. The barn can only be viewed from the outside.

PAXTON

12 miles E of Duns just off the B6460 and close to the Tweed

Near the village stands **Paxton House**, built in 1758 by Patrick Home, later the 13th Laird of Wedderburn. When he was 19 he went to Leipzig in Germany, and from there went to Berlin, where he was admitted to the court of Frederick the Great of Prussia. Here he fell in love with Sophie de Brandt, illegitimate daughter of Frederick and Lady-in-Waiting to Elizabeth Christina, Frederick's wife.

He returned home, and in anticipation of his marriage to Sophie, built Paxton House. Alas, the marriage never took place, though a pair of kid gloves given to Patrick by Sophie is on display.

The house was designed by John and James Adam, with plasterwork by their brother Robert, and it is reckoned to be the best Palladian mansion in Britain. It houses the finest collection of Chippendale furniture in Scotland, and the art gallery (added to the house in 1811) is the largest private gallery in the country. It now houses paintings from the National Galleries of Scotland.

The house sits in 80 acres of grounds designed by Robert Robinson in the 18th century, and has nature trails, woodland walks and a "Paxton Ted" teddy bear

trail. From the award-winning red squirrel hide you can catch glimpses of what is rapidly becoming one of Scotland's rarest mammals. There is also a tearoom and shop, and in the Victorian boathouse on the banks of the Tweed is a museum dedicated to salmon net fishing. Well behaved dogs are welcome if kept on a lead.

Close by is the **Union Suspension Bridge** across the Tweed, connecting Scotland and England. It was built in 1820 by Sir Samuel Browne, who also invented the wrought-iron chain links used in its construction. It is 480 feet long and was Britain's first major suspension bridge to carry vehicular traffic as well as pedestrians.

LADYKIRK

7 miles SE of Duns on a minor road off the B6470 and close to the Tweed

The **Parish Church of St Mary** dates from 1500, with a tower added in 1743. It is built entirely of stone to prevent it being burnt down by the English. It is supposed to owe its origins to James IV, who had it built in thanksgiving for his rescue from drowning while trying to cross the Tweed. At the same time he changed the name of the village from Upsettington to Ladykirk.

COLDSTREAM

12 miles S of Duns on the A697

The town sits on the north bank of the Tweed at a point where the river forms the border between Scotland and England. **Coldstream Bridge**, joining the two countries, was built in 1766, and replaced a ford that had been a natural crossing point for centuries. On the bridge is a plaque that commemorates the fact that Robert Burns entered England by this route in 1787. In the 19th century, Coldstream rivalled Gretna

Green as a place for runaway marriages. At the Scottish end of the bridge is the **Old Toll House**, where, in a 13-year period during the 19th century, 1,466 marriages were conducted.

General Monk founded the **Coldstream Guards** in 1659. It is the only regiment in Britain to take its name from a town, and within **Henderson Park** is a memorial stone which commemorates the regiment's foundation. The **Coldstream Museum** in Market Square houses extensive displays on its history. It also has a children's section and a courtyard with fountain and picnic area.

A mile north of the town is **The Hirsel**, home of the Earls of Home since 1611. Sir Alec Douglas Home, the British prime minister, lived here. Though the house is not open to the public, the grounds can be explored. There is also a small museum, a crafts centre, a gem display and a tearoom.

And three miles north of the town, just off the A697, are the ruins of **Castlelaw**, built on a mote small hill. The former castle on the site was home to the Drienchester, or Darnchester,

River Tweed, Coldstream

family, but was pulled down in the 16th century to make way for the present building. Which itself was partially dismantled in 1818. From the mote there are some good views of the surrounding countryside.

Eccles

7 miles SW of Duns on the B6461

In the mid-12th century, a Cistercian nunnery was founded here by the Earl of Dunbar. Remnants of it have been built into the wall surrounding the graveyard of the present **Eccles Parish Church**, built in 1774. The nunnery was badly damaged during English raids in the 1540s.

FOGO

3 miles S of Duns off the B6460

Fogo litterally means the "foggage pit", foggage being the grass, or moss, that grows in a field after the hay has been cut. **Fogo Church** dates from the 17th and 18th centuries, though parts of it - especially the lower courses of its masonry - date from the 13th century or earlier. On the north wall are traces of built up arches. The church bell dates from 1644, and within the vestry is one of the oldest gravestones in Berwickshire, dating from the 14th century. The church's communion cups are the oldest still in use, and date from 1662. They were presented to the church by George Trotter of Charterhall. On the outside wall of the church are stairs leading to private lofts, where the gentry once worshipped.

The picturesque lych gate is now a war memorial, and in the kirkyard are the war graves of 16 airmen from World War II.

Hume Castle, Greenlaw

GREENLAW

7 miles SW of Duns on the A697

Greenlaw was the county town of Berwickshire from 1696 to 1853, when Duns replaced it. It formerly stood near the "green law", or hill, a little to the southwest, and was given its burgh charter in 1596. The picturesque **Market Cross** dates from 1696, and the Parish Church dates from the 17th century, with a later tower that was once used as a jail. There are many fine buildings within the town, including a town hall built in 1829. Three miles south are the impressive ruins of **Hume Castle**, ancient seat of the Hume family. The original castle was built in the 13th century, dismantled in 1515 and rebuilt in 1519. Over the years it was captured by the English and retaken by the Scots many times over. Eventually it was captured by Cromwell in 1651 and demolished. What you see now is a folly built in 1770 by the Earl of Marchmont. It sits 600 feet above sea level, and makes an excellent viewpoint.

LAUDER

17 miles W of Duns on the A68

To the east of the town is **Thirlestane Castle**, which is open to the public. It's a flamboyant place, with turrets, pinnacles and towers, giving it the appearance of a French château. It was originally built in the 13th century, but was extended and refurbished in the 16th century for the Maitland family, whose most famous member was John Maitland, second Earl and later first (and only) Duke of Lauderdale, who lived between 1616 and 1682. He was a close friend of Charles II and a member of the famous but unpopular "Cabal Cabinet". The word "cabal" comes from the initials of the five men who comprised it, Maitland's being "L" for Lauderdale. So powerful was he that he was soon regarded as the uncrowned king of Scotland. His ghost is said to haunt the castle.

Lauder Parish Church was built in 1673 to the designs of Sir William Bruce, and is in the form of a Greek cross. The medieval church stood in the grounds of Thirlestane Castle, and legend states that the Duke had it removed in the 17th century to improve his view. He instructed a bowman to fire an arrow westwards from the castle steps. Wherever the arrow landed the Duke would build a new church. That is why the church now stands within the town of Lauder itself.

GALASHIELS

Galashiels (known locally as "Gala") sits on the Gala Water, and is a manufacturing town at one time noted for its tweed and woollen mills. As a reflection of this, the motto of the Galashiels Manufacturer's Corporation was "We dye to live and live to die".

The **Lochcarron of Scotland Cashmere and Wool Centre** is located within the Waverley Mill in Huddersfield Street, and offers tours which explain the

THIRLESTANE CASTLE

Lauder, Berwickshire TD2 6RU
Tel: 01578 722430 Fax: 01578 722761
e-mail: enquiries@thirlestanecastle.co.uk
website: www.thirlestanecastle.co.uk

Thirlestane, one of the oldest and finest castles in Scotland is set in lovely Border hills at Lauder, 28 miles south of Edinburgh and 68 miles north of Newcastle, on the A68. Built originally as a defensive fort in the 13th century it was re-built in the 16th century as the home of the Maitlands. As the seat of the Earls and Duke of Lauderdale it was enlarged and embellished over the centuries

but it still remains home to the Maitland family. The Duke's ghost is said to haunt the castle.

See the Panelled Room and the Library with their defensive walls up to 13 feet thick. Absorb the atmosphere of the Billiard Room with its fascinating salmon fly screen. Climb the ancient turnpike stair to the Duke's Suite, including the incomparable 17th century plasterwork ceilings. Relish the

splendour of the Green Drawing Room and the Ante Drawing Room with their exquisite ceilings and joinery. Meet the Maitlands through the portrait collection in the State Dining Room and discover some of their fascinating treasures. Sink into nostalgia as you enter the Family Nurseries with their unique collection of historic toys. Some are in replica form for children to use and dipping into the dressing up chest can create some memorable moments on a family holiday. Discover the old Kitchens and Laundries, and explore the Border Country Life exhibitions showing domestic, sporting and agricultural life over the centuries.

FLAT CAT GALLERY

2 Market Place, Lauder, Berwickshire TD2 6SR
Tel: 01578 722808
website: www.flatcatgallery.co.uk

The Flat Cat Gallery is situated in the heart of lauder. Established in 1998, it offers changing exhibitions of paintings, ceramics, sculpture, furniture, textiles and jewellery. With a resident Middle East rug restorer, there are regular exhibitions of tribal rugs, textiles and artefacts. There is also a coffee shop serving excellent coffee, light lunches and wicked cakes, and here you can sit on (and enjoy!) the furniture made by the Workshop of Tim Stead.

BANK HOUSE

1 East High Street, Lauder, Berwickshire TD2 6SS
Tel/Fax: 01578 722877
e-mail: shop@bankhouselauder.co.uk
website: www.bankhouselauder.co.uk

The moment you enter the door of **Bank House**, perfect present and fabric frenzy takes over! The shop is full of incredibly discounted colourful linen, chintz, voile and cotton with patterns that take in everything from roses and butterflies to stripes, checks, honeysuckle and birds. The place is alive with colour, especially in the back room, where there are curtains to die for. If that's not enough, there are also gifts galore with everything at affordable prices.

BLACK BULL

Market Place, Lauder, Berwickshire TD2 6SR
Tel: 01578 722208 Fax: 01578 722419
e-mail: enquiries@bl;ackbull-lauder.com
website: www.blackbull-lauder.com

The **Black Bull** is a former 18th century coaching inn that offers stylish accommodation, great food and drink and a warm Scottish welcome. With eight en suite rooms, it oozes charm and warmth, just right for a break in the Romantic Borders Country, even though it is only half an hour from Edinburgh. Have a relaxing drink in the Harness Room Bar, or a meal in one of the superb dining areas. You won't be disappointed.

WORKSHOP OF TIM STEAD

The Steading, Blainslie, Galashiels TD1 2PR
Tel/Fax: 01896 860266
e-mail: timstead@virgin.net
website: www.timsteadfurniture.co.uk

The **Workshop of Tim Stead** is internationally renowned, and has been established for over 25 years. It produces superb, individualistic pieces of furniture made from native hardwoods, the design of each piece being based on the qualities of the wood used, with prices reflecting this accordingly. The skilled craftsmen are more than happy to give you an estimate for any piece you want made. Furniture can be bought directly from the workshop, though guided tours are by appointment only.

processes involved in the manufacture of woollens and tweeds.

However, the town is very old (the first mention of cloth mills was in 1588), and every year, in July, it holds the **Brae Lads Gathering**, which celebrates its long history. On the coat of arms of the old burgh appears the words "soor plooms" (sour plums), which refers to an incident in 1337, when some English troops were killed after crossing the border and found stealing plums in the town. In 1503, the betrothal of James IV to Margaret Tudor, Henry VII's daughter, took place at the town's old **Mercat Cross**. It's successor dates from 1695.

Old Gala House dates from the 15th century with later additions, and at one time was the town house of the Pringles, Lairds of Gala. It is now a museum and art gallery, and its gardens have recently been re-established, with a pond, spring bulbs and rhododendrons. Exhibitions of local art are sometimes held in the house. In Bank Street are the **Bank Street Gardens**, laid out shortly after World War II. In front of the town's war memorial (described by H.V. Morton as "the most perfect town memorial in the British Isles") is a reminder of the area's bloody past - a bronze statue of a border reiver, armed and on horseback.

Two miles south of the town, on the banks of the Tweed, is **Abbotsford**, the home of **Sir Walter Scott**, writer and lawyer. Scott had it built between 1817 and 1822, and he lived in it until he died in 1832. Behind it is the Tweed, and here the monks of Melrose Abbey made a ford across the river, so Scott decided to call it Abbotsford. It is built in the Scottish Baronial style, and is crammed with mementoes and objects that reflected the great man's passion for Scottish history, such as a tumbler on which Burns had etched some verses, a lock of Charles Edward Stuart's hair, and a piece of oatcake found in the pocket of a Highlander killed at Culloden. There is more than a hint of Gothic about the interior, especially the panelled hallway, which contains a carriage clock - still keeping good time - once owned by Marie Antoinette.

The main focus of the house is Scott's austere study, where many of his books were written. A gallery runs round the room, and in one corner is a door with a stairway behind it. Early each morning Scott descended these stairs from his dressing room to write for a few hours before heading for the courthouse in Selkirk.

Perhaps the most poignant room in the house is the dining room. Having returned from a trip abroad in September 1832, Scott knew that his end was near, and called for his bed to be set up at the window so that he could look out towards the Tweed. On September 21st he died. He had never got over the death of his wife Charlotte in 1826, and at about the same time a publishing firm in which he

Abbotsford

was a partner went bankrupt. He decided to write his way out of debt, even though he still had his duties at Selkirk Sheriff Court to attend to. It eventually ruined his health, and he now lies beside his wife among the ruins of Dryburgh Abbey.

The Southern Upland Way passes through Galashiels, and you can also join the 89-mile-long **Tweed Cycle Way**, which passes close by. It starts at Biggar in Lanarkshire and ends up in Berwick-upon-Tweed.

AROUND GALASHIELS

CLOVENFORDS
3 miles W of Galashiels on the A72

Clovenfords sits about a mile north of the Tweed, and is home to the **School of Casting, Salmon and Trout Fishing**. It offers weekly courses throughout the season. In 1803 William and Dorothy Wordsworth stayed at a local inn while touring the Scottish Borders.

In the 19th century the village became famous for something you do not normally associate with Scotland - a vineyard. Grape growing was introduced into the village by William Thomson, who grew the fruit under glass at his Tweed Vineyards. Soon the grapes became famous throughout Britain and Western Europe, and no less a person than the Emperor of France presented him with a gold medal for their quality. He died in 1895.

STOW
5 miles N of Galashiels on the A7

Stow (sometimes called Stow-of-Wedale) is a delightful village on the Gala Water. The imposing **St Mary of Wedale Parish Church** has a spire over 140 feet high. To the west of the village are the lonely Moorfoot Hills, and to the east is some

Stow

further moorland which separates it from Lauderdale. The B6362 leaves Stow and climbs up onto the moorland, reaching a height of 1,100 feet before descending through Lauder Common into the small town of Lauder.

Our Lady's Well sits just south of the village, and was rebuilt in the year 2000 by a local man. Legend says that King Arthur fought a bloody battle nearby against the Angles, and in gratitude for his victory had an image of the Virgin Mary brought to the village and put on display.

The **Pack Bridge** across the Gala Water dates from 1655, and was the first bridge ever built across the river. Before that fords were used.

GORDON
11 miles NE of Galashiels on the A6089

This pleasant village is the cradle of the Gordon clan, which moved north into Aberdeenshire in the 13th century, when

Robert the Bruce granted them the lands of Strathbogie, which had been forfeited by the Earl of Atholl (see Huntly). The village sits on a crossroads, and to the north are the well-preserved ruins of **Greenknowe Tower**, built in 1581 by James Seton of Touch and his wife Janet Edmonstone. It is a typical L-shaped tower house, built originally as a fortified home. The Pringles, one of the great Borders families, later acquired it.

MELLERSTAIN

10 miles E of Galashiels, on an unmarked road between the A6089 and the B6397

Mellerstain is a grand mansion originally designed by William Adam in the 1720s, and completed by his son Robert in the 1790s. It is one of the grandest Georgian houses in Britain, and holds a collection

Mellerstain House

of fine furniture, as well as paintings by Van Dyck, Naismith, Gainsborough and Ramsey. The Italian terraces were laid out in 1909 by Sir Reginald Blomfield, and give excellent views out over a small artificial loch towards the Cheviots.

MELROSE

3 miles SE of Galashiels just off the A6091

Melrose sits in the shadow of the triple peaks of the **Eildon Hills**, which have a waymarked path leading to their summits. Legend states that **King Arthur** and his knights lie buried beneath one of them, and indeed there is an old folk tale which tells of a man called Canonbie Dick who actually found the cave, thanks to a mysterious stranger, and saw the knights slumbering. A great wind rose up and blew Dick out of the cave, and no one has ever been able to find it since.

Another legend says that the entrance to the Fairy Kingdom lies among the Eildon Hills, and that Thomas the Rhymer (see Earlston) used it to visit the his lover, the Fairy Queen, for years at a time.

At the summit of Eildon Hill North are the remains of the largest hill fort in Scotland, which dates to the 10th century BC. When the Romans came, they built a watch tower within it.

Melrose, which is on the Southern Upland Way, is mainly visited nowadays to view the ruins of **Melrose Abbey** (Historic Scotland), surely the loveliest of all the Borders abbeys. It was founded in 1136 by David I for the Cistercian Order, and rose to become one of the most important in Scotland. The ruins that the visitor sees nowadays date mainly from the late 14th and early 15th centuries, thanks to the English army of Richard II, which destroyed the earlier buildings. It was here that the heart of Robert the Bruce,

Melrose Abbey

Scotland's great hero during the Wars of Independence, was buried. On his death bed in 1329, the king had told Sir James Douglas (known as the "Good Sir James" to the Scots, and the "Black Douglas" to the English) to place his heart in a casket after his death and take it to the Holy Land. But in 1330, on his way to the Holy Land, Sir James was killed at Teba in Spain fighting the Moors. His friends didn't want him buried on foreign soil, so they boiled his body in vinegar so that his flesh would fall from his bones. The flesh was buried in Spain and his bones, along with the casket, were brought back to Scotland (see also Cardross, Dunfermline and Threave Castle). In the late 1990s, during some restoration work on the abbey, the lead casket containing his heart was rediscovered and subsequently reburied within the abbey grounds. A plaque in the grounds

HARMONY GARDEN

St Mary's Road, Melrose, Borders TD6 9LJ
website: www.nts.org.uk

A delightfully tranquil walled garden comprising lawns, herbaceous and mixed borders, vegetable and fruit areas, and a rich display of spring bulbs. The garden is set around an early 19th century house (not open to the public), built by Melrose joiner Robert Waugh, who named it 'Harmony' after the Jamaican pimento plantation where he had made his fortune, Harmony Garden has excellent views of Melrose Abbey and the Eildon Hills and is situated near Priorwood Garden (see below).

PRIORWOOD GARDEN & DRIED FLOWER SHOP

Melrose, Borders, TD6 9PX
Tel : 01896 822493 Fax: 01896 823181 Shop: Tel: 01896 822965
e-mail priorwooddriedflowers@nts.org.uk
website: www.nts.org.uk

A specialist garden where most of the plants grown are suitable for drying. The colourful and imaginative selection ensures variety for the dried flower arrangements made here. Visitors can enjoy a stroll through the orchard which includes historic varieties of apples that are organically grown. Enjoy the different blossoms in spring, a picnic here in the summer, and catch a glimpse of the impressive ruins of Melrose Abbey which overlook the garden. Priorwood Garden is a short walk from Harmony Garden (see above). For information on day courses throughout the year, please contact the property.

now marks its resting place (see also Cardross and Dunfermline).

On a bend in the Tweed, two miles east of the town, is the site of **Old Melrose** (then called Mailros, meaning "bare moor"), where, in about AD 650, Celtic monks from Iona established a monastery. It was near here, in about AD 635, that a young shepherd, who was later to become **St Cuthbert**, was born. In AD 651, following a vision in which he saw the soul of St Aidan of Lindisfarne ascending to heaven, he entered the monastery to train as a monk. He eventually became Bishop of Lindisfarne, and died in 687. He now lies buried in Durham Cathedral. A 62-mile walking route called **St Cuthbert's Way** links Melrose and Lindisfarne.

River Tweed, Melrose

Close to the abbey ruins is **Priorwood Gardens** (National Trust for Scotland). It specialises in plants which are suitable for drying and arranging, and classes are organised to teach the techniques involved. There is also a shop. **Harmony Garden**, also run by the Trust, is close by. It is set around a 19th century house which is not open to the public, and has excellent views of the Eildon Hills. There are herbaceous borders, well tended lawns and vegetable and fruit areas. It is renowned for its sense of peace and tranquillity. The house and small estate was built by Robert Waugh, a Melrose joiner, in the early 19th century after making his fortune from a Jamaica plantation called "Harmony". It was sold to the Pitman family in 1820, and was bequeathed to the NTS in 1996 by Mrs Christian Pitman..

The **100 Aker Wood Visitor Centre** is on the old Melrose to Newstead road, and has woodland walks, a childrens'

play area, a coffee shop and car park.

A mile east of Melrose is **Newstead**, where there are the remains of **Trimontium Roman Fort**, covering 15 acres, and named after the three peaks of the Eildons. It was occupied between the late first century well into the second, and was the most important Roman settlement of the northern frontier. At its height it housed 1,500 Roman soldiers, and supported a large town which covered a further 200 acres. **The Three Hills Roman Heritage Centre**, in the Ormiston Institute in Melrose's Market Square, has displays on what life was like within a Roman settlement, and has artefacts that were found there. On Thursday afternoons (and Tuesday afternoons in July and August) a guided five mile, four hour walk to the fort leaves from the Centre.

The Scottish Borders is a rugby playing area, and at Melrose that version of the game known as "rugby sevens" was invented.

EARLSTON
8 miles E of Galashiels on the A68

The small town of Earlston is dominated by **Black Hill**, which gives a good view of the surrounding countryside. One of Scotland's earliest poets, **Thomas Learmont of Earlston,** was born here in about 1220. Also known as Thomas the Rhymer, Thomas of Erceldoune or True Thomas, he attained an almost supernatural status, as he was also a seer who could predict the future. Some ruins in the town are supposed be of his home, **Rhymer's Tower**.

It didn't take much in those days for a man to gain a reputation for having mythical and prophetic powers, and no doubt Thomas's many trips abroad accounted for the stories of him going off to live with the Fairy Queen under the Eildon Hills for years at a time (see also Melrose). His prophecies included Alexander III's death in 1285, the victory of Bruce over the English at Bannockburn in 1314 and Scotland's defeat by the English at Flodden in 1513. However, like most prophesies, they are all too easy to explain after the event.

SMAILHOLM
10 miles E of Galashiels on the B6397

Smailholm Tower (Historic Scotland) seems to grow out of a low, rocky outcrop, and is a four square 60 feet high tower which was once surrounded by a wall. It was originally a Pringle stronghold, but was sold to the Scott family in 1645. Within it you can see a collection of costumed figures and tapestries connected with Scott's Minstrelsy of the Scottish Borders. Scott, as a child, spent a lot of time with his grandparents at the nearby farm of Sandyknowe, and knew the tower well.

TOM DAVIDSON GALLERY

High Street, Earlston, Berwickshire TD4 6BU
Tel: 01896 848898
website: www.tomdavidson.co.uk

Tom Davidson is a renowned printmaker living in the heart of the Borders. He opened the **Tom Davidson Gallery** in 1995 to showcase his work, which has since become a favourite stopping place for many people touring the area. Although print making is his main activity, Tom also paints in various media - watercolour, acrylic and gouache, and you can see and buy his work when you visit the gallery.

All of his prints - lino-cuts, etchings or silk screen - are in limited editions of no more than 50, so if you buy a piece of his artwork, you know you are getting something special. So highly is he thought of that his work is to be found in private collections around the world, as well as in the Houses of Parliament, Floors Castle, Durham University and Paintings in Hospitals (Scotland), an organisation which, as its name suggests, places works of art in hospitals throughout Scotland.

Tom's gallery also has a small selection of hand-turned wood and ceramic items, with everything realistically priced. You can even watch Tom at work, and see the fascinating print-making processes he uses to create his works of art. He undertakes commissions, and one of his prints would make the ideal gift or souvenir of your time in the lovely Scottish Borders.

Smailholm Tower

KELSO

16 miles E of Galashiels on the A698

Kelso is a gracious town with a large, cobbled **Market Square** (said to be the largest in Scotland) that would not look out of place in France or Belgium. Surrounding it are imposing 18th and 19th century buildings, with the supremely elegant **Town House** of 1816, which now houses the tourism information centre, as its centrepiece.

The town sits at the junction of the Tweed and the Teviot. **Kelso Abbey** (Historic Scotland) was founded in 1128, after David I, who had founded an abbey at Selkirk and brought over 13 monks from France, decided that Kelso was a much better place for it, as the strategically positioned Roxburgh Castle was already there to offer it protection. It

was the biggest of the border abbeys, and during a siege by the English under the Earl of Hertford in 1545, it was almost totally destroyed. Now all that remains of the church are the transepts, part of the tower, two nave bays and part of the west end.

But the ruins are still dramatic and imposing, and are well worth a visit. A town trail has been laid out which takes you round the town's architectural gems.

The **War Memorial Garden** is in Bridge Street, and formed part of the former abbey grounds. It has helped Kelso to win the Beautiful Scotland and Britain in Bloom competitions on several occasions, and was gifted to the town by the Duke of Roxburgh in 1921.

In July every year the **Kelso Civic Week** takes place, with many events that echo similar ceremonies in other Borders towns. On the banks of the Teviot, three miles south west of the town, once stood the proud **Royal Burgh of Roxburgh**. This was probably founded about 1113, and was a thriving walled town in medieval times with no less than four churches, but nothing now survives above ground, thanks to the repeated attentions of succeeding English armies. It was one of Scotland's original "four burghs".

Where the Teviot and the Tweed meet is a high defensive mound, the site up until 1550 of **Roxburgh Castle**. It was during a siege of the castle in 1460 that James II was killed outright when a cannon accidentally blew up in his face. The place has been suggested as yet another possible site for King Arthur's magnificent capital of **Camelot** (see also Ayr). To the west of Kelso, within parkland overlooking the Tweed, stands the magnificent **Floors Castle**, Scotland's largest inhabited castle. It is home to the Duke and Duchess of Roxburgh, and has a huge collection of works of art and furniture.

The **Millenium Viewpoint**, on the other side of the Tweed and close to Maxwellheugh, was constructed in the year 2000, and is a vantage point for great views of the town and surrounding area.

Rennie's Bridge is a handsome, five-arched bridge spanning the Tweed - the first in the country to feature elliptical aches rather than round or pointed. It was designed by John Rennie the Scottish civil engineer, and was built in 1803 to replace an older bridge destroyed by floods. Rennie based his design for Waterloo Bridge in London on it (see also East Linton). The broad expanse of grass beside the river is known as **The Cobby**.

The bridge was the scene of a riot in 1854, when people objected to paying tolls to cross it, even though all the building costs had been met. So bad was it that the Riot Act was read. However, it took another three years before the tolls were withdrawn.

Horse racing in Kelso began in 1822, and **Kelso Race Course** (known as the "Friendly Course") hosts horse racing all year.

Ruins of Kelso Abbey

EDNAM
21 miles E of Galashiels on the B6461

The village stands on the Eden, a tributary of the Tweed, and was the birthplace of two famous men. The first was **James Thomson**, born in September 1700, who wrote the words to *Rule Britannia*. It was written about 1740 for a masque called *Alfred*, and was soon adopted as a patriotic song. The other was **Henry Francis Lyte**, born in June 1793, who wrote *Abide with Me*. A memorial to Thomson has been erected at Ferniehill, to the south of the village, and the bridge over the river has a plaque commemorating Lyte, who died in Nice in France in1847.

Kelso Town Centre

MAXTON

8 miles SE of Galashiels on the A699

Maxton Parish Church was rebuilt in 1812, though it contains fragments of an earlier, medieval building. **Maxton Cross**, on the tiny village green, partially dates from the 14th century, though the main part was replaced in 1881.

DRYBURGH

7 miles SE of Galashiels off the B6356

The ruins of **Dryburgh Abbey** (Historic Scotland) must be the most romantically situated in all of Scotland, sitting as it does on a loop of the Tweed, which surrounds it on three sides. Nothing much remains of the great abbey church, except for the west door and parts of the north and south transepts. However, the substantial ruins of the other abbey buildings (including a fine chapter house) can still be explored. Within the north transept is buried Sir Walter Scott and his wife Charlotte, as well as **Field Marshall Earl Haig of Bemersyde**. He was Commander-in-Chief of the British Expeditionary forces in France and Flanders during World War I.

The Premonstratensian abbey was founded in 1150 by Hugh de Moreville, Constable of Scotland. The site had already been a sacred one, as it was here that **St Modan**, a Celtic monk, set up a monastery in about 600AD. In 1322, during the Wars of Independence, Edward II's army, after a successful invasion of Scotland, set fire to the place. This was the first of many sackings, including the one of 1544, when 700 English soldiers reduced it to ruins. It was abandoned soon after.

It now forms part of the 55-mile-long **Abbeys Cycle Route**, taking in the other three great Borders abbeys of Melrose, Kelso and Jedburgh. A short walk from the abbey is the 31 feet high (including

Dryburgh Abbey

pedestal) **William Wallace Statue**. He spent a lot of time in the Borders hiding from the English in Ettrick Forest. The Earl of Buchan commissioned the statue in 1814.

North of Dryburgh is **Scott's View**, which gives an amazing panorama of the Eildon Hills. Sir Walter Scott used to ride up here to get inspiration, and when his funeral cortege was making its way to Dryburgh, the hearse stopped for a short while. It is best accessed from the A68, where it is signposted from the Leaderfoot Viaduct that spans the Tweed.

ST. BOSWELLS

7 miles SE of Galashiels on the A68

This village is named after **St Boisil**, who was an abbot of the Celtic monastery at Old Melrose in the 7th century. The centrepiece of the village is its green,

Continued on page 28

St Boswells, River Tweed and Dryburgh Abbey

Distance:	5.0 miles (8.0 kilometres)
Typical time:	180 mins
Height gain:	33 metres
Map:	Explorer 338 and 339
Walk:	www.walkingworld.com ID:2917
Contributor:	Mark and Tracey Douglas

Access Information:

The walk starts in St Boswells at the bus station.St Boswells is accessible by bus from most border towns and Edinburgh. There is a small carpark at the bus station and in front of the adjacent village hall. On street parking is available within the vicinity. There are no parking charges.

Description:

A beautiful walk along the banks of the River Tweed. The walk starts in the small charming village of St Boswells, and after an initial section on St Cuthbert's Way the walk joins the banks of the River Tweed.

The middle part of the walk takes in the hamlet of Dryburgh. Here you will pass the ruins of the 12th Century Dryburgh Abbey, which is open to visitors all year round and is the last resting place of Sir Walter Scott.

A short detour from Dryburgh will take you the Wallace Monument; a large statue in memory of the 12th Century Scottish Warrior which offers commanding views over the surrounding countryside and the Eildon Hills. The final section of the walk rejoins St Cuthberts way along the banks of the Tweed back into St Boswells.

Wildlife is in abundance and you may also see the odd salmon rising particularly in the Autumn months at the salmon ladder at

Mertoun Mill as they make the journey upstream to their spawning grounds.

Additional Information

Dryburgh Abbey was founded in the 12th century by King David I and run by the monks of the Premonstratensian Order. With its location on the Scottish Frontier, the Abbey, like all the other Border Abbeys, was prone to attack and was destroyed in 1322, 1385 and finally in 1544.

Now in the ownership of Historic Scotland, the Abbey is open to the public all year round.

Facilities

There are toilets in St Boswells and outside Dryburgh Abbey.The Buccleuch Hotel in St Boswells in open to non-residents and serves food all day. There are a couple of small convenience shops in St Boswells.

Features:

River, Toilets, Wildlife, Birds, Great Views, Gift Shop, Food Shop, Mostly Flat, Public Transport, Ancient Monument

Walk Directions:

1 From the bus station, turn right along the main street passing in front of the small row of shops. Just past the last shop (The Village Shop) turn left up the lane (The Wynd) and continue up passing the Air Cadet Hut until you meet a small track. Carry on and after about 50m take a right at the path junction. Go along this track ignoring the turn off to the right and within 200m the track will fork. Take the right fork up the flight of wooden steps and continue along this track for about 150m until you meet a tarmac road. Continue straight ahead on this road for about 150m until you reach the top of the Golf Course brae.

2 Turn left down the golf course brae, continue past the clubhouse and once you reach the course turn right. Keeping the fence to your right you will shortly join a footpath. Continue along the path which is part of St Cuthberts Way, keeping the fence to your right and the golf course to your left - be aware of golf being played! After about 1km you will reach the end of the golf course. Carry on along the path and you will shortly have the River Tweed on your left. Continue along the path passing the Cauld and Salmon Ladder until you reach Mertoun Bridge.

3 Climb the wooden staircase onto Mertoun Bridge. Be careful of traffic as you step out onto the road. Turn left and cross the bridge. Take great care crossing the bridge, face oncoming traffic. On reaching the end of the bridge turn left on to a track and head for the cottages at Mertoun Mill. Pass in front of the cottages and the old mill buildings and you will reach a set of steps.

4 Climb the steps, cross over the stile at the top and turn left along the field keeping the fence to your left, at the end of the field go through a gate and carry on down the track which will eventually take you down to the banks of the River Tweed. Carry on upstream,(you will observe the Golf Course on the opposite bank) for about 1km , cross a stile and carry on along the grass track keeping on straight ahead until you meet a small ladder stile.

5 Cross the ladder stile and turn right along the road. Within 200m you will pass the

entrance to Dryburgh Abbey. (You will have passed a toilet block on your right). Carry on straight ahead passing the parking area, the road will curve to the left and within 100m you will arrive at the entrance gate to Dryburgh Abbey Hotel.

6 If you wish to visit the monument, turn right and follow the road up the gentle hill for about 250m. Once you pass the final house on the left 'Newmains' turn left up the track which is signposted for the Wallace Statue. Carry on along this track for 500m before turning right up to the Monument. You will enjoy commanding views of the surrounding countryside and the Eildon Hills. (If you don't wish to visit the Wallace Monument, carry on direct to Waymark 8 by carrying on straight ahead down the road signposted as a dead-end towards the Tweed.)

7 Retrace your steps to take you back to Waymark 6 by turning right before the gates of Dryburgh Abbey Hotel. Carry on down this road for 300m to the suspension bridge which will shortly come into view.

8 You may wish to make a short visit to the Temple of the Muses which you will observe on the small hill on your right next to the bridge. Cross the suspension bridge and then turn immediately left down the track - you are now re-joining St Cuthberts Way. Follow this track for 1.5km following the signs for St Cuthberts Way and keeping the River Tweed on your left until you arrive at a footbridge crossing a small stream.

9 Cross the small bridge and follow the track right up the hill. Ignore the paths which turn off to the left and keep on until you reach a tarmac road, turn right along this road and then first left which will take you back into St Boswells before turning left to the Bus Station.

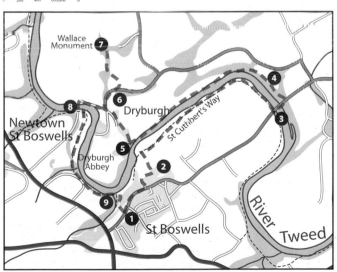

which hosts a fair on July 18th (St Boisil's Day) each year. In past times, this fair was one of the largest in the country, and attracted people - especially gypsies - from all over the Borders and beyond. At one time over 1,000 horses were offered for sale at the fair.

A mile or so to the east are **Mertoun House Gardens**. Though the house is not open to the public, the 26-acre gardens can be visited between April and September. **Mertoun Kirk**, in the grounds of the house, is open on alternate Sundays for church services. The original kirk was built in 1241, though the present building dates from 1658.

SELKIRK

5 miles S of Galashiels on the A7

Once the county town of Selkirkshire, Selkirk is now a quiet royal burgh on the edge of the Ettrick Forest. It was the site of the first abbey in the Borders, which was founded in 1113 by David I. However, 15 years later, before one stone was laid, David moved the monks to Kelso, where the abbey was finally built.

The Ettrick Water, a tributary of the Tweed, flows to the west of the town, and it is joined a couple of miles out of town by the Yarrow Water. The Vale of Yarrow is very scenic, with the hamlet of **Yarrow** itself, about eight miles west of Selkirk, being very picturesque. Scott's

great-grandfather was once minister of **Yarrow Parish Church**. It was built about 1640 to replace the medieval St Mary's Church, which stood above St Mary's Loch.

In Selkirk's High Street, outside the **Old Courthouse** where he presided, there is a statute of Sir Walter Scott, who was sheriff-depute here from 1804 until his death in 1832. Within the courtroom is an audiovisual display telling of his associations with the area. Another statue in the High Street commemorates **Mungo Park**, the explorer and surgeon, who was born in Yarrow in 1771. The oldest building in the town is **Halliwell's House and Robson Gallery**, just off the market square, where there is a small museum on the ground floor and art gallery on the upper floor. **Robert D. Clapperton Photographic** in Scotts Place is a working museum and photographic archive. It dates from 1867, and here, the good citizens of Selkirk posed stiffly in Victorian times while having their photograph taken. At the **Selkirk Glass Visitor Centre** at Dunsdalehaugh you can see glass paperweights being made.

In common with many Borders town, Selkirk has its **Common Riding Ceremony**, held annually in June, when over 500 riders regularly set out to patrol the marches, or boundaries, of the town lands. But the ceremony also commemorates the darkest day in the town's history. In 1513, Selkirk sent 80 of its bravest men to fight alongside James IV at Flodden, taking with them the town flag. The battle was a disaster for Scotland, with the flower of Scottish manhood, including the king himself, being killed. Only one Selkirk man, named Fletcher, returned, without the Selkirk flag but bearing a bloodstained English one, which can be seen in Halliwell's House. A memorial to the fallen can be found outside the Victoria Halls in the High Street.

Overlooking Selkirk

The **Scottish Borders Archive and Local History Centre** is within St Mary's Mill, and offers research facilities on local history, geography and genealogy, including the records of the old counties of Berwickshire, Selkirkshire, Roxburghshire and Peeblesshire.

Three miles west of the town is **Bowhill**, the Borders home of the Duke of Queensberry and Buccleuch. It is a fine early 19th century mansion, and in its grounds is **Bowhill Little Theatre**, which presents many professional plays. A **James Hogg Exhibition** is housed in a building off the courtyard (see St Mary's Loch). There is also a visitors centre, rural walks, a restored Victorian kitchen and a display of fire engines.

The ruins of **Newark Castle** is also within its grounds, dating from about 1450. In 1645 the **Battle of Philiphaugh** took place nearby, when Leslie's Covenanting army met and defeated a royal army commanded by Montrose. Leslie's army was triumphant, and prisoners were taken to Newark Castle. it was here, on September 13th 1645, that

several hundred soldiers and camp followers of the Montrose's army were savagely butchered. In 1810, when excavations were taking place beside the castle, bones were uncovered in a field known as "Slain Men's Lea". The tower can only be viewed from the outside.

Aikwood Tower, (not open to the public), home of Sir David Steel, was once the home of Michael Scott the legendary wizard. He lived from about 1175 to 1230, and was one of the cleverest men of his age. He was credited with dividing the Eildon Hills (see Melrose) into three, though the Roman name for the hills (Trimontium) shows that they always had three peaks. He was educated at Durham Cathedral School and later Oxford, Paris and Bologna, where he studied mathematics, law and theology. In his day he was known as the "wonder of the world", and his reputation spread all over Europe as a man who had learned everything there was to know in the Christian world.

He is also said to have dabbled in alchemy, and some of the legends attached to him and his so-called "wizardry" (such as his "demon horse" and "demon ship") were no doubt borrowed from the story of Merlin the

Magician. He probably died in Italy (some say after being hit by a piece of masonry that had fallen from a church) and was buried there.

The tower was granted to Master Michael Scott, a descendant of the wizard, by the infant James V in 1517. Previously it had been held by the crown.

ST. MARY'S LOCH

The loch is in a truly beautiful setting of rounded, green hills. Both Scott and William Wordsworth have sung its praises, but no words can adequately describe this delightful sheet of water. A narrow spit of land separates it from the smaller **Loch of the Lowes**, with **Tibbie Shiel's Inn**, now an angling hostelry, situated between them. It was opened in 1824, and is named after Isabella Shiels, the woman who ran it until 1878. Her visitor's book is still in existence, and records such names as R.L. Stevenson, Gladstone and Thomas Carlyle. It is a favourite stopping point on the Southern Upland Way, which passes close by.

James Hogg, nicknamed "The Ettrick Shepherd", was also a frequent visitor. He was born at Altrive Lake (not a lake, but a farm) nearby in 1770, and wrote *Confessions of a Justified Sinner*, one of the great books of the 19th century (see also Selkirk).

HAWICK

Hawick is the largest town in the Borders, and is famous for the quality of its knitwear, with names like Pringle and Lyle and Scott being known worldwide.

The **Hawick Common Riding** takes place in June each year, and commemorates yet another skirmish between the English and the Scots. This occurred in 1514, when some Hawick men beat off English soldiers camped near the town at Hornshole and captured their banner. A disagreement of a different kind took place in the mid-1990s, when two women riders tried to join what had traditionally been an all-male occasion. Their participation provoked hostile opposition, even from some women. It took a court case to establish that women had the right to join in, though even today some people still tolerate their presence rather than welcome it.

St Mary's Parish Church was built in 1763, and replaced an earlier, 13th century church. The town's oldest building is the 16th century **Drumlanrig's Tower**. In 1570 it survived a raid by English troops which destroyed the rest of Hawick, and was once a typical moated L-shaped Borders tower house before the area between the two "legs" was filled in to convert it into an elegant town house. At one time it

belonged to the Douglases of Drumlanrig, in Dumfriesshire, and it was here that Anna, Duchess of Buccleuch, and wife of the executed Duke of Monmouth, once stayed. The basement was later used as a prison, and finally a wine cellar when it became a hotel. Now the tower has been restored and houses the town's visitor information centre and an exhibition explaining the history of the Borders.

The award-winning **Wilton Lodge Park** sits by the banks of the Teviot, and has 107 acres of riverside walks, gardens, a tropical glasshouse, recreational facilities and a café. Within it is the **Hawick Museum and Scott Art Gallery**, which explains the history of the town and its industries. The gallery has a collection of 19th and 20th century Scottish paintings, and regularly hosts exhibitions of works by local and national artists. Many of the mills in the town, such as **Peter Scott and Company** in Buccleuch Street and **Wrights of Trowmill** outside the town have visitor centres and guided tours. The **Hawick Cashmere Company**, based in Trinity Mills in Duke Street, has a viewing gallery and shop. And if Duns has its Jim Clark Memorial Trophy Room, Hawick has its **Jimmy Guthrie Statue**. Andrew James Guthrie was a local TT rider who won six Tourist Trophy races on the Isle of Man. He was killed in 1937 while competing in the German Grand Prix at Chemnitz.

AROUND HAWICK

MINTO
5 miles NE of Hawick off the B6405

Minto was founded in the late 18th century as a planned village by the 2nd Earl of Minto. It was laid out by the architect William Playfair. The **Parish Church** was completed in 1831, and replaced an earlier building dating from the 13th century.

On top of Minto Crags sits the curiously named **Fatlips Castle**, built in the 16th century for the Turnbull family. It was restored in 1857 and used as a shooting lodge and private museum, though it is now ruinous.

To the east of Fatlips are the ruins of **Barnhills Tower**, another Turnbull stronghold. It was built in the 16th century, but now only a few decayed walls are left standing.

DENHOLM
4 miles NE of Hawick on the A698

In 1775 this pleasant village, with its village green, was the birthplace of John Leyden, poet, doctor, linguist and friend of Sir Walter Scott. He was educated at the local school, and so gifted was he

THE CELTIC GOLDSMITH AT THE JOHNNIE ARMSTRONG GALLERY

Teviothead, by Hawick, Roxburghshire TD9 0LF
Tel/Fax: 01450 850237
website: www.thecelticgoldsmith.com

The Celtic Goldsmith is a family business specialising in the research, design and manufacture of high quality gold and silver jewellery, in Scottish, Celtic and Viking styles.

The Moffatt family have lived in the Border hills since 1978, honing their art, perfecting their skills and immersing themselves in the history, mythology and legends of the North. Each piece they make is a tiny handcrafted work of art, with its own story to tell. They remain a unique business, producing genuine "Native Scottish designs" in small quantities, and selling exclusively from their own premises direct to their clients.

Pieces from their workshops can be found in the collections of connoisseurs the world over, many of whom regard their jewellery as an art investment for future generations.

The range is being expanded to include bronze sculptures, ranging from small ornaments for the shelf, to medium sized pieces for indoor display. Production will be carried out only in foundry bronze, and once again the theme will be Northern myth and legend. The jewellery and bronze collections are displayed alongside genuine historic artifacts relating to their design.

that he entered Edinburgh University when only 15 years old. The **John Leyden Memorial**, which stands on the green, commemorates the great man, who died in 1811 on the island of Java. He was the son of a local farmer, and in 1806 had settled in Calcutta, where he became assay master to the local mint. Here he wrote about the local languages.

Also born in the village was **Sir James Murray** (1837-1915), who undertook the tremendous task of editing the *New English Dictionary on Historical Principles*, forerunner of the *Oxford English Dictionary*.

JEDBURGH
14 miles NE of Hawick on the A68

The route of the present day A68 was at one time the main route from Edinburgh to England, so Jedburgh saw many armies passing along its streets when Scotland and England were constantly at war with each other. The local's once called the town "Jethart", and it is still remembered in the expression "Jethart justice", meaning hang first and try later, a throwback to the bad old days of the reivers.

Every year at Candlemas (February 2nd) the **Fastern Even Handba'** game is played in the town, when the "Uppies" play the "Doonies" and chase beribboned balls through the streets of the town. Though the present game dates from the 18th century, it is thought that it had its origins in the 16th century, when the severed heads of English reivers were used instead of balls.

It is an attractive small town with gaily-painted houses, especially in the Market Place and the Canongate, and it regularly wins awards in "Beautiful Scotland in Bloom" competitions. **Jedburgh Abbey** (Historic Scotland), on the banks of the Jed Water, was founded in 1138 by David I for the Augustinians. It was destroyed nine times by the invading English. Each time, save for the last one, the monks painstakingly rebuilt it. It is the most complete of all the Border abbeys, amd a visitor centre explains its story, with one of its more intriguing exhibits being the "Jedburgh Comb", found during excavations. Part of the church building was used as a parish church up until 1875. The **Cloister Garden** was planted in 1986, and shows what a typical monastic garden would have looked like in her early 16th century

Not far from the abbey is **Mary Queen of Scots House**. Here, in October 1566, Mary Stuart stayed for four weeks when presiding at local courts in the Borders. While she was there she made an arduous journey to Hermitage Castle to visit her lover, the Earl of Bothwell, which nearly killed her. When Elizabeth I held her in captivity, she declared that she would have preferred to have died in Jedburgh than England. Now it is a museum and visitors centre with displays on the tragic queen's life (see also Hermitage Castle).

Jedburgh Castle Jail, in Castlegate, was a 19th century reform prison which now houses a display about the history of the town. Four miles northeast of Jedburgh are the **Monteviot House Gardens**,

Mary Queen of Scots House, Jedburgh

which has a pinetum, a herb garden and a riverside garden linked by bridges.

Five miles northeast of Jedburgh, off the A698, are the **Teviot Water Gardens**, situated on three levels above the River Tweed. There are three riverside walks, a bird hide and a café.

Jedforest Deer and Farm Park is five miles south of Jedburgh on the Mervinslaw Estate, just off the A68. It is a

modern working farm with a deer herd and rare breeds. There are also birds of prey demonstrations using eagles, owls and hawks, and plenty of ranger-led activities.

Four miles beyond the Farm Park, the A68 reaches the English border at **Carter Bar**, which is 1370 feet above sea level in the Cheviots. From here there is a wonderful view northwards, and it almost seems that the whole of Southern Scotland is spread out before you. In the 18th century herds of sheep and cattle were driven over this route towards the markets in the south.

The last Borders skirmish, known as the **Redeswire Raid**, took place here in 1575. It took the arrival of a contingent of Jedburgh men to turn what was going to be a Scots defeat into a victory.

ANCRUM
10 miles NE of Hawick on the B6400

Ancrum is a typical Borders village, to the north of which was fought the **Battle of Ancrum Moor** in 1545. It was part of what was known as the "Rough Wooing", when Henry VIII tried to force the Scots into allowing the young Mary Queen of Scots to marry his son Edward. 3,000 English and Scottish horsemen under Lord Eure were ambushed by a hastily assembled army of Borderers. During the battle, the Scots horsemen changed sides when they saw that the Borderers were gaining the upper hand, resulting in a total rout.

Ancrum Parish Church was built in 1890, though the ruins of the earlier 18th century church still survive in the graveyard. It is thought that the original Ancrum church was built in the 12th century.

Two miles east of the village, on Peniel Haugh, is the 150 feet high **Waterloo Monument**, erected by the Marquis of Lothian between 1817 and 1824 to commemorate the Battle of Waterloo. Though there are stairs within the tower, it is not open to the public. The best way to reach it is to walk from the **Harestanes Countryside Visitor Centre**, which is nearby. The Centre has countryside walks, activities and displays, all with a countryside theme, as well as a car park, gift shop and tearoom.

MOREBATTLE
18 miles NE of Hawick on the B6401

This little village sits on the St Cuthbert's Way, close to the Kale Water. It's name comes from the "botl", or dwelling, beside the mere, which was a small loch. In the 19th century the loch was drained to provide more agricultural land. The surrounding area was once a hiding place for Covenanters fleeing the persecution of Charles II's troops in the 17th century.

To the north of the village is **Linton Church**, which has Norman details, a fine Norman font and a belfry dated 1697. One Norman survival is the tympanum above the door, which commemorates the killing of the **Linton Worm** by John Somerville in the 13th century. The Linton Worm was 12 feet long, and lived in a cave below the church. It terrorised the district, and the local people were powerless against it. John noticed that when it saw anything it wanted to eat, it opened its mouth wide. So he made a special spear that had inflammable materials instead of a point, and when he approached the worm on horseback with the spear blazing, it duly opened its mouth to devour him. John stuck the spear down the worm's throat, and the worm was killed. For this act the king granted him the lands of Linton.

The church sits on a low mound of fine sand, which is almost certainly a natural feature. However, a local legend tells a different story. It seems that a young man was once condemned to death for murdering a priest. His two sisters pleaded for his life, saying they would carry out a specific task to atone for his crime. They would sieve tons of sand, removing all large grains, and from the small grains build a mound on which a church building could stand. The church authorities agreed to this, and the women set to work. Eventually, after many years, a mound of sand was created, and a church was indeed built on it.

The ruins of the L-shaped **Cessford Castle**, which surrendered to the English in 1545, lie two miles to the southwest. It was built by the Kerrs in about 1450, and was once one of the most important castles in the Borders.

KIRK YETHOLM
22 miles NE of Hawick on the B6352

This village, lying within the Bowmont Valley, is at the northern end of the **Pennine Way**, with St Cuthbert's Way passing close by as well. It got its name from the Scottish word "yett", meaning a gate, as it was one of the gateways into England. It, and to a lesser extent its twin village of **Town Yetholm**, were famous at one time as being where the kings and queens of the Scottish gypsies lived. The most famous queen was Esther Faa Blyth, who ruled in the 19th century. In 1898 Charles Faa Blyth, her son, was crowned king at Yetholm. Though the title had lost much of its meaning by this time, the coronation was attended by an estimated 10,000 people. A small cottage is still pointed out as his "palace". St Cuthbert's Way passes through the village, and the the Pennine Way, which snakes over the Pennines in England, ends at **Yetholm Parish Church**, an elegant building with a small tower. It was built in 1836 and has a Burgerhuys bell cast in 1643.

NEWCASTLETON
20 miles S of Hawick, on the B6357

Newcastleton, in Liddesdale, is a planned village, founded by the third Duke of Buccleuch in 1793 as a handloom-weaving centre. The **Liddesdale Heritage Centre Museum** is in the old Townfoot Kirk in South Hermitage Street, and has attractive displays about the history of the area and its people.

This is the heartland of the great Borders families of Kerr, Armstrong and Elliot, and was always a place of unrest before Scotland and England were united. The border with England follows the Liddel Water then, about three miles south of Newcastleton, strikes east along the Kershope Burn for a mile before turning northeast. At Kershopefoot, where the Kershope Burn meets the Liddel Water, the Wardens of the Western Marches of both Scotland and England met regularly to settle arguments and seek redress for crimes committed by both sides. A jury of 12 men settled the disputes, with the Scots choosing the six English, and the English choosing the six Scots. However, even these meetings were known to result in violence, and many a Scottish or English warden and his entourage were chased far into their own territory if redress was not forthcoming.

Every year, in July, the village holds the **Newcastleton Traditional Music Festival**, one of the oldest such festivals in Scotland. It was founded in 1970, and has concerts, ceilidhs and competitions. There are many informal music sessions held throughout the village. On the last day of the festival is the "Grand Winners Concert".

A mile from the village, off the Canonbie road, is the **Millholm Cross**. It has the initials AA and MA carved on it. The AA is thought to be Alexander

GRAPES HOTEL

16 Douglas Square,
Newcastleton TD 9 0QD
Tel: 01387 375245/375680
Fax: 01387 375896
e-mail: info@the-grapes-hotel.com
website: www.the-grapes-hotel.com

Newcastleton is a lovely, stone-built village nestling in the Borders. It was built in 1793 by the Duke of Buccleuch to house handloom weavers, and is now a centre for exploring this beautiful part of Scotland. Situated in the heart of the village in Douglas Square, the **Grapes Hotel** is one of the best hostelries in the Borders, and offers unrivalled food, drink and accommodation. Value for money and high standards of service are the watchwords here, and the establishment has earned itself a fine reputation for its hospitality and attention to detail. The Grapes is owned and managed by Trevor Cambridge, and he is determined to maintain its high standards and its great reputation.

There are six guest rooms on offer, each one comfortable and tastefully decorated. Two doubles, a single and a twin are fully en suite, while two family rooms share a bathroom and toilet. Each comes with TV and tea/coffee making facilities. The furniture is traditional/modern, and reflects the tradition and history attached to the hotel

There is a fine range of drinks available, including beer, spirits, wines and liqueurs, with, of course, soft drinks always on offer if you're driving. The Nichol Bar is on the ground floor, and has an open air look due to its central glass atrium, that lets light flood in. Bar meals, snacks, teas and coffees are served here. The lounge bar is cosy and warm, and here you can enjoy morning coffee and afternoon teas, as well as snacks and drinks. The Reivers Bar also on the ground floor, is popular with its two pool tables and games facility. The Douglas Room, the upper bar - is a relaxing place of low beams where you can have a drink or bar meal. It is also ideal for that special occasion, such as a wedding reception, private party, christening or small business meeting.

The food in the Grapes Hotel is, as you would expect, outstanding. The Vine is the à la carte restaurant, and offers fine cuisine in stylish yet comfortable surroundings. So popular is it that you are advised to book in advance. The highly acclaimed chef uses only the finest and freshest of local produce wherever possible, and many people return again and again to sample the wonderful dishes on the menu. This is the place for that special and romantic meal to celebrate an anniversary, a birthday or some other special occasion

Armstrong, reiver from nearby Mangerton Tower.

The **Dykescroft Information Centre and Newcastleton Historic Forest Walk** lies to the south of the village, off a minor road. It is closed in February and March each year. One walk ends at Priest Hill, where there is a 200-year-old hill fort.

Five miles north of Newcastleton is the massive bulk of **Hermitage Castle** (Historic Scotland). It dates from the 14th century, and its imposing walls and stout defences reflect the bloody warfare that was common in this area before the union of Scotland and England. It belonged to the de Soulis family, who built the original castle of wood in the mid-13th century. However, in 1320 William de Soulis was found guilty of plotting against Robert the Bruce, his lands and property were confiscated by the crown. It later became a Douglas stronghold.

While staying in Jedburgh, Mary Stuart covered the 50 miles between there and Hermitage and back again in one day to visit the Earl of Bothwell, whom she later married. During her journey, she lost a watch, which was recovered in the 19th century (see also Jedburgh).

A few miles north of the village is **Castleton**, the site of a lost village. All that remains of the medieval St Martin's Church is the kirkyard, and a series of earthworks marks where a castle belonging to the Soulis family once stood. The village also had a green, and this is marked by a commemorative stone.

PEEBLES

Peebles sits on the banks of the River Tweed, and though it looks peaceful enough nowadays, its history is anything but. It was burnt to the ground by the English in 1545, occupied by Cromwell in 1649, and again by Charles Edward Stuart in 1745.

In June each year the Town holds its **Beltane Week**, with the crowning of the Beltane Queen. The ceremony's origins go right back to pagan times, though the present Beltane Week celebrations date only from the 19th century, when they were revived. The Chambers Institute was founded in 1859 by local man William Chambers, who, with his brother Robert, went on to found the great Chambers publishing house in Edinburgh. Within it is the **Tweeddale Museum and Gallery**, where the history of the town is explained. Here you can also see the extraordinary classical frieze commissioned by William Chambers which is based on parts of the Parthenon Frieze in the British Museum and on the Alexander Frieze commissioned in 1812 by Napoleon Bonaparte. On Innerleithen Road, opposite the Park Hotel, is the unusual **Cornice Museum of Ornamental Plasterwork**, dedicated to displaying and explaining ornate plasterwork.

The ruins of the **Cross Kirk** (Historic Scotland), founded in 1261 as the church of a Trinitarian Friary, are to the west of the town. The Trinitarians were a monastic order founded in 1198 by St John of Math, a Frenchman, to redeem captives taken by the Saracens in the Holy Land during the Crusades. The tower of the former **St Andrews Church** still survives just off Neidpath Road. The present **Peebles Parish Church** is an imposing Victorian building at the west end of the High Street, a short distance from the quaintly named **Cuddy Bridge** over the Eddleston Water, a tributary of the Tweed. One of the hidden places of the town is to be found beyond an archway leading from the high street - the **Quadrangle**. Surrounding the town's war memorial are well laid out, colourful gardens.

Eastgate Theatre and Arts Centre is housed in a 19th century church. It has a programme of drama and exhibitions throughout the year, and there is a small café.

Glentress Forest lies one mile east of Peebles off the A72. It is now the most visited tourist attraction in the Scottish Borders, and is said to have the country's best mountain biking course.

Peebles

AROUND PEEBLES

NEIDPATH CASTLE
1 mile W of Peebles on the A72

Neidpath Castle stands on the banks of the Tweed. The previous castle that stood here was built by the Fraser family in the 14th century. It subsequently passed to the Hays when the daughter of Sir Simon Hay married Gilbert de Hay of Yester. It was probably Gilbert who built the present castle.

In 1685 William Douglas, the first Duke of Queensberry, bought it and it remained a Douglas property until 1810,

LYNE FARMHOUSE B&B

Lyne Farm, Peebles Peeblesshire EH45 8NR
Tel & Fax: 01721 740255
Email: lynefarmhouse@btinternet.com
Website: www.lynefarm.co.uk

The three-star **Lyne Farmhouse** is four miles from Peebles, and has magnificent views out over the Stobo valley. It offers two double rooms and a twin, and is a solid, Victorian building dating from 1850. The rooms are both comfortable and elegant, and the full Scottish breakfasts are beautifully cooked. There is also a self-catering cottage with four bedrooms. Evening meals are available by prior arrangement. A warm welcome awaits you at Lyne Farmhouse!

Neidpath Castle

when it passed to the Earl of Wemyss. Sir Walter Scott visited it frequently when his friend, Adam Ferguson, rented it at the end of the 18th century.

It is the epitome of a Scottish tower house, and originally consisted of three great vaulted halls, one above the other (though the top vault was subsequently removed and replaced by a timber roof), reached by winding stone staircases. There is a genuine dungeon below what was the guardroom which prisoners were sometimes lowered into and in many cases forgotten about. Mary Stuart and James VI both visited the castle, reflecting the importance of the Hay family in the 16th century. The castle is privately owned, and is open to the public. Wall hangings depict the tragic life of Mary Stuart.

KAILZIE GARDENS

3 miles E of Peebles on the B7062

Extending to 14 acres, Kailzie Gardens sit on the banks of the Tweed, surrounded by hills. The main part is contained in an old walled garden, plus there is a 15-acre wild garden and woodland walks among rhododendrons and azeleas. There is also a restaurant, gift shop and 18-hole putting green.

INNERLEITHEN

6 miles E of Peebles on the A72

Innerleithen is a small town which was the original for Sir Walter Scott's St Ronan's Well. It used to be a spa town, and the **St. Ronan's Well Interpretive Centre** at Well's Brae explains the history of the wells, whose waters were full of sulphur and other minerals. You can even sample the water if you're brave enough. In the High Street is **Robert Smail's Printing Works** (National Trust for Scotland). This was a genuine print works that still retained many of its original features and fittings when taken over by the Trust in 1987. Now you can see how things were printed at the turn of the century, and even have a go yourself.

TRAQUAIR

6 miles SE of Peebles on the B709

Traquair is a small village visited mostly for the magnificent **Traquair House**. It is reputed to be the oldest continuously inhabited house in Scotland, and has its origins in a royal hunting lodge built on the banks of the Tweed in about AD 950. In its time, 27 kings and queens have visited the place, including Alexander I in the 11th century, Edward I of England (known as the "Hammer of the Scots") in the 13th, and Mary Stuart in the 16th. One laird of Traquair fell with his king at Flodden, and in the 18th century the then laird, the fifth Earl of Traquair, supported the Jacobite cause.

Charles Edward Stuart visited in 1745, and when he left, the laird closed the **Bear Gates** at the end of the long drive, vowing that they would never be opened until a Stuart ascended the British throne once more. They have remained closed ever since. Within the house itself are secret passages and priests' holes, as the owners reverted to Roman Catholicism in the early 17th century. It is still the family home of the Maxwell Stuart family.

In 1965 the then laird renovated the brewhouse which lies beneath the private chapel, and the **Traquair House Brewery** now produces a fine range of ales which can be bought in the estate shop. It is said that when Charles Edward Stuart visited, he too enjoyed a glass or two of Traquair Ale.

At the beginning of August each year the **Traquair Fair** is held, with music, dance, theatre, puppetry and children's entertainment.

DRUMELZIER
8 miles SW of Peebles, on the B712

It is reputed that one of King Arthur's knights lies buried where the Drumelzier Burn joins the Tweed, just north of the village. At Drumelzier Haugh is an old standing stone known as **Merlin's Stone**, and on Tinnis Hill there is a stone circle. At one time **Drumelzier Castle**, owned by the Tweedie family, stood close to the village, but now little remains above ground. In the graveyard of **Drumelzier Parish Church** is an old burial vault of the Tweedies.

LYNE
4 miles W of Peebles on the A72

Lyne Church, perched picturesquely on a hillside above the road, is said to be the smallest parish church in Scotland. A

Traquair House

chapel has stood here since the 122th century at least, but the present church was built about 1645. It contains a pulpit and two pews reputed to be of Dutch workmanship.

STOBO
5 miles W of Peebles on the B712

Stobo Kirk, one of the oldest and most beautiful in the area, has a Norman tower, nave and chancel, with some later features and additions. **Stobo Castle** is set in some lovely grounds, and is now one of Scotland's most luxurious health farms and spas. Two miles south, along the B712, is the **Dawyck Botanic Garden and Arboretum**, an outpost of the National Botanic Gardens in Edinburgh. It sits on the Scrape Burn, a tributary of the Tweed, and houses a unique collection of conifers, rhododendrons and other tree species within its 50 acres.

The original garden was laid out in the lte 17th century by Sir James Naesmyth, who imported trees and shrubs from North America. In 1832 the garden was landscaped by Italian gardeners, who built bridges, terraces and steps.

BROUGHTON
10 miles W of Peebles, on the A701

Broughton is forever associated with the

SKIRLING HOUSE

Skirling, by Biggar, Lanarkshire ML12 6HD
Tel: 01899 860274 e-mail: enquiry@skirlinghouse.com.
Fax: 01899 860255 website: www.skirlinghouse.com

Skirling House provides high quality accommodation and fine dining amid luxurious surroundings of beautiful paintings, rich fabrics and antiques. The house was designed by the Arts & Crafts architect Ramsay Traquair in, in 1908 for Lord Charmichael, a prominent art collector at the time. Used as his country retreat, it contained his art collection, inlcuing a magnificent 16th century Florentine carved wooden ceiling, which can now be seen in the drawing room. The Arts & Crafts influence can also be seen in the ornate wrought ironwork and the decorative carvings.

Bob Hunter is the proprietor and chef of this house, set amid lovely Borders scenery, and is helped by his wife, Isobel when she is not at work in Edinburgh. The five en-suite bedrooms are large and comfortable with TV's and hospitality trays, and the breakfasts are delicious, including dishes such as scrambled eggs with smoked salmon. The dinner menu is imaginative and beautifully presented, with the emphasis on fresh local produce including meat, fish and cheese. The vegetables, as much as possible, are grown in the house garden. A good wine list ensures the perfect accompaniment to your meal. In summer drinks can be taken in the garden and in winter, afternoon tea can be taken in the drawing room with its comfortable sofas and open log fire, making this a perfect place to relax, take a stroll in the countryside or explore the local historic attractions.

author and Governor-General of Canada, John Buchan, whose most famous work is undoubtedly *The Thirty Nine Steps*. Though born in Perth, his maternal grandparents farmed nearby, and his father, a Free Church minister, married his mother in the village. The old tree kirk is now the **John Buchan Centre**, with displays about his life and writings. The village is also home to the famous **Broughton Ales**.

WEST LINTON

14 miles NW of Peebles, just off the A702

West Linton is a delightful village, and one of the hidden gems of Peeblesshire. The picturesque **St Andrews Parish Church** of 1781 stands in the middle of the village, and the surrounding gravestones testify to the craftsmanship of the many stone carvers who used to live in the area. The local **Whipman** ceremonies take place in June each year. They originated in 1803, when some local agricultural workers decided to form a benevolent society known as the "Whipmen of Linton". Now the weeklong festivities include honouring the Whipman (meaning a carter) and his Lass. In the centre of the village stands **Lady Gifford's Well**, with a stone carving of 1666 on one of its sides.

One of the many streets is quaintly called Teapot Lane, as a tap once stood here where the women of the village drew water into teapots to make tea.

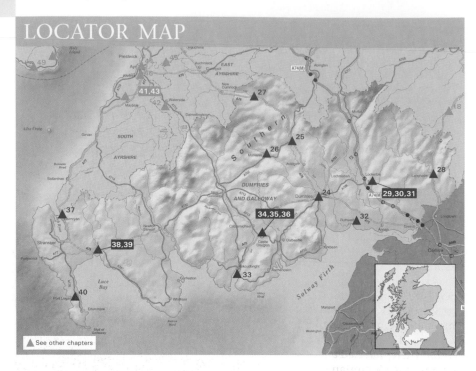

LOCATOR MAP

See other chapters

ADVERTISERS AND PLACES OF INTEREST

People scurrying north along the M74 rarely turn off at Gretna and head for Dumfries and Galloway. This is a pity, as it is a wonderful area that can match anything in Scotland for beautiful scenery, grandeur and history. There are over 200 miles of coastline with small coves, neat fishing ports, towering cliffs and wonderful sandy beaches. There also are beautiful villages, old abbeys and castles, vibrant towns and country roads that meander through soft, verdant scenery or climb up into bleak moorland landscapes that were made for walking. In the fields you will see herds of the region's own indigenous cattle - the Belted Galloways, so called because they have a wide white band running round their bodies.

Dumfries is the largest town in the area, and is a lovely place, full of old red sandstone buildings and great shopping facilities. It is also where Scotland's national poet, Robert Burns, is buried, and any trip to Scotland should include a visit to St Michael's Kirkyard to see his mausoleum. Kirkcudbright, because of the quality of light found there, has had an artist's colony since Victorian times, and is a gracious place, full of Regency and Georgian buildings. Wigtown is Scotland's official book town, and Stranraer, with its ferries, is a gateway to Northern Ireland. Then there's Lockerbie, forever associated with the disaster of 1988.

The area contains three former counties - Dumfriesshire, Kirkcudbrightshire and Wigtownshire, and each one has its own particular charm. You can explore beautiful Nithsdale in Dumfriesshire, for instance, and visit Drumlanrig Castle, one of the homes of the Duke of Queensberry and Buccleuch. Kirkcudbrightshire was the

Cliff Top Walk, Portpatrick

birthplace of John Paul Jones, founder of the American navy, and Wigtownshire was where Christianity was introduced into Scotland.

Surrounding the fertile fields and picturesque towns of coastal Galloway are the high hills and bleak moorland, which cut off Dumfries and Galloway from the rest of Scotland. Because of this, the area was almost independent of Scottish kings in medieval times, and was ruled by a succession of families, from the ancient Lords of Galloway to the mighty Douglases. All have left their mark in stone, such as Devorgilla's Bridge in Dumfries and the mighty Threave Castle, built on an island in the River Dee.

Then there are the abbeys, for, like the Borders, this was an area much favoured by medieval monks. At New Abbey are the ruins of a monastery that gave the word "sweetheart" to the English language; at Glenluce - a word which means "valley of light" - are the wonderful ruins of Glenluce Abbey; and south of Kirkcudbright is Dundrennan, where Mary Stuart - better known as Mary Queen of Scots - spent her last night on Scottish soil. The castles are equally as impressive. Drumlanrig - Threave - Cardoness - Caerlaverock; the names trip off the tongue, and go to the very heart of Scotland's history.

From the middle of August to the end of October each year the area holds its "Gael Force Festival", bringing together musical events, literary festivals, traditional Scottish entertainment, concerts, drama and art.

This part of Scotland has a mild climate, and at one time the coastline was nicknamed the "Scottish Riviera". First-time visitors are always surprised to see palm trees flourishing in cottage gardens near the coast, or in the grand, formal gardens such as Logan Botanic Garden or Castle Kennedy Garden in Wigtownshire. But then, Dumfries and Galloway has always been full of surprises.

DUMFRIES

The Royal Burgh of Dumfries certainly lives up to its nickname of the "Queen of the South". It has a lovely location on the banks of the River Nith, and was once voted the town with the best quality of life in Britain.

The town is forever associated with Scotland's national poet, Robert Burns. Though born in Ayrshire, he died in Dumfries, and lies in the **Burns Mausoleum** within the kirkyard that surrounds **St Michael's Parish Church**, built in the 1740s. Also buried there are his wife, Jean Armour, and five of their family. Burns had a family pew in St Michael's (marked by a plaque), and long after his death his wife was a regular attender. The mausoleum was built in 1815, in Grecian style, and in that year Burns' remains were transferred there. Also in the kirkyard are the graves of many of his friends. (see also Alloway).

Not far away is Burns Street (formerly called Mill Vennel), where **Burns' House** is situated. He lived here from 1793 until he died in 1796 at the early age of 37. It is open to the public, and though not a grand house, it was nonetheless a substantial building for its day, showing that by the end of his life Burns had achieved some form of financial stability due to his work as an exciseman. On display are letters and manuscripts, the pistol he carried with him on his rounds and the chair in which he sat when he wrote his last poems.

The **Globe Inn** was the poet's "howff", and it can still be visited. It was established in 1610, and is situated down a narrow passage off the main street.

On the west bank of the Nith is the **Robert Burns Centre**, which tells the full story of the poet and his connections with the town. Within it are displays and exhibits, including a model of the Dumfries that Burns would have known in the late 18th century. There is also a cinema.

The history of Dumfries goes much further back than Robert Burns, however. It is an ancient town, with a royal charter from William I dated 1186, and it was here, in 1306, that Robert the Bruce murdered the Red Comyn, a rival contender for the throne of Scotland. The deed took place before the high altar of Greyfriar's Monastery, a deed for which he was excommunicated by the Pope. However, this didn't seem to worry the man, as he immediately had himself crowned king of Scotland at Scone in Perthshire in the presence of Scottish bishops, who continued to give him communion. Nothing now remains of the monastery, though the present **Greyfriar's Kirk**, a flamboyant building in red sandstone, is close to where it stood.

In the High Street stands the **Midsteeple**, built of red sandstone in 1707. It was formerly the town hall and jail, and on its south face is a carving of an ell, an old Scots cloth measurement of about 37 inches. There is also a table of distances from Dumfries to various important Scottish towns. One of the towns however, is in England - Huntingdon. Three successive Scottish

kings in medieval times held the earldom of Huntingdon, and it was one of the places where Scottish drovers took cattle to market in the 17th and 18th centuries.

In Shakespeare Street stands, rather appropriately, the famous **Theatre Royal**, one of the oldest theatres in Scotland, dating from 1792. Burns regularly attended performances. Between September 2005 and May 2007 it will be closed for refurbishment. In contrast, Dumfries's newest attraction is **Organised Chaos** on Lockerbie Road. This activity centre has a paint ball arena and a purpose-built, all terrain 800 metre track for off-road buggies.

Dumfries proper sits on the east bank of the Nith. On the west, up until it was amalgamated into Dumfries in 1929, was the separate burgh of **Maxwelltown**,

Robert Burns Statue, Dumfries

which was in Kirkcudbrightshire. Joining the two towns is **Devorgilla's Bridge**. Though the present bridge dates from 1431, the original structure was built by Devorgilla, Lady of Galloway, in the 13th century. Her husband was John Balliol, who founded Balliol College in Oxford (see also New Abbey).

At the Maxwellton end of the bridge is the **Old Bridge House Museum**, with exhibits and displays illustrating everyday life in the town. The museum building dates from 1660, and is built into the structure of the bridge. Also on the Maxwellton side of the river is **Dumfries Museum**, housed in an 18th century windmill, and with a **Camera Obscura** that gives fascinating views of the town.

On the northern outskirts of the town, but now surrounded by modern housing, are the beautiful red sandstone remains of **Lincluden College** (Historic Scotland). Built originally in 1164 as a Benedictine nunnery by Uchtred, Lord of Galloway, it was suppressed in the late 14th century by **Archibald the Grim**, third Earl of Douglas, and replaced by a collegiate church. The present ruins date from that time. One of its main features is the elaborate canopied tomb of Princess Margaret, daughter of Robert III and widow of the Earl of Douglas (see also Threave Castle). Adjoining the site is the Norman **Lincluden Motte**, which was later terraced and incorporated into a garden. The adjoining tower house was built in the late 16th century, after the Reformation, by the commendator of the college, William Stewart.

To the east of the town at Heathhall is the **Dumfries and Galloway Aviation Museum**, run by a group of amateur enthusiasts. It has three floors of displays in what was the control tower of the old airfield of RAF Tinwald Downs, and holds a fascinating collection of military aircraft, both propeller and jet driven, as well as engines, memorabilia and photographs. Within what was Crichton Royal Hospital in Bankend Road, is the cathedralesque **Crichton Memorial Church**, designed by Sydney Mitchell and built between 1890-1897 as part of a mental hospital. For those interested in genealogy, the **Dumfries and Galloway Family History Research Centre** in Glasgow Street must be visited. There are archives, fiches and books about local history and families, though there is a modest fee for the use of the facilities.

The hamlet of **Holywood** sits just off the A76, two miles north of Dumfries. The present **Holywood Parish Church** of 1779 (with a tower dating to 1821) was partly built from the stones of a great medieval abbey which once stood here, of which nothing now remains

above ground. To the west, on the other side of the A76, is a stone circle known as the **Twelve Apostles**, though one massive stone is now missing.

Another writer associated with Dumfries is J.M. Barrie (see also Kirriemuir). Though not born here, he attended **Dumfries Academy**, a handsome building in Academy Street. While at the school, he stayed in a house in George Street, and later admitted that the games of pirates he and his friends played in the garden sloping down to the Nith gave him the idea for Peter Pan and Captain Hook.

AROUND DUMFRIES

DALSWINTON

6 miles N of Dumfries on a minor road off the A76

The hamlet of Dalswinton is no more than two rows of cottages on either side of the road. But it is an attractive place, built as an estate village. When Robert Burns was living locally at Ellisland Farm, Patrick Millar owned Dalswinton House, in the grounds of which (not open to the public) is **Dalswinton Loch**. Patrick encouraged William Symington, originally from Leadhills, to experiment with his steam-driven boat on the waters of the loch in the late 18th century, and it is thought that Burns may have been a passenger on one of the sailings (see also Leadhills).

ELLISLAND

6 miles N of Dumfries on the A76

Robert Burns brought his family south from Mauchline to Ellisland in June 1788. However, there was no farmhouse at the time, and he had to have one built, meaning that he couldn't move in properly until the following year. He leased the 170-acre farm from Patrick

Millar of Dalswinton, but found the soil to be infertile and stony. So much so that by 1791 he gave up the unequal struggle to make a living from it, and moved with his family to Dumfries.

The farm sits in a beautiful spot beside the Nith, and it was this romantic location which had made Burns choose it in the first place. Here he wrote some of his best poetry, including *Auld Lang Syne* and his masterpiece of the comic/macabre, *Tam o' Shanter*. Burns used to recount that Tam o' Shanter was conceived while walking the banks of the Nith, and he laughed out loud as he thought up his hero's adventures with the witches. Now the farmhouse houses a lively museum dedicated to his memory. To the north is **Hermitage Cottage**, which Burns used as a place to muse and write poetry.

AE

8 miles N of Dumfries on a minor road off the A701

The small village of Ae is famous for having the shortest name of any town or village in Britain, and for having the only place name with no consonant in it. It takes its name from the Water of Ae, and was founded in 1947 to house forestry workers. It is set in a great conifer forest which has some good walks and footpaths.

CLOSEBURN

11 miles N of Dumfries on the A76

Closeburn sits in one of the most beautiful parts of Dumfriesshire - Nithsdale. To the north of the village the wooded dale closes in on either side, with the River Nith tumbling through it. To the south, it gradually opens out into a wide, fertile strath, dotted with green fields and old, whitewashed farms. The **Parish Church of Closeburn** sits some distance away from the village, and is an

ANGELS PORTION

19 East Morton Street, Thornhill, Dumfriesshire DG3 5LZ
Tel: 01848 331553 Fax: 01848 331552
e-mail: dorothy@chintzandchina.co.uk
website: www.angelsportion.co.uk

Angel's Portion is situated in what was the Old Parish Hall in Thornhill, deep in Nithdale. It is one of the most historic buildings in the village, and is an apt location for a special shop that offers a wide range of designer-led goods that are just right for that special souvenir or gift. The place is rich in colour, light and texture, and there is sure to be something that catches your eye. The owner, Dorothy Hill, personally searches the world for the finest items to include in her eclectic stock.The shop takes its name from the small amount of whisky that is lost while the spirit is maturing in casks within bonded warehouses. It's a mysterious process, and one that is aptly named.

Glassware - houseware - prints - tableware - cards - cookware

- jewellery - ceramics -perfumes - it has them all! Take your time when browsing round the showroom. Most items are from an artistic background, and many are hard to find elsewhere. Some are exclusive to the Angel's Portion, which shows the shop's commitment to good design, superb craftsmanship and value for money.

The jewellery, for instance, encompasses the timeless beauty of Corona Silver as well as the striking and colourful hand-turned wooden beads of the internationally renowned local craftswoman Denise Zygadlo. Plus, if it's pottery you're after, the shop stocks two ranges of Stephen Pearce's renowned earthenware - the classic 'Traditional' in terracotta and creamy white, and the striking 'Shanagarry' range in black and white. The 'Shanagarry' pieces are handmade and hand-decorated at a pottery near Shanagarry in Ireland, and are as as practical as they are beautiful.

Upstairs from the main shop is The Gallery, featuring paintings, sculpture, furniture, casts. etchings and other objet d'art from both local and national artists and craftspersons. These represent the cream of good design, and range from turned bowls by Glen Lucas to Sheryl Brown's silver castings. You're sure to find something that will inspire and captivate you.

And while you're visiting Angels Portion why not relax and treat yourself to a coffee or tea in the coffee shop? Or even a fruit juice? There is also delicious home baking, and all food items are available as a 'carry out'.

Thornhill is a beautiful village, and well worth exploring. You will notice, as you enter the shop, a small bust of Thornhill's own writer - Jospeh Laing Waugh. He wrote books in lowland Scots, and the people of the village are justly proud of him.

Just as they are of the Angels Portion. It's a wonderful shop, and entering it is an adventure that you just can't miss. So if you're in beautiful Nithsdale, be sure to call in.

attractive Victorian building with a slim tower. Fragments of the older church, which date from 1741, can be seen in the kirkyard. **Closeburn Castle** (not open to the public) has been continuously inhabited since the 14th century, when it was built by the Kirkparticks, who were closely associated with Robert I.

A small road winds up eastwards from just south of Closeburn into the moorland above the village. It makes an interesting drive, and takes you past the small but picturesque **Loch Ettrick**.

THORNHILL

13 miles N of Dumfries on the A76

This lovely village, with its wide main street and pollarded trees, has a French feel to it, and was laid out in 1714 by the Duke of Queensberry. At the crossroads in the middle of the village is a monument surmounted by a winged horse, a symbol of the Queensberry family. In a field to the west of the village, and close to the bridge over the Nith, is the 15th century **Boatford Cross**, associated with the ferry and ford that preceded the bridge.

Three miles north of the village, and to the west of the A702, are the remains of 15th century **Morton Castle**, situated romantically on a tongue of land jutting out into Morton Loch. A castle of some kind has stood here since the 12th century, though the present castle was built by the Douglases, who were the Earls of Morton. In 1588 the castle was sacked by the troops of James VI, who were conducting a campaign against the Maxwells.

Against the wall of a building in East Morton Street is the bust of Joseph Laing Waugh, Thornhill's own novelist and poet, who set some of his books, written in lowland Scots, in and around the village.

DRUMLANRIG CASTLE

16 miles N of Dumfries on a minor road off the A76

Drumlanrig Castle is set in a 120,000-acre estate, and is the Dumfriesshire home of the Duke of Queensberry and Buccleuch. It was built by William Douglas, 1st Duke of Queensberry, and completed in 1691. It sits on the site of an earlier Douglas castle, and contains many fine paintings, including works by Gainsborough, Rembrandt and Hans Holbein. Its name comes from the word "drum", meaning a low hill, on a "lang", or long, "rig", or ridge. Therefore it is the low hill on the long ridge.

In the summer of 2003 it was the scene of a daring burglary when a painting by Leonardo da Vinci worth millions of pounds was stolen from it in broad daylight. Within the estate is a country park and gardens, the ruins of **Tibbers Castle**, and some of the outbuildings have been converted into craft workshops. The **Drumlanrig Sycamore** is one of the largest sycamores in the country, and there is also the first Douglas fir ever planted in the United Kingdom.

DURISDEER

19 miles N of Dumfries on a minor road off the A702

The tiny hamlet of Durisdeer sits at the end of a narrow road leading off the A702, with not many people knowing about it. It consists of a handful of cottages and a **Parish Church** built in 1699, and the church is unusual in that it has, attached to it, the former parish school. It is also surprisingly large for such a small hamlet, but this is due to the fact that it is the church for the Queensberry estate. But it also hides a secret which makes it special - the wonderful **Durisdeer Marbles**. They are, in fact, an elaborate funerary monument constructed in 1713 to the 2nd Duke of Queensberry and his wife, who lie buried in the crypt beneath. They were carved in marble by the Flemish sculptor Jan Nost, and are said to be the best of their kind in the country.

PENPONT

13 miles N of Dumfries on the A702

This small, attractive village is well worth a visit in the summer months to see the colourful gardens that surround some of the old picturesque cottages. The cathedralesque **Parish Church** is Victorian, and seems far too large for such a small place.

Durisdeer Church

Penpont was, in 1858, the birthplace of **Joseph Thomson** the African explorer, after whom Thomson's gazelle is named. He studied at Edinburgh University and joined an expedition to Africa in 1878, thus starting a long association with the continent. He died at the young age of 37 in 1895, his body wasted by the many diseases he had contracted.

On a slight rise in a field just off the road to Moniaive is a piece of sculpture shaped like an egg. This is the work of **Andy Goldsworthy** the famous sculptor, who was born in Cheshire but now lives in the village.

KEIR

12 miles N of Dumfries on a minor road off the A702

Keir is no more than a hamlet with a small **Parish Church** dating mainly from 1814. It was near here that **Kirkpatrick MacMillan**, inventor of the modern bicycle, was born in 1813, and while his brothers all went on to become successful in their careers, Kirkpatrick was content to stay at home and ply the trade of a blacksmith.

Hobbyhorses, which relied on riders pushing themselves forward with their feet, had been around since the early part of the 19th century, but Kirkpatrick MacMillan's bicycle was the first to incorporate revolving pedals. On June 6th 1842 he set out on a 70-mile ride to Glasgow on his bicycle, and was greeted by crowds when he arrived there. However, while passing through the Gorbals, he knocked down a young girl, and even though she wasn't badly injured, he was fined five shillings by a Glasgow magistrate, the first recorded case of a cyclist being fined for a traffic offence. However, rumour has it that the magistrate offered to pay the fine out of his own pocket if Kirkpatrick would allow him to have a ride on the bicycle.

TYNRON

15 miles N of Dumfries on a minor road off the A702

This small, pretty conservation village has only one building dating after 1900. The **Parish Church**, which looks as if it is far too big for such a small place, was built in 1837, and was one of the last in Scotland to be lit by oil lamps. Early in the 20th century a distillery which had a contract to supply the Palace of Westminster was situated here.

DUNSCORE

8 miles NW of Dumfries on the B729

Dunscore (pronounced "Dunsker") is a small, attractive village with a neat, whitewashed **Parish Church** dating from 1823. When Robert Burns and his family stayed at Ellisland Farm, four miles to the east, they used to worship in its predecessor.

Not far from Dunscore is Lochenhead Farm, birthplace in 1897 of **Jane Haining**, the only British person to have died at Auschwitz during World War II. While still young she joined the Church of Scotland's Jewish Mission Service, and was eventually appointed matron of the Jewish Mission in Budapest in 1932. In 1944 she was arrested, purportedly because she had been listening to BBC broadcasts, but actually because she had been working among the Jews. She was taken to Auschwitz, and on July 17th 1944 died there. Her death certificate gave the cause of death as cachexia, a wasting illness sometimes associated with cancer, but there is no doubt she was gassed.

The isolated farm of **Craigenputtock**, where Thomas Carlyle lived while writing *Sartor Resartus*, lies off an unmarked road five miles to the west (see also Ecclefechan). It was here that an unusual - not to say hilarious - event took place concerning a small religious sect known as the Buchanites, founded by Mother Buchan in Irvine, Ayrshire, in the 18th century. She attracted a wide following, claiming she could bestow immortality on a person by breathing on them, and that she herself was immortal.

She also claimed that her followers would ascend to heaven in bodily form, without the inconvenience of death. The cult was eventually hounded from Irvine by the town magistrates, and it headed south towards Dumfries. In a large field near Craigenputtock she decided that it was time her followers went to heaven. So she had a wooden platform set up in a field at Craigenputtock, and she and her followers assembled on it, their heads shaved apart form a small tuft that the angels would grasp to lift them up into God's kingdom. However, in the middle of the service the platform collapsed, throwing her followers to the ground. The sect eventually broke up when Elspeth had the nerve to die a natural death (see also Irvine and Crocketford).

Out of doors at **Glenkiln**, beside Glenkiln Reservoir four miles (as the crow flies) south west of Dunscore, is a collection of sculptures by Henry Moore and Rodin.

MONIAIVE

16 miles NW of Dumfries on the A 702

Moniaive, caught in a fold of the hills at the head of Glencairn, through which the Cairn Water flows to join the Nith, must surely be one of the prettiest villages in Dumfriesshire. It is actually two villages, Moniaive itself and Dunreggan, on the northeast side of the river. Within the village is the **Renwick Monument**, which commemorates a Covenanting martyr who died in 1688.

James Paterson was a painter who was a member of that group known as the "Glasgow Boys". In 1882 he settled in the village with his wife, and lived there until 1906, when he moved to Edinburgh. Several of his paintings show scenes in and around the village.

Three miles east is the great mansion of **Maxwelton House** (not open to the public), formerly known as Glencairn Castle. It was here that Anna (her real name) Laurie, of **Bonnie Annie Laurie** fame, was born in 1682. The song was written by William Douglas of Fingland, though he later jilted her and joined the Jacobite army. Anna herself went on to

GLENLUIART HOLIDAY COTTAGES

Glenluiart House, Moniaive, Dumfriesshire DG3 4JA
Tel: 01848 200331 Fax: 01848 200675
e-mail: sue@badpress.demon.co.uk
website: www.moniaive.com

Set close to one of the most picturesque villages in Scotland,
Glenluiart Holiday Cottages offer accommodation for those who
appreciate quiet country life and beautiful scenery. The four
cottages (one with four bedrooms, one with two bedrooms and
two with one bedroom), are set around a shared courtyard only half a mile from Moniaive with all its
amenities, and make an ideal base for exploring this historic and scenic part of Scotland.

marry Alexander Fergusson, 14th Laird
of Craigdarroch (see also Sanquhar).

Every September the village hosts the
Scottish Comic Festival, with displays
and exhibitions, as well as talks by
cartoonists and comic illustrators. There
is also the **Moniaive Folk Festival** in
May each year.

WANLOCKHEAD

25 miles N of Dumfries on the B797

People are usually surprised to discover
that Scotland's highest village isn't in the
Highlands, but in the Lowlands.
Wanlockhead, in the Lowther Hills, is
1,531 feet above sea level, and is a former
lead mining village which is right on the
Southern Upland Way. It is best
approached from the A76, passing
through one of the most beautiful and
majestic glens in southern Scotland - the
Mennock Pass. As you drive up, keep
your eyes open for a small cross laid flat
into the grass on the north side of the
road. It commemorates Kate Anderson, a
nurse who was killed here in 1925 when
she was returning to Sanquhar after
attending a patient. She fell off her
bicycle in a snowstorm and broke her
neck.

In the middle of Wanlockhead, in
what was the village smithy, you'll find
the **Museum of Lead Mining**, which
explains all about the industry, and gives
you the opportunity to go down the

Lochnell Mine, a former working mine.
The **Miners' Library** is situated on a rise
above the museum, and was founded in
1756 by 35 men. At the height of its
popularity it had 3,000 books on its
shelves. Within the village you'll also
find the **Beam Engine**, which has
recently been restored. It used to pump
water from one of the mines using,
curiously enough, water to power it.
Straitsteps Cottages shows the living
conditions of the lead miners in the 18th
and 19th centuries.

The **Leadhills and Wanlockhead
Light Railway** is Britain's highest
adhesion railway, reaching 1,498 feet
above sea level. It was originally built to
take refined lead to Scotland's central
belt, but finally closed in 1938. Now a
length of two-feet gauge track has been
re-opened between Wanlockhead and its
twin village of Leadhills, and trips are
available at weekends during the summer.

Lead is not the only metal associated
with Wanlockhead. In olden days, this
whole area was known as "God's Treasure
House in Scotland" because of the gold
found there. In fact, the Scottish crown
was refashioned for James V in the 16th
century from gold mined here. The
largest nugget of gold ever discovered in
the UK was found close to Wanlockhead.
It weighed all of two pounds, and was
the size of a cricket ball. Gold panning is
still a popular activity in the local

streams, and the **UK National Gold Panning Championships** are held here every May.

Sanquhar

28 miles N of Dumfries on the A76

Sanquhar (pronounced San-kar) is a small town in Upper Nithsdale that was created a royal burgh in 1598. The name comes from the language of the ancient Britons, and means "Old Fort". The site of this fort was on a small hill to the north of the town, close to **St Bride's Parish Church**, built in 1824 on the site of a much older church. Within the church is a small collection of stone carvings, including one of St Nicholas and a medieval cross.

The **Sanquhar Tolbooth** was built to the designs of William Adam in 1735 as a town hall, schoolroom and jail, and now houses a small museum. It was in a house opposite the Tolbooth that William Boyd, 4th Earl of Kilmarnock, lodged while on his way south to be tried and executed for his part in the Jacobite uprising, and there is a plaque on the wall commemorating his stay. In Main Street is **Sanquhar Post Office**, dating from 1712, the oldest continuously used post office in the world. The Southern Upland Way passes through the burgh, and the **Sanquhar Historic Walk** takes you round many of the town's attractions and historic sites.

To the south of Sanquhar are the ruins of **Sanquhar Castle**, originally an old Crichton stronghold. It fell into the hands of the Douglases, and it was here that William Douglas, who wrote the original version of the song *Annie Laurie*, was born in 1672 (see Maxwelton House). The castle was founded in the 11th century, though what you see now dates from much later.

In the 17th century, Sanquhar was a Covenanting stronghold. Charles II had imposed bishops on the Church of Scotland, and the Covenanters took up arms to keep the church Presbyterian. These times were known as the "Killing Times", and many people were executed for following the dictates of their conscience. One of the most militant Covenanters was **Richard Cameron**, who rode into Sanquhar in 1680 and attached what became known as the "**Sanquhar Declaration**" to the Market Cross. This disowned the king, which was effectively treason. Cameron was subsequently killed at the Battle of Airds Moss in the same year (see also Falkland).

The **Riding of the Marches** is an ancient ceremony, and takes place every August. The burgh boundaries are ridden by horse riders to ensure that adjoining landowners have not encroached onto burgh or common land - a common occurrence in olden times.

One of the more unusual cottage

industries in Sanquhar during the 18th and 19th centuries was the hand knitting of gloves, and the intricate patterns soon made the gloves popular throughout the country. Up until the 1950s these patterns had never been published. Now it is possible once more to buy both hand and machine knitted gloves and garments made from the distinctive patterns.

A series of plaques on various buildings takes you on a historic walk round the town, with a leaflet being available in the local tourist office.

ELIOCK HOUSE

26 miles N of Dumfries on a side road running parallel to the A76

Set deep in the heart of Nithsdale off a minor road, Eliock House (not open to the public) was the birthplace in 1560 of **James Crichton**, better known as the "Admirable Crichton". He was the son of the then Lord Advocate of Scotland, and was educated at St Andrews University. He travelled extensively in Europe, where he followed careers in soldiering and lecturing at universities. Though a young man, he could speak 12 languages fluently, and was one of the best swordsmen of his day. However, this didn't prevent him from being killed in Mantua in Italy in 1582 while a lecturer at the university there.

The story goes that he was returning from a party one evening when he was set upon by a gang of robbers, and defeated each one in a sword fight. He then realised that one of the robbers was a pupil at the university, Vincentio di Gonzaga, son of the Duke of Mantua, ruler of the city. Realising what he had done, he handed Vincentio his sword and asked forgiveness. Vincentio, however, was a nasty piece of work. He took the sword and stabbed the defenceless James through the heart, killing him outright.

KIRKCONNEL (UPPER NITHSDALE)

31 miles N of Dumfries on the A76

This former mining village in upper Nithsdale is not to be confused with Kirkconnell House near New Abbey or Kirkconnel graveyard in Annandale. **St Connel's Parish Church** dates from 1729, and is a fine looking building to the west of the village.

High on the hills above the village are the scant remains of an even earlier church, which may date from before the 11th century. Near the present parish church is a monument to **Alexander Anderson**, a local poet who wrote under the name of "The Surfaceman". Though born in lowly circumstances, he rose to become chief librarian at Edinburgh University and subsequently the secretary of the Edinburgh Philosophical Union.

The **Kirkconnel Miners Memorial** commemorates the men who lost their lives in the Upper Nithsdale mining industry between 1872 and 1968.

MOFFAT

20 miles NE of Dumfries on the A701

Sheep farming has always been important in **Annandale**, and this is illustrated by the ram that surmounts the **Colvin Fountain** in the middle of the wide High Street. The town is situated in a fertile bowl surrounded by low green hills, and at one time was a spa, thanks to a mineral spring discovered on its outskirts in the 17th century. By 1827 the sulphurous water was being pumped into the town, and by Victorian times it had become a fashionable place to visit and "take the waters".

Moffat was the birthplace, in 1882, of **Air Chief Marshal Lord Dowding**, architect of the Battle of Britain. A statue of him can be found in **Station Park**. Though he wasn't born in the town, **John Loudon McAdam**, the great road builder, is buried in the old kirkyard at the south end of the High Street. He lived at Dumcrieff House, outside the town, and died in 1836 (see also Ayr, Carsphairn and Muirkirk). Though born in Edinburgh, Dorothy Emily Stevenson, better known as the novelist **DE Stevenson**, lived in Moffat, and died there in 1973. She is buried in the local cemetery. The small **Moffat Museum** at The Neuk, Church Gate, charts the history of the town and the people associated with it, including Dowding, McAdam and Stevenson.

The **Black Bull Inn** is one of the oldest in Dumfriesshire, and dates from 1568. Burns was a regular visitor, and Graham of Claverhouse used it as his headquarters while hunting Covenanters in the district. Another hostelry in Moffat that has a claim to fame, albeit a more unusual one, is the **Star Hotel** in the High Street. It is only 20 feet wide, making it the narrowest hotel in Britain. On the other side of the road is the former **Moffat House**, designed by John Adam for the Earl of Hopetoun and dating from 1750s. It, too, is now a hotel.

Two miles east of the town, on the A708, are **Craiglochan Gardens**, which are open during the summer months. They extend to four acres, and there is a small nursery.

GREY MARE'S TAIL
28 miles NE of Dumfries just off the A708

The A708 winds northeast from the town, and takes you past St Mary's Loch as you head for Selkirk. About eight miles along the road is a waterfall called The Grey Mare's Tail (National Trust for Scotland), fed by the waters of tiny Loch Skeen, high in the hills. The surrounding area has changed little since the 17th century, when it was a hiding place for Covenanters. It is now a 2,150-acre nature reserve, and is rich in fauna and

Grey Mare's Tail Waterfall

flora, including a herd of wild goats. During the summer months there is a programme of guided walks starting from the visitor centre.

TWEEDSWELL
26 miles NE of Dumfries, well off the A701

Tweedswell is the source of the Tweed, and sits 1,250 feet above sea level. It seems strange that within an area of no more than a few square miles, three rivers rise. The Tweed flows east, the Annan flows south, and the Clyde flows north.

Here also is a great hollowed-out area among the hills known as the **Devil's Beef Tub**. Here, in olden times, border reivers used to hide their stolen cattle. To the east towers the 2,651 feet high **Hartfell**, supposedly the seat of **Merlin the Magician** in Arthurian days.

ESKDALEMUIR

23 miles NE of Dumfries on the B709

Eskdalemuir, high in the hills, holds one of Dumfriesshire's hidden gems. The **Samye Ling Centre**, founded in 1967 by two refugee Tibetan abbots, is the largest Tibetan Buddhist monastery in Western Europe. Not only is it a monastery, it is a place where Tibetan culture, customs and

Langholm

art is preserved. To see its colourful Eastern buildings, its flags flying and its prayer wheels revolving in what is a typical Scottish moorland setting, comes as a great surprise.

Close by is **Eskdalemuir Geomagnetic Observatory**, opened in 1908. It was built here for an unusual reason. The observatory was originally at Kew in London, but the sensitive geomagnetic instruments used to measure the earth's magnetic field were affected by the overhead electricity lines used to power trams. It was at Eskdalemuir in June 1953 that the highest short-term rainfall for Scotland was recorded - 3.15 inches in half an hour. This represents about 15 per cent of Scotland's average annual rainfall.

LANGHOLM

24 miles NE of Dumfries on the A7

Though within Dumfriesshire, the "muckle toon" of Langholm, in Eskdale, is more of a Borders town than a Dumfries and Galloway one. It was here, in 1892, that Christopher Murray Grieve the poet - better known as **Hugh McDiarmid** - was born (see also Biggar), though it took many years for the people of the town to formally acknowledge his undoubted contribution to Scottish literature. Also born in the town, but not a native, was **James Robertson Justice**

ESKDALE TOWN & COUNTRY

82-84 High Street, Langholm, Dumfriesshire DG13 0DH
Tel: 01387 380619
e-mail: eskdaletandc@hotmail.co.uk

The whole of Eskdale, in the Scottish Borders, is famous for fishing and shooting, and you can observe a huge variety of wildlife, including roe deer, red squirrels and buzzards. In **Town & Country**, just off the market square, you will find everything you need for a holiday based on country pursuits. The shop carries a wide range of brand-name equipment and clothing for anglers and shooting enthusiasts, and has a staff that is both friendly and knowledgeable.

the actor. His mother was passing through and was forced to stop at the Crown Hotel, where he was delivered.

This is Armstrong country, and when Neil Armstrong, the first man to set foot on the moon, came to Langholm in 1972. he given the freedom of the burgh. The **Armstrong Clan Museum** at Lodge Walk in Castleholm traces the history of one of the greatest Borders family. **Langholm Castle**, which is ruinous (though there has been some restoration work done on it) dates from the 16th century, and stands at the confluence of the River Esk and the Ewes Water. It can be accessed from the car park beside the museum. On the last Friday in July the annual **Common Riding Ceremony** is held in the town.

On a hillside to the east of the town is the **Malcolm Monument**, in memory of Sir John Malcolm, who died in 1833. He was born at Burnfoot, a farm near Langholm, in 1769, and became a major-general who distinguished himself in India.

WESTERKIRK

29 miles NE of Dumfries on the B709

The parish of Westerkirk lies a few miles north west of the Langholm, and it was here that **Thomas Telford** the great civil engineer was born in 1757. The son of a shepherd, he left school at 14 and was apprenticed to a stone mason in Langholm. However, he was destined for greater things, and rose to be the greatest civil engineer of his generation, building the Ellesmere Canal, the Caledonian Canal and the Menai Straits Bridge in Wales. Within the parish is the unique **Bentpath Library**, founded in 1793 for the use of the antimony miners who used to work in the nearby Meggat Valley. It is still in use today, though only the people of the local parishes may borrow from its stock of 8,000 books. On his death in 1834, Thomas Telford bequeathed money to it.

LOCKERBIE

10 miles NE of Dumfries off the M74

This quiet market town in Annandale is remembered for one thing - the **Lockerbie Disaster** of 1988. On the evening of December 21st, Pan Am flight 103 exploded in mid air after a terrorist bomb was detonated within its hold. The cockpit crashed into a field at Tundergarth, two and-a-half miles east of the town, and its fuselage crashed into the town itself, killing all the passengers and crew, as well as 11 people on the ground. **Remembrance Garden** is situated within the town cemetery to the west of the motorway on the A709. It is a peaceful spot, though there is still an air of raw emotion about the place, and no one visits without developing a lump in the throat.

On December 6th, 1593 the **Battle of**

QUEENS HOTEL

Annan Road, Lockerbie, Dumfriesshire DG11 2RB
Tel: 01576 202415   Fax: 01567 203901
e-mail: queens_hotel@hotmail.com
website: www.queenshotellockerbie.co.uk

Situated conveniently close to the M74, the **Queens Hotel** sits in three acres of landscaped gardens. There are 21 comfortable en-suite bedrooms, each one having a colour TV, hair dryer, direct dial telephone, shaver point, complimentary toiletries and tea/coffee making facilities.

The food is outstanding, with all culinary tastes catered for, and is served in the stylish and spacious restaurant. Why not relax in the oak-lined lounge bar and enjoy a quiet drink after a hard day's driving? The cocktail area serves a wide range of drinks, including beers, wines, single malts and soft

drinks, or you can order coffees and teas in the coffee lounge area.

The hotel boasts a leisure complex where hotel guests can enjoy the swimming pool, sauna, jacuzzi and full-size snooker table, while the more energetic can have a work-out in the well equipped gym.

Lockerbie makes the ideal base from which to explore Dumfries and Galloway and the Scottish Borders. It sits 14 miles from Gretna, 23 miles from Carlisle, 72 miles from Glasgow and 73 miles from Edinburgh making it an ideal stopping off point as you head north or south.

CHARIOTS OF FIRE

Boreland, Lockerbie, Dumfriesshire DG11 2LL
Tel: 01576 610248
e-mail: amanda@chariots.org.uk
website: www.chariots.org.uk

The aptly named **Chariots of Fire** is a three star, top quality equestrian centre that specialises in dressage and chariot driving. Here you will find the Chariots of Fire Stunt Team. The centre was set up in 1995 and expanded in 1998 into a driving centre where tuition is available in both disciplines. There is stabling and grazing for over 40 horses and ponies, an indoor arena, outdoor menage and purpose-built driving hazards; along with miles of wonderful driving in the surrounding picturesque countryside to improve fitness. The centre specialises in competition preparation and schooling, both ridden and driven, from novice to advanced.

In the typically Scottish farmhouse of Nether Boreland, clients stay in excellent bed and breakfast

accommodation. There are two double rooms, both en-suite, each with TV, tea/coffee making facilities, clock radio, hair dryer and so on. Even with all these extras, charges are surprisingly reasonable. After a hearty Scottish breakfast you can take advantage of all the surrounding countryside has to offer. There's golf, fishing and quad bike riding, and the farm is on a number of recognised walking and cycling routes. You can even bring your own horse and also take advantage of the excellent four legged accommodation.

Dryfe Sands took place on the banks of the Dryfe Water north of the town. The two great families in the area - the Maxwells and the Johnstones - were forever fighting about who should be the dominant family on the western border. Eventually the Maxwells brought things to a head by marching into Johnstone territory with 2,000 men. The Johnstones could only muster 400, and a Maxwell victory seemed to be a foregone conclusion. However, when they met in battle at Dryfe Sands, the Johnstones won the day, killing over 700 Maxwells.

To the south of the town is **Burnswark**, where 2nd century Roman forts are built on the site of an Iron Age fort.

HIGHTAE
0 miles E of Dumfries on a minor road off the B7020

Rammerscales House is an 18th century manor house (not open to the public) with fine views from its grounds. There is a walled garden and a woodland walk. It is only open in August each year.

LOCHMABEN
8 miles NE of Dumfries on the A709

Lochmaben is a small royal burgh in Annandale. In the vicinity are many small lochs in which is found the vendace, a rare species of fish. Near the Castle Loch stand the scant remains of Lochmaben Castle (Historic Scotland), which originally covered 16 acres. It can only be viewed from the outside. An earlier 12th century castle (now no more that a small earthwork on the local golf course) was the home of the Bruce family, Lords of Annandale, and is said to be the birthplace of Robert the Bruce (later Robert I), though Turnberry in Ayrshire lays a similar, and perhaps more likely, claim (see also Turnberry).

About three miles to the southwest is Skipmyre, where **William Paterson** was born. He was the driving force behind the ill-fated Darien Scheme of 1698, which sought to establish a Scottish colony in modern day Panama. Many Scots who went to Central America perished there, and it almost bankrupted the country. He was more successful in another venture - he founded the Bank of England in 1694 (see also New Abbey).

TORTHORWALD
4 miles E of Dumfries on the A709

Within the village, on a narrow road off the A709, is the **Cruck Cottage**, an early 18th century example of a thatched cottage made in the traditional way, with "crucks", or thick, curved wooden supports. They were placed some yards apart within holes in the ground so that they leaned towards each other, forming the shape of an "A". The ruined 14th century **Torthorwald Castle** was once a stronghold of the Carlyle and Kirkpatrick families. In 1544 Lord Carlyle destroyed the castle during a dispute with his sister-in-law.

CAERLAVEROCK
7 miles S of Dumfries on the B725

Think of an old, romantic, turreted medieval castle surrounded by a water-filled moat, and you could be thinking of **Caerlaverock Castle** (Historic Scotland). An earlier castle was built by the Maxwells as their main seat to the southeast of the present castle, but this was soon abandoned in favour of the present site. It dates from the 13th century, and was attacked by Edward I in 1300 during the Wars of Independence. It is triangular in shape, with a turret at two corners and a double turret at the other, where the entrance is located. It was attacked by Covenanters in 1640 and dismantled, though in the early 1600s the then Earl of Nithsdale had some fine courtyard buildings constructed within the walls in the Renaissance style.

Caerlaverock Wildfowl and Wetlands Trust is about three miles west of the castle, and is situated in a 1,400-acre nature reserve. Here a wide variety of wildlife can be observed, including swans and barnacle geese. If you're

Caerlaverock Castle

lucky, you may also come across the extremely rare natterjack toad. There are three observation towers, 20 hides and a wild swan observatory linked by nature trails and screen approaches. There are also picnic areas, a gift shop, refreshments and binocular hire. Some facilities are wheelchair friendly.

The place is on the well-signposted **Solway Coast Heritage Trail**, which stretches from Gretna in the east to Stranraer in the west.

ANNAN

14 miles E of Dumfries, on the A75

The picturesque old Royal Burgh of Annan, even though it is a mile from the coast, was once a thriving seaport, and had a boat-building yard. Even today there is a small, silted up quay on the River Annan. The **Burns Cairn** stands nearby commemorating the fact that Robert Burns visited here as an excise man.

The predominant stone in the town is red sandstone, epitomised by the handsome **Town Hall** of 1878, which dominates the High Street.

Edward Irving, the founder of the Catholic Apostolic Church, which thrived on elaborate ceremony and a

complicated hierarchy of ministers and priests, was born here in 1792. He started his career as a clergyman in the Church of Scotland church in Regent Square, London, and earned a great reputation as a preacher and what we would now call a "Pentecostal" scholar, for which he was ejected from the Chruch of Scotland in 1833.

Four years earlier, **Hugh Clapperton** the explorer had been born in the town. At the age of 13 he became a cabin boy on a ship sailing between Liverpool and North America, and later went to the Mediterranean after being press ganged into the Royal Navy. He died in Nigeria in 1827 while searching for the source of the Niger. His notebooks and diaries have been published under the name *Difficult and Dangerous Roads*. Another Annan man was **Thomas Blacklock**, born in 1721. He was the first blind man to be ordained a minister in the Church of Scotland. **Annan Parish Church** in the High Street, with its stumpy spire, dates from 1786. The place has associations with the Bruce family, who were Lords of Annandale. In Bank Street is the **Historic Resources Centre**, a small museum that puts on a programme of displays and exhibitions.

Haaf Net Fishing is a means of catching fish that stretches back to Viking times, and it is still carried out at the mouth of the River Annan from April to August each year. The fishermen stand chest deep in the water wielding large haaf nets, which are attached to long wooden frames. In 1538 James V granted the haaf net fishermen of Annan a royal charter. In 1992 the rights of the fishermen were challenged in court by the owners of a time-share development further up the river, but the judge took the view that the charter still held good today.

South of the town, at one time, was the **Solway Viaduct**, a railway bridge that connected Dumfriesshire to Cumbria across the Solway Firth. It was opened for passenger trains in 1870, and at the time was the longest railway bridge across water in Britain. In 1881 parts of the bridge were damaged when great ice flows smashed into its stanchions. The then keeper of the bridge, John Welch, plus two colleagues, remained in their cabin on the bridge as the lumps of ice, some as big as 27 yards square, careered into the bridge's supports. At 3.30 in the morning, when disaster seemed imminent, they were ordered to leave. Two lengths of the bridge, one 50 feet long, and one 300 feet long, collapsed into the firth, and 37 girders and 45 pillars were smashed beyond repair. However, unlike the Tay Bridge disaster, there was no loss of life. Finally, in 1934, the bridge was dismantled, and all that is left to see nowadays are the approaches on both shores, and a stump in the middle of the water.

To the northeast of the town is the outline of **Chapelcross Nuclear Power Station**, opened in 1959, making it one of the oldest in the country.

RUTHWELL
10 miles SE of Dumfries off the B724

Within the **Parish Church** of 1800 is the famous 18-feet high **Ruthwell Cross**. It dates from about AD 800, when this part of Scotland was within the Anglian kingdom of Northumbria. The carvings show scenes from the Gospels, twining vines and verses from an old poem called The Dream of the Rood, at one time thought to have been written by Caedmon of Whitby.

In 1810, the Revd Henry Duncan founded the world's first savings bank in the village, and the small **Savings Bank Museum** has displays and artefacts about the savings bank movement.

POWFOOT
13 miles SE of Dumfries on a minor road off the B724

Today Powfoot is a quiet village on the Solway coast. But in the late 19th and

---

SAVINGS BANK MUSEUM

Ruthwell, Dumfries DG1 4NN
Tel: 01387 870640 e-mail: info@savingsbankmuseum.co.uk
website: www.savingsbankmuseum.co.uk
Dr Henry Duncan was an accomplished artist and some of his work is displayed in the museum, but he is best remembered as the man who identified the first fossil footprints in Britain. Minister of the Ruthwell parish church for 50 years, he opened the world's first commercial savings bank in 1810. The museum also houses a large collection of early home savings boxes, coins and bank notes from many parts of the world.Open 10am to 4pm Tuesday to Saturday and Monday Bank Holidays. Admission free.

early 20th centuries plans were laid to make it a grand holiday resort, with hotels, formal gardens, woodland walks, a promenade, a pier, golf courses and bowling greens. The whole scheme eventually collapsed, though some of the attractions were actually built. Now the village is famous for its red brick housing and terraces, which look incongruous on the shores of the Solway, but wouldn't look out of place in Lancashire.

EASTRIGGS

18 miles E of Dumfries on the A75

A huge government works manufacturing explosives and gunpowder once stretched from Longtown in the east to Annan in the west, a total of nine miles. The **Eastriggs Heritage Project**, in St John's Church on Dunedin Road, traces the lives of the 30,000 workers who manufactured what Sir Arthur Conan Doyle called "The Devil's Porridge". At its height the whole complex employed over 30,000 people from all over the United Kingdom.

GRETNA GREEN

23 miles E of Dumfries off the M74

This small village, just across the border from England, is the "romance" capital of Britain. In the 18th century it was the first stopping place in Scotland for coaches travelling north, so was the ideal place for English runaways to get married.

In 1754 irregular marriages in England were made illegal, and the legal age at which people could get married without parental consent was set at 21. However, this didn't apply in Scotland, and soon a roaring trade in runaway marriages got underway in the village. The actual border between Scotland and England is the River Sark, and one of the places where marriages took place was the **Old Toll House**

(now bypassed by the M74) on the Scottish side of the river. Another place was **Gretna Hall**. Dating from 1710, this is now a hotel.

But perhaps the most famous was the **Old Blacksmith's Shop**, built in about 1712. A wedding ceremony in front of the anvil became the popular means of tying the knot, and the Anvil Priests, as they became known, charged anything from a dram of whisky to a guinea to conduct what was a perfectly legal ceremony. By 1856, the number of weddings had dropped, due to what was called the "Lord Brougham Act", which required that at least one of the parties to the marriage had to have been resident in Scotland for the previous 21 days. This act was only repealed in 1979.

However, couples still come from all over the world to get married before the anvil in Gretna Green, though the ceremony is no more than a confirmation of vows taken earlier in the registry office. The Old Blacksmith's Shop is still open,

Piper, Gretna Green

and houses an exhibition on the irregular marriage trade.

Gretna Green was within the **Debatable Lands**, a stretch of land which, as its name implies, was claimed by both Scotland and England. It was therefore a lawless area in the 15th and 16th centuries, as no country's laws were recognised, and no one could adequately police it. About a mile to the southwest is the **Lochmaben Stone**, a huge rock where representatives from the two countries met to air grievances and seek justice. It is also sometimes known as the "Clochmaben" Stone, Maben being a shadowy figure associated with King Arthur.

In the nearby village of **Gretna** is the **Gretna Gateway Outlet Village**, a complex of shops selling designer label fashions.

ECCLEFECHAN

14 miles E of Dumfries on the B7076

This small village's rather curious name means the church of St Fechan or Fechin, a 7th century Irish saint. Within it you will find **Carlyle's Birthplace** (National Trust for Scotland), where Thomas Carlyle was born in 1795. Called "The Arched House", it was built on the main street by Thomas's father and uncle, who were both master masons. Within it is a collection of memorabilia about the great man (see also Dunscore). At the time of writing, the house was closed to the public, though this may change. Please check.

DALTON

9 miles E of Dumfries on the B7020

This little village has picturesque cottages dating from the mid-18th century. The parish church dates from the late 19th century, though the remains of an earlier church, with some medieval fragments, stands in the kirkyard. Half a mile west, on a minor road, is **Dalton Pottery**, which sells a range of porcelain gittware. Young and old alike can also have fun decorating pots and tiles using ceramic felt-tipped pens, which are fired in a small kiln and ready to take away the same day. You can also throw a pot on a wheel, though you have to return to collect it some time later.

KIRKCONNEL (KIRTLEBRIDGE)

17 mile E of Dumfries off the M74

In the kirkyard of the ruined Kirkconnel Church are said to be the graves of **Fair Helen of Kirkconnel Lee** and her lover **Adam Fleming**. Their story is a romantic one, and a famous ballad was written about it. Helen Irving was loved by two men, Adam Fleming and a man named Bell (whose first name isn't known) of nearby Bonshawe Tower. Helen found herself drawn towards Adam, and Bell was consumed with jealousy. He therefore decided to kill his rival. He waylaid the couple close to the kirkyard, and pulled out a pistol. As he fired, Helen threw herself in front of her lover, and was shot dead. There are two versions of the story after this. One says that Adam killed Bell where he stood, and another says he pursued him to Madrid, where he killed him. Either way, he was inconsolable, and joined the army. But he could never forget Helen, and one day he returned to Kirkconnel, lay on her tombstone, and died of a broken heart. He was buried beside her. It's a poignant tale, but there is no proof that the events actually took place.

KIRKPATRICK FLEMING

20 miles E of Dumfries off the M74

This pleasant little village is visited mainly to see **Robert the Bruce's Cave**, where the great man is supposed to have seen the spider, though similar claims are made for other caves in both Scotland and Ireland. Sir William Irving hid Robert the Bruce here for three months while he was being hunted by the English.

CANONBIE

26 miles E of Dumfries on the B6357

Canonbie means the "town of the canons", because a priory once stood here. The English destroyed it in 1542, and some of the stones may have been used in the building of **Hollows Bridge** across the River Esk, Scotland's second fastest flowing river. This is the heart of the Debatable Lands, and was a safe haven for reivers. Beyond the bridge, and marked by a stone and plaque, is the site of **Gilnockie Castle**, home of **Johnnie Armstrong**, one of the greatest reivers of them all. So much of a threat was he to the relationship between Scotland and England that James V hanged him in 1530. The story goes that Johnnie and his men were invited to a great gathering at Carlanrig in Teviotdale where they would meet the king, who promised them safe passage. Taking him at his word, Johnnie and a band of men set out. However, when they got there, James had them all strung up on the spot. Perhaps the most amazing aspect of this tale is that the king was no world-weary warrior, but an 18-year-old lad at the time. Some of the castle's stones also went into building Hollows Bridge.

    Gilnockie Tower, which dates from the 16th century, was a roofless ruin until 1980, but now it houses a small museum and Clan Armstrong library.

The **Scots Dyke**, two miles south of the village, was erected in the 16th century in an attempt to delineate the boundary between Scotland and England. It consists of a "dyke", or low, earthen wall and an accompanying ditch.

NEW ABBEY

6 miles S of Dumfries on the A710

This attractive little village sits in the shadow of **The Criffel**, a 1,866 feet high hill that can be seen from miles around. Within the village you'll find the beautiful red sandstone ruins of **Sweetheart Abbey** (Historic Scotland), which date from the 13th and 14th centuries. It was founded for the Cistercians in 1273 by Devorgilla, Lady of Galloway in her own right (see also Dumfries). Her husband was John Balliol of Barnard Castle in County Durham, who founded Balliol College in Oxford. After his death she carried his embalmed heart around with her in a small casket, and when she herself died in 1289, she was buried along with the heart in front of the abbey's high altar. The Cistercian monks gave the name "Dolce Cor" to the abbey, and thus was born the word

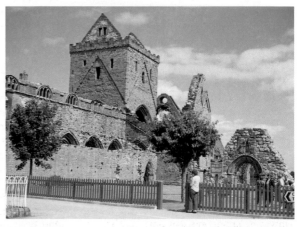

Sweetheart Abbey, New Abbey

"sweetheart". In its graveyard lies William Paterson, founder of the Bank of England and chief proponent of the Darien Scheme in 1698 (see also Lochmaben).

At the other end of the village is the **New Abbey Corn Mill** (Historic Scotland), dating from the late 18th century. It is in full working order, and there are regular demonstrations on how a water powered mill works. The original mill on the site is thought to have belonged to the monks of Sweetheart Abbey. The millpond behind the mill is thought to have been constructed by them.

Shambellie House is a large mansion designed by David Bryce on the outskirts of New Abbey, which houses the **Shambellie House Museum of Costume**, part of the National Museums of Scotland. The house and its collection were given to the National Museums in 1977 by the then owner, Charles Stewart, and most of the costumes, which range from Victorian to the 1930s, are now displayed in appropriate settings.

KIRKBEAN
6 miles SW of Dumfries, on the A710

About two miles south of the village is the estate of **Arbigland**, birthplace in 1747 of the founder of the American navy, **John Paul Jones** (see also Kirkcudbright). Paul was the son of an Arbigland gardener, and went to sea when he was about 13 years old. The cottage in which he was born is now a small museum. **Kirkbean Parish Church** was built in 1776, and inside is a font presented by the American Navy in 1945. To continue the American theme, **Dr James Craik**, Physician General of the United States Army during the American Revolution, was also born on the estate. However, James was not born in the

same humble circumstances as John Paul Jones. His father Robert was a Member of Parliament, and owned the estate.

BEESWING
9 miles W of Dumfries, on the A711

This small village was laid out in the 19th century. The only remarkable thing about it is its name. It must be the only village in Scotland that is named after a horse. Beeswing was one of the most famous horses in the early 19th century, its finest performance being in the Doncaster Cup, which it won in 1840. A local man won so much money on the race that he opened an inn called The Beeswing, and the village grew up round it.

CROCKETFORD
9 miles W of Dumfries, on the A75

It was at Crocketford that the sorry tale of Elspeth Buchan, who founded a religious sect called the Buchanites, came to a macabre end. Part of the sect's beliefs was that Elspeth was immortal, and that she could bestow immortality on others by breathing on them. After having been driven out of Irvine, she and her followers headed south towards Dumfriesshire and settled there. Alas, Elspeth disappointed her followers by dying a natural death, and the sect broke up.

But one man, who lived in Crocketford, still believed in her immortality, and that she would rise from the dead. He therefore acquired her body and kept it in a cupboard at the top of the stairs in his cottage, where it gradually mummified. Eventually he built an extension to the cottage, on the other side of the wall from the fireplace, and kept the corpse there. He even had a small opening cut through the wall so that he could examine the corpse every day to see if it had come alive again. Of course, it didn't. though, this never shook his belief in her resurection, and the body remained in the cottage with him until his own death. (see also Dunscore and Irvine).

KIRKCUDBRIGHT

Kirkcudbright (pronounced "Kirk-coo-bray") is one of the loveliest small towns in Scotland, Its name simply means the kirk of St Cuthbert, as the original church built here was dedicated to that saint. It was an established town by the 11th century, and has been a royal burgh since at least 1455. It sits close to the mouth of the Dee, and is still a working port with a small fishing fleet.

Kirkcudbright was once the county town of Kirkcudbrightshire, also known as the "Stewartry of Kirkcudbright". It is a place of brightly painted Georgian, Regency and Victorian houses, making it

a colourful and interesting place to explore. This part of Galloway has a very mild climate, thanks to the Gulf Stream washing its shores, and this, as well as the quality of light to be found here, encouraged the founding of an artists' colony. On a summer's morning, the edge between light and shadow can be as sharp as a knife, whereas during the day it becomes diffused and soft, and artists have been reaching for their paints and palettes for years to try and capture these two qualities. Even today, straw-hatted artists can still be seen at the harbour-side, trying to capture the scene.

It is said that St Cuthbert himself founded the first church here, which was located within the cemetery to the east of the town. Down through the years, gravediggers have often turned up carved stones that belonged to it. Within the graveyard is **Billy Marshall's Grave**. Billy was known as the "King of Galloway Tinkers", and the gravestone states that he died in 1792 aged 120 years. Don't be surprised to see coins lying on top of the gravestone. It's supposed to be an old gypsy custom, whereby a passing gypsy or tinker without money could use the coins to buy food. The money nowadays is usually left by tourists, with the main beneficiaries being local children.

The present **Parish Church** is a grand affair in red sandstone near the centre of the town, and dates from 1838. Parts of a much older church are to be found near the harbour. **Greyfriar's Kirk** is all that is left of a 16th century Franciscan monastery that stood here, though it has been largely rebuilt over the

Kirkcudbright

GALLOWAY HYDROS VISITOR CENTRE

Tangland Power Station, Kirkudbright
Tel: 01557 330114 e-mail: visit.galloway@scottishpower.com

A guided tour of Galloway Hydros will give you an insight into the force of nature that is captured, channelled and released back into the environment, enabling Scottish Power to produce pure, clean energy. The Visitor Centre tells the story of the construction of the Galloway Hydros in the 1930s and the tour takes you into the power station, the control room and the turbine hall. You will learn about the operation of the power stations and how they contribute to the national electricity grid system. Close by is the impressive Tongland Dam and Reservoir - the power source. Here, you might catch a glimpse of a migrating salmon. A picnic area and refreshments room allow you to relax.

years. Within it is the grand tomb of **Sir Thomas MacLellan of Bombie** and his wife Grizzell Maxwell, which was erected in 1597. But the tomb isn't all it seems. The couple's son, in an effort to save money, used effigies from an earlier tomb within what is essentially a Renaissance canopy. The friary is thought to have been founded in 1224 by Alan, Lord of Galloway and father of Devorgilla, who founded Sweetheart Abbey. The kirk sits on a slight rise known as the **Moat Brae**, where Roland, Lord of Galloway in the 12th century, may have had a castle.

Nearby, in Castle Street, are the substantial ruins of **MacLellan's Castle** (Historic Scotland), built by the same Sir Thomas who lies in the Greyfriar's Kirk. It isn't really a castle, but a grand town house, and Sir Thomas, who was obviously his son's role model where thrift was concerned, used the stones from the friary as building material. Sir Thomas was a local magnate and favourite of the king who became Provost of Kirkcudbright. The castle is open to the public. Watch out for the small room behind the fireplace in the Great Hall. Sir Thomas used to hide himself there and listen to what was being said about him in the Great Hall through a small opening in the wall called the "Laird's Lug".

Walk up the side of the castle into Castle Bank, passing the whitewashed

Harbour Cottage Gallery, where there are regular exhibitions of work by local artists, and you arrive at the **High Street**. This must be one of the most charming and colourful streets in Scotland. The elegant Georgian and Regency houses - some of them quite substantial - are painted in bright, uncompromising colours, such as yellow, green and pink. **Auchingool House** is the oldest, having been built in 1617 for the McCullochs of Auchengool. **Broughton House**, dating from the 18th century, is now owned by the National Trust for Scotland, and was the home of A.E. Hornel the artist. He was one of the Glasgow Boys, and died in 1933. The house is very much as it was when he lived there. Behind the house is the marvellous **Japanese Gardens**, influenced by trips that Hornel made to the Far East.

Further along the street is **Greengates Close**, (not open to the public) which was the home of Jessie M. King, another artist. A few yards further on the High Street takes a dog leg to the east, and here stands the early 17th century **Tolbooth**, which has been refurbished and now houses a museum and art gallery telling the story of the artists' colony. The Queen opened it in 1993. This was the former town house and jail, and John Paul Jones, founder of the American navy, was imprisoned here at one time for murder. He got his revenge in later years when he returned to the town aboard an American ship and shelled the nearby **St Mary's Isle**, where the seat of the Earl of Selkirk was located and a medieval priory of nuns once stood.

This "isle" is in fact a peninsula, and to confuse matters even further, one of the smaller bays in Kirkcudbright Bay (itself an inlet of the Solway Firth) is called **Manxman's Lake**, one of the few instances in Scotland of a natural stretch of water being called a lake rather than a loch (see also Lake of Menteith, Stenton and Ellon). A walk up St Mary's Wynd beside the Tolbooth and past the modern school takes you to **Castledykes**, where once stood a royal castle. Edward I stayed here, as did Henry VI and Queen Margaret after their defeat at the Battle of Towton in 1461 during the Wars of the Roses, and James IV used it as a staging post on his many pilgrimages to Whithorn. In St Mary's Street is the **Stewartry Museum**, which has many artefacts and displays on the history of the Stewartry of Kirkcudbright. On the opposite side of the street is the **Town Hall**, where themed painting exhibitions are held every year.

The town also has its literary associations. **Dorothy L. Sayers** set her Lord Peter Wimsey whodunit *Five Red Herrings* among the artists' colony. It's not one of her best, as it over-relies on a detailed knowledge of train times between Kirkcudbrightshire and Ayrshire, and of the paints found on an artist's palette. **Ronald Searle** also knew the town, and he based his **St Trinians** innocents on St Trinian's School in Edinburgh, attended by the daughters of Kirkcudbright artist W. Miles Johnston.

Kirkcudbright was where the village scenes in the cult movie **The Wicker Man** were filmed, and indeed many locations in Dumfries and Galloway -

and even Ayrshire - stood in for the fictional Summerisles, where the action is supposed to have taken place.

AROUND KIRKCUDBRIGHT

TONGLAND
2 miles N of Kirkcudbright on the A711

The small village of Tongland was once the site of the great **Tongland Abbey**, founded in 1218 by Fergus, Lord of Galloway, and the scant remains - no more than a medieval archway in a piece of preserved wall - can still be seen in the kirkyard. The abbey's most famous inmate was Abbot John Damien, known as the "Frenzied Friar of Tongland", who achieved fame by jumping off the ramparts of Stirling Castle in an attempt to fly like a bird (see also Stirling). Tours are available of **Tongland Power Station**, the largest generating station in the great Galloway hydroelectric scheme built in the 1930s. Close by is **Tongland Bridge**, a graceful structure across the Dee designed by Thomas Telford and built in 1805.

LOCH KEN
9 miles N of Kirkcudbright between the A713 and the A762

Loch Ken is a narrow stretch of water almost nine miles long, and nowhere wider than a mile. It was created in the 1930s as the result of the great Galloway hydroelectric scheme, with the turbines being housed in the power station at Tongland, further down the Dee. Other schemes were constructed at Clatteringshaws and Loch Doon.

Loch Ken is a favourite spot for bird watching and sports such as sailing, fishing and water skiing, and round the shores are small nature reserves. Details about using the loch are available from the **Loch Ken Marina**, off the A713 on the eastern shore. At the Marina you can also find the Loch Ken Water Ski School.

NEW GALLOWAY

17 miles N of Kirkcudbright on the A762

Though New Galloway is a small village with a population of about 300, it is still a proud royal burgh - the smallest in Scotland, boasting a town hall - and a picturesque place. It is a planned burgh, having been laid out in the early 1600s by Viscount Kenmure. This part of Kirkcudbrightshire is known as the **Glenkens**, an area combining the high drama of lonely moorland with fertile, wooded valleys. Within **Kells Churchyard**, north of the town, is the grave of a Covenanter, shot in 1685.

A mile to the south, near Loch Ken, are the ruins of Kenmure Castle, which belonged to the Gordon family. To say that the building is unlucky would be an understatement, as it has been burnt down three times and rebuilt twice. After the last burning in the 1880s, it was left as a shell.

Each year in early August New Galloway plays host to the **Scottish Alternative Games**. It's a refreshing antidote to all the traditional games held in Scotland, where tossing the caber, throwing the hammer, shot putting and Highland dancing take place. Instead there are sports such as gird and cleek (hoop and stick) racing, hurlin' (throwing) the curlin' stane, snail racing, flingin' the herd's bunnet (throwing the herdsman's bonnet) and tossin' the sheaf.

BALMACLELLAN

18 miles N of Kirkcudbright off the A712

This attractive little village was the home of **Robert Paterson**, a stonemason who was the model for Old Mortality in Scott's book of the same name. He travelled Scotland cleaning up the monuments and gravestones of the Covenanters, a group of men and women who fought Charles II's attempts to impose bishops on the Church of Scotland. Eventually he left home for good to concentrate on this work, leaving behind a no doubt angry wife and five children. Up to his death in 1800, he continued to travel the country, usually on an old grey pony. A statue of him and his horse sits inside the kirkyard of the whitewashed parish church

Just outside the village you will find **The Balmaclellan Clog and Shoe Workshop**, where 20 styles of footwear are made by hand. Visitors can look round the workshop and see shoes and clogs being made.

ST JOHN'S TOWN OF DALRY

19 miles N of Kirkcudbright on the A713

St John's Town of Dalry, sometimes known simply as Dalry, lies on the Southern Uplands Way, and is a picturesque Glenkens village with many old cottages. It got its name from the Knights Hospitaller of the Order of St John of Jerusalem, an order of military monks which owned the surrounding lands in medieval times.

Within the village is a curious chair-shaped stone known as **St John's Stone**. Local tradition says that John the Baptist rested in it. In the kirkyard is the **Gordon Aisle**, part of the medieval church that stood here before the present church of 1832. When a reservoir was created at lonely **Lochinvar** near Dalry in 1968, the waters of the loch were raised, covering the scant ruins of a castle owned by the Gordons. This was the home of the famous Young Lochinvar, written about by Scott in his famous lines from

Marmion:

*"O, young Lochinvar is come out of
the west,*
*Through all the wide border his steed
was the best..."*

A cairn by the loch side, which is reached by a narrow track, records the existence of the castle. It was built using stones from the castle ruins.

Earlston Castle, overlooking Earlston Loch to the north of the village, was also a Gordon stronghold. It was the birthplace of Catherine Gordon, later Mrs Catherine Stewart, who befriended Burns and encouraged him to write poetry when she lived in Stair Castle in Ayrshire. She was buried, along with two daughters, in Stair kirkyard in Ayrshire (see also Stair).

Carlingwark Loch, Castle Douglas

CARSPHAIRN

27 miles N of Kirkcudbright on the A713

Close to this quiet village there used to be lead mines. John Loudon MacAdam the roads pioneer, whose father came from near the village, experimented on his revolutionary road surfaces on the A713 north of the village (see also Ayr and Moffat). The **Carsphairn Heritage Centre** has displays and exhibits on the history of the village.

CASTLE DOUGLAS

9 miles NE of Kirkcudbright off the A75

Castle Douglas is a pleasant town based round what was a small village known as "Carlingwark". It was founded in the 18th century by William Douglas, a local merchant who earned his money trading with Virginia and the West Indies. He wanted to establish a thriving manufacturing town based on the woollen industry, and though he was only partly successful, he did lay the foundations for a charming town where

MARKET INN HOTEL

6/7 Queen Street, Castle Douglas, Dumfries & Galloway DG7 1HX
Tel/Fax: 01556 502105
e-mail: chris@themarkethotel.co.uk website: www.themarkethotel.co.uk
Good food and a warm welcome awaits you at the **Market Inn Hotel** in
Castle Douglas, Scotland's food town. It is a friendly, family-owned
establishment boasting nine extremely comfortable and fully en suite

rooms, all non-smoking. There are three bars within the hotel, and here you can relax and unwind after a hard day exploring an area that is renowned for its history and beauty. All the food is home-cooked, and there is a wide ranging menu featuring everything from a snack to à la carte. Well behaved pets are welcome by prior arrangement.

In House Chocolates & Deli

128 King street, Castle Douglas, Kirkcudbrightshire DG7 1LU
Tel: 01556 503037 e-mail: mail@inhousechocolates.co.uk
Fax: 01556 504430 website: www.inhousechocolates.co.uk

Set in the old picturesque burgh of Castle Douglas, the **In House Chocolate & Deli** not only produces delicious, award-winning hand-crafted chocolates, but sells a wide range of pâtes, preserves, cheeses and beers. It has earned an enviable reputation for the quality of its produce, and you can even see how the chocolates are produced on the premises using only the finest ingredients. It's a fascinating process, and if you're holidaying in Dumfries and Galloway, or just passing through, you can't afford to miss this wonderful shop.

some of his original 18th century buildings can still be seen. On the edge of the town is **Carlingwark Loch**, where crannogs (dwellings built on artificial islands) have been discovered. It was joined to the River Dee in 1765 by **Carlingwark Lane**, a narrow canal. Marl, a limey clay used as manure, was dug from the bed of the loch and taken down river to Kirkcudbright on barges.

In Market Street is the **Castle Douglas Art Gallery**, gifted to the town in 1938 by the artist Ethel Bristowe. There is a continuing programme of painting, sculpture and craft exhibitions.

Castle Douglas is Scotland's food town, and offers real Scottish produce, such as meat, fish, vegetables, baking and drinks in its many small, specialist shops. The **Sulworth Brewery** is in King Street, and

here you can see the brewing process from barley to beer, and enjoy a complimentary half pint of Criffel or Knockendoch real ale. The **Ken Dee Marches Nature Reserve** follows the woodland and marshes along the River Dee and Loch Ken, north west of the town.

Threave Castle

8 miles N of Kirkcudbright, close to the A75

On an island in the River Dee stand the magnificent ruins of Threave Castle (Historic Scotland), reached by a small ferry that answers the call of a bell on a jetty on the riverbank. It was built by Archibald Douglas, 3rd Earl of Douglas - known as Archibald the Grim - soon after he became Lord of Galloway in 1369. It was Archibald's father, the "Good Sir James", who died while on his way to the Holy Land with the heart of Robert the Bruce (see also Melrose, Cardross and Dunfermline). When Archibald died at Threave in 1400, he was the most powerful man in southern Scotland, and almost independent of the king, Robert III. It was Archibald's son, also called Archibald, who married Princess Margaret, daughter of

Threave Castle

THREAVE

Castle Douglas, Dumfries & Galloway, DG7 I RX
Tel: 01556 502575 Fax: 01556 502683
Ranger/natural ist: tel (01556) 503702
e-mail threave@nts.org.uk website: www.nts.org.uk

Threave Garden is delightful in all seasons. It is best known for its spectacular springtime daffodils (nearly 200 varieties), but herbaceous beds are colourful in summer and trees and the heather garden are striking in autumn. The Victorian house is home to the Trust's School of Practical Gardening. The principal rooms in **Threave House** opened to the public for the first time in 2002 and have attracted great interest ever since. The interiors have been restored to their appearance in the 1930s, and from the house visitors can enjoy impressive vistas of the Galloway countryside. Guided walks. Maxwell Collection of local bygones in the Visitor Centre on show. Plant Centre.

Threave Estate is a wildfowl refuge and is designated a Special Protection Area for its breeding waders and wintering wildfowl. The important wetlands are designated an Area of Special Scientific Interest. Threave provides a good example of integrated management of the land, taking account of agriculture, forestry and nature conservation. Marked walks include a 2.5 km estate trail through this variety of landscapes, and hides provide good cover to observe bird activity. A Countryside Centre in the old stables highlights nature conservation, forestry and agriculture at Threave.

Robert III (see also Dumfries). When James II laid siege to the castle in 1455 to curtail the power of the Douglases, it took two months before the occupants finally surrendered.

THREAVE GARDENS

7 miles NE of Kirkcudbright, on the A75

Threave Gardens and Estate (National Trust for Scotland) surround a house built in 1872 by William Gordon, a Liverpool businessman. In 1948 the estate was given to the National Trust for Scotland by William's grandson. The gardens were created from scratch, and now house the Trust's School of Practical Gardening. The house itself is open to the public, with its interiors restored to how they would have looked when the

place was owned by the Gordon family. The Maxwell Collection of local bygones is on display within the visitor centre.

KIPPFORD

10 miles NE of Kirkcudbright off the A710

The tides in the Solway Firth are among the fastest in Britain, but this hasn't prevented the picturesque village of Kippford from becoming a great yachting centre. It was once a thriving port and fishing village, and it even had its own shipyard. Like its neighbour Rockcliffe, five miles away, it was also once a smuggling village.

PALNACKIE

10 miles NE of Kirkcudbright on the A711

This small, attractive village on the west

bank of the Water of Urr is a mile from the sea, though at one time it was a thriving port. However, the meanderings of the river meant that ships were usually towed upstream by teams of horses. Each year, in summer, it hosts one of the most unusual competitions in Great Britain - the annual **World Flounder Tramping Championships**, held at the end of July. People come from all over the world to compete, making it a truly international event. The object is to walk out onto the mud flats south of the village at low tide, feeling for flounders hiding beneath the mud with your toes as you go. The person who collects the largest weight of flounders wins the championship. It may seem a light hearted and eccentric competition, but it has a firm basis in local history, as this was a recognised way of catching fish in olden times.

The **North Glen Gallery** features glassblowing and interior and exterior design. It is also a good place to get advice on local walks and wildlife. A mile south west is **Orchardton Tower**, the only round tower house in Scotland; it dates from the middle of the 15th century, and was built by John Cairns in the late 16th century as a home after his retirement. In the 17th century it passed to the Maxwells, who in turn sold the estate on which it stood to James Douglas, brother of William, who founded the town of Castle Douglas.

DALBEATTIE
11 miles NE of Kirkcudbright on the A711

This small town stands just east of the Water of Urr, which at one time was navigable as far up-river as here. Ships of up to 60 tons could make the six-mile trip from the open sea beyond Rough Island, pulled by teams of horses. Now the "Pool of Dalbeattie" (the name given to the port area) is derelict, and the river has silted up.

Dalbeattie was a planned town, founded in the 1790s as a textile centre by two landowners - George Maxwell and Alexander Copland, who sold feus, or tenancies, to various people so that they could build houses. Close by there were easily worked deposits of granite which also provided employment. The granite was of high quality, and was used in the building of Sydney Harbour Bridge, Liverpool Docks and the Thames enbankment.

In Southwick Road you'll find the **Dalbeattie Museum**, and this has displays and exhibits about the history of the town. It has a particularly fine collection of Victoriana. Within Colliston Park is the **Dalbeattie Granite Garden**, designed by Solway Heritage to celebrate the beauty of the stone and the workers and craftsmen who mined it.

On the west bank of the Urr, about a mile from the town, is all that remains of **Buittle Castle and Bailey**, home to John Balliol, son of Devorgilla, whom Edward I placed on the throne of Scotland as a puppet king. Robert I established a burgh here in 1325, and a recent archaeological dig has revealed that the castle's large bailey (an enclosed space next to the castle) may have housed it. A later tower house, the **Old Buittle Tower**, stands close by. It has occasional displays of arms and armour.

On the wall of the former town hall is the Murdoch Memorial to **Lt William Murdoch**, who was the First Officer aboard the Titanic when it sank in 1912. Through the years he has been unfairly accused of being, among other things, a coward who shot passengers attempting to leave the ship. He was also accused of not allowing third class passengers near the lifeboats and of accepting bribes from first class passengers to let them board lifeboats to which they were not entitled.

The recent film also treated him unfairly, though the witness statements presented at the later official Board of Trade Enquiry cleared him of all these charges. In 1996 his name was finally and officially cleared of any wrongdoing.

Three miles north of Dalbeattie is the **Motte of Urr**, a 12th century motte-hill and bailey that is the largest non-industrial man-made hill in Scotland. At its summit at one time would have been a large, wooden castle, supposedly built by William de Berkeley. It stands close to the Water of Urr, and at one time the river flowed by on either side, creating an island that was easily defended. Tradition says that Robert the Bruce fought an English knight called Sir Walter Selby at the Motte of Urr. The wife of a man called Sprotte who at that time lived within the motte saw the fight, and observed that Selby was gaining the upper hand. So she rushed out and jumped on him, bringing him to his knees in front of the Scottish king.

However, Bruce chose to spare Selby, and both men retired to the woman's house. She produced one bowl of porridge and placed it before Robert, saying that she would not feed an Englishman. However, Robert told her to go outside and run as fast as she could. He would grant her and her husband all the land she could cover. The woman did so, and Robert and Walter finished off the porridge between them. Robert, however, kept his promise, and the Sprottes were granted 20 acres of land. They owned the land for over 500 years, with the condition that if a Scottish king were to pass by, they were to give him a bowl of porridge.

Five miles southwest of Dalbeattie is **Scree Hill**, with marked walks through forest and woodland to its top, from which there are excellent views.

ROCKCLIFFE

10 miles E of Kirkcudbright on a minor road off the A710

Rockcliffe was at one time a great smuggling centre, but is now a quiet resort sitting on the **Rough Firth**, one of the smallest firths in Scotland. Off the coast is **Rough Island** (National Trust for Scotland), a bird sanctuary. It can be accessed at low tide. Close to the village is the great **Mote of Mark** (National Trust for Scotland), the site of a 5th century fort. Mark was a king featured in the story of Tristan and Isolde, though there is no proof that the fort was ever his. It is more likely to have been built by a powerful Dark Ages chief.

There are a number of footpaths connecting Rockcliffe with Kippford, the two-mile long **Jubilee Path** (National

Rockcliffe

Trust for Scotland) being the main one. There is a programme of ranger-guided walks along it in the summer months. **Castlehill Point**, a mile south of the village on a clifftop, can be reached by a pathway. It has the remains of an old fort.

DUNDRENNAN

4 miles SE of Kirkcudbright on the A711

This quiet village is now visited mainly because of the ruins of the once substantial **Dundrennan Abbey** (Historic Scotland). It was founded in 1142 by David I and Fergus, Lord of Galloway for the Cistercian monks of Rievaulx in Yorkshire, and was where Mary Stuart spent her last night on Scottish soil in 1568 before sailing for England and her eventual execution. Little of the grand abbey church now remains, though the chapter house and some of the other buildings are well worth seeing, as are some interesting grave slabs.

TWYNHOLM

3 miles NW of Kirkcudbright on the A75

Twynholm is the home village of David Coulthard the racing driver, and within the **David Coulthard Museum** in Dumfries you can learn about the man's life. There is also a gift shop and tearoom.

GATEHOUSE OF FLEET

6 miles NW of Kirkcudbright off the A75

This neat little town was the original for the "Kippletringan" of Scott's *Guy Mannering*. It sits on the Water of Fleet, about a mile from Fleet Bay, and was at one time a port, thanks to the canalisation of the river in 1823 by a local landowner, Alexander Murray of Cally House. The port area was known as **Port MacAdam**, though the site has now been grassed over. Cally House is now a hotel, though next to it are the **Cally Gardens**, housed in a two-and-a-half acre walled garden.

Gatehouse of Fleet was laid out in the 1760s as a cotton-weaving centre by James Murray of Broughton, and today it remains more or less the way he planned it. He wished to create a great industrial town, though nowadays it is hard to imagine "dark satanic mills" in such an idyllic setting. Within one of the former cotton mills is a museum called the **Mill on the Fleet**, which tells the story of the town's former weaving industry.

It was supposedly in Gatehouse of Fleet, in the **Murray Arms**, that Burns set down the words to *Scots Wha Hae*. About a mile west of the town stands the substantial ruins of 15th century **Cardoness Castle** (Historic Scotland), former home of the McCullochs of Galloway. It stands on a rocky platform above the road, and is open to the public.

The small hamlet of Anworth stands just off the A75 to the west of the town. The ruins of the ancient **Anworth Parish Church** can be seen, set in a small kirkyard. The Revd Samuael Rutherford was the minister here in the 17th century. He is best remembered for being exiled from his parish to Aberdeen because of his opposition to a Church of Scotland with bishops. After he was admitted back into the church, he became a professor of theology at st Andrews University.

CAIRNHOLY

11 miles W of Kirkcudbright off the A75

Cairn Holy (Historic Scotland) comprises two chambered cairns dating from between 2000 and 3000 BC. The most remarkable thing about their construction is how our ancestors managed to raise such huge stones. The

Cairnholy Tomb

place is supposed to be the mark the grave of an ancient, mythical king of Scotland called Caldus. About a mile north of the cairns are the ruins of **Carsluith Castle**, dating from the 16th century. The castle was built by the Browns of Carsluith.

CREETOWN

14 miles NW of Kirkcudbright on the A75

Set at the mouth of the River Cree, the neat village of Creetown was once a centre for the mining of granite. Now it is visited chiefly because of the **Creetown Gem Rock Museum**, housed in a former school. It was established in 1971, and since then has amassed a remarkable collection of gemstones and minerals from all over the world. There are also exhibitions on geology and on the formation of our landscapes from earliest times. It even has an "erupting

volcano".

The **Creetown Exhibition Centre** in St John's Street has exhibits on local history and wildlife, as well as occasional exhibitions by local artists. Over a weekend in September each year, the **Creetown Country Music Weekend** takes place, featuring the best in country music. There is also a street fair, parades and children's activities.

STRANRAER

Sitting at the head of Loch Ryan, and on the edge of the **Rhinns of Galloway**, that hammer shaped peninsula that juts out into the Irish Sea, Stranraer is a royal burgh and was at one time the only Scottish port serving Northern Ireland. It was granted its royal burgh charter in 1617, and is a town of narrow streets and old alleyways.

In the centre of the town is the **Castle of St John**, a tower house built by the Adair family in the 16th century. Claverhouse used it as a base while hunting down Covenanters in the area, and it was later used as the town jail. It is now a museum and interpretation centre. There is another museum in the **Old Town Hall**, which explains the history of the town and the county of Wigtownshire.

North West Castle is now a hotel, but at one time it was the home of **Sir John Ross** (1777-1856), who explored the legendary North West Passage north of Canada connecting the Atlantic and the northern Pacific. He was born near Kirkcolm, son of a minister, and joined the navy at the age of nine, reaching the rank of commander by the time he was 35 years old. On one of his expeditions he discovered the Boothia Peninsula, mainland America's northernmost point. He later served as British consul in Stockholm.

Ferry at Stranraer

On the sea front is the **Princess Victoria Monument**, which commemorates the sinking of the car ferry Princess Victoria on January 31st, 1953. It had left Stranraer bound for Larne with 127 passengers and 49 crew, and on leaving the shelter of Loch Ryan encountered a horrific gale. Though lifeboats were launched, it eventually sank with the loss of 134 lives.

Three miles east of Stranraer are the magnificent **Castle Kennedy Gardens**. They cover 75 acres between two small lochs, and are laid out around the ivy-clad ruins of Castle Kennedy, destroyed by fire in 1710. The 2nd Earl of Stair began creating the gardens in 1733, and being a field marshal under the Duke of

Marlborough, he used soldiers to construct some of it. Also within the gardens is the relatively modern **Lochinch Castle**, the present home of the Earl and Countess of Stair. It is not open to the public.

South of the A75 is Soulseat Loch, where there is good fishing. A narrow peninsula with a few bumps and indentations on it juts out into the water - the site of **Soulseat Abbey**, of which not a stone now remains above ground. It was founded for the Premonstratensian Order of canons by Fergus, Lord of Galloway, in 1148 and dedicated to St Mary and St John the Baptist.

Three miles beyond Castle Kennedy on the A75 is the village of Dunragit, where you'll find **Glenwhan Gardens**, overlooking beautiful Luce Bay. They were started from scratch in 1979, and now cover 12 acres.

AROUND STRANRAER

CAIRNRYAN

6 miles N of Stranraer on the A77

Cairnryan is strung out along the coast of Loch Ryan. Between the main road and the coast is a complex of car parks,

Castle Kennedy

ALBANNACH GUEST HOUSE

Main Street, Cairnryan, Dumfries and Galloway DG9 8QX
Tel: 01581 200624

Albannach Guest House is a comfortable, family-run guest house
that offers superb accommodation in three fully en suite rooms.
The house itself is picturesque and four-square, and is a former
manse built over 100 years ago of warm, local stone. There are
tea/coffee making facilities in each room, as well as a TV, hair
dryer and trouser press. Each one has wonderful views. Cairnryan
is the ferry terminal for the P&O ferries to and from Northern Ireland, so the village makes the perfect
stopping off point at the beginning or end of a holiday.

piers, jetties and offices, as this small
village is the Scottish terminus of the
ferries to Northern Ireland. It was
developed as a port during World War II,
and had a breaker's yard. It was here that
the famous aircraft carrier **HMS Ark
Royal** was scrapped.

The Atlantic U boat fleet surrendered
in Loch Ryan in 1945, and were berthed
at Cairnryan before being taken out
into the Atlantic and sunk.

GLENTROOL

**20 miles NE of Stranraer on a minor road
which leaves the A714 at Bargrennan**

It was here, close to the lovely but
lonely waters of Loch Trool, that
Robert I defeated an English army in
1307, a year after his coronation. His
soldiers had hidden themselves in
the hills above the loch, and when
the English troops went past, they
rolled great boulders down on them
before attacking. It was a turning
point in the Wars of Independence,
as up until then Robert had had little
success. **Bruce's Stone** above the
loch commemorates the event. It is
said that Bruce rested here after the
battle was over. The **Glentrool
Visitor Centre**, three miles away,
offers information about the
surrounding forest walks, and has a
small tearoom and gift shop.

GLENLUCE

8 miles E of Stranraer off the A75

The attractive little village of Glenluce
has been bypassed by the A75, one of the
main routes from southern Scotland and
Northern England to the Irish ferries at
Stranraer and Cairnryan. At one time it
was the home of **Alexander Agnew**,
nicknamed the "Devil of Luce". He was a

Bruce's Stone, Glentrool

beggar who, in the mid 1600s, asked for alms from a weaver named Campbell in the village, but was refused. He thereupon cursed the family and its dwelling, and strange things began to happen. Stones were thrown at thr doors and windows when there was no one about, and stones came down the chimney. The bedclothes were even ripped from the children's beds as they slept. If this wasn't bad enough, Andrews was heard to say that there was no God but salt, meal and water - a clear case of atheism. He was eventually hanged for blasphemy at Dumfries.

A mile to the northwest are the ruins of **Glenluce Abbey** (Historic Scotland), founded in 1190 by Roland, Lord of Galloway for Cistercian monks from Dundrennan Abbey. It's best preserved feature is its chapter house. The end of the abbey came in 1560, with the advent of the Reformation. However, the monks

Glenluce Abbey

ANTIQUE CENTRE AT GLENLUCE

Dervaid Farm, Glenluce, Dumfries & Galloway DG8 0LF
Tel: 01581 300540
e-mail: chris@jones2701.freeserve.co.uk

When visiting Wigtownshire in Dumfries & Galloway, you must visit the **Antique Centre at Glenluce**. It is a fascinating place dating from the 16th century, and has antiques and collectables ranging from Jacobean to the 20th century. There is glass, china, silver, paintings, furniture, brass as well as architectural and garden antiques, displayed in a series of rooms. The business has been in the family for 40 years and current owner Chris Jones has been involved since he was nine. The antiques are keenly priced and make excellent souvenirs of a visit to this lovely part of Scotland.

KELVIN HOUSE HOTEL

53 main street, Glenluce, Wigtownshire DG8 0PP
Tel/Fax: 01581 300303
e-mail: mail@kelvin-house.co.uk website: www.kelvin-house.co.uk

The **Kelvin House Hotel** is one of the best establishments of its kind in Wigtownshire, and boasts six spacious rooms, all with private facilities, TV, tea/coffee making facilities and individually controlled central heating. Owned by Jenny and Ray Dyer, it is famous for its fine cuisine (Jenny being the chef) and its relaxing, family atmosphere. Whether it's an overnight stay, or something a bit longer, you're assured of a warm Galloway welcome. And watch out for the resident ghost - a friendly character in full deerstalker outfit and smelling of sandalwood.

Larg Hill and Bruntis Loch

Distance:	4.0 miles (6.4 kilometres)
Typical time:	120 mins
Height gain:	25 metres
Map:	Explorer 319
Walk:	www.walkingworld.com ID:2365
Contributor:	Tony Brotherton

Access Information:

Turn off the A75 at Palnure, three miles east of Newton Stewart, then follow signs for Galloway Forest Park and park in the Kirroughtree Visitor Centre car park. Bus Service 500 runs Monday to Saturday along the A75 between Stranraer and Newton Stewart to the west and Gatehouse of Fleet, Castle Douglas and Dumfries to the east; alight at Palnure and walk the mile or so via Stronord to the Visitor Centre's car park.

Description:

When the Scots find a name they like, they tend to use it liberally. Thus in Galloway, there are no fewer than three mountains which include the name 'Cairnsmore'. Similarly, there are several hills named 'Larg', two of which are within sight of each other; confusingly, one Larg 'Hill' is actually a mountain of over 2,000ft. Set within the Galloway Forest Park, this pleasant walk follows Forestry Commission Scotland's trail around the 'other' Larg Hill, a more modest 561ft (171m). The route starts from Kirroughtree Visitor Centre and is mainly level or of easy gradients and along good paths, tracks and forest roads. It skirts lovely Bruntis Loch and follows the course of a tumbling burn back to the Visitor Centre. There are occasional views across open countryside and of mountains and the Solway Firth.

Facilities

The Visitor Centre is open daily from Easter to the end of October, from 10.30 am until 5.30 pm.

Features:

Hills or Fells, Mountains, Lake/Loch, Sea, Toilets, Play Area, Wildlife, Birds, Flowers, Great Views, Butterflies, Cafe, Gift Shop, Food Shop, Good for Kids, Mostly Flat, Public Transport, Nature Trail, Tea Shop, Waterfall, Woodland

Walk Directions:

1 From car park, walk towards Visitor Centre but follow 'forest walks' sign to pass behind white Daltamie House and locate start of various forest trails indicated by three posts. Follow 'blue' trail. Take rising woodland path and presently an isolated building will appear on left.

2 Further on, path momentarily runs alongside Old Military Road before veering right and left into woodland, then joining road.

3 Now walk right along road. Ignore rising forest road off to right, marked 'no unauthorised vehicles', then take next turn right.

4 Where track comes in from right, bear left past blue-banded post.

5 Continue along woodland track to bench-seat and a view across country to Newton Stewart. Further along track is a view towards larger Larg Hill and other mountains of the Minnigaff Group.

6 Carry on and go right as per arrow, onto forest road. Hereabouts is your glimpse of sea.

7 Continue along road, passing by turn-off signed to Auchlannochy. Further on, look for a turn-off left. Follow descending path through trees and at crossing forest road, where to go right leads to Little Bruntis Loch, turn left. Through trees, Cairnsmore of Fleet (2,231ft - 711m) may be seen here.

8 Route follows road until a turn-off right. (Tracks, paths etc for this and following three points are not marked on map, so just keep following blue-banded marker-posts).

9 Path leads along to a road, where you again turn right. Along the road, Bruntis Loch may be glimpsed through trees to left; turn down path to reach its shore. Rest awhile on a handy perch, courtesy of John Crosbie; several more such seats are secreted throughout Galloway Forest Park, part of its commissioned art programme. Further opportunity to rest is provided by a picnic table-seat at the southern end of Bruntis Loch.

10 To continue, drop down on path and turn left along track, soon to follow this delightful burn.

11 Branch right at a marker-post and rejoin Brunton Burn by this waterfall.

12 Finally, return to start via 'all walkers path to car parks' command and reward yourself with refreshments and array of cakes at Visitor Centre and gift shop.

were allowed to live on within the abbey, the last one dying in 1602. Mary Stuart once visited, as did James 1V and Robert the Bruce. **Castle of Park** is an imposing tower house built in about 1590 by Thomas Hay, son of the last abbot of Glenluce. A stone over the door commemorates the event. It is now owned by the Landmark Trust, and used as rented holiday accommodation.

Immediately after the Reformation, the then Earl of Cassillis, head of the great Kennedy family, claimed the property and lands of Glenluce. He persuaded one of the monks to forge the abbot's signature on a document granting him the lands, then had the monk murdered. He then executed the men who had done the foul deed on his behalf in the name of justice.

NEWTON STEWART

22 miles E of Stranraer on the A75

The burgh of Newton Stewart sits on the River Cree, close to where it enters Wigtown Bay. It is a pleasant, clean town, founded in the 17th century by William Steweart, son of the Earl of Galloway. A ford once stood where the present bridge crosses the Cree, and it was used by pilgrims to Whithorn and St Ninian's shrine. **Newton Stewart Museum** is within a former church in York Road, and has displays and exhibits about the history of the town and immediate area. In Queen Street you'll find an unusual but internationally known little museum called **Sophie's Puppenstube and Dolls House Museum**, which has 50 beautifully made doll's houses and room settings. The scale is 1:12, and all the exhibits are behind glass. There is also a collection of over 200 exquisitely dressed dolls.

The **Wood of Cree Nature Reserve** is owned and managed by the Royal Society for the Protection of Birds, and lies four miles north of the town on a

minor road running parallel to the A714.
It has the largest ancient woodland in
Southern Scotland, and here you can see
redstarts, pied flycatchers, wood warblers
and so on. There is a picnic area and
nature trails.

Six miles west of Newton Stewart is the
picturesque village of **Kirkcowan**, which
has a church dating from 1834 with
external stairs to the gallery.

WIGTOWN
23 miles E of Stranraer on the A714

This small royal burgh has achieved fame
as being **Scotland's Book Town**, and has
many bookshops and publishing houses.
The focus for book activity, apart from
the shops, are the **County Buildings** of
1863, and during the two book fairs held
here every year - one in May and one in
September - many of the readings, talks
and events take place within them.

In the kirkyard of Wigtown Parish
Church are the remains of the medieval
church, dedicated to St Machuto, who is
known in France as St Malo, and gave his
name to the French port. Also in the
kirkyard are the **Martyrs' Graves**. In
1685, during the time of the Covenanters,
two women - one aged 18 and one aged
63 - were tied to stakes at the mouth of
the River Bladnoch for adhering to the
Covenant and renouncing Charles as the
head of the church. Rather than give up
their principles, they drowned as the tide
rose over their heads. The spot where the
martyrdom took place is marked by the
small **Martyrs Monument** on what are
now salt marshes (see also Stirling). On a
small hill behind the town is another
Covenanters' Monument, this time a
slender column.

One mile west of the town is **Bladnoch
Distillery**, Scotland's most southerly
whisky distillery. There is a visitor centre
and shop, and guided tours are available
showing the distilling process.

Four miles west of the town, reached
by the B733, is the Bronze Age **Torhouse
Stone Circle**, built about 2000BC to
1500BC. It consists of 19 boulders
forming a circle, with three other
boulders in a line within it. It is of a
type more commonly found in
Aberdeenshire and north east Scotland.

CHAPEL FINIAN
16 miles SE of Stranraer on the A747

Beside the road that runs along the
western shore of **The Machars**, the name
given to that great peninsula that sticks
out into the Irish Sea between Luce and
Wigtown Bays, you'll find the
foundations of a small church. The most
interesting thing about them is their
great age, as they probably date from the
10th century. Later on the chapel was
probably used as a stopping off point for
people making a pilgrimage to St
Ninian's Shrine at Whithorn, 12 miles to
the southeast. The chapel was dedicated
to St Finian of Moville lived during the
6th century, and had founded a great
monastic school in Northern Ireland
where St Columba studied.

Four miles inland from the chapel, and
reached by a minor road off the A7005,
is the **Old Place of Mochrum**, on the
northern edge of lonely Mochrum Loch.
It was originally built in in the 16th
century by the Dunbar family, and was
restored by the Marquis of Bute between
1876 and 1911. The gardens are
particularly fine.

MONREITH
23 miles SE of Stranraer on the A746

This small village lies on Monreith Bay.
The ruins of the old church of
KirkMaiden-in-Fernis can still be seen,
the chancel now a burial place for the
Maxwells of Monreith.

The **Animal World & Gavin Maxwell
Museum** has displays about local

wildlife. It is named after Gavin Maxwell, author of *Ring of Bright Water*, who was born at nearby Elrig, which features in his book *The House of Elrig*.

WHITHORN

26 miles SE of Stranraer on the A746

This tiny royal burgh (no bigger than a village) is often called the "Cradle of Scottish Christianity". A century before Columba came to Iona, a monk called **St Ninian** set up a monastery here. He is a shadowy figure who may have been born in either Galloway or Cumbria , the son of a tribal chief. He almost certainly visited Rome, and stayed with St Martin of Tours, whom he greatly admired. Some sources say he died in AD432.

The monastery would have been a typical Celtic foundation, with a high circular bank, or "rath", enclosing an area of monks' cells, workshops and chapels. This monastery was different in one respect, however. The main church was made of stone, not the more common wood, and was painted white. For this reason it was called **Candida Casa**, or "White House". When this part of Scotland was later absorbed into the kingdom of Northumbria, the name was translated into Anglo Saxon as "Hwit

Aerne", from which Whithorn is derived.

The place was subsequently an important ecclesiastical and trading centre. In the 12th century Fergus, Lord of Galloway, founded **Whithorn Priory** (Historic Scotland), and its church became the cathedral for the diocese of Galloway. All that is left of the priory church is its nave and crypt. To the east of the crypt may be seen some scant foundations which may be all that is left of Ninian's original whitewashed church. The cathedral, with its relics of St Ninian, eventually became a place of pilgrimage, and many Scottish monarchs, especially James IV, made pilgrimages to pray there.

The town's main street, George Street, is wide and spacious, with many small Georgian, Regency and Victorian houses. **The Pend**, dating from about 1500, is an archway leading to the priory ruins, and above it are the royal arms of Scotland. Close to the priory is the **Priory Museum** (Historic Scotland), with a collection of stones on which are carved early Christian symbols. One of them, the **Latinus Stone**, dates from the 5th century, and may be the earliest carved Christian stone in Scotland. Some years ago, excavations were undertaken at Whithorn, and at the **Whithorn Visitors Centre**, owned by the Whithorn Trust, you can learn about the excavations and what was found there.

St Ninian's Cave is on the shore three miles southwest of the town. It has incised crosses on its walls, and a legend states that St Ninian himself came to this cave to seek solitude and pray. At Glasserton, two miles west

Whithorn Priory

of Whithorn, are the **Woodfall Gardens**, covering three acres within an old walled garden. They were laid out in the 18th century by Keith Stewart, second son of the earl of Galloway an admiral in the British navy when he was given the 2,000 acres of the barony of Glassertion in 1767. And at Garlieston, four miles north of the town, are the **Galloway House Gardens**, laid out informally at the ruined Cruggleton Castle, and with walks leading down to the shores of Cruggleton Bay. The medieval **Cruggleton Church** sits by itself in a field, and was built as a chapel for the castle. It was restored in the 19th century by the Marquis of Bute, and a key for it is available at nearby Crugleton farm.

Three miles to the southeast is the tiny fishing village of **Isle of Whithorn**. On a headland are the 13th century ruins of the tiny **St Ninian's Chapel**. Though it sits on the mainland, the small area surrounding it may at one time have been an island, giving the village its name. It was probably built for pilgrims to Whithorn Priory who came by sea.

KIRKMADRINE

8 miles S of Stranraer on a minor road off the A716

In the porch of what was the tiny parish church of Toskerton are the **Kirkmadrine Stones**, thought to be the oldest inscribed stones in Scotland after those at Whithorn. They were discovered when the church was being rebuilt and converted into a burial chamber by a local family, the McTaggarts of Ardwell. Parts of the former medieval church have been incorporated into it, though it is thought that there has been a church here since the 6th century.

ARDWELL

10 miles S of Stranraer on the A716

Ardwell Gardens are grouped round the 18th century Ardwell House. They feature azaleas, camellias and rhododendrons, and are a testimony to the mildness of the climate in these parts, and feature a woodland and a formal garden, as well as good views out over Luce Bay from the pond.

PORT LOGAN

12 miles S of Stranraer on the B7065

Port Logan is a small fishing village situated on Port Logan Bay. Close by is the **Logan Fish Pond**, a remarkable tidal pond famous for its tame sea fish, which can be fed by hand. It was constructed in about 1800 as a source of fresh fish for the tables of nearby Logan House.

If anywhere illustrates the mildness of the climate in this part of Scotland, it is **Logan Botanic Garden**, part of the National Botanic Gardens of Scotland. Here, growing quite freely, are exotic plants and trees such as the tree fern (which can normally only survive in glass houses in Britain), the eucalyptus, palm trees, magnolias and passionflowers. In fact, over 40 per cent of all the plants and trees at Logan come from the Southern hemisphere. Within the garden is the Discovery Centre, which gives an insight into the plants that grow here.

The village achieved national fame when the TV series *2,000 Acres of Sky*, supposedly set on a Hebridean island, was filmed in and around Port Logan.

KIRKMAIDEN

15 miles S of Stranraer on the B7065

Kirkmaiden is Scotoand's most southerly parish. Four miles south of the village is the **Mull of Galloway**, Scotland's most southerly point. It comes as a surprise to some people when they learn that places like Durham in England are further north. The lighthouse was built in 1828 to the designs of Robert Stevenson, and sits on the massive cliffs, 270 feet above

---

LOGAN FISH POND

Port Logan, Stranraer
Tel/Fax: 01776 860300
website: www.loganfishpond.co.uk

The first time visitor to **Logan Fish Pond** is often amazed and surprised by what they see. Not until they enter through the original Fish Keepers Cottage and have their first glimpse of the pond below do they have any idea of what this unique and historic attraction holds. In 1788 Andrew McDouall Laird of Logan decided to create a Fish Larder for storing live sea fish by adapting a natural rock formation in the form of a blow hole, formed during the last ice-age. The work took 12 years and was finished in 1800. Many visitors return year after year and indeed some have been doing so for 50 or 60 years, feeding the fish today as they remember doing so as children.

In the springtime, the area around the pond is a carpet of daffodils, primroses and bluebells and later in the year these are replaced with an abundance of wild flowers, including thrift and sea campion. On the rocks next to the fish pond is a restored Victorian bathing hut which adjoins a bathing pool. Recent additions to the original pond include Touch Pools, Cave Aquarium and Gift Shop. Open 1st February to 30th September 10am to 5pm and 1st October to early November 11am to 4pm. Some disabled access.

the sea. In Drummore, half a mile to the east of the village, is the **Kirkmaiden information Centre**, which has displays and exhibitions about the area.

PORTPATRICK

6 miles SW of Stranraer on the A77

This lovely little village is at the western end of the Southern Upland Way. At one time it was the main Scottish port for Northern Ireland, but was in such an exposed position that Stranraer eventually took over. It sits round a little harbour that is always busy, and, with its old cottages and craft shops, has become a small holiday resort.

On a headland to the south of the village are the ruins of **Dunskey Castle**, built in the early 16th century by the Adair family. The recently re-established **Dunskey Garden and Woodland Walk** is well worth visiting. Every Wednesday afternoon in summer, there are guided tours conducted by the gardener. Within the village is the ruined **Portpatrick Parish Church**. It was built in the 17th century, and unusually, has a round tower.

Built as a hunting lodge in 1869 by lady Hunter Blair, **Knockinaam Lodge** stands to the south of the village. It is now a hotel, but it was here, during the closing stages of the Second World War, that Churchill and Eisenhower planned the Allied strategy.

Portpatrick

LOCATOR MAP

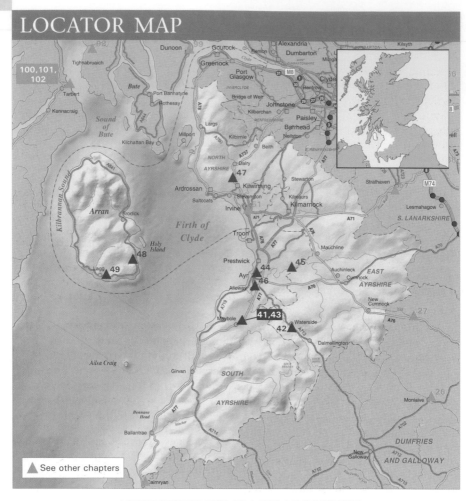

See other chapters

ADVERTISERS AND PLACES OF INTEREST

AYRSHIRE & ARRAN 3

Ayrshire was at one time Scotland's largest Lowland county. Facing the Firth of Clyde, it is ringed by moorland and hills which slope down to a rich agricultural patchwork of small fields, country lanes, woodland and picturesque villages. The poet Keats, when he made his pilgrimage in 1818 to the birthplace of Robert Burns in Alloway, compared its scenery to that of Devon. Indeed, in places you almost feel you are in an English rural landscape.

The county was formerly divided into three parts. Carrick is the most southerly, and owes a lot to neighbouring Galloway. It is separated from Kyle, a rich dairying area where the native Ayrshire cattle can be seen dotting the fields, by the River Doon. To the north, beyond the River Irvine, is Cunninghame, which at one time was the most industrialised of the three, though it managed this without losing too much of its rural aspect.

Kyle itself was divided by the River Ayr into Kyle Regal and Kyle Stewart, reflecting the fact that one section was ruled directly by the king while the other was ruled by high stewards of Scotland, who eventually went on to be kings in their own right.

Ayrshire and Robert Burns, known to all Scottish people as "Rabbie" (never, ever *Robbie*!) are inextricably linked. He was born in Alloway, which nowadays is a well-off suburb of Ayr, and spent the first 29 years of his life in the county before moving south to Dumfriesshire. We know a lot about the man, and all the places in Ayrshire where he lived, drank, courted and caroused are well signposted. A full week could easily be spent meandering along the main roads and narrow lanes of the county, visiting such towns and villages as Tarbolton, Mauchline, Ayr, Kilmarnock, Irvine, Failford and Kirkoswald. Every year in May the **Burns an' a' That Festival** takes place throughout Ayrshire to celebrate his life and work. Venues include pubs, concert halls, theatres, museums and churches. The most spectacular concert is held out of doors at Culzean Castle.

There are three main towns in the county - Ayr, Kilmarnock and Irvine. Irvine is the largest, though it was not always so. In the 1960s it was designated a new town, and took an overspill population from Glasgow. Industrial estates were built, factories were opened and new housing established. However, its central core is still worth exploring. Kilmarnock is traditionally the industrial centre, though it is an ancient town, and Ayr was the administrative and commercial capital before Ayrshire ceased to exist as a local government unit in the 1970s.

Up until the 1960s, when more exotic places took over, the Ayrshire coast was Glasgow's holiday playground. Known as the "Costa del Clyde", it attracted thousands of people each year who flocked to such holiday resorts as Troon, Largs, Prestwick, Girvan and Ayr itself. These halcyon days are gone, though it is still a popular place for day trips and for people to retire to, giving it a new nickname - the "Costa Geriatrica". The coastline is also famous for golf. The first British Open Golf Championship was held at Prestwick in 1860, and both Troon and Turnberry have regularly hosted the tournament in modern times.

Ayrshire is also a county of castles, from the spectacular Culzean (pronounced "Cull-ane") perched on a cliff top above the sea, to Kelburn near Largs or Dean Castle in Kilmarnock, with its collection of rare musical instruments.

The Ayrshire coalfield used to employ thousands of people, though nowadays not a deep mine remains. But even at its height, the industry never did as

Robert Burns Monument, Alloway

much damage to the environment as in, say, South Yorkshire or the Welsh valleys. Now you would never suspect that the industry ever existed at all, and a day just motoring round the quiet lanes is a relaxing experience in itself.

Twenty miles offshore is the island of Arran, at one time within the county of Bute, but now more associated with Ayrshire. It has been called "Scotland in Miniature", and is a wonderful blend of wild scenery, pastoral views and rocky coastlines. Its history stretches right back into the mists of time, as the many standing stones and ancient burial cairns testify. It is properly part of the Highlands, and Gaelic used to be the predominant language. A ferry connects it to Ardrossan on the Ayrshire coast.

Also within Bute were two other islands - Great and Little Cumbrae. Little Cumbrae is largely uninhabited, apart from one or two houses, but on Great Cumbrae is the town of Millport, a gem of a holiday resort. Within Millport is another gem - Cumbrae Cathedral, the smallest cathedral in Britain. A short ferry crossibng from largs takes you to the island.

MAYBOLE

This small, quiet town is the capital of Carrick, and sits on a hillside about four miles inland from the coast. It was here that Burns's parents, William Burnes (he later changed the name to Burns) and Agnes Broun met in 1756.

In 1562, a famous meeting took place in Maybole between John Knox, the Scottish reformer, and Abbot Quentin Kennedy of nearby Crossraguel Abbey. The purpose of the meeting was to debate the significance and doctrine of the Mass, and it attracted a huge crowd of people, even though it was held in a small room of the house where the provost of the town's collegiate church lived. Forty people from each side were allowed in to hear the debate, which lasted for three days. It only broke up - with no conclusion reached - when the town ran out of food to feed the thronging masses round the door (see also Kirkoswald).

The ruins of **Maybole Collegiate Church** (Historic Scotland) can still be viewed, though they are not open to the public. The church, dedicated to St Mary, was founded by Sir John Kennedy of Dunure in 1371 for the saying of daily prayers for himself, his wife Mary and their children. The clergy consisted of one clerk and three chaplains, who said the prayers daily. The present ruins date from a rebuilding in the 15th century, when it became a full collegiate church with a provost and a "college" of priests. The present **Parish Church** dates from 1808, and has an unusual stepped spire.

At one time Maybole had no less that 28 lairds' town houses, each one referred to as a "castle". Now there are only two left, one at each end of the main street. The "upper" one is now part of the **Town Hall**, and was the 17th century town house of the lairds of Blairquhan

Castle, about five miles to the east. The other is still referred to as **Maybole Castle** (see panel on page 90), though it too was a town house, this time for the Earls of Cassillis. It dates from the late 16th century, and there is a curious legend attached to the building.

A few miles west of Maybole, near the farm of Drumshang, is the curiously named **Electric Brae**, on the A719 road between Ayr and Turnberry. Stop your car on the convenient layby at the side of the road, put it out of gear, let off the brake, and be amazed as it rolls uphill. Better still, lay a football on the layby's surface, and watch it roll uphill as well. The phenomenon has nothing to do with electricity, lay lines, earth magic, the "unseen world" of the earth's energy system or the same power displayed by poltergeists when they move objects (as someone once declared), and everything to do with an optical illusion. The surrounding land makes you think that the road rises towards the west when it fact it descends.

AROUND MAYBOLE

KIRKMICHAEL
3 miles E of Maybole on the B7045

Like its neighbour Crosshill, Kirkmichael is a former weaving village. However, its roots go deep into Scottish history. The **Parish Church** dates from 1790, and the picturesque lych-gate from about 1700. Within the kirkyard is the grave of a Covenanter called Gilbert MacAdam, shot in 1686 by Archibald Kennedy.

Kirkmichael is the scene, every May, of the **Kirkmichael International Guitar Festival**, which draws musicians from all over the world. It covers everything from jazz to pop and country to classical. Huge marquees are erected, and local pubs host impromptu jamming sessions

MAYBOLE CASTLE

Maybole, Ayrshire

Maybole Castle is the oldest inhabited house in the town having been built about the middle of the 16th century (believed to be around 1560). It was the town house of the Earls of Cassillis who spent most of the winter months in Maybole, and was the largest and finest of the 28 lairds' houses written about by Abercrummie in 1696. It was built in the style of a typical Scottish castle, with square tower and round turrets, and strong enough to protect its occupants from unfriendly neighbours, of whom there were many at that time. The main hall was above vaulted cellars which still remain and above the hall were the sleeping apartments. The retainers' quarters were on the other side of a gateway which gave entrance into the castle yard, built round the well, locally known as "The Pump".

The tower is capped by a lovely little oriel window with heads carved round it which local people wrongly believe represent the heads of Johnnie Faa and his gypsies. The corbels to the roof of the little room at the top of the tower (known as the Countess's Room) are carved with male and female heads and symbols of fertility. The walls are extremely thick (in some places about seven feet) and it must have been a safe retreat in troublesome times when the Earls lived here, with their own men around them in the small township clustered on the hillside below it.

It was from Maybole Castle that the Earl of Cassillis and his men sallied forth to the fight at Ladycross in December 1601, when young Bargany was killed in the bitter feud between the Cassillis and Bargany families. Locally there is an old tale of the Countess of Cassillis being imprisoned at the top of the tower, after she had allegedly eloped with Johnnie Faa, King of the Gypsies, but while the story is a delightful one, facts disprove it.

As years passed the Earls spent less of their time in Maybole, and gradually the old Castle fell into disrepair and was practically abandoned except for a few old retainers who lived in outbuildings. In 1805 the Earl of Cassillis agreed with the town council that the part sited where the Post Office now stands could be demolished to allow a road to be formed from the foot of the High Street to Duncanland Toll at the bottom of Redbrae. When the old buildings were removed the Earl decided to repair the Castle and in 1812 reroofed it and built some additions. The gardens and park had walls erected round them and from 1812 the Castle has remained as it is now, apart from repairs to the roof following a fire in 1919.

The Historical Society has been very active in promoting Maybole Castle since May-Tag (founded by the Community Council in 1986 as a training company to promote local unemployment) moved out and has said, "The Castle goes from strength to strength and we have a very good relationship with the factor and through him the Estate and Trustee. We are putting together proposals and plans for opening the castle regularly to the public; improving and expanding the display material in the castle; and the future of the castle as a heritage centre."

and folk concerts. It was founded by the internationally renowned jazz guitarist Martin Taylor, who lives locally.

DALMELLINGTON

11 miles E of Maybole on the A713

This former mining village sits on the banks of the Doon. Over the last few years, it has exploited its rich heritage, and created some visitor centres and museums that explain the village's industrial past. The **Dunaskin Open Air Museum** (see panel below), which covers 110 acres, has many facets, and each one is well worth exploring. The **Dalmellington Iron Works** were first opened in the 1840s, and are now the largest restored Victorian Ironworks in Europe. Other attractions include the **Brickworks** and the **Scottish Industrial Railway Centre**, where steam trains run on a restored track. The **Cathcartson Centre** in the village is housed in

weaving cottages dating from the 18th century, and shows how weavers lived long ago.

Dalmellington is the starting point for the new **Scottish Coal Cycle Route** which will stretch between Dalmellington and Coalburn, 66km away in Lanarkshire. It will became part of the National Cycle Network.

A couple of miles beyond Dalmellington is a minor road that takes you to lovely **Loch Doon**, surrounded by lonely hills and moorland, and the source of the river that Burns wrote about. It was here, during World War I, that a **School of Aerial Gunnery** was proposed. Millions of pounds were wasted on it before the plans were finally abandoned. When a hydroelectric scheme was built in the 1930s, the water level of the loch was raised. **Loch Doon Castle**, which stood on an island in the loch, was dismantled stone by stone and

THE DUNASKIN HERITAGE CENTRE

Dalmellington Road, Waterside, Patna, Ayrshire
Tel: 01292 531144
website: www.dunaskin.org.uk

The Dalmellington Iron Company was founded in 1848, at the height of the Industrial Revolution. At its zenith, the company's eight furnaces worked day and

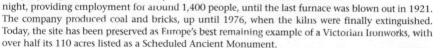

night, providing employment for around 1,400 people, until the last furnace was blown out in 1921. The company produced coal and bricks, up until 1976, when the kilns were finally extinguished. Today, the site has been preserved as Europe's best remaining example of a Victorian Ironworks, with over half its 110 acres listed as a Scheduled Ancient Monument.

Dunaskin is a visitor attraction for all the family. The Dunaskin Experience lets you explore the past as it was actually lived by Ayrshire people. An open air, living museum set amidst beautiful rolling countryside, it follows the story of the people and places of the Doon Valley through the Industrial Revolution, two World Wars and right up to modern times. There's the Mary Gallagher Experience: an audio visual which recreates Ayrshire life in the 19th and early 20th centuries. For younger children there's the Furnace Play Tower. Teenagers can interact with Billy the Brick Computer Quiz.

Everyone will enjoy the delightful walks, including Dunaskin Glen which is a designated Site of Special Scientific Interest. There's a period cottage and industrial machinery. You can even feel what it was like to work in a coal mine. Finally you can break your visit and meet the welcoming staff at Chimneys Restaurant and Coffee Shop and browse in the Gift Shop.

reassembled on the shore, where it can still be seen.

In 1306 it was besieged by the English when Sir Christopher Seton, Robert the Bruce's brother-in-law, took refuge there after the Scottish army's defeat at the Battle of Methven. However, the governor of the castle, Sir Gilbert de Carrick, feared that the Bruce's cause was lost, and surrendered to the English troops. Seton was executed at Dumfries and Gilbert de Carrick was spared. The castle was again besieged in 1446 by the Douglases, who were trying to usurp the Kennedys in Carrick. However, the siege failed, thanks to the McLellans of Dumfriesshire. It was again besieged in 1510, this timke by the Crawfords, but the castle held firm.

In the late 1970s it was announced that 32 deep tunnels would be bored in the hills surrounding the loch to store most of Britain's radioactive waste. After many protests by local people, the idea was abandoned.

CROSSHILL
3 miles SE of Maybole, on the B7023

Crosshill is a former handloom-weaving village established in about 1808, with many small, attractive cottages. Many of the weavers were Irish, attracted to the place by the prospect of work. There are no outstanding buildings, nor does it have much history or legend attached to it. But it is a conservation village with a quiet charm, and well worth visiting because of this alone. Some of the original cottages built by the Irish immigrants in the early 19th century can still be seen in Dalhowan Street.

STRAITON
6 miles SE of Maybole on the B741

A narrow road runs south from this lovely village called the **Nick o' the**

Balloch. It doesn't go through the Carrick of gentle fields or verdant valleys, but over the wild hills and moorland that make the edges of this area so beautiful, and finally drops down into Glentrool.

Straiton itself sits on the water of Girvan, and has picturesque little cottages facing each other across a main street some with roses growing round the door. It was a planned village, laid out in 1760 by the Earl of Cassillis on the site of a small hamlet. The local pub, The Black Bull, dates from 1766, while parts of **St Cuthbert's Parish Church** date back to 1510.

Close to the village is **Blairquhan** (pronounced "Blair-whan"), a Tudor-Gothic mansion built between 1821 and 1824 to the designs of the famous Scottish architect William Burn. It sits on the site of an earlier tower house dating to 1346 that was once a McWhirter stronghold before passing to the Kennedys. It is now owned by the Hunter Blair family, and is open to the public in summer. It has a fine collection of paintings by the Scottish Colourists. On a hill above the village stands the **Hunter Blair Monument**, built in 1856 to commemorate James Hunter Blair, killed at the Battle of Inkerman.

Many of the scenes in the film *The Match* (also called *The Big Game*) were shot in Straiton, which became the fictional Highland village Inverdoune.

OLD DAILLY
9 miles S of Maybole on the B734

Old Dailly was originally called Dalmakerran, and was once an important village, with many cottages, a manse for the minister and a mill. Now it is a row of council houses and the ruins of 14th century **Old Dailly Parish**

Church . Within the kirkyard are two hefty stones called the **Charter Stones**, which men tried to lift in bygone days during trials of strength.

Buried in the kirkyard is the pre-Raphaelite artist **William Bell Scott**, who was staying at nearby **Penkill Castle** (not open to the public) when he died. Many members of the pre-Raphaelite Brotherhood visited the place, including **Dante Gabriel Rossetti**. Close by is the 17th century **Bargany House**, with its marvellous gardens, once a Kennedy stronghold. The mining village of **New Dailly**, with its T-shaped **New Dailly Parish Church** of 1766 is three miles to the east. Close by, on the opposite side of the Girvan Water, are the substantial ruins of **Dalquharran Castle**. It was designed by Robert Adam and built between 1780 and 1791 for Kennedy of Dunure. Plans were announced in 2004 to turn it and its estate into a luxury hotel and golf resort, with Jack Nicklaus designing the golf course. The ruins of the 15th century **Old Dalquharran Castle** are close by.

BARR

11 miles S of Maybole on the B734

Tucked in a fold of the Carrick hills, Barr is an idyllic village that was once the site of the wonderfully named **Kirkdandie Fair**. It was the largest annual fair in Southern Scotland during the late 18th and early 19th centuries, and was held on a strip of land where stood the long gone Kirkdandie (or Kirkdominae) Church. Its main claim to fame was the fighting that took place there every year, and it soon became known as the "Donnybrook of Scotland". People even came over from Ireland to participate in the great pitched battles. So famous did it become that a ballad was written about it, describing at least 63 tents, the sound of pipes and people socialising, dancing, drinking and eating.

Above Barr is the estate of Changue (pronounced "Shang"), to which an old legend is attached. The cruel and wicked **Laird of Changue** was a smuggler and distiller of illicit whisky who enjoyed the fruits of his own still a bit to much and was therefore always penniless. One day, while walking through his estates, Satan appeared and offered him a deal. If he handed over his soul when he died, he would become rich. The laird, who was a young man, agreed, and duly prospered. But as he grew older he began to regret his rashness, and when Satan at last appeared before him to claim his soul - at the same spot where he had appeared all these years before - the laird refused to keep his side of the bargain.

Instead he challenged the Devil to fight for it. Drawing a large circle on the ground round both of them, he said that the first person to be forced out of it would be the loser. After a bitter struggle, the laird cut off the end of Satan's tail with his sword, and he jumped out of the circle in pain. The laird had won. Up until the end of the 19th century, a great bare circle on some grassland was shown as the place where all this took place. It's a wonderful story, but no one has ever managed to put a name or date to this mysterious laird. And it has often been pointed out that if Satan had bided his time, he would have had the soul of the laird in the usual way, so wicked was he.

COLMONELL

19 Miles S of Maybole on the B734

The River Stinchar is the southernmost of Ayrshire's major rivers, and flows through a lovely glen bordered on both sides by high moorland and hills. In this valley, four miles from the sea, sits Colmonell. It's an attractive village of small cottages, with the romantic ruins of the old Kennedy stronghold of **Kirkhill Castle** close by. **Knockdolian Hill**, two miles west, was at one time called the "false Ailsa Craig" because of its resemblance to the volcanic island out in the Firth of Clyde.

BALLANTRAE

22 miles S of Maybole on the A77

When on a walking tour of Carrick in 1876, R.L. Stevenson spent a night in Ballantrae, a small fishing village. However, dour villagers took exception to his way of dressing, and almost ran him out of town. He got his revenge by writing "The Master of Ballantrae", which confused everyone by having no connection with the place whatsoever.

In the churchyard is the **Bargany Aisle**, containing the ornate tomb of Gilbert Kennedy, laird of Bargany and Ardstinchar, who was killed by the Earl of Cassillis (also a Kennedy) in 1601. A bitter feud between the Cassillis and Bargany branches of the Kennedy family had been going on right through the 16th century, with no quarter given or taken. Matters came to a head when the two branches met near Ayr, and Bargany was killed. The power of the Bargany branch was broken forever, and the feud fizzled out. The ruins of **Ardstinchar Castle**, Bargany's main stronghold, can still be seen beside the river. It was built in 1421, and in August 1566 Mary Stuart stayed there.

Glenapp Castle, a few miles south of the village just off the A77, was designed in 1870 by the noted Victorian architect David Bryce for James Hunter, the Deputy Lord Lieutenant of Ayrshire. It is now a luxury hotel surrounded by 30 acres of grounds and gardens.

LENDALFOOT

18 miles S of Maybole on the A77

Carleton Castle, now in ruins, was the home of Sir John Carleton, who, legend states, had a neat way of earning a living. He married ladies of wealth then enticed them to **Gamesloup**, a nearby rocky eminence, where he pushed them to their deaths and inherited their wealth. Sir John went through seven or eight wives before meeting the daughter of Kennedy of Culzean. After marrying her, he took her to Gamesloup, but instead of him pushing her over, she pushed him over, and lived happily ever after on his accumulated wealth. It is said that you can still occasionally hear the screams of the women as they were pushed to their death.

But if it's a gruesome tale you're after, then you should head for **Sawney Bean's Cave** a few miles south of the village, on the shoreline north of Bennane Head, and easily reached by a footpath from a layby on the A77. Here, in the 16th century, lived a family of cannibals led by Sawney Bean ("Sawny" being Scots for "Sandy"), which waylaid strangers, robbed them, and ate their flesh. They evaded capture for many years until a troop of men sent by James VI trapped them in their cave. They were taken to Edinburgh and executed. It's a wonderful story, but no documentary proof has ever been unearthed to prove that it really happened.

KIRKOSWALD

4 miles SW of Maybole on the A77

It was to Kirkoswald, in 1775, that Burns came for one term to learn surveying. Though his poem *Tam o' Shanter* is set in Alloway, all the characters in it have their origins in the parish of Kirkoswald, which was where his maternal grandparents came from.

Kirkoswald Parish Church dates from 1777, and was designed by Robert Adam while he was working on Culzean Castle. Dwight D. Eisenhower worshipped here twice, one of the occasions being when he was president of the United States (see also Culzean Castle on page 96). Another visitor is not so well known, though the airline he helped to found is. The late Randolph Fields, together with Richard Branson, founded Virgin Airlines. Randolph loved this part of Ayrshire, and when he died in 1997, he left some money for the restoration of the church. A year later his widow presented the church with a small table, on which is a plaque commemorating his donation.

Old Parish Church of St Oswald lies at the heart of the village. It is a ruin now, but it was here, in 1562, that Abbot Quentin Kennedy of Crossraguel Abbey preached forcefully against the Reformation and in favour of the sacrifice of the mass, he challenged anyone to debate the matter with him, and John Knox, who was in the area, agreed to take him on. They met in nearby Maybole, where the two of them debated over three days without resolving the issue (see also Maybole). In its kirkyard are the graves of many people associated with Burns, including David Graham of Shanter Farm near Maidens, the real life "Tam o' Shanter".

The church also contains one interesting relic - **Robert the Bruce's Baptismal Font.** Both Lochmaben in Dumfriesshire and Turnberry Castle, within the parish of Kirkoswald, claim to have been the birthplace of Robert the Bruce. Turnberry is the more likely, as it was the ancestral home of the Countess of Carrick, Bruce's mother, and it is known that she was living there at about the time of the birth. The story goes that the baby was premature, and that he was rushed to Crossraguel Abbey for baptism

in case he died. The abbey's font was used, and when Crossraguel was abandoned after the Reformation, the people of Kirkoswald rescued the font and put it in their own church (see also Lochmaben).

Within the village you'll also find **Souter Johnnie's Cottage** (National Trust for Scotland). John Davidson was a "souter", or cobbler, and featured in *Tam o' Shanter*. Now his thatched cottage has been turned into a small museum.

CROSSRAGUEL ABBEY
2 miles SW of Maybole, on the A77

These romantic ruins (Historic Scotland) sit complacently beside the main Ayr-Stranraer road. They are very well preserved, and give a wonderful idea of the layout of a medieval abbey. Some of the architecture and stone carving, such as that in the chapter house, is well worth seeking out. Duncan, Earl of Carrick, founded it in 1244 for Cluniac monks from Paisley Abbey, though most of what you see nowadays dates from after the 13th century. The name is supposed to come from an old cross which stood here before the abbey was built, and it may mean the regal, or royal cross, or the cross of Riaghail, possibly a local chief.

To the north are the ruins of **Baltersan Castle**, an old fortified 16th century tower house built either for John Kennedy of Pennyglen and his wife Margaret Cathcart or as the residence of Quentin Kennedy, the Abbot of Crossraguel from 1548 until 1564.

TURNBERRY
7 miles SW of Maybole on the A719

Very little now survives of the 12th century **Turnberry Castle**, where Robert the Bruce is supposed to have been born. The story of how his parents met is an

CULZEAN CASTLE AND COUNTRY PARK

Maybole, South Ayrshire, KA19 8LE
Functions, events and Eisenhower Apartment:
Tel: 01655 884455 Fax 01655 884503
Group/school bookings, ranger service, Country
Park information:
Tel: 01655 884400 Fax 01655 884522.
e-mail: culzean@nts.org.uk
website: www.culzeancastle.net

Robert Adam converted a rather ordinary fortified
tower house into this elegant bachelor residence
for David Kennedy, 10th Earl of Cassillis, between
1777 and 1792. He also built a 'Roman' viaduct
and Ruined Arch to add drama to this Italianate
castle in its spectacular clifftop setting. Both the
exterior stonework and the interior of the castle
have been restored by the National Trust for
Scotland. It contains a fine collection of paintings
and furniture, and a display of weapons in the
Armoury. The Circular Saloon has a superb
panoramic view over the Firth of Clyde and the beautiful Oval Staircase is Robert Adam's final
masterpiece of interior design.

In 1945 the top floor was given to General Eisenhower as a token of Scotland's recognition of his
role during World War II. His apartment is now run as a small country house hotel, and an Eisenhower
Exhibition in the castle tells something of Ike the man and his visits to Culzean. The Georgian Kitchen
gives a glimpse of life below stairs 200 years ago. Educational programmes and tours are available.
Through the Clocktower Courtyard, a coach house and stables have been converted into the Castle
Shop and Old Stables Coffee House.

The Country Park - Scotland's first country park, created in 1969 and consisting of 563 acres
contains a wealth of natural and historical interest. Miles of woodland walks take the visitor to the
Deer Park, along the Cliff Walk or to the many restored estate buildings, such as the Ruined Arch and
Viaduct, beautiful Camellia House and unique Pagoda. Garden areas include the terraced Fountain
Court and the Walled Garden with its redesigned pleasure garden and impressive reconstructed
Victorian Vinery. The exciting adventure playground introduces children to the wildlife of the park
and makes the Swan Pond a perfect spot for a family picnic.

The Visitor Centre, formerly the Home Farm, is the focus for the main visitor facilities. These
include the Home Farm Restaurant, the Home Farm Shop, the Country Park Shop and Plant Centre.
The new auditorium and exhibition at the Visitor Centre explain the history of Culzean and the

Trust's conservation work,
and there are smaller
interpretive centres at the Gas
House, Ice House and Swan
Pond. Three miles of coastline
provide panoramic views
across the Firth of Clyde and
improved facilities have been
provided at Croy Shore - 1½
miles of beach - accessed from
the A719. The ranger service
provides an extensive
environmental education
service and interpretive
programme.

unusual one. Marjorie Countess of Carrick, the young widow of Adam de Kilconquhar, saw a knight passing by her castle at Turnberry. She immediately became infatuated with him, and had him kidnapped and brought into her presence. He turned out to be Robert de Brus, son of the Lord of Annandale, and she persuaded him to marry her. The result of the marriage was Robert the Bruce, who himself became Earl of Carrick on his mother's death. Because Robert ascended the throne of Scotland as Robert I, the earldom became a royal one, and the present Earl of Carrick is Prince Charles.

Built onto the scant ruins of the castle is **Turnberry Lighthouse**, surrounded on three sides by the championship golf course. The elegant five star **Turnberry Hotel** is situated south east of the castle, just off the main road, and is one of the premier hotels in Scotland. It even has its own small runway for aircraft, and at one time had its own railway line from Ayr to bring guests. During World Wars I and II, all this area was an airfield, and the runways can still be seen. There is a **War Memorial** on the golf course dedicated to the men of the airfield who died in World War I. It is in the shape of a double Celtic cross, and was erected by the people of Kirkoswald parish in 1923. In 1990 the monument was altered so that the names of the airmen killed during World War II could be added.

GIRVAN

10 miles SW of Maybole on the A77

This pleasant little town is the main holiday resort in Carrick. It is also a thriving fishing port, with many boats in the harbour at the mouth of the Water of Girvan. Though there is a long, sandy beach, a boating pond and a small funfair in summer the town is a quiet place

overlooked by the bulk of **Byne Hill** to the south. From the top there is a fine view of the Firth of Clyde, and on a clear day the coast of Northern Ireland can be seen. The small **Crauford Monument** above Ardmillan House, on the western side, commemorates Major A.C.B. Crauford, who took part in the capture of the Cape of Good Hope in 1795.

Out in the Firth of Clyde the bulk of **Ailsa Craig** rises sheer from the water. It is the plug of an ancient volcano, and is now a bird sanctuary. Trips round it are available from Girvan harbour.

Within the town, in Knockcushan Street, is a small, curious building with a short spire which has been given the nickname **Auld Stumpy**. It dates from the 18th century, and at one time was attached to the later McMaster Hall, which burnt down in 1939. Behind Knockcushan House, near the harbour, are **Knockcushan Gardens**, the site of a court held by Robert the Bruce in 1328. At the **McKechnie Institute** in Dalrymple Street art exhibitions are sometimes held.

CULZEAN CASTLE

4 miles W of Maybole off the A719

Culzean Castle (National Trust for Scotland - see panel opposite), perched on a cliff above the Firth of Clyde is possibly the most spectacularly sited castle in Scotland. It was designed by Robert Adam in 1777, and built round an old keep for the 10th Earl of Cassillis. It has some wonderful features, such as the Oval Staircase and the Circular Saloon with its views out over the Firth. Surrounding the castle is **Culzean Country Park**, with such attractions as a Walled Garden, the Swan Pond, the Deer Park and the Fountain Court.

In gratitude for his part in World War II, the National Trust for Scotland

Continued on page 100

Croy to Maidens via Culzean Country Park

Distance:	3.4 miles (5.4 kilometres)
Typical time:	120 mins
Height gain:	0 metres
Map:	Explorer 326 Ayr & Troon
Walk:	www.walkingworld.com ID:799
Contributor:	Joyce and Dougie Howat

Access Information:

Take the A719 south from Ayr. Soon after Croy Brae take the road to the right to Croy Beach. There is a choice of parking either at the top or bottom of the hill. Ideally this is a one-way walk, so drop your passengers at the top of this road and they can walk to the lower car park, while a second car is taken to the finish location at Maidens. To drive to the finishing car park, continue south on the A719. Turn right at the T-junction (towards Culzean Country Park). Continue past the park entrance to Maidens. At a sharp 90-degree bend in the road to the left, take the small road to the right. The car parking is along this road.

The walk can easily be altered to become a circular walk should this be preferred. Once you reach the swan pond in Culzean Country Park (Waymark 9) take any of the paths signposted towards the Home Farm, then return along the coast.

Additional Information:

This walk is good for kids and other features include woodland and a country house. It is worth stopping in the lay-by at Croy Brae. The road here is an optical illusion. Going south the road looks as though it is downhill, when in fact it is uphill. Take your foot off the brake and see the car freewheel the wrong way!

Description:

A coastal walk which takes in part of the rugged headland by Culzean Castle (a National Trust for Scotland property). Starting outside the park boundaries at Croy Shore, the walk takes you along the coast to reach the castle. This can be seen from a long distance away, sitting high up on the headland with its impressive vantage point. Having passed through the ornamental gardens of the castle, the walk continues back down onto the shore. As some of the bays are very rocky (and under water at high tide), the walk turns inland to take in the cliff walk within the park boundaries. This path has magnificent views to the west and south - on a good day both the Mull of Kintyre and Northern Ireland can be seen from the section of path (not to mention the nearer island of Arran).

Features:

Sea, Pub, Toilets, Museum, Play Area, Castle, National Trust/NTS, Wildlife, Birds, Flowers, Great Views

Walk Directions:

1 Leave the top car park and follow the road down to the lower car park. Wait here for the drivers to join you.

2 Turn left onto the beach at the shore car park. Walk along the beach until you reach some small cottages which are right on the shore at Seganwell.

3 There are steps here which lead up to the Culzean Home Farm with restaurant, shop and toilets. However, the coastal walk continues in woodland parallel to the shore.

4 At the next bay take the path away from the shore, past the Gas House and Gas Keeper's Cottage. There are interesting exhibits here, showing how the gas was made in the past to light the castle. The coast becomes very rocky here so it is worth entering Culzean Park; the entry is free from the coast. Follow the path up through the trees towards the castle. At the top of the steps, this is the view back towards Croy and the start of the walk. Follow the path to the right towards the castle.

5 Branch left towards the castle's forecourt. There are toilets and a shop in the old stables. The castle is also worth a visit, but it takes some time and there is a charge to the Scottish National Trust. Take the gate to the left of the castle and follow the path along the side.

6 Descend the steps to the gardens and Fountain Court. The Orangery always has interesting flowers, protected from the frost. Continue through the gardens in a southerly direction.

7 Continue south through a gap in the wall, into a grassy field. There are many routes through the park. All will take you towards Maidens if you chose southerly directions. Cut across the field directly towards the sea, to reach some wooden steps. Follow the wooden steps down past the cannons, to the boathouse beach and past the Dolphin House (under renovation at the moment).

8 Turn left and continue along the coast in a southerly direction. Take care as you will need to pick your way over some rocks at the end of this bay. Continue along the next bay to reach another set of wooden steps. Take the steps and wooden walkway through the marshy area, back to a T-junction on a well-trodden path. Turn right and follow the path.

9 Turn right again at the 'Cliff Walk' sign. This path is high above the sea, with magnificent views. The path eventually turns inland and descends to the Swan Pond.

10 Turn to the right at the side of the pond, but only walk a few metres, to reach a junction with a smaller path off to the right. Now leave the main path for a smaller one signposted 'Port Carrick, Barwhin Hill'. Alternatively, continue on the main path to toilets and a children's play area.

11 Take the fork to the left which leads down to the beach, out of the park to Maidens Shore.

12 Follow the path down to reach the shore. Turn left and continue along the beach to reach the Maidens car park.

13 The end of the walk and hopefully where you have a car dropped off to take you back. Nearby is the Bruce Hotel, should its services be required.

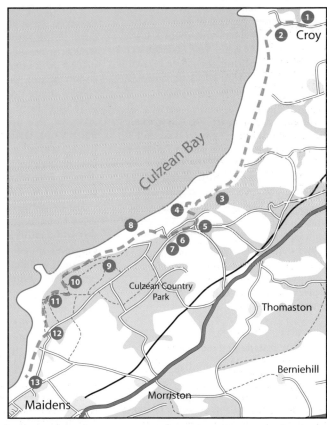

Culzean Castle

harbour.

To the south of the village are the ruins of **Dunure Castle**, perched on the coastline. This is the original castle of the Kennedys, and dates mostly from the 14th century. It was here that the famous **Roasting of the Abbot** took place in 1570. The Kennedys were at the height of their powers, and Gilbert Kennedy, 4th Earl of Cassillis, owned most of the land in Carrick. He was, as his contemporaries observed, "ane very greedy man", and coveted the lands of Crossraguel Abbey, which, at the Reformation, had been placed in the hands of Allan Stewart, commendator, or lay abbot, of the abbey. Gilbert invited Allan to Dunure Castle for a huge feast, and when Allan accepted, had him incarcerated in the Black Vault. He then stripped him and placed him on a spit over a great open fire, turning him occasionally like a side of beef. Eventually Allan signed away the lands, and was released.

But he immediately protested to the Privy Council and the Regent (James VI was still a child at the time), which ordered Kennedy to pay for the lands. But such was Kennedy's power that he ignored the order.

presented General Eisenhower with the life tenure of a flat in Culzean. Eisenhower accepted, and spent a few golfing holidays here. The **Eisenhower Presentation**, within the castle, explains his connections with the area, and has exhibits about D-Day (see also Kirkoswald).

On the shoreline are the **Gasworks**, which produced coal gas to heat and light the castle. At one time a small boat-building yard stood on the shore immediately to the south of the castle, and many fine yachts were built there.

The caves beneath the castle were at one time used by smugglers. A recent archaeological dig unearthed human bones dating form the Bronze Age, showing that the caves have been occupied for thousands of years. However, access to them is barred, as they can be dangerous.

DUNURE

5 miles NW of Maybole off the A 719

This pretty little fishing village would not look out of place in Cornwall. Arriving by car, you drop down towards it, giving excellent views of the cottages and pub, all grouped round a small

AYR

Ayr is the major holiday resort on the Ayrshire coast. It stands at the mouth of the River Ayr, on the south bank, and was formerly the county town of Ayrshire. Always an important place, it was granted its royal charter in the early 1200s, and is the old capital of the Kyle district. Its most distinctive feature is the tall, elegant steeple of the **Town Hall**, built between 1827 and 1832 to the designs of Thomas Hamilton. Seen from the north, it blends beautifully with a cluster of fine Georgian buildings beside the river.

After the Battle of Bannockburn, Bruce held his first parliament here, in the ancient kirk of St John the Baptist, to decide on the royal succession after he died. This kirk is no longer there save for the tower, now called **St John's Tower**, which stands among Edwardian villas near the shore. Oliver Cromwell dismantled the church and used the stone to build **Ayr Citadel**, which has now gone as well, save for a few feet of wall near the river and an arch in a side street. To compensate, he gave the burgh £600 to build a new church, which is now known as the **Auld Parish Kirk**, situated on the banks of the river where

a friary once stood. It dates from the mid-1600s, and is a mellow old T-plan building surrounded by tottering gravestones. Within the lych gate can be seen a couple of mortsafes, which were placed over fresh graves to prevent grave robbing in the early 19th century.

Ayr was the starting off point for Tam o' Shanter's drunken and macabre ride home after spending the evening at an inn, as portrayed in Burns's poem of the same name. In the High Street is the thatched **Tam o' Shanter Inn**, where the ride was supposed to have started. At one time it was a small museum, but now it has thankfully reverted to its original purpose, and you can enjoy a drink within its walls.

Robert Burns and Ayr are inseparable. He was born in a village to the south of the town which has now become a well-heeled suburb, and his influences are everywhere. Off the High Street is the

Auld Brig o' Ayr, which dates from the 14th century, and down river is the **New Bridge**, dating from 1878. In a poem called *The Twa Brigs* Burns accurately forecast that the Auld Brig would outlast the new one. He was right - the New Bridge of Burns's time was swept away in a flood, to be replaced by the present New Bridge, while the Auld Brig still survives.

The second oldest building in the town is **Loudoun Hall**, in the Boat Vennel close to the New Bridge. It was built about 1513 as a fine town house for the Campbells of Loudoun, hereditary sheriffs of Ayr. It was due for demolition just after the war, but was saved when its importance was realised. South of Loudoun Hall, in the Sandgate, is **Lady Cathcart's House**, a tenement building which dates from the 17th century. Within it, in 1756, John Loudon McAdam, the roads engineer, was supposed to have been born (see also Muirkirk, Moffat and Carsphairn).

The bridges of Ayr take you to **Newton upon Ayr** on the north bank of the river, which was once a separate burgh with a charter dated to 1446, but now part of the town. Part of its old tolbooth survives as **Newton Tower**, caught in an island in the middle of the street.

The **Belleisle Estate and Gardens** are to the south of the town, with parkland, deer park, aviary and pets corner. Nearby is **Rozelle House Galleries and Gardens**. There are art exhibitions within the mansion house, plus a tearoom and craft shop.

Also south of the town, perched precariously on a cliff top and always seeming to be in imminent danger of collapsing into the sea, is **Greenan Castle**, a 17th century tower house. It was built in 1603 for John Kennedy of Baltersan and his third wife Florence MacDowell, who owned the lands of Greenan. However, an earlier castle may have stood here, and it may also have been the site of an Iron Age fort. It is typical of many such tower houses in Ayrshire, but some experts believe it has one unique claim to fame - it may mark the real spot where King Arthur's **Camelot** once stood (see also Kelso).

Ayr Racecourse is Scotland's leading racecourse, and is the venue for the Scottish Grand National in April and the Scottish Derby in July.

AROUND AYR

PRESTWICK

2 miles N of Ayr town centre, on the A79

Prestwick is one of the oldest towns in Scotland, having been granted its original burgh charter in the 12th century. It was also one of the most popular holiday resorts for Glaswegians until Spain and Florida took over, and has a long, sandy beach.

To the north of the town is **Prestwick International Airport**, at one time the main transatlantic airport for Glasgow. It is still a busy place, being a favourite starting point for those holidays in warmer climes that eventually saw off Prestwick as a holiday resort. On March 2nd 1960, the airport had possibly its most famous visitor - **Elvis Presley**. Having been discharged from the American army, his plane touched down at the airport for refuelling when he was returning home from Germany. He stayed at the American air force base (now gone) for just under an hour, and then re-boarded his flight. It was the only time that "The King" ever set foot in Britain. A plaque in the airport commemorates his visit, and people still turn up from all over Europe to pay their respects. In later life, someone asked Elvis what country he would like to visit, and he replied that he would like to go back to Scotland, possibly also because he had Scottish ancestors.

The name Prestwick means "priest's burgh", and the ruins of the ancient **Parish Church of St Nicholas** are near the coastline. At **Kingcase** was a lazar house where Robert the Bruce went to seek a cure for his leprosy. **Bruce's Well** can still be seen there.

The very first British Open golf Championship was held at Prestwick in 1860 (with eight competitors) and for 12 years after, and a cairn near the golf course, unveiled in 1977 by Henry Cotton, commemorates the event.

MONKTON

4 miles N of Ayr on the A79

Traffic between Glasgow and Ayr used to thunder through Monkton, but now it is more or less bypassed. It sits on the edge of Prestwick Airport, and at one time the main road cut right across the main runway. This meant that traffic was held up every time an aircraft took off or landed - a magnificent site, but inconvenient for cars and buses. The ruins of 13th century **St Cuthbert's Church** sit at the heart of the village, and at one time the Rev. Thomas Burns, Robert Burns's nephew, was minister here. A church has certainly stood here since 1227, when it is mentioned in a charter of Walter, Bishop of Glasgow, as belonging to Paisley Abbey. In 1834 Monkton parish was united with Prestwick, with a new church being built to serve both communities.

William Wallace, it is said, once fell asleep in the church, and had a dream in which an old man presented him with a sword and a young woman presented him with a wand. He took it to mean

that he must continue his struggle for Scotland's freedom.

The **Muckle Stane** is an "erratic" (a boulder brought by an ice flow towards the end of the last Ice Age), and previously stood in a field outside the village. In 1998 it was relocated within the village.

To the north of the village is a curious monument known as **MacRae's Monument**. It commemorates James MacRae, Governor of Madras in the early 18th century. He was born in Ochiltree in humble circumstances, his father having died before he was born. He was then brought up by a carpenter called Hugh McGuire, and when MacRae returned from India in 1731 a rich man he bought the Orangefield estate (which stood where part of Prestwick Airport now stands). He also found his old benefactor living in poverty. He bought him the estate of Drumdow at Stair, east of Monkton, and introduced his daughters into polite society, each of them making good marriages, one of them even becoming the Countess of Glencairn. MacRae was buried in the churchyard at Monkton, though no stone now marks his grave. A curious tale tells of a gravedigger who once inadvertently dug up MacRae's coffin in the 19th century, and stripped it of its lead. However, the silver plaque on the coffin lid he gave to the authorities in Ayr.

The estate of Ladykirk is to be found a few miles east of Monkton. It was here, in **Ladykirk Chapel** (which has all but vanished), that Robert II (the first Stewart king) married his first wife, Elizabeth Mure of Rowallan, in 1347. It was a marriage that some people considered unlawful, as the couple were related. But later in the year Pope Clement VI declared it a lawful marriage.

From it came Robert III, Robert II's successor.

TROON
6 miles N of Ayr, on the A759

This seaside resort is synonymous with golf, and the British Open has been held here many times. It is a young town, having been laid out in the early 1800s by the 4th Duke of Portland, who wished to create a harbour from which to export the coal from his Ayrshire coalfields. It formed the western terminus of Scotland's earliest rail line, the **Troon/ Kilmarnock Railway**, which was opened in 1812. In 1816 the Duke introduced a steam locomotive onto the line, and it started pulling passenger trains (see also Kilmarnock). The town is now the Scottish terminal for the Scotland/ Ireland P&O express ferry service.

On the shoreline is the **Ballast Bank**, created over the years by ships which discharged their ballast before taking on coal for Ireland. Behind Troon a narrow road climbs up into the **Dundonald Hills**, from where a magnificent view of the Firth of Clyde can be obtained.

SYMINGTON
6 miles N of Ayr off the A77

Symington is a pleasant village of old cottages, though a large estate of council housing on its northern edge has somewhat marred its picturesqueness. It is named after its Norman founder, Simon Lockhart, and at its heart is **Symington Parish Church**, Ayrshire's oldest church still in use. This Norman building, formerly dedicated to the Holy Trinity, was originally built about 1150, and has in its east wall a trio of delightful Norman windows. It has its original piscina in the south wall, and an ancient timbered roof. On a hillside to the west of the village, at a spot called

Barnweil, is the Victorian **Barnweil Monument**, looking for all the world like a church tower without a church. This marks the spot where Wallace watched the "barns o' Ayr burn weel" after he set fire to them. Next to it are the scant ruins of **Barnweil Church**, where John Knox once preached. The parish of Barnweil was suppressed in 1673, and the church, which may have been one of the oldest in Ayrshire, gradually became ruinous.

DUNDONALD
8 miles N of Ayr on the B730

Dundonald Castle (Historic Scotland) is one of Scotland's royal castles, and sits on a high hill overlooking the village. The hill has been occupied for at least 3,000 years, and has been the site of at least three medieval castles. What you see nowadays are the remains of the third castle, built in the 14th century by Robert II, grandson of Robert the Bruce and the first Stewart king of Scotland, to mark his accession to the throne in 1371. It was here, in his favourite residence, that Robert died in 1390. When Boswell and Dr Johnson visited the castle in 1773 during their Scottish journey, Johnson was much amused by the humble home of "Good King Bob", though in the 14th century the castle was much larger than it is now, having stables, a brew house and a blacksmith's workshop. Over the years, the castle has been owned by many families, including the Wallaces and the Cochranes, who later became Earls of Dundonald.

At the top, now reached by a metal staircase, are what would have been the royal apartments, and it is here that Robert II no doubt died. There are fine views northwards and eastwards over central Ayrshire.

TARBOLTON

6 miles NE of Ayr on the B744

When Burns stayed at nearby **Lochlee Farm** (not open to the public) both he and his brother Gilbert looked to Tarbolton for leisure activities. In 1780 they founded a debating society, which met in a thatched house in Sandgate Street in the village. This house is now the **Bachelors' Club** (National Trust for Scotland). It was here that Burns also took dancing lessons, something of which his father William did not approve. Round the fireplace in the upper room you'll see a helical pattern drawn in chalk - an old Ayrshire custom to prevent the Devil from entering the house by way of the chimney.

The farm of Lochlee (also known as Lochlea) sat beside a now drained loch to the west of the village, and had poor soil. When Burns's father died in 1784, the family moved to Mossgiel near Mauchline. In 1779 Burns wrote *The Tarbolton Lassies*, which praises the young women of the village.

Tarbolton Parish Church is an elegant, imposing building of 1821 standing on a low hill.

MAUCHLINE

10 miles NE of Ayr on the A76

When Burns's father died at Lochlee near Tarbolton, the Burns family moved to **Mossgiel Farm** near the village of Mauchline. The farm that Burns knew is no more, but its successor still stands to the north of the village, with its farmhouse looking considerably more prosperous than the one Burns knew. It was in Mauchline that he met Jean Armour, his future wife, and it was here that they first settled down. Jean lived in a house (now gone) in the Cowgate, daughter to a prosperous stone mason who, not surprisingly, originally

disapproved of Jean seeing a penniless failed farmer who had a deserved reputation as a womaniser and who wrote verse. So much so that Jean's mother packed Jean off to her uncle in Paisley, even though the couple had signed a marriage pact that was legal under Scots law of the time. Not only that - she was pregnant.

But eventually the Armours bowed to the inevitable, and Jean and Robert set up home in Castle Street (which at that time was the main street of the village and was called Back Causeway). Their home now houses the **Burns House Museum**. The red sandstone building actually had four families living in it in the 18th century, but it has now been converted so that various displays and exhibitions can be accommodated. Robert and Jean's apartment has been furnished in much the same way as it would have been in 1788 when they moved in. Across from it, but now a private house, was **Nance Tinnock's Inn**, Burns's favourite drinking place.

Burns lived in Mauchline from 1784 until 1788, when he and his family moved to Dumfriesshire. The four years were the most productive in his life, and to his time in Mauchline we owe *To a Mountain Daisy, To a Mouse, Holy Willie's Prayer* and *The Holy Fair*. But it was also troubled times for him, and while trying to eke a living from the poor soil of Mossgiel, he contemplated emigrating to Jamaica. However, the success of his first book of verse, now called the Kilmarnock Edition, made him change his mind. It also, to some extent, softened the Armours' opinion of him.

The **Parish Church** you see today is not the one that Burns knew. The old Norman church of St Michael was pulled down and rebuilt in 1826, though the kirkyard still has many graves connected

NURSERIES DIRECT GARDEN CENTRE

Trabboch Road, Stair, Mauchline, Ayrshire KA5 5JD
Tel: 01292 591900 Fax: 01292 591080
e-mail: staff@nurseriesdirect.co.ok
website: www.nurseriesdirect.co.uk

Set in the heart of the soft, green Ayrshire countryside, **Nurseries Direct** is one of the best garden centres in southwest Scotland. Enclosed within its 4,500 square metres of land is all you will ever need to create and maintain a stunning and colourful garden. There are bedding plants, seeds, tools, books, garden furniture, gifts such as toys, games, kitchenware, pottery and a range of foods such as chutney, sauces and conserves.

In fact, Nurseries Direct is more than just a garden centre - it is a great day out for all the family. The coffee shop sells a wide range of home baking, soups, sandwiches, coffees and teas, all made fresh every day on the premises. There's also a daily specials board, with the food made to order using only fresh local produce wherever possible. And for the kids there's a well-equipped and safe play area, with swings, slide and climbing frame. The prices are always reasonable, and the range is huge, which

guarantees that you're sure to find something that appeals. Catering for the expert and the beginner alike, the knowledgeable and friendly staff is always ready to help and advise.

The centre is near the hamlet of Stair, with its picturesque inn and old church, and through the trees you can even catch a glimpse of historic Stair Castle. So perhaps you'd like to combine a day out exploring the area with a visit to the Garden Centre? You won't be disappointed!

with the poet (including the graves of four of his children). A chart on the church wall explains where each one is. One to look out for is that of **William Fisher**. William was an elder in Mauchline Kirk, and the butt of Burns's satirical poem *Holy Willie's Prayer*, in which he attacks the cant and hypocrisy of the church. Willie asks God's forgiveness for his own, understandable sins, while asking that he severely punish the sins of others. Opposite the church is **Poosie Nansy's Inn**. Though not a great frequenter of this inn, the poet still drank there occasionally, and Burns enthusiasts can still drink there today.

To the north of the village is the **Burns Memorial**, built in 1897. It is a tall, red sandstone tower with a small museum inside. From the top, you get good views of the rich agricultural lands of Ayrshire. Beside the memorial, and forming part of

it, are some pleasant alms cottages for old people.

Gavin Hamilton was Burns's friend and landlord. His house can still be seen, attached to the 15th century **Abbot Hunter's Tower**. The tower looks like a small castle, but was in fact the monastic headquarters, or grange, of the Ayrshire estates owned by Melrose Abbey.

The **Ballochmyle Viaduct**, to the south of the village, carries the Glasgow to Dumfries line across the River Ayr, and is considered to be one of the finest railway bridges in the world. Work started on it in 1843, and it is still Britain's highest stone and brick railway bridge, being 163 feet above the river. It has three smaller arches at either end, and one long, graceful arch in the middle that spans 181 feet. One of the main scenes from the film *Mission Impossible* was filmed there with Tom Cruise, though in the film it was supposed to be on the London to Paris line. And during the First World War a pilot is supposed to have flown under the main arch.

The **Ballochmyle** estate, which stood to the south of the village, is no more. Up until recently it was the site of a hospital, but even that has been pulled down. When Burns first came to Mauchline it was owned by the Whitefoords, who had lost everything when the Douglas Heron Bank of Ayr collapsed in 1773. They eventually sold it to Claud Alexander and his family to pay off their huge debts.

Burns had been used to wandering the Ballochmyle estates, which sit on the banks of the River Ayr, and one day in about 1786 when he was strolling along the banks, he saw Miss Wilhelmina Alexander, Claud's sister. He was so taken by her that he wrote *The Lass o' Ballochmyle*, one of his most famous works, in her honour. He sent it to her, but so angry was she that she never replied. However, the anger was more to do with the fact that she was in her 40s at the time, and thought that Burns was having a joke at her expense. In later years, however, she cherished the poem.

FAILFORD

7 miles E of Ayr on the B743

Near this little village, in 1786, Burns took his farewell of Highland Mary, who would die soon after in Greenock (see also Greenock and Dunoon). Burns, disillusioned by his treatment at the hands of Jean Armour's parents, had asked her to accompany him to Jamaica. They exchanged Bibles, which was seen as a marriage contract, and Mary set off home to Dunoon to prepare for the voyage. However, en route she died in Greenock. The **Failford Monument**, on a slight rise, commemorates the meeting.

A mile east of Failford, in a field, are the remains of a tumulus known as **King Cole's Grave**. Legend tells us that Old King Cole of nursery rhyme fame was a real person - a British king called Coel or Coilus, who ruled in Ayrshire. In the Dark Ages, he fought a great battle against the Scots under their king, Fergus. Cole's army was routed, and he fled the battlefield. Eventually he was captured and killed. His supporters later cremated his body and buried it with some pomp at the spot where he died (see also Coylton). The Kyle area of Ayrshire is supposed to be named after him.

The tumulus was opened in 1837, and some cremated bones were discovered in two small urns. Up until not so long ago the nearby stream was referred to locally as the "Bloody Burn", and one field beside the stream was known as "Deadmen's Holm", as that is where those killed in the battle were supposedly buried. Tales were often told of bits of human bone and armour being turned up by men ploughing the field.

It is in the Failford Inn that the guide centre for the new **River Ayr Way**, a long-distance footpath that follows the course of the River Ayr from Glenbuck to the sea, will be set up in 2005.

OCHILTREE

11 miles E of Ayr on the A70

Ochiltree was the birthplace of yet another Ayrshire writer, **George Douglas Brown**, who was born here in 1869, the illegitimate son of a local farmer and a serving girl. He and went on to write *The House with the Green Shutters*, a hard, unrelenting book about life in Scotland in the late 19th century. He wanted to banish the "kailyard school" of writing, which saw Scotland's countryside as being comfortable and innocent, full of couthy, happy people of unquestionable worth. He set his book in the fictional town of "Barbie", which is a thinly disguised Ochiltree, and not many characters in the book have redeeming features. One of the village's cottages (not open to the public) now has green shutters, and is itself known as the "House with the Green Shutters".

AUCHINLECK

13 miles E of Ayr off the A76

Burns is not the only famous literary person associated with Ayrshire. Though born in Edinburgh, **James Boswell** was the son of a Court of Session judge who lived in **Auchinleck House**, near what became the mining village of Auchinleck. He had the house built in about 1760 as his country seat, and Boswell brought the great Dr Johnson there to meet him when the pair were touring Scotland. They didn't hit it off.

Boswell himself died in 1795, and now lies in a small mausoleum attached to the old **Auchinleck Kirk**, which is no longer used for worship, but instead houses a museum dedicated to the writer and biographer.

SORN

14 miles E of Ayr on the B743

Sorn is one of the most picturesque villages in the county, and has won national and international awards for its tidiness and well kept gardens. It sits on the River Ayr, with an 18th century bridge spanning it, and has many delightful cottages. **Sorn Parish Church** dates from 1658, and the lofts, or galleries, are reached by stairs on the outside of the walls. **Sorn Castle** dates from the 14th century, with later additions. It was built by a branch of the Hamilton family, and James VI once

visited on horseback in the depths of winter to attend the wedding of Isobel Hamilton, the daughter of his Treasurer, to Lord Seton. James VI's journey to Sorn so sickened him that he later said that if he were to play a trick on the devil, he would send him from Glasgow to Sorn on a cold winter's day (see also Kilmarnock). It is open to the public from mid July to early August each year.

Alexander Peden was born at Auchincloich near Sorn in 1626. Known as **Prophet Peden**, he was a Covenanter who held secret conventicles, or prayer meetings, at lonely spots all over central Ayrshire. The whole area abounds with places that have been named after him, such as "Peden's Pulpit" and "Peden's Table". There is even a field called "Preaching Peden".

CUMNOCK

15 miles E of Ayr off the A76

Cumnock is a small industrial town which was granted its burgh charter in 1509. In the middle of its square sits **Cumnock Old Parish Church**, built in the mid 1800s. It's a foursquare building that seems to sprout transepts, apses and porches in all directions. Two miles west of the town, at Lugar, is **Bello Mill** (not open to the public), birthplace in 1754 of William Murdoch, discoverer of gas lighting and, believe it or not, the man who invented the wooden top hat. He conducted his gas experiments in a cave on the banks of the Lugar Water upstream from Bello.

Dumfries House (not open to the public), one mile west of Cumnock, was designed for the 4th Earl of Dumfries in the mid 1700s by John and Robert Adam. It is said that James Armour, Robert Burns's father-in-law, was one of the masons who worked on the building of the house.

At the north end of the town is the house that **James Keir Hardie**, the founder of the Scottish Labour Party, built for himself. Though born in Lanarkshire, he considered himself to be a Cumnock man. He was first of all MP for West Ham in London, and later for Merthyr Tydfil in Wales. His bust can be found outside the Town Hall.

MUIRKIRK
23 miles E of Ayr on the A70

This former mining and iron-working town is surrounded by bleak but lovely moorland. To the west is the site of the **Battle of Airds Moss**, fought in 1680 and marked by a memorial. A Covenanting army was heavily defeated by Government troops. Just south of the town, and along an unmarked road, is a small monument to John Loudon McAdam the road builder, who owned a tar works in the vicinity. A mile-long canal was dug here in 1789, which served the former iron works (see also Ayr, Moffat and Carsphairn).

NEW CUMNOCK
18 miles E of Ayr on the A76

The parish of New Cumnock was carved from the much older parish of Cumnock in 1650, with a church being built on the site of Cumnock Castle, once owned by the Dunbars, and once visited by Edward II of England during his campaign to subjugate Scotland. The ruins of this church can still be seen. It was near here that the **Knockshinnoch Mining Disaster** took place in 1950. 129 miners were trapped underground when a slurry of mud and peat filled some workings that were close to the surface. 116 were eventually brought out alive, and great bravery was shown by the rescuers. A feature film, *The Brave Don't Cry*, was made about the disaster in 1952. To the south of the village is **Glen Afton**,

through which flows the Afton Water. A cairn marks the spot where Burns was inspired to write *Flow Gently Sweet Afton*.

DALRYMPLE
5 miles SE of Ayr on the B7034

In this quiet little village of weavers' cottages Burns first received an education. While staying at Mount Oliphant, he and his brother Gilbert attended the Parish School on alternate weeks. The village sits on the Doon, and has a small **Parish Church** built in 1849.

Some people say it was the inspiration for the musical *Brigadoon*, about a mysterious Scottish village that only appears every 100 years. Alan Jay Lerner, who wrote the words, was looking for a way of turning a German fairy tale about a magical village called *Germelshausen* into a musical, and one day while in Scotland he suddenly happened upon Dalrymple, which sits in a small glen, hidden until you're almost upon it. He immediately thought of locating his musical in Scotland, and called it Brigadoon because there really is a bridge over the River Doon in the village. He also called one of the characters Charlie Dalrymple.

Two miles south, and straight out of a fairy tale as well, is **Cassillis Castle** (not open to the public), the home of the Marquis of Ailsa, head of Clan Kennedy. It is a wonderful concoction of pepper pot turrets and towers built originally in the 15th century but added to throughout the years. It is here that the hanging of Johnny Faa and his men from the Dule Tree is supposed to have taken place. (see also Maybole).

ALLOWAY
2 miles S of Ayr town centre on the B7024

Robert Burns was not the uneducated "ploughman poet" from the peasant classes that his more romantic admirers

Alloway

sighted father. He knew his Classics, he could speak French and some Latin, he could read music, he took dancing lessons, and he could play both the fiddle and, surprisingly, the guitar. When he went to Edinburgh in later life, he was possibly better educated than some of the gentry who patronised him. Two of his sons, James Glencairn Burns and W. Nicol Burns, attained the ranks of Lieutenant Colonel and Colonel respectively in the British Army.

would have us believe. His father was a tenant farmer, and although not well off, still managed to employ workmen and serving girls on his farm.

Burns himself was a highly educated man for his time, thanks to his far-

At one time, Alloway was a small country village. Now it forms part of Ayr, and is full of large, impressive houses which illustrate the relative affluence of

TWENTY-SEVEN ALLOWAY

27 Alloway, Alloway, Ayrshire KA7 4PY
Tel/Fax: 01292 440202
e-mail: 27alloway@btconnect.com
website: www.27alloway.co.uk

You could spend a whole afternoon at Twenty-Seven Alloway, an innovative and fascinating shop in the village where Scotland's national poet, Robert Burns, was born. In fact it sits opposite Burns' Cottage, in an elegant Georgian style building.

Owned and personally managed by Linda Singh and Amber Thom, this modern, chic shop overflows with

thoughtful gifts and accessories for all occasions. There are candles, prints, cards, furnishings, pottery and a host of objects that would make a perfect souvenir of your visit. Twenty-Seven Alloway can even supply fresh flowers seven days a week for that special occasion or just to brighten up your room. There are also lamps, canvasses and glass, with the shop being laid out in such a way that everything is bright, cheerful and yet elegantly displayed.

Linda and Amber are determined to stock only the best in inspirational and cutting edge giftware, while at the same time offering keen prices that are sure to impress. There is ample parking close by.

this part of Ayrshire. It was here, in 1759, that Robert Burns was born in a cottage that his father built with his own hands. Now **Burns Cottage** is a place of pilgrimage, and people come from all over the world to pay their respects. Within the grounds of the cottage is the **Burns Museum**, containing many of his manuscripts, letters and possessions.

Robert Burns Cottage

Alloway Kirk is where Robert's father, William Burns, is buried, and it was the main setting for the poem *Tam o' Shanter*. It dates from the early 16th century, but even in Burns's day it was a ruin. Across the road, within some beautiful gardens, is the Grecian **Burns Monument**, built in the 1820s. Inside is a small museum.

Spanning the Doon is the graceful **Brig o' Doon**, a single arched bridge dating from the 15th century or possibly earlier. It was across the Brig o' Doon that Tam o' Shanter was chased by the witches he disturbed in Alloway Kirk. However, he managed to gain the keystone of the bridge and escaped unharmed, as witches cannot cross running water, even though his horse lost its tail. In Burn's day it lay on the main road south into Carrick, but a newer, wider bridge now carries traffic south.

Across the road from Alloway Kirk is the **Tam o' Shanter Experience**, a visitor centre with two audiovisual shows within its large auditorium. One illustrates Burns's life and times, and the other recreates what happened to Tam o' Shanter after he left the inn and made his fateful ride south from Ayr.

East of Alloway is **Mount Oliphant Farm** (not open to the public) to which Burns and his family moved when he was seven years old.

St Quivox

2 miles NE of Ayr just off the A77

The tiny **Parish Church** is a small gem of a building. Though altered beyond recognition over the years, its basic fabric is still medieval, and it takes its name from a shadowy Celtic saint called variously St Kevock, St Kennocha, St Kenochis, St Cavocks and St Evox. It was restored by Lord Cathcart of Auchincruive - and no doubt altered to suit Protestant services - in 1595.

To the east is **Oswald Hall**, designed by Robert Adam for James Oswald in 1767. It is now a conference centre. The surrounding Auchincruive estate is one of the campuses of the Scottish Agricultural College.

The **Hannah Research Institute**, close to the village, carries out research work on agricultural animals as well as cells, organs and body tissue. It is one of the leading scientific centres in the world working in this sphere.

KILMARNOCK

Though it is largely an industrial town, Kilmarnock was granted its burgh charter in 1592, so its roots go deep into Scottish history. Legend says it grew up round a church founded by St Marnock, a Celtic saint, in the 7th century. The present **Laigh Kirk** (now called The Laigh West High Kirk) in Bank Street dates from 1802. It has a 17th century steeple (a date stone on it says 1410, but this may refer to an earlier building), and is supposed to stand on the site of the earlier church. In 1801, during a service, 29 people were trampled to deaths when plasterwork started falling off the ceiling of the previous kirk, causing a mad rush for the doors. When it was rebuilt, it was given 13 exits in case it ever happened again. The town's other old church is the **Old High Kirk**, which dates from the early 1730s.

Kilmarnock has many Burns associations, and the first edition of his poems was published in the town, at Star Inn Close (now gone) in 1786. Now a copy is worth many thousands of pounds. A stone marking the spot can be found in the small shopping mall. Also in the mall is a stone marking the spot where Covenanting martyr **John Nesbit** was executed in 1683. His grave can be seen in the kirkyard of the Laigh and West High Kirk.

Burns Statue, unveiled in the mid 1990s by the Princess Royal, stands at Kilmarnock Cross. It is the work of Sandy Stoddard, whose other works include the statue of David Hume on Edinburgh's Royal Mile and the sculptured friezes in the Queen's Gallery in Buckingham Palace.

In truth, Kilmarnock's shopping centre, notably Kilmarnock Cross and King Street, is dull and unattractive, due to uninspired modern developments. But if you go down Cheapside towards Bank Street and the narrow streets round the Laigh and West High Kirk, you get an idea of what the 18th century town looked like.

It was in a shop in King Street that Johnnie Walker first started bottling and selling whisky in 1820. The **Johnnie Walker Bottling Plant** in Hill Street is now one of the largest plants of its kind in the world. Johnnie Walker himself lies in the kirk yard of St Andrew's Glencairn Church (no longer used for worship) to the south of the town centre, and his statue can be found in the Strand.

One place not to be missed is the **Dick Institute**, the town's museum, art gallery and library. It is housed in a grand classical building, and has impressive collections featuring geology, archaeology, biology and local history. The gallery is also impressive, with paintings by Corot, Constable, Turner and Kilmarnock's own painter, Robert Colquhoun. The area around the Dick Institute is particularly attractive, with a war memorial, Victorian houses, and the richly decorated façade of the old technical college, now being converted into flats. Across from the Dick Institute is the statue of Kilmarnock's own Dick Whittington - **James Shaw** (known affectionately in the town as "Jimmy Shaw") who became Lord Mayor of London in 1805.

To the north east of the town centre is the town's oldest building, **Dean Castle**. It was the home of the Boyd family, who became Earls of Kilmarnock, and is in fact two castles within a curtain wall - the 14th century Keep and the later Palace. Both are open to the public, and house wonderful collections of tapestries, musical instruments and armour. Surrounding it is **Dean Castle Country**

Park with many walks and a small children's zoo.

The Boyd family rose to become the most important family in Scotland in the 1460s, when Sir Robert Boyd became Regent of Scotland. In 1746 the last earl was beheaded in London for fighting alongside Charles Edward Stuart at Culloden, and all his lands and titles were forfeited.

During his trial in London, his young wife, the Countess of Kilmarnock, stayed at the Boyd's other residence in the town - Kilmarnock House (now gone). Daily she walked its grounds, awaiting news of his fate. These grounds are now the **Howard Park**, which has a tree lined avenue known as **Lady's Walk**. The Countess herself died shortly after her husband, and some people say that her ghost still haunts the park (see also Falkirk).

Kilmarnock Academy, which stands on an eminence overlooking the town centre, is said to be one of the few schools in the world that has produced two Nobel Prize winners - Lord Boyd Orr (see also Kilmaurs) and Sir Alexander Fleming (see also Darvel).

Across from the new sheriff court building near the park is the **Old Sheriff Court** of 1852, an attractive building in neoclassical style. It sits on the site of one of the termini of Scotland's first railway, the Troon/Kilmarnock Railway, built by the Duke of Portland in 1812 (see also Troon). Two miles west of the town is the **Gatehead Viaduct**, built in 1807 to take the railway over the River Irvine. Though it no longer carries a railway line, it is still Scotland's oldest railway bridge.

Though Elderslie in Renfrewshire seems a likelier location, there are those who claim that **William Wallace** was born at Ellerslie, west of Riccarton, a suburb of Kilmarnock (and named after Sir Richard Wallace, a relation of William). There was certainly a Wallace castle in the area, and young William is known to have had his first skirmish with English troops on the banks of the River Irvine within the town.

In 1862, at Crosshouse, a mining village west of Kilmarnock, was born **Andrew Fisher**, who rose to become Prime Minister of Australia on three separate occasions.

A few miles north of Kilmarnock, on the A77 (now bypassed by a motorway) is the farm of Kingswell. It was here, in the late 16th century, that James VI stopped to drink the waters of the well that once stood here. He was on his way to Sorn Castle to attend a wedding in the middle of winter, and found the journey harrowing (see also Sorn).

AROUND KILMARNOCK

FENWICK

4 miles N of Kilmarnock off the A77

Fenwick (pronounced "Fennick") is really two villages - High Fenwick and Laigh Fenwick. They lie on the edge of the Fenwick Moors, which separate the farmlands of Ayrshire from Glasgow and its suburbs, and were originally weaving villages. Some of the cottages still show their weaving origins, with two windows on one side of the door to allow plenty of light to enter the room containing the loom and one window on the other. **Fenwick Parish Church**, which dates from 1643, is an attractive whitewashed building with a Greek cross plan. On one wall hangs the original **jougs**, where wrongdoers were chained by their necks to the wall.

Two miles south east of the village is the quaintly named, and often photographed, hamlet of **Moscow** (pronounced "Moss-cow" rather than "Moss-coe"), which actually has a burn called the Volga flowing through it. And five miles to the north, off the B764, is **Lochgoin Farm**, which has a small museum commemorating the Covenanters.

Fenwick was the birthplace, in 1803, of John Fulton, a shoemaker who gained considerable fame throughout Scotland by making orreries - working models of the solar system where the planets revolve round the sun and satellites revolve round the planets, all synchronised by the use of gearing. Fulton built three such orreries, and one of them is still on show in the Kelvin Galleries in Glasgow (temporarily closed for refurbishment)

KILMAURS

2 miles NW of Kilmarnock, on the A735

Kilmaurs is a former weaving village, and though only a few fields separate it from Kilmarnock's suburbs, it is still a small, self-contained community with many small cottages. At its centre is the old 17th century **Tolbooth**, still with the jougs attached, which were placed round wrongdoers' necks as a punishment.

St Maurs Glencairn Church dates from 1888, and replaced an earlier medieval collegiate church founded by the Earls of Glencairn, who lived close by. **Glencairn Aisle**, the 16th century burial vault of the Earls of Glencairn, still stands to the rear of the church, however, and it has an ornate monument inside to the 7th Earl and his family. It dates from around 1600, and carries an inscription that reads "nothing is surer than death, be therefore sober and watch in prayer"

The village takes its name from St Maura, daughter of a Scottish chieftain

on the island of Little Cumbrae in the Firth of Clyde. **John Boyd Orr**, first director of the United Nations Food and Agricultural Organisation and Nobel prize-winner, was born in Kilmaurs in 1880.

Kilmaurs Place (not open to the public) dates from the 17th century, and was built as a replacement for the earlier Kilmaurs Castle. It was the home of the Earls of Glencairn and later of the powerful Montgomery family.

STEWARTON

5 miles N of Kilmarnock on the A735

Stewarton is famous as being the home of bonnet making in Ayrshire. It was the birthplace, in 1739, of **David Dale**, the industrialist and social reformer who founded New Lanark (see also Lanark). The **Parish Church of St Columba** dates originally from 1696, though it has been much altered.

DUNLOP

7 miles N of Kilmarnock on the A735

Dunlop is a delightful village of small weavers' cottages. The **Parish Church** dates from 1835, though it has fragments from the earlier church incorporated into the north aisle. In the kirkyard is the ornate early 17th century **Hans Hamilton Tomb**, contained within a small mausoleum. Hamilton was Dunlop's first Protestant minister, and was made Viscount Clandeboye by James VI. The small **Clandeboye Hall**, beside the mausoleum, dates from the 17th century, and was the village's first school.

It was in a farm near the village that the famous Dunlop cheese was first manufactured in the 17th century by a farmer's wife called Barbara Gilmour. It is made from the milk of Ayrshire cattle, and closely resembles a Cheddar. Barbara now lies buried in the kirkyard, and her grave can still be seen. Cheese making was recently revived in the village, and Dunlop cheese, which is harder than the original variety, is made by Dunlop Dairy.

GALSTON

4 miles E of Kilmarnock on the A71

This pleasant little town in the Irvine Valley has a splendid **Parish Church** dating from 1808. One of its ministers, Perthshire-born **Robert Stirling**, was the inventor of the Stirling Engine. He died in 1878.

Another church not to be missed is **St Sophia's RC Church**, modelled on the Hagia St Sophia in Istanbul. **Barr Castle** is a solid, 15th century tower house once owned by the Lockhart family. William Wallace is said to have taken refuge within the walls of a previous castle on the site in the 13th century, and when the English troops surrounded it he escaped by jumping from a window onto a tree. John Knox preached in 1556. An ancient game of handball used to be played against its walls by the locals. The castle is now a small museum with many exhibits relating to local history.

To the north of the town are the impressive ruins of **Loudoun Castle**, ancestral home of the Campbells of Loudoun. It was burnt down in 1941, and in its time entertained so lavishly that it was called the "Windsor of Scotland". Three ghosts reputedly haunt it - a Grey Lady, a Phantom Piper and a Benevolent Monk. At one time the great sword of William Wallace was kept within the castle, but it was sold in 1930. Beside its walls is the **Auld Yew Tree**, under which Hugh, 3rd Earl of Loudoun, prepared the draft of the Treaty of Union between Scotland and England. Today

the **Loudoun Castle Theme Park** fills the grounds of the castle.

Loudoun Castle was the birthplace of **Lady Flora Hastings**, who shook the monarchy and government to its core in 1839. Queen Victoria was 20 years old at the time, and had been on the throne for just two years. Lady Flora was a Lady of the Bedchamber who contracted a disease which so swelled her abdomen that she appeared pregnant. Gossip raged through the court, and she was shunned, even though doctors whom she consulted confirmed that she wasn't pregnant but ill, and had an enlarged liver.

Neither the government nor the Queen did anything to dispel the rumours, and people began to sympathise with the young woman. Soon it was the Queen's turn to be shunned, and she was shocked when people turned their back on her as she proceeded through London by coach. It wasn't until Lady Flora was on her deathbed in 1833 in Buckingham Palace that a grudging reconciliation took place, though no apology was ever given. The Campbells were so incensed by Flora's treatment that when postage stamps were introduced bearing Victoria's image, family members stuck them onto envelopes upside down (see also Newmilns).

A mile or so away from Loudoun Castle are the ruins of the medieval **Loudoun Kirk**, at one time dedicated to St Michael. Flora now lies in the choir, which has been converted into a burial vault for the Campbells of Loudoun, and a slim monument stands in the kirkyard to her memory. Their coat-of-arms can still be seen on the choir walls, above the entrance to the vault. The church seems isolated today, but this was not always so. Up until just after the Second World War, a village stood here as well. However, the houses had no running water, electricity or sewage services, so were demolished, though the outlines of many gardens can still be seen.

Attached to a wall of the ruined kirk is a plaque which commemorates the Belgian paratroopers who trained at Loudoun Castle during the Second World War.

NEWMILNS
7 miles E of Kilmarnock on the A71

Newmilns is a small lace making and weaving town in the Irvine Valley, which was granted its charter in 1490, making it the oldest inland burgh in Ayrshire. The small crow stepped **Town House**, or Tolbooth, dates from 1739, and behind the Loudoun Arms, which itself dates from the 18th century, is **Newmilns Tower**, an early 16th century tower house built by Sir Hugh Campbell, Earl of Loudoun. Sir Hugh was perhaps the most tragic member of the Campbell of Loudon family. After being involved in the murder of a member of the powerful Kennedy family during an ongoing feud, his wife and nine children were killed when the Kennedys besieged Loudoun Castle, a few miles away.

The **Lady Flora Institute**, built in 1877 as a girl's school, commemorates the tragic Lady Flora Hastings, a lady-in-waiting to Queen Victoria (see also Galston). The institute is now private housing.

During the American Civil War, the weavers of Newmilns sent a message of support to Abraham Lincoln, and he in turn sent back an American flag. This was subsequently lost, but in 1949 the American Embassy gave the town a replacement, which is now housed in the early 19th century **Parish Church** in the main street.

DARVEL
8 miles E of Kilmarnock, on the A71

Situated in the lovely Irvine Valley, Darvel is a small, attractive town which was laid out in the late 18th and early 19th centuries. Like its neighbour Newmilns, it is a lace making town, the skills having been brought here by the Dutch in the 17th century. It was in Lochfield, near Darvel, that **Sir Alexander Fleming**, the discoverer of penicillin, was born in 1881. To the east of the town is the immense bulk of **Loudoun Hill**, the plug of a former volcano. A Roman fort was built here in about AD60, and finally abandoned 100 years later. Nothing now remains of it due to sand and gravel excavation. Both William Wallace and Robert the Bruce fought battles at Loudoun Hill against the English, in 1297 and 1307 respectively. South of the town is the quaintly named **Distinkhorn**, the highest hill in the area.

IRVINE
7 miles W of Kilmarnock on the A71

Irvine is an ancient seaport and royal burgh which, in the 1960s, was designated as Britain's first seaside new town. It is a mixture of old and new, and has many unattractive industrial estates surrounding it. However, the historical core has been preserved, though a brutally modern and totally unnecessary shopping mall straddling the River Irvine dominates it. Robert Burns learned flax dressing in Irvine in 1781, and lodged in a house in the cobbled **Glasgow Vennel**. A small museum has been created within both it and the heckling shop behind it.

Irvine has other, more unexpected, literary associations, however. In 1815 the American writer **Edgar Allan Poe**, spent a couple of months in the town, attending the local school. It is said that part of his lessons was to copy the epitaphs from the tombstones in the kirkyard of the **Parish Kirk**, which may have prepared him for some of the macabre tales he wrote in later life (see also Saltcoats). Irvine was also the birthplace of the writer **John Galt**, a relative of the man who adopted Edgar Allan Poe in the United States. **Alexander MacMillan**, who founded the great publishing house, was also a native of the town.

In the nearby village of **Dreghorn** was born in 1840 yet another famous Ayrshireman - **John Boyd Dunlop**, who invented the pneumatic tyre. Born in 1840, he came from a farming background, and graduated from Edinburgh University as a veterinary surgeon. He practised in Edinburgh and then Belfast. He found the roads of Ulster to be stony and rough, and eventually invented an inflatable tyre to overcome the discomfort of travelling on them. Unfortunately, unknown to him, another Scot, Robert William Thomson, had patented the idea before him, and only after a court case could he set up the Dunlop Rubber Company.

Dreghorn Parish Church, built in 1780, is unusual in that it is six-sided in plan. It was built by Archibald, the 11th Earl of Eglinton, and used to have the nickname of the "threepenny church", as its shape reminded people of the old threepenny bit.

The ruins of **Seagate Castle** date from the early 16th century, and it is said that Mary Stuart lodged here briefly in 1563. Every August the town has its **Marymass Week**, which supposedly commemorates her visit. However, the celebrations probably have more to do with a pre-Reformation religious festival, as the parish church was formerly dedicated to St Mary.

In the 18th century, Irvine saw the founding of perhaps the most unusual religious cult ever seen in Scotland - the Buchanites. Elspet Buchan was the daughter of a publican, and claimed she could bestow immortality on a person by breathing on them, and that she herself was immortal. She attracted a wide following, including a gullible Irvine clergyman, but was hounded, along with her followers, from the town. She eventually died a natural death, and the cult broke up (see also Dunscore and Crocketford).

Down by the harbour side is the **Magnum Leisure Centre**, one of the biggest centres of its kind in Scotland. It has a theatre and concert hall, an indoor bowling green, an ice rink, swimming pool and fitness and coaching areas.

Near the Magnum Centre is one of the three sites of the **Scottish Maritime Museum** (see also Dumbarton and Glasgow). It houses a wide collection of ships and small craft. There's also the Linthouse Engine Works, which houses a vast collection of maritime machinery, such as engines, winding gear and so on. In the Ship worker's Tenement Flat, a typical "room and kitchen" flat dating from the 1920s has been re-created, showing how shipyard workers lived in those days. Visitors can also board the *Spartan*, one of the last puffers in Scotland. These small cargo boats, immortalised in the *Para Handy* tales by Neil Munro, sailed the west coast of Scotland for many years.

Irvine was the setting, in 1839, of the grand **Eglinton Tournament**, organised by the 13th Earl of Eglinton at his home, Eglinton Castle, on the outskirts of the town. Here, a great medieval tournament was to be re-created, with jousting, horse riding and other knightly pursuits for the great and the good. They attended from all over Europe, but alas, the three-day event was a wash out due to colossal rainstorms. Little remains of the castle, but the grounds have been turned into **Eglinton Country Park**.

KILWINNING

9 miles NW of Kilmarnock on the A737

Though nowadays a continuation of Irvine, Kilwinning was, up until 1975, a separate burgh. Its former name was Segtoune, meaning the "saint's town", as it was founded in the 7th century by St Winnin, whom some people associate with St Finnan of Moville, who taught St Columba in Ireland. In the 12th century the great Tironensian **Kilwinning Abbey** was built on the site, and its ruins still dominate the town centre, though they are not as extensive as those of Ayrshire's other great abbey, Crossraguel. It was founded by Hugh de Morville, High

Constable of Scotland and a relation of Richard de Morville, one of the murderers of Thomas à Becket at Canterbury. The tower you see nowadays was built in 1815, and replaced the original medieval one, which fell down the year before. The Ancient Society of Kilwinning Archers is one of the oldest archery organisations in the world, and each year in August it holds the **Papingo Shoot**, where archers shoot upwards at a target (the papingo) held from a window of the tower. The papingo is usually a wooden pigeon, and such shoots were once common throughout Britain. **Kilwinning Parish Church**, which sits within the ruins of the abbey, was built in 1775. The town is the home of Freemasonry in Scotland.

A few miles out of town, on the A737, is **Dalgarven Mill** (see panel below) dating from about 1620. It is now a museum dedicated to country life in Ayrshire.

ARDROSSAN, SALTCOATS & STEVENSTON

11 miles W of Kilmarnock on the A78

These towns form a trio of holiday resorts on the Ayrshire coast. Ardrossan

DALGARVEN MILL

Dalgarven, Kilwinning KA13 6PL
Tel: 01294 552448
website: www.dalgarvenmill.org.uk

There has been a mill on the site since the 14th century, set up by the monks of Kilwinning Abbey. The present mill was erected in 1640 and rebuilt in 1880 after being damaged by fire. The Garnock waters power a six metre diameter breast shot wheel that drives the French millstones through cast iron gearing. Traditional methods of producing flour can be traced and the wheel turns when possible. The three storey grain store has been converted to house an extensive collection of Ayrshire farming and domestic memorabilia and there is an exhibition drawn from a collection of over 6,000 costumes and accessories ranging from 1775 to 1980. The top floor is a re-creation of the mill owner's house as it would have been in the 1880s. There are delightful walks by the river, a coffee shop in a farmhouse kitchen setting and an antique shop to complete your visit.

is the most industrialised, and is the ferry terminal for Arran. It is a planned town, with its core being laid out in the early 19th century by the 12th Earl of Eglinton. The ruins of 15th century **Ardrossan Castle**, once a stronghold of the Montgomeries, sit on Castle Hill overlooking the main streets. Cromwell is said to have plundered some of its masonry to build the Citadel at Ayr. The ruins and the land surrounding them were given to the town by the Earl of Eglinton as a public park. The **Obelisk** at the highest point on the hill commemorates a local doctor, Alexander McFadzean, who promoted piped water and gas supplies in the town. At the foot of the hill stands **St Peter in Chains**, designed by Jack Coia, one of Scotland's best-known architects, and built in 1938. It is reckoned to be one of the finest modern churches in Ayrshire.

Just off the coast is **Horse Island**, an RSPB reserve. Though it looks peaceful enough, it has been the scene of many shipwrecks over the years, and many sailors have found themselves marooned on it after their ships struck its submerged reefs. At the **Clyde Marina** is a sculpture park featuring works by the Japanese artist Hideo Furuta, who lives and works in Scotland.

Ardrossan Docks, up until the 1930s, was one of the main supply ports for the Hudson Bay Company, and the harbour was crammed with ships loading supplies for North America and unloading furs, fish and sometimes animals.

At Saltcoats the **North Ayrshire Museum**, housed in a former church, has an interesting local history collection. A gravestone in the kirkyard may be that of an ancestor of Edgar Allan Poe (see also Irvine). The town has a fine beach, and its name is a reminder of the times when salt was produced here from seawater.

The small harbour dates from the late 17th century with later alterations, and at low tide fossilised trees can be seen on the harbour floor. It was in Saltcoats, in 1793, that **Betsy Miller**, the only woman ever to have become a registered ship's captain, was born.

Stevenston is a straggling town, with a **High Church** that dates from 1832. It has a good beach, though it is some way from the centre of the town. Nearby, at Ardeer, the British Dynamite Company established a factory in 1873. It later became Nobel's Explosives Company, and in 1926 became part of ICI.

On the seawall of the beach is a portrait of Robert Burns which is 25 feet high and about 16 feet wide.

DALRY

11 miles NW of Kilmarnock on the A737

This small industrial town's square is dominated by the **Parish Church of St Margaret**, dating from the 1870s. The town's name comes from the Gaelic "Dal Righe", meaning the "King's Field", which shows that at one time it must have had royal connections. To the south east of the town is **Blair**, a large mansion centred on what was a typical Scottish tower house of the 12th century. The parkland, which surrounds it, was laid out by William Blair in the 1760s. It is the home of Clan Blair, who were supporters of both Bruce and Wallace. It was at one time the home of the daughter of the English King John, who had married William de Blare. Now the mansion can be hired as a venue for conferences and seminars.

BEITH

11 miles NW of Kilmarnock off the A737

Beith is a small attractive town, and at 500 feet is the highest town in Ayrshire. The remains of the **Auld Kirk** date from the late 16th century, while the impressive **High Church** dates from the early 19th century. **Eglinton Street** is the most attractive part of the town, with small, neat two-storey buildings dating from the late 18th and 19th centuries.

KILBIRNIE
12 miles NW of Kilmarnock on the A760

Kilbirnie literally means the "kil" or "cell" of St Birinus or Birinie, a West Saxon monk who died at Dorchester in Dorset in 650AD. Within the town you'll find the **Barony Parish Church**, dating from the 15th century. Inside is some wonderfully exuberant woodwork from the 17th and 18th centuries, including the extravagant Crawford Loft and the Cunninghame Aisle. In medieval times it was dedicated to St Brendan of Clonfert in Ireland. Standing next to the golf course are the ruins of the **Place of Kilbirnie**, a former castle of the Crawford family dating from the 15th century.

WEST KILBRIDE
16 miles NW of Kilmarnock off the A78

West Kilbride is a sedate village of Glasgow commuters, perched above its twin village of **Seamill**, on the coast. **Law Castle** was built in the 15th century for Princess Mary, sister of James III, on her marriage to Thomas Boyd of Kilmarnock, who became the Earl of Arran. However, the marriage was later annulled and he had to flee to the Continent, where he died in Antwerp. Mary eventually remarried, this time to James Hamilton, first Lord Hamilton, and the Earlship of Arran passed to their son.

At the hamlet of Portencross, out on a headland beyond Seamill, are the substantial ruins of 14th century **Portencross Castle**, another Boyd stronghold. Also on the headland is **Hunterston Castle** (not open to the public), ancestral home of Clan Hunter, and **Hunterston Nuclear Power Station**.

THE CUMBRAES
19 miles NW of Kilmarnock, in the Firth of Clyde

These two islands - **Little Cumbrae** and **Great Cumbrae** - were once in the county of Bute. Little Cumbrae is privately owned, but Great Cumbrae can be visited by a frequent ferry from Largs, the crossing taking only ten minutes.

The only town on the island is **Millport**, a small, attractive holiday resort with a unique feature - the **Cathedral of the Isles**, Britain's smallest cathedral. It is sometimes referred to as Europe's smallest, but this honour is held by an even smaller cathedral in Greece. Nevertheless it is a real gem, and was completed in 1851 as part of a theological complex funded by the George Boyle, who later became the 6th Earl of Glasgow. Its nave is 40 feet by 20 feet, and can only seat 100 people. It was designed by William Butterfield, who also designed Keble College, Oxford. The ceiling is painted with all the wild flowers found on the island.

Crocodile Rock is on the beach. It is, as the name suggests, a rock shaped like a crocodile's head, and it has been painted with eyes and teeth so that the crocodile features are even more evident. It is said that the rock got its name after a Millport town councillor, on leaving a pub where a council meeting had just finished, remarked that the rock on the foreshore resembled a crocodile.

On the eastern shore of the island, facing the mainland, is the **University Marine Biological Station**. It is an institution of both Glasgow and London Universities, and offers students research facilities, tuition in diving, and tuition in marine biology. It houses a museum, which is open to the public.

The **Museum of the Cumbraes** can be found at The Garrison, just off the seafront. There are exhibits and displays on Millport's heyday as one of the Clyde holiday resorts.

LARGS

19 miles NW of Kilmarnock on the A78

Largs is the epitome of the Ayrshire seaside town. During the last fortnight in July, hordes of Glaswegians used to descend on places like this for their annual fortnight's holiday. These days are gone, but the towns themselves have adapted, and now cater for retired people and day-trippers. In fact, the town of Largs is possibly the favourite retirement town in Scotland.

But the town is still a lively, attractive place, and is the mainland terminal for the Cumbrae Ferry. It was south of here that the **Battle of Largs** took place in 1263, when the Scots defeated a force led by King Haakon IV of Norway and finally threw off the Norse yolk (see also Lerwick). A tall thin monument south of the town affectionately known as the **Pencil** commemorates the event. Within the town you'll find **Vikingar!** a museum and interpretation centre that explains the life and travels of the Vikings all these years ago.

Largs Museum, with its local history collection, is also worth a visit, as is the **Skelmorlie Aisle** (Historic Scotland). It was built in 1636, and sits in the old kirkyard in the centre of the town. It was built as a transept of the former medieval parish church. Within it is the mausoleum of Sir Robert Montgomery of Skelmorlie and his wife, Dame Margaret Douglas. It is a Renaissance-style tomb with wonderful stone carving. **Sir Thomas Brisbane**, was born in Largs in 1773. After a distinguished military career, he was appointed Governor of New South Wales in 1820, and gave his name to the city of Brisbane and the Brisbane River. There is also a crater on the moon named after him. He died in 1860, and lies in the Brisbane Vault next to Skelmorlie Aisle. In the local cemetery is buried **Sir William Burrell**, shipping magnate and millionaire, who gave the Burrell Collection to the city of Glasgow in 1944 (see also Hutton).

"The Waverley", World's Last Sea Going Paddle Steamer, Largs

Kelburn Castle stands to the south of the town, overlooking the Firth of clyde, of which it has spectacular views. It is the ancestral home of the Boyles, Earls of Glasgow, and parts of it date back to the 13th century. Its grounds are now a country park, with gardens, an adventure playground, woodland walks, a pet's corner and craft workshops.

ISLE OF ARRAN

Arran (13 miles and 55 minutes from Ardrossan by ferry) is called "Scotland in miniature", as it is mountainous in the north, low lying in the middle and rises again towards the south. It is 19 miles long by about ten miles across at its widest, and within its 165 square miles it has history and spectacular scenery aplenty. This is an island of Celtic saints, mysterious standing stones, craft workshops, cairns and old castles. It was a Gaelic speaking island up until the early 19th century, though the place names owe as much to the language of the Norsemen who settled here in the 10th and 11th centuries as they do to Gaelic. In fact, Brodick, one of the main settlements, comes from the Norse for "broad bay".

The northern portion can be every bit as spectacular as the Highlands, and for those with the stamina, a climb to the summit of **Goat Fell**, at 2,866 feet the island's highest peak, is a must. There are two recognised routes to the top, with both routes eventually converging, and information on each can be had at the tourist office in Brodick.

Just north of Brodick is the **Arran Brewery**, which has a visitor centre and shop. There are also viewing galleries where you can see the brewing process. And at Home Farm, also near Brodick, is **Arran Aromatics**, Scotland's leading producer of body care products and scented candles. Again, you can watch the manufacturing processes from a viewing gallery.

Beneath Goat Fell, is **Brodick Castle** (National Trust for Scotland). This former Hamilton family stronghold (the Hamiltons became the Earls of Arran after the title was forfeited by the Boyds of Kilmarnock) sits in a wonderful location, surrounded by mature gardens. There has been a castle of sorts here since the Dark Ages, and it is known that a Norse fort also stood on the site. The present building dates from the 16th century and later, and inside there is a collection of paintings and furniture. In about 1844 the tenth Duke of Hamilton and his wife, Princess Marie of Baden, engaged on a building project that

almost doubled the size of the castle.

On the northern outskirts of the village is the **Isle of Arran Heritage Museum**, which is well worth a visit, as it shows the history of the island's ordinary people. North of Brodick, on the A841 is the beautiful village of **Corrie**, with its small harbour, whitewashed cottages and gardens aflame with colour in the summer months.

The road from Corrie follows the coast north, then turns north west and goes through the bleak but extremely

Goat Fell and Brodick Castle, Arran

beautiful Glen Chalmadale before bringing you to **Lochranza** ("Loch of the rowan tree river"). On the shores of this small village are the imposing ruins of **Lochranza Castle** (Historic Scotland),

---

THE GRANARY & CREAGENROIN

Kilmory, Isle of Arran KA27 8PH
Tel: 01770 870263
e-mail: papicken@hotmail.com
website: www.pickenhouses.fsnet.co.uk

The Granary, on Lenamhor Farm at the southern end of the beautiful island of Arran, was opened in 2003, and is one of the best self-catering cottages on the whole of the island. It is a wheelchair-friendly, modern bungalow that offers all the features and facilities you would expect from the top end of the market. It has an open plan living room and kitchen area (with all modern conveniences), a conservatory and a shower room with full wheelchair access. Qualified respite care packages are available on request. It enjoys beautiful, panoramic views out over the Firth of Clyde, Argyll and the Irish coast.

Creagenroin Cottage sits right beside the romantic ruins of Kildonan Castle, again at the southern most point of the Isle of Arran. It boasts two bedrooms - a double and a twin, as well as a spacious lounge/dining area, well-equipped kitchen and a bathroom. This is a superb get-away-from-it-all cottage, and makes an ideal base from which to explore the many attractions of an island that has been called "Scotland in miniature" The patio doors open out onto a large patio and well-tended lawn where you can relax on warm summer evenings. If it's not so warm, however, there is central heating throughout and a multi-fuel stove in the lounge, which also has a colour TV and video. The cottage has ample parking, as well as a large secure garden. Grocery starter packs and towels can be arranged for a small fee, and pets are welcome by arrangement.

Lochranza Castle, Arran

built in the 16th century on the site of an earlier castle. It started life as a hunting lodge for the Scottish kings before passing first to the Campbells and then the Montgomeries, Earls of Eglinton.

At the entrance to the village is the **Isle of Arran Whisky Distillery**, which has guided tours and a visitor centre. In the summer months a small car ferry runs from the Mull of Kintyre to Lochranza, the crossing taking about 35 minutes.

Beyond Lochranza is the small village of **Catacol**, with a row of identical whitewashed cottages known as **The Twelve Apostles**. They were built in the 19th century to accommodate islanders cleared from Glen Catacol in favour of deer. From here you get a good view across to the Mull of Kintyre, which is only four miles away.

Further on, and inland from Machrie Bay, is the wonderful **Auchagallon Stone Circle**, a Bronze Age burial cairn with a circle of 15 upright slabs surrounding it. There are several ancient monuments in the area, including the **Machrie Moor Stone Circle** and the **Moss Farm Road Stone Circle**. It is said that this part of Arran has more stone circles per square mile than anywhere else in Scotland.

The magnificent cliffs at **Drumadoon** stand high above a raised beach, and are spectacular. The **King's Cave** is close to the shore, and is supposed to be the cave where Robert the Bruce saw his spider, (though many other places in Scotland

and Ireland make a similar claim). From the village of **Blackwaterfoot**, south of Machrie Bay, a road called **The String** cuts across the centre of the island towards Brodick. The village of **Shiskine**, on The String, has the lovely **St Molas Church**, with an ancient stone carving of the saint embedded in its wall. The **Balmichael Visitor Centre** is within a converted mill complex, has speciality shops and facilities for various outdoor activities.

South of Blackwaterfoot the road continues on towards **Lagg**, and if you need convincing about the mildness of the climate hereabouts, the palm trees in the gardens of the Lagg Inn should do the trick. The **Torrylinn Creamery**, which makes traditional Dunlop cheese in the old fashioned way, has a viewing gallery and shop. The tiny island of **Pladda**, with its lighthouse of 1790, can be seen about a mile from the coast before the road turns north once more

towards **Whiting Bay**, another small village and holiday resort. At one time it was a fishing port, and it takes its name from the whiting that were caught in the bay. A splendid walk starts from south of the village towards **Glenashdale Falls** and the prehistoric burial cairns known as the **Giant's Graves**.

Lamlash sits on Lamlash Bay. Having the local high school, the hospital and the local government offices, it is the island's capital. In the bay sits the magnificent bulk of **Holy Island**, so called because the Celtic St Molas lived a life of austerity here in the 6th and 7th centuries. Nowadays it has regained its religious significance, as it is home to a Tibetan Buddhist monastery and retreat. Near Lamlash is the factory **Arran Provisions**, the island's biggest employer. It makes a wide range of mustards, jams and preserves, and has a visitor centre and shop.

LOCATOR MAP

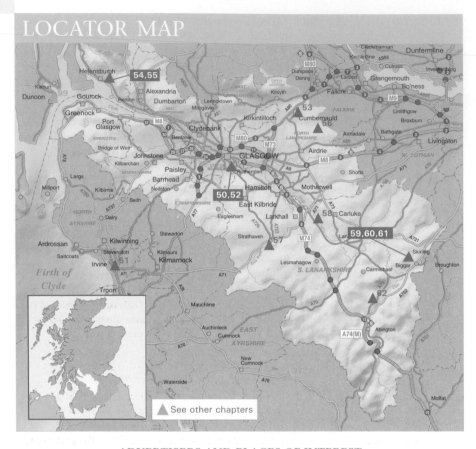

▲ See other chapters

ADVERTISERS AND PLACES OF INTEREST

GLASGOW AND WEST CENTRAL SCOTLAND 4

Glasgow and West Central Scotland was at one time the country's industrial hub. Heavy engineering, shipbuilding, coal mining and steelworks predominated, providing work for thousands and fortunes for the favoured few. As well as the city of Glasgow, the area takes in the former counties of Dunbartonshire, Renfrewshire and Lanarkshire, which all played their part in Scotland's rich industrial history. But while it is still Scotland's most populous area, and where the bulk of its industry and commerce is located, it is now clean and attractive, with much to do and see.

The scenery can be outstanding, from the upper reaches of the Clyde, with its quiet pastoral scenery and cosy villages surrounded by high, lonely moorland, to the hills above Greenock and of course, the bonnie banks of Loch Lomond. Then there's Glasgow. Once a gritty working class city with an image problem, it has burgeoned into a sophisticated, cosmopolitan city with a lively café society (at least once during a visit, do what the locals do - sit at a pavement café sipping coffee while people watch you watching them). There are art galleries and museums galore, bars, shops and shopping malls, (it is the second largest shopping centre in Britain), award-winning restaurants, glitzy hotels, concert halls and nightclubs.

It is home to Scottish Opera, The Royal Scottish National Orchestra, Scottish Ballet, and a string of theatres where you can see anything from serious drama to variety shows. It is also one of Britain's best dressed cities, and it is reckoned that there are more Armani and Versace outfits worn here than anywhere else in Britain outside London.

That area of the West End known as Kelvinside is the city's wealthiest area. It isn't just a place of trendy flats and apartments, though these abound. It also has some seriously large mansions in the streets north and south of Great Western Road. These are occupied by professional people such as TV personalities, doctors, writers and lawyers, who appreciate the leafy elegance of the area.

And in the centre of Glasgow is the Merchant City, once run down and seedy, but now home to the city's café society. New apartment

River Kelvin, Glasgow

blocks have recently been built and older properties have been converted into flats.

But there is still the quirky Glasgow - the city of fish and chips shops, betting shops, working men's pubs, raucous laughter and street markets, including the famous Barras, held every Saturday and Sunday in the east end. The city is ringed by enormous council estates that took the families who used to live in the teeming tenements. It may not be the image of Glasgow that some people would like to project, but they are still there, and in their own way they have as much to do with the city's character as the smart bars, restaurants, concert halls and theatres.

Glasgow has always been an easy place to get out of. Within half an hour of the city centre you can be admiring the grandeur of bens, glens and lochs, taking it easy in some wonderfully bucolic pastoral scenery, or strolling along a lonely beach, which has a backdrop of magnificent hills.

Loch Lomond is renowned the world over. A train can take you straight to its bonnie banks in just under an hour, and it's a journey thousands of Glaswegians make. We're on the edge of the Highlands here, and indeed the Highland Boundary Fault, which separates the Highland from the Lowlands, passes through the loch.

The River Clyde has traditionally been a working river, its banks once ringing to the sound of shipbuilding. But there is another Clyde, one that isn't so well known. The upper reaches of the river, in rural Lanarkshire, present an altogether different picture. Within the verdant Clyde Valley, you'll find quiet orchards, green fields, woodland, small attractive villages and cosy pubs. The area around Lanark is green and pleasant, with small farms, woodland, low rounded hills and quiet country roads. And the lonely moorland where the river rises has a gaunt but compelling beauty.

The towns also have their attractions. Helensburgh, Gourock and Dumbarton (once the capital of the Kingdom of Strathclyde) sit on the shores of the Firth of Clyde. Hamilton, Paisley, Lanark, Motherwell and the new town of East Kilbride are inland towns, and each has its attractions, such as the magnificent Paisley Abbey or the marvellous shopping malls (the largest in Scotland) in East Kilbride. In some towns close to Glasgow, such as Motherwell, Airdrie or Coatbridge, the excesses of industry once blighted the landscape, but these have been cleaned up, and some places, such as Summerlee at Coatbridge, have taken this industrial heritage and turned it into a tourist attraction.

This whole area was once the powerhouse of Scotland. It is not ashamed of the fact, nor should it be. Coal was mined here, steel was produced, heavy industry sent smoke pluming into the sky, ships were built, deals were struck and money made. Money is still being made in the area, but now it comes from electronics, banking, tourism, broadcasting and publishing. But the people haven't changed. They have remained hardworking and friendly, with a pride in the past and a great faith in the future.

GLASGOW

Glasgow has worked hard on its image over the last few years. Gone are the constant references to gang fights, organised crime, drunkenness, ugly industrial townscapes and bad housing. Now people talk of trendy nightspots, theatres, restaurants, pavement cafés and art galleries.

The city has changed its image more than once over the years. It was founded in the 7th century by St Kentigern, also known as St Mungo, and started life in early medieval times as a small religious community grouped round a cathedral. In the 17th and 18th centuries it became a city of trade, dealing with the American colonies in such commodities as tobacco and cotton, which made many people very rich indeed. In the 19th century it became a city of industry, with shipyards and heavy engineering works. Now it relies mostly on tourism, the media, service industries and the arts for employment.

The area round the Cathedral of St Mungo (Historic Scotland) is where it all started. This was where St Kentigern, or Mungo, established a small church in the 6th century. The present cathedral was founded in the 12th century by David I, and the building shows work from this period onwards. It is the only Scottish mainland cathedral that escaped the Reformation of 1560 more or less intact. In its crypt is the **Tomb of St Mungo**, once a place of

pilgrimage, but now visited by pilgrims of a different sort - tourists. The **Blackadder Aisle** is a wonderful piece of architecture added by Archbishop Robert Blackadder in about 1500.

Behind the Cathedral, on a hill, is the **Necropolis**, Glasgow's ancient burial ground, and in front of the cathedral is the modern (and looking anything but modern) **St Mungo Museum of Religious Life and Art**. Across from it is Glasgow's oldest house, **Provand's Lordship**, built in 1471 as a manse for the former St Nicholas Hospital.

"The Clyde made Glasgow, and Glasgow made the Clyde", runs an old, but true, saying. In the 17th century, the city was seen as being wholly inland, and the river was so shallow that people could wade across it. But in 1768 a man called John Golborne began canalising and deepening it to allow large ships to sail right up into the city. The **Tall Ship**

Conference Centre, Glasgow

THE TALL SHIP AT GLASGOW HARBOUR

100 Stobcross Road, Glasgow G3 8QQ
Tel: 0141 222 2513
e-mail: info@thetallship.com   website: www.thetallship.com

Sail through 100 years of maritime history at the Tall Ship at Glasgow Harbour. Follow the remarkable restoration of the Glenlee from an abandoned hulk in Seville harbour to her fullyrigged splendour today and learn about the living conditions aboard a deep sea trading ship. Explore the cargo hold where you will see what goods she carried, the deck house where the crew lived, the poop deck and the galley. Also in the harbour is the Pier 17 restaurant, a gift shop and various exhibitions and events. Phone for details.

at Glasgow Harbour (see panel above) at Stobcross Road tells the story of the river and the industries it spawned. The centrepiece is the tall ship itself, the S.V. Glenlee, built in 1896. At Braehead, on the south side of the river, and a few miles downstream, is another museum, which celebrates the Clyde - the award-winning **Clydebuilt**. It is part of the Scottish Maritime Museum (see also Irvine and Dumbarton), and tells the river's story from the 1700s up to the present day.

The **Clyde Waterbus Service** takes you on a boat trip along the Clyde from the city centre to Braehead, with a commentary on the history of the river as you go.

Close to the Tall Ship is the **Scottish Exhibition and Conference Centre**, a mammoth complex of halls and auditoriums, including what Glaswegians now refer to as the **Armadillo**, a metal and glass creation whose design owes more than a little to Sydney Opera House. And across the river from it is the city's newest attraction, the **Glasgow Science Centre**. Built on the site of the Glasgow Garden Festival, it is a combination of museum, laboratory and hands-on exhibition area that explores science and discovery, and has four floors featuring over 300 exhibits. The accompanying **Glasgow Tower** is Scotland's tallest freestanding structure at 412 feet, and

there's also an **IMAX Theatre**.

Glasgow has always been a city of museums and art galleries, even when it relied on industry for its employment. Like most large cities, its **West End** is where the well off built their mansions, as the prevailing south westerly winds carried the smells of the city away from them. Here you'll find the **Kelvingrove Art Gallery and Museum** (closed for renovations until 2006), housed in a grand red sandstone building that froths with detail. It has internationally important collections on archaeology, botany, zoology, geology and all the other ologies you can think of. There are Egyptian mummies, fossils, stuffed animals, dinosaur skeletons, clothing and uniforms from all over the world, weapons, and a host of other material. The art collection is stunning, and is possibly the most comprehensive civic collection in Europe. While the Kelvingrove is closed, some of the paintings can now be seen in the **McLellan Galleries** in Sauchiehall Street, while some of the exhibits are on display at the **Glasgow Museums Resource Centre** in Nitshill, on the south side of the river. Access to the stores is by guided tours only.

The **Glasgow Museum of Transport**, with trains, carriages, motorcars and a marvellous collection of model ships, sits opposite the Kelvingrove Art Gallery and

Museum. Perhaps the most striking display is the one on Glasgow's "underground" system. The system forms a simple loop round the city centre and West End, and in the late '70s was upgraded, with orange trains taking the place of the much-loved wood and metal ones. The Glaswegians immediately dubbed it the "Clockwork Orange" and the name has stuck. More properly, it is known as the **Glasgow Subway**, rather than "underground" or "metro".

City Chambers, Glasgow

Also in the West End, just off Byres Road (the area's trendiest street) are the **Hunterian Museum** and the **Hunterian Art Gallery**, which form part of Glasgow University. The museum has fine collections covering geology and numismatics, while the gallery has paintings, furniture and interior design by Mackintosh and Whistler. At the top of Byres Road is the **Glasgow Botanic Gardens**, with at its centre the **Kibble Palace**, a huge greenhouse with plants from all over the world. It is named after its builder John Kibble, who erected it beside his house on the banks of Loch Long. It was rebuilt here in 1873, after being dismantled and sailed up the Clyde.

Within Victoria Park, further to the west, is the **Fossil Grove** (open between April and September only), undoubtedly the city's most ancient attraction. It consists of fragments of an ancient forest over 330 million years old, which was discovered in 1887. They are housed within a small building to protect them.

The heart of Glasgow nowadays is

George Square, a huge open space in front of the Victorian **City Chambers** (conducted tours available). There are statues galore, and it is a favourite place for city workers to relax in the sun. The City Chambers themselves reflect Glasgow's wealth and confidence in Victorian times, and so opulent are the interiors that they stood in for the Vatican in the film *Heavenly Pursuits*. Round the corner you'll find **Hutcheson's Hall** (National Trust for Scotland), founded in 1641 as a hospice, though the building itself is 18th century. It was designed by David Hamilton, and has a small exhibition about the **Merchant City**, that area that housed the homes and offices of the rich 17th and 18th century merchants who traded with America. Nowadays it is an area of expensive apartment blocks, smart bars, restaurants and pubs. Not far away, in Queen Street, is the **Gallery of Modern Art**, with four floors of work by modern artists such as Christine Borland and Toby Paterson. In Buccleuch Street near Charing Cross, is the **Tenement House** (National Trust for Scotland). Built in the late 19th century, it re-

War Memorial, Kelvingrove Park

The **Glasgow Police Museum** is in St Andrews Square (to the east of Glasgow Cross), with exhibits highlighting the Glasgow Police Force between 1800 and 1975. And at the Cross itself is the old **Glasgow Tolbooth Steeple**, dating from the 1620s. At one time it provided offices for the City Council, and had a jail incorporated into it.

Glasgow Green, a huge area of parkland in the city's east end, is "Glasgow's lung". It has been common land for centuries, and it was here that Charles Edward Stuart mustered his troops during the Jacobite Uprising when he occupied the city. Now it is the city's largest park, with its centrepiece being the **People's Palace and Winter Gardens**, a museum and glasshouse complex which tells the city's own story. Close to it is the **Doulton Fountain**, at 46 feet high and 70 feet wide the world's largest terracotta fountain. It was recently refurbished at a cost of £3.75m. On the eastern edge of Glasgow Green is one of the city's most colourful buildings - **Templeton's Carpet Factory** (now a

creates the genteel tenement living conditions that were common among Glasgow's lower middle classes in the early 20th century. It is open between March and October. The **Centre for Contemporary Arts** (CCA) is at 320 Sauchiehall Street, and has a changing programme of events, performances and exhibitions. There are six galleries, small cinema, bookshop and bar/restaurant

The **Mitchell Library** is an imposing domed building in North Street, not far from Charing Cross. It is Britain's largest municipal library, and has collections covering Scottish and local history, genealogy, and Robert Burns.

SCOTTISH MARITIME MUSEUM

Harbourside, Irvine KA12 8QE
Tel: 01294 278283 Fax: 01294 313211
website: www.scottishmaritimemuseum.org

The museum is sited in three locations - the Scottish Maritime Museum at Irvine, Clydebuilt at Braehead and the Denny Ship Model Experiment at Dumbarton. At Irvine you will have the opportunity for a guided tour which includes a restored 1920s shipyard workers Tenement Flat and a collection of moored vessels in the harbour, some of which can be boarded. Trips are occasionally available for visitors. The museum shop stocks a wide selection of souvenirs and light meals, snacks and drinks are served at the Puffers Coffee Shop on the wharf. Check website for opening times.

business centre). It is based on a Venetian design, with walls that incorporate multi-coloured bricks.

Glasgow is synonymous with football, and at the redeveloped Hampden Park, on the south side of the Clyde, is the **Scottish Football Museum**. It reveals the sights, sounds and stories of the world's most popular game, and tells how it almost shaped the history of Glasgow in the late 19th and 20th centuries. You can see such things as the oldest football ticket in the world, the Scottish Cup trophy and Kenny Dalglish's 100th Scottish cap.

At Celtic Park in the Parkhead area of the city is the **Celtic Visitor Centre**, which traces the history of Celtic Football Club, one of Glasgow's "big two" football clubs. There are exhibits, a stadium tour and a shop selling Celtic memorabilia. Rangers Football Club is Glasgow's other major team, with Ibrox, in Govan, to the south of the river. The **Rangers Tour Experience** takes you on a guided tour of the stadium, including the Trophy Room.

If you want to immerse yourself in something typically Scottish, then the **National Piping Centre** in Otago Street has a small museum dedicated to Scotland's national instrument. Within the Caledonian University on Cowcaddens Road, not far away, is the **Heatherbank Museum of Social Work**. It has displays on housing, health and childcare, and looks at how socially excluded people were cared for in the past.

Charles Rennie Mackintosh is the most famous of Glasgow's architects, and was born in 1868. He designed a number of buildings in Glasgow, and there are organised tours taking you to the best of them arranged by the Charles Rennie Mackintosh Society. His most famous building is the **Glasgow School of Art** in

Glasgow University

Renfrew Street. It is still a working college, though tours are only available by appointment. On the south side of the river is the **Scotland Street School**, now a museum dedicated to education. Another school is the **Martyr's Public School** in Parson Street, (no longer used as a school) and it is open to the public. The **Willow Tea Rooms** in Sauchiehall Street still sells traditional Scottish "high teas" amid Mackintosh's designs, and the **Queen's Cross Church** on Garscube Road is now the headquarters of the Charles Rennie Mackintosh Society. At Bellahouston Park, on the south side, is the **House for an Art Lover**, which interprets some of the incomplete designs Mackintosh submitted to a competition in a German magazine. **The Lighthouse**, Scotland's centre for architecture, design and the city, is in Mitchell Lane and has a Mackintosh interpretation centre. It is housed in a

Mackintosh-designed building that was once the home of Glasgow's daily newspaper, the Herald. In the Hunterian Art Gallery there is also the **Mackintosh House**, featuring the principal rooms from Mackintosh's own house, together with a collection of designs and watercolours.

Another Glasgow architect, formerly overshadowed by Mackintosh but now more widely known, was Alexander Thomson, known as **"Greek" Thomson** because of the Greek influences in his work (see also Balfron). He lived in the 19th century, and designed **St Vincent Street Church**, as well as **Holmwood House** (National Trust for Scotland) in Netherlee Road, in the southern suburbs.

Perhaps Glasgow's most famous modern attraction is the **Burrell Collection**, housed in a purpose built complex of galleries in **Pollok Country Park**, south of the river. William Burrell (see also Largs and Hutton Castle) gifted a huge collection of art and historical objects to the city of Glasgow, and now over 8,000 of them are on display. A whole day could be spent going round the collection. Also in the park is **Pollok House** (National Trust for Scotland), a Georgian mansion that houses the Stirling Maxwell collection of decorative arts (see panel below).

Glasgow is Britain's second largest shopping centre, the three main shopping streets being Argyle Street, Sauchiehall Street and Buchanan Street. There are also enormous shopping malls. The **St Enoch Centre** is just off Argyle Street, the **Buchanan Galleries** are at the corner of Buchanan Street and Sauchiehall Street, while the **Braehead Shopping Centre** is south of the river on the city's western fringes, near Renfrew.

POLLOK HOUSE

Pollok Country Park, 2060 Pollokshaws Road,
Glasgow G43 1AT
Tel: 0141 616 6410 Fax: 014) 616 6521
e-mail pollokhouse@nts.org.uk
website: www.nts.org.uk

Visit **Pollok House** and capture the flavour of one of Scotland's grandest Edwardian country houses. It is the ancestral home of the Maxwells of Pollok, who have lived on this site for 700 years. The present house, which replaced

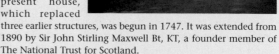

three earlier structures, was begun in 1747. It was extended from 1890 by Sir John Stirling Maxwell Bt, KT, a founder member of The National Trust for Scotland.

The house contains much original furniture as well as some of the finest Spanish paintings in Britain. A rare survival is the magnificent suite of servants' quarters, which shows the scale of country house life around 1900. These contain the popular Edwardian Kitchen Restaurant, renowned for its lunch menu and home baking, and the shop in the Housekeeper's Room. At weekends, visitors can see a reconstruction, of the way the house might have been run at the turn of the last century. Pollok House is set amid formal and walled gardens at the heart of **Pollok Country Park**.

There's also the **Forge** at Parkhead, in the east end.

Within the city centre there are two exclusive retail developments. **Princes Square**, off Buchanan Street, is a mix of upmarket shops and cafés, while the **Italian Centre** is where you'll find the designer labels.

In Sauchiehall Street is the **Regimental Museum of the Royal Highland Fusiliers**. It is Scotland's second oldest infantry regiment, and was formed in the 1960s when the Highland Light Infantry amalgamated with the Royal Scottish Fusiliers.

AROUND GLASGOW

KIRKINTILLOCH

7 miles NE of Glasgow city centre on the A803

The old burgh of Kirkintilloch sits on the **Forth and Clyde Canal**, which has recently been re-opened after a multi-million pound refurbishment. It connects the Firth of Clyde and the Firth of Forth, with a further canal, the Union Canal, connecting it to Edinburgh. The **Auld Kirk Museum** is housed in the former parish church, which dates from 1644. In **Peel Park** are some Roman remains from the Antonine Wall.

Craft Daft (On a Raft) is a craft studio on a canal boat moored in the Forth and Clyde Canal at Glasgow Bridge.

CUMBERNAULD

12 miles NE of Glasgow off the A80

Cumbernauld is one of Scotland's new towns, and the setting for the 1981 film *Gregory's Girl*. It sits on a hill above the A80, and has an indoor shopping centre. **Palacerigg Country Park** covers 750 acres, and is to the south east of the

CHERISHED DOLLS & CERAMICS AT GREENACRES HOUSE AND POTTERY

Greenacres, Palaceriggs, Cumbernauld G67 3HU
Tel: 01236 724281 e-mail: sandra.russells@lineone.net
website: www.palaceriggbedandbrek.com

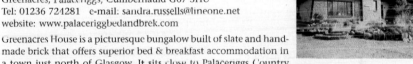

Greenacres House is a picturesque bungalow built of slate and hand-made brick that offers superior bed & breakfast accommodation in a town just north of Glasgow. It sits close to Palaceriggs Country Park, and is the ideal place to stay while exploring both Glasgow and the surrounding countryside. It boasts two comfortable bedrooms that each has a TV, radio alarm clock, hair dryer, tea/coffee making facilities and trouser press. They are both beautifully furnished and decorated, and overlook quiet fields. The B&B caters for families, and has many toys, games and books for younger people to enjoy when they stay here. A cot is also available, as are drying facilities. The breakfast is hearty and filling, though lighter options are also available. Why not try the American pancakes with maple syrup? Delicious! The owners, being interested in history, are always on hand to offer advise as to places to visit and things to see in the area, and can sometimes even organise excursions.

Why not come to a craft session at the Greenacres' pottery and ceramics studio, **Cherished Dolls and Ceramics**? It has been established since 1995, making both pots and ceramic dolls, and there have been many satisfied customers who are still taking an interest in painting on ceramics such as plates and pots. There are also quilting classes, throwing pots on a wheel, and a host of other activities that will appeal to young and old alike. Greenacres House sits just off the A80 main road connecting Glasgow with Inverness, so a quick detour should take you to it. The accommodation is comfortable and reasonable priced, and the workshops are always enjoyable!

town. The town was established in the 1950s partly on what was an old country estate. Though it sits to the north east of Glasgow, Cumbernauld, like Kirkintilloch, was once in a detached part of Dunbartonshire.

KILSYTH

11miles Ne of Glasgow on the A809

The **Battle of Kilsyth** was fought on the 15th August 1645, when the 1st Marquis of Montrose routed a Covenanting army led by William Bailiie of Letham. A reservoir is now located where Montrose's army camped, and a cairn marks the spot where the battle took place.

RUTHERGLEN

2 miles SE of Glasgow city centre on the A749

This royal burgh is one of the oldest in Scotland, having been granted its royal charter by David I in the 12th century. For a short while the burgh was incorporated into the city of Glasgow, something that was greatly resented by some of its citizens, but since 1997 has formed part of the local authority area of South Lanarkshire. A gable of its medieval **Parish Church** survives in the kirkyard of its more modern successor. Robbie Coltrane (Hagrid in the Harry potter films) was born here, and for a short while Stan Laurel lived in the town and went to a local school.

NEWTON MEARNS

7 miles S of Glasgow on the A77

Newton Mearns is a commuter town of smart bungalows and substantial houses. The foursquare Parish Church dates from

River Clyde

1755, and close by is **Greenbank House** (National Trust for Scotland) surrounded by beautiful gardens. The house is not open to the public.

CLYDEBANK

7 miles W of Glasgow city centre on the A814

Clydebank is a former shipbuilding town, and it was here that the *Queen Mary*, the *Queen Elizabeth* and the *Queen Elizabeth II* were built. The town suffered more damage in proportion to its size than any other British town from air raids in World War II. In early 1941, during the Clydebank Blitz, the centre of the town was flattened, other parts severely damaged and many people were killed. The **Clydebank Museum** at the Town Hall in Dumbarton Road has exhibits devoted to the Blitz, as well as to the famous Singer sewing machine factory which once stood in the town.

PAISLEY

5 miles W of Glasgow city centre on the A761

The large town of Paisley is centred on the great Abbey Church of Saints Mary the Virgin, James the Greater of Compostella, Mirin and Milburga, otherwise known as **Paisley Abbey**. It was founded in the 12th century by Walter FitzAlan, first High Steward of Scotland and progenitor of the Stewart dynasty. Within its walls are the tombs of most of the non-royal High Stewards, as well as that of Princess Marjory, daughter of Robert the Bruce, who married Walter, the sixth High Steward, and their grandson Robert III. It can legitimately claim to be the birthplace of the Stewart dynasty, because Robert II, the first Stewart king, was born here in 1316. Marjory had been seriously injured in a riding accident at Knock, a nearby hill, and she was brought to the abbey, where she died soon after giving birth to her son.

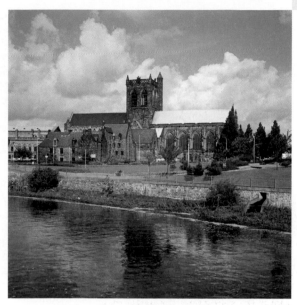

Paisley Abbey

The building as you see it now was built from the 12th century onwards, though the bulk dates from the 15th century. The choir was rebuilt in the early 1900s. Within the abbey is a memorial to **John Witherspoon**, a former minister of the Laigh Kirk, who signed the American Declaration of Independence. A statue of him can also be found in front of **Paisley University** (see also Gifford).

Another famous Paisley church is the Baptist **Thomas Coats Memorial Church**, sometimes known as the "Baptist Cathedral" because of its size. It was built in 1894 in memory of Thomas Coats of the Coats and Clark thread making firm. The same Thomas Coats gifted the **Coats Observatory** to the town's Philosophical Institution in 1883. It is now open to the public. Adjacent is **Paisley Museum and Art Galleries**, with displays of Paisley shawls and other memorabilia.

Paisley was the birthplace of many famous people. **Tom Conti** the actor was born here, as was **John Byrne** the artist and writer (whose most famous work is undoubtedly the TV series *Tutti Frutti*), **Andrew Neill**, now editor of the *Scotsman*, **Gerry Rafferty** the singer and **Fulton Mackay** of *Porridge* fame.

At the corner of Shuttle Street and George Place are the 18th and 19th century weaving cottages known as **Sma' Shot Cottages**, housing an interpretation centre which gives an insight into the living conditions of Paisley weaving families in the past. Nearby, in New Street, is **Paisley Arts Centre**, housed in the former Laigh Kirk of 1738.

In the 18th century, the town was famed for its poets, the most famous being Robert Tannahill, who was born in **Tannahill Cottage** in Queen Street in 1774. He was a silk weaver who wrote the words to such beautiful songs as *Jessie the*

Flower o' Dunblane and *The Braes o' Gleniffer*. The actual braes themselves now form part of the 1,300 acre **Gleniffer Braes Country Park**, to the south of the town. There are spectacular views from the Robertson Car Park, and guiodde tours are available.

Jenny's Well Local Nature Reserve, on the south bank of the White Cart Water, is less than a mile from the centre of the town, and is locked between a council estate and a chemicals factory. For all that, it is a haven for wildlife with some pleasant walks. To the north of Paisley, on the other side of the M8, is **Glasgow International Airport**.

The village of Elderslie, a mile west of the town, is the supposed birthplace of William Wallace, and the **Wallace Memorial**, built in 1912, explains his exploits.

LOCHWINNOCH

16 miles SW of Glasgow on the B786

The **Clyde Muirshiel Regional Park** covers 106 square miles of magnificent countryside from Greenock to Inverkip and down into Ayrshire. It is ideal for walking, cycling, fishing and observing wildlife. There is also sailing on Castle Semple Loch. Near its shores are the ruins of **Castle Semple Church**, founded in the early 16th century by John Semple. He was later killed at the Battle of Flodden in 1513, and his tomb can be seen at the east end of the church.

The **Lochwinnoch Nature Reserve** is run by the RSPB, and has nature trails through woodland, with viewing aeas and a visitor centre.

KILBARCHAN

11 miles SW of Glasgow, off the A761

This is undoubtedly the most picturesque village in Renfrewshire, and is a huddle of old 18th century weaving cottages.

The Weaver's Cottage (National Trust for Scotland) dates from 1723, and shows what a typical weaver's cottage (complete with working loom) was like.

In a niche on the wall of the Steeple Hall of 1755 is a statute to **Habbie Simpson**, the village's famous 17th century piper. It is a bronze reproduction of one made from wood by Archibald Simpson in 1822.

RENFREW

5 miles W of Glasgow on the A8

The ancient burgh of Renfrew was granted its charter in 1143, making it one of the oldest in Scotland. It was here, in 1164, that one of the lesser-known, but still important, Scottish battles took place - the **Battle of Renfrew**. It was fought between Somerled, Lord of the Isles, and the royal army of Malcolm IV led by Walter FitzAlan, founder of Paisley Abbey and first High Steward of Scotland, who had been granted the lands of Renfrew by the king. This battle brought the Western Isles fully under the control of the Scottish monarchy. The story of the battle is an intriguing one. Somerled had sailed up the Clyde the previous year with 15,000 troops carried in over 160 great warships. One version of the story says that the king had bribed Somerled's nephew to murder him, and this was duly carried out, causing the troops to return home. Another version - probably the true one - says that Somerled was killed during the battle along with his heir, and they were carried off to be buried in Saddell Abbey on the Mull of Kintyre (see also Saddell).

The **Renfrew Community Museum** in the Brown Institute in Canal Street was opened in 1997 to coincide with the 600th anniversary of the town being granted royal burgh status. It has displays of local history.

6 miles NW of Glasgow city centre on the A809 and A81

These two prosperous towns are firmly within Glasgow's inner commuting belt, and are full of large Victorian and Edwardian mansions as well as the more modest bungalows of the 1930s. The **Antonine Wall** (named after Roman Emperor Antoninus Pius) passes close by (see also Falkirk). It was built of turf in the 2nd century to keep out the warring tribesmen of the north, and stretched for 37 miles between the Clyde and the Forth. In Bearsden there are the remains of a **Roman Bathhouse.**

Mugdock Country Park sits off the A81 north of Milngavie (pronounced "Mull-guy"), which is the starting point for the 95-mile long **West Highland Way**, which connects the Glasgow conurbation with Fort William.

The Lillie Art Gallery, in Station Road, Milngavie, was founded by banker and amateur artist Robert Lillie, and opened in 1962. It has a collection of 20th century Scottish paintings, including works by the Scottish Colourists, Joan Eardley and Philip Reves.

DUMBARTON

The town sits where the River Leven, fed by Loch Lomond, enters the Clyde, is dominated by **Dumbarton Castle** (Historic Scotland), high on a volcanic plug 240 feet above the Firth of Clyde. It is one of the oldest fortified sites in Britain, and from the 8th to the early 11th centuries was the capital of the ancient kingdom of Strathclyde. It was incorporated into Scotland in 1034, when its king, Duncan, also assumed the throne of Scotland. The name itself means the "Fort of the Britons", and though the town is called Dumbarton, the former county is Dunbartonshire, with an "n". The castle now mainly consists of modern barracks, but there is still plenty to see, including a 12th century gateway, a dungeon and a museum. From the top there is a splendid view out over the Firth of Clyde. It was from Dumbarton in 1548 that Mary Queen of Scots set sail for France and her eventual marriage to Francis, the Dauphin. This was considered to be much safer than leaving from an east coast port, as Henry VIII's ships were patrolling the North Sea. The English king had wanted Mary to marry his son Henry, and when the Scottish parliament refused to ratify such an agreement, Henry tried unsuccessfully to force the marriage, a period known as the "Rough Wooing".

The **Denny Tank Museum** in Castle Street forms part of the Scottish Maritime Museum (see also Glasgow and Irvine). It is the oldest

Dumbarton Castle

experimental water tank in the world, and is the length of a football pitch. It was built in 1882 as part of Denny's shipyard (whose most famous ship was undoubtedly the tea clipper the "Cutty Sark"), and it was here that hull shapes were tested in water using carefully crafted models before the ships themselves were built. On display are many of the models built by Denny craftsmen.

Duck Bay, Loch Lomond

Though Denny was famous for its ships, it also has a place in aircraft history, as it built the world's first hovercraft, as well as the first helicopter capable of flight in 1909.

In Church Street is an old archway called the **College Bow** once part of the long gone Collegiate Church of St Mary. On the hillside above the town is the beautiful **Overtoun Estate**, with wonderful views over the Firth. It was bequeathed to the people of Dumbarton by Douglas White, a London doctor, in 1939. **Old Kilpatrick**, to the west of the town, is supposed to be the birthplace of St Patrick, who was captured by raiders and taken to Ireland in the 4th century.

AROUND DUMBARTON

BALLOCH

4 miles N of Dumbarton on the A811

This pleasant town sits at the point where the River Leven (at five miles long, Scotland's shortest river) leaves **Loch Lomond** on its way to Dumbarton and

the Clyde. The loch is recognised as Scotland's largest and most beautiful sheet of water, covering over 27 square miles. The **Loch Lomond and the Trossachs National Park** was Scotland's first national park, opened in 2002, and **Lomond Shores** at Balloch includes the National Park Gateway.

The loch is at its widest to the south. It gradually narrows and gets deeper as it goes north, and at some points it reaches a depth of over 600 feet, making it the third deepest loch in Scotland. Many songs have been written about this stretch of water, the most famous being the *Bonnie, Bonnie Banks o' Loch Lomond*. It was written by a Jacobite prisoner held in Carlisle Castle who was due to be executed. He is telling a fellow prisoner whose life had been spared that he (the condemned man) will be in Scotland before him because he will take the "low road", i.e., the road of death, while his colleague will take the "high road", or the road of life.

At the nearby village of **Gartocharn** is **Duncryne Hill** (nicknamed "The Dumpling" by locals), where you get a marvellous view, not just of the loch, but also of the surrounding countryside. The **Highland Boundary Fault**, which separates the Lowlands of Scotland from the Highlands, passes through Loch Lomond from Glen Fruin on the west to Balmaha on the east. The **Balloch Castle Country Park**, north east of Balloch, has lochside walks, gardens and a visitor centre. South from the town you can follow the **Leven Valley Heritage Trail**, taking you down the valley of the Leven to Dumbarton, passing such small industrial towns as **Alexandria** and **Renton**.

In Alexandria is the **Antartex Village Visitor Centre**. It incorporates a factory making sheepskin coats (with factory tours available), a mill shop and a small craft village. Close by is the **Loch Lomond Factory Outlets and Motoring Memories Museum**, housed in a magnificent building where one of Scotland's former makes of car, the "Argyll", was manufactured.

Renton has a special place in the hearts of all Scottish football supporters. Not only was Renton Football Club responsible for the founding of the Scottish League, it became "champions of the United Kingdom and the world" in 1888 when it beat West Bromwich Albion at Hampden Park.

CARDROSS

4 miles W of Dumbarton on the A814

Geilston Gardens (National Trust for Scotland) surround a late 17th century house (not open to the public) to the east of the town. Also at Cardross, in Darleith Road, is **St Mahew's Chapel**, dating from

1467, though a church of some kind has stood here since the 7th century. It was at Cardross Castle (now gone) that Robert the Bruce died of leprosy in 1329 (see also Dunfermline and Melrose).

HELENSBURGH

9 miles W of Dumbarton on the A814

Helensburgh now finds itself within Argyll, though at one time it was in Dunbartonshire. It was founded in the 18th century by Sir James Colquhoun of Luss, and named after his wife Helen. **John Logie Baird**, the inventor of television, was born herein 1888. It is one of the ports of call in July and August for the **PS Waverley**, the world's last ocean-going paddle steamer.

In Upper Colquhoun Street you'll find one of Charles Rennie Mackintosh's masterpieces - the **Hill House**. It was commissioned by Walter Blackie, the Glasgow publisher, in 1902, and contains some of Mackintosh's finest work. For not only did he design the building, he also designed the interior decoration, the fittings and most of the furniture. There are also gardens surrounding the house.

North of Helensburgh is **Glen Fruin**, which has a narrow road that takes you over to Loch Lomond. It was the scene of

Memorial to John Logie Baird, Helensburgh

AVA LODGE

44 Glasgow Street, Helensburgh G84 8YH
Tel/Fax: 01436 677751
website: www.stayatlochlomond.com
e-mail: david.cantello@homecall.co.uk

Ava Lodge is a high class, four star guest house in the small Clyde resort of Helensburgh. It was built in 1850 for a successful sea captain, and has many original features. It sits only a five minutes walk from the centre of town and about 600 yeards from the seafront. It is now one of the best guest houses in the area and owners Norma and David Cantello are justly proud. There are two fully en-suite rooms on offer which boast tea/coffee making facilities and colour TVs, and are furnished and decorated to an exceptional standard.

Breakfast is served in the dining room, with its huge, 12 by six foot mirror, and are filling and hearty, setting you up for a day exploring. You can chose from a full Scottish or have a lighter option,

which includes cereal, yogurts and fruits, with some of the produce coming from Ava Lodge's own gardens. Vegetarians can be accommodated, and breakfast comes complete with jams, marmalades and oatcakes. In the winter months, the fire in the dining area is lit to give a cosy, intimate atmosphere. The house sits amidst well-tended and colourful gardens and there are garden ponds and seating areas where you can enjoy a glass of wine of a cup of coffee. For the comfort of guests, this is a no smoking establishment, and pets are not allowed.

THE HILL HOUSE

Upper Colquhoun Street, Helensburgh G84 9AJ
Tel: 01436 673900 Fax: 01436 674685
website: www.nts.org.uk

The finest of Charles Rennie Mackintosh's domestic creations, **The Hill House** sits high above the Clyde, commanding fine views over the river estuary. Walter Blackie, director of the well-known Glasgow publishers, commissioned not only the house and garden but much of the furniture and all the interior fittings and decorative schemes. Mackintosh's wife, Margaret MacDonald, contributed fabric designs and a unique gesso overmantel. The overall effect is daring, but restrained in its elegance: the result, timeless rooms, as modern today as they must have been in 1904 when the Blackie family moved in.

An information room interprets the special relationship between architect and patron and provides a historical context for Inspirations, a dazzling exhibition in the upper east wing and the gardens. It brings together exceptional pieces of domestic design by great living designers, all of whom, in some way, pay homage to Mackintosh's elegance and invention. Inspiring comparisons may be drawn between the work of Mackintosh, now recognised as one of the geniuses of the early 20th century, and pieces that themselves have become 21st century icons.

The gardens have been restored to their former glory, and reflect features common to Mackintosh's architectural designs. They also contain a kinetic sculpture given to the house by the artist George Rickey.

a battle in 1602 when the MacGregors defeated the Colquhouns with much loss of life. Two members of Clan McGregor were returning to Loch Rannoch from Glasgow in early winter, and stopped near the Loch Lomond end of Glen Fruin to ask for hospitality from the Colquhouns. This was refused, a blatant breach of the rules of Highland hospitality, so the two McGregors killed and cooked and ate a sheep. On finding out, the Colquhoun chief ordered that the two men be executed, even though they had offered to pay for the animal.

The execution was duly carried out, and when word reached the McGregor chief, Alasdair of Glenstrae, he decided to seek revenge. A party of 80 men set out for Glen Fruin, where they killed two Colqhuouns and drove off some sheep and cattle. The two clans eventually met in battle at the east end of the glen, near Loch Lomond.

RHU

10 miles W of Dumbarton on the A814

Rhu (pronounced "roo") is a small, attractive village at the entrance to the Gair Loch. It was originally called Row,

and in the 18th century was one of the ports on the Rhu - Roseneath ferry. **Glenarn Gardens** off Glenarn Road is a sheltered woodland garden famous for its rhododendrons.

LUSS

11 miles N of Dumbarton off the A82

This beautiful little village - one of the loveliest in Scotland - was once the setting for Scottish Television's soap opera *High Road*, where it was called Glendarroch. It's an estate village built by the Colquhoun family of nearby Rossdhu Castle, and sits on the banks of Loch Lomond. On the opposite shore, the mighty bulk of **Ben Lomond** can be seen. It is the most southerly of Scotland's "Munros", or mountains over 3,000 feet, and is a comfortable climb if you're reasonably fit and active. The **Parish Church of St MacKessog**, built in 1875 on the site of a much older church, is well worth a visit.

GARELOCHHEAD

14 miles NW of Dumbarton off the A814

This old village at the head of the beautiful **Gare Loch** now finds itself in Argyll for administrative purposes. However, along with the picturesque **Rosneath Peninsula**, it was once part of the old county of Dunbartonshire, and it is to Dumbarton that it still looks for shopping and other services. It makes a fine centre for hill walking, bird watching and yachting. At Cove, on the Rosneath Peninsula, are the **Linn Botanical Gardens**.

Rhu

GREENOCK

Situated on the south bank of the Firth of Clyde, at a point known as **The Tail of the Bank**, Greenock is a bustling industrial town and port. It was the birthplace, in 1736, of **James Watt**, who perfected the steam engine. Hills pile up behind the town, and on the slopes of Lyle Hill is a huge **Cross of Lorraine** mounted on an anchor, which was built in 1946. It commemorates the Free French sailors who sailed from Greenock and lost their lives on the Atlantic during World War II. There are excellent views out over the Firth of Clyde and as far north as Ben Lomond.

Customhouse Quay was the departure point for thousands of Scottish emigrants sailing away to America in the 19th and early 20th centuries. The magnificent **Custom House**, built in 1810, reflects the port's importance in bygone days, and it now houses a museum dedicated to the work of HM Customs and Excise. Another museum is the **McLean Museum and Art Gallery** on Kelly Street, which features exhibits on local history as well as paintings by Courbin, Boudin and the Scottish Colourists. The **Watt Library** in union street is named after the town's most famous son, and is the place to go for genealogical information.

In Greenock cemetery is the grave of **Highland Mary**, whose real name was Mary Campbell (see also Failford and Dunoon). Burns had met her at a low point in his life in Mauchline, and had asked her to accompany him to the West Indies when he thought of emigrating. However, on a trip home to Dunoon to make arrangements for her departure, she died. She was previously buried in the kirkyard of the former Old West Kirk, but was exhumed and reburied in 1920.

When the Old West Kirk, which dated from the late 16th century, was dismantled in 1926, some of its stones were used to build the new **Old West Kirk**, on the Esplanade. It has some wonderful stained glass and woodcarving.

AROUND GREENOCK

PORT GLASGOW

4 miles E of Greenock on the A8

Before the Clyde at Glasgow was canalised and deepened, this town was Glasgow's main port. **Newark Castle** (Historic Scotland) lies close to the riverbank, and dates from the 16th and 17th centuries. Up until the 1980s the castle was completely surrounded by shipyards, testament to the importance of this industry to the town at one time.

It was originally built by George Maxwell in the late 15th century, and upgraded in 1597 to what you see today by its most notorious owner, Sir Patrick Maxwell. He was an unsavoury man who was always quarrelling with other families, most notably the Montgomerys of Skelmorlie near Largs. In fact he murdered two of them - Montgomery himself and his eldest son - in the one day. He also treated his wife Margaret abominably. In 1632, in front of the local minister, he struck her on the face so hard that she had to take to her bed for six months. As soon as she had recovered, he attacked her again, this time with a sword.

Many times Margaret had resorted to the law to have her husband restrained. Patrick even had his son ejected from the castle when he tried to intervene. Eventually, after 44 years of marriage and 16 children, Margaret left him, choosing a life of abject poverty rather than suffer any more. This caused the authorities to take an interest in his conduct, but before he could be brought to trial in Edinburgh he died of natural causes.

Two miles west of Port Glasgow is the **Finlaystone Estate**, where the present head of the Clan Macmillan lives. It is open to the public, and features gardens and 140 acres of woodland, which can be explored. Finlaystone House, at the heart of the estate, dates back to the 14th century, though it has been extended over the centuries. It can be visited by special arrangement.

GOUROCK

2 miles W of Greenock town centre on the A770

This little holiday resort is now more or less a suburb of Greenock, though at one time it was a separate burgh. It is on a most attractive part of the Clyde, opposite Kilcreggan, the Gareloch and the entrance to Loch Long, where the mountains tumble down towards the sea. The Firth of Clyde is a famous yachting area, and the town is the home of the **Royal Gourock Yacht Club**, which is situated near the Promenade. At Cloch Point, four miles to the southwest, is the **Cloch Lighthouse** of 1797, a famous landmark for ships sailing on the Clyde. Between Castle Gardens and Kempock Street in the town is the curiously named **Granny Kempock's Stone**, which dates from prehistoric times. It is shaped like a cloaked figure, and to walk round it is said to bring good luck. However, it also has associations with witchcraft. In 1662 a young woman was burnt to death after she admitted that she was going to use supernatural powers to throw the stone into the waters of the Firth of Clyde and cause shipwrecks

The town is the one of the ferry terminals for Dunoon, across the Clyde in Argyll.

HAMILTON

Hamilton was once the county town of Lanarkshire, Scotland's most populous and industrialised county. It became a royal burgh in 1548, though it lost this status in 1669. It is very much connected with one of the most important families in Scotland, the Dukes of Hamilton, Scotland's premier dukes. Up until medieval times, the town was known as Cadzow, but gradually Hamilton took over as the family grew in importance. By the 1920s, when it was demolished, the immense Hamilton Palace, home to the dukes, was the grandest non-royal residence in Britain.

Not a stone now remains of it above ground, though the Hamilton's burial place, the grandiose **Hamilton Mausoleum**, still remains. It is a curious building with an immense dome, and is full of Masonic symbolism. It consists of a chapel above and a crypt below, and was built in the mid 19th century for Alexander, the 10th Duke (nicknamed "Il Magnifico"), who had his ancestors removed from the ruins (now gone completely) of the old Collegiate Church of Hamilton and re-interred in the crypt. When he himself died, he was laid to rest in the sarcophagus of an Egyptian princess, and this was placed in the upper chapel. A curious tale tells of how the duke was found to be too tall to fit into the sarcophagus when he died. Therefore his legs were broken and folded over. However, that's all it is - a tale. The duke was indeed too big for the sarcophagus, but he knew this long before he died, as he used to lie in it. So he had stonemasons enlarge it.

The crypt is entered through the middle arch of three arches. Above each arch is a carved head, representing life, death and immortality.

The bodies were all removed from the mausoleum in 1921, and the place can now be visited. It was never used as a chapel, however, as it is reckoned to have the longest echo of any building in Britain. One thing to note is that the crypt doors lock from the inside. The reason is simple - once a month a servant was sent from the palace to dust and clean the huge coffins. To prevent ghoulish sightseers, a policeman was stationed outside and she locked herself in.

A two-mile long Grand Avenue once stretched from the palace all the way to **Chatelherault**, pronounced "Shattly-row"), a Hamilton hunting lodge east of the town. Most of the avenue is gone, but Chatelherault survives, having been refurbished in the 1980s in the largest refurbishment project of its time in Britain and then officially opened in September 1987 by the Duke of Gloucester. It was originally designed by William Adam and dates from the 1730s. The lodge once also housed the Duke's hunting dogs, and was therefore known as the "Dog Kennels". Now it houses a museum and interpretation centre. The lodge got its name because the Dukes of Hamilton were also the Dukes of Chatelherault (the French spelling of the name) near Poitou in France. The title was bestowed in 1548 by Henry II of France in recognition of the part the family played in arranging the marriage of Mary Stuart to his son Francis, the Dauphin. The spelling of the name changed over the years, and Chatellerault gradually became Chatelherault. Surrounding the lodge is **Chatelherault Country Park**, with over ten miles of woodland walks. The ruins of **Cadzow Castle**, the original home of the Hamiltons, and where Mary Stuart once stayed, can be see within the park. There are also the remains of an old **Iron Age Fort** and the **Cadzow Oaks**, which are very old. In a field in front of Chatelherault is a small but famous herd of **White Cattle**.

Hamilton Parish Church, within the town, was designed by William Adam in the early 1730s at the same time as he was designing Chatelherault. It is an elegant building in the shape of a Greek cross, with a cupola over the crossing. The pre-Norman **Netherton Cross** stands at the church entrance, and in the kirkyard is the **Heads Monument**, commemorating four Covenanters beheaded in Edinburgh after the Pentland Rising of 1666.

In Almada Street you'll find the town's most prominent landmark - the **County Buildings**. They were built in the 1960s for the then Lanarkshire County Council, and were modelled on the United Nations building in New York. It is one of the few 1960s buildings in Scotland to be listed.

Based in an old 17th century coaching inn once known as the Hamilton Arms is the **Low Parks Museum**, which has displays and memorabilia on local history. It also houses a large display on Lanarkshire's own regiment - the **Cameronians (Scottish Rifles)**. Raised as a Covenanting force in 1689, it took its name from Richard Cameron, a Covenanting minister who opposed bishops in the Church of Scotland and the king being its head. It chose to disband itself in 1968 rather than amalgamate with another regiment (see also Douglas). Most of the Low Parks, which at one time formed some of Hamilton Palace's parkland, has been given over to a huge retail development that includes a multi-screen cinema and supermarket

In the Bent Cemetery is the simple grave of one of Scotland's best-known entertainers, **Sir Harry Lauder**. Born in Portobello near Edinburgh in 1870, he at one time he worked in the coalmines in Quarter, a village near Hamilton. He died in 1950 (see also Strathaven). Nearby is the plot where the members of the Hamilton family who formerly lay in the mausoleum are now buried. The 10th Duke, who had the mausoleum built, still lies in his Egyptian sarcophagus.

Hamilton is the start of one of Scotland's ten national tourist routes, the **Clyde Valley Tourist Route**. It follows the Clyde Valley all the way south to Abington on the M74.

AROUND HAMILTON

AIRDRIE AND COATBRIDGE

7 miles N of Hamilton on the A89

The twin towns of Airdrie and Coatbridge are industrial in character. In Coatbridge, in 1889, was born **John Reith**, first general manager of what was then the British Broadcasting Company. Single-handedly he shaped the character of the organisation.

The town is home to the **Summerlee Heritage Centre**, built on the site of the old Summerlee Ironworks, which traces the history of the area's old industries - steel making, coalmining and the manufacture of heavy plant. Tramlines have been laid out in it, and there is a small collection of trams from all over Europe. There is also a short section of the Summerlee branch of the **Monklands Canal** (now closed), which ran from Glasgow to the Lanarkshire coalfields. The canal was built between 1770 and 1794, and at one time was the most profitable in Scotland. **The North Calder Heritage Trail** runs from Summerlee to Hillend Reservoir, and passes many sites connected with the

past industry of the area.

The **Time Capsule** is one of the largest leisure centres in the area. In the **Drumpellier Country Park** there is a visitor centre, butterfly house, formal gardens, golf course and pets' corner.

MOTHERWELL AND WISHAW
3 miles E of Hamilton on the A721

The twin towns of Motherwell and Wishaw were, up until 1975, included in the one burgh. They were steel making towns, though the steelworks at Ravenscraig have now gone. The award-winning **Motherwell Heritage Centre** on High Road has a number of exhibitions, and hosts varied activities with a heritage theme. To the west of Motherwell, adjoining the M74, is the 1,100 acres of **Strathclyde Country Park**, built on waste ground in the early '70s. Within it there is an international-sized rowing lake where the rowing events of the 1986 Commonwealth Games were held. On its banks are the remains of a **Roman Bathhouse**. There are guided walks throughout the year, as well as nature trails and a camping and caravanning site. **M&D's Theme Park** is located near the north banks of the loch.

A mile north east of Motherwell is the small industrial village of Carfin, where you will find the Lourdes-inspired **Carfin Pilgrimage Centre and Grotto**, created in the 1920s by Fr. Thomas Nimmo Taylor the local priest helped by out-of-work miners. There are displays and exhibits that help explain the notion of pilgrimage, not just in the Roman Catholic religion, but also in all major religions.

The **Shotts Heritage Centre** is in Benhar Road in Shotts, eight miles to the west of Motherwell and Wishaw. There are displays on the history of this former mining town. **Kirk o' Shotts**, built in 1820, lies to the east of the town, and can easily be seen from the M8 motorway. Its future is in jeopardy, as it is badly in need of restoration. Within its kirkyard is a gravestone marking the last resting place of William Smith, a Covenanter who fought at Rullion Green in 1666.

DALSERF
7 miles SE of Hamilton town centre off the A72

Once a sizeable village with inns and a ferry across the Clyde, Dalserf has now shrunk to no more than a few cottages and a church. **Dalserf Parish Church**, with its whitewashed walls, looks more like a house than a place of worship, and dates from 1655, though an ancient chapel dedicated to St Serf stood here before that. The building is a rare survivor of a mid-17th century Scottish church. Most from that period were simply built, with earth floors and a thatched roof. In the 18th and 19th centuries they were usually demolished to make way for something more imposing. Dalserf has lasted because the parish was a poor one, and couldn't afford to rebuild, preferring instead to upgrade whenever it could. In the kirkyard is a pre-Norman "hogs back" grave slab, which was dug up in 1897, and also a memorial to the **Revd John Macmillan**, sometimes called "the last of the Covenanters". He died in 1753.

STONEHOUSE
6 miles S of Hamilton on the A71

This former weaving village still has rows of 18th and 19th century weaving cottages. On one side of the main door is a large window, which allows plenty of light into the room which housed the loom, and on the other is small window, which allowed light to enter the main living quarters.

Patrick Hamilton, Scotland's first Protestant martyr, was born in Stonehouse in about 1503. He was burned at the stake in St Andrews in 1527 (see also St Andrews). The **Alexander Hamilton Memorial Park** was opened in 1925, the gift of a local man. It has a bandstand, which was originally made for the Great Glasgow Exhibition of 1911.

The remains of the **Old St Ninian's Parish Church** are to the north of the village, surrounded by an old kirkyard. A prehistoric burial kist was once dug up in the kirkyard, showing that the site may have had a religious significance long before Christianity came to the area.

STRATHAVEN

7 miles S of Hamilton on the A723

Strathaven (pronounced "Stray-ven") is a real gem of a small town that sits at the heart of Avondale. The ruins of **Strathaven Castle** (also known as Avondale Castle) are all that is left of a once large and powerful 14th century stronghold. It was built by the Douglas family, then passed to the Stewarts, who became Earls of Avondale, and eventually came into the hands of the Hamiltons. A legend says that before the Reformation, a wife of one of the owners was walled up alive in the castle, and when parts of a wall fell down in the 19th century, human bones were found

among the rubble. On the edge of the **John Hastie Park** is the **John Hastie Museum**, which has local history collections.

Close to the cemetery is the **James Wilson Monument**. James was born in Strathaven in 1760, his father being a weaver. He was a free thinker on the matter of religion, and was also a radical reformer, something of which the local landowners did not approve. In 1820 a band of reformers, of which he was a member, posted a bill on the streets of Glasgow that was held to be treasonable. He was arrested near Falkirk and executed in 1820.

To the west of the town, at Drumclog, was fought the **Battle of Drumclog**, where an army of Covenanters overcame government troops in 1679. A memorial on a minor road off the A71 commemorates the event. At the small village of Sandford, two miles to the south, are the lovely 50-feet high **Spectacle E'e Falls** on the Kype Water, a tributary of the Avon.

EAST KILBRIDE

5 miles W of Hamilton on the A726

East Kilbride is the largest and undoubtedly the most successful of Scotland's new towns. Work started on laying it out in 1947 round an old village, and now it has a population of

about 70,000. It is renowned for its shopping facilities, and has four shopping malls, **Princes Mall**, the **Plaza**, the **Olympia Centre** and **Centre West**, which together make up the largest undercover shopping area in Scotland.

In the Calderwood area of the town is **Hunter House**, birthplace in the 18th century of the Hunter brothers, John and William, pioneering surgeons and anatomists who worked in both Glasgow and London. The house has a small display and museum about the two men and their lives The Hunterian Museum in Glasgow is one of their legacies.

On the outskirts of the town is **Calderglen Country Park**, based on Torrance House (not open to the public). It has play areas, nature trails and a children's zoo. To the north of the town is the **James Hamilton Heritage Park**, with a 16-acre boating loch. Behind it is the restored **Mains Castle** (not open to the public), which was built by the Lindsay family in the early 15th century and subsequently sold to the Stuarts of Torrance. Up until the 1970s it was a ruin. Close by is the **Scottish Museum of Country Life** is based around Wester Kittochside Farm, which had been home to the Reid family since the 16th century. In 1992, the last of the family, Margaret Reid, gifted it to the National Trust for Scotland. Run jointly by the National Museums of Scotland and the National Trust, it explains rural life in Scotland throughout the ages, and has a huge collection of farm implements and machinery. The elegant farmhouse of Wester Kittochside, which dates from 1783, is also open to the public.

EAGLESHAM

9 miles W of Hamilton on the B764

The conservation village of Eaglesham was planned and built by the Earl of Eglinton in the mid 1700s. It is shaped like a huge "A", with the point facing the moorland to the west of the village. Between the two arms of the "A" is a large village green area known as the "Orry", on which once stood a cotton mill. The lovely period cottages and houses in the village make a perfect picture of Scottish rural life, though the village has largely been colonised by commuters from Glasgow and Lanarkshire. The **Parish Church**, which dates from 1788, has the look of an Alpine church about it, and it is reckoned that while planning Eaglesham the 10th Earl was influenced by villages he had admired in northern Italy.

It was in a field near Eaglesham in 1941 that **Rudolph Hess**, Hitler's deputy, landed after he parachuted from an ME 110. He was found by a local farmer called David McLean, who took him home and treated him firmly but politely. Hess gave his name as Alfred Horn, but it was soon established that he was Hitler's deputy. He said he was on a secret mission to speak to the Duke of Hamilton, and a map he possessed showed that he had been trying to reach Dungavel House, one of the Duke's hunting lodges near Strathaven.

He was then taken to Maryhill Barracks in Glasgow, where he was sometimes in the custody of Corporal William Ross, who went on to become the Secretary of State for Scotland in the Wilson government. Hess was later moved to Buchanan Castle near Drymen in Stirlingshire, where he was interrogated (see also Drymen).

BOTHWELL

2 miles NW of Hamilton off the M74

In the centre of this small town is **St Bride's Parish Church**, with a chancel dating from 1398. It was built as part of a collegiate church by Archibald the Grim, 3rd Earl of Douglas, and has a roof made entirely of stone. A year after it was built, it was the scene of a royal wedding when David, son of Robert III, married Archibald the Grim's daughter Marjory. Outside the west end of the Victorian nave is a monument to **Joanna Baillie**, a playwright and poetess born at Bothwell manse in 1762. She was praised by Scott as being one of the finest writers of the 18th century. Her work, though at times filled with humour, is dark and sometimes violent, with murderous, paranoid characters, and more than one critic has wondered where a seemingly prim daughter of a minister found the material write such stuff.

On the banks of the Clyde, some distance from the town, are the massive and impressive remains of **Bothwell Castle** (Historic Scotland), which historians have rated as one of the most important secular medieval buildings in Scotland. It was most likely built in the 13th century by Walter de Moravia, who was granted the lands of Bothwell by Alexander II. It later passed to the Douglas family, who rebuilt and strengthened most of it. In the 15th century, when James II overthrew the Douglases, it passed to the crown Upstream is Bothwell Bridge, scene, in 1679, of the **Battle of Bothwell Bridge** between the Royalist forces of the Duke of Monmouth and a Covenanting army. The Covenanters were heavily defeated, with over 500 being killed and 1,200 taken prisoner. The bridge you see today is basically the same bridge, though much altered and widened. A memorial on the Bothwell side of the bridge commemorates the event.

Blantyre

3 miles NW of Hamilton on the A724

Blantyre is a former mining town, which nowadays is visited because of the **David Livingstone Centre** (National Trust for Scotland). Here, at Shuttle Row, was born in 1813 the African explorer and missionary David Livingstone. A great cotton mill once stood here, and Shuttle Row was a tenement block that housed some of the workers. The great man was born in a one-room flat, though the whole tenement has now been given over to housing displays and mementos about his life and work.

Within the centre there is also an art gallery, social history museum, African play park, tearoom and gift shop.

LANARK

Set above the Clyde Valley near the upper reaches of the Clyde, the ancient royal burgh of Lanark received its royal charter in about 1140, making it one of the oldest towns in Scotland. But even before this it was an important place, because in AD978 Kenneth II of Scotland held the very first recorded meeting of a Scottish parliament here.

Every year, in June, the town celebrates **Lanimer Day**, which originated as a ceremony of riding the boundaries of the burgh. And on March 1 each year is held the **Whuppity Scoorie** celebrations, when the children of the town race round the 18th century **St Nicholas's Church** waving paper balls above their head, and then scrambling for coins thrown at them. Noways it is the opening event in the Whuppity Scoorie Storytelling Festival, but it may have had its origins in pagan times, when it celebrated the arrival of Spring.

Another custom is the **Het Pint**, held on January 1st each year. Citizens of the town meet at 10am and are given a glass of mulled wine. Anyone wishing to do so can also claim a pound. The tradition goes back to the 17th century, when Lord Hyndford gave money to the town to be used each year for pious or educational purposes.

High on a wall of St Nicholas's Church is a statue of William Wallace the Scottish freedom fighter. It recalls an event which took place when the town's castle (now gone) was garrisoned by English troops. Wallace committed some misdemeanour that brought him to the attention of the English sheriff of Lanark, Sir William Hesselrig. He fled, and when Wallace's wife Marion Braidfute (some versions refer to her as his "lemman", or girlfriend) refused to divulge where he was, Hesselrig killed her and her household. Wallace later returned and killed the sheriff in revenge. The supposed site of **Wallace's House** is now marked by a plaque near the church.

In the Westport you'll find the **Royal Burgh of Lanark Museum**, which explains the incident, as well as the town's history. Near the centre of the town are the ruins of the original place of worship, **St Kentigern's Church**. It is said that William married Marion Braidfute within the church, though there is no proof of this. However, there certainly was a real Marion Braidfute living in the area at the time, referred to as the "heiress of Lamington", a village to the south of Lanark.

In St Kentigern's kirkyard is buried **William Smellie** (pronounced Smillie), the father of modern midwifery. He was born in Lanark in 1697, and was the first obstetrician to teach midwifery on a formal basis as a branch of medicine. He also pioneered the use of forceps. He began life as a doctor in Lanark, but then studied in Glasgow and Paris before establishing a practise in London, where he also lectured. He was a kindly man, and frequently delivered the babies of the poor of London without charging them. He died in 1763.

ROSEBANK GARDEN CENTRE

By Carluke, Lanarkshire ML8 5QA
Tel: 01555 860221

The lovely Clyde Valley in Lanarkshire is the setting for one of the best garden centres in Scotland - the **Rosebank Garden Centre**. It was established over 100 years ago, and has been on the present site over 60 years. Throughout this time is has remained a family-run business that is committed to quality, value for money and friendly service. A visit to the place will confirm that this is no idle boast. It will also confirm that the range of plants and products on offer is staggering - everything from bedding plants, seeds and tubs to garden furniture, cane furniture, tools, stoneware, books, gifts and shrubs.

There is also a highly popular coffee shop that serves a wide range of hot and cold drinks, as well as home baking and light lunches. In the summer months you can sit outside as you eat, savouring the vibrant colours and textures of a garden centre that has become one of the best known in Scotland.

From October to December each year the Rosebank Garden Centre gives itself over to all things Christmas, with gifts, winter plants, artificial flowers, lighting and decorations to the fore. The centre is just a short detour from the M74, the main motorway between Glasgow and England. So if you're heading north or south along it, why not call in at Rosebank and be prepared to be astounded at the colourful displays and the astonishing array of gardening equipment on offer.

On the banks of the Clyde below Lanark lies the village and UNESCO World Heritage Site of **New Lanark**. It was here, in 1785, that David Dale (see also Stewarton) founded a cotton mill and village of 2,500 people that became a model for social reform. Under Dale's son-in-law **Robert Owen**, who was manager, there were good working conditions, decent homes, fair wages, schools and health care in the village.

The mills were still in production up to 1968. Under the care of the New Lanark Conservation Trust, it has become one of the most popular tourist destinations in Scotland, even though people still live in some of the original tenements and cottages.

Attractions include a **Visitors Centre** (including a Textile Machinery Exhibition and the New Millennium Ride that introduces you to Robert Owen's original vision), the **Millworker's House**, the **Village Store Exhibition** and **Robert Owen's House**. Other buildings have been converted into craft workshops, and there is also a hotel housed in a former mill. A presentation called **Annie McLeod's Story** is shown in what was **Robert Owen's School**, and uses the latest in 3-D technology. The "ghost" of 18th century mill girl Annie Macleod returns to tell the story of her life in the days of Robert Owen. Also in the village is a **Scottish Wildlife Trust Visitors Centre**.

The mills were at one time powered by the Clyde, and close by are the **Falls of Clyde** waterfalls, the most famous being Cora Linn and Bonnington. A hydroelectric scheme now harnesses the power of the water, and the falls are only seen at their most spectacular at certain times of the year.

A few miles north of the town is **Carluke**, which stands above the Clyde Valley. It is noted for its orchards, introduced in medieval times by the monks of Lesmahagow Priory. The bell tower of the former parish church, built in 1715, still stands.

AROUND LANARK

BIGGAR
10 miles SE of Lanark on the A702

Biggar is a small, attractive market town that still has its original medieval layout. It sits among the rich agricultural lands of South Lanarkshire, and was granted its burgh charter in 1451.

It must have more museums per head of population than any other place in Britain. The **Biggar Gas Works Museum**, housed in the town's former gas works dating from 1839, explains how gas was produced from coal in former times, and the **Moat Park Heritage Centre** has exhibits and displays about the town and

its immediate area from the time the landscape was formed millions of years ago right up until the present day. **Greenhill Covenanter's House** used to stand at Wiston, 10 miles away, but was transported to Biggar stone by stone, and is now dedicated to the memory of the Covenanters. These were men and women who, in the 17th century, resisted the Stuart monarchs' attempts to impose bishops on the Church of Scotland, and sometimes paid with their lives. The **Gladstone Court Museum** has re-created a Victorian street, with a dressmaker's shop, boot maker's shop and even a schoolroom.

The Albion Building houses the **Albion Motors Archives**, which are the records of the Albion Motor Company, started up locally in 1899 by Norman Fulton and T.B. Murray before moving production to Glasgow. It soon grew to

ELPHINSTONE HOTEL

145 High Street, Biggar, Lanarkshire ML12 6DL
Tel: 01889 220044
e-mail: robert@the-elph-fsworld.co.uk

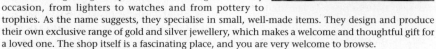

The **Elphinstone Hotel** is a picturesque, whitewashed building (some parts over 400 years old) standing in Biggar's wide main street. Here you will find outstanding accommodation and very reasonable prices in four recently refurbished rooms, all fully en suite and with tea/ coffee making facilities, TV and phone. The restaurant is very popular, with the chef only using fresh local produce in season wherever possible. This, coupled with the quiet lounge bar where you can enjoy a drink, makes it a great base from which to explore the area.

MINIATURES AND MINDINGS

123 High Street, Biggar, Lanarkshire ML12 6DL
Tel: 01899 221569
e-mail: morag@namechains.co.uk
website: www.namechains.co.uk

Established in 1994, **Miniatures and Mindings** is a small family-run business in the market town of Biggar. Here you will find a huge range of special and unusual gifts for every occasion, from lighters to watches and from pottery to trophies. As the name suggests, they specialise in small, well-made items. They design and produce their own exclusive range of gold and silver jewellery, which makes a welcome and thoughtful gift for a loved one. The shop itself is a fascinating place, and you are very welcome to browse.

They are especially proud of their range of Scottish produced jigsaw puzzles, which make ideal gifts for the young and not-so-young. Something else they are very proud of is their extensive range of steam model engines from Mamod and Wilesco. Why not treat someone to a superb Zippo lighter or

a stylish watch. A state-of-the-art engraving service using the latest computer technology is available to have your purchases personalised at very little extra cost. If you're looking for something for your wife, fiancée or mother, then the stock includes a range of Russian dolls which they are sure to love.

Biggar is said to have more museums per head of population than any other town in Scotland. Miniatures and Mindings are proud to be part of the town, and look forward to welcoming you to their fascinating shop.

be the largest manufacturer of commercial vehicles in the British Empire.

At Brownsbank Cottage, a mile-and-a-half from the town, lived the Scottish poet Christopher Grieve, better known as **Hugh McDiarmid** (see also Langholm). He died in 1978, and his wife Valda continued to live there until her death in 1989. Now it has been restored to exactly how it looked when the poet lived there, and it is home to a writer-in-residence. It can be visited by appointment only.

In Broughton Road is the professionally run **Biggar Puppet Theatre**, which has a Victorian-style theatre seating up to 100 people, plus a museum. Purves Puppets, which owns it, is Scotland's largest puppet company, and regularly presents shows all over Britain.

St Mary's Church was founded in 1546 by Malcolm, Lord Fleming, Chancellor of Scotland. It was formerly collegiate, and is a graceful, cruciform building. It was the last church to be built in Scotland before the Reformation. In the kirkyard is a gravestone commemorating the Gladstone family, forebears of William Ewart Gladstone, British prime minister during Victorian times.

To the west of the town, just off the M74, are the twin settlements of **Abington** and **Crawford**, which have a number of services, and make ideal stopping off places when heading north or south along the motorway.

LEADHILLS

18 miles S of Lanark on the B797

Like its neighbour Wanlockhead (which is in Dumfriesshire), Leadhills is a former lead mining village. It has the highest golf course in Scotland, and is full of old

SUNNYSIDE ANTIQUES

Castledykes, Wiston, By Biggar, Lanarkshire ML12 6HT
Tel: 01899 850552
e-mail: info@periodantiques.net
website: www.periodantiques.net

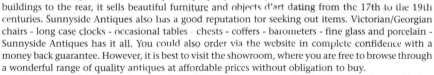

Set in the heart of rural Lanarkshire on the A73, an easy 50-minute drive from Edinburgh or Glasgow and just five miles southwest of the small, attractive market town of Biggar, **Sunnyside Antiques** is well worth seeking out. Housed in a period property with adjacent buildings to the rear, it sells beautiful furniture and objects d'art dating from the 17th to the 19th centuries. Sunnyside Antiques also has a good reputation for seeking out items. Victorian/Georgian chairs - long case clocks - occasional tables - chests - coffers - barometers - fine glass and porcelain - Sunnyside Antiques has it all. You could also order via the website in complete confidence with a money back guarantee. However, it is best to visit the showroom, where you are free to browse through a wonderful range of quality antiques at affordable prices without obligation to buy.

Sunnyside Antiques is a family-run business and managed by Mark Attwood, who has a wealth of experience in the antiques trade, and many satisfied customers. As well as selling antiques it also offers a fully copmprehensive professional restoration service for 17th to 19th century furniture, including French polishing, cabinet making, veneering and upholstery. Mark takes pride in restoring furniture to its former glory without making it look new. Situated in some of Scotland's most stunning scenery at the bottom of Tinto Hill makes a visit truly worthwhile.

18th and 19th century lead miners' cottages. It forms one terminus for the Leadhills and Wanlockhead Light Railway (see also Wanlockhead). The **Allan Ramsay Library** is the oldest subscription Library in Scotland, and is named after the famous poet born here in 1684 (see also Penicuik). In the graveyard is the grave of **John Taylor**, a lead miner who lived to be 137 years old. Next to the cemetery is a monument to **William Symington**, who was born in the village in 1764. He worked as an engineer in the mines, and was a pioneer of steam propulsion in ships. His paddleboat the *Charlotte Dundas* was launched at Grangemouth in 1802 (see also Dalswinton).

CARMICHAEL
4 miles S of Lanark on a minor road west of the A73

The small **Carmichael Parish Church** dates from 1750, and has an interesting laird's loft. One of the past lairds, the Earl of Hyndford, left a sum of money called the Hyndford Mortification to provide the local schoolmasters with a yearly pair of trousers and a supply of whisky. The **Carmichael Visitor Centre** is situated on the Carmichael Estate, and has a display of waxwork models (formerly housed in Edinburgh) that illustrate Scotland's history from the year AD 1000 to the present day. There are also displays about the history of the Carmichael family, which has owned the lands of Carmichael since the 13th century, and about wind energy.

DOUGLAS
8 miles SW of Lanark on the A70

It was in Douglas, in 1968, that the Cameronians (Scottish Rifles), a proud Scottish regiment, was disbanded (see also Hamilton). The ceremony took

place in the grounds of **Castle Dangerous**, ancestral home of the Douglases, of which only a tower now survives. It was here, in 1689, that the regiment was raised by **James, Earl of Angus**. His statue now stands in the village.

The centre of Douglas is a conservation area, with many old cottages and houses. **The Sun Inn** of 1621 was once the village's Tolbooth, where justice was meted out. **Old St Bride's** is the choir of the former parish church dating from the 14th century. Within it are memorials to members of the Douglas family, including Archibald, the 5th Earl of Angus. He was killed at Flodden in 1513, and had the curious nickname of "**Bell the Cat**". There is also a memorial to "the Good Sir James of Douglas", killed by the Moors in Spain while taking Robert the Bruce's heart to the Holy Land for burial. The clock in the clock tower was gifted to the church by Mary Stuart in 1565, and is the oldest working public clock in Scotland.

Douglas Heritage Museum, in Bell's Wynd, is situated in the former dower house of the castle. It is open on Saturdays and Sundays by prior appointment. It has displays on the Douglas family and on the Cameroonians (Scottish Rifles).

CROSSFORD
4 miles NW of Lanark on the A72

This lovely little village sits in the heart of the Clyde Valley, on the banks of the river. Above it you'll find the substantial ruins of **Craignethan Castle** (Historic Scotland), where Mary Stuart once stayed. It was built in the 1530s by Sir James Hamilton of Finnart, illegitimate son of James Hamilton, 1st Earl of Arran and ancestor of the present Dukes of Hamilton. He was the master of works to

Crossford

James V, who gave him the lands of Draffan on which the castle was built. However, the king later suspected that Hamilton had been plotting against him (which was probabl;y not true), and had him executed.

The castle then passed to the crown, and subsequently given to the 2nd Earl of Arran, Sir James's half-brother and the Regent of Scotland.

Sir Walter Scott is reputed to have used the castle as a model for his "Tillietudlem Castle" in *Old Mortality*, though he later denied any link.

LOCATOR MAP

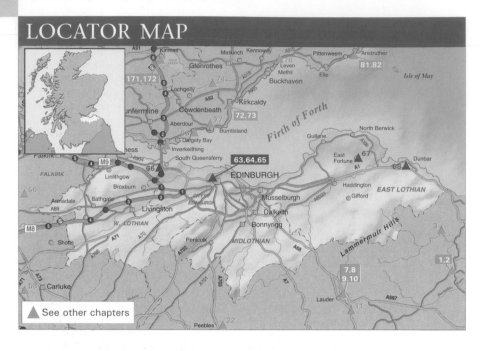

See other chapters

ADVERTISERS AND PLACES OF INTEREST

EDINBURGH & THE LOTHIANS 5

The Lothians consist of the three former counties of East Lothian, Midlothian and West Lothian. The land is generally low lying to the north, rising to moorland and hills in the south, with areas of industry to the west and areas of good arable farmland to the east. Being close to Edinburgh, this area is at the heart of Scottish history, full of castles, grand houses and churches. It is also a place of quiet, pastoral villages and marvellous scenery. The only towns that could possibly be said to be industrial are Dalkeith, Bo'ness, Armadale and Bathgate, and even here industry never intrudes too much.

Dominating it all is the city of Edinburgh, which probably has more history per square mile than any other comparable place in the world. But it's a compact city, and its suburbs haven't yet gobbled up too much countryside. Behind the city are the Pentland Hills, a lonely area of high moorland stretching south west towards the Lanarkshire boundary, and to the south and south east are the Moorfoot and Lammermuir Hills respectively, which thrust down into the Borders.

East Lothian (formerly "Haddingtonshire") is a farming county, and is a patchwork of fields and woodland dotted all over with small, neat villages. The quiet country lanes cry out to be explored by car, and though there is none of the grandeur of the Highlands here - indeed, the scenery has, like Ayrshire. an almost rural English feel to it - it is still a beautiful area. The county rises to the south, where it meets the Lammermuir Hills, and here the landscape changes, though it never loses it gentle aspect. Haddington is the county town, and is full of old

buildings. The main Edinburgh-London railway line bypassed it, so it never developed as a place of industry. The town's main building is the cathedralesque St Mary's Church, the tower of which is sometimes called the "Lamp of the Lothians". A succession of small resorts and golfing centres ring the coastline, though none have been commercialised to any great extent.

Mid Lothian was at one time called "Edinburghshire". Towards the south it meets the Moorfoot Hills, and has a string

Edinburgh Castle

of small towns sitting like satellites round Edinburgh itself. Coalmining was once important here, though all vestiges of the industry have now gone. It is home to such places as Dalkeith and Bonnyrigg, which have never been overwhelmed by industry. Plus, of course, it has the world famous Rosslyn Chapel, which, people claim (and Dan Brown's novel *The Da Vinci Code* backs up this claim), conceals a mystery that goes right to the heart of Christianity.

Before 1975, the county town of West Lothian was Linlithgow. It is an ancient burgh with a royal palace where Mary Stuart, better known as Mary Queen of Scots, was born. West Lothian is more industrial in character than the other two Lothians, and at one time had coal and shale mines, the latter being used to produce oil. Both industries have gone, though the occasional red shale spoil heap (called a "bing" hereabouts) can still be seen.

But there are still plenty of tranquil places to be visited, such as Torphichen, with its preceptory of St John, and South Queensferry, in the shadow of the two Forth bridges. A full day could be taken up exploring Linlithgow itself, with its royal palace, medieval church, canal basin and old, stone buildings. Then there are the county's grand houses, such as Hopetoun and The Binns, which deserve to be visited and explored.

EDINBURGH

Edinburgh, the cultural and administrative capital of Scotland, is one of the great cities of the world. It used to be called the "Athens of the North", and a full week would not be enough to see everything it has to offer the tourist. Whereas Glasgow has worked hard at building a new image, Edinburgh has never needed to do so, though this has led to a certain amount of complacency at times.

With the advent of the Scottish Parliament, the world has rediscovered Edinburgh, and it now has all the feel and buzz of a great capital city once more. It is the sixth most important financial capital in Europe, and both the Church of Scotland and the Scottish law courts have their headquarters here.

The name "Edinburgh" has two possible origins. It either comes from the old Brithonic "eiden burg", meaning "fortress on the hill slope", or "Edwin's Burgh", from a 7th century Anglo Saxon king of Northumbria who built a fort where the castle now stands, though there was no doubt a fort here even before this.

Whatever the explanation, there's no denying that **Edinburgh Castle** (Historic Scotland) is where it all began. It sits on a volcanic plug (the core of a volcano which has solidified), with a narrow ridge running east from it on which sits the old town. There has been a fortification of some kind on the site for thousands of years, though the first stone castle was probably built by Malcom III in the 11th century. The castle as you see it now dates from all periods, with the oldest part being **St Margaret's Chapel**, which dates from the 12th century. St Margaret was the wife of Malcolm III, and it was thanks to her that the Scottish Church came under the jurisdiction of Rome and swept away the last vestiges of Celtic monasticism (see also Dunfermline). Her son David may have built the chapel in her memory. Every year in August the **Castle**

Esplanade hosts the **Edinburgh Military Tattoo**, an extravaganza of military uniforms, marching, music and spectacle that is known the world over. The **Ensign Ewart Tomb** on the esplanade contains the body of Charles Ewart of the 2nd (Scots Greys), who captured the eagle and standard of the French 45th Regiment of the Line at the Battle of Waterloo on 18th June 1815. A curious story once circulated that the Castle Esplanade had become part of the Scottish colony of Nova Scotia, now in Canada, in the 17th century. This was so that the newly created barons of Nova Scotia could set foot in the colony and legally claim their titles. The story was completely untrue, though there is a plaque on the esplanade which states that in 1625 Sir William Alexander took possession of the colony of Nova Scotia "by the ancient and symbolic ceremony of delivery of earth and stone" (see also Menstrie and Stirling)

Edinburgh City Centre

Overlooking the Esplanade and the entrance to the castle is the **Half Moon Battery**, built by Regent Morton in the 16th century, and behind it is the **National War Memorial**, designed by Sir Robert Lorimer and converted from an old barracks block between 1924 and 1927. The **King's Lodging** opposite originally dates from the 15th century, and it was here that the monarch had his personal apartments. One of the rooms, **Queen Mary's Room**, is where, in June 1566, Mary Stuart gave birth to her son James, who later became James VI of Scotland and I of Britain.

There are two curious story about this birth. One says that the Earl of Bothwell, and not Lord Darnley, Mary's husband, was the father of the baby, which would have made him illegitimate. The other says that Mary's baby was stillborn, and that another baby - the son of the Earl of Mar - was substituted in its place. At a later date, when the room was being refurbished, workmen are supposed to have found an infant's bones within the walls of the room (see also Alloa).

In the **Crown Chamber** can be seen the Scottish crown jewels, known as the **Honours of Scotland**, and the **Stone of Destiny** (see also Dunadd and Scone), supposed to be the pillow on which Jacob slept, and on which the ancient kings of Ireland and Scotland were crowned. It was taken from Scone near Perth by Edward I in 1297, and lay in Westminster Abbey for 700 years. Some people claim, however, that it is merely a copy, and that the monks of Scone gave Edward a worthless drain cover and hid the real one. Others claim that, when the Stone was "liberated" from Westminster Abbey in 1953 by Scottish Nationalists, the perpetrators substituted another stone in its place when it was returned. Whatever is the truth of the matter, there is no doubt that it is a potent symbol of Scottish nationhood. The **National War Museum of Scotland** is also within the castle, and explores military service over the last 400 years. Another museum within the castle is the regimental **Museum of the Royal Scots Dragoon Guards**, which is at present based in Germany. The regiment is Scotland's only cavalry regiment, and was formed in 1971 when older regiments amalgamated.

From the castle every day except Sunday is fired the **One o' Clock Gun**. It booms out over the city, frightening tourists who are visiting the castle at the time.

Edinburgh Castle

Another gun associated with the castle is **Mons Meg**. It is one of two huge siege guns presented to James II in 1457 by the Duke of Burgundy. Some people imagine that it is Mons Meg which is fired at one o' clock, but it is in fact a 25lb gun situated on Hill Mount Battery.

Leading from Edinburgh Castle down to the **Palace of Holyroodhouse** is the **Royal Mile**, one of the most famous streets in the world. It follows the crest of a ridge that slopes down from the castle, and was the heart of the old Edinburgh. It is actually four streets - Castlehill, Lawnmarket, the High Street and the Canongate, and each one had tall tenements on either side. The city was surprisingly egalitarian in olden days, and the gentry and the poor lived in the same tenement blocks, the rich at the top, the professional classes in the middle, and the poor at the bottom.

The **Tolbooth Church** was built in 1844, and was for a time the annual meeting place of the General Assembly of

the Church of Scotland, the kirk's governing body. It was designed by James Gillespie Graham and Augustus Welby Pugin, and has a 240-foot spire, which is the highest point in the city centre.

The **Scotch Whisky Heritage Centre** on Castlehill tells the story of Scotch, and brings three hundred years of its history to life. You'll learn about how it's made, and every Sunday afternoon there is a tasting session.

Between July and September, Edinburgh plays host to many festivals, the most important being the **Edinburgh International Festival** (with its attendant **Fringe Festival**) in August. The Royal Mile then becomes a colourful open-air theatre, where Fringe performers and buskers take over every inch of pavement to present drama, juggling, classical music, magicians, jazz, piping, folk music and a host of other activities.

Edinburgh has often been called the "medieval Manhattan", as the 16th and 17th century tenement blocks on the

Royal Mile, which looked no more than four of five storeys high, were in fact up to 12 storeys high, due to the steep slope on which they were built. **Gladstone's Land** (National Trust for Scotland), in the Lawnmarket, belonged to Thomas Gledstone, a rich merchant. It was built about 1620, has painted ceilings, and is furnished in the way it would have been in the 17th century. In Lady Stair's House, off the Lawnmarket, you'll find the **Writer's Museum**, with displays on Scotland's trio of great writers, Burns, Scott and Stevenson. The house is named after Lady Stair, who owned the house in the 18th century.

The glory of the Royal Mile is **St Giles Cathedral**. Originally the High Kirk of Edinburgh, it was only a cathedral for a short while in the 17th century when the Church of Scotland embraced bishops. It is now the spiritual home of Presbyterianism in Scotland. The first church in Edinburgh was built in the 9th century by monks from Lindisfarne, and St Giles is its direct descendant. It dates mainly from the 15th century, with a magnificent crown steeple, which is, along with the castle, one of Edinburgh's icons. At one time, in the Preston Aisle, an arm bone of St Giles was kept as a holy relic.

Attached to the cathedral is the ornate **Thistle Chapel**, designed by Sir Robert Lorimer and built in 1911. It is the home of the **Most Ancient and Noble Order of the Thistle**, which is said (erroneously, some people claim) to have been founded by Alexander II when he came to the

throne in 1249. We do know, however, that James VII instituted the modern order in 1867, and it consists of 16 knights (who may be female) and the sovereign. There is provision also for certain "extra" knights, who may be members of the British or foreign royal families. Its motto is *nemo me impune lacissit*, which means "no one provokes me with impunity". However, it is usually expressed in Lowland Scots as "wha daur meddle wi me?", meaning "who dares meddle with me?" One of the delights of the chapel is a woodcarving of an angel playing the bagpipes. Behind the cathedral is **Parliament House**, where Scotland's parliament met up until the Treaty of Union in 1707. The building itself dates from the late 17th century, though the façade was added in 1829.

Across from the cathedral are the **Edinburgh City Chambers**, home to the city council. It started life as a royal exchange, and was built between 1753 and 1761 to designs by John Adam, brother of the better-known Robert. Though it appears to have only two or

Ainslie Place

three storeys if seen from the Royal Mile, it actually has 12 storeys, which tumble down the slope at the back. Under the Chambers is the **Real Mary King's Close**, a narrow Edinburgh street which was closed off and built over after the bubonic plague visited the city in 1645. Conducted tours of this most moving of places are available, though participants are advise to seek out a pub afterwards to steady the nerves, as the place is suppose to be haunted. The most moving ghost is said to be that of a young girl, and people still leave gifts for her, such as sweets and dolls.

The old **Tron Church**, built in 1648, was in use as a church up until 1952. It is now a visitor information centre. An archaeological dig inside the church in 1974 revealed the foundations of shops and cellars from a medieval street called Marlin's Wynd, and these can now be seen.

Further down the Royal Mile is the **Museum of Childhood**, a nostalgic trip down memory lane for most adults. It features toys, games and books, and even medicines such as castor oil. **John Knox House** is almost opposite. It dates from the 15th century, and though there is no real proof that he lived in the house, he may well have died here. Eastwards from John Knox's House the Royal Mile becomes the **Canongate**, so called because it is the "gate" or street, of the canons of Holyrood Abbey. Up until 1865 Canongate was a separate burgh with its own officials and councillors, and the **Canongate Tolbooth** of 1591, which held the council chamber, courtroom and burgh jail, is a curious building with a clock that projects out over the pavement. It contains the **Museum of Edinburgh**, which gives an insight into the history of the city itself, and is packed with exhibits from its colourful past.

The **Canongate Church** of 1688 has Dutch influences, and in the kirkyard is buried **Adam Smith** the famous economist, **Agnes McLehose** for whom Burns wrote *Ae Fond Kiss*, and **Robert Fergusson** the poet. He was Burns's hero, and died aged 24 in a madhouse. When Burns visited his grave, he was disgusted to see that there was no grave marker, so he paid for the tombstone over the grave that we see now. **White Horse Close**, beyond the church, is the most picturesque of Edinburgh's closes, and it was from the White Horse Inn that the horse-drawn coaches left for London and York.

The Palace of Holyroodhouse is the Queen's official residence in Scotland. It grew out of the Abbey of Holyrood, of which only the ruined nave remains. Legend says that while out hunting, David I was injured by a stag, and while he fought with it he found himself

Holyrood House

grasping, not the stag's antlers, but a holy cross or "rood". As an act of thanksgiving he founded the abbey in 1128 for Augustinian canons. It became a favourite residence for Scottish kings, being much less draughty than the castle up the hill. It was here that Mary Stuart set up court on her return from France in the 16th century, and it was here that the murder of Rizzio, her Italian secretary took place (see also Seton).

The picture gallery contains portraits of over 100 Scottish kings. The recently opened **Queen's Gallery** is the first permanent exhibition space for the royal collection of paintings and sculpture in Scotland. It was designed by Benjamin Tindall Architects, and is housed in the former Holyrood Free Church and Duchess of Gordon's School at the entrance to the grounds.

Close to Holyrood is the new **Scottish Parliament Building**, designed by the late Catalan architect Enric Miralles. Officially opened in October 2004 by HM the Queen, it is a controversial building, having cost ten times the original estimate and opened four years late. It's appearance has also divided the nation, with some people loving it and others loathing it. Guided tours are available, and while Parliament is in session you can sit in the public galleries and watch the proceedings. In Holyrood Road is **Our Dynamic Earth**, an exhibition and visitors centre that takes you on a journey through the history of the universe, from the beginning of time and on into the future. It features dinosaurs, earthquakes, lava flows and tropical rainstorms.

To the south of the Royal Mile, in Chambers Street behind Edinburgh University, are the **Royal Museum** and the new **Museum of Scotland** (see panel below). They house internationally

MUSEUM OF SCOTLAND

Chambers Street, Edinburgh EH1 1JF
Tel: 0131 247 4422
website: www.nms.ac.uk

The Museum of Scotland tells the remarkable story of a remarkable country. From the geological dawn of time to modern day life in Scotland, you'll discover the roots of a nation - a land steeped in fascinating cultures and terrible wars, passionate religion and scientific invention. A land of creative struggle - and occasionally of glorious failure. In a unique and purpose-built museum are gathered together the treasured inheritance and cultural icons which tell Scotland's many stories. The people, the land, the events that have shaped the way they live now.

If you weren't aware of the extraordinary history and impressive achievements of this small country, then it's time to find out. Because after more than 3,000 million years of Scotland's story, there is the perfect place in which to celebrate it - the Museum of Scotland. The exhibits include the earliest

known fossil reptile found in Bathgate, dating back to 338 million years BC, artifacts from around 8000 BC when the first settlers arrived and a tiny shrine thought to date from AD750.

The museum shop sells a wide variety of souvenirs and a cafe and restaurant ensure that all appetites are catered for. Guides are available and there is a rooftop garden with spectacular views. Open Monday to Saturday 10am-5pm and Sunday 12 noon-5pm. Disabled access.

important collections relating to natural history, science, the arts and history. On Nicolson Street is the **Surgeon's Hall Museum**, owned and run by the Royal College of Surgeons of Edinburgh.

One of Edinburgh's hidden gems can be found in the Cowgate - the **Magdalen Chapel** of 1547. It was built by Michael McQueen and his wife Janet Rynd, who are buried within it. It then passed to the Guild of Hammermen. The chapel contains pre-Reformation stained glass, and was where the very first General Assembly of the Church of Scotland was held in 1560, with 42 churchmen attending.

Another famous church south of the Royal Mile is **Greyfriars**. Built in 1612, it was here that the National Covenant rejecting bishops in the Church of Scotland was signed in 1638. From this, the adherents of Presbyterianism in the 17th century got the name "Covenanters". In nearby Candlemaker Row is the famous **Greyfriars Bobby** statue. It commemorates a terrier that faithfully kept guard over the grave of John Gray, his former master, who died in 1858 of tuberculosis. He did this for 14 years, until he too died in 1872. Bobby became famous after an American author, Eleanor Stackhouse Atkinson,

wrote a book about it and Disney turned it into a film. However, she embellished the story somewhat by stating that Gray was a simple shepherd, when in fact he was a policeman.

North of the Royal Mile is Edinburgh's **New Town**. In the late 18th and early 19th centuries the medieval city was overcrowded and unhealthy, so the New Town was laid out in a series of elegant streets and squares to a plan by James Craig. **Princes Street** was one of these streets, and is now the city's main shopping area. It faces **Princes Street Gardens**, created from the drained bed of the old Nor' Loch.

Within the new town's Charlotte Square you'll find the **Georgian House** (National Trust for Scotland - see panel below), which re-creates the interiors found in the New Town when it was being built. At **No. 28 Charlotte Square** is the National Trust for Scotland's headquarters and an art gallery. And within the Square gardens each August is held the **Edinburgh Book Festival**. At the west end of the New Town is one of Edinburgh's most spectacular churches - **St Mary's Cathedral**. It was built in Victorian times as the cathedral for the Episcopalian diocese of Edinburgh, and is as large and grand as a medieval

THE GEORGIAN HOUSE

7 Charlotte Square, Edinburgh EH2 4DR
Tel/Fax: 0131 226 3318
or Tel: 0131 225 2160
e-mail: thegeorgianhouse@nts.org.uk
website: www.nts.org.uk

The Georgian House is part of Robert Adam's masterpiece of urban design, Charlotte Square. It dates from 1796, when those who could afford it began to escape from the cramped, squalid conditions of Edinburgh's Old Town to settle in the fashionable New Town. The house's beautiful china, shining silver, exquisite paintings and furniture all reflect the domestic surroundings and social conditions of the times. Video programme. New touch screen programme featuring a virtual tour of the house.

cathedral, with three soaring spires that have become Edinburgh landmarks. It was designed by the eminent architect Sir George Glibert Scott and built in the 1870s, though the spires were added in the early 20th century. Beside the cathedral is the much altered 17th century manor house of **Easter Coates House**, now part of the choir school.

The **National Gallery of Scotland** on the Mound, the **Scottish National Portrait Gallery** (combined with the **Scottish National Photography Collection**) in Queen Street, the **Dean Gallery** and the **Scottish National Gallery of Modern Art** in Belford Road are all within, or close to, the New Town. A bus service runs between all four. The **City Art Centre** is in Market street, behind Waverley Station. It houses the city's own art collection, and houses major exhibitions, not just of art. The **Talbot Rice Gallery**, part of Edinburgh

University, is in the Old College on South Bridge. The **City Art Gallery**, on Market Street, behind Waverley Station, houses the city's own art collection, and holds many exhibitions throughout the year. Also in Market Street is **The Edinburgh Dungeon**, which aims to bring Scotland's bloody past to life.

The **Scottish Genealogy Society Library and Family History Centre** is in Victoria Terrace off George IV Bridge. At the east end of Princes Street you'll find **Register House**, where the National Archives of Scotland are stored. It was designed by Robert Adam, with the foundation stone being laid in 1774. In front of it is an equestrian statue of the Duke of Wellington by Sir John Steell. Also in Princes Street is Scotland's official memorial to one of its greatest writers, the Gothic **Scott Monument**, which soars to over 200 feet, and offers a marvellous view from the top. It was

designed by George Meikle Kemp, with work beginning in 1840. In August 1846 it opened to the public.

On Calton Hill, to the east of Princes Street is the 106-feet high **Nelson Monument**, from the top of which are views out over the city. It commemorates Nelson's death at the Battle of Trafalgar in 1805, and was designed by the architect Robert Burn. A time signal is installed at the top, consisting of a ball which drops at 12 noon in winter and 1pm in summer. It allowed ship's captains on the Forth to set their watches accurately.

Further north, off Inverleith Row, are the **Royal Botanic Gardens**, 70 acres of greenery and colour surrounded by the bustle of the city. They were founded in 1670 as a "physic garden" at Holyrood, but were transferred here in 1823. And at Leith, up until the 1920s a separate burgh, you'll find the **Royal Yacht Britannia** (see panel on page 167) moored at the **Ocean Terminal**, a leisure and entertainment complex. The ship is open to the public.

In Pier Place in Newhaven, to the west of Leith, is the **Newhaven Heritage Museum** explaining the history of this former fishing village. It was in Newhaven that the largest fighting ship of its day, the Great Michael was built

Royal Botanic Gardens

between 1507 and 1513 for James IV's Scottish navy. It is said that the whole fleet which sailed to America with Columbus in 1492 could fit comfortably into her hull. It was the envy of Europe, and Henry VIII even demanded that it be handed over to him, as it was far too good for the Scots. In charge of the building project was Scotland's Admiral of the Fleet Sir Andrew Wood (see also Largo).

Granton sits further west, and at one time was a busy harbour and industrial area, with a huge gas works. It is now undergoing a major redevelopment, though one of the huge gasometers has been preserved. At its centre is **Caroline Park**, an elegant mansion dating from the 17th century (not open to the public).

Further to the west, at Corstorphine, are the **Edinburgh Zoological Gardens**, set in 80 acres. The zoo is famous for its penguins, and the daily "penguin parade" when the penguins march round part of the zoo. However, the parade taking place or not depends on the weather and the whim of the penguins themselves, who sometimes choose not to hold it.

Craigmillar Castle (Historic Scotland) is on the southeast outskirts of the city. The extensive ruins date from the 14th century, with many later additions. Mary Stuart stayed here for a short while after her Italian secretary Rizzio was murdered. **Lauriston Castle**, near Davidson's Mains, is also worth visiting. It is set in 30 acres of parkland. One of its owners was the father of **John Napier**, who invented logarithms. It now has a collection of furniture and decorative arts. Napier's own home, **Merchiston Tower**, is now part of Napier University. The **Royal Observatory** sits on

Craigmillar Castle

Blackford Hill, south of the city centre, and has displays and exhibits relating to astronomy

AROUND EDINBURGH

MUSSELBURGH

6 miles E of Edinburgh on the A199

Musselburgh got its name from the beds of mussels that once lay at the mouth of the River Esk, on which the town stands. Now it is a dormitory town for Edinburgh. The **Tolbooth** dates from the 1590s, and was built of stones from the former Chapel of Our Lady of Loretto, which in pre-Reformation times was served by a hermit. **Inveresk Lodge Gardens** (National Trust for Scotland), with their terraces and walled garden, illustrates methods and plants that can be used in a home garden. The **Battle of Pinkie**, the last battle fought between Scottish and English national armies, took place near Musselburgh in 1547 during the "Rough Wooing", when Henry VIII was trying to force the Scottish parliament to agree to a marriage between his son and the infant Mary Stuart. The Scots were defeated due to the incompetence of the Earl of Arran,

Scotland's commander, though Mary herself eventually married the Dauphin of France, heir to the French throne.

PRESTONPANS

7 miles E of Edinburgh on the B1348

At the **Battle of Prestonpans** in 1745 the Jacobite army of Charles Edward Stuart defeated a Hanoverian army under Sir John Cope. The whole battle only took 15 minutes, with many of the Hanovarian troops being trapped against a high wall (which can still be seen) surrounding **Prestongrange House**. Contemporary accounts tell of terrified Hanovarian troops trying to scale the wall and dropping into the comparative safety of the house's grounds. Even though it took place in the early 18th century, the site was largely an industrial one, with even a primitive tramway for hauling coal crossing the battle field. The Jacobite song *Hey Johnnie Cope* lampoons the English commander, though he was not wholly to blame for the Hanovarian defeat.

The **Prestongrange Museum** is at Morrison's Haven, and tells the story of the local industries through the ages.

PORT SETON

9 miles E of Edinburgh on the B1348

Port Seton Collegiate Church (Historic Scotland) was built, but never completed, in the 14th century as a collegiate church served by a college of priests. It is dedicated to St Mary and the Holy Cross, and has some tombs of the Seton family, as well as fine vaulting. In 1544 it was looted and stripped by the Earl of Hertford and his English army. **Seton Castle** dates from 1790, and was designed by Robert Adam. It replaces the former Seton Palace, one of the grandest Scottish buildings of its time. Mary Stuart visited the Palace after the murder of Rizzio by her second husband, Lord Darnley (see also Edinburgh).

DALKEITH
7 miles SE of Edinburgh on the A68

This pleasant town is nowadays a dormitory for Edinburgh, but at one time was an important market town on the main road south from Edinburgh to England. **Dalkeith Palace** was built around the medieval Dalkeith Castle for Anne, Duchess of Monmouth and Buccleuch in the early 18th century. It became known as the "grandest of all classical houses in Scotland", and its 2,000 acre grounds are now a country park.

Anne's husband James Scott, Duke of Monmouth, was an illegitimate son of Charles II who had defeated a Covenanting army at Bothwell Bridge. However, he later plotted to usurp his father, and had himself declared king on June 20th 1685. He was defeated at the Battle of Sedgemoor (the last battle fought on English, rather than British soil) on July 6th, and was executed on

Tower Hill in London nine days later. Anne had been Duchess of Buccleuch in her own right, and was allowed to keep her title, though the Monmouth title was suppressed.

St Nicholas Buccleuch Church is a large building - formerly a collegiate church - with, attached to it, the ruins of an old apse in which lie the remains of Anne, who died in 1732. Also buried there are the first Earl of Morton and his wife Joanna, daughter to James I of Scotland.

NEWTONGRANGE
8 miles SE of Edinburgh on the A7

The monks of Newbattle Abbey started coal mining in the Lothians in the 13th century, so the industry has a long history in the area. The Lady Victoria Colliery in Newtongrange houses the **Scottish Mining Museum**, which tells the story of coal mining in Scotland from those days right up until the present. There is a re-created coalface, as well as the original winding engines and a visitor's centre. The Lady Victoria is one of the finest surviving Victorian collieries in Europe. It opened in the 1890s and closed in 1981. At its peak, it employed over 2,000 men.

ARNISTON
9 miles SE of Edinburgh off the A7

Arniston House has been the home of the Dundas family for over 400 years. It was built between 1726 and the 1750s to the designs of William and John Adam on the site of an old tower house. The interior detail is wonderful, and there is also a fine collection of paintings by artists such as Raeburn and Ramsay. In the 17th century the Dundas family was one of the most powerful in Scotland, and

Scottish Mining Museum, Newtongrange

held many important posts in the Scottish legal system. The house is open to the public, though dates and times should be checked, as they vary throughout the summer.

BORTHWICK

11 miles SE of Edinburgh off the A7

Borthwick Castle is a massive twin-towered castle built by Sir William Borthwick in about 1430 on the site of an earlier tower house. It was to this castle that Mary Stuart and Bothwell came after their marriage in 1567. It was a marriage which displeased the Scottish people, and over 1,000 Scottish nobles cornered the couple there. They demanded that Mary hand over Bothwell for his part in the murder of Lord Darnley, Mary's second husband. However, Bothwell escaped and fled to Dunbar.

On hearing of his escape, they immediately retired from the Queen's presence, thinking that she had seen through his treachery. However, no sooner had they left her than she tore off her fine gowns and put on breeches and a pageboy's shirt, and made her escape so that she could rejoin her husband. The Red Room is said to be haunted by her ghost.

The Borthwicks were a powerful family, and when they took prisoners one of the games they played was to tie the prisoners' hands behind their backs and make them jump the 12 feet from the top of one tower to the other. If they succeeded they were set free.

In 1650 the castle was attacked by Oliver Cromwell's Parliamentarian army, and it was abandoned not long after. In the early 20th century it was restored, and during World War II it was secretly used to store national treasures. It is now a hotel.

The modern **Borthwick Parish Church** has a 15th century aisle with effigies of the first Lord and Lady Borthwick.

CRICHTON

11 miles SE of Edinburgh on the B6367

Crichton Castle (Historic Scotland) was probably built in the late 14th century by John de Crichton. It consisted of a simple tower house typical of the period, but was added to by his son William, an ambitious and unscrupulous man who became Lord Chancellor of Scotland. During the minority of James II, Archibald the 5th Earl of Douglas was appointed regent, but he died two years after James ascended the throne. Both Crichton and Sir Alexander Livingstone competed to take Archibald's place, fearing that a Douglas might be appointed again.

They invited the 6th Earl of Douglas, who was only 16, to a banquet at Edinburgh Castle in 1440, along with his brother and a friend. The head of a black bull was brought to the table, and at this sign the Earl, his brother and their friend were murdered. The affair became known as the *Black Dinner*.

Crichton Collegiate Church was built in 1449 by William Crichton. **Vogrie Country Park** lies to the north of the castle, and is centred on Vogrie House. It has woodland walks, picnic areas and a golf course.

SOUTRA

15 miles SE of Edinburgh off the A68

From Soutra, high in the Lammermuir Hills, it is reckoned that you get the best view in Central Scotland. On a clear day you can see the full sweep of the Firth of Forth with Fife beyond, and at least 60 Highland peaks. **Soutra Aisle** is all that remains of a medieval hospital. It was dedicated to the Holy Trinity, and it was here that Augustinian monks looked after travellers, pilgrims and the sick and wounded. A recent archaeological dig uncovered evidence of surgery and the treatment of patients by herbal remedies. Some pieces of bandage with human tissue still attached to them were even recovered.

ROSSLYN

7 miles S of Edinburgh on the B7006

Rosslyn (also known as Roslin), has gained world renown through *The Da Vinci Code*, a thriller written by American author Dan Brown. According to some people, it is the most important place in Christendom, all due to **Rosslyn Church**, an extravaganza of a building on which work began in 1446. Its founder was Sir William St Clair, third and last Prince of Orkney, who lived at nearby **Rosslyn Castle**. In the choir of this unfinished church (still in use) are carvings with both Masonic and Knights Templar associations (see also Kirkwall).

The carving in the interior is spectacular, and shows plants that only grow in the New World, even though Columbus had not yet sailed across the Atlantic when it was built. There are also pagan carvings of "The Green Man", as well as the famous **Apprentice Pillar**. This was said to have been carved by an apprentice when the master mason working on the church was on the Continent seeking inspiration. When he returned and saw the workmanship, the mason is supposed to have murdered the apprentice in a fit of jealousy.

Legends abound about the church. One theory says that the writings of Christ lie in its unopened vaults. Another says that the bodies of Knights Templar lie in the unopened crypt, fully dressed in armour. A third says that the

Holy Grail is embedded in one of the pillars. And yet another says it is a re-creation of **Solomon's Temple** in Jerusalem.

There's even a theory that the body of Christ himself lies in the vaults. Whatever the truth of the matter, and the theories seem to get wilder and wilder with every new book written about it, there's no denying that it is one of the most beautiful buildings in Britain. There is certainly an aura about the place that can almost be felt (see also Kilmartin).

Nearby is the **Roslin Glen Country Park**, with woodland walks that go past old gunpowder works.

PENICUIK

9 miles S of Edinburgh on the A701

Penicuik was once a mining and paper making town, founded in 1770 by its laird, Sir James Clerk of Penicuik. To the west of the town rise the Pentland Hills, with **Scald Law** being the highest peak at 1,898 feet. In the grounds of Penicuik House stands the **Allan Ramsay Obelisk**, dedicated to the memory of Allan Ramsay, who was born in Leadhills in Lanarkshire in 1685. Ramsay visited the town often, as he was a friend of Sir James Clerk, who raised the obelisk, and had a house nearby (see also Leadhills). **St Mungo's Parish Church** dates from 1771, and has a 12th century detached belfry. The **Edinburgh Crystal Visitor Centre** at Eastfield has displays and exhibits about the history of crystal and glass making in Scotland, plus factory tours.

CRAMOND

5 miles W of Edinburgh on a minor road off the A90

Cramond is a charming village of old whitewashed cottages on the banks of the River Almond where it enters the Firth of Forth. The **Parish Church** of

CRAIGBRAE FARMHOUSE

By Kirkliston, West Lothian EH29 9EL
Tel: 0131 331 1205 Fax: 0131 319 1476
e-mail: louise@craigbrae.com website: www.craigbrae.com

Situated only seven miles from the heart of Edinburgh, yet in the countryside with a 15-minute rail link to Edinburgh just two miles away at Dalmeny, Craigbrae farmhouse is an excellent, comfortable B&B offering the best in Scottish hospitality. It has three superb guest rooms, the Blue and Yellow rooms can be either twin or double and the Double has a beautiful en suite bathroom. There are two other bathrooms and also a separate toilet. The house is cosy and always welcoming and all the rooms have views out over the countryside. You can choose either a hearty Scottish breakfast or a lighter option with fruit from the garden and homemade jam.

1656, with its medieval tower, sits within the ruins of a **Roman Fort** built about AD 142. The Rev. Robert Walker, who was painted by Raeburn skating on Duddingston Loch in the 18th century, was minister here.

Cramond Tower (not open to the public) dates from the 15th century, And **Cramond House** (not open to the public) dates from 1680. At one time, the village was famous for the manufacture of nails. **Cramond Island** sits one mile offshore, and it is possible to walk to it via a causeway at low tide, though walkers should heed the notices about tide times before setting off.

INGLISTON

7 miles W of Edinburgh off the A8

Almost in the shadow of Edinburgh International Airport at Turnhouse is the **Royal Showground**, home each year of the Royal Highland Show, Scotland's premier country and farming fair. The **Cars of the Stars Motor Museum**, opened in 2003, features vehicles used in films. It features two of the cars used in James Bond films.

BALERNO

7 miles SW of Edinburgh off the A70

Malleny Garden (National Trust for Scotland) is a walled garden beside the

17th century Malleny House (not open to the public) extending to three acres and dominated by 400-year-old clipped yew trees. There are herbaceous borders, a fine collection of old-fashioned roses, and it houses the National Bonsai Collection for Scotland. The house was built for Sir James Murray of Kilbaberton.

RATHO

0 miles W of Edinburgh on a minor road off the A8

Ratho sits on the Union Canal, and from the **Edinburgh Canal Centre**, opened in 1989, canal cruises are available. Parts of **Ratho Parish Church** dates from the 12th century, though little of this can now be seen due to restorations over the years.

The **Adventure Centre** is billed as the "gateway to adventure", with the National Rock Climbing Centre having 2,400 square metres of artificial wall surfaces, the largest climbing arena in the world. One other feature is the Airpark, Europe's largest suspended aerial adventure ropes ride.

SOUTH QUEENSFERRY

9 miles W of Edinburgh city centre off the A90

South Queensferry is named after St Margaret, Malcolm III's queen, who founded a ferry here in the 11th century to carry pilgrims across the Forth to

South Queensferry and Dalmeny

Distance:	5.2 miles (8.3 kilometres)
Typical time:	120 mins
Height gain:	60 metres
Map:	Explorer 350
Walk:	www.walkingworld.com ID:2522
Contributor:	Fiona Dick

Access Information:

By car; leave Edinburgh on A90. After leaving the built-up area, take the second exit onto the B924, signposted Dalmeny. Follow signs to the village and drive to the west end (past the war memorial). Where the road swings round to the left into Standingstone Road, carry straight on into the cul-de-sac and park opposite Wester Dalmeny Farmhouse.

By public transport: there are three buses an hour to Dalmeny Village from Princes Street in the yellow taxibus.

Additional Information:

Dalmeny Village has a delightful small church (Norman doorway). Dalmeny House is home to the Earls of Rosebury and can be visited in the summer season (furniture, tapestries, paintings, small golf course). South Queensferry is an historic town that used to be the jumping-off point for travellers to the north of Scotland; there are still boat trips out to Inchcolm Island (birds, ruined abbey). As well as a museum and harbour, it can offer toilets (open even in winter), cafes, restaurants and pubs, of which the most famous is the Hawes Inn, featured in Robert Louis Stevenson's *Kidnapped*. Glorious views of the Forth Rail and Road Bridges, as well as down the estuary and back to Edinburgh. And all this within the boundaries of the City of Edinburgh.

Description:

A level walk passing through a country estate that juts out into the Forth Estuary, thus combining seashore and country. Easy going underfoot; you could just about get around with a buggy if you were prepared to lift it at a couple of places. Some walking on minor roads, but there is pavement throughout.

There are better views out to sea when the trees are bare, lots of daffodils in the spring and a lovely mix of specimen trees in the summer.

Features:

Sea, Pub, Toilets, Church, Stately Home, Birds, Flowers, Great Views, Cafe, Food Shop, Good for Kids, Mostly Flat, Public Transport, Restaurants, Woodland

Walk Directions:

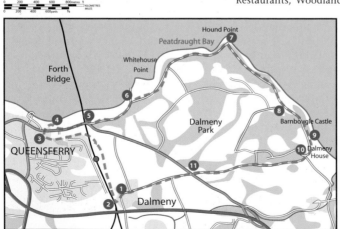

1 Walk straight ahead (west) to the old railway bridge. At the blue sign take the path to the left alongside houses. Take steps down to the old railway line.

2 Turn right between three big stones onto the tarmac cycle path and go under the railway bridge. After the second bridge there is a view of the

Forth Rail Bridge. Carry on under several bridges and round a left-hand bend.

3 Just before the houses on the left-hand side, turn right onto an earth path towards a white house. At the house, turn right down the path onto the shore road.

4 Cross over and turn right towards the Forth Rail Bridge, passing underneath it, with the Hawes Inn on the opposite side of the road.

5 As the road bends round to the right, take the lower path that runs alongside the water, with a low white building on the left-hand side (ices in summer). Carry on round the shore path - don't forget to look back for more great views of the rail bridge.

6 At Long Craig Gate (white) and cottage, go through into the Dalmeny Estate (information board). Path now becomes hard-surfaced track. Carry on through the estate, following signs to Cramond Ferry, past the large tanker berth in the estuary. Ignore all side turnings.

7 At Hound Point the track turns right. Here it is worth making a small detour onto the sand to admire the views.

8 On meeting a tarmac road coming in from the right, carry straight on towards Dalmeny House, which you shortly see.

9 Ignore a sign off to left to the shore walk (although it is worth going to the edge of the golf course for the view). Instead, keep on the hard path curving round to the right past the house and the statue of a horse.

10 At a five-way junction, go straight ahead up the slope with a field and fence to your left. Shortly cross a cattle grid and make your way through the estate on the road (occasional cars).

11 At the estate exit, cross the road with care and go straight ahead (signposted 'Dalmeny'). Pass a farm with a converted doocot on the left and carry on into the village, with more views of the bridges over the hedges. Continue through the village back to your car.

Dunfermline Abbey and St Andrew's Cathedral. When she herself died she was buried in the abbey and later canonised, with her shrine becoming a place of pilgrimage as well. Now the ferry has been replaced by the **Forth Rail Bridge** and the **Forth Road Bridge**, two mammoth pieces of civil engineering. The rail bridge was built between 1883 and 1890 to link Edinburgh and Aberdeen, and the road bridge was completed in 1964. In the shadow of the Rail Bridge is the historic **Hawes Inn** of 1683, which features in R.L. Stevenson's *Kidnapped*. Opposite is the slipway from which the former ferry sailed.

The town has a glorious mix of cottages and houses dating from the 16th century onwards. **Plewlands House** (National Trust for Scotland) dates from 1643, and has been converted into private flats. The

Queensferry Museum, in the High Street, has exhibits and displays on local history. There are also wonderful views of the two bridges from it. The church of the former **Carmelite Friary** in Rose Lane dates from the 15th century, and is now an Episcopalian church.

Each year in early August the quaint custom of the **Burry Man** takes place. Dressed from head to toe in plant burrs,

Forth Rail Bridge, South Queensferry

he spends nine hours walking about the town on a Friday. While everyone agrees it is an ancient custom, no on knows how it originated or what purpose it served.

Dalmeny House, to the east of the town, overlooks the Firth of Forth. It is the home of the Primrose family, who are Earls of Roseberry, and was built in the 1820s. There is an excellent collection of tapestries and furniture. **Dalmeny Church**, dedicated to St Cuthbert, is one of the best-preserved Norman churches in Britain. The south doorway is richly carved, as is the chancel and apse.

HADDINGTON

The royal burgh of Haddington received its royal charter in the 12th century from David I, and is thought to be the birthplace in 1505 of John Knox. It sits on the River Tyne (but not the one that flows through Newcastle), and at one time it was the fourth largest town in Scotland. It was in **St Martin's Church** (all that is left of an old nunnery that stood in Nungate, outside the then burgh boundaries) that the Scottish and French parliaments met in 1548 to sanction Mary Stuart's marriage to the Dauphin of France. Members of both the French and Scottish nobility attended, and put an end to the Henry VIII's plans to have Mary marry his son Edward.

It is a quiet town of old buildings, including the quite superb cathedralesque **Parish Church of St Mary.** It was formerly collegiate, and dates from the 15th century. It stood outside the burgh boundaries at that time, and when the parliament was meeting at St Martin's, the Scots were laying siege to the town, as it was occupied by the English. Mary of Guise (Mary Stuart's mother) attended the

parliament, and when she climbed to the top of St Mary's tower to view the English defences she was shot at. The ruined choir was restored in the early part of the 20th century, and such is the church's size and beauty (it is the longest parish church in Scotland) that some people erroneously think it is the church of a former abbey. In the choir is the burial place of **Jane Welsh** (Thomas Carlyle's wife), who was born in the town, in a house that can still be seen. The **Lauderdale Aisle**, owned by the Earls of Lauderdale, is unique in that it is a small Episcopalian chapel within a Presbyterian Church. This ecumenicalism continues every year in May with the **Whitekirk and Haddington Pilgrimage**, when people from all the main Christian religions in Scotland walk between the two towns (see also Whitekirk).

St Mary's is one of the few Church of Scotland churches to have a full peel of bells, which were installed in 1999. The 16th century **Nungate Bridge** over the Tyne is behind St Mary's, and is named after the nunnery where the Scottish parliament met.

The writer **Samuel Smiles** was born in Haddington in 1812. Though he wrote many books, he is best known for *Self Help*. Alexander II and William the Lion may also have been born here, in a royal castle that has long gone.

The **Town House**, with its graceful spire, was designed by William Adam and built in the late 1740s, though the spire was added in 1831. Close to Haddington is **Lennoxlove**, home to the Dukes of Hamilton since 1946. It houses the death mask of Mary Stuart, which shows her to have been, as many contemporaries observed, an extremely beautiful woman. The origins of the house go back to at least the 13th century, when it was called Lethington Hall, and the home of the Maitland family.

About four miles east of Haddington is **Traprain Law**, from the top of which there are superb views. The summit was occupied from Neolithic times right up until the Dark Ages, and the outline of a fort can clearly be seen. It was the capital of a tribe the Romans called the Votadini, which roughly translated means "the farmers". More Roman finds have been made here, including a horde of Roman silver, than anywhere else in Scotland.

AROUND HADDINGTON

GULLANE
6 miles N of Haddington on the A198

This village sits inland from the Firth of Forth, but has fine views north towards Fife. Nowadays it is a small golfing resort with many large, imposing villas. The British Open is held here regularly, and the course at **Muirfield** is home to the Honourable Company of Edinburgh Golfers. The **Heritage of Golf** exhibition on the West Links Road traces the golfing history of the area.

The ruins of the **St Andrew's Church** can be seen at the west end of the main street. They date from the 12th century, and were abandoned in 1612. On Gullane Bay, and signposted from the main street, is **Gullane Bents**, one of the best beaches on the Firth of Forth.

DIRLETON
6 miles N of Haddington off the A198

The impressive ruins of **Dirleton Castle** (Historic Scotland) dominate this pleasant village. The oldest parts date to the end of the 13th century, though there have been extensive additions and alterations over the years. The castle was taken by Edward I of England in 1298, but was back in Scottish hands by 1311. It was built by the Norman family of de

Vaux, though it has also been owned by the Halyburtons and the Ruthvens. The third Lord Ruthven was implicated in the murder of Mary Stuart's Italian secretary Rizzio in Holyroodhouse. To the west of the castle are some formal terraced gardens, which are in the Guinness Book of Records as having the longest herbaceous border in the world.

ABERLADY
6 miles N of Haddington on the A198

This pleasant village was the port for Haddington until the bay silted up. The **Aberlady Bay Nature Reserve** covers 1439 acres of foreshore and dunes, and is popular with bird watchers. The village was home to one of Scotland's most popular historical novelists, **Nigel Tranter**, who died in the year 2000. There is a small cairn to his memory close to Quarry House, where he used to live.

Myreton Motor Museum contains displays of motorcars, cycles and military vehicles. **Aberlady Parish Church** was remodelled in the 19th century, though an interesting 16th century tower still stands. In the High Street is the old **Mercat Cross** of 1780. To the east of the village is **Luffness Castle**, once the ancestral home of the Hepburns, and now a hotel.

ATHELSTANEFORD
2 miles NE of Haddington on the B1343

Athelstaneford has a special place in Scottish history. It was here that the Scottish flag, the **Saltire**, or St Andrew's Cross, was first adopted. Athelstan was a king of Northumbria who fought a combined army of Picts and Scots at Athelstaneford in AD832. The Pictish leader, Angus mac Fergus, on the day before the battle, saw a huge white cross made of clouds in the sky, and took it as an omen. Athelstane was duly defeated, and a white cross on a blue background was adopted as the flag of Scotland, making it the oldest national flag in Europe.

This is why the Saltire on its own should be white and sky blue, whereas when it is incorporated into the Union Jack the blue darkens. The **National Flag Centre** in an old doocot ("dovecot") in the village explains the story of the battle and the flag.

NORTH BERWICK
7 miles NE of Haddington on the A198

North Berwick is one of Scotland's best-known holiday and golfing resorts. It is a clean, attractive town, which was granted a royal charter by Robert II in 1373. **North Berwick Law**, a volcanic plug, rises to a height of 613 feet behind the town, and makes a wonderful viewpoint. Two miles off the coast lies the **Bass Rock**, another volcanic plug that broods over the waters of the Firth of Forth. Over 150,000 sea birds nest each year on the 350-feet high cliffs and on other, smaller islands such as Fidra and Craigleith. From the **Scottish Seabird Centre** on a promontory near the old harbour you can use remote controlled cameras which are situated on the islands to study them without disturbing the colonies. There are also powerful telescopes on a viewing deck, a film about Scotland's sea birds, and a café restaurant.

In the 8th century the Bass Rock was home to the hermit **St Baldred**, who evangelised this part of Scotland (though he not to be confused with another St Baldred who succeeded St Mungo as Bishop of Glasgow, and who lived a century earlier). In later times it also served as a prison for Jacobites and Covenanters, and there are traces of old fortifications on it.

Also on the promontory are the scant ruins of the **St Andrew's Auld Kirk**, which date from the 12th century onwards. It was finally abandoned in the 17th century due to coastal erosion, and when the Seabird Centre was being built, over 30 well-preserved skeletons from the old graveyard were uncovered, the earliest one dating back to the 7th century. In School Road is the **North Berwick Museum**, housed in a former school, which has displays and memorabilia about local history, wildlife and golf.

In the 16th century the town was supposed to have been the home of a notorious **Witches Coven**, and a well-publicised trial took place in 1595. One of the accusations made was that the witches had caused a terrible storm to rise up when James VI's ship was returning from Denmark with his new bride.

It all started when a poor serving girl called Gelie Duncan was found to have remarkable healing powers, which aroused suspicion. Her master, David Seaton, tried to extract a confession of witchcraft from her using thumbscrews, and when this failed he had her body examined for the "marks of the devil". These were duly found on her throat, and she confessed and was thrown in jail.

On being tortured further, Gelie claimed to be one of 200 witches and warlocks in the town who, at the behest of the Earl of Bothwell, David Seaton's sworn enemy, were trying to harm the king. At Hallowe'en in 1590, Gelie told them, the witches convened at the Auld Kirk, where Satan appeared to them and preached a sermon from the pulpit. King James had all the women identified by Gelie put to death, including one Agnes Sampson and a schoolmaster from

Prestonpans called John Fian. Gelie herself was burnt on the Castle Esplanade in Edinburgh.

Though people have subsequently claimed that the Earl of Bothwell dressed up as Satan to take part in the Hallowe'en coven in the kirk, there's little doubt that Gelie made up the stories to save herself from further torture, and many innocent people were executed because of this. There is also no doubt that David Seaton had no interest in the women as such - he merely wanted to harm the Earl of Bothwell.

East of North Berwick is **Tantallon Castle** (Historic Scotland). Its substantial and romantic ruins stand on a cliff top above the Firth of Forth, almost opposite the Bass Rock. It was a Douglas stronghold, built in the 14th century by William, 1st Earl of Douglas. Cromwell ordered General Monk to take the castle, and in 1651, after a 12-day siege, he destroyed it.

WHITEKIRK

7 miles NE of Haddington off the A198

St Mary's Parish Church dates from the 15th century, and is the eastern end of the annual Whitekirk to Haddington Pilgrimage (see also Haddington). However, Whitekirk had been a place of pilgrimage long before this. In pre Reformation times, people came to the village to seek cures at the Well of Our Lady, which used to be located nearby. An account of 1413 relates that over 15,000 people of all nationalities visited yearly. Close to the church is the 16th century **Tithe Barn**, built to store the "tithes" (a tithe being a tenth part) given to the church as offerings from the parishioners' agricultural produce.

The place's most famous pilgrim - but one who did not come seeking a cure - was a young Italian nobleman called **Aeneas Sylvius Piccolomini**. He had set out from Rome in the winter of 1435 as an envoy to the court of James I, and during the sea crossing he was blown off course by a raging gale. Aeneas vowed that if he made it to dry land he would offer thanksgiving at the nearest church dedicated to Our Lady. The boat was eventually shipwrecked between North Berwick and Dunbar, and Aeneas survived. He therefore set out on a ten-mile pilgrimage in a snowstorm to Whitekirk, where he duly offered prayers of thanks. While in Scotland, he fell in love with a young woman, and made a pledge of love to her. However, he was ambitious, and soon gave her up. Twenty years later, Aeneas became Pope Pious II.

EAST LINTON

6 miles E of Haddington off the A1

Anyone travelling along the A1 should make a small detour to view this picturesque village. To the east is **Phantassie**, the mansion where **John Rennie** the civil engineer was born He designed Waterloo, London and Southwark bridges over the Thames, and Rennie's Bridge at Kelso (see also Kelso).

Preston Mill (National Trust for Scotland) is an old, quaint water mill that has been restored to full working order. It sits in an idyllic rural spot, and dates from the 18th century, though a mill has stood on the spot for centuries. With its conical roofed kiln and red pantiles, it is a favourite subject for painters and photographers. Close by is **Phantassie Doocot** (National Trust for Scotland), which belonged to Phantassie House, and could hold 500 birds. Also close by is **Prestonkirk**, a small, attractive church. It was built in 1770, though the 13th century chancel still stands, as it was used as a mausoleum for the Hepburn family.

MUSEUM OF FLIGHT

East Fortune Airfield, East Lothian, EH39 5LF
Tel: 01620 880308   Fax: 01620 880355   website: nms.ac.uk/flight

The Museum of Flight is based at East Fortune Airfield, a Scheduled Ancient Monument and one of the most famous sites in world aviation history. It tells the history of East Fortune (established in 1915 as a fighter base to protect Scotland from Zeppelin attacks) and of the Scottish built airship R34 which left East Fortune and flew to Long Island, New York, becoming the first return transatlantic flight. The Museum collection is housed in the original hangars and restoration work can be seen in progress. A large selection of models, toys and books is on sale in the shop and the Parachute Cafe serves light refreshments.

The ruins of **Hailes Castle** lie to the west of East Linton. Its earliest masonry dates from the 13th century, though it was much altered in later years by the Hepburns, who acquired the castle in the 14th century. It was to Hailes Castle that James Hepburn, Earl of Bothwell, brought Mary Stuart after seizing her at Fountainbridge in 1567. He was later to become her third husband.

The **Scottish Museum of Flight** (see panel above) is situated at East Fortune, to the north east of the village. Formerly a World War II airfield, it now houses a collection of aircraft, rockets, models and memorabilia. The most famous exhibit is Concorde, brought to the museum in 2004. Another is a Prestwick Pioneer, the only aircraft ever to have been wholly designed and built in Scotland. Also on display are a Soviet MIG, a Blue Streak rocket and a Lightning.

STENTON

7 miles E of Haddington on the B6370

This small conservation village still retains its old **Tron**, on which wool brought to the Stenton Fair by local sheep farmers was weighed. To the south of the village is **Pressmennan Lake**, one of the few lakes, as opposed to lochs, in Scotland (see also Lake of Menteith, Ellon and Kirkcudbright). This one,

however, is artificial, created in 1819 by the local landowner. The **Pressmennan Forest Trail** runs along its southern shore, and from the highest point you can see Arthur's Seat in Edinburgh and the Bass Rock in the Firth of Forth.

Stenton Kirk is a handsome building designed by the noted architect William Burn in 1829. In the kirkyard is the **Old Kirk**, dating probably from the 14th century.

TYNINGHAME

7 miles E of Haddington on the B1407

Originally the lands of Tyninghame belonged to the Archbishops of St Andrews, but in 1628 they were acquired by the Earls of Haddington. Tyninghame itself is a small conservation village which formerly stood in what are now the grounds of **Tyninghame House**, which has been divided up into private flats. In 1761 it was moved to its present position by the then Earl of Haddington to improve the view from his house, though the remains of the former parish kirk, dedicated to St Baldred, still stand there.

DUNBAR

11 miles E of Haddington on the A1087

The Royal Burgh of Dunbar received its royal charter in 1445. It is a former fishing and whaling port, though its main industries are now brewing and tourism. It was near here, in 1650, that the **Battle of Dunbar** took place between the troops of Cromwell and a Covenanting army under General Leslie. The Covenanters were resoundingly beaten when General Leslie's advice not to confront Cromwell was ignored by the Scottish ministers. A stone commemorates the event.

The ruins of **Dunbar Castle** overlook the harbour, and date back to the 12th century. The castle was originally built for the Cospatrick family, which

Dunbar

later changed its name to Dunbar. It was to Dunbar Castle that Edward II fled after his defeat at Bannockburn. He then boarded a boat for Berwick-upon-Tweed. In 1338 the Countess of Dunbar, known as "Black Agnes", held the castle for five months against an English army before being relieved by a small contingent of Scots. On the orders of the Scottish Parliament, the castle was dismantled after Mary Stuart abdicated.

The old **Town House** in the High Street dates from about 1620 and houses a small museum on local history and archaeology. A much newer "attraction" is situated south of the town, near the shore. **Torness Nuclear Power Station** was built in the early '80s, and has a

visitor centre that explains how electricity is produced from nuclear power.

John Muir, founder of the American national parks system, was born in Dunbar in 1838. His birthplace in the High Street is now the **John Muir Centre**, with displays on his travels and his work. The **John Muir Country Park** is to the north west of the town. Established in 1976, this was the first park of its kind in Scotland, and covers 1,760 acres.

Two miles south of the town, off the A1, is **Doonhill Homestead** (Historic Scotland), where once an Anglian hall dating from the 7th - 8th century stood. It is marked out on the grass, and shows

Dunbar Church

that this area of Scotland was once part of the mighty Anglian kingdom of Northumbria.

GARVALD
6 miles SE of Haddington off the B6370

This tiny red sandstone village lies on the northern slopes of the Lammermuir Hills. **Garvald Parish Church** dates partly from the 12th century, and has a sundial dated 1633. It is surprisingly light and airy inside. South east of the village is the mansion of **Nunraw**, in whose grounds Cistercian monks, who arrived here in 1946, began building the Abbey of Sancta Maria in 1952. It was the first Cistercian monastery in Scotland since the Reformation, and was colonised by monks form Tipperary in Ireland. A Cistercian nunnery, founded by nuns from Haddington, had previously been founded here in about 1158.

GIFFORD
4 miles S of Haddington on the B6369

Gifford was laid out in the 18th century, and is a pretty village with views of the Lammermuir Hills to the south. The whitewashed **Yester Parish Church**, which has Dutch influences, was built in 1708, and has a medieval bell. It was in Gifford that John Witherspoon, the only clergyman to sign the American Declaration of Independence, was born in 1723 (see also Paisley).

Southeast of the village is **Yester House**, designed by James Smith and dating from 1745. The interiors were later re-styled by Robert Adam in 1789. Beyond it are the ruins of **Yester Castle**, built by Hugo de Gifford in the late 13th century. He was known as the "Wizard of Yester", and beneath the castle is a chamber known as **Goblin Ha'** where he is supposed to have practised magic and called up goblins and demons. Scott mentions him in *Marmion*.

The narrow road from Gifford up into the Lammermuir Hills is a fine drive, and takes you past Whiteadder reservoir and down into Berwickshire.

PENCAITLAND
6 miles SW of Haddington on the A6093

The oldest part of **Pencaitland Parish Church** is the Winton Aisle, which dates from the 13th century. Close to the village is the 500-year-old **Winton House**. It was built for the Seton family by the king's master mason, and is famous for its "twisted chimneys". It overlooks the Tyne, and has lovely terraced gardens. **Glenkinchie Distillery**, to the south of the village, was opened in 1837, and has a small exhibition. It offers tours showing how whisky is distilled.

LINLITHGOW

This ancient royal burgh was granted its royal charter in 1138. It is a lovely place, with many historic buildings in its old High Street, and has played a central role in Scotland's history. **Linlithgow Palace** (Historic Scotland), situated on the banks of **Linlithgow Loch**, dates originally from the reign of James I, who ruled in the early 15th century. It replaced an older castle where Edward I once stayed when he invaded Scotland in support of John Balliol's claim to the Scottish throne.

It was a favourite of many Scottish kings and queens, and it was here, in 1512, that James V was born. It was also the birthplace, in 1542, of his daughter, the tragic Mary Stuart. The birth room was most probably the **Queen's Bedchamber** in the northwest tower. Her association with Linlithgow Palace lasted only seven months, as her mother, Mary of Guise, later took her to the more secure Stirling Castle. When Mary Stuart returned from France in 1561 after the death of her husband King Francis II, she

Linlithgow Palace

only stayed briefly at the castle, and it was allowed to decay.

Cromwell stayed here briefly in 1650 when he invaded Scotland after its parliament had declared Charles II king of Britain. Then, in 1745, Charles Edward Stuart stayed in the Palace. A year later the troops of the Duke of Cumberland moved in, and when they moved out they left their straw bedding too close to the fires. The whole place caught fire, and soon the whole building was ablaze, leaving it roofless and uninhabitable.

In the castle courtyard is the **King's Fountain**, built between 1536 and 1538 for James V and now being restored to full working order. It is the oldest fountain in Britain, and is in three tiers, with elaborate carving that symbolises his reign, and was badly damaged during the fire. A restoration scheme of the 1930s used concrete to replace some of the carvings, and this introduced salts into the structure, which began its decay.

The **Outer Gateway** to the palace still stands, and on it are the coats of arms of the four orders of chivalry to which James V belonged - the Garter of England, the Thistle of Scotland, the Golden Fleece of Burgundy and St Michael of France.

Opposite the Palace is **St Michael's Parish Church**, one of the most important medieval churches in Scotland. It dates from the 15th century, though a church had stood here long before that. Within the church one of the most unusual incidents in Scottish history took place. The church was especially dear to James IV, who worshipped there regularly. In 1514, he had decided to take a large army into England in support of France, which had been invaded by Henry VIII's troops. Most of the Scottish court was against the idea, as was James's wife Margaret, sister of the English king.

But James held firm, and a few days before he and his army set out, he was at mass in St Michael's Church with his courtiers. A strange man with long, fair hair suddenly appeared in the church dressed in a blue gown tied with a white band and carrying a staff. Pushing aside the courtiers, he approached James and spoke to him. He had been sent "by his mother", he said, to tell James that no good would come of the invasion of England. Furthermore, he was not to meddle with other women.

Some of the courtiers tried to grab him, but before they could the old man made good his escape. Confusion reigned, and people immediately took the man to be a ghost. The reference to his mother, they said, meant that he had been sent by Our Lady (of whom James was especially fond). James took no heed, and marched into England. He, and all the flower of Scottish manhood, were wiped out on the field at Flodden. The "ghost's" prophecy came true.

People nowadays discount the ghost theory, and say that the whole thing had been orchestrated by James's wife with the help of some of the court. The reference to the king's meddling with other women was the Queen's own contribution to the event, as James was renowned for his philandering.

One of the courtiers was Sir David Lyndsay, Lord Lyon and playwright, who knew all the tricks of the stage, and he may have been involved as well. There is a theory that says that Margaret had been put up to it by her brother Henry

Linlithgow

VIII, who was totally unprepared for a Scottish invasion, though this is now discounted. All she wanted to do was protect him from his own folly.

The **Town House**, in the centre of the town, dates from 1668, and replaces an earlier building destroyed by Oliver Cromwell in 1650. The **Cross Well** dates from 1807, and replaces an earlier structure.

It was in Linlithgow that the Earl of Moray, Regent of Scotland, was assassinated in the street by James Hamilton of Bothwellhaugh, who later escaped to France. A plaque on the old **County Buildings** commemorates the event. In Annet House in the High Street is the **Linlithgow Story**, with displays and exhibits explaining the history of the town. There are also herb, fruit tree and flower gardens. At the **Linlithgow Canal Centre** in Manse Road is a small museum dedicated to the Union Canal, which links the Forth and Clyde Canal at Falkirk with Edinburgh. Trips along the canal are also available. **Beecraigs Country Park**, to the south of the town, is set in 913 acres of land near the Bathgate Hills. It has a loch where you can fish, a deer farm and a camping and caravan park.

To the north of the town is the **House of the Binns** (National Trust for Scotland), ancestral home of the Dalyell family, the best known member of which is Tam Dalyell the former MP. In 1601 the Edinburgh butter merchant Thomas Dalyell married Janet, daughter of the first Baron Kinloss, and bought the lands of Binns. Between 1621 and 1630 he enlarged the house, and the present building has at its core that 17ᵗʰ century structure. It represents possibly the best example of the transition from a fortified castle to a comfortable home in Scotland.

His son was also Thomas, though he earned an unsavoury reputation as "Bluidie Tam Dalyel", scourge of the Covenanters. He was every inch a king's man, and when Charles I was executed in 1649, he vowed never to cut his hair until there was a king on the throne once more. And indeed, Bloody Tam's portrait in The Binns shows a man with hair flowing down past his shoulders. Tam also helped the Tsar of Russia reorganise the Russian army, and was made a nobleman of Russia. For that reason he also had another nickname - "The Bluidie Muscovite".

Another stately home near Linlithgow is **Hopetoun House**, possibly the grandest "big house" in Scotland, and certainly the best example of a Georgian house in the country. It sits almost on the banks of the Forth, and is home to the Marquis of Linlithgow. It was started in 1699 by the 1st Earl of Hopetoun, ancestor of the present Marquis, and designed by Sir William Bruce with enlargements by William Adam, who

introduced the sweeping curves. The inside is spectacular and opulent, with ornate plasterwork, tapestries, furnishings and paintings. Surrounding the house is magnificent parkland extending to 150 acres, with a deer park and spring garden. The main approach to the house is by the Royal Drive, which can only be used by royalty. George IV used it when he visited Scotland in 1822, and Elizabeth II also used it in 1988.

AROUND LINLITHGOW

BO'NESS
3 miles N of Linlithgow on the A904

The town's real name is Borrowstoneness, though it is always referred to nowadays by its shortened name. It is an industrial town, and was formerly one of Scotland's leading whaling ports. It was near here that the eastern end of the Antonine Wall terminated. Near the town is the Kinneil Estate, with, at its centre, **Kinneil House**. It was built by the Hamilton family in the 16th and 17th centuries. It isn't open to the public, though it can be viewed from the outside. However, within the house's 17th century stable block is the **Kinneil Museum**, which tells the story of Bo'ness over the last 2,000 years. There is also an exhibition called "Rome's Northern Frontier", which highlights the Antonine Wall and the Roman soldiers who manned it. The ruins of **Kinneil Church** lie near the house, and probably date from the 13th century with later additions. It was abandoned as a place of worship in 1669, when a new parish church was built at Corbie Hall. It was accidentally destroyed by fire in 1745 by a troop of dragoons stationed at the house.

The town's main attraction is the **Bo'ness and Kinneil Railway**, which has been developed since 1979 by the Scottish Railway Preservation Society. There is a

Scottish railway exhibition as well as workshops and a working station. Trips on the steam trains, which run between Bo'ness and Birkhill Station are popular with the public, and trains can also be chartered for special occasions. At Birkhill are the caverns of the former **Birkhill Fireclay Mine**, which can be explored.

BLACKNESS

4 miles NE of Linlithgow on the B903

Blackness Castle (Historic Scotland) must be the most unusually shaped castle in Scotland. It sits on a promontory jutting out into the Firth of Forth, and from the air looks like a huge ship. It was a Crichton stronghold, with the first castle on the site being built in about 1449 by Sir George Crichton, Sheriff of Linlithgow and Admiral of Scotland. However, there is an intriguing but untrue story about how the castle eventually came to look like a ship.

By the early 16th century the castle had passed to the Douglases. James V appointed Archibald Douglas as Lord High Admiral of the Scottish fleet, but soon discovered that he had made a mistake, as every time Archibald went to sea he became sea sick.

The young James was enraged, and threatened to dismiss him. Archibald, who was making a fortune out of selling commissions in the navy, wanted to retain his position. So he promised his king that if he was allowed to keep his job, he would build him a ship that the English couldn't sink and on which he would never be sick. Mollified, the king agreed, and Douglas built Blackness Castle. However, a more mundane explanation of its shape is the restricted shape of the site on which it was built.

The castle was subsequently besieged by Cromwell's army in 1650, and was later used as a prison for Covenanters.

During the Napoleonic wars, it was again used as a prison, this time for French prisoners-of-war. After that it was used as an ammunition dump, and was finally restored and opened to the public.

TORPHICHEN

3 miles S of Linlithgow on the B792

The unusual name of this picturesque village comes from Gaelic "Torr Phigheainn", meaning the "hill of the magpies", and is pronounced "Tor fichen". It is an ancient place, with its history going back to the founding of a church dedicated to St Ninian in the 6th century.

The Knights of the Order of St John of Jerusalem, or the Knights Hospitallers as they were more commonly called, was a monastic order of soldier monks formed in the 11th century to look after St John's Hospital in Jerusalem, and to offer hospitality and protection to pilgrims travelling to the Holy Land. **Torphichen Preceptory** (Historic Scotland) was one of only two such establishments in Britain, the other one being in London. It was founded in about 1124, when the lands of Torphichen were given to the monks by David I. The head of a Knights Hospitaller monastery was called a "preceptor", and for this reason a monastery was always known as a "preceptory". During the Wars of Independence, the then preceptor supported Edward I of England, and after Bannockburn the monks had to flee. However, they later returned.

The only parts left standing of the original preceptory are the transepts and crossing of the monastic church. Above the crossing is a tower, which, no doubt because of the Knights' military role, looks more like a castle than a church tower. Within a small room is a display about the modern Order of St John, which was refounded in 1947 as a separate order in Scotland by George VI. Nowadays it runs old folks homes, mountain rescue units and hospitals in Scotland. Where the nave once stood is now **Torphichen Parish Church**, which dates from 1756, though it incorporates masonry from the earlier building.

Livingston

6 miles S of Linlithgow off the M8

Livingston is one of Scotland's new towns, built round an historic village which has the **Livingston Parish Church** of 1732. At the 20-acre **Almond Valley Heritage Centre** in Millfield the visitor can find out about local history and the environment, including the Scottish shale industry, which once thrived in West Lothian. There is also an 18th century water mill, a small railway line, a farm, a picnic area and teahouse.

The **Almondell and Calderwood Country Park** is three miles east of the town centre, and has woodland and riverside walks. Almondell was originally a private estate, which belonged to the Erskine family, and many items from Kirkhill House, with which it was associated, have been relocated within the park, such as the entrance gates and the astronomical pillar. Calderwood was also a private estate, and belonged to the barons of Torphichen. This area has been deliberately left undeveloped to encourage wildlife. The **Oakbank Shale Bings** are a reminder of the shale industry, and have been landscaped. A good view of the surrounding countryside, and even up into Fife, is available from the top.

Mid Calder

8 miles SE of Linlithgow on the B8046

The Kirk of Mid Calder has an apse built in the 16th century. One of the 17th century ministers of the church was Hew Kennedy, who was zealous in his persecution of witches. In 1644 several of them were burnt at the stake.

While staying at **Calder House** (not open to the public) in 1556 (four years before the Scottish Reformation) John Knox first administered Holy Communion using the new reformed liturgy. In 1848 the Polish pianist Chopin also stayed here.

Bathgate

6 miles S of Linlithgow on the A89

Bathgate is a substantial industrial town, and was formerly a centre for the shale oil industry. **Sir James Young Simpson**, who introduced chloroform into midwifery, was the son of a Bathgate baker, and he was born here in 1811, as was **James "Paraffin" Young**, who opened the world's first oil refinery in 1850, extracting paraffin from the local shale. **Cairnpapple Hill** (Historic Scotland), to the north of the town, is 1,017 feet high, and was the site of a temple built about 2000 - 2500 BC. Fragments of bone and pottery have been found. The view from the top is magnificent, and on a clear day both the Bass Rock in the Firth of Forth and the mountains of Arran in the Firth of Clyde can be seen.

In Mansefield Street is the **Bennie Museum**, which contains collections relating to local history. **Polkemmet Country Park** is four miles west of the town, and has a golf course, a driving range, bowling green and picnic areas. The whole area was owned at one time by the Baillie family, and a mausoleum, built by Robert Baillie, fourth Lord Polkemmet, can still be seen.

LOCATOR MAP

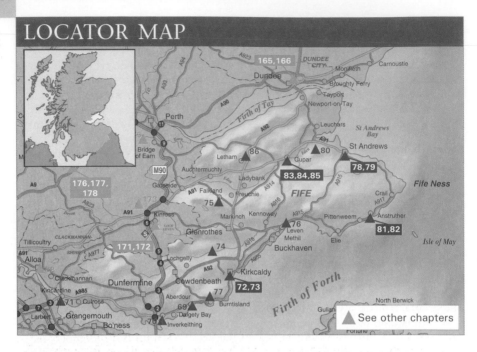

ADVERTISERS AND PLACES OF INTEREST

FIFE 6

The county of Fife consists of a long peninsula bounded on the south by the Firth of Forth and on the north by the Firth of Tay. It is steeped in history, and for that reason is sometimes referred to as the "Kingdom of Fife". James II, who ruled from 1437 to 1460, once called it a "fringe of gold on a beggar's mantle", meaning that, in his day, it had prosperous coastal towns and a barren interior. During the Cold War years, Fife was where Scotland would be governed from in the event of a nuclear attack. The underground Secret Bunker, as it is now known. was located on a farm near St Andrews.

Dunfermline, still an important town, was Scotland's capital before Edinburgh took over, and on the coast there were small prosperous seaports which traded with Europe. You can still see the European influence today. Some of the older buildings in the coastal towns have a distinctly Low Countries feel to them, and some houses have red pantiles - brought in as ballast from the Netherlands and the Baltic countries - instead of slates. These ports, with names such as Crail, Pittenweem and Anstruther, are still there, though now they rely on tourism rather than trade.

Of all the towns on the county's east coast the most famous is surely St Andrews. Seen from a distance, it shimmers with spires and towers, and is crammed with old buildings and historical associations. It was formerly a place of pilgrimage because of its great cathedral, the impressive ruins of which still overlook the shore. In it were kept the relics of St Andrew, Scotland's national saint, and this made it the country's ecclesiastical capital in pre Reformation days.

It was also the seat of an archbishop, and was where Scotland's first university was founded. Even today students can be seen dressed in their traditional red gowns as they scurry to lectures during term time. And the place still attracts pilgrims, though now they come in the name of sport, for the town - or perhaps we should call it a small city - is the recognised home of golf.

The county's largest town is Kirkcaldy, famous for the manufacture of linoleum. So much so that people used to say that

St Andrews

you could always tell when you were approaching the town by its "queer-like smell". But this royal burgh, which was granted its charter in 1644, is much more that a manufacturing centre, and has many historical associations. At one time it was known as the "Lang Toun", because it appeared to consist of one long street, though it has now spread inland. And it can lay fair claim to being the birthplace of economics, because, in 1728, Adam Smith was born here.

To the west of the county another industry held sway - coal mining. The Fife coalfields used to employ thousands of men, but now it has all but gone, leaving in its wake many small mining villages that are proud and fiercely independent. Dunfermline is the largest town in this area - another Fife royal burgh whose roots go deep into Scotland's history, having been granted its royal charter in 1124. It's abbey, like the cathedral at St Andrews, was once a place of pilgrimage due to the tomb of St Margaret, and is now the resting place of one of Scotland's great heroes, Robert the Bruce. And, like Kirkcaldy, it too has its famous sons. Charles I was born here in 1600, as was, in 1835, Andrew Carnegie the millionaire philanthropist.

Mining has given way to electronics as an employer, and this part of Fife is well and truly part of "silicon glen". But the area hasn't lost its attractiveness, and one of the places that must be visited is Culross, surely one of the loveliest and most historic small towns in Scotland.

Since the opening of the Tay Road Bridge in 1966, the towns and villages of northern Fife, such as Newport-on-Tay, Tayport, Leuchars and Wormit, have become dormitory towns for Dundee, across the firth. Even before this people were commuting, thanks to the Tay Rail Bridge, opened in 1887 after the first bridge collapsed into the firth in 1879 with much loss of life.

DUNFERMLINE

Now an important industrial town, Dunfermline was at one time the capital of Scotland, and still has many reminders of its past glories. It was here that Malcolm III (known as "Malcolm Canmore", meaning "bighead") and his second queen, later to become **St Margaret of Scotland**, held court in the 11th century.

Malcolm and Margaret married in 1070, and their reign was a turning point in Scotland's history. Margaret was the daughter of Edgar Aetheling, heir-apparent to the English throne, and was half Saxon and half Hungarian. When she came to the Scottish court in about

1067, she was shocked at what she found, and, with her husband's consent, set about changing things. The Scottish church, though nominally subservient to Rome, was still observing the old Celtic rites, which she found abhorrent. So the church was the first thing she changed. A Culdee (from the Irish céli dé, meaning "servants of God") monastery manned by Celtic/Irish priests had previously been established in Dunfermline, and she suppressed it, founding a Benedictine priory (later to become Dunfermline Abbey) in its place and inviting monks from Durham to serve in it. When she died in 1093, she was buried before the High Altar within the abbey.

In 1250 she was canonised by Pope

Innocent IV, and it is said that Mary Queen of Scots owned her skull as a religious relic. It later passed to the monks of Douai in France, and was lost during the French Revolution.

Scotland in the 11th century was a small kingdom, perched precariously on the edge of the known world. It was Margaret who brought refinement to the court and made the country think of itself as an integral part of Europe. Under Margaret and Malcolm, who was also a driving force, trade with the continent flourished. Malcolm revelled in this, as though he could neither read nor write, he hankered after refinement and culture, and had only a few years before moved Scotland's capital from Perthshire to Dunfermline to be nearer the Fife ports that traded with Europe. Under Margaret, the centre of power shifted once more - this time to Edinburgh, which later became the nation's capital.

One other innovation is attributed to St Margaret - buttons on the sleeves of men's jackets. She had been disgusted to see that Scottish courtiers - in common with courtiers throughout Europe - wiped their noses on their sleeves, so set about making this habit as uncomfortable as possible. The buttons eventually became fashionable, and the fashion spread throughout Europe.

She died soon after her husband and son were killed in Northumberland in 1093, and was buried in the abbey she had founded. Soon a cult grew up round her, and her burial spot became a place of pilgrimage. The remains of her shrine, destroyed during the Reformation, can still be seen.

Dunfermline Abbey as we see it today is a mixture of dates. The heavily buttressed nave is Norman, and is reminiscent of Durham Cathedral. Beneath it lie the remains of the original church. The choir was rebuilt in the early 19th century as the parish church, and it was during its construction that workmen came across the skeleton of a man lying within a stone coffin and wrapped with gold cloth. It was immediately recognised as that of Robert the Bruce, King of Scots, as the breastbone and ribs had been sawn away. After he died, Bruce's heart had been removed from his body so that it could be taken to the Holy Land (see also Melrose, Cardross and Threave Castle). It was re-interred with due reverence, and now a brass plate beneath the pulpit marks the spot. Around the battlements of the abbey tower are the words "King Robert the Bruce".

The **Dunfermline Abbey and Palace Visitors Centre** (Historic Scotland) tells of the history of the abbey and of the later palace that was built on the site of the monastic buildings. A

Dunfermline Abbey and Royal Palace

magnificent 200-feet long buttressed wall is all that now remains of the palace where Charles I was born.

To the west of the abbey is a great mound known as **Malcolm's Tower**, all that remains of Malcolm's fortress. The town takes part of its name from the mound, as *Dunfermline* literally means "fort on the hill by the crooked stream".

It sits within **Pittencrieff Park** (famous for its peacocks), which was gifted to the town by Andrew Carnegie in 1908. The park had always fascinated him as a boy, and as it was privately owned at the time, he was always denied access. So when he had the money, he bought it and threw it open to the people of the town. Also in the park is **Pittencrieff House Museum**, based in a 17th century mansion, which has an art gallery and displays on local history.

The **Abbot House Heritage Centre** is housed in a 14th - 16th century house to the north of the abbey in Maygate. It was formerly the Abbot's Lodgings for the great Benedictine monastery, as well as its administrative centre. Poets, kings and bishops visited, and it played its part in some of the great events in Scottish history.

St Margaret's Shrine has been reconstructed with its wall, showing just how rich the interior of the abbey was when it was at the height of its powers. In all, over 1,000 years of history can be seen, from the Picts right up until the present day.

Near Chalmers Street Car Park, about a quarter of a mile north of Abbot House, can be found **St Margaret's Cave**, where the pious queen prayed in solitude. A legend has it that Malcolm became suspicious of his wife's unexplained absences from court, and fearing that she had a lover, followed her to the cave one day, where he found her kneeling in prayer. It's fortunate that the cave still exists, as in the 1960s the local council wanted to cover it in concrete as part of a car park.

Andrew Carnegie was, in the 19th century, the richest man in the world. He was born in Dunfermline in 1835, and emigrated with his parents to the United States in 1848. By the 1880s, he had amassed a fortune through iron and steel making, and retired from business in 1901 to distribute his wealth. His humble birthplace in Moodie Street, a former weaver's cottage, is now the central feature of the **Andrew Carnegie Birthplace Museum**. It tells the story of the great man from his humble origins to his death in 1919. In Pittencrief Park, close to the **Louise Carnegie Gates** (named after his wife) is a statue of the great man.

It is not only New York that has a **Carnegie Hall** - Dunfermline has one as well, housing a theatre and concert hall. It can be found in East Port, near the **Dunfermline Museum and Small Gallery** in Viewfield. Here the history of the town is explained, including its time as a centre of manufacture for linen and silk, which continued right up until the 20th century. There are special displays from the Dunfermline Linen Damask Collection.

To the north of the town, at Lathalmond, is the **Scottish Vintage Bus Museum**, housed in a former Royal Navy Stores depot. It is possibly the largest collection of vintage buses in Britain, and has been open since 1995.

AROUND DUNFERMLINE

COWDENBEATH
5 miles NE of Dunfermline, off the A909

This small town was at the centre of the Fife coalfields, and though the mines have long gone, it still has the feel of a mining community about it. Its football team has perhaps the most unusual nickname of any senior team in Scotland - the "Blue Brazils". **Racewall Cowdenbeath** has stock car racing every Saturday evening from March to November.

LOCHGELLY
7 miles NE of Dunfermline on the B981

Lochgelly is a small mining town, famous throughout Scotland at one time for the manufacture of the "Lochgelly", the leather strap used to punish children in school. Near the town is the **Lochore Meadows Country Park**, set in 1,200 acres of reclaimed industrial land. The last pits closed here in 1966, with the park being created on the site in the early '70s. The area is now a haven for wildlife, and at the west end of the loch is a bird hide with disabled access.

The 260-acre Loch Ore, created as a result of mining subsidence, is stocked with brown trout. It can also be used for water sports.

SALINE
6 miles NW of Dunfermline on the B913

The Knockhill Racing Circuit is Scotland's national motor sports centre for cars and motorbikes, and has meetings on most Sundays from April to October.

ABERDOUR
6 miles E of Dunfermline on the A921

Aberdour is a small coastal burgh that received its charter in 1500. The restored **St Fillan's Church** is partly Norman, with fragments that may date back to at least 1123, and has what is known as a "leper window". This was a window looking on to the altar through which lepers could see from a private room the mass being celebrated. It is said that Robert the Bruce, himself suffering from leprosy, used the window after his victory at Bannockburn in 1314.

In 1790 the church was abandoned, and gradually fell into disrepair. However, in 1925 work began on restoring it, and it now open for services once more. The town has two beaches, one of which, **Silver Sands**, has won a European blue flag for its cleanliness. **Aberdour Castle** (Historic Scotland), close to the church, dates from the 14th century, when it was built by the Mortimer family, with later additions being made in the 16th and 17th century. It was later owned by James Douglas, 4th Earl of Morton and Regent of Scotland between 1572 and 1578. In 1580 he was executed for his part in the murder of Mary Stuart's second husband, Lord Darnley. The **Aberdour Festival** is held every year at the end of July.

CEDAR INN

Shore Road, Aberdour, Fife KY3 0TR
Tel: 01383 860310 e-mail: cedarinnaberdour@supanet.com
Fax: 01383 860004 website: www.cedarinn.co.uk

The **Cedar Inn** is a family-run hotel with a great reputation in the lovely village of Aberdour on the shores of the Firth of Forth, and close to golf courses and a picturesque harbour and beach. With nine comfortable rooms, all of them with en suite facilities, it is the ideal base from which to explore one of Scotland's most historic areas. The popular restaurant offers the very best in traditional Scottish cuisine, and the public bar (which is popular with the locals) offers six hand-pulled real ales as well as a wide range of single malts. The atmosphere is informal and friendly, and the owners, Gillian and Richard Anthistle, will offer you a warm Scottish welcome.

Continued on page 195

Aberdour and Silversands Bay

Distance:	3.7 miles (5.9 kilometres)
Typical time:	120 mins
Height gain:	80 metres
Map:	Explorer 367
Walk:	www.walkingworld.com ID:1860
Contributor:	Oliver O'Brien

Access Information:

By train there are very regular services to Aberdour from Edinburgh (half-hourly via the 'Inner Circle' and the spectacular Forth Rail Bridge) and limited services from Aberdeen, Dundee and Perth. By bus, Stagecoach in Fife Service Number 7 runs past the walk start, at Aberdour Station. By road, the start is on the A921 Inverkeithing – Kirkcaldy road.

Additonal Information:

Part of the walk follows the Fife Coastal Path, which stretches over many miles from the Forth Road Bridge at North Queensferry, to the Tay Bridge, across the water from Dundee. Aberdour has a castle and gardens owned by Historic Scotland and open for public visiting.

Description:

This walk takes in a short section of the Fife Coastal Path, passing through a picturesque Aberdour Village and its harbour, with views south over the Firth of Forth to Edinburgh. It continues past Hawkcraig Point with more spectacular views and passes the appropriately named Silversands Beach, which has an award for a 'Premium' British beach. The route then follows the railway line below 50m-high cliffs, the route passing through woodlands with a rocky beach only a few metres away, visiting a pleasant cascade at Bendameer, before striking uphill and returning on a smaller, pleasant high path through deciduous woodland The Heughs, back to Aberdour Village. There is a

dramatic clifftop view at one point near the end.

Features:

Sea, Pub, Toilets, Play Area, Castle, Wildlife, Birds, Flowers, Great Views, Butterflies, Cafe, Gift Shop, Food Shop, Good for Kids, Public Transport, Nature Trail, Restaurant, Tea Shop, Waterfall, Woodland

Walk Directions:

1 (If arriving on a train from Edinburgh, cross over by the footbridge). Leave the station car park and turn left off the main road, passing the entrance to Aberdour Castle, open to the public. Continue straight ahead, follow the road around to the right, pass a pub on your right and turn left, off Livingston Lane. Follow the narrow, walled road down to the seafront.

2 There is a great view to Inchcolm Island here. The sign indicates the route of the Fife Coastal Path, so bear left and follow the promenade beside the road, to the harbour entrance.

3 The road carries on down to the harbour. Bear left here onto the raised path, passing to the left of the building marked 'CAFÉ.' Follow the path around the harbour, crossing a small bridge annd passing toilets.

4 There is a choice here. Either head left, climb the steps and continue along the road, passing a large car park on your right, down into Silversands car park. Or carry straight on, following the path round (watching out for cliffs!) to Hawkcraig Point. Pick up the access road and follow it around to the left, leading into Silversands car park.

5 Head along beside the appropriately named Silversands Beach, passing a playground at the far end. There are a couple of waymarks on the track beside the beach, indicating the continuation of the Fife Coastal Path.

6 Pass through this gap in the wall, turn right and follow the path beside the railway line. This is the longest and most pleasant section of this walk, with the rocky beach never far away. There is a dramatic rock formation on your left at one point and later on a path down to a short, attractive section of the beach. The industry of Burntisland can be seen ahead on the horizon.

7 Follow the path underneath the railway sign and continue along the path, passing a turning to the left (you'll come back here shortly)

8 This is a rather attractive cascade, best viewed from the bridge itself. Bendameer House is just ahead, but not visible from here. Although the Fife Coastal Path continues onwards, the next few miles are rather unpleasant as they thread through the industrialised Burntisland. So instead turn around and retrace your steps back to that signpost you passed.

9 This signpost indicates 'Aberdour by The Heughs and Burntisland by the A921'. Turn right here and climb up the steep steps. The path becomes small but is easy to follow and continues upwards through very pleasant woodland, as views back down to the coastline become more impressive.

10 Turn left at the signpost here and follow the widening path, that begins gradually to descend through the woodland.

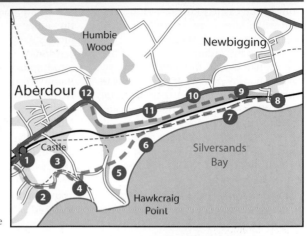

11 The view here, to the left of the path, opens out suddenly. There is a sheer 50m drop in front and Silversands and Hawkcraig Point can be clearly seen. The route continues along the path, descending slowly and bearing to the right. Ignore a small path to the left.

12 The path meets the main road here, at the edge of Aberdour. Turn left and continue along the pavement, through the village and back to Aberdour Station and the walk start.

DALGETY BAY

4 miles SE of Dunfermline off the A921

The ivy-clad ruins of **St Bridget's Church**, once the burial place of the Earls of Dunfermline, date from the 12th century, and was first mentioned in a Papal Bull of 1178. It was near Dalgety Bay that the murder of James Stewart, the **2nd Earl of Moray**, took place, an event which is remembered in one of the best known of Scottish songs, *The Bonnie Earl o' Moray*. Moray was the grandson of Regent Morton, regent of Scotland when Mary Stuart abdicated in favour of her infant son, later to be James VI, and was a popular nobleman, dashing and

handsome. But he was a staunch Protestant, and was always feuding with the Earls of Huntly, one of the great Catholic families of the time, and was implicated in a coup to overthrow James VI, though he probably had no involvement.

But Huntly saw his chance, and armed with a king's warrant and a troop of soldiers, set out to seize the young earl. He eventually found him at his mother's castle at Donibristle, in what is now Dalgety Bay. He demanded that he give himself up, but Moray refused.

The troops therefore set fire to the building. Some men ran out from the front of the castle to distract Huntly's men while Moray ran out the back way, hoping to hide near the shore. Unfortunately, unknown to Moray, his bonnet had caught fire, and the smoke gave him away. He was hacked to death, with Huntly, it is said, striking the fatal blow. When James VI found out about the murder, he feigned outrage, though when the crowds later discovered that Huntly had been armed with a king's warrant, James had to flee to Glasgow to escape their wrath.

It was a death that touched the pulse of the common people of Scotland at a time when the country was in turmoil, not knowing if the Reformation would take hold or whether Roman Catholicism would make a return. Huntly spent a few weeks in Blackness Castle as a punishment, and was then released.

INCHCOLM
6 miles SE of Dunfermline, in the Firth of Forth

This small island was at one time known as the "Iona of the East". On it are the substantial ruins of **Inchcolm Abbey** (Historic Scotland), dedicated to St Columba. The story goes that Alexander I, son of Malcolm III and Queen Margaret, was crossing the Forth in 1123 when a storm blew up and the royal party had to seek refuge on the island, which had, for many years, supported a succession of hermits. The hermit of the time shared his meagre provisions with his guests for three days until the storm subsided. When Alexander reached the shore he vowed to build a monastery dedicated to St Columba on the island in thanksgiving for his safe passage, but before he could put his plans into effect he died. His younger brother David I, who succeeded him, founded a priory, which eventually became the Abbey of Inchcolm in 1223.

A small stone building to the west of the abbey may have been the original monks' cell, though it has been much restored over the years. The abbey buildings as we see them now date mainly from the 15th century, and represent the most complete medieval abbey in Scotland, with most of the buildings remaining intact.

In the late 18th century, a military hospital was set up on the island to look after wounded sailors from the Russian fleet, which was using the Firth of Forth as a base. In the 20th century it was fortified as part of the United Kingdom's sea defences, and some of these can still be seen. Over 500 troops were stationed on the island, and the first air raid of World War II took place close by, when German bombers, in 1939, dropped bombs not far from the Forth Rail Bridge.

INVERKEITHING
3 miles S of Dunfermline off the A90

Inverkeithing is an ancient royal burgh which received its royal charter from William the Lion in about 1193. In medieval times it was a walled town with four "ports", or gates, though the walls were pulled down in the 16th century. It sits close to the Forth Road and Rail Bridges, and has many old buildings. The **Mercat Cross** is 16th century, and the **Old Town Hall** opposite, with its outside staircase, dates from 1770. Of the 15th century **St Peter's Church**, only the tower remains, as the rest dates from 1826. Two other old buildings are **Thomsoun's House** dating from 1617 and **Fordell's Lodging** dating from 1670. **Inverkeithing Museum** (see panel opposite), housed in the hospitum of an old friary, tells the story of Inverkeithing and of **Admiral Sir Samuel Greig**, a local man born in 1735 in what is now the Royal Hotel in the High Street who

INVERKEITHING MUSEUM

The Friary, Queen Street, Inverkeithing, Fife KY11 1LS
Tel: 01383 313594

Inverkeithing Museum is housed in the upper floor of a wonderful 14th century friary guest house, standing amidst well tended gardens. The gallery is only small but has a lovely collection of local photographs, paintings and artefacts, illustrating the history of the area. Admiral Greig, Inverkeithing's most famous son - the "Father of the Russian Navy", is featured. Open Thursday, Friday, Saturday and Sunday 11am to 12.30 pm and 1pm to 4pm. Admission is free but access is by stairs only and so is not suitable for the disabled.

entered the service of Tsarina Catherine of Russia in 1764. He largely created the modern Russian navy, manning it initially with Scottish officers. He died in 1788 aged only 53.

Near the town, in 1651, was fought the **Battle of Inverkeithing** between a Royalist force under Sir Hector MacLean of Duart and the Parliamentarian forces of Cromwell. The result was a victory for the Parliamentarians, and the death of MacLean. As a result of the battle the towns of Inverkeithing and Dunfermline were plundered, and the long-term result was the ascendancy of Cromwell in Scotland. A small cairn by the roadside opposite **Pitreavy Castle** (not open to the public), erected by the Clan MacLean, commemorates the event.

In the 14th century Pitreavy Castle was owned by Christina Bruce, Robert the Bruce's sister. It later passed to the Kellock family and the Wardlaws, who rebuilt it. From World War II until 1996 a bunker beneath the castle was the naval operations HQ for Scotland.

It is reputedly haunted by three ghosts: the Grey Lady, the Green Lady and a headless Highlander who is said to moan in anguish.

NORTH QUEENSFERRY

4 miles S of Dunfermline off the A90

This small town was the northern terminus for the ferry that plied across the Forth from South Queensferry in West Lothian, originally founded by Queen Margaret (hence the town's name) in the 11th century. It sits on a small peninsula, which juts out into the Forth where the river has its narrowest point until the Kincardine Bridge is reached. The **Forth Bridges Visitors Centre** is housed within the Queensferry Lodge Hotel, and tells the story of the two bridges spanning the Forth. There is a magnificent scale model of the Firth of Forth, as well as photographs, documents and artefacts.

Deep Sea World is billed as "Scotland's Aquarium", and takes you on a walk along the "ocean floor", thanks to the world's longest underwater tunnel made of specially toughened glass. Fish swim above and beside you in a specially made sea containing a million gallons of water. As you stand within it you can see sharks, stingrays and electric eels. A special touch pool allows you to touch sharks, sea urchins and anemones. One of the most popular experiences on offer at the aquarium is the chance to dive with sharks.

North Queensferry is the start of the **Fife Coastal Path**, a 78-mile long pathway that eventually takes you through most of the small picturesque towns and villages on the Fife coast, ending at the

Tay Bridge on the Firth of Tay.

CHARLESTOWN
3 miles SW of Dunfermline on a minor road off the A985

This small village was established in 1756 by Charles Bruce, 5th Earl of Elgin, to exploit the large deposits of limestone in the area, including an easily worked crag facing the sea. It was Scotland's first planned industrial village, though Bruce died before

Charlestown

the work was finished. It was finally completed by the 7th Earl (of Elgin Marbles fame). There were nine kilns here at one time producing lime for building, agriculture and the making of iron and glass. It was a self-sufficient community, with its own harbour, shops and school, and the houses were arranged in the shape of the founder's initials - CE, meaning Charles Elgin.

The works closed in 1956, having produced in their 200 years of existence over 11 million tons of quicklime. Now guided walks round the complex are available in the summer months thanks to the Scottish Lime Centre in the Granary Building in Rocks Road. Nearby is the village of **Limekilns**, which was once a port for the monks of Dunfermline Abbey.

CULROSS
7 miles W of Dunfermline on a minor road off the A985

If you wish to see what a Scottish burgh looked like in the 16th, 17th and 18th centuries, then the royal burgh of Culross is the place to do it. It was granted its royal charter in 1592, and though having a population of no more than a few hundred, it had its own town

council and provost up until local government reorganisation in 1975.

It is undoubtedly the most picturesque of Fife's old burghs - a situation that owes a lot to the town's relative poverty in the 18th, 19th and early 20th centuries when there was no money for modernisation. In the 16th century it was a prosperous port that traded with the Low Countries, but when this trade dried up it sunk into poverty. Now it is largely owned by the National Trust or Scotland.

It is a thriving and lively community with most of the quaint crow-step gabled houses occupied. The streets are cobbled, and those around the old **Mercat Cross** (dating from 1588) have a feature known as the "crown o' the causie", a raised portion in the middle where only the wealthy were allowed to walk, while the rest of the townsfolk had to walk on the edges where water and dirt accumulated.

The town's main industries were coalmining, salt panning and the making of baking girdles. Coal mining had been introduced by the monks of Culross Abbey at a time when coal was little known about, and wondrous tales spread round Scotland about the "stones that could burn". After the Reformation, the mines were taken over by Sir George

Bruce, a descendant of Robert the Bruce. Between 1575 and his death 50 years later he revolutionised the industry. He was the first man to extend a coal mine beneath the sea, something which is taken for granted today. One of his mines had a tunnel out under the waters of the Firth of Forth for over a mile. It eventually came up to sea level, surrounded by a stone wall to keep the water out. James VI was fascinated by Culross's industry, and paid a visit. Sir George took him on a tour of the mine, and led the unsuspecting king along the tunnel. When he emerged and found himself surrounded on all four sides by water, he panicked, shouting "treason!"

Culross

As an offshoot of the mining industry, salt panning became another major occupation in the town. It is reckoned that at one time there were 50 saltpans along the coast, all using inferior coal to heat salt water from the sea. Another industry was the making of iron girdles for cooking. Culross blacksmiths are said to have invented these round, flat utensils for frying and cooking after Robert the Bruce, in the 14th century, ordered that each one of his troops be given a flat pan for cooking oatcakes.

Nothing remains of Sir George's mining ventures. However, his home, now called **Culross Palace**, still stands, and is open to the public. Work started on it in 1597, and is a typical residence of its time for someone of Sir George's standing in society. It has splendid kitchen gardens. Along from it is the **Town House**, built in 1625 and gifted to the National Trust for Scotland in 1975 when Culross Town Council was wound up. At one time the ground floor was a debtors' prison, while the attic was used

as a prison for witches. It now houses the local tourist information centre.

Beside the Mercat Cross is **The Study**. It was built about 1610, and after the Palace, is Culross's grandest house. When the Church of Scotland was Episcopalian, the town formed part of the diocese of Dunblane, and it was here that Bishop Robert Leighton stayed on his visits. The quaint Outlook Tower housed his actual study, hence the name of the house. If you continue past The Study, along Tanhouse Brae and into Kirk Street, you will eventually reach **Culross Abbey**, dedicated to St Serf and St Mary. The choir of the church (restored in 1633) still stands, and is used as the parish church, though the other buildings have either completely disappeared or are in ruins. It was founded in 1217 by Malcolm, Earl of Fife, and housed a Cistercian order of monks who left Kinloss Abbey. It is likely that the site of the abbey is where St Serf founded a monastery in the 6th century. Off the north transept is the Bruce Vault, where there is an impressive monument to Sir George Bruce of Carnock, his wife and their eight children.

Culross was the birthplace, in AD 514, of St Kentigern, patron saint of Glasgow. In 1503 Archbishop Blackadder of Glasgow erected a small chapel on the spot where the birth is supposed to have taken place, and its ruins can still be seen to the east of the village. The story goes that he was the son of Thenew (also known as Enoch), a princess of the kingdom of the Lothians. When her father Loth (after which the Lothians was supposedly named) discovered that she was pregnant, he banished her from his kingdom, and she set sail in a boat across the Firth of Forth. She landed at Culross, and here gave birth to her son, who was taken into care by a monk called Serf (later St Serf), who had established a monastic school there. It is now known that St Serf lived in the century following Kentigern's birth, so the story is doubtful.

But Culross's attractions aren't all historical. Close to the town is **Longannet Power Station**, one of Scotland's largest. There are organised tours (which have to be pre-booked), and you can see the huge turbine hall from a viewing platform, as well as tour the visitors centre, which shows how coal produces electricity.

Stretching from Longannet past Culross to Combie Point on the shores of the Firth of Forth is the **Torry Bay Local Nature Reserve**, where there is series of artificial lagoons built from the waste ash from Longannet. Here you can see many species of birds, such as shelduck, greenshank and great crested grebe.

KINCARDINE-ON-FORTH
10 miles W of Dunfermline, on the A985

This small burgh, which received its charter in 1663, sits at the north end of the **Kincardine Bridge**. Up until the Forth Road Bridge opened in 1964, this was the only road crossing of the Forth downstream from Stirling. Opened in 1936, the middle section used to swivel to allow ships to pass up the river. It was controlled from a control room above the swivel section, and was, at the time, the largest swivel bridge in Europe. It allowed ships to sail up to Alloa, but has not opened since the 1980s, when Alloa declined as a port.

The town is full of small, old-fashioned cottages with red pantiled roofs, and there are the ruins of the 17th century **Tulliallan Church**. The burgh's **Mercat Cross** dates from the 17th century, and it was in the town, in 1842, that Sir James Dewar, inventor of the vacuum flask and co-inventor of cordite was born. It was not until 1904, however, that the

---

FELT HEAD TO TOE

25 Glebe road, Kincardine-on-Forth, Clackmannanshire FK10 4QB
Tel & Fax: 01259 730779
e-mail: ewa@feltheadtotoe.co.uk   website: www.feltheadtotoe.co.uk

The owner of **Felt Head to Toe**, Ewa Kuniczak, is famous as a designer and maker of fashion items in hand-made seamless felt for children, adults and the home. Established in 1994 Ewa sells throughout Britain as well as in Japan and the USA. She uses only the finest hand-dyed Merino wool for her creations, which include hats, bags, waistcoats, scarves, shawls, cushions, tea cosies and interior drapes. The showroom is a fascinating place, full of colour and texture and should never be missed if you're in the area. The prices are remarkably reasonable, and the quality is always high. By appointment only.

vacuum, or Thermos, flask was produced commercially by a firm in Germany. The term "Thermos" was coined in Munich, and comes from the Greek word *therme*, which means "hot". To the west of the town is **Tulliallan Castle**, now the main police training college in Scotland.

KIRKCALDY

Kirkcaldy is the largest town in Fife, and is famous for the manufacture of linoleum. At one time it was known as the "Lang Toun", due to the fact that it appeared to stretch out along one main street. It was created a royal burgh in 1644, and one of the famous events held here every year in April is the **Links Market**, reckoned to be the longest street fair in Europe. The town's Esplanade is cordoned off from traffic and taken over by swings, roundabouts, dodgems, carousels, hoopla stalls and all the other attractions of a modern funfair. The very first Links Market took place in 1306 in Links Street in the town, hence its name.

Within **Kirkcaldy Museum and Art Gallery** at the War Memorial Gardens is an exhibition devoted to Wemyss Ware, a form of earthenware pottery that was produced in the town by the firm of Robert Heron and Son between 1882 and 1930. It is now much collected, and is possibly the most sought after pottery ever to have been made in Scotland. Its

most distinctive feature was its decoration, which was bold, simple and direct. The firing methods caused a lot of waste, which meant that the pottery was always expensive. The museum also houses a local history collection, plus an extensive collection of Scottish paintings.

The ruins of **Ravenscraig Castle** sit on a promontory to the east of the town centre. It was built in the 15th century by James II for his queen, Mary of Gueldres, who died there in 1463. James had a passion for weaponry - especially guns - and had it built so that it could withstand the latest artillery. In 1470 it passed to William Sinclair, Earl of Orkney, who had to give up his earldom and Kirkwall Castle to acquire it. Overlooking the town harbour is the 15th century **Sailor's Walk**, the town's oldest house. The **Old Parish Church** sits at the top of Kirk Wynd, and dates from 1808. However, its tower is medieval.

Beyond Ravenscraig Castle is **Dysart**, which, up until 1930, was a separate burgh. Its harbour area is very picturesque, with whitewashed cottages and houses dating from the 16th, 17th and 18th centuries. At one time this was a salt panning area, and **Pan Ha'** (meaning "Pan Haugh") is a group of particularly fine 17th century buildings with red pantiled roofs (not open to the public). **St Serf's Tower** is the tower of the former parish church, and dates from the 15th

century. It looks more like a castle than a tower, and reflects the area's troubled times when English ships prowled the Forth. In Rectory Lane is the **John McDouall Stuart Museum**, dedicated to the life of a locally born explorer who, in 1861-62, made the first return journey across the Australian continent.

Adam Smith, the founder of the science of economics, was born in Kirkcaldy in 1723. He went on to occupy the chair of moral philosophy at Glasgow University, and his famous book, *The Wealth of Nations*, was partly written in his mother's house (now gone) in the town's High Street. Also born in the town were **William Adam** the architect, and his son, **Robert Adam**.

In the town's Abbotshall Kirkyard stands a statue to another person born in Kirkcaldy, but an unusual one. **Marjory Fleming** was a child writer whose nickname was "Pet Marjory". She died in 1811, and yet her writings have intrigued and delighted people down through the ages. She kept a journal, in which she jotted down thoughts, poems and biographical scraps. She was, by all accounts, a "handful", and when her mother gave birth to another girl in 1809, Marjory was sent to live with her aunt in Edinburgh. This is where her writing began, encouraged by her cousin Isa, and she eventually filled three notebooks. Nobody knows what she might have achieved in adulthood, because, one month short of her ninth birthday, and after she had returned to Kirkcaldy, she tragically died of meningitis. Her last piece of writing was a touching poem addressed to her beloved cousin. Her writings were subsequently published, and found great favour with the Victorians, though some frowned on the absolute honesty she displayed when it came to describing her tantrums and innermost thoughts.

ELOISE

26 Hunter Street, Kirkcaldy, Fife KY1 1ED
Tel: 01592 643147

Eloise is a fascinating shop in Kirkcaldy that sells high fashion lingerie, jewellery, designer shoes and handbags, furniture, lamps and mirrors. It also sells children's jewellery, crystals and glassware, and there is an in-shop coffee house serving delicious coffees and teas. The place is ideal for browsing, and for buying a present for a loved one or souvenir of your trip to Scotland.

It is run and managed by Louise Canny, who has brought a wealth of experience in the retail trade to the shop. In fact, she started her "career" when she was ten years old, buying and selling antiques, and she opened her first shop when she was 16! Since then she has always been determined to offer the best of everything at competitive prices, and scours the country - and souks, bazaars and markets abroad - to source her stock. She won't reveal the names of her suppliers - they come from every continent, are a closely guarded secret, and most of the items are available no-where else in Scotland, something she is very proud of.

Kirkcaldy is a town well worth exploring with a superb shopping centre and people come from all over Scotland to visit Louise's shop. She will gladly admit that she sees no need to open branches in the big cities of Edinburgh and Glasgow - the items she sells attracts people in their droves to the Fife town.

ELITE FALCONRY

Cluny Mains, By Kirkcaldy, Fife KY2 6QU
Tel & Fax: 01592 722 143
e-mail: elitefalconry@btopenworld.com

Elite Falconry is owned and managed by Janet Cooper and Barry Blyther, who are very proud of their falconry centre, and are very keen to share their knowledge of these fascinating and graceful birds of prey with people who want to experience the thrill of working with them. As you arrive at the centre you will be surprised by what you see. Outside the barn, (except in foul weather), on the weathering lawn you will see up to 25 magnificent birds soaking up the sun or taking a gentle bath. The collection is not the largest but is probably the most unusual in Scotland. You will be captivated. More birds can be seen in spacious aviaries inside the barn.

The falconry experience days on offer are all very much hands on. You will start your experience flying a great grey owl in her aviary; she is a stunning, gentle delight. As your day progresses you will take to the outdoors and enjoy a walk out when you will fly a harris hawk, be stunned by the incredible speed and agility of a falcon going through its paces and perhaps be awestruck as an eagle drops to your fist from over 1,000 ft at phenomenal speed. Another possibility is for you to join the exclusive Gathering of Eagles that takes place every January in the mountains of Scotland. This unique opportunity to see Golden Eagles and others in their own very special environments as they hunt mountain hares. If speed and falcons are your thing again you can be thrilled as Elite Falconry will take you grouse hawking with peregrine falcons when you can witness the fastest creature on the planet as the falcon stoops in excess of 200mph in pursuit of red grouse.

Janet and Barry established Elite Falconry some six years ago based on many years of experience and have since developed an enviable reputation for the value for money and the exciting and unique falconry opportunities they offer. If you are planning a visit to Scotland or the Kingdom of Fife, give them a call and book a visit or experience.

AROUND KIRKCALDY

GLENROTHES
5 miles N of Kirkcaldy on the A92

Glenrothes was one of the new towns established in Scotland in the late 1940s. In **Balbirnie Park**, which extends to 416 acres, is a late Neolithic stone circle dating from about 3000 BC. It was moved to its present site in 1971-1972 when the A92 was widened. The park was created in the estate of Balbirnie House, once owned by the Balfours.

FALKLAND
10 miles N of Kirkcaldy on the A912

This little royal burgh sits in the shadow of the **Lomond Hills**. There are two distinct peaks - East Lomond, at 1,471 feet, and West Lomond at 1,713 feet, the highest point in Fife. It has quaint old cobbled streets lined with 17th and 18th century cottages, and was the first conservation area in Scotland. It was a favourite place of the Scottish kings, and **Falkland Palace** (National Trust for Scotland - see panel on page 204) was built in the 15th century by the Duke of Albany on the site of an earlier castle owned by the Earls of Fife. James V later employed stonemasons to turn it into a magnificent Renaissance palace.

It was never an important castle like Edinburgh or Stirling. Rather it was a country retreat for Stuart kings to hunt deer and boar and get away from the affairs of state. James V died in Falkland Palace in 1542, and his daughter Mary Stuart, it is said, spent the best years of her tragic life at Falkland.

Mary was born a few days before James

V died, and the story is told that when he was on his deathbed, aged only 30, and told about the birth of a daughter and heir, he exclaimed: "It cam' wi' a lass, and it'll gang wi' a lass!", meaning that the House of Stuart had started with Marjory, daughter of Robert the Bruce, and it would die out with his own daughter. In this prediction, he was both right and wrong. It did die out "wi' a lass", but not Mary Stuart. The last Stuart monarch was Queen Ann, who died in 1715. The Palace is still nominally the property of the monarch, and its chapel, housed in what was the banqueting hall in the South Range, is the only Roman Catholic Church in Britain within royal property. In 1654 Cromwell burnt the Great Hall to the ground, and it was never rebuilt.

Both Charles I and Charles II visited Falkland, and it was in the Palace, in 1650, that Charles II founded the Scots Guards. His father Charles I had founded a regiment in 1642 called "Argyll's Regiment" to act as his personal bodyguard in Ireland, and this had later merged with nine small regiments to form the Irish Companies. While at Falkland Charles II renamed this regiment The King's Lyfeguard of Foot, and proclaimed it to be his bodyguard. It was later renamed the Scots Guards.

In the East Range can be seen the King's Bedchamber and the Queen's Room, and within the Gatehouse are the Keeper's Apartments. The gardens were laid out in the mid-20th century, and have magnificent herbaceous borders. Within the gardens is the **Royal Tennis Court**, which dates from the early 16th century, and the oldest in the country

FALKLAND PALACE, GARDEN AND OLD BURGH

Falkland, Cupar, Fife KY15 7BU
Tel: 01337 857397 Fax: 01337 857980
Tel shop: 01337 857918
website: www.nts.org.uk

The **Royal Palace of Falkland** was the country residence of Stuart kings and queens when they hunted deer and wild boar in the Fife forest. Mary, Queen of Scots spent some of the happiest days of her tragic life here, 'playing the country girl in the woods and parks'. The Palace was built between 1501 and 1541 by James IV and James V, replacing earlier castle and palace buildings

dating from the 12th century, traces of which can still be seen in the grounds. The roofed South Range contains the Chapel Royal, and the East Range the King's Bedchamber and the Queen's Room, both restored by the Trust. The Keeper's Apartments in the Gatehouse are now also on display. The palace contains fine portraits of the Stuart monarchs and two sets of 17th century tapestry hangings.

The garden, designed and built by Percy Cane between 1947 and 1952, contains three herbaceous borders enclosing a wide lawn with many varieties of shrubs and trees. Here also is the original Royal Tennis Court the oldest in Britain still in use built in 1539. There is also a small herb garden border featuring quotations from John Gerard's book *Herboll* (1597). Exhibitions at Royal Tennis Court and at Town Hall.

still in use. Here "real tennis" is played, with the roofs of the "lean tos" on either side of the court playing an integral part in the game. Tennis is still played here today, and there is a thriving club. The word "real" simply means royal, and it was a favourite sport of kings throughout Europe at one time. It is said that it dates back to at least the 11th century, when monks played it in the cloisters of their abbeys and priories. In the 14th century the Pope banned the playing of the game, but by this time it had become popular among the nobility.

At the beginning of the 19th century the Keepership of the Palace was in the hands of Professor John Bruce of Edinburgh University. For six years he spent a lot of his own money on rebuilding and refurbishment, and when he died in 1826 he left the Keepership to his niece Margaret and to an Indian lady. In 1828 Margaret married a Bristol lawyer with the delightful name of Onesiphorus Tyndall, who added Bruce to his name to become Onesiphorus Tyndall-Bruce, whose statue stands in the town. The Keepership later passed to John Crichton Stuart, Marquis of Bute., and his descendants still hold it.

The burgh's **Town Hall**, which dates from 1805, houses an exhibition about the town. Close to it, in the square, is a house with a plaque which commemorates Richard Cameron, a local schoolmaster and Covenanter, who was killed at the Battle of Airds Moss in Ayrshire in 1680 (see also Sanquhar).

WEMYSS

4 miles NE of Kirkcaldy on the A955

Below the substantial ruins of **MacDuff Castle**, near the shoreline, are some caves in the sandstone cliffs with old carvings on the walls. They date mainly from between AD400 to AD800, though some may go back to before Christ. It has been claimed that there are more carvings within these caves than in all the other caves in Britain put together. However, due to erosion and subsidence, most of the caves can no longer be entered, though they may be viewed from the shore.

BUCKHAVEN AND METHIL

7 miles NE of Kirkcaldy on the B931

Buckhaven and Methil constituted one burgh which was created in 1891. Its motto was Carbone Carbasoque, which means "By Coal and by Sail", reflecting the fact that it used to export coal. As with other Fife ports, it also had saltpans, and by 1677 three pans were in operation, fuelled by coal. The Methil docks were opened in 1887. In Lower Methil's High Street is the **Methil Heritage Centre**, a lively community museum that explains the history of the area.

Buckhaven, to the west, was never as industrialised as Methil. It was once a fishing port and ferry terminal, and has some old, quaint cottages. In College Street there is the **Buckhaven Museum**, which has displays about the town's industries, including fishing.

Wemyss Castle dates from the 13th century, and was where Mary Stuart first met Lord Darnley, her second husband, in 1565.

LARGO

11 miles NE of Kirkcaldy on the A915

There are two Largos - Lower Largo on the shores of the Forth and Upper Largo about half a mile inland, where the **Parish Church**, some parts of which date from the early 17th century, stands. It was here that Scotland's greatest seafarer and one time Admiral of the Fleet, **Sir Andrew Wood**, had his home. He died in

LORNE HOUSE

Largo Road, Leven, Fife KY8 4TB
Tel: 01333 423255   e-mail: lornehouseleven@aol.com
website: www.lornehouseleven.com

With three guest bedrooms - two fully en suite doubles and a twin
with private bathroom - **Lorne House** is one of the best and most
comfortable B&Bs in Fife. All rooms have TVs, mini fridges, and
tea/coffee making facilities. It has a four-star rating, and sits on
the outskirts of Leven, a town with plenty of shops, beaches and a
large leisure centre. The guest lounge, with Sky TV, is spacious and welcoming, as is the dining room,
which has individual tables.

1515, and was buried in the kirkyard. He
oversaw the building in Newhaven of the
largest and most magnificent fighting
ship of its day, the **Great Michael**,
flagship of the Scottish fleet (see also
Edinburgh). Nothing now remains of
Wood's castle but a tower.

Alexander Selkirk was another
seafaring man who came from Largo. He
was born in 1676, and was the seventh
son of a local shoemaker. At the age of
19 the Kirk Session ordered him to
appear before it after fighting with his
brother, but instead of appearing he fled
to sea, where he eventually became a
privateer, or legalised pirate working for
the British king.

By all accounts he was a short-
tempered, unpleasant man, and while
sailing on a ship called the
Cinque Ports in 1704, he
quarrelled with the captain,
who put him ashore (at
Selkirks's request) on the
uninhabited island of Juan
Fernandez in the Pacific
Ocean. He remained there
until 1709, when he was
rescued. Daniel Defoe,
though he never met Selkirk,
based his novel *Robinson
Crusoe* on his adventures. A
statue of Selkirk can be
found near the harbour.

KINGHORN
4 miles SW of Kirkcaldy on the A921

This quiet little royal burgh saw one of
the most decisive events in Scottish
history. At the **Pettycur Crags** to the
west of the town Alexander III was killed,
throwing Scotland into turmoil. He was
the last of the country's Celtic kings, and
had previously married Princess
Margaret, daughter of Henry III of
England, who had borne him two sons.
But Margaret and the sons died; so, at
the age of 45, Alexander married again,
this time Yolande, daughter of the Count
of Dreux in France, in the hope of
continuing the direct royal line.

After a meeting of his nobles at
Edinburgh in 1286, Alexander was

Lower Largo

anxious to return to his queen, who was staying at Kinghorn Castle (now gone). The weather was stormy, and some of his men tried to dissuade him from crossing the Forth. However, he was adamant, and was taken across to Fife. But while riding along the Pettycur Crags, almost in sight of the castle where his wife awaited him, his horse stumbled, sending him over the cliffs to his death. It is said that the spot is haunted by the ghost of Yolande, still waiting for her husband to return to her arms.

The heir to the Scottish throne was now three-year-old Margaret, known as the "Maid of Norway". She was the daughter of Alexander's own daughter, who had married Eric II of Norway. But while crossing from Norway to Scotland, Margaret also died, leaving the country without an heir. In the resultant vacuum, noblemen jockeyed for position, putting forward many claimants to the throne. Edward I of England was asked to intercede, and he saw his chance. He tried to incorporate Scotland into his own kingdom by installing a puppet king, and thus began the Wars of Independence.

A tall monument at the side of the road, erected in 1886, marks the spot where Alexander was killed.

Kinghorn Parish Church dates from 1774, though there are partial remains of an earlier church dating from 1243 in the kirkyard. **Earthship Fife**, at Kinghorn Loch, is an unusual building made of used car tyres and soft drink cans. It has its own heating, lighting, water supply and sewage works, and explains all about eco-buildings and sustainable lifestyles.

BURNTISLAND
6 miles SW of Kirkcaldy on the A921

This small royal burgh, called Portus Gratiae, or "Port of Grace" by the Romans, is overlooked by a 632-feet high hill called **The Binn**. In medieval times it was the second most important port on the Forth after Leith, and in Victorian times exported coal from the Fife coalfields. **St Columba's Parish Church** is a four square building dating from 1592, and is possibly based on a Dutch design. It was the first church built in Scotland after the Reformation which is still in use today, and has a wealth of detail inside, including elaborate lofts and pews. The nave sits at the centre of the church, with the altar, or "Holy Table", sitting in the middle. The pews face it on four sides, emphasising the "equality of all believers". It is the birthplace of the **Authorised Version of the Bible**, as James VI attended a General Assembly of the Church of Scotland here in May 1601, and put forward the proposal for a translation of the Bible into English. The suggestion

PRESENT TIME
175 High Street, Burntisland, Fife KY3 9AE
Tel: 01592 873914

Present Time is a light, airy shop selling a wide range of gifts for weddings engagements, baby birthdays and so on. It is a family-run business which has over 30 years experience in the gift trade, making it the ideal place to buy that special souvenir of gift for yourself. You are free to browse the huge range of clocks, jewellery, barometers, handbags, glassware and cards for every occasion. The staff are friendly and knowledgeable, and shopping here is a real pleasure.

was enthusiastically received, but it was not until James had assumed the throne of Britain that work began.

The **Burntisland Edwardian Fair Museum** is in the High Street, and features displays about Edwardian fairgrounds and local history. Off the coast of the town, in 1633, Charles I lost most of his treasure, estimated to be worth over £20m in today's money, when his baggage ship, the *Blessing of Burntisland*, foundered and sank. Nineteen witches, who, it was claimed, put a curse on the ship, were executed. In 1999 the wreckage was finally located, lying in a few metres of silt. Plans are afoot to explore the wreckage.

The restored **Rossend Castle**, at the western end of the town, was the scene of a bizarre incident concerning Mary Stuart and a love struck French poet who broke into her room to declare his undying love for her. As he had attempted it once before at Holyrood, he was later executed (see also St Andrews).

ST ANDREWS

St Andrews is one of the most important and historic towns in Britain. Perhaps one should call it a city, as it was, in pre Reformation times, Scotland's ecclesiastical capital on account of its huge cathedral, which was Scotland's largest building in medieval times. It is also a university town, and the home of golf.

St Andrews Cathedral (Historic Scotland) was begun by Bishop Arnold in 1160, though the magnificent ruins you see nowadays date from many periods. The choir was the first part to be built, and

shows both Norman and Gothic details. The nave was completed in the late 13th century, though the great west front was blown down in a gale and had to be rebuilt. The whole building was finally consecrated in July 1318 in the presence of Robert the Bruce. As well as being a cathedral, it was also a priory served by Augustinian canons.

This wasn't the first cathedral on the site. In about 1127 a more modest church was built, a remnant of which still remains. This is **St Rule's Tower** and its attached chancel, to the south of the ruins. From its top, there's a magnificent view of the town.

Legend tells us that St Rule (or Regulus) came from Patras in Greece in the 4th century, carrying with him the bones of St Andrew. He set up a shrine for them on the Fife coast, at what was then called Kilrimont - present day St Andrews. A more likely story is that the bones were brought here by Bishop Acca of Hexham in AD 732. The relics were eventually transferred to the later building, housed in a shrine behind the high altar. St Andrews soon became a place of pilgrimage, with people coming from all over Europe to pray at the shrine. However, in 1559 John Knox

St Andrews

preached a sermon in the town, which resulted in reformers sacking the cathedral and destroying the fittings and altars. Though there were plans to restore the building, by 1600 it was being used as a quarry for building material.

To the east of the cathedral and outside its precincts are the scant ruins of another church, **St Mary on the Rock**. When the cathedral was being built, there were still Culdee monks of the old Celtic church at St Andrews, and they refused to join the cathedral priory. In the 13th century they built this church for themselves, which became the first collegiate church in Scotland. However, the monks gradually adopted the rites of the Catholic Church, and its priests were soon allowed a place in the cathedral chapter.

St Andrews Castle was the archbishop's residence. It too sits on the coast, and its ruins are sturdy yet picturesque. The first castle on the site was probably built in the early 13th century, though this has been rebuilt and altered over the years. It was here, in 1546, that **Cardinal David Beaton**, Archbishop of St Andrews, was murdered. In March of that year, George Wishart the Protestant reformer had been burnt at the stake in front of the castle on Beaton's authority, which made him many enemies (see also Dundee and Montrose). In May a group of Fife lairds broke into the castle and murdered him in his bedroom, hanging the corpse from the window. There then followed a long siege of the castle, during which sappers working for the Earl of Arran dug a tunnel beneath the fortifications to gain entry. These tunnels can still be seen today.

Beaton was not the only Archbishop of St Andrews to have been murdered. The other one was **Archbishop James Sharp**,

---

St Andrews Art And Music Shop

138 South Street, St Andrews, Fife KY16 9EQ
Tel & Fax: 01334 478625

St Andrews, with its university (which has 6,500 students), cathedral ruins and golf courses, is one of the most historic towns in Scotland. In South Street you'll find the **St Andrews Art and Music Shop**, selling a wide range of goods to do with both art and music. Owned and managed by Catherine Sharp, it sits next to the ancient West Port - originally one of the gates into the town - and has a blue and white frontage that is both smart and bright.

Catherine bought a small music shop in 2003. A year later she bought a nearby art shop, and combined the two, creating one of the most intriguing shops in town. The interior is bright and fascinating, with everything the discerning musician or artist could ever need. There are ranges of oil paints, acrylics and watercolours. And there are brushes, easels, canvases, crayons, craft materials, inks, pens, drawing paper, sketch books and a whole lot more. Plus, for the musician there is everything

from strings, music stands and musical instruments to CDs, sheet music, score books and plectrums. There are even musical gifts that would make the ideal souvenir of your visit to the town.

The staff are friendly and approachable, and Catherine herself is always available to offer advice and help. You should make this your first stop when you visit St Andrews - there is plenty of pay and display parking in South Street, and all of the town's historical sites and features are a short walk away.

the Protestant archbishop when the
Church of Scotland was Episcopalian. He
had embarked upon a savage and bloody
persecution of Covenanters, those people
who wished the church to remain
Presbyterian, and so was a hated man. In
May 1679 he was returning to St
Andrews from Edinburgh in a coach with
his daughter. At Magus Muir, near the
city, he was waylaid by Covenanters. Not
averse to acts of unspeakable cruelty
themselves when it suited them, they
stabbed the archbishop to death in front
of his daughter. This was not the first
attempt on his life. In 1668 a man called
James Mitchell attempted to murder
him, and he was captured six years later
and executed. Perhaps the most amazing
thing about James Sharp was that he
himself had once been sympathetic to
the Covenanting cause.

Wishart was not the only Protestant to
have been executed in the town. There
were others, including **Patrick
Hamilton**, who was burnt at the stake in
1528 (see also Stonehouse). The spot is
marked by his initials incorporated into
the cobbles outside **St Salvator's Church**
in North Street, part of **St Salvator's
College**. The church was founded in
1450 by Bishop James Kennedy, not only
to serve the college, but as a place of
worship for the people of the town.

It was on August 28th 1413 that Pope
Benedict XIII issued six papal bulls

authorising the founding of the
university. At first the classes were held
in the cathedral, but this was found to be
unsatisfactory. In 1450 Bishop Kennedy
founded St Salvator's College, and classes
moved there. In the 16th century two
others were founded, **St Leonard's
College** and **St Mary's College**. St
Leonard's was eventually incorporated
into St Salvator's, and a girl's school now
stands on the site where it once stood. **St
Leonard's Chapel** still exists, however,
and the earliest parts date from the 12th
century, showing it had been built long
before the college came into being.

St Mary's College is undoubtedly the
loveliest of today's colleges. Step through
the arch from South Street and you are
in a grassed quadrangle surrounded by
old, mellow buildings from the 16th
century onwards. At the foot of the Stair
Tower is **Queen Mary's Thorn**, said to
have been planted by Mary Stuart in
1565. She visited the town five times,
and possibly lodged at what is now
known as **Queen Mary's House** in South
Street. It dates from about 1525, and was
built by one of the cathedral's canons.
Charles II also stayed in it in 1650.

In February 1563 a French poet called
Pierre de Châtelard was executed in
Market Street. He had accompanied Mary
when she returned from France, and
swore undying love for her. However, he
went too far, twice breaking into Mary's

bedroom - once in Holyrood and once at Rossend Castle near Burntisland. He was taken to St Andrews Castle, and there imprisoned. On February 22nd he was brought to trial and condemned to death. On the scaffold, he read out a poem called *Hymn to Death*, then cried out "Farewell cruel dame!" (see also Burntisland).

Many people made political capital out of the incidents, saying he had been in the pay of the French, or that Mary had been his mistress. John Knox even claimed that when the poet had said "cruel dame" he had actually meant "cruel mistress", showing that Mary and he were closer than was proper for a queen and a commoner. However, there is little doubt that he was just a foolish young man who had unwisely fallen in love with a queen.

Further along South Street, in front of **Madras College**, one of the town's schools, is all that remains of the **Dominican Friary**. This is the 16th century north transept of the friary church, with some wonderful tracery in its windows. The friary was originally founded in the 13th century by Bishop William Wishart.

Almost across from it is **Holy Trinity Parish Church**. It was founded in the 15th century, though the building as we see it today dates largely from a rebuilding early in the 20th century. The only surviving parts of the medieval building are to be found in the west wall, some pillars and the tower. It contains a memorial to Archbishop Sharp, slain in 1679, though his body no longer rests under it. No doubt it had been removed and disposed of as soon as the Scottish

St Andrews Golf Course

church reverted to Presbyterianism.

At the west end of South Street can be found the **West Port**, one of the original gates into the town. It was built about 1589 on the site of an earlier port. In North Street is the **St Andrews Preservation Trust Museum and Garden**, housed in a charming building dating from the 16th century. It has displays and artefacts illustrating the town's history. The **St Andrews Museum** at Kinburn Park also celebrates the town's heritage.

At the Scores, down near the shore, you'll find the **St Andrews Aquarium**, which not only lets you see lots of fish and animals from sea horses to seals and piranha to sharks, but lets you touch some as well. Also on the Scores is the **Martyr's Monument**, which commemorates the Protestant martyrs who were executed in St Andrews. It is a tall, needle-like monument, erected in 1842. Close by is the **British Golf Museum**, which illustrates the history of a game that Scotland gave to the world, with a particular focus on St Andrews. It has an array of exhibits from over 500 years of golfing history, and gives an insight into "surprising facts and striking feats".

St Andrews and golf are inseparable. The town is still a place of pilgrimage, only today the pilgrims come wearing Pringle sweaters and weighed down by golf bags. **The Royal and Ancient Golf Club** is the world's ruling body on the game (with the exception of the United States), and formulates its rules as well as organising the yearly British Open Championship. The most famous of the town's courses is the **Old Course**, and it is here, in the clubhouse, that the Royal and Ancient has its headquarters.

Two of the greatest names in golf were born in St Andrews - **Tom Morris** and his

Martyr's Monument

son, also called Tom. Old Tom was made green keeper at the Old Course in 1865, and was one of the best golfers of his

---

KINCAPLE LODGE

Kincaple, St Andrews, Fife KY16 9SH
Tel & Fax: 01334 850217
e-mail: jim@woodlandholidays.co.uk
website: www.woodlandholidays.co.uk

For a relaxing woodland holiday, you can't beat Woodland Holidays at **Kincaple Lodge**. It has nine superb wooden Scandinavian lodges on offer three miles from the beautiful and historic town of St Andrews. Each lodge has a good-sized living and dining area, a fully equipped kitchen, two bedrooms with wash hand basins and a bathroom with heated towel rail. The lodges have wonderful views out over fields towards the Eden estuary and St Andrews itself, and come complete with bed linen, towels, electric blankets, verandah with garden chairs and covered washing line. This is the ideal location to unwind after a hard day's sightseeing in this delightful part of Fife, which has so much to offer. Z-beds are available, there is a laundry room and telephone on site, and Kincaple also offers a baby sitting service. The lodges are fully insulated, and are open all year round. Unfortunately, pets are not allowed.

Kincaple House, within the site, also offers superb four star B&B accommodation. You will appreciate the warm Scottish welcome you get here, as well as the comfortable, well-furnished rooms that are all en suite. There is ample paring, and a tennis court that guests can use. Breakfasts are beautifully cooked, and you can chose from a hearty Scottish breakfast or a lighter, Continental option. All the produce is sourced locally so that it is as fresh as possible. This part of Fife is full of history and heritage, and the city of Dundee is only ten miles away. If you are visiting, you can't afford not to stay at the lodges or Kincaple House.

day. His son, however, was even better, and won the Open Championship three times in a row while still a teenager. He eventually died in 1875, aged only 24, some say of a broken heart after his wife died in childbirth. Memorials to both men can be seen in the cathedral graveyard.

The **Crawford Arts Centre**, originally part of the university, is in North Street, and has regular exhibitions of art and craftwork by living artists. **Craigton Country Park** sits about a mile outside the town to the southwest. It has a small boating loch, miniature railway, aviary, pet's corner, glasshouses, restaurant and café. **Cambo Gardens** is a two-and-a-half acre walled garden within the Cambo estate at Kingsbarns. Cambo has been the home of the Erskine family since 1688, though the present mansion dates from 1881. There is also 70 acres of woodland, which is famous for its snowdrops.

Crail

AROUND ST ANDREWS

CRAIL
8 miles SE of St Andrews on the A917

The royal burgh of Crail is one of the oldest ports in the East Neuk ("East Corner"), as this area of Fife is known. It is also possibly the most picturesque, and the small harbour has featured on countless calendars and post cards. Artists flock to the place because of the light and the quaint buildings. The **Tolbooth** dates from the early 16th century with a tower dated 1776, and has Dutch influences. In the Marketgate is the **Crail Museum and Heritage Centre**, which traces the history of the town and its industries.

At Troywood, three miles west of the town, off the B9131, is perhaps the most unusual visitor attraction in Scotland. The **Secret Bunker** was Scotland's underground command centre in event of a nuclear attack. It has an amazing 24,000 square feet of accommodation on two levels, 100 feet underground and encased in 15 feet thick concrete walls. It was from here that the country was to have been run in the event of war with the Soviet Union. It is entered by an innocent looking farmhouse, and guarded by three tons of blast proof doors. As well as operations rooms, living quarters and six dormitories, it also contains two cinemas, a café and a BBC sound studio. Several similar bunkers were built around the country, and this is one of the largest. It came off the Official Secrets list in 1993 at the end of the Cold War.

JUST FOR YOU

2 Rodger Street, Anstruther, Fife KY10 3DU
Tel: 01333 312106

When in the small, picturesque town of Anstruther, treat yourself to a new outfit in **Just For You**, one of the best fashion shops in Fife. It is owned and managed for 16 years by Jean Frame, who is always on hand to help you choose an ensemble that flatters and is just right for that special occasion, such as a wedding or party. The premises are large, bright and airy, with a colourful frontage in blue and white that just can't be missed. There are two areas within the shop - one for formal and evening wear and one for casual yet elegant fashions. Jean

stocks sizes from 10 to 24, and many of her lines are unavailable elsewhere, meaning that satisfied customers come from all over the UK to buy an outfit for that special occasion. Lines include Slimma, Libra, Whimsy, Personal Choice, Pomodoro, Finn Karelia, Emreco and a whole lot more.

Plus Jean stocks a wide range of accessories that means you can be clothed from top to toe. There are splendid hats for every occasion, as well as jewellery, shoes, bags and wraps that complement any fashion ensemble. If alterations are needed, then this service is available as well. At the front of the shop there is parking for two to three cars, and there is plenty of street parking not far away. So when you visit the East Neuk of Fife, and especially Anstruther (and don't forger to pronounce it "Anster", like the locals do), pay a visit to Just for You. You're sure to find something that is flattering and elegant.

SCOTTISH FISHERIES MUSEUM

St. Ayles, Harbourhead, Anstruther, Fife KY10 3AB
Tel/Fax: 01333 310628
e-mail: enquiries@scotfishmuseum.org
website: www.scotfishmuseum.org

Fishing has always been important to the small villages that fringe the East Neuk of Fife and in the **Scottish Fisheries Museum** you can learn all about the industry, not just in Fife, but throughout Scotland. It is a truly fascinating place, and is housed in buildings dating from the 16th to the 19th centuries. There are displays on many facets of the industry, and a trip round makes a great day out for children and adults alike. It begins by examining a replica dug-out canoe dating from AD500, created in the museum workshop to illustrate that fishing in Scotland goes back to ancient times. After it was made in 1991, it was tested in Anstruther Harbour, and performed beautifully.

There are many galleries, each one highlighting a facet of the industry. There is an area on whaling, for example, plus a gallery called 'The Herring Market', with a net-loft where nets were repaired, a fish merchant's office, and lively herring lassies gutting and packing the catch. There are also, of course,

fishing boats, and you can see and touch the craft that took hardy fishermen out into the seas round Britain in days gone by. One of the most fascinating galleries is the one dedicated to Zulu fishing boats. How did they get their name? What key role did they play in the industry? There is also a tearoom, a room which you can book to enjoy your packed lunch, and a shop, where you can pick up well-crafted souvenirs to remind you of your trip to one of the most interesting and enjoyable museums in Scotland. It is wheelchair friendly, and special themed visits can also be arranged.

The four star **Jerdan Gallery**, in Marketgate South, has a wide variety of paintings and craftwork from the 19th and 20th centuries, with exhibits changing on a monthly basis.

ANSTRUTHER

9 miles S of St Andrews off the A917

Anstruther (sometimes pronounced "(Ainster") is a former herring fishing port. It comprises two ancient royal burghs, Anstruther Easter and Anstruther Wester, and is a picturesque place full of old white washed cottages with red pantiled roofs and crow stepped gables.

There is a story that, after the English defeated the Spanish Armada in 1588, one of the ships of the Spanish fleet put in at Anstruther and was civilly received by the people of the town. The ship's commander was one Jan Gomez de Midini, and he and his crew were offered hospitality (this at a time when Scotland and England were still independent countries). A few years later the Spaniard repaid his debt when he discovered fishermen from Anstruther marooned in a foreign port after their boat had been wrecked. He re-equipped them and sent them homewards once more.

Located in 16th century St Ayles House, once a lodging house for the monks from Balmerino Abbey, is the **Scottish Fisheries Museum**, which was opened in 1969. Here you can follow the fleet with the "herring lassies", explore a typical fishing family's cottage and see skilled craftsmen at work. Also on display are two boats - a 78-feet long "Zulu" built in the early 1900s and based on an original African design, and the *Reaper*, a "fifie" herring drifter built in 1901. In a small private chapel is the poignant Memorial to Scottish Fishermen Lost at Sea.

Six miles southeast of Anstruther, in the Firth of Forth, is the **Isle of May**, measuring just over a mile long by a quarter of a mile wide at its widest. There are the scant remains of an old Augustinian priory, dedicated to St Oran and St Colman, which was founded by David I and colonised from reading abbey in England. In 1996 an archaeological investigation uncovered the remains of a 9th century church - one of the oldest on Scotland's east coast. The whole place is now a national nature reserve managed by Scottish Natural Heritage. It was on this island that Scotland's first lighthouse was built in 1635. It was no more than a small stone tower with a brazier atop it, which burnt coal. Trips to the island are available from the pier at Anstruther.

Anstruther

KILRENNY

9 miles S of St Andrews on the A917

Kilrenny Parish Church has a tower dating from the 15th century, though the rest is early 19th century. In the Kirk yard is a mausoleum to the Scotts of Balcomie. There are many picturesque 18th and 19th century cottages, formerly the homes of fishermen. The name "Kilrenny" actually means "the church of the bracken", and the village may be one of the earliest settlements in the area.

PITTENWEEM

9 miles S of St Andrews on the A917

The older houses in this small royal burgh crowd round the picturesque fishing harbour, which is now the busiest of all the fishing harbours in the area. Like most of the houses in the East Neuk, they are whitewashed with red pantiled roofs and crow step gables. An Augustinian Priory was founded here in the 12th century by monks from the Isle of May, though very little of it now remains. The **Parish Church** has a substantial tower (which looks more like a small castle than a piece of ecclesiastical architecture) dating from the 16th century, while the rest is Victorian.

Pittenweem means "the place of the cave", and the cave in question is **St Fillan's Cave** in Cave Wynd, which is supposed to be where St Fillan, an 8th century missionary to the Picts, used to go for private prayer (see also Tyndrum, Madderty and St Fillans). It was renovated and re-dedicated in 1935. There are also many art galleries and antique shops, a testimony to the popularity of this area with artists and retired people.

Kellie Castle (National Trust for Scotland) dates from the 14th century, and is one of the best examples in the Lowlands of the secular architecture of the time. It contains superb plaster ceilings, murals, painted panelling and furniture designed by Sir Robert Lorimer, who refurbished the place in the late 19th century. There are fine gardens with old roses and herbaceous borders.

ST MONANS

10 miles S of St Andrews on the A917

This little fishing port's motto is Mare Vivimus, meaning "From the Sea we Have Life". It is famous for the **Parish Church of St Monans**, built by David II, son of Robert the Bruce, in thanksgiving after he survived a shipwreck on the Forth. It stands almost on the shoreline, and is a substantial building consisting of a nave, transepts and stumpy spire atop a tower. The chancel was never built.

The ruins of 15th century **Newark Castle** can also be seen near the shore. It originally belonged to the Newark family, but perhaps its most famous owner was

Pittenweem

St Monans Windmill

General General David Leslie, who fought for Cromwell in the 17th century.

Salt panning was once an important industry in the town, and the 18th century **St Monans Windmill** at one time formed part of a small industrial complex, which produced salt from seawater.

EARLSFERRY AND ELIE
10 miles S of St Andrews off the A917

These two villages are small holiday resorts surrounding a sandy bay. The older of the two is Earlsferry, which is a royal burgh. It was once the northern terminal for ferries which plied between it and ports on the south bank of the Forth. The "earl" in its name comes from an incident concerning Macduff, who was the Earl of Fife. In 1054 he escaped from King Macbeth, took refuge in a cave at Kincraig Point near the town, and was then ferried across the Forth to Dunbar. **Gillespie House**, in Elie, dates from the 17th century, and has a fine carved doorway. **Elie Parish Church** dates from 1639, though the unusual tower was added in 1729. At Ruby Bay are the scant

remains of **Lady's Tower**, built in the late 18th century as a changing room for Lady Anstruther, who bathed in the sea here.

At one time an old track called the "Cadgers Road" led from Earlsferry to Falkland, and it was along this that supplies of fresh fish were taken to feed the king when he stayed there.

CUPAR
8 miles W of St Andrews on the A91

This small town, sitting on the River Eden, was once the county town of Fife. It is a pleasant place, and well worth strolling round just to see and appreciate its many old buildings. The **Mercat Cross**, topped with a unicorn, was moved from Tarvit Hill to its present location in 1897 to commemorate Queen Victoria's Diamond Jubilee. In Duffus Park is the **Douglas Bader Garden**, designed with

Earlsferry and Elie

NUMBER FIVE

56 Bonnygate, Cupar, Fife KY15 4LD
Tel/Fax: 01334 657784
e-mail: jsh_bruce@yahoo.co.uk
website: www.clairedonald.com

Your eyes are always drawn to the windows of **Number Five**, a shop in Cupar's Bonnygate. It sells exquisite jewellery based on the designs of a number of jewellers, including internationally experienced designer, jeweller and goldsmith Claire Donald, who trained in Scotland, London and Paris.

Entering the shop is to step into a world where beauty, fashion and craftsmanship fuse to create objects both beautiful in themselves and which add elegance to any ensemble. Imagine entering a gallery where you see all the desirable pieces of jewellery in other galleries collected at one location. There is everything from simple stainless steel and titanium designs to bold acrylic pieces, traditional settings and truly inspiring pieces in the noble metals - gold, silver and platinum. They all represent remarkable value for money, and make the ideal gift for someone special, to mark a wedding, engagement or anniversary, or simply a unique token of love.

The pieces showcased are not limited to those produced by Claire Donald but also include the work of other top British designers from up and down the country. Their creations show a wide and varied range of different styles and techniques in traditional and contemporary materials.

To quote one admirer the designs are "deliciously seductive". The craftsmanship as you would expect is of the highest order. So successful has Number Five been that, having at first been renowned for its silverware, it now carries many fine pieces in 18 carat gold and other metals. Claire Donald has created many beautiful engagement and wedding rings, including white and yellow gold rings set with sparkling precious stones.

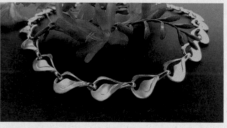

Claire likes to offer real choice to her customers, and not sell ranges that are too limited. Her pieces aren't just about shape or colour, but about the juxtaposition of textures and the contrast between various materials. For this reason, many pendants are sold separately from chains so that customers can bring their own tastes to an object, and stamp it with their own personality.

Number Five has a base of regular customers who return again and again. However, if you just want to buy one piece you are more than welcome to come along and browse in the shop. It is gaining a reputation throughout Scotland as a place where craftsmanship is showcased, keeping alive crafts that go deep into the heart of Scottish culture. It sells pieces that are at the top end of the range - the perfect accessories for the fashion conscious.

CAIRNIE FRUIT FARM & MEGA MAZE

Cupar, Fife   Open 7 days 9.30-6.00pm July-Sept
Tel: 01334 655610 website: www.cairniefruitfarm.co.uk

Strawberries, raspberries, black & redcurrants, gooseberries & tayberries all available to pick or to purchase ready-picked. At the Farm Shop they also sell seasonal fresh produce, local honey & their own home produced range of Cairnie Fruit Farm jams. Their Tearoom Garden boasts the best home baking in Fife. They are particularly well known for their super fresh scones, giant strawberry tarts and melt-in- the-mouth shortbread. Their speciality strawberry and raspberry swirl ice-cream is a real treat too. They also feature a six acre Mega Maze which changes each season. A Mega Maze ticket holder has unlimited use of the "Funyard" within the Maze which features a fantastic straw bale climbing fortress, a giant sand box with diggers, go-carts, trampolines, maze puzzles and lots of other surprises. A great day out.

PEAT INN

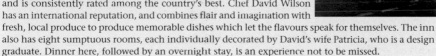

Cupar, Fife KY15 5LH
Tel: 01334 840206 Fax: 01334 840530
e-mail: reception@thepeatinn.co.uk
website: www.thepeatinn.co.uk

The **Peat Inn** is renowned all over Britain for the quality of its cuisine, and is consistently rated among the country's best. Chef David Wilson has an international reputation, and combines flair and imagination with fresh, local produce to produce memorable dishes which let the flavours speak for themselves. The inn also has eight sumptuous rooms, each individually decorated by David's wife Patricia, who is a design graduate. Dinner here, followed by an overnight stay, is an experience not to be missed.

the disabled in mind. The **Old Parish Church** dates from 1785, though the tower is medieval.

Hill of Tarvit Mansionhouse (National Trust for Scotland) is a fine Edwardian mansion that lies two miles south of the town, and was designed by Sir Robert Lorimer in 1906. It has French, Scottish and Chippendale furniture, a collection of paintings, an Edwardian laundry and fine gardens.

Close by is **Scotstarvit Tower** (Historic Scotland). It was built by the Inglis family around 1487 when they were granted the lands of Tarvit. In 1612 it was bought by Sir John Scott. He was an advocate who was deprived of his twin positions in the Scottish judiciary as judge and director of chancery by Cromwell in the 17th century, and retired to Scotstarvit, where he was visited by many eminent men of the time.

FERNIE CASTLE HOTEL

Letham, near Cupar, Fife KY15 7RU
Tel: 01337 810381 e-mail: mail@ferniecastle.demon.co.uk
Fax: 01337 810422 website: www.ferniecastle.demon.co.uk

Fernie Castle was first recorded in 1353, with the present building being over 450 years old. Now it is the four star **Fernie Castle Hotel** that offers all the romance and character of Scotland's turbulent past coupled with modern amenities. There are 20 individually designed en suite rooms equipped to the highest standards. Dining can take place in the vaulted Keep Bar or in the elegant Auld Alliance Room. The food is superb, and afterwards guests can relax over a quiet drink or coffee in the Wallace Lounge, with its turret snuggery. Weddings or corporate events can be held in the Balfour Suite, and private dinner rooms are also available.

A few miles west of Cupar, at Rankeilor Park, is the **Scottish Deer Centre** and **Raptor World**. At the Deer Centre you can see - and even feed - both species of deer native to Scotland, the roe and the red deer, plus other species from around the world. At the Raptor Centre there are exhibitions about birds of prey such as owls, hawks and falcons, plus there are spectacular flying demonstrations. There is also a small shopping court, an indoor adventure play area and picnic areas.

CERES
7 miles W of St Andrews on the B939

Ceres gets its name from the family which once owned the lands surrounding the vilage - the de Syras family. It is a small picturesque village with a village green and the hump-backed, medieval **Bishop's Bridge**. The **Parish Church** contains some medieval tombs of the Earls of Crawford, and in the **Fife Folk Museum** you can find out about what everyday life was like in Fife in bygone days.

Two miles southwest of Ceres are the ruins of 14th century **Struthers Castle**. It has been owned by the de Ochters, the Keiths, the Lindsays and the Crawfords. At one time the lands belonging to the castle were called "Outhirothistrodyr", from which the word "Struther" comes.

The village's **Bannockburn Monument** is close by the Bishop's Bridge, and was erected in 1914, 600 years after the Battle of Bannockburn took place, to commemorate the archers of Ceres who fell in it. The **Parish Church** was built in 1806 on the site of a much older church. Its most unusual features are the communion tables, which run the full length of the church. Built into a wall on the main street is a curious carving known as **The Provost**, said to have been the Revd Thomas Buchanan, the last holder of the title in 1578.

NEWBURGH
16 miles W of St Andrews on the A913

This small royal burgh stands on the banks of the Tay. Close to it are the red sandstone ruins of **Lindores Abbey**, founded by David I in 1178 for Tironenisan monks. It was the first abbey in Scotland to be sacked by Protestant sympathisers, 17 years before Scotland officially became a Protestant country. And the very first mention of whisky production in Scotland is contained in a document of 1494, when James IV commissioned John Cor, a monk at the abbey, to make the equivalent of 400 bottles of "aquavitae" for the king's table.

The **Laing Museum** in the High Street has displays on Newburgh's history from medieval burgh to industrial town.

AUCHTERMUCHTY
16 miles W of St Andrews on the A91

Auchtermuchty is a typical inland Fife town. It is small and compact, and sits in a fertile area known as the Howe of Fife ("Hollow of Fife"). The **Tolbooth** dates from 1728, and it was here that the TV series *Dr Finlay* was filmed, its town centre being turned into a typical townscape of the 1930s.

Though born in East Wemyss, **Jimmy Shand**, the well known Scottish dance band leader, lived in the town for many years. There is a statue of him, complete with kilt, at Upper Glens in the town.

LEUCHARS
4 miles NW of St Andrews, on the A919

Every September, the Royal Air Force puts on the **Leuchars Air Show**, held in one of Scotland's biggest RAF bases. The village is also famous for it's **Parish Church of St Athernase**, said by some to be the second finest Norman church in Britain. It was built in the late 12th century by Robert de Quinci, who lived in Leuchars Castle. The best parts are the finely carved chancel and apse, with the rather plain nave being Victorian. A bell tower was added to the apse in the 17th century. St Athernase is also known as St Ethernesc, and he was a companion of St Columba who travelled and preached throughout Fife.

St Athernase Church, Leuchars

Earlshall Castle (not open to the public) was started in 1546 by Sir William Bruce, and completed by his descendant of the same name in 1617. It subsequently fell into disrepair, but was rebuilt in 1891 under the direction of Sir Robert Lorimer. **Tentsmuir Forest**, to the north of Leuchars, is a 3,700-acre pine forest planted on sand dunes on the shores of the North Sea and the Firth of Tay. The whole area is rich in wildlife.

NEWPORT-ON-TAY

9 miles NW of St Andrews on the A92

This little town sits at the southern end of the Tay Road Bridge, and at **Wormit**, about a mile to the west, is the start of the Tay Rail Bridge. The ruins of **Balmerino Abbey** (National Trust for Scotland) sit five miles to the west. It was founded in 1229 by Queen Ermengarde, widow of William the Lion, king of Scotland, and colonised by Cistercian monks from Melrose. The ruins are not open to the public, but can be viewed from close by.

LOCATOR MAP

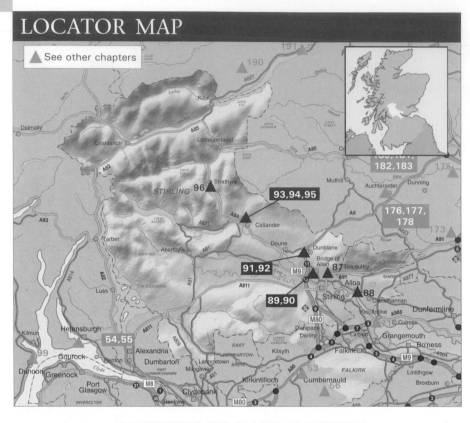

▲ See other chapters

STIRLING 96▲

93,94,95

182,183

176,177, 178

91,92   87

89,90   88

54,55

99

ADVERTISERS AND PLACES OF INTEREST

STIRLINGSHIRE & CLACKMANNANSHIRE 7

That area of Scotland between the Firths of Clyde and Forth has always been strategically important. It is often referred to as Scotland's "waist", and before the Kincardine Bridge was built in 1936, the bridge at Stirling was the lowest crossing point of the River Forth. To the west of the town are the Campsie and Kilsyth Hills, and these, along with marshy bogland such as Flanders Moss, formed another natural barrier, so the bridge at Stirling became the gateway to Perthshire and the Highlands.

That's why so many battles have been fought in and around Stirling and Falkirk, including Scotland's most important, the Battle of Bannockburn, which secured Scotland's future as an independent nation. It is also the reason why Stirling Castle was built. This royal castle sits sentinel on a great rocky outcrop, with the town of Stirling laid out below it to the west. In medieval times it was almost impregnable, and from its top an approaching army could easily be seen even if it was miles away.

This is an area, which has witnessed great changes over the years due to local government reorganisations. Dunblane, to the north of Stirling, was at one time in Perthshire, as was Callander and Port of Menteith. For a while, Clackmannanshire ceased to exist (though it remained alive in the hearts of all those born there). Now it has come back, and still proudly proclaims itself to be Scotland's smallest county, with an area of only 55 square miles. It sits in the shelter of the Ochil Hills to the north, which rise to well over 2,000 feet in places, and was a centre for woollens and textiles. The string of "hillfoot villages" at the foot of the Ochils are all picturesque and well worth visiting for this alone.

Around Falkirk and Grangemouth, Stirlingshire is unashamedly industrial. This is the heart of Scotland's petrochemical industry, with great

Loch Drunkie, Trossachs

refineries lining the shores of the Forth, which is still tidal at this point. It was also at one time a coal mining area, though the mines have long gone.

Travel northwest from Stirling however, and you enter another world - the Trossachs, one of Scotland's most beautiful areas. Though its hills are not as high as those of the Grampians or the Cairngorms, and don't have that brooding majesty we tend to associate with Highland scenery, it is still Highland in character. The hills slip down to the wooded banks of lochs such as Loch Katrine, Loch Venachar and the wonderfully named Loch Drunkie, which are among the most picturesque in Scotland, and the skies seem endless and sweeping. The Loch Lomond and Trossachs National Park (see also Balloch) takes in most of the Trossachs in its 720 square miles. It was the country's first national park, opened in 2002.

The town of Stirling is one of the most historic in Scotland, and has played a leading role in shaping the country's destiny. The castle has been fought over countless times by the Scottish and the English, and eventually became a favourite royal residence. Mary Queen of Scots stayed there, and her son, who became James VI, had his coronation in the town's Church of the Holy Rood. Falkirk, though more industrial in character, is also an ancient town, and has witnessed two important battles as Scotland's history was played out. Alloa, Clackmannanshire's largest town, is also industrial in character, though it too has history aplenty. At one time it was a thriving port, and Scotland's brewing capital, though only one brewery now remains.

For those interested in architecture, the whole area offers some memorable buildings. Stirling Castle itself was given a Renaissance makeover by James IV. Dunblane Cathedral, Alloa Tower, the ruins of Camubuskenneth Priory, the Wallace Monument, and both Doune Castle and Castle Campbell are also well worth visiting.

CLACKMANNAN

This small town was granted its burgh charter in 1550. It was once a small port on the Black Devon, a tributary of the Forth, but the river silted up years ago, leaving it high and dry. In the centre of the town is the belfry of the old **Tolbooth**, built by William Menteith in 1592. He was the sheriff of the town, and objected strongly to holding felons in his own home, so he built the Tolbooth to hold them instead.

Beside it stands the **Mannau Stone**. Legend states that when St Serf came to this part of Scotland in the 6th century to convert it to Christianity, he found the locals worshipping the sea god Mannau, or Mannan, in the form of the stone (known as the "clach mannau"). From this, the town supposedly got its name. Another legend states that the name derives from an incident in the life of Robert the Bruce. It seems that he once rested close to the stone, and on remounting his horse, left his glove lying on it. He ordered one of his servants to return to the "clach" (stone) and retrieve his "mannan" (glove). The stone can still be seen on top of a column close to the

Tolbooth and the **Mercat Cross**, which dates from the 1600s.

Clackmannan Tower, on King's Seat Hill, where once a royal hunting lodge built by David I stood, dates from the 14th century, with later alterations, and was once owned by Robert the Bruce. Though in the care of Historic Scotland, it can only be viewed from the outside at present. Robert Burns visited the area in 1787, and was "knighted" by a direct descendant of Robert the Bruce, a Mrs Bruce, who lived in a mansion house (demolished in 1791) near the castle. She was in her nineties at the time, and a woman of "hospitality and urbanity". She still possessed her ancestor's helmet and two-handed sword, and she used the sword to carry out the ceremony, declaring that she had a better right to confer knighthoods than "some people" (meaning the Hanovarian kings who were on the throne in London).

Clackmannan's **Parish Church** dates from 1815, though St Serf may have founded the original church in the 6th century. Inside is the beautiful Coronation Window, gifted to the church by its congregation to mark the coronation of Elizabeth II in 1953. The Queen visited the church specially to view it in 1997, so it seems that the loyalty of at least some Clackmannan people towards the monarchy in London is not in doubt any more.

Two miles north of the town is the **Gartmorn Dam Country Park**. It is centred on the 170-acre Gartmorn Dam, the oldest man made reservoir in Scotland. It was constructed in the early 1700s by John Erskine, 6th Earl of Mar, to power the pumps which pumped water out of his coal mines at nearby Sauchie. Now a nature reserve, the park is popular with walkers and nature lovers, and the reservoir itself is stocked with brown trout.

AROUND CLACKMANNAN

TILLICOULTRY
4 miles N of Clackmannan on the A91

Tillicoultry is one of the "hillfoot villages" which relied on water tumbling down from the Ochils to power the mills in which most people were employed. It became a town in 1871, and behind it is the picturesque **Tillicoultry Glen**, whose waters once powered eight mills in the town.

An old story says that the town got its unusual name from a Highlander who was driving some cattle along a road where the town now stands. He stropped at a stream to allow the cattle to drink. However, none of the cattle did so, and he exclaimed, "there's tiel a coo try", meaning "devil a cow is thirsty!" However, a more prosaic explanation of the name is that it comes from the Gaelic, and means "hill in the back land".

DOLLAR
5 miles NE of Clackmannan on the A91

Dollar is another "hillfoot village", famous as the home of **Dollar Academy**. This private school (the equivalent of an English public school) was founded in the early 19th century thanks to a bequest by Captain John McNabb, a local herd boy born in 1732 who amassed a fortune in London as a merchant before his death in 1802. Eighteen years later the academy had been built, though if he came back today he might be puzzled to see it, for he had intended it to be a school for the children of the poor in Dollar parish. The elegant, colonnaded building was designed by the eminent architect William Playfair, and was opened in 1819. In the 1930s McNabb's coffin was rediscovered in a London crypt. The remains were cremated, and the ashes now rest in a niche above the bronze doors of the school.

Within an old woollen mill now called Castle Campbell Hall in Dollar is the small **Dollar Museum**, which has displays on the history of the village and on the Devon Valley railway. Above the town, and reached through the wooded **Dollar Glen** (National Trust for Scotland), is **Castle Campbell** (National Trust for Scotland). It was one of Clan Campbell's Lowland homes, and was formerly known as "Castle Gloom". Close by are two burns called Care and Sorrow, and even the name Dollar itself is said to derive from "dolour", meaning sadness. It seems strange that such a beautiful spot should have such depressing names. The castle dates essentially from the 15th century, with some later additions. Both John Knox and Mary Stuart have stayed there.

Castle Campbell, Dollar

ALVA
3 miles NW of Clackmannan on the A91

Alva sits at the foot of the Ochils, and is one of the "hillfoot villages" where weaving and spinning were the main industries. It's name means "rocky plain", as does that of its near neighbour Alloa. To the northeast is the Ochil Hills' highest peak, the 2,363-feet **Ben Cleuch**. At the **Mill Trail Visitor Centre**, housed in the former Glentana Mill building of 1887, there are displays and exhibits that explain what life was like in mill factories over the last 150 years. There is also a shop and a café. **The Mill Trail** itself is a signposted route taking you to many mills with retail outlets. **The Ochil Hills Woodland Park** has attractive walks and a visitor centre. It is centred on what were the grounds of the long gone Alva House.

Alva

Alva Glen, also called the "Silver Glen", is very picturesque. Silver was once mined here in the 18th century, and **St Serf's Parish Church**, which dates from 1815, has some communion vessels made from local silver. It was the Erskine family that mined the silver, and according to them it was a hit or miss affair. A story is told of one member of the family, Sir John Erskine, showing two of the mines to a friend. "Out of that hole there I earned £50,000," he told him. "And in that hole there I lost it all again."

BLAIRLOGIE

6 miles NW of Clackmannan on the A91

Blairlogie is possibly the most beautiful of the "hillfoot villages", and was the first conservation village in Scotland. It sits in the shadow of the 1,373-feet **Dumyat**, which has the remains of a hilltop fort on its summit. The name derives from Dun Maetae, meaning the fort of the Maetae, a Pictish tribe. At the summit there are memorials to the Argyll and Sutherland Highlanders, and superb views as far as Edinburgh.

MENSTRIE

4 miles NW of Clackmannan on the A91

Sir William Alexander, 1st Earl of Stirling, was born in **Menstrie Castle** in 1567. He was the founder of Nova Scotia, Scotland's only real colony in North America. The only part of the castle open to the public is the Nova Scotia Commemoration Room, which has displays about the colony. There are also the armorial bearings of the Nova Scotia baronetcies created in Scotland at the beginning of the 17th century. The baronetcies had nothing to do with chivalry or valour, but all to do with

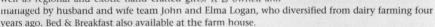

money.,as they were offered for sale at 3,000 Scots merks each.

In 1621 Sir William persuaded James VI to create the baronetcies, and when James realised how much money he could make from it, he readily agreed. In 1624, while at Windsor, he began the money making scheme. A year later he was dead, and his son Charles I, not unnaturally, continued the practise. By the end of 1625 the first 22 titles had been conferred. Even today there are 109 titles still in existence. Sir William died penniless in London in 1644, and now lies buried in the Church of the Holy Rood in Stirling. (see also Edinburgh and Stirling).

The castle itself was built in the late 16th century, and was a stronghold of Clan McAllister, a family that changed its name to Alexander as it adopted English customs. It gradually fell into a state of disrepair, but was refurbished in the 1950s.

Sir Ralph Abercromby, who commanded the British troops at the Battle of Alexandria in 1801, was born in Menstrie in 1734. He died at Alexandria in 1801 of wounds received during the battle.

ALLOA
2 miles W of Clackmannan on the A907

With a population of about 15,000, Alloa is the largest town in Scotland's smallest county. Though an inland town, it sits on the River Forth at a point where it is still tidal, and its name is supposed to mean "rocky plain". It was traditionally an engineering, brewing and glass-making town, though today these industries are less important than they once were.

St Mungo's Parish Church dates from 1817, though it incorporates the 17th century tower of an earlier church. **Alloa Tower** (National Trust for Scotland) dates from the 14th century, and is all that is left of the ancestral home of the Erskines, one of the most important families in Scotland. They eventually became the Earls of Mar, and as such were (and still are as the Earls of Mar and Kellie) Hereditary Keepers of Stirling Castle. The tower was built for Alexander Erskine, the 3rd Lord Erskine, in the late 15th century, and later remodelled by the 6th Earl of Mar in the 18th century. It has the original oak roof beams,

ALLOA TOWER

Alloa Park, Alloa, Clackmannanshire, FK10 1PP
Tel: 01259 211701 Fax: 01259 218744
website: www.nts.org.uk

Alloa Tower, the largest surviving keep in Scotland, dates from the 14th century. It was home to successive generations of the Earls of Mar, who played host to and were guardians of many Scots monarchs. Here, so legend has it, Mary, Queen of Scots was reconciled with Darnley and shortly thereafter granted the 5th Lord Erskine the much coveted earldom in 1565. One tradition holds that Mary's infant son, later James VI and I, died shortly after his birth and was replaced by the baby son of the Earl of Mar.

The Tower has seen six major alterations, the most dramatic being the sweeping Italianate staircase and dome added in the early 1700s by the 6th Earl of Mar. But it still retains original medieval features such as the dungeon, first floor well and magnificent oak roof timbers. Fully restored and furnished to a high standard, the Tower contains a unique collection of family portraits and silver on loan from the present Earl of Mar and Kellie.

medieval vaulting and a dungeon.

The Erskines were custodians of Mary Stuart during her infancy, and she lived in the tower for a time. An old story says that when Mary gave birth to James VI in Edinburgh Castle in 1566, the baby was stillborn, and the Earl of Mar's infant son was substituted (see also Edinburgh). Certainly, while still a boy, James stayed here, as did his mother.

The 6th Earl was an ardent Jacobite, and after the 1715 Uprising he was sent into exile. The story of the Erskines is told within the tower, and the present Earl has loaned a superb collection of paintings, including works by Raeburn and Kneller.

Alloa Museum and Gallery, in the Speirs Centre in Primrose Street, has exhibits tracing the history of the town.

TULLIBODY
4 miles W of Clackmannan on the B9140

Legend says that Tullibody was founded by King Kenneth McAlpine, the first king of Scots, who united the kingdoms of Dalriada and the Picts in AD 843. He called it "Tirlbothy", meaning the "oath of the crofts", as he and his followers made an oath there that they would not lay down their arms until their enemies or themselves were killed. A stone once stood at Baingle Brae where the oath was made.

Tullibody Auld Brig, which spans the River Devon, was built about 1535 by James Spittal, tailor to the royal family (see also Doune). In January 1560 the eastern most arch of the bridge was dismantled by Kirkcaldy of Grange to impede a French army, which was in Scotland in support of Mary of Guise, mother of Mary Stuart and widow of James V. However, the French army dismantled the roof of **Tullibody Auld Kirk**, which dated from the early 16th

century, and made a new bridge. In 1697. Thomas Bauchop, a local mason, was commissioned by John, 6th Earl of Mar, to build a new eastern arch.

Robert Dick, the eminent, but self taught, botanist was born in Tullibody in 1811.

FALKIRK

Falkirk is Stirlingshire's largest town, and received its burgh charter in 1600. It sits at an important point on the road from Edinburgh to Stirling, and nearby **Stenhousemuir** was once the meeting place of various drove roads coming down from the Highlands. Here great herds of cattle were kept before being sold at "trysts" and taken further south to the markets of Northern England. It has been estimated that over 24,000 head of cattle were sold annually at the three trysts held each year.

Falkirk, like Stirling, is located in an important part of Scotland. Here the country narrows, with the Firth of Forth to the east and the Campsie and Kilsyth Hills to the west. This meant that any army trying to march north from the Lowlands or south from the Highlands had to pass close to the town. For that reason, there have been two battles fought at Falkirk. One was in 1298, when William Wallace and his Scottish army were defeated by the English army of Edward I.

The second **Battle of Falkirk** was fought in 1746, when a Jacobite army defeated a Hanovarian army led by Lieutenant General Henry Hawley. After the defeat, Hawley was replaced by the Duke of Cumberland.

The name of the town means the "kirk of mottled stone", a reference to its first stone built medieval church. The present **Old Parish Church** dates from 1810, and incorporates fragments of an earlier church. Its tower dates from 1734. The church was the burial place for many prominent local families, and buried in the churchyard is said to be Sir John de Graeme, who was killed at the Battle of Falkirk fighting in William Wallace's army.

The **Town Steeple** was built in 1814, and was designed by the famous architect David Hamilton. It replaced an earlier building, which dated from the 17th century, and has traditionally been a meeting place for the people of the town. In 1927 the upper portion of the steeple was struck by lightning and had to be rebuilt.

Near Falkirk the two great Lowland canals - the Forth and Clyde and the Union Canal - meet. Thanks to the £84.5 million Millennium Link Project, they have recently been restored, and the magnificent new 120-feet high **Falkirk Wheel** at Rough Castle, which has become a tourist attraction in its own right, carries boats between one canal and the other (which are on different levels), within water filled "gondolas". It is the world's first (and as yet only) rotating lift for boats. It replaced a series of locks built in the early 19th century but which had been abandoned as the canals fell into disuse.

Centred on the village of Bonnybridge, two miles west of Falkirk, is the **Bonnybridge Triangle**, so called because there have been more sightings of UFOs and unexplained phenomena in this area than anywhere else in the UK. It all started in 1992 when a cross shaped cluster of lights was seen hovering above a road, and it has continued up until the present day, with mysterious football-sized lights, delta shaped craft and even spaceships with opening doors being seen as well.

The town sits on the line of the Antonine Wall, a massive turf wall on a stone base built on the orders of the Roman emperor Antonius Pius just after AD 138 (see also Bearsden and Milngavie). It stretched the 38 miles from the Firth of Clyde at Bowling to the Firth of Forth west of Bo'ness. **Rough Castle** (National Trust for Scotland) five miles from the town, is one of the best preserved of the wall's fortifications. Parts of the wall can be seen in the town's **Callendar Park**, in which you will also find **Callendar House**. This magnificent building, modelled on a French château, has played a major role in Scotland's history. In 1293 Alexander II granted land to one Malcolm de Kalynter, and he may have built a wooden castle. A descendant of Malcolm became involved in plots against David II in 1345, and the estates were forfeited and given to Sir William Livingstone, whose descendants lived there until the 18th century.

The Livingstones were close to Mary Stuart, and the queen visited the estate many times. In 1600 James VI rewarded the family by making them Earls of Linlithgow. But with the rise of the Jacobites, the family's fortunes went into decline. The 5th Earl was forced into exile for siding with the Old Pretender in 1715, and his daughter, Lady Anne married the ill-fated Earl of Kilmarnock, who was beheaded in London for his part in the 1745 Uprising (see also Kilmarnock). A story is told that on the evening before the Battle of Falkirk, the commander of the Hanovarian troops, General Hawley, dined at Callendar House with Lady Anne. He so enjoyed her company that he ignored requests to leave early to be appraised of the Jacobite movements. His troops were soundly beaten the following day.

In 1783 the house and estate were bought by the businessman William Forbes, whose descendants lived there for almost 200 years. It has now been restored by the local council as a heritage centre and museum, with a working Georgian kitchen, printer's and clockmaker's workrooms and a general store. In the Victorian library is an extensive archive of books, documents and photographs on the history of the area, and the Major William Forbes Falkirk exhibition traces the history of the town. The **Park Gallery**, which runs a series of art exhibitions and workshop activities, is also located in Callendar Park.

The Pineapple

AROUND FALKIRK

AIRTH

5 miles N of Falkirk on the A905

It is hard to imagine that a huge royal dockyard founded by James IV once stood close to this small village in the 15th and 16th centuries. Now it is visited mainly because of one of the most unusual buildings in Scotland - **The Pineapple** (National Trust for Scotland) in Dunmore Park. It is a summerhouse, built in 1761, and on top of it is a huge, 45-feet high pineapple made of stone. It is heated using an early form of central heating, as passages and cavities within the stone walls carry hot air through them. It can be rented as a holiday home. Also at Dunmore are 16 acres of gardens.

Parts of the nearby **Airth Castle** (now a hotel) date from the 14th century. An earlier castle stood on the site, and it was here that William Wallace's uncle, a priest, was held prisoner by the English before Wallace rescued him. The castle frontage as seen today dates from 1810, and was designed by David Hamilton.

Close to the castle are the ruins of a 16th century church.

GRANGEMOUTH

3 miles E of Falkirk on the A904

Grangemouth is a modern town, and the centre of Scotland's petrochemical industry. It was one of the country's first planned towns, having been established by Sir Laurence Dundas in the late 18th century to be the eastern terminus of the Forth and Clyde Canal. His son Thomas continued the work.

On Bo'ness Road is the **Grangemouth Museum**, which traces the history of the town up to the present day. The **Jupiter Urban Wildlife Garden** is off Wood Street, and was established in 1990 by

Zeneca (formerly ICI) and the Scottish Wildlife Trust on a piece of land that was once a railway marshalling yard. Surrounded by industrial buildings and smokestacks, this oasis of green shows how derelict industrial land can be cleaned up and reclaimed for nature. It has four ponds, an area of scrub birch known as The Wilderness, a wildlife plant nursery and a formal wildlife garden, as well as meadows, marshland and reed beds.

Stirling Castle

Zetland Park is the town's main open area, and offers putting, crazy golf, an adventure playground, a boating pond and tennis courts.

STIRLING

Stirling is one of the most strategically placed towns in Scotland, and was granted its royal charter in 1226. It sits astride the main route north from the Lowlands at Scotland's narrowest point, which is why it is so important. On the craggy plug of an ancient volcano a fort was build in prehistoric times, which evolved over the years to become a castle and royal residence. At the same time, a settlement grew on the eastern slope of the hill to cater for its needs. Now it is Scotland's newest city, as in 2002 it was granted city status as part of the Queen's Golden jubilee celebrations.

The old town is a mixture of buildings dating from the 15th century onwards, and a day could be spent walking about and admiring them. **Stirling Castle** (Historic Scotland) is a mixture of styles and dates. Some form of fortification has no doubt stood here from at last pre-Christian times, and it is one of the many sites in Scotland associated with King Arthur. It entered recorded history in the early 12th century, when Alexander I dedicated a chapel. There must also have been a palace of some kind, as Alexander died here in 1124. We next hear of it in 1174, when William the Lion was compelled to hand over various Scottish castles to Henry II of England, Stirling included.

During the Wars of Independence in the 13th and 14th centuries, Stirling Castle played a leading role. By this time it was back in Scottish hands, and Edward I was outraged by the fact that it was the last Lowland castle to hold out against his conquest of the country, and a barrier to further conquest in the north. So, in 1304, he set out to besiege it, and it eventually fell. For the next ten years the English garrisoned it. In 1313 Edward Bruce, brother of Robert I, laid siege to it, and its commander, Sir Philip Mowbray, agreed to surrender if the castle on June 24th 1314 if it was not relieved by an English army.

By this time Edward I was dead, and his son Edward II was on the throne. He did not want to lose Stirling, so he came north with a great army to relieve it. The Scots met this army at Bannockburn, and secured a great victory - one that sealed Scotland's independence.

All traces of the castle as it was at the time of Bannockburn have long gone. Most of the buildings now date from the 15th century and later. James III was the first of the Scottish kings to take an interest in its architecture, and built the Great Hall as a meeting place of the Scottish parliament and for great ceremonial occasions. James IV then began building a new palace in the Renaissance style, with his son James V finishing the work. In 1594 James VI had the Chapel Royal built, and these three buildings represent the most important architectural elements in the castle. It was within the Chapel Royal, on September 9th 1543, when she was barely nine months old, that Mary Stuart, later known as Mary, Queen of Scots, was crowned in a ceremony that was curiously lacking in pomp or majesty.

A curious tale is told of Stirling Castle. It concerns James IV and John Damien, the Abbot of Tongland in Kirkcudbrightshire, who earned the nickname of the **Frenzied Friar of Tongland** (see also Tongland). He was an Italian, and a learned man who spent a lot of time at court. In 1507 he convinced James IV that man could fly, and to prove it, he told him that he would jump from the walls of the castle and soar like a bird.

A date was set for the

flight to take place, and a bemused James IV and his court assembled on the battlements. Meanwhile, Abbot Damien had told his servants to amass a large collection of feathers from flying birds and construct a large pair of wings from them. However, his servants could not collect enough feathers of the right kind in time, so incorporated some chicken feathers as well. The Abbot duly presented himself on the battlements of the castle with the wings strapped to his back and wrists. No mention is made in contemporary accounts of how the king and the court viewed this unusual sight, but there must have been a few suppressed sniggers.

Damien stood on the battlements, made a short speech, and began flapping his wings. He then jumped - and fell like a stone, landing in the castle midden, on which more than the castle's kitchen scraps were deposited. His fall couldn't

Continued on page 235

Robert Burns Statue, Stirling

Around Stirling

Distance:	6.5 miles (10.4 kilometres)
Typical time:	195 mins
Height gain:	180 metres
Map:	Explorer 366
Walk:	www.walkingworld.com ID:2938
Contributor:	Tony Brotherton

Access Information:

Park in one of the streets behind the Tourist Information Centre in Dumbarton Road (any one of Allan Park, Park Road, Glebe Road, Victoria Square, Clarendon Place etc). These are beautifully laid out and prime examples of fine town planning and worth an admiring stroll around in their own right.

Description:

'Scotland's newest city' says the blurb (and surely more deserving than other contenders I've heard proposed for city status recently, in what has become an unseemly 'dash for cash') Given its historical and strategic importance, it is surprising that Stirling wasn't a city long before now. The walk follows part of the Historic Trail around the Old Town and visits Stirling Castle and the Beheading Stone, crosses the Forth via Stirling Auld Brig and takes in the Wallace Monument and Cambuskenneth Abbey.

Features:

Hills or Fells, River, Pub, Toilets, Museum, Play Area, Church, Castle, Wildlife, Birds, Flowers, Great Views, Butterflies, Cafe, Gift Shop, Food Shop, Good for Kids, Industrial Archaeology, Public Transport, Nature Trail, Restaurant, Tea Shop, Woodland, Ancient Monument

Walk Directions:

1 Starting from the TIC in Dumbarton Road, cross and turn left to reach Robert Burns' statue standing this side of Albert Halls. Turn right up road (Corn Exchange) to find statue of Rob Roy. Passing Rob Roy, turn left into Back Walk.

2 Walk uphill alongside town wall ('best preserved in Scotland').

3 Divert to visit Old Town at the sign for Church of the Holy Rude. Opposite church is Cowane's Hospital, with a representation of its founder above entrance. It originally provided accommodation for 'twelve decayed guild brethren'. Continue to road and turn left. On left is ruinous Mar's Wark, former palace built in 1570s by Earl of Mar. Turn downhill along Broad Street, centre of Old Town. Here is found Darnley's House, Tolbooth (music and arts centre) and Mercat Cross.

4 Walk down to pair of cannons. Turn left into St Mary's Wynd. Walk down to Settle Inn of 1733. To resume route along Upper Back Walk, retrace your steps to Waymark 3 and turn right. Continue up to Ladies' Rock. Here castle ladies would sit to watch tournaments (so 'tis said). Alternatively, you can take short cut to castle by turning back up St Mary's Wynd for few yards and then cutting up steep alleyway on right. This is unsigned but leads directly onto Castle Esplanade.

5 By nearby seat on left, one may look down on The King's Knot. This formal garden was laid out for King Charles I. Now it is grassed over, but symmetrical earthworks remain. Continue uphill through cemetery to reach Stirling Castle, 'the Key to the Kingdom'. Seven battle sites may be seen from its ramparts. Mary, Queen of Scots, once lived here, as did many Stuart kings. There are displays and exhibitions, guided tours and Argyll and Sutherland Highlanders' Regimental Museum.

6 Now take Castle Esplanade downhill to just before visitors' centre (free). Turn left down steps and along footpath to meet road. Here turn left. Walk down road with castle on left, to arrive at Ballengeich Cemetery gates. Pass through gates and bear right. Walk across cemetery and exit at far side onto gravel track curving downhill.

7 Keep on main path and aim for cannons on top of Mote Hill ahead. Climb hill to reach cannons and find Beheading Stone.

8 Retrace steps and turn left to descend to road. Cross with care into Union Street straight ahead. At large roundabout, turn left. With Laurencecroft Roundabout ahead, take underpass and bear right to reach Stirling Auld Brig. This was setting for William Wallace's victory in Battle of Stirling Bridge in 1297. Present-day bridge dates from late 15th Century.

9 Cross River Forth via Auld Brig. At road ahead, cross at lights and pass under railway bridge to walk along A9 road towards Wallace Monument, prominent atop its crag. Continue to Causewayhead Roundabout, then turn right along A907 for short distance, to reach children's play area in park.

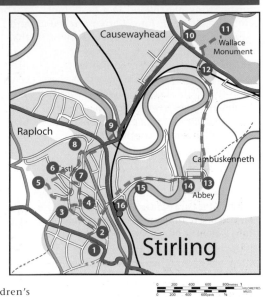

10 Walk across playground and take path leading to steps uphill.

11 Climb Abbey Craig to reach Wallace Monument. Resuming walk, retrace steps to road and turn left. Cross and turn right into Ladysneuk Road.

12 On reaching this level crossing, keep on along road soon to meet loop of river and distant view of castle.

13 Continue into Cambuskenneth Village and reach abbey, founded in 1147 for David I. Robert the Bruce held parliament here in 1326 and James III and Margaret of Denmark are buried in grounds. Today only its 14th Century belfry survives.

14 Retrace steps and turn left along South Street to reach footbridge over river.

15 Back in Stirling, bear left and follow road, forking left to meet river again. Keep ahead along pathway and then along road to reach Stirling Station.

16 Cross railway bridge. Now cross road in front of station and turn left to reach main shops and enter pedestrianised area. Follow signs for tourist information centre along Port Street and turn right into Dumbarton Road.

have been that far, as all he succeeded in doing was breaking a leg. When he later discovered that his servants had incorporated chicken feathers in the wings, he blamed this for the failure of his flight. The court poet William Dunbar was present at this attempt at the world's first manned flight, and wrote some verses about it.

The **Church of the Holy Rude** on St John Street is Stirling's parish church. The word "rude" in this context means "cross", and is also found in Holyrood Abbey in Edinburgh. It dates from the 15th century, and was built on the site of an earlier place of worship at the command of James IV, who, tradition says, worked alongside the masons during its construction. It is one of the finest medieval churches in Scotland, and has its original oak roof. Within the church, in 1567, the infant James VI was crowned king of Scotland in a Protestant ceremony at which John Knox preached a sermon and without the attendance of his mother, Mary Stuart, who was being held prisoner in Loch Leven Castle. What is not generally known is that James (who later became James VI and I of England and Great Britain) had been christened Charles. James was chosen as his "royal" name to continue the tradition of having a "James" on the Scottish throne.

It is one of only two still functioning churches in Great Britain to have witnessed a coronation, the other one being Westminster Abbey. From just after the reformation until the 1930s a wall divided the church in two, with two independent congregations worshipping at the same time.

The kirkyard was once the castle's tilting ground, where great tournaments of jousting and horsemanship were held. One of the monuments in the kirkyard is the **Martyr's Monument**, commemorating two women who were drowned for their religious beliefs at Wigtown in 1685 (see also Wigtown). The **Star Pyramid** also commemorates the Covenanting martyrs of the 17th century. A local legend says that a man was interred within it, sitting at a table laden with food. **Lady's Rock** is next to the kirkyard, and was where the ladies of the court sat and watched staged events take place on the fields below. Close by is **Cowane's Hospital**, on which work started in 1637 and finished in 1649. It is named after John Cowane, a Stirling merchant, who bequeathed funds to establish an almshouse for 12 unsuccessful merchants, or "decayed guildsmen" of the town. It was later used as a school and an epidemic hospital, and is now a venue for ceilidhs and concerts. Above the door is a statue of Cowane himself.

The **King's Knot** sits beneath the castle and church, on the south side, and is all that is left of a formal garden, originally planted in the 1490s, though the knot itself is much older - possibly early 14th century. It is in the shape of an octagonal stepped mound nine feet high, now grassed over. Near it used to be the **King's Park** (where houses now stand), once a favourite hunting ground for the Scottish kings.

The **Old Town Jail**, down the slope in the city itself, was opened in 1847 to take the prisoners that were formerly held in the Tolbooth. From 1888 until 1935 it was used as a military prison. Now it has been reopened as a tourist attraction, and shows what life was like for prisoners and wardens in the 19th century. You'll also meet a character called Jock Rankin, who was the town's hangman. If, during your visit, a prisoner should try to escape, you should remain calm and follow the advice of the warden!

The intriguingly named **Mar's Wark** is in Broad Street, close to the parish church. It was the "wark" (meaning work, or building) of the sixth Earl of Mar, Regent of Scotland and guardian of the young James VI. In 1570 he began building a new Renaissance palace using French masons that would reflect his status and power, and Mar's Wark was the result. In the 18th century it became a military hospital, but soon after fell into disrepair. Now all that is left of the building is a façade along the street front.

On the opposite side of the street is **Argyll's Lodging** (Historic Scotland), a Renaissance-style mansion built about 1630 by Sir William Alexander, the founder of Nova Scotia (see also Edinburgh and Menstrie). It was further enlarged by the 9th Earl of Argyll in the 1670s, and is possibly the best example of a 17th century town house in Scotland. Most of the rooms have been restored, showing what life would have been like when the Earl lived there.

Stirling is one of the few Scottish towns with parts of its **Town Wall** still standing. It was built in 1547 as a defence against the English armies of Henry VIII when he was trying to force a marriage between his son Edward and Mary Stuart (a time known as the "Rough Wooing"). The remaining parts stretch along the south side of the town, from near the Old Town Jail to Dumbarton Road. Incorporated into the Thistle Shopping Mall is the 16th century **Bastion**, one of the wall's defensive towers. It contains a vaulted guardroom above an underground chamber, and has a small display about the history of the town. There was no wall to the north of the town, as attacks never came from that quarter, though people who lived there were supposed to build thick, high walls at the backs of their gardens as a defence, and keep them in good repair.

One bloody association with Scotland's past is to be found at the **Beheading Stone**, well to the north of the castle. It was here, in 1425, that James I took his revenge on Murdoch, Duke of Albany, his two sons and the Earl of Lennox his father-in-law by having them beheaded. The Duke's father had controlled Scotland for 18 years while the English held James captive, and he and his cronies had brought the country to its knees by their greed and cruelty. Their lands were forfeited to the crown, and James gave them to his supporters.

The **Tolbooth** sits at the heart of the old town. It was built in 1704 by Sir William Bruce, and was where the town council met and looked after the affairs of the burgh. A courthouse and jail were added in 1809. It is now used as a venue for concerts and rehearsals. The **Mercat Cross**, close to the Tolbooth, has the figure of a unicorn on top, and this is known locally as the "puggy".

Two famous battles have been fought near Stirling. The **Battle of Stirling Bridge** took place in 1297, when William Wallace defeated an English army under John de Warenne, Earl of Surrey, and Hugh de Cressingham. Wallace, who was a guerrilla fighter and a master tactician, used the bridge to divide the English forces - leaving one contingent on each bank - before launching his attack. It was a major set back for Edward I, and he more or less had to start his conquest of the country all over again. The bridge in those days was a wooden one, and the present **Old Stirling Bridge**, which stands upstream from the original, was built in the late 15th century. Up until 1831, when **Stirling New Bridge** was built downstream, this was the lowest crossing point of the Forth, which made it one of the most important bridges in Scotland

The other famous battle was the **Battle of Bannockburn**, fought to the south of the town in 1314. The actual site of the battle still arouses much debate, but there is no doubt that it was a defining moment in Scotland's history. Edward I had died by this time, and his son Edward II, a much weaker man, was in charge of the English army, which was trying to reach Stirling Castle to relieve it. Robert the Bruce, one of Scotland's great heroes, achieved a stunning victory - one that secured the country's status as an independent nation. The **Bannockburn Heritage Centre** (National Trust for Scotland), on the A872 two miles south of the town, commemorates this victory. There are exhibitions, an audiovisual display and a huge statue of Bruce on his warhorse.

CLIVE RAMSAY

26-28 Henderson Street, Bridge of Allan,
Stirlingshire FK9 4HR
Tel: 01786 831616 Shop: 01786 833903
e-mail: jonnymitvhell@aol.com
website: www.cliveramsay.com

Bridge of Allan sits just off the M9 motorway connecting Central Scotland with Inverness and the north. So if you're travelling along it, why not make a detour into the affluent and historic town of Bridge of Allan? There you will find one of the best delicatessens and restaurants in the country - **Clive Ramsay**. It was founded in 1984 by Clive and his wife Violet, and since that time has earned an enviable reputation throughout central Scotland as a first class restaurant and purveyor of fine foods.

In fact, over the years it has won many awards, including the BBC Good Food Shop of the Year Award in 1991 and the McClennan Scottish Cheese Award three times running. This is all down to Clive's specialist knowledge and love of good food and fresh produce. He scours not just Great Britain, but the world in search of new products and lines that will enhance his reputation even further, and entice customers into his shop.

The lines carried by the shop are extensive. Clive sells the Best of Taste Company's range of hand-made coulis dessert sauces, for instance, which use natural ingredients throughout. The flavours range from apricot, damson with sloe gin and Raspberry to black cherry with kirsch, wild blueberry and strawberry. Each one is delicious and wholesome. He also stocks Innocent Smoothies, a range of drinks made from 100 per cent fresh juice. Choose from such flavours as strawberries and raspberries, blackberries and blueberries, oranges, bananas and pineapples and mangoes and passion fruit. They are delicious and refreshing, with each smoothie containing over three quarters of a pound of fruit.

Or how about Clive Ramsay's range of Bar B Bar barbecue sauces? Or the Tipsage Farm of Tunbridge Wells Gin Collection? Or even the full range of Blinding's cooking sauces? All are here, and a whole lot more besides. And the delicatessen has recently expanded its services by opening a café next door, where the food is all freshly made using the finest local produce wherever possible, and often using some of the products found in the shop. The Café is licensed and open seven days a week from 8am until late. A breakfast menu is served until 11.30am after which an extensive main menu is available. This offers mouthwatering choices such as Pot Roast Highland Beef with Oriental Glaze or Ricotta Ravioli, as well as a large selection of fish dishes which include Prawn Tagliatelli or Chargrilled Swordfish with Pecorino Sauce.

You can't afford to miss this establishment. The service is friendly and the prices represent great value for money.

National Wallace Monument

Scotland's other national hero, of course, is William Wallace, and on Abbey Craig, to the east of the town and across the river, is the **National Wallace Monument**. This spectacular tower is 220 feet high, with 246 steps, and from the top you get a panoramic view that takes in the Forth Bridges to the east and Ben Lomond to the west. Here you can learn about the Battle of Stirling Bridge, plus see a re-creation of Wallace's travesty of a trial at Westminster, when he was charged with of treason, even though he wasn't English. You can even gaze on his great two-handed broadsword, which is five feet six inches long.

The scant ruins of **Cambuskenneth Abbey** (Historic Scotland) also lie on the eastern banks of the Forth. David I founded it as an abbey in 1140 for Augustinian monks, and in 1326 Robert the Bruce held an important parliament here. It suffered greatly at the hands of various English armies, and by 1378 was in ruins. It was rebuilt in the early 15th century through royal patronage. The detached bell tower of the abbey is more or less complete, though only the foundations of the rest of the buildings survive. James III and his queen, Margaret of Denmark, are buried before the high altar, and a monument marks the spot. In 1488 the king had been assassinated near Bannockburn after his defeat at the Battle of Sauchieburn, where his son, the future James IV, was on the opposing side.

The **Smith Art Gallery and Museum** in Albert Place chronicles Stirling's long history through displays, exhibitions and artefacts. It has a fine collection of paintings, including ones by Naysmith and Sir George Harvey, who painted great works depicting Scottish history. One of the more unusual exhibits in the museum is the world's oldest football, found in Mary Stuart's bedchamber in Stirling Castle and dated to the late 16th century.

AROUND STIRLING

BRIDGE OF ALLAN
2 miles N of Stirling off the M9

Bridge of Allan, which is almost a suburb of Stirling nowadays, was once a small spa town and watering place with a pump room and baths. Now it is chiefly known for being the home of Stirling University, based in the grounds of the **Airthrie Estate**, with its picturesque loch. In 1617, James VI wanted to establish a college or university at Stirling, but it was not until 1967 that his wish came true, when the first 180 students enrolled. Now it has over 9,000 students, and is one of the premier

COLLECTIONS

58 Henderson Street, Bridge of Allan,
Stirlingshire FK9 4HS
Tel: 01786 833295 Fax: 01786 471324

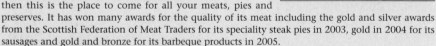

Set in the town of Bridge of Allan, just off the M9 motorway
north of Stirling, **Collections** is a shop selling a wonderful
range of gifts, cards and home ideas that are sure to appeal to
the most discerning of tastes. There are fantastic cards, photo
frames, beautiful and unusual jewellery, lots of candles,
Crabtree and Evelyn toiletries, pot pourri, ceramics, flowers,
soft toys, children's gifts and baby items to mention but a few. Plus there are handbags and purses by
Tula and jewellery by well known designer Kit Heath.

The shop is owned and managed by Isobel Taylor, who brings a wealth of experience to selling
quality items at affordable prices. She and her staff are always on hand to offer knowledgeable and

helpful advice should you need it. No pressure
will be put upon you should you choose to
browse, and indeed before you buy anything, you
are well advised to browse, as the full range of
items on sale is huge! To the south of Bridge of
Allan is Stirling, Scotland's newest city, a place
that is well worth exploring as it crammed with
history and heritage. When visiting, why not
take a trip north to Collections in Bridge of Allan,
and see for yourself the huge range of items that
are on offer. You won't be disappointed.

DAVID BENNETT & SON

82 High Street, Dunblane FK15 0AY
Tel: 01786 823212
website: www.bennettsthebutcher.co.uk

David Bennett and Son has been trading in Dunblane since
1901, and today its reputation is as high as ever. If you're
enjoying a self-catering, caravan or camping holiday in the area,
then this is the place to come for all your meats, pies and
preserves. It has won many awards for the quality of its meat including the gold and silver awards
from the Scottish Federation of Meat Traders for its speciality steak pies in 2003, gold in 2004 for its
sausages and gold and bronze for its barbeque products in 2005.

For over 20 years, the beef at David Bennett and Son has been sourced
locally from one farm ensuring the highest quality linked to competitive
prices. The farmer who rears the beef even comes into the shop every
Monday morning to check that the quality is being maintained. It is
Aberdeen Angus cross and the animals are monitored daily, so traceability
and quality of the meat is assured.

The wide range of sausages, burgers and cooked meats are all freshly
made daily on the premises. The shop also stocks its own range of tasty
preserves, marinades and chutneys. Special freezer orders can be catered
for, as can individually seasoned or marinated meats for the barbeque.
The staff are friendly and experienced, and can help you choose the right
cut of meat for your needs. The present owner is Graham Fleming, great
grandson of the shop's founder, and he is determined to maintain the
high standards set all those years ago.

universities in Scotland.

Airthrie was owned by Sir Robert Abercrombie, who was instrumental in setting up the village as a spa, having had the waters of a local spring analysed. In 1844 the estate was bought by a Major Henderson, who developed the town even further. The **Fountain of Ninevah** on Fountain Road was built by him in 1851 to commemorate the archaeological excavations going on at Nineveh at the time. Though healing waters are no longer taken, other, equally interesting, liquids are most certainly consumed. **The Bridge of Allan Brewery Company**, a microbrewery in Queens Lane, has tours showing how beer is produced.

Bridge of Allan Parish Church (formerly know as Holy Trinity Church) was built in 1860, and inside it are some furnishings designed by the Glasgow architect Charles Rennie Mackintosh.

DUNBLANE

5 miles N of Stirling off the M9

Before local government reorganisation, Dunblane (and most of the area north and north west of Stirling) was in Perthshire. This small town, or more properly city, is famous for two things. The first is the horrific shooting that took place here in 1996 when 16 schoolchildren and their teacher were killed in a local school. The **Dunblane Memorial Garden**, built in 1998, commemorates the victims, and is within Dunblane Cemetery.

The second is the **Cathedral Church of St Blane and St Lawrence** (Historic Scotland) sits on the site of Celtic monastery founded by St Blane in about AD602. He had been born on Bute, and had founded a great monastery there as well (see also Bute). Dunblane monastery would have been a cleared space

GRAHAM STEWART

91-95 High Street, Dunblane, Perthshire FK15 0ER
Tel: 01786 825244 Fax: 01786 825993
e-mail: info@grahamstewartsilversmith.co.uk
website: www.grahamstewartsilversmith.co.uk

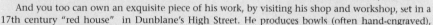

Set in the small, attractive city of Dunblane, a few miles north of Stirling, **Graham Stewart** is a well established and highly respected designer and maker of fine silver and jewellery. His beautiful work is collected widely, and can be found in many public collections. He was even asked to design and produce the "Honours of Scotland" sculpture presented to the new Scottish Parliament by the Queen.

And you too can own an exquisite piece of his work, by visiting his shop and workshop, set in a 17th century "red house" in Dunblane's High Street. He produces bowls (often hand-engraved),

tumblers, centre pieces, candlesticks, traditional Scottish quaichs, spoons etc and a range of wonderful jewellery. Graham also sells a range of items manufactured by other silversmiths, all personally chosen by him to reflect the best in craftsmanship and value for money. And if it's ceramics, glass, furniture, paintings, wood carvings, rugs, ironwork and toys you want, Graham sells these as well.

Graham is a graduate of Gray's School of Art in Aberdeen, and in 1999 was awarded the "best crafts/shopping" award from the local tourist office. As well as himself, he now employs three full time craftsmen to realise his exciting designs. You will get plenty of friendly advice, and if you want to commission an individual piece, Graham will be happy to advise. His shop has often been called an "Aladdin's Cave" and this is no idle boast. Visit it and see for yourself.

surrounded by a low wall, or "rath", within which would have been wooden churches, monks' cells, school rooms, brewhouses and workshops.

What you see nowadays dates mainly from the 13th century, and was built by Bishop Clement, who was elected bishop in 1233. He decided that the only part of the previous 12th century Norman church which would be left standing was the tower, though two extra storeys were added to it in the 15th century. It is not a cathedral in the style of Elgin, St Andrews or any of the great English establishments. Rather it is an intimate church with no side aisles or transepts.

View to Dunblane Cathedral

The diocese was established in about 1150 by the Earl of Strahearn, and a simple stone cathedral built. However, the diocese was a poor one, and the Pope eventually authorised the bishops of Dunkeld and Glasgow to give a fourth of their income to help establish it properly. With this income, Clement managed to build most of the cathedral we see today before his death in 1258.

In the 16th century, with the arrival of Protestantism, only the choir was used for worship, and the nave fell into decay, with the roof collapsing about 1600. The city also fell into decay, and it became a small weaving centre. In 1898 the whole building was restored under the direction of Sir Rowand Anderson, a noted Scottish architect, and in 1914 Sir Robert Lorimer did further work on the choir, with the present choir stalls - one of the glories of the cathedral - being designed by him.

Within the **Dean's House**, built in 1624 by Dean James Pearson during the time the Church of Scotland was episcopal, is a small museum, which explains the history of the city and its cathedral. **Bishop Leighton's Library** is housed in a building that dates from 1681 and contains over 4,000 books, some of them priceless.

With the coming of the railways, Dunblane became a popular place in which to holiday, and it regained some of its former prosperity. **Dunblane Hydro** was built in 1875 to cash in on the tourist boom, and it is still a luxury hotel to this day.

About three miles north east of the town is the site of the **Battle of Sheriffmuir** (see also Callander), one of the deciding battles in the 1715 Jacobite Uprising. It took place on November 13th 1715, and was an unusual battle in that the outcome was a stalemate. The

Jacobite forces were led by John Erskine, 11th Earl of Mar, and the Government forces by John Campbell, 2nd Duke of Argyll.

FINTRY
12 miles SW of Stirling on the B818

This charming village sits on the northern slopes of the **Campsies**, that great range of hills that forms a northern backdrop for the city of Glasgow. There are some fine walks on the hills, which are popular with Glaswegians at weekends and holidays. The **Loup of Fintry**, east of the village, is a fine waterfall caused by the Endrick Water tumbling down a 94-feet high slope.

Culcreuch Castle (now a country house hotel) is a 700 year old tower house within a large estate that was once owned by the Galbraiths. The last Galbraith chieftain to live there was Robert Galbraith, who fled to Ireland in 1630 after killing a guest in his home. **Carron Valley Reservoir**, to the east of the village, was built in the 19th century to supply Falkirk and Grangemouth with a water supply. It now offers trout fishing (permit required).

Fintry Parish Church dates from 1823, and its method of building was unusual. The former church was too small for the growing congregation, so the present church was built around it. Only when it was complete was the earlier church, which had continued in use, demolished.

KIPPEN
9 miles W of Stirling on the B822

This attractive little village sits to the south of that expanse of flat land called **Flanders Moss**. At one time it was peat bog, then, in the 18th century, Lord Kames, a law lord and agricultural improver, began removing the peat to get at the fertile bands of clay beneath (see also Blair Drummond). There are still a few remnants of the original peat bog left, and they have been declared Areas of Special Scientific Interest.

It has, in **Kippen Parish Church**, built in 1825, one of the finest post Reformation churches in Scotland. The Carmichael Memorial Window was installed in 1985, and is the work of John K. Clarke. The ruins of the old church, built in 1691, still survive, surrounded by an old graveyard.

In 1891, a man called Duncan Buchanan planted a vineyard in Kippen within a glasshouse, and one of the vines, later to be called the **Kippen Vine**, grew to be the largest in the world. When fully grown, it had an annual crop of over 2,000 bunches of table grapes, and in 1958 created a record by producing 2,956 bunches. By this time it was enormous, covering an area of 5,000 square feet and stretching for 300 feet within four large greenhouses. It became a tourist attraction, and people came from all over Scotland and abroad to see it.

But alas, the vinery closed down in 1964 (when it could also boast the second and third largest vines in the world) and the Kippen Vine was unceremoniously chopped down by Selby Buchanan, Duncan's son. The land was later used for housing.

ARNPRIOR
10 miles W of Sterling on the A811

In the early 16th century, a man called John Buchanan, who had styled himself the **King of Kippen**, lived in this small village. One day a party of hunters was returning to Stirling Castle with some venison for James V's court, and passed John's castle. John captured them and confiscated the venison. The hunters told him that the meat was for the king, but John merely replied that if James was King of Scotland, then he was King of Kippen.

The king was duly informed of this, and instead of being angry, found the incident amusing. He and some courtiers rode out from Stirling one day to pay the King of Kippen a visit. He approached John's castle, and demanded that he be allowed to enter. His demand was refused by a guard, who told the king that John Buchanan was at dinner, and could not be disturbed.

James V had a habit of dressing up in peasant's clothes and slipping out of his palaces alone to meet and speak to his subjects and gauge their opinions of their king and country. When he did this, he assumed the guise of the "Guidman of Ballengeich" (meaning "The Goodman of Ballengeich"), Ballengeich being the name of a pathway he always took down from Stirling Castle when in disguise.

He therefore told the guard to tell Buchanan that the Guidman of Ballengeich was at his door, and he humbly requested an audience with the King of Kippen. When informed, John Buchanan knew who his visitor was, and rushed out in trepidation. But James greeted him cordially, and laughed at the escapade of the venison. Buchanan invited the king into his home to dine, and the king agreed. Soon the company was merry, and the king told Buchanan that he could take as much venison as he liked from the royal hunters that passed his door. He also invited the King of Kippen to visit his brother monarch at Stirling any time he liked. The "king" was later killed at the Battle of Pinkie in 1547.

To the east of Kippen, and off the A811, is the village of **Gargunnock**, with a picturesque parish church built in 1774.

PORT OF MENTEITH
14 miles W of Stirling on the B8034

This little village sits on the shore of the **Lake of Menteith**, sometimes erroneously called the only lake (as opposed to loch) in Scotland. However, there are several bodies of water in Scotland - some natural, some man made - which are referred to as lakes (see also Kirkcudbright, Stenton and Ellon).

But there is no doubting that the Lake of Menteith is one of Scotland's most beautiful stretches of water. It is only a mile wide by a mile-and-a-half long, with low hills sloping down towards it northern shores. Its name is probably a corruption of Laigh (meaning a flat piece of land) of Menteith, as the land to the south of the lake, Flanders Moss, is flat.

On the island of Inchmahome are the beautiful ruins of **Inchmahome Priory** (Historic Scotland), within which Mary Stuart was kept after the Battle of Pinkie in 1547. Within the re-roofed chapter house are many carved effigies and tombstones. The priory was founded in 1238 by Walter Comyn, Earl of Menteith, for Augustinian canons. In 1306, 1308 and 1310, Robert the Bruce visited the place, as the then prior had sworn allegiance to Edward I of England. No doubt Robert was pressurising him to change his mind.

On the nearby **Inchtulla** the Menteiths had their castle, and on **Dog Island** the Earl kept his hunting dogs.

The priory can be reached by a small ferry from the jetty at Port of Menteith.

ABERFOYLE
17 miles W of Stirling on the A821

Aberfoyle has been called the Gateway to the Trossachs (see also Callander), and sits on the River Forth after it emerges from beautiful Loch Ard. The six-mile long **Duke's Road** (named after a Duke

The Trossachs

of Montrose who laid out the road in 1886) goes north from the village to the Trossachs proper, and has some good views over Lochs Drunkie and Venachar.

Standing close to the village's main road is a gnarled oak known as the **Poker Tree**. In Scott's novel *Rob Roy*, Baillie Nicol Jarvie, a Glasgow magistrate and cousin of Rob Roy, gets involved in a fight with a Highlander at a local inn, and draws the red hot poker from the fire to defend himself. A poker was later hung from the tree to remind people of the escapade.

The **Scottish Wool Centre** is situated within the village, and tells the story of Scottish wool. You can visit the Spinner's Cottage, and have a go at spinning wool into yarn. There are also occasional visits from local shepherds, who put on sheepdog demonstrations. There is also a shop where woollen items - from coats to blankets - can be bought.

It was in Aberfoyle that the famous and mysterious disappearance of the

Rev. Robert Kirk, minister at Aberfoyle Parish Church, took place. He was born in 1644, and had an abiding interest in fairies, even writing a book called *The Secret Commonwealth of Elves, Fauns and Fairies*.

Legend states that the fairies were none too pleased that Robert had revealed their secrets. In 1692, while walking on Doon Hill, well known in the area as one of the entrances to the fairy realm, Robert disappeared. People claimed that he had been taken to the fairy kingdom, and that one day he would come back, looking no older than he did when he disappeared. To this day, he has not returned.

Another legend states that Robert's wife was given the chance of getting her husband back. He would appear, she was told, during Sunday service in the kirk, and she had to throw a knife at him, which should penetrate his flesh. Robert did appear during the service, but his wife could not bring herself to throw the knife, so he disappeared once more.

Robert Kirk was indeed a minister in Aberfoyle in the 17th century, and he did indeed disappear one day while out walking. Did the fairies take him? Or was he the victim of a more earthly crime? No one will ever know - unless he turns up again to give his account of what happened!

South of Aberfoyle, near the conservation village of **Gartmore**, is the **Cunninghame Graham Memorial** (National Trust for Scotland). Robert Cunninghame Graham of Ardoch (born Robert Bontine) was a Scottish author and politician who died in 1936. The memorial once stood at Castlehill in Dumbarton, but was moved here in 1980.

KILLEARN

18 miles W of Stirling on the A875

Killearn Glen is a picturesque area of deciduous woodland over 250 years old with narrow footpaths. The village was the birthplace, in 1506, of George Buchanan, Protestant reformer and tutor to James VI, who greatly admired him. He was a noted linguist, and could speak Latin, Greek, French, Gaelic, Spanish, Hebrew and Italian. He also wrote plays, mostly in Latin, and now lies buried in the Greyfriars kirkyard in Edinburgh. The **Buchanan Monument**, built in 1788, commemorates him.

DRYMEN

20 miles W of Stirling off the A811

During World War II, **Buchanan Castle** was a military hospital. Its most famous patient was Rudolph Hess, Hitler's deputy, who was kept here after he parachuted into Scotland in 1941 on a secret mission to see the Duke of Hamilton (see also Eaglesham). The castle itself dates from 1855, and was built by the 4th Duke of Montrose after the former castle was destroyed by fire three years previously. The roof was removed in 1955 to prevent the paying of taxes on it, and it is now partly ruinous, though it can be viewed from the outside.

Drymen is on the West Highland Way, the footpath that stretches from Milngavie on the outskirts of Glasgow to Fort William. It is also the gateway to the eastern, and less busy, shores of Loch Lomond, which lie three miles away. The

small village of **Balmaha** (also on the West Highland Way) sits on the shore of the loch, and should be visited for the wonderful views it gives of Britain's largest sheet of water. **Balfron**, four miles east of Drymen, is an attractive village with a parish church that dates from 1832. Alexander "Greek" Thomson, the noted architect whose work can bee seen in Glasgow, was born in Balfron in 1817.

BLAIR DRUMMOND

6 miles NW of Stirling on the A84

Blair Drummond Safari and Leisure Park is one of the most visited tourist attractions in Scotland. You can tour the 1,500-acre park by car or coach, and see animals such as elephants, lions, zebras, giraffes, white rhino and ostriches in conditions that allow them plenty of freedom. You can take a boat trip round Chimp Island, watch the sea lion show or glide above the lake on the "Flying Fox".

In the 18th century Blair Drummond was the home of Henry Home, a law lord who sat in the High Court as Lord Kames (see also Kippen).

Ploughing at Balfron

DOUNE

6 miles NW of Stirling on the A84

The bridge across the River Teith in this picturesque village was built by James Spittal, tailor to James IV (see also Tullibody). Legend has it that he arrived at the ferry that once operated where the bridge now stands without any money, and the ferryman refused to take him across. So, out of spite, he had the bridge built to deprive the ferryman of a livelihood.

Doune Castle (Historic Scotland) is one of the best preserved 14th century castles in Scotland, and was the seat of the Earls of Moray. It stands where the River Ardoch meets the Teith, and was originally built for Robert Stewart, Duke of Albany, son of Robert II and Regent of Scotland during the minority of James I. Later James had the Duke's son executed for plotting against the crown, and the castle passed to him. Later the castle was acquired by Sir James Stewart, the first Lord Doune, and then by the Morays. It has two main towers connected by a Great Hall with a high wooden ceiling. In 1883 the 14th Earl of Moray restored the castle. It is visited each year by many fans of Monty Python, as some of the scenes in *Monty Python and the Holy Grail* were filmed here.

The village itself gained its burgh charter in 1611, and originally stood close to the castle. In the early 1700s, however, the village and its 17th century **Mercat Cross** were moved to their present position. The village was, at one time, famous as a centre of pistol making. The industry was started in about 1646 by a man called Thomas Cadell, and so accurate and well made were his guns that they soon became prized possessions. By the 18th century Cadell's descendants were all involved in making guns, and began exporting them to the Continent. It is said that the first pistol fired in the American War of Independence was made in Doune.

On the B824 between Doune and Dunblane is the **Sir David Stirling Memorial Statue**, commemorating the founder member of the Special Air Services (better known as the SAS) during World War II.

DEANSTON

8 miles NW of Stirling on the B8032

Deanston is a village on the banks of the River Teith, built round the Adephi Cotton Mill, founded in 1785 and designed by Sir Richard Arkwright. It passed through several hands before finally closing in 1965. Now the mill houses the **Deanston Distillery**, which makes a range of whiskies, using the same water that once powered the weaving machines. It is not open to the public.

CALLANDER

13 miles NW of Stirling on the A84

This pleasant holiday town stands to the east of the Trossachs, and has some

Watchman's House, Callander

DESIRABLES

33 Main Street, Callander, Perthshire FK17 8DO
Tel:01877 330331
e-mail: desirablesbyval@aol.com   website: www.desirablesbyval.co.uk

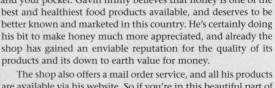

Opened in September 2004, **Desirables** has, in that short time, earned an enviable reputation as a place for the very best in stylish and up to the minute fashion. It is set in the picturesque town of Callander, and is owned and personally managed by Valerie Gray, who brings a wealth of experience to selling only the best clothes and accessories available. She offers friendly and impartial advice on the clothing that is just right for you. The shop stocks a wide range of fashion labels, day wear by

Olsen, quirky stylish Oska seperates and trendy Jocavi and Elisa Cortes. Smart linen and knitwear seperates by Orla of Ireland. Eveningwear/cocktail wear by After Six. For the mother/bride/groom they have a fabulous selection from Presen of Barcelona, Condici and danish designer Elinette for the wedding guests.

And to complement the fashion clothing, Desirables also stocks a wide range of accessories that are elegant and exciting. The range of hats, for instance, is hard to find anywhere else, and includes creations by local milliner and designer Clare Workman. You can choose from jewellery by such designers and manufacturers as Ted Lapidus, Yaron Morhaim (from Israel) and Chartage, from Belgium, plus many more. There are also scarves, wraps, Radley Tula bags and, of course, shoes that offer not only comfort and style, but value for money as well. So why not head to Desirables and treat your loved one - or yourself - to a new stunning outfit? You won't be disappointed.

HONEY ET CETERA

2 Cross Street, Callander, Perthshire FK17 8EA
Tel: 01877 339033
website: www.getyourhoneyhere.com

Gavin Millar has always been interested in honey, bees and beekeeping. He worked in retail and hotel management before spending time in the USA and UK with commercial honey farmers. Now he has set up on his own in the lovely town of Callander selling a range of honeys that are delicious and represent great value for money. Tasters are available.

And it's not just honey that **Honey Et Cetera** sells. There is also a wide range of items ranging from beeswax products, including polishes and cosmetics, to jams, chutneys, biscuits, salad dressings and so on. You could spend a happy hour or two just browsing the many fascinating products sold here!

The honey sold in Honey Et Cetera comes from abroad as well as from Scotland and there is sure to be a honey that suits both your taste and your pocket. Gavin firmly believes that honey is one of the

best and healthiest food products available, and deserves to be better known and marketed in this country. He's certainly doing his bit to make honey much more appreciated, and already the shop has gained an enviable reputation for the quality of its products and its down to earth value for money.

The shop also offers a mail order service, and all his products are available via his website. So if you're in this beautiful part of Perthshire, be sure to visit Callander and call in at one of the most fascinating shops in the area - Honey Et Cetera.

wonderful walking country on its doorstep. It is home to the **Rob Roy and Trossachs Visitor Centre**, housed in a former church in Ancaster Square, and, as the name suggests, tells the story of both the Trossachs and its most famous son, Rob Roy MacGregor (see also Balquhidder). His real name was Robert MacGregor (1671-1734) and even today people still cannot agree on whether he was a crook, a freedom fighter or the Scottish Robin Hood (though you don't have to guess which opinion the Visitor Centre prefers).

The Duke of Montrose confiscated his lands in 1712, and he was imprisoned by the English in the 1720s. He was made famous by two books - Daniel Defoe's *Highland Rogue* and Sir Walter Scott's *Rob Roy*, as well as by the recent film starring Liam Neeson and Jessica Lange. An earlier film, *Rob Roy the Highland Rogue*, was made in 1953, starring Richard Todd and Glynis Johns.

There's no denying that the man was an outstanding leader who could read and write in English and Gaelic, and possessed a large library. It was Sir Walter Scott who made him behave

River Teith, Callander

dishonourably at the Battle of Sheriffmuir (see Dunblane), when in fact he acquitted himself with courage and honour fighting for the Jacobites. At his funeral on New Year's Day 1735, people came from all over Scotland to pay their respects.

Also in Callander is the **Hamilton Toy Museum**, five rooms of model cars, planes, dolls, teddy bears and such TV collectables as Thunderbird, Star Trek and Star Wars figures.

DELI ECOSSE

10 North Ancaster Square, Callander, Stirlingshire FK17 8ED
Tel: 01877 331220

There's always a warm welcome at the **Deli Ecosse**. It stocks a wide range of hand-made Scottish produce, as well as Continental and fresh-baked bread, ready made meals, tasty sweets and savouries, wines and ales. If you're camping or having a self-catering holiday, head here for all your food needs. There is also a small café where you can relax over a cup of coffee and something special from the deli's range. Lunch boxes and hampers can be made up to order. There's something to suit everyone at Deli Ecosse.

LOCH KATRINE
23 miles NW of Stirling close to the A821

There is no doubt that Loch Katrine is one of the most beautiful lochs in Scotland. It is surrounded by craggy hills, which in autumn blaze with orange and gold. But the loch as you see it today has more to do with man than nature. In the mid-19th century, the loch became a huge reservoir for the city of Glasgow, and the depth of the water was increased considerably. In 1859 Queen Victoria opened the new reservoir, and 90 million gallons of water a day flowed towards Glasgow, over 30 miles away.

The engineering that made this happen was well ahead of its time, and consisted of tunnels and aqueducts that relied purely on gravity to carry the water towards the city. The engineering surrounding the loch was equally as spectacular. The water from **Loch Arklet**, high in the hills between Lochs Katrine and Lomond, used to flow west into Loch Lomond. By the use of dams, this was changed so that it flowed east into Loch Katrine. The whole scheme was the largest of its kind in the world for many years, and even today, Glasgow still gets its water from Loch Katrine.

Loch Katrine

The loch's name comes from the early welsh "cethern", meaning "furious", a reference to the many mountain torrents found in the area. It was made famous by Sir Walter Scott, who set his poem *The Lady of the Lake* here. And at **Glengyle**, at the western end of the loch, Rob Roy MacGregor was born. It is still a remote place, and cannot be reached by car.

CREAGAN HOUSE

Strathyre, Perthshire FK18 8ND
Tel: 01877 384638 Fax: 01877 384319
e-mail: eatandstay@creaganhouse.co.uk
website: www.creaganhouse.co.uk

Set in beautiful Strathyre, **Creagan House** dates from the 17th century, and has been restored to provide an establishment that offers fine dining as well as comfortable accommodation in five charming fully en suite bedrooms, one of which has a four poster bed. Each room has tea/coffee making facilities, CD/radio alarm and many thoughtful extras. Good food is at the heart of Creagan House, with only the finest and freshest of local produce being used wherever possible. Owners Cherry and Gordon Gunn have created a superb restaurant with accommodation, and they offer you a warm welcome.

The steamer **Sir Walter Scott** has been sailing the waters of the loch from the beginning of the 20th century, and it still does so today. It was built in Dumbarton, and people always wonder how it got from there to the loch, The answer is that it was transported by barge up the river Leven onto Loch Lomond, then dragged overland by horses from Inversnaid. When it reached Loch Katrine, the engines were fitted.

The steamship takes you from the pier at the east end of the loch towards **Stronachlachar**, six miles away. The small islet at Stronachlachan is known as

Ruins of the Old Kirk, Balquidder

the **Factor's Island**, and recalls one of Rob Roy's exploits. He captured the Duke of Montrose's factor, who was collecting rents in the area, and imprisoned him on the island. He then sent a ransom note to the Duke, but none came. So Rob Roy calmly relieved the man of the £3,000 he was carrying and sent him on his way.

This is the heart of the Trossachs (the name translates as "bristly" or "prickly"), and there are other equally as attractive lochs nearby. **Loch Lubnaig**, to the east, is the largest. **Loch Venachar**, **Loch Achray** and **Loch Drunkie** (which can only be reached by a footpath through the forest) are well worth visiting. At the southern end of Loch Lubnaig are the spectacular **Falls of Leny**.

BALQUHIDDER
24 miles NW of Stirling on a minor road off the A84

This small village sits to the east of the picturesque **Loch Voil**. It lies in that area

of Scotland known as **Breadalbane** ("uplands of Alban", as Alban is the ancient name for Scotland), and in the heart of Clan MacGregor country. In the kirkyard of the roofless kirk is **Rob Roy MacGregor's Grave** (see also Callander), plus those of some of his family including his wife.

Rob's real name was Robert McGregor, the "Roy" coming from the Gaelic *ruadh*, meaning red-haired. He died in 1734 a free man, having received a royal pardon for his misdeeds (if indeed they were misdeeds) in 1726.

KILLIN
30 miles NW of Stirling on the A827

Killin sits close to the western end of **Loch Tay**, which stretches for 15 miles north eastwards into Perthshire. The best views of the loch are from the wooded south shore road, though the northern road is wider and straighter.

Loch Tay

The **Falls of Dochart**, a series of cascades on the River Dochart as it enters Loch Tay, are within the village, and next to them is the **Breadalbane Folklore Centre**, housed in an old mill, which gives an insight into life and legends of the area. Three miles north on a minor road are the **Falls of Lochay** on the River Lochay, though care should be taken when approaching them. The **Moirlanich Longhouse** (National Trust for Scotland) on the Glen Lochay road dates from the 19th century, and is a rare surviving example of a cruck-frame Scottish longhouse, where a family and their livestock lived under the one roof. In an adjacent shed is a display of working clothes found in the longhouse, along with displays, which explain the building's history and restoration.

The ruins of **Finlarig Castle**, which date from the late 16th century, are to the north of the village. The castle was once a Campbell stronghold, and was built by Black Duncan, one of the most notorious members of the clan. Within its grounds are the remains of a beheading pit and a Campbell mausoleum built in 1829.

LOCHEARNHEAD

21 miles NW of Stirling on the A84

This small, attractive village is at the western end of Loch Earn, and is a centre for such pursuits as sailing, fishing, water skiing and diving. East of the village is **Edinample Castle** (not open to the public), owned by Black Duncan Campbell of Glenorchy in the 16th century. It was originally a McGregor stronghold, and is associated with tales of black deeds, doom and gloom. It is said that in the 6th century St Blane cursed the lands around the castle. Another tale says that the castle was doomed as it was built using old gravestones.

CRIANLARICH

32 miles NW of Stirling on the A82

The name of this small village comes from the Gaelic for "low pass", and sits on the southern edge of Breadalbane. Surrounding it is some marvellous walking and climbing country, with the West Highland Way passing close to the village. The twin peaks of Ben More (3,843 feet) and Stobinian (3,821 feet) are to the south east, while the picturesque **Falls of Falloch** (with a small car park close by) lie four miles to the southwest on the A82.

TYNDRUM

40 miles NW of Stirling on the A82

This little village has a population of no more than 100 people, and yet has two railway stations - one on the line from Glasgow to Oban and the other on the line from Glasgow to Fort William. It sits at the head of **Strath Fillan**, which snakes south towards Crianlarich and carrying the West Highland Way. At **Dalrigh** (meaning "the field of the king"), in 1306, Robert the Bruce was defeated in battle. Nearby is the site of **Strathfillan Priory**, founded by Bruce in 1318. St Fillan was an Irish monk who lived during the 8th century

Farmland near Tyndrum

and founded a Celtic monastery in the vicinity (see also Pittenweem, Madderty and St Fillans). It is said that while building the monastery, a wolf attacked and killed one of the oxen used to bring materials to the site. St Fillan then prayed, and a miracle occurred - the wolf took the place of the ox. St Fillian's relics were paraded before the Scottish army at the Battle of Bannockburn, and the subsequent victory endeared the saint to the Scottish king.

LOCATOR MAP

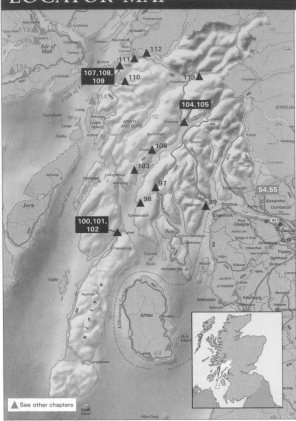

See other chapters

ADVERTISERS AND PLACES OF INTEREST

Argyll (sometimes also called Argyllshire) is one of the most diverse and beautiful counties in Scotland. It sits on the country's western seaboard, where long sea lochs penetrate deep into the interior and mountains tumble down towards fertile glens.

The name "Argyll" comes from the Gaelic *Earraghaidheal*, meaning the "coastline of the Gaels". It can truly claim to be the cradle of Scotland, for this was, at one time, the kingdom of Dalriada, founded by the "Scotti" who originally came from Ireland in the 6th century. Here, at the fortress of Dunadd, they established their capital. From Dunadd, in 843, Kenneth MacAlpin, King of Dalriada, set off towards Scone in Perthshire (taking the Stone of Destiny with him) to claim the throne of the Picts through his mother's family, thus uniting the two great northern kingdoms and creating an embryonic Scotland, at that time called Alba. In the 11th century, the Lothians (centred on Edinburgh) and Strathclyde (centred on Dumbarton) were absorbed, and Scotland as we largely know it today was formed.

The other great Dalriadan centre was at what is now Dunstaffnage, north of Oban. The site is nowadays occupied by Dunstaffnage Castle, one of the most spectacular fortifications on Scotland's western seaboard. And the 12th century Castle Sween, on the shores of Loch Sween, is reckoned to be the oldest surviving stone built castle on the Scottish mainland.

Though it has attractive towns such as Oban, Lochgilphead, Inveraray and Campbeltown, Argyll is sparsely populated. There are few clogged highways, (though Oban can get very busy in the summer months), and driving is a pleasure. New vistas are constantly being opened up as you drive along roads such as the one from Lochgilphead to Oban, and even on overcast days (which are not unknown in this part of Scotland) they are a constant source of wonder and delight. The climate is mild, thanks to

Inveraray Pier

the Gulf Stream, and the place has many fine gardens to explore, such as Ardkinglas, Crarae and Arduaine, some with palm trees and other species you would not expect to thrive so far north.

Strictly speaking, Argyll lies north of the Highland Boundary Fault, which means that it comes within the Scottish Highlands, though not within the local government area now known as the Highlands. Man has lived in Argyll for centuries, and around Kilmartin there are cairns and standing stones built long before the ancient Egyptians built the pyramids. A museum in the village of Kilmartin itself explains the history of the area, and explains the many cairns, standing stones, stone circles, graves and henges that abound in the area.

Argyll is also a place of intriguing legends. When that great order of monastic soldiers called the Knights Templar was suppressed by Pope Clement V in 1307, it was to this part of Scotland, we are told, that the remaining knights fled. Robert the Bruce, the Scots king, had been excommunicated by the Pope, so Papal authority did not extend to this part of Europe, and here the warrior monks could settle in peace. Their legacy, some people claim, are the wonderfully carved tombstones with Templar symbols on them found in such places as Kilmichael Glassary and Kilmartin. Legend also says that a troop of Knights Templar from this area even helped Robert the Bruce defeat the English at Bannockburn.

The Argyll coastline is rugged and rocky, though there are some marvellous, glistening beaches which are invariably empty. And, while the landscapes are rugged and romantic, there are also lush meadows and farmlands where heavily-horned Highland cattle can be seen.

The island of Bute, in the Firth of Clyde, also forms part of Argyll. Along with Arran and the Cumbraes, it used to form the county of Bute, but local government reorganisation in the '70s meant its demise as an administrative unit, sharing it out its islands between Argyll and Ayrshire.

Local government reorganisation also took Morvern, Sunart and the Ardnamurchan peninsula from Argyll, and today they form part of the Highlands local government area. But at the same time parts of what were formerly Dunbartonshire, such as the town of Helensburgh and the Rosneath Peninsula, came within Argyll, although they are dealt with in another section of the book.

That great peninsula known as the Mull of Kintyre, which hangs down into the Atlantic like an arm, is also in Argyll. This is a remote part of Scotland. It forms part of the mainland yet is as isolated as any island. Though Glasgow is only 60 miles from Campbeltown as the crow flies, it takes the average driver three or four hours over twisting, loch-girt roads to reach it. This is the area made famous by Sir Paul McCartney's song *Mull of Kintyre*, where he sings of "mists rolling in from the sea".

BUTE

The island of Bute is the second largest of the islands in the Firth of Clyde, and used to be part of the small county of the same name, which also took in Arran and the Cumbraes. It is about 15 miles long by five miles wide, and though it now comes under Argyll, the Highland Boundary Fault passes right through the island's capital, Rothesay, and the 175-acre **Loch Fad**, in the heart of the island. This means that the larger northern part is in the Highlands while the smaller southern part is in the Lowlands. The scenery reflects this, with the north being rugged, while the south is pastoral, with many small farms and settlements.

There are two ferries connecting Bute to the mainland. The main one is from Wemyss Bay in Renfrewshire to Rothesay, while another, smaller one, runs between Ardentraive on the Cowal Peninsula and Rhubodach on the north east tip of the island. The latter crossing takes only about five minutes, with the distance being only a third of a mile. At one time cattle, instead of being transported between the Bute and the mainland, were made to swim the crossing.

The main town is **Rothesay**, an ancient royal burgh that was given its charter in 1401. It is one of the most famous holiday resorts on the Firth of Clyde, and at one time attracted thousands of Glasgow tourists during the "Glasgow Fair", which is always the last two weeks in July. Fine Victorian mansions line the front, built to take Glasgow merchants who would descend on the town, complete with family and servants, for weeks at a time. There were also more modest B&Bs and guest houses that took in the working classes for what was their one and only holiday of the year. It eventually earned the nickname of "Scotland's Madeira", not just because it was on an island, but also because palm trees flourish here due to the influence of the Gulf Stream.

The gentleness of the climate can best be appreciated at **Ardencraig Gardens** in Ardencraig Lane, which were bought by Rothesay Town Council in 1970. They formed part of the original gardens designed by Percy Cane for the owners of Ardencraig House. Every summer it shimmers with colour, and is a popular spot with holidaymakers. Another popular spot is **Canada Hill**, to the south of the town, where there are spectacular views of the Firth of Clyde. From here, people used to watch ships sailing down the Clyde taking Scottish emigrants to a new life in North America, hence its name. On the sea front is a memorial to people who left Rothesay but never

Rothesay, Bute

Rothesay

on his eldest son. Ever since, all royal heirs bear the title, with Prince Charles being the present duke. The whole building was in a ruinous state until 1816, when it was partly rebuilt by the 2nd Marquis of Bute.

In Stuart Street, close to the castle, is the **Bute Museum**, which has displays and artefacts about Rothesay, the Firth of Clyde and the island of Bute itself. The ruins of **Church of St Mary** (Historic Scotland), on the southern outskirts of the town, is next to the present High Kirk built in 1796. It dates mainly from the 13th and 14th centuries and has two canopied tombs. One contains the effigy of a woman and child, and the other the effigy of a man. There is also the grave slab of an unknown Norman knight on the floor. The church has been recently re-roofed to protect them.

The **Isle of Bute Discovery Centre** is housed in the town's Winter Garden (built in 1924), on the front. It houses an exhibition highlighting life on the island through interactive displays and plasma screens, as well as a cinema/theatre.

Rothesay has more unusual attractions, such as the **Victorian Toilets** at the end of the pier, which date from 1899. They still work perfectly, and are full of ornate design. They were recently voted the second best place in the world to spend a penny. If you want the best place, you'll have to go to Hong Kong. Women can view the toilets at quiet times.

Scotland's first long distance island footpath, the 30-mile long **West Island Way**, starts at Kilchattan Bay and finishes

returned - the six hundred Bute bowmen who fought alongside William Wallace at the Battle of Falkirk in 1298.

Rothesay Castle (Historic Scotland) is one of the oldest in Scotland. It is a royal castle with an unusual circular curtain wall and a water-filled moat, and was probably built in the 13th century by Walter, third steward of the royal household. Not long after, the Vikings besieged it. King Haakon of Norway took it in 1263, but afterwards was defeated at the Battle of Largs. The Treaty of Perth, signed in 1266, gave Scotland the Inner Hebrides and the island of Bute, and it became a favourite residence of the first Stuart king, Robert II, and his son, Robert III, who may have died there. The courtyard contains the remains of a royal chapel, dedicated to St Michael the Archangel.

It was Robert III who created the dukedom of Rothesay (the first such dukedom in Scotland), and conferred it at Port Bannatyne. Full details of the trail are available from the Isle of Bute Discovery Centre in Rothesay.

Close to Kilchattan Bay, at Kingarth, is **St Blane's Chapel**. The ruins of this Norman structure sit within what was a Celtic monastery, founded by St Blane in the sixth century (see also Dunblane). The whole area shows how such a monastery would have been laid out. The rath, or cashel, a low wall surrounding the monastery, can still be seen, as can the foundations of various beehive cells in which the monks lived. There are two old graveyards - one for men, and one for women. Close by is the **Dunagoil Vitrified Fort**, which dates from the Iron Age. Vitrified forts are so called because at one time they were exposed to great heat, turning the surface of the stone used in their construction to a glass-like substance.

There are lots of other religious sites on Bute, some dating from the Dark Ages. At **Straad** (a name which tells you that the island once belonged to the Vikings) there are the scant remains of **St Ninian's Chapel**, which may go back at least 1,500 years, and at **Kilmichael** there are the ruins of the old **St Macaille Chapel**.

Mount Stuart House, near the lovely village of **Kerrycroy**, is the ancestral home of the Marquis of Bute. In 1877 a fire destroyed most of the old house, built during the reign of Queen Anne, and the third Marquis employed Robert Rowand Anderson to design the present Victorian Gothic one. It is an immense house, full of treasures, and reflects the history and importance of the family who owned it. When built, it was full of technological wonders. It was the first house in Scotland to be lit by electricity, and the first private house to have a heated indoor swimming pool. Surrounding the house are 300 acres of delightful gardens. The house achieved international fame in 2003 when Stella McCartney, daughter of Paul, got married here

Near Port Bannatyne, north of Rothesay, is **Kames Castle**, dating from the 14th century. Neither it nor its beautiful gardens are open to the public, but they can be viewed from the road. One place, which can be visited, however, is **Ascog Hall Fernery and Garden**, three miles south of Rothesay. It was built about 1870, and has a sunken fern house which houses over 80 sub-tropical fern species. It was awarded the first ever Scottish prize by the Historic Gardens Foundation, which promotes historic gardens and parks throughout the world.

Off the west coast of Bute is the small privately owned island of **Inchmarnock**, no more than two miles long by half a mile wide. Its name means "Marnock's

KILFINAN HOTEL

Near Tighnabruich, Argyll PA21 2EP
Tel: 01700 821201 e-mail: info@kilfinan.com
Fax: 01700 821205   website: www.kilfinan.com

Situated on the beautiful Cowal Peninsula in Argyll, the **Kilfinan Hotel** is a three star establishment that offers the very best in Scottish hospitality. It is the perfect place to chill out and makes a wonderful base from which to explore an area that is both historic and scenic, with Oban, Inveraray, Lochgilphead, the Mull of Kintyre, Dunoon and the Crinan Canal being no more than an hour's drive away. And it's so easy to reach by ferry from Gourock.

The hotel Sits within the 6,000-acre Otter Estate, and has been welcoming guests since before the 18th century. It has ten guest bedrooms, each one fully en suite, with central heating, colour TV and direct dial telephone. They are cosy and comfortable, and are furnished and decorated to an exceedingly high standard. And the same care and attention has been paid to the public rooms, which have blazing log fires in the colder months. Eating at the hotel is an experience not to be missed. The menu contains many dishes that have been cooked with imagination and flare, combining good, fresh local produce with the highest standards of Scottish cooking. Fresh locally caught crabs, scallops and lobster are available to order. There is everything from the traditional haddock and chips to poached Loch Duart salmon, Highland rib-eye steak, lamb cutlets and the ever popular "haggis, neeps and tatties". The chef may even prepare your own special menu to order. There is a good selection of wines, as well as single malts and brandies to complete your meal.

The hotel sits in the clan lands of Clan Lamont, Clan Lachlan and Clan McEwan, and there is so much to do and see in the area. The opportunities for walking and climbing start almost at the hotel's front door, plus there is fishing, sailing on nearby Loch Fyne, golf and nature study. The newly-restored Church of Kilfinan, founded in the 7th century is close by, and there are many other historical sites that can be explored as well.

island", the Marnock in question being a Celtic saint whose name is also found in other Scottish place names such as Kilmarnock. There are the ruins of an ancient chapel.

DUNOON

Dunoon is one of the best-known Clyde holiday resorts. It sits opposite the Renfrewshire coast, and an all year ferry connects it to Gourock, with a further ferry going from Hunter's Quay, to the north of the town, to the mainland. Each year in August the town hosts the **Cowal Highland Gathering**, one of the largest in Scotland, where competitors take part in tossing the caber, throwing the hammer and other Scottish events.

The **Castle House Museum** is in the Castle Gardens, and has an exhibition entitled "Dunoon and Cowal Past and Present". There are models, artefacts and photographs, which bring the Dunoon of yesteryear to life. There are also furnished Victorian rooms and a shop. The statue of **Highland Mary**, erected in 1896, is close by (see also Failford and Greenock). She was a native of Dunoon, and worked as a maid in a large house near Mauchline in Ayrshire. Burns met her there, and asked her to accompany him to the West Indies when he was thinking of emigrating. She agreed, but on a trip home to Dunoon to make arrangements, she died and was buried in Greenock.

Little now remains of **Dunoon Castle**. It was built in the 12th century, and

Mary Stuart is said to have stayed in it for a short while. On Tom-a-Mhoid Road, in West Bay, is the **Lamont Memorial**, erected in 1906 to commemorate the massacre of the Lamonts by the Campbells in 1646 (see also Toward). Three miles north of Dunoon, on the A815, is **Adam's Grave**, the popular name for a 3,500-year-old neolithic burial cairn, which still has two portals and a capstone intact at its entrance. It sits close to the **Holy Loch**, at one time an American nuclear submarine base. It was chosen as a base not just because of its deep water, but because this part of Argyll has a cloud covering for most of the year, thwarting satellite and aerial photography. The Americans left in 1992, taking with them their large American cars and their accents, which were once common in the streets of the town. At Sandbank, on the shores of the loch, is the two-mile long **Ardnadam Heritage Trail**, with a climb up to a viewpoint at Dunan. The **Cowal Bird Garden** at Sandbank is open from Easter to October every year, and has parrots, exotic birds, donkeys, rabbits and other birds and animals. Details of the 47-mile long **Cowal Way**, a footpath which runs from Portavadie to Artgartan, can be had at the local tourist office.

AROUND DUNOON

KILMUN

3 miles N of Dunoon on the A880

Kilmun Church, dedicated to St Munn, was a collegiate church founded in 1442 by Sir Duncan Campbell of Lochawe, ancestor of the present Dukes of Argyll. All that remains is the tower, now roofless. In 1794 a Campbell mausoleum was built close to the present church of St Munn, built in 1841 to designs by Thomas Burns, and in the kirkyard is the grave of **Elizabeth Blackwell**, who, in 1849, was the first woman to graduate in medicine. Born in Bristol in 1821, she studied in Geneva (where she graduated), in the United States and at Paris and London. After returning to the United States, she opened (despite intense opposition) the first hospital staffed entirely by women. She died in 1910, and was buried in the churchyard as she regularly holidayed in the area. Close by is the grave of the **Revd Alexander Robinson**, a former minister who was deposed after writing *The Saviour in the Newer Light*, a book that put forward opinions which brought accusations of heresy.

On a hillside is the **Kilmun Arboretum**, extending to 180 acres. First planted in 1930, it has a wide range of trees - some rare - from all over the world, and is maintained by the Forestry Commission, which does research work here.

BENMORE

6 miles N of Dunoon off the A815

The **Younger Botanic Garden** (see panel on page 262) is a specialist sector of the Royal Botanic Garden in Edinburgh, and in its 140 acres you can see a wide collection of trees and shrubs from all over the world. There are 250 species of rhododendron, an avenue of giant redwoods from America and a formal garden. Within the Glen Massan Arboretum are some of the tallest trees in Scotland, including a Douglas fir over 178 feet high. From the top of Benmore Hill there is a magnificent view across the Holy Loch to the Firth of Clyde and the Renfrewshire coast. **Puck's Glen** was once part of the Benmore Estate, but is now a delightful walk with great views and picnic areas.

To the north of Benmore is the seven mile long **Loch Eck**, with the A815

BENMORE BOTANIC GARDEN

Dunoon, Argyll PA23 8QU
Tel: 01369 706261 website: www.rbge.org.uk

A member of the National Botanic Gardens of Scotland, Benmore
Botanic Garden is famous for its collection of trees and shrubs. Set
amid dramatic scenery, the west coast climate provides ideal growing
conditions for some of the finest Himalayan rhododendrons. Guided
walks are available to discover the secrets of this sensational garden, including the historic formal
garden with Puck's Hut and established conifers. There is something of interest all year round and
autumn provides a beautiful array of colours. There is a cafe for refreshments and a shop to buy gifts
and plants, whilst various exhibitions and events take place in the Courtyard Gallery. Phone for details.

following its eastern shores towards
Strachur on Loch Fyne. Near the head of
the loch is Tom-a-Chorachasich, a low
hill where, legend says, a Viking prince
was once slain.

ARDENTINNY

7 miles N of Dunoon on a minor road

Ardentinny sits on the shores of Loch
Long, and is a small, attractive village
made famous by the Sir Harry Lauder
song *O'er the Hill to Ardentinny*. The mile-
long **Flowers of the Forest Trail** takes
you through oak woodland, where you
can discover some of the native flowers
and plants of the area.

Inland from the village is **Glenfinart**,
where a skirmish took place between
Norsemen and Gaels prior to the
Norsemen's defeat at the Battle of Largs
in 1263.

TOWARD

6 miles S of Dunoon on the A815

The ruins of **Toward Castle** date mainly
from the 15th century. It was a
stronghold of the Lamonts, who
supported the MacDonalds and Charles
II in his attempts to impose bishops on
the Church of Scotland, while the
Campbells were Covenanters, and
bitterly opposed to episcopacy. Mary
Stuart stayed at the castle in 1563.

An episode in 1646 shows just how the
Scottish clans took matters into their

own hands when dispensing justice. The
Campbells laid siege to the castle, and
after unsuccessfully trying to blow it up,
offered safe passage as far as Dunoon to
the Lamonts sheltering within.

The Lamonts duly left the castle, and
were immediately rounded up and taken
to Tom-a-Mhoid ("Hill of Justice") in
Dunoon, where 36 clansmen were hung
(see also Dunoon). It wasn't just political
or religious differences that prompted
the massacre. Previously, the Lamonts
themselves had slaughtered Campbells at
Strachur and attacked and slaughtered
the villagers of Kilmun, who were hiding
in their church.

CAMPBELTOWN

Campbeltown has the reputation of
being the most isolated town on the
British mainland. It sits on the Mull of
Kintyre, that great peninsula hanging
down from the main body of Argyll. It
received its royal charter in 1700,
making it the second youngest royal
burgh in Scotland. Though 140 miles
from Glasgow by road, it is only 30 miles
from Ballycastle in Northern Ireland. It
also has the distinction of being the
most southerly town in the Scottish
Highlands, and is 25 miles further south
than Berwick-upon-Tweed.

At one time the main industries were
fishing and distilling, but the fishing fleet

has gone now, and only three distilleries remain of the 30 or so that once produced over two million gallons of whisky a year. There are conducted tours, by appointment only, round **Springbank Distillery**, established in 1828. At the **Campbeltown Heritage Centre**, in an old kirk, there are displays and exhibits about South Kintyre, including photos of the light railway that once connected the town with Machrihanish on the peninsula's west coast, where the town's airport now stands. The airport has one of the longest runways in Europe, though only one flight uses it - a Loganair flight to Glasgow. The **Campbeltown Museum** in Hall Street has exhibits on the geology, wildlife and archaeology of the Kintyre Peninsula.

The town sits on Campbeltown Loch, which is guarded by the small island of **Davaar**. Within a cave on the island is a famous painting of the Crucifixion by local artist David MacKinnon from 1887. The island can be reached on foot at low tide by a long shingle beach known as The Doirlinn. **Campbeltown Cross**, erected near the harbour, dates from the 14th century. It was used as the mercat cross after the town became a royal burgh. In the grounds of Campbeltown

Library are the **Lady Linda McCartney Memorial Gardens**, named after the late wife of Sir Paul McCartney, who has a holiday home on Kintyre. Campbeltown Picture House was built in 1913, and is the oldest purpose-cinema still functioning in Scotland.

AROUND CAMPBELTOWN

SOUTHEND
8 miles S of Campbeltown on the B842

This is the most southerly village in Argyll. It was near here, at **Keil**, that St Columba is supposed to have first set foot on Scottish soil before sailing north towards Iona. In the ancient churchyard at Keil are footprints, which are said to mark the spot. It was near here also that a massacre of 300 MacDonald clansmen under Sir Alasdair MacDonald took place in 1647. The nine feet tall **Knockstapple Standing Stone** can be seen from the Campbeltown - Southend Road. The remote **Sanda Island**, two miles south of the village, can be reached by boat from Campbeltown. Though it is remote, it still has a pub - the Byron Darnton Tavern.

SADDELL
9 miles N of Campbeltown on the B842

Saddell Abbey (Historic Scotland) was founded by Somerled, Lord of the Isles in 1148 for Cistercian monks, and completed by his son Reginald, who also founded Iona Abbey and Nunnery. Only scant remains can now be seen, most notably the presbytery and the north transept. As at other places in Argyll, stone carving once flourished

Campbeltown

COLUMBA HOTEL

East Pier Road, Tarbert, Loch Fyne, Argyll PA29 6UF
Tel: 01880 820808 Fax: 01880 821129
e-mail: info@columba.com
website: www.columbahotel.com

Within the conservation village of Tarbert, on the Mull of
Kintyre, you'll find the three-star **Columba Hotel**, which is
surely one of Scotland's best kept secrets. It overlooks the
entrance to Tarbert harbour, a haven for yachtsmen and the
home base for an active fishing fleet. Here you can unwind
in comfort, knowing that you are in a hotel that values tradition and high standards of service. The
staff are friendly and approachable, and all are knowledgeable about the area.

Each of the hotel's ten bedrooms has an individual character,
offering fully en suite facilities and a high standard of décor and
furnishings. The Columba Restaurant has a three course table d'hote
menu that features only the finest and freshest of local produce
wherever possible. The Taste of Scotland, Scotland's "food watchdog",
describes it as "modern Scottish cooking which makes an imaginative
use of excellent local produce". For this reason, it is essential to book a
table in advance during the summer months. Being a fishing port,
seafood - especially shellfish - is a speciality. There is also a great bar
menu for the hotel's tasty bar meals. The wine list contains over 40
fine wines and 30 delicate single malts, so you are sure to find
something to complement your meal beautifully.

STRUAN HOUSE

Harbour Street, Tarbert, Argyll PA29 6UD
Tel: 01880 820190
e-mail: moleatstruan@btopenworld.com
website: www.struan-house-lochfyne.co.uk

Now you can enjoy all the amenities of superior bed and
breakfast accommodation while enjoying a superb holiday
beside Loch Fyne in Argyll. **Struan House**, in the small, beautiful
fishing village of Tarbert, offers excellent accommodation during
the holiday season from April to October each year.

It sits close to the quay, in the heart of the village, close to
pubs, quality shops and good restaurants. It boasts three double bedrooms which have been tastefully
furnished and decorated to make them comfortable and inviting, and each one has washing facilities.
Breakfasts are served in the colourful and atmospheric dining room, and you can choose from the full
Scottish - always hearty, and always ready to set you up for the
day - or lighter options.

The owners Lin and Pete both have a deep love of art with
Pete being a professional sculptor. They have recently opened
their own studios where guests can create their own ceramic
masterpiece to take home. The couple also own a traditional
Scottish boat which is a wonderful way to view Loch Fyne,
perhaps taking your sketch pad on board? (wine and seafood
supplied). So why not come and relax at Struan and dip into
the art of Scotland's beautiful west coast.

here, and no fewer than 11 beautiful grave slabs, each one showing a knight in full armour or a monk, can be seen. After the Battle of Renfrew in 1164, the bodies of Somerled and his heir were brought to Saddell for burial (see also Renfrew). **Saddell Castle** (not open to the public) was built in 1508 for the Bishop of Argyll.

CARRADALE

12 miles N of Campbeltown on the B879

This quiet fishing village lies opposite Arran, on the east coast of the Mull of Kintyre. The **Network Carradale Heritage Centre**, in an old school, has displays about fishing, farming and forestry in the area, as well as hands-on activities for children. Carradale House dates from the 18th century, but was extended in 1804 for the then owner Richard Campbell. In its grounds are gardens noted for their rhododendrons, of which there are over 100 varieties.

Torrisdale Castle, which has been converted into holiday accommodation, was built in 1815, and has a tannery which can be visited

GLENBARR

10 miles N of Campbeltown on the A83

At the **Clan Macalister Centre** in Glenbarr Abbey (not an abbey but a mansion house) are exhibits tracing the history of Clan Macalister as far back as Somerled, Lord of the Isles, nearly 900 years ago. The castle was presented to the clan in 1984 by Angus C. Macalister, 5th Laird of Glenbarr. The mansion

house itself is open to the public between Easter and mid October each year.

TARBERT

31 miles N of Campbeltown on the A83

This small fishing port sits at a point where Kintyre is no more than a mile wide, and is the gateway to the peninsula. To the east is the small East Loch Tarbert, and to the west is the eight-mile long West Loch Tarbert, where, at **Kennacraig**, ferries leave for Islay and Jura. In 1093 King Magnus Barelegs of Norway is said to have been dragged in his galley across the narrow isthmus, proving to his own satisfaction that the Mull of Kintyre was an island, and he was entitled to add it to his empire. **An Tairbeart**, to the south of the village, is a heritage centre that tells of the place's history and people. **Tarbert Castle**, which is now ruinous, dates originally from the 13th century. Robert the Bruce later added further defences. The ruins as we see them today date from the late 15th century. It can be reached along a footpath from Harbour Street.

North of the village is Stonefield Castle, built in 1837 and now a hotel.

Tarbert

ANCHORAGE SEAFOOD RESTAURANT

Harbour Street, Tarbert, Argyll PA29 6UD
Tel/Fax: 01880 820881
e-mail: anchoragetarbert@aol.com

With an international reputation, the **Anchorage Seafood Restaurant** is one of the best places to eat in Scotland. Step inside and be charmed by its modern décor with just a hint of tradition - the crisp linen, the sparkling cutlery and the elegant seating. Be charmed by its high standards of service and attention to detail, and then be completely won over by the high quality of its cuisine, just as many famous people have before (as the guest book will testify). It has featured in the *London Times*, *Time Out* magazine and many other publications.

Situated near the harbour in Tarbert on Loch Fyne, a loch famous for the quality of its fish, seafood predominates on the menu although other dishes are also available. All the produce used is fresh and sourced locally, from the seafood itself to game, cheeses and meats. The

restaurant is also committed to conservation and good ecological practice, and uses locally farmed salmon of the highest quality to ensure that wild salmon stocks are maintained. All the dishes combine good, Scottish cooking with imagination and flair and dishes include halibut with wild mushroom and a mussel sauce, red mullet with cod, and frittered king scallops served with Irish champ and mornay sauce. The owner and chef, Trevor Kelso, took over in August 2004, and is determined to maintain and even increase the high standards the restaurant has continuously enjoyed.

LOCHGAIR HOTEL

Lochgair, Near Lochgilphead, Argyll PA31 8SA
Tel: 01546 886333 Fax: 01546 886217
e-mail: info@lochgair.com

Situated north of Lochgilphead, Lochgair is a small, picturesque village on the A83. And it is here that you will find the family-run **Lochgair Hotel**, surely one of the finest hotels in the area. Its owners, Lesley and Leslie Grant-Pavitt, are proud of its friendly, informal atmosphere and high standards of service and care. The handsome, whitewashed building sits just a few yards from Loch Fyne, and makes an ideal base from which to explore Kilmartin Glen, Inveraray, the Mull of Kintyre and beautiful Knapdale. All the wonderful gardens of Argyll are also within easy reach.

There are ten bedrooms (eight doubles and two twins), all with en suite facilities that were completely updated in 2005. They also have colour TVs and tea/coffee making facilities. Each one is comfortable, and furnished and decorated to a high standard.

The hotel's reception area is a warm, inviting place, and hints at the high standards of service that await the guest. It is carpeted in tartan, and has a traditional fireplace which is in use during the winter months. The bar is just as inviting, and makes the ideal place to enjoy a refreshing drink. The bar stocks over 30 single malts, as well as beers, wines, spirits and liqueurs. And, of course, the food is outstanding. Leslie is a chef trained to Michelin standards, and uses only fresh local produce in season wherever possible.

Attached is **Stonefield Castle Garden**, which is open to the public. As with so many gardens in the area, it is famous for its rhododendrons. There are also plants from Chile and New Zealand, and conifers such as the sierra redwood.

Seven miles south of Tarbert is **Skipness Castle** (Historic Scotland), which dates originally from the 13th century. The first historical mention of it is in 1261 when the McSweens owned it, though it later came into the possession of Walter Stewart, Earl of Menteith. It finally came into the possession of the Campbells, and was abandoned in the late 17th century, when a newer, more comfortable house was built close by. The ruins of **Kilbrannan Chapel**, near the foreshore, dates from the 13th century, and were dedicated to St Brendan. Five medieval grave slabs are to be found inside the chapel walls and in the kirkyard. The church replaced an earlier building dedicated to St Columba.

Crinan Canal

LOCHGILPHEAD

Lochgilphead, as the name suggests, stands at the head of Loch Gilp, a small inlet of Loch Fyne. It is a planned town, and was laid out in about 1790, and is the main shopping centre for a wide area known as Knapdale, that portion of Argyll from which the long "arm" of the Mull of Kintyre descends. Knapdale is steeped in history, and though it now seems to be on the edge of things, at one time it was at the crossroads of a great communications network. Ireland was to the southwest, the Isle of Man was to the south, the Hebrides were to the north, the bulk of Scotland itself was to the east, and all could be easily reached by

boat.

Kilmory Woodland Park, off the A83, surrounds Kilmory Castle, which has been turned into local government offices. The park contains many rare trees, plus a garden and woodland walks.

The **Crinan Canal** (known as "Scotland's most beautiful shortcut") starts at **Ardrishaig**, a couple of miles south of Lochgiplhead, and skirts the town as it heads across the peninsula towards the village of Crinan on the west coast. Work started on the canal in 1794. However, it was beset with problems, and finally opened, albeit in an incomplete form, in 1801. By 1804 it still wasn't complete and had debts of £140,000. Then, in 1805, some of the canal banks collapsed and had to be rebuilt. It was finally opened in 1809, though in 1815 Thomas Telford, the civil engineer, inspected it and declared that even more work needed doing. In 1817 it reopened, this time to everyone's satisfaction.

It is nine miles long, has a mean depth

of nine feet six inches and rises to 65 feet above sea level. it has, in this short length, 15 locks. In 1847 it got the royal seal of approval when Queen Victoria sailed its full length as she was making a tour of the Highlands. Perhaps the most unusual craft to have used it were midget submarines during World War II.

AROUND LOCHGILPHEAD

DUNADD
4 miles N of Lochgilphead off the A816

Dunadd (Historic Scotland) is one of the most important historical sites in Scotland. This great rock rises to a height of 175 feet from a flat area of land called Crinan Moss, and is where the ancient kings of **Dalriada** had their royal fort and capital. From here, they ruled a kingdom that took in all of modern day Argyll. It was founded by immigrants from Antrim in present day Northern Ireland in the 5th century, and gradually grew in importance. With them from Ireland they brought that great icon of Scottish nationhood, the Stone of Destiny (see also Scone and Edinburgh).

A climb to the top of Dunadd gives a wonderful view over the surrounding countryside, which is the reason the fort was established here in the first place. Parts of the ramparts can still be seen, and near the top, on a flat outcrop of rock, are some carvings of a boar, a footprint, a bowl and some ogham writing, which may have been connected to the inauguration of the Dalriadan kings.

The kings of Dalriada were special. Before this time, kings were looked upon more as great tribal leaders and warriors than as men set apart to rule a kingdom. But one man changed all that - St Columba. His monastery on Iona was within Dalriada, and on that island he conducted the first Christian "coronation" in Britain. In AD 574 he anointed Aidan king of the Dalriadans in a ceremony that relied on Biblical precedents. It also contained an element that is still used in today's coronations, when the assembled crowds shouted out "God Save the King!" in unison. There is no doubt that Aidan sat on the Stone of Destiny during the ceremony.

Though it may now look austere and lonely, Dunadd, in its heyday, would have been a busy place, as excavations have shown that it traded with the kingdoms of present day England and the Continent. When the king was in residence, great flags would have fluttered from the wooden buildings, colourful banners and pennants would have hung from the ramparts and soldiers would have stood guard at its entrance. The River Add, no more than a couple of feet deep nowadays, winds its way round the base of the rock before entering the sea at Loch Crinan. In olden days, before Crinan Moss was drained for agriculture, it would have been navigable right up to the rock itself. Boats would have been tied up at its banks, and there would have been a small township to house the king's retainers. There would also have been storerooms, stables and workshops where jewellery and weapons were crafted, cloth woven and pots made.

The other great kingdom north of the Forth and Clyde was the kingdom of the Picts, and for years it and Dalriada traded, fought, mingled and intermarried. Eventually, in AD 843, because of this intermarriage, Kenneth MacAlpin, king of Dalriada, also inherited the throne of the Picts. By this time the centres of power had moved to the west because of constant Norse raids, so Kenneth MacAlpin set off for Scone in present day Perthshire (taking the Stone of Destiny with him) and established his capital there. Thus was born the kingdom of Scotland, or Alba as it was known then, though it would be another 200 years before the kingdoms of the Lowlands - the Angles of the Lothians and the British of Strathclyde - were incorporated as well.

Dunadd survived for a few years after Kenneth left, but it was no longer an important place, and by the 12th century was largely abandoned.

KILMICHAEL GLASSARY

4 miles N of Lochgilphead on a minor road off the A816

In common with many other kirkyards in this part of Argyll, the kirkyard of the attractive 19th century **Parish Church** has a fine collection of carved, medieval and later, grave slabs.

The **Cup and Ring Rock** (Historic Scotland) lies within a small fenced off area in the village, and has some ancient cup and ring markings carved into it. No one knows the significance of such carvings, though there are many throughout Scotland.

KILMARTIN

8 miles N of Lochgilphead on the A816

The area surrounding Kilmartin is said to be Scotland's richest prehistoric landscape. Within a six-mile radius of the village over 150 prehistoric and 200 later monuments are to be found. The whole place is awash with standing stones, stone circles, cairns, henges, burial mounds, forts, crannogs, cup and ring markings, castles, carved grave slabs and crosses.

A church has stood in the village for centuries, though the present **Parish Church** was

only built in 1835. Its former dedication to St Martin shows that a church has stood here since at least the Dark Ages, as St Martin was a favourite saint of Celtic monks. Within it is a decorated cross that dates from about the 9th century, and within the kirkyard are three further crosses, dating also from the 9th century. Also in the kirkyard is the finest collection of carved medieval grave slabs in Western Scotland. Most date from the 14th or 15th century, though there are some, which might be older. They might come as a surprise to people who imagine Scottish warriors to be wild Highlanders in kilts who brandish broadswords as they dash across the heather. These warriors are dressed in the kind of sophisticated armour found all over Europe at the time. Only the well-off could have afforded it, and the other carvings on the slabs, such as swords, coats-of-arms and crosses, bear out their aristocratic lineage.

Some people have suggested that the carvings show Knights Templar, those warrior monks whose order was suppressed by Pope Clement V in 1307, egged on by Philip le Bel, king of France,

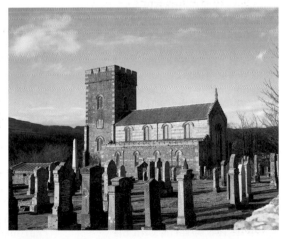

Kilmartin Church

who wanted his hands on the order's fabled treasure.

A great Templar fleet left La Rochelle in France soon after the order was suppressed - supposedly carrying the Templar's treasure - and were never heard of again. Not long before, the Pope had excommunicated Robert the Bruce for his murder of the Red Comyn in a friary in Dumfries, and people believe the Templars were heading for Scotland. The Pope's influence in the country was minimal, and indeed the clergy was ignoring the Pope, still giving communion to Bruce. So it would certainly have made sense for the Templars to make for Scotland, bringing their treasure with them. Edward I was forever bemoaning the fact that the Scots seemed to have unlimited funds to defend themselves.

An even more intriguing theory has been put forward that the treasure was in the form of a great secret regarding Jesus, who either survived the crucifixion or married Mary Magdalene. Whatever the truth, many books have been written linking this part of Argyll - and other parts of Scotland - with the Knights Templar (see also Rosslyn).

Behind the church is the **Glebe Cairn**, a circular mound of stones dating from 1500-2000 BC. It forms part of what is known as the linear cemetery, a collection of such cairns, which stretches for a mile along the floor of Kilmartin Glen. The others are **Nether Largie North Cairn**, **Nether Largie Mid Cairn**, **Nether Largie South Cairn** and **Ri Cruin Cairn**. All are accessible by foot. In addition, there is the **Dunchraigaig Cairn**, just off the A816, which doesn't form part of the linear cemetery.

The **Temple Wood Circles**, south of Kilmartin, date from about 3500 BC. There are two of them, with the

northern one possibly being used as a solar observatory when agriculture was introduced into the area. Burials were introduced at a later date. The **Nether Largie Standing Stones** are close to the Temple Wood Circle, and the **Ballymeanoch Standing Stones** are to the south of them. Of the seven stones, only six now survive in their original positions.

To the north of Kilmartin are the substantial ruins of **Carnassarie Castle** (Historic Scotland), dating from the 16th century. It was built for John Carswell, Protestant Bishop of the Isles and the man who translated Knox's Book of Common Order (his liturgy for the reformed church) into Gaelic. It was the first book ever to be printed in that language.

If you find all these stone circles, cairns, castles, carvings and burial mounds hard to comprehend, then you should visit the award winning **Kilmartin House Museum** next to the church in the village. Using maps, photographs, displays and artefacts it explains the whole chronology of the area from about 7000 BC right up until 1100 AD.

KILMORY

13 miles SW of Lochgilphead on a minor road off the B8025

North of Kilmory, on the shores of Loch Sween, stands the bulky ruins of **Castle Sween**, mainland Scotland's oldest surviving stone castle. Four massive, thick walls surround a courtyard where originally wood and thatch lean-tos would have housed stables, workshops and a brewery. It was started by one Suibhne (pronounced "Sween"), ancestor of the MacSweens, in about 1100, and in later years became a centre of craftsmanship and artistry. This is shown by the **Kilmory Sculptured Stones**, at the 700-year-old Kilmory Knap chapel, a few miles south west of the castle. There was a thriving settlement here in medieval times, and within the ruins of the chapel is a remarkable collection of carved stones collected from the kirkyard, some going back at least 1,000 years. The symbols on them include men in armour, blacksmiths' and woodworkers' tools, swords and crosses. They probably all marked the graves of craftsmen and warriors associated with Castle Sween over the years.

The most spectacular stone is **MacMillan's Cross**, which dates from the 15th century. On one side it shows the Crucifixion, and on the other a hunting scene. There is a Latin inscription that translates, "This is the cross of Alexander MacMillan". Across Loch Sween, at the end of the B8025, is **Keills Chapel**, which has another fine collection of grave slabs.

KILBERRY

10 miles SW of Lochgilphead on the B8024

At Kilberry Castle are some late medieval sculptured stones (Historic Scotland), which were gathered from the Kilberry estate.

KILMARIE

On the B8002 10 miles NW of Lochgilphead

If you take the B8002 a few miles north of Kilmartin, you will find yourself on the Craignish Peninsula. Beyond the attractive village of **Ardfern**, a popular haven for yachtsmen is **Kilmarie Old Parish Church**. This roofless ruin, dedicated to St Maelrubha, dates from the 13th century, and

contains a wonderful collection of carved grave slabs dating from the 14th and 15th centuries.

INVERARAY

Standing on the western shores of Loch Fyne, Inveraray is a perfect example of a planned Scottish town. It was built between 1753 and 1776 by the 3rd Duke of Argyll, who had pulled down his decaying castle and replaced it with a grander one, which would reflect his important position in society. At that time the small clachan, or hamlet, of Inveraray stood in front of the castle, and the duke wanted to improve the castle's view out over Loch Fyne, so he had the old township, which stood east of the castle, demolished. He then built a new town to the immediate south, which became a royal burgh thanks to a charter of 1648 granted by Charles I. The result is an elegant town with wide streets and well-proportioned, whitewashed houses. It is actually no bigger than a village, but so well planned is it that it has all the feel of a busy metropolis, and indeed in the summer months tourists flock to it, making it an extremely busy place.

Inveraray Castle

Inveraray Castle (see panel below) sits to the north, and is an elegant, foursquare stately home. With its four turrets - one at each corner of the building - it looks more like a grand French château than a Highland castle, but this was the intention. It was designed to tell the world that the Campbells, Dukes of Argyll, belonged to one of the most powerful families in the land - one which had always supported the Protestant cause and the Hanovarian dynasty against the Jacobites. It was designed by Roger Morris and Robert Mylne, and contains a famous armoury, French tapestries, Scottish and European furniture, and a genealogy room that traces the history of Clan Campbell.

There are two churches within the town - the **Parish Church**, which dates from 1794, and the Episcopalian **Church of All Saints**. The Parish Church was designed by Robert Mylne, and is divided in two so that services could be held in both English and Gaelic, though this is seldom done nowadays. All Saints Church, which dates from 1886, has a bell tower with the second heaviest ring of ten bells in the world. Each bell is named after a saint, and has the name inscribed on it. Ringers can sometimes be watched in action, and visiting ringers can practise by appointment.

Being the main town for a large area, Inveraray was the place where justice was

INVERARAY CASTLE

Castle Estate Office, Inveraray, Argyll PA32 8XE
Tel: 01499 302203 Fax: 01499 302421
e-mail: enquire@inveraray-castle.com
website: www.inveraray-castle.com

Inveraray Castle is the ancestral home of the chief of Clan Campbell. It is situated on the shores of picturesque Loch Fyne and close to Inveraray, surely one of the most interesting small towns in Scotland. Though it is first and foremost the well-loved family home of the 13th Duke and Duchess of Argyll, it is also a treasure house of fine furniture, paintings, tapestries, porcelain and other objets d'art that recall a more elegant time. It is open to the public, and you too can marvel at the weapons in the armoury, the family portraits, the ornate plasterwork, the four poster beds, the old kitchen and so on. Or you can explore the gardens and grounds, and admire the outside of a castle that was built in the 18th century, and owes more than a little to the elegance of the great French châteaux of the Loire Valley.

The Campbells have been at the heart of Scottish history for centuries, and are descended from solid British stock that once lived in the ancient Kingdom of Strathclyde, arriving in Argyllshire as part of a royal expedition in about 1220. The 11th Earl of Argyll became a duke in 1701, and each duke since has been a loyal king's man - supporting the House of Hanover during the Jacobite Uprisings of 1715 and 1745 and sometimes serving with distinction in the British Army. There is a fascinating "Clan Room", where Campbells from all over the world come to learn about the family. But even if you're not a Campbell, Inveraray Castle is still worth visiting.

meted out. **Inveraray Jail** (see panel below) takes you on a trip through Scotland's penal system in the 1800s, and here you can see what the living conditions were like in cells that housed murderers and thieves. There are two prison blocks, one built in 1820 and one in 1848, the latter having more "enlightened" conditions. You can also see the branding irons, thumb screws and whips that passed for justice before the 18th century, and see what life is like in prison today. There is also a courtroom where a tableau, complete with sound, shows how a trial was conducted before a High Court judge.

Inveraray

Within the Arctic Penguin, a three-masted schooner built in 1911, is the **Inveraray Maritime Museum**. Here the maritime history of Scotland's western seaboard is vividly brought to life. There's an on board cinema with an archive of old film, and people can see what conditions were like aboard a ship taking them to a new life in America. The latest addition to the museum is the *Eilean Eisdeal*, a typical puffer built in Hull in 1944.

One of the area's most famous sons was **Neil Munro** (1863-1930), the writer and journalist who wrote the ever-popular *Para Handy* books. On the A819 through Glen Aray towards Loch Awe is a monument that commemorates him. It stands close to his birthplace at Carnus.

AROUND INVERARAY

CAIRNDOW
6 miles NE of Inveraray across the loch on the A83

This small village stands at the western end of Glen Kinglas, on the shores of Loch Fyne. Within the Arkinglas Estate is the 25-acre **Arkinglas Woodland**

INVERARAY JAIL

Church Square, Inveraray, Argyll PA32 8TX
Tel: 01499 302381 Fax: 01499 302195
e-mail: info@inverarayjail.co.uk
website: www.inverarayjail.co.uk

Inveraray Jail, the former County Courthouse and prison for Argyll, tells the story of the men, women and children who were tried and served their sentences here. Fascinating displays give an insight into the harshness of prison life in the 19th century, including cells where murderers, madmen and children were crammed in together, the courtroom where trials took place and the airing yards where prisoners were allowed to take an hour's exercise each day. An exhibition of items such as branding irons and thumb screws illustrates punishments inflicted before the days of prisons. There is an excellent range of gifts and souvenirs available at the Jail Shop. Ring for details.

Garden. High annual rainfall, a mild climate and light, sandy soil have created the right conditions for a collection of coniferous trees. The Callander family established the collection in about 1875, and it has seven champion trees that are either the tallest or widest in Britain. There is also one of the best collections of rhododendrons in the country. Arkinglas House itself, designed by Robert Lorimer in 1907, is not open to the public.

At Clachan Farm near Arkinglas you'll find the **Clachan Farm Woodland Walks**, which allow you to see many species of native tree, such as oak, hazel and birch. The walks vary from a few hundred yards in length to two-and-a-half miles, and even takes in the old burial ground of Kilmorich.

STRACHUR
4 miles S of Inveraray across the loch on the A815

Strachur sits on the shores of Long Fyne, on the opposite bank from Inveraray. **Strachur Smiddy** (meaning "smithy") dates from 1791, and finally closed in the 1950s.It has now been restored as a small museum and craft shop, and has some original tools and implements used by blacksmiths and farriers. **Glenbranter**, which was once owned by Sir Harry Lauder, has three short walks through mature woodlands. In the kirkyard at Strachur is buried **Sir Fitzroy MacLean**, diplomat and spy, who died in 1996, and said to be the inspiration for Ian Fleming's James Bond.

Lachlan Castle (not open to the public), ancestral home of the MacLachlans, lies six miles south of Strachur on the B8000. The older 15th century castle, which is in ruins, is close by. Nine miles south of the castle, still on the B8000, is **Otter Ferry**. As the name implies, this village was once the eastern terminal of a ferry that crossed Loch Fyne, but it is long gone. The word "otter" comes from the Gaelic "oitir", meaning a gravel bank, and has nothing to do with the animal.

A single lane track, the **Ballochandrain**, leaves Otter Ferry and rises to over 1,000 feet before descending to Glendaruel. It has some wonderful views towards the Inner Hebrides.

South of Otter Ferry is the small, peaceful clachan of Kilfinan. The ruined **St Finan's Chapel**, dedicated to St Finian, a 6th century Irish saint, dates from about the 12th century and has some old burial stones. Five miles further on at Millhouse is a turn off to the right along an unmarked road for **Portavadie**, where the Portavadie-Tarbert ferry will take you onto the Mull of Kintyre (summer only). If you turn left at the same junction and head north again, you pass through **Tighnabruaich** on the Kyles of Bute, and eventually arrive at **Glendaruel**, the site of a battle in about 1110 between Norsemen led by Mekan, son of Magnis Barefoot, and native Gaels, in which the Vikings were defeated. The name translates from the Gaelic as the "glen of red blood", as the defeated Norsemen were thrown into a local burn whose water turned red with their blood. The road hugs the shoreline most of the way, and gives some wonderful views of sea and hill. At Glendaruel are the **Kilmodan Sculptured Stones**, within the graveyard of Kilmodan Parish Church

ARROCHAR
13 miles E of Inveraray on the A83

Arrochar sits at the head of Loch Long. Two miles to the west is the small village of **Tarbet**, which sits on the shores of Loch Lomond. It sometimes surprises people who don't know the area that Britain's largest sheet of fresh water is so close to the sea. From the jetty at Tarbet

Loch Long, near Arrochar

hundred feet below the road at some points.

Near the Jubilee Well in Arrochar are the **Cruach Tairbeirt Walks**. These footpaths (totalling just over a mile and a half in length) give some wonderful views over Loch Lomond and Loch Long. Though well surfaced, they are quite steep in some places.

AUCHINDRAIN

5 miles S of Inveraray on the A83

small ships offer cruises on the loch. **Arrochar Parish Church** is a whitewashed building dating from 1847, and it was recently saved from demolition by the concerted effort of the villagers.

Some of Argyll's finest mountains are to be found close by, such as **Ben Narnain** (3,036 feet) and **Ben Ime** (3,318 feet). This area could fairly claim to be the homeland of Scottish mountaineering, as the first mountaineering club in the country, the Cobbler Club, was established here in 1865. The road westwards towards Inveraray climbs up past the 2,891 feet Ben Arthur, better known as **The Cobbler**, and over the wonderfully named **Rest and Be Thankful** until it drops down again through Glen Kinglas to the shores of Loch Fyne. It is a wonderful drive, with the floor of Glen Croe several

Auchindrain Township is an original West Highland village which has been brought back to life as an outdoor museum and interpretation centre. Once common throughout the Highlands, many of these settlements were abandoned at the time of the Clearances, while others were abandoned as people headed for cities such as Glasgow and Edinburgh to find work. Queen Victoria visited Auchindrain in 1875 when it was inhabited, and you can now see what she

Auchindrain Highland Township

CRARAE GARDEN

Crarae, Inveraray, Argyll PA32 8YA
Tel/Fax: (Visitor Centre) 01546 886614
website: www.nts.org.uk

The main garden at Crarae is unique, with a strong 'sense of place'. Set on a hillside down which tumbles the Crarae Burn, the scene is reminiscent of a Himalayan gorge. The surrounding tree and shrub collections are rich and diverse, planted for artistic and naturalistic effect. The garden contains one of the best collections of the genus Rhododendron in Scotland, unusually rich in cultivars, as well as part of the National Collection of Nothofagus and particularly good representations of Acer, Eucalyptus, Eucryphia and Sorbus. The autumn colours of the leaves and berries are a perfect balance to the earlier blooming rhododendrons and azaleas.

Extending to around 25 hectares, the garden was traditionally accessed by a network of paths that criss crossed the burn via a series of footbridges. The Trust intends to reinstate these routes as part of a phased programme of repairs to allow visitors full access once again.

saw. Most of the cottages and other buildings have been restored and furnished to explain the living conditions of the Highlanders in past centuries. The visitor centre also has displays on West Highland life, showing many farming and household implements.

CRARAE

10 miles S of Inveraray on the A83

Crarae Garden (National Trust for Scotland - see panel above) was started by Lady Campbell in 1912, and includes the national collection of southern beech, as well as eucalyptus and Eucryphia. It is one of the finest woodland gardens in Scotland, with rare trees and exotic shrubs thriving in the mild climate, and over 400 species of rhododendron and azaleas providing a colourful display in spring and summer. A fine collection of deciduous trees adding colour and fire to autumn. There are sheltered woodland walks and a spectacular gorge. The Scottish Clan Garden features a selection of plants associated with various Argyll clans.

OBAN

Seeing Oban nowadays, it is hard to imagine that in the 18th century this

BOLLIWOOD

3 Albany Street, Oban, Argyll PA34 4AR
Tel: 01631 570999 e-mail: sales@bolliwood.co.uk
website: www.bolliwood.co.uk

Situated opposite Oban Tourist Information, Bolliwood is a small shop specialising in imported crafts and jewellery. A selection of these include, walnut furniture and furnishings, carvings, plain and embroidered pashmina, chain stitch rugs and duvet covers hand-made from exquisite sari material. You can also purchase a unique piece of silver jewellery from an extensive range. There is an enormous selection of semi precious stone set jewellery, with designs and prices to suit most tastes, including some celtic. It is a fascination shop where you are made welcome and are free to browse the many delightful objects on display. It is an experience shopping in Bolliwood, where each item is carefully selected and imported into this country by owner Fiona Fraser . Realistic prices are coupled with great craftsmanship.

bustling holiday resort was no more than a village, with only a handful of cottages built round a small bay. It got its original burgh charter in 1811, but even then it was an unimportant place. With the coming of the railway in 1880, the town blossomed as people discovered its charms. Great Victorian and Edwardian villas were built by prosperous Glasgow merchants, and local people began to open hotels, guest houses and B&Bs.

Now it is the capital of the Western Highlands, and known as the "Gateway to the Western Isles". It has two cathedrals, the Roman Catholic **Cathedral of St Columba**, built in 1930 of granite and the town's largest church, and the Episcopalian Cathedral Church of St John the Divine in George Street, built in the 19th century but never fully completed.

Dominating the town is **McCaig's Folly**, a vast coliseum of a building that was begun in 1897. To call it a folly is a misnomer, because the man who built it, Oban banker John Stuart McCaig, wanted to establish a museum and art gallery inside it, but he died before it was completed. As the town had a lot of

Oban

unemployed people at the time, he also wanted to create work for them. In his will he left money for a series of large statues of himself and his family to be erected around the parapet, but these were never carried out.

The oldest building in Oban is **Dunollie Castle**, the ruins of which can be seen on the northern outskirts of the town beyond the Corran Esplanade. It was built on a site that has been fortified since the Dark Ages, and was a

---

MacDougall stronghold. It was finally abandoned as a dwelling house in the early 1700s, when a new McDougall mansion was built. It soon became a quarry for the people of the area. North of the ruins, near the beach at Ganavan, is the *Clach a' Choin*, or **Dog's Stone**, where, legend has it, the giant Fingal tied up his dog Bran. The groove at the base is supposed to be where the leash wore away the stone.

Armaddy Castle Garden, eight miles south of Oban off the B844 road for Seil Island, is another of the local gardens that benefit from the area's mild climate.

The pier is where most of the ferries leave for the Western Isles. From here you can sail for Lismore, Mull, Coll, Tiree, Colonsay, Barra and South Uist, and one of the joys of Oban is sitting on

---

THE BARRIEMORE

Corran Esplanade, Oban, Argyll PA34 5AQ
Tel: 01631 566356 Fax: 01631 571084
e-mail:reception@barriemore-hotel.co.uk
website: www.barriemore-hotel.co.uk

"At the end of the day... location matters".

From its vantage point on the Corran Esplanade, the four star **Barriemore Hotel** enjoys a splendid reputation in Oban. It has magnificent vistas over the bay, towards the town and the islands of Kerrera, Mull and Lismore, which can be enjoyed from many of its rooms.

The is fine and imposing house was built in 1895 for John Stuart McCaig, a wealthy banker who financed Oban's most famous landmark - McCaig's Tower, which dominates the town's skyline. The Barriemore is elegant and opulent, with spacious, comfortable bedrooms that are individually furnished and decorated to an exceptional standard. Each room is fully en suite, with hospitality tray, radio alarm clock, colour TV (many have video or DVD facilities) and hairdryers. Attention to detail are the watchwords here.

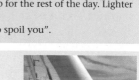

The guests' lounge boasts an open fire place, a wide range of books, magazines, local information and board games, and here you can relax over a cup of tea, coffee or something stronger as you watch sea going vessels of all types and sizes sail past, or plan your next excursion.

The breakfasts are outstanding, with full Scottish being a favourite along with locally smoked fish and assorted Scottish produce. It is hearty and filling, and will set you up for the rest of the day. Lighter choices are also available.

"This is your holiday...allow us to spoil you".

CORRYVRECKAN

Dal an Eas, Kilmore, Oban, Argyllshire PA34 4XU
Tel/Fax: 01631 770246 e-mail: yacht.corryvreckan@virgin.net
website: www.corryvreckan.co.uk

Beginner or expert, you're sure to enjoy a sailing holiday aboard the **Corryvreckan**, a yacht that sails among the sheltered lochs and remote islands of the west coast of Scotland. It's an experience not to be missed Join in the yachting life as you learn to hoist and set the sails or discover the art of navigation, all in an exciting but safe environment. Come beachcombing, bird watching and whale spotting or just relax on deck and enjoy the dramatic scenery. The yacht is big, blue, and beautiful, and owned and run by Douglas and Mary Lindsay, who have a wealth of yachting experience. In addition, Mary is a first class cook, and your on-board dinners will be long remembered.

the pier watching the graceful ferries entering and leaving Oban Bay.

The **Oban Distillery** in Stafford Street produces a whisky that is one of the six "classic malts" of Scotland, and has tours showing the distillery at work. The whisky is a lightly peated malt, and the tour includes a free dram. On the Corran Esplanade is the **Oban War and Peace Museum**, which has photographs and military memorabilia. There is also a model of a flying boat with a 14 feet wingspan.

The **Oban Rare Breeds Farm Park** at Glencruitten has, in addition to rare breeds, a pets corner, a woodland walk, tearoom and shop. And at Upper Soroba is the **Oban Zoological World**, a small family-run zoo specialising in small mammals and reptiles. The **Puffin Dive Centre** at Port Gallanach is an award winning activity centre where you can learn to scuba dive in some remarkably clear water.

AROUND OBAN

CONNEL BRIDGE
4 miles NE of Oban off the A828

Connel Bridge is a one-time a railway bridge which now it carries the A828 over the entrance to Loch Etive. The entrance to this sea loch is very shallow, and when the tide ebbs, the water pours out of the loch into the Firth of Lorne over the **Falls of Lora**.

DUNSTAFFNAGE
3 miles N of Oban off the A85

On a promontory sticking out into Ardmuchnish Bay, in the Firth of Lorne, is the substantial **Dunstaffnage Castle** (Historic Scotland). Seen from the east, it has a glorious setting, with the island of Lismore and the hills of Morvern behind it. And the setting is not just beautiful. This must be one of the most strategic places in Argyll as far as sea travel is concerned, as many important sea routes converge here. The castle was originally built in the 13th century by either Ewan or Duncan MacDougall, Lords of Lorne, on the site of a Dalriadan royal fort and settlement, though the castle as seen today dates from all periods up to the 19th century. In 1309 the castle fell into the hands of Robert the Bruce, and he gave it to the Stewarts. In 1470 Colin Campbell, the first Earl of Argyll, was created hereditary captain, or keeper of Dunstaffnage.

In 1363 a dark deed was carried out here. The then Stewart owner was set upon outside the castle and murdered by a troop of MacDougalls, who still considered the castle theirs. The troop then attacked the castle, and it fell into their hands once more. A few months later a force of men sent by David II,

Robert the Bruce's son, retook it. In 1746, Flora MacDonald was held captive here for a short while.

The castle's resident ghost is called the **Ell Maid**, and sometimes on stormy nights she can be heard wandering through the ruins, her footsteps clanging off the stone as if shod in iron. If she is heard laughing, it means that there will be good news for the castle. If she shrieks and sobs, it means the opposite.

Dunstaffnage Chapel sits outside the castle, and also dates from the 13th century. It is unusual in that chapels were usually within the defensive walls of a castle. A small burial aisle built in 1740 for the Campbells of Dunstaffnage forms an eastern extension.

BENDERLOCH
8 miles N of Oban on the A828

The **Oban Seal and Marine Centre** is Scotland's leading marine animal rescue centre, and it looks after dozens of injured or orphaned seal pups before returning them back into the wild.

Barcaldine Castle has associations with the Appin murder and the Massacre of Glencoe. There are secret passages and a bottle dungeon, and the castle is said to be haunted by a Blue Lady. Though not open to the public, it offers B&B accommodation. **Tralee Beech** is one of the best beeches in the area. It lies off the unmarked road to South Shian and Eriska.

ARDCHATTAN
8 miles NE of Oban on a minor road on the north shore of Loch Etive

Ardchattan Priory (Historic Scotland) was built in about 1230 by Duncan McDougall, Lord of Lorne, for the Valliscaulian order of monks. The ruins of the church can still be seen, though the rest of the priory, including the nave

BLARCREEN HOUSE

Ardchattan, Oban, Argyll PA37 1RG
Tel: 01631 750272 Fax: 01631 750132
e-mail: info@blarcreenhouse.com
website: www.blarcreenhouse.com

Standing on the shores of Loch Etive, **Blarcreen House** is an elegant Victorian farmhouse dating from 1886 within the historic Ardchattan Estate. A house has stood here for at least 400 years, so the place is full of history and heritage, and makes the ideal base from which to explore the area. It has four coveted stars from VisitScotland, five diamonds from the AA. Food is important at Blarcreen House. Fresh Scottish produce of the highest quality is always used, and three-course candlelit dinners are available with prior notice. There is also a fine selection of wines and spirits.

There are three comfortable rooms on offer, all en-suite and all decorated and furnished to an extremely high standard. The Loch Etive Room has stunning views out over Loch Etive, and features a king-sized solid mahogany four-poster bed and a private dressing room. The Henderson Room is spacious and well appointed, also with king-sized four poster bed and views of Loch Etive. The Moffat Room enjoys the morning sun, and has an oak panelled queen-size bed, with loch and mountain views.

The dining room is spacious and elegant, and the public rooms are all comfortable and informal - the perfect places to relax and possibly enjoy a drink after a hard day's sightseeing.

and cloisters, was incorporated into Ardchattan House in the 17th century by John Campbell, who took over the priory at the Reformation. There are some old grave slabs which mark McDougall graves. **Ardchattan Priory Garden** is open to the public, and has herbaceous borders, roses, a rockery and a wild flower meadow.

KINLOCHLAICH GARDENS

11 miles N of Oban on the A828

This old walled garden was created in 1790 by John Campbell. It sits on the shores of Loch Linnhe, in an area known as Appin, and it has one of Scotland's largest plant and nursery centres.

DRUIMNEIL HOUSE GARDEN

10 miles N of Oban on a minor road off the A828

The garden has a fine display of rhododendrons, shrubs and trees, plus a garden centre. It is open from Easter to October each year under the Scottish gardens Scheme. Teas and coffees are available.

TAYNUILT

9 miles E of Oban on the A85

Taynuilt lies close to the shores of Loch Etiven and is on the 128-mile long **Coast to Coast Walk** from Oban to St Andrews. Nearby, at Inverawe, is the **Bonawe Furnace**, which dates from 1753. Ironworking was carried out here for over 100 years, and the furnace made many of the cannonballs used by Nelson's navy. In 1805 the workers erected a statue to Nelson, the first in Britain, and it can still be seen today near Muchairn Church.

At Barguillean Farm you will find **Barguillean's Angus Garden**, established in 1957 on the shores of Loch Angus. It extends to nine acres, and was created in memory of Angus Macdonald, a journalist who was killed in Cyprus in 1956.

LOCH AWE

16 miles E of Oban on the A85

If you take the road east from Dunstaffnage Castle, passing near the shores of Loch Etive and going through the Pass of Brander, you will come to Scotland's longest loch, Loch Awe. This is its northern shore, and it snakes southwest for a distance of nearly 25½ miles until it almost reaches Kilmartin. Twenty crannogs, or artificial islands, have been discovered in the loch. On them defensive houses were built of wood, with a causeway connecting them to the mainland. They were in use in the Highlands from about 3000BC right up until the 16th century. Near the village of Lochawe are the impressive ruins of **Kilchurn Castle** (Historic Scotland), right on the shores of the loch. It was built by Sir Colin Campbell, who came from a cadet branch of the great Campbell family, in about 1450. They were eventually elevated to the peerage as the Earls of Breadalbane. In the 1680s Sir John Campbell converted the castle into a barracks to house troops fighting the Jacobites. However, it was never used as such.

Loch Awe

St Conan's Kirk, also on the banks of the loch, is reckoned to be one of the most beautiful churches in Scotland, though it dates only from the 1880s, with later additions. It was built by Walter Douglas Campbell, who had built a mansion house nearby. The story goes that his mother disliked the long drive to the parish church at Dalmally, so in 1881 Walter decided to built a church on the shores of Loch Awe. Not only did he commission it, he designed it and also carved some of the woodwork. The church was completed in 1887, but it proved too small for him, so in 1907 he began extending it. He died in 1914 before he could complete it, and it was finally finished in its present state in 1930. It has a superb chancel, an ambulatory, a nave with a south aisle, various chapels and, curiously for a small church, cloisters. The Bruce Chapel commemorates a skirmish near the church, when a small force of men loyal to Robert the Bruce defeated John of Lorne, who had sworn allegiance to Edward I of England. The chapel contains a small fragment of bone from Bruce's tomb in Dunfermline Abbey.

The waters of Loch Cruachan, high on Ben Cruachan above Loch Awe, have been harnessed for one of the most ambitious hydroelectric schemes in Scotland. Not only does the **Cruachan Power Station** (see panel below) produce electricity from the waters of Loch Cruachan as they tumble down through pipes into its turbines and then into Loch Awe, it can actually pump 120 tons of water a second from Loch Awe back up the pipes towards Loch Cruachan by putting the turbines into reverse. This it does during the night, using the excess electricity produced by conventional power stations. In this way, power is

CRUACHAN VISITOR CENTRE

Dalmally, Argyll PA33 1AN
Tel: 01866 822618 Fax: 01866 822509
e-mail: visit.cruachan@scottishpower.com
website: www.scottishpower.com/cruachan/

Hidden deep within the mountain of Ben Cruachan on the shores of Loch Awe is Cruachan Power Station. Here, a short distance from Oban, you can discover one of the hidden wonders of the Highlands. A power station buried one kilometre below ground. At its centre lies a massive cavern, high enough to house the Tower of London. Here enormous turbines convert the power of water into electricity, available to you in your home at the flick of a switch. Take an unforgettable journey into Ben Cruachan and find out how power is generated. Experienced guides will lead you along a tunnel cut from solid rock. A coach will transport you into a different world, a place so warm that sub-tropical plants grow.

Find the nerve centre of the station and understand how the power of water from Loch Awe is harnessed to provide a rapid response to sharp rises in demand for electricity such as at mealtimes. A generator can go from standstill to an output of 100,000 kilowatts in two minutes to provide as much electricity as necessary.

Back on the surface, the visitor centre has many things to see and do. The Exhibition includes touch screens and demonstrates the way in which power will continue to be generated in the future. To finish off, there is a lochside cafeteria and gift shop. Open Easter to mid November 9.30am-5pm; August 9,30am-6pm.

stored so that it can be released when demand is high, and it was the first station in the world to use the technology, though nowadays it is commonplace.

The turbine halls are in huge artificial caves beneath the mountain, and there is an exhibition explaining the technology. Tours are also available taking you round one of the wonders of Scottish civil engineering - one that can produce enough electricity to supply a city the size of Edinburgh.

KILMELFORD

11 miles S of Oban on the A816

To the west of this little village, near the shores of Loch Melfort, there was once a gunpowder mill, one of the many small industries that once dotted Argyll. In the kirkyard of the small **Parish Church** of 1785 are some gravestones marking the burial places of people killed while making the "black porridge".

It was at Loch Melfort, in 1821, that one Scotland's most unusual weather phenomenons occurred - it rained herrings. The likeliest explanation is that the brisk south westerly which was blowing at the time lifted the herring from the loch and deposited them on dry land.

ARDUAINE

15 miles S of Oban on the A816

The 50-acre **Arduaine Gardens** (National Trust for Scotland) are situated on a south-facing slope overlooking Asknish Bay. They are another testimony to the mildness of the climate on Argyll's coast, and have a wonderful collection of rhododendrons. There are also great trees, herbaceous borders and a diversity of plants from all over the world. They were laid out by James Arthur Campbell, who built a home here in 1898 and called it Arduaine, which means "green point". It was acquired by the NTS in 1992.

ARDANAISEIG GARDEN

14 miles E of Oban on a minor road off the B845 on the banks of Loch Awe

Ardanaiseig is a large, 100-acre woodland garden with a large herbaceous border. The garden is closed from January to mid February each year.

DALAVICH

13 miles SE of Oban on a minor road off the B845 on the banks of Loch Awe

If you follow the B845 south from Taynuilt, then turn south west onto a minor road near Kilchrenan, you will eventually reach the **Dalavich Oakwood Trail**. It is a two-mile long walk laid out by the Forestry Commission, with not only oaks, but also alder, hazel, downy birch and juniper. There are also small sites where 18th and 19th century charcoal burners produced charcoal for the Bonawe Iron Furnace near Taynuilt. Other woodland trails are the **Timber Walk** and the **Loch Avich.**

Kilmelford

LOCATOR MAP

ADVERTISERS AND PLACES OF INTEREST

INNER HEBRIDES 9

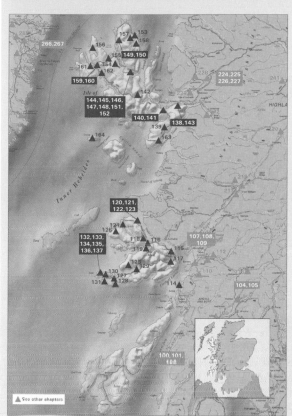

The Inner Hebrides, unlike the Western Isles, is not a compact geographical unit. Rather it is a collection of disparate islands lying off the Argyll coast, and forming part of that county (apart from Skye, which is part of the Highlands). Each island has its own distinct character, with sizes ranging from the 87,800 hectares of Mull (the third largest of Scotland's islands) to the 33 hectares of Staffa and the 877 hectares of Iona.

Not all the islands are inhabited, and of those that are, most have seen a drop in population over the years. Some of the uninhabited ones were inhabited at one time, and the remains of cottages and even old chapels are still to be found. The names trip off the tongue like a litany, and some, to English speakers, are decidedly unusual. Mull; Muck; Rum; Eigg; Coll; Canna; Tiree; Islay; Jura; Colonsay. All have their origins in Gaelic, and in some cases Norse.

And each island is different. Lismore, for instance, is flat and fertile, while Jura is mountainous. Mull is easily accessible from the mainland, while Canna, beyond Rum, is remote. Islay (pronounced "Eyelah") and Jura are the most southerly, and lie off the western coast of the Mull of Kintyre, from where they are reached by ferry. Islay is where you will find, at Finlagan, the capital of the ancient Lordship of the Isles. It is also an island famous for its distilleries, which make a peaty, dark malt. Tiree is said to be the sunniest spot in Britain, though it is also one of the wettest and windiest. It is low lying, so much so that its name in Gaelic, "Tir an Eorna" actually means "the land below the sea". It is now famous for its surfing beaches, and many championships are held here.

Even though most of the islands lie well away from the mainland, they have still been influenced by Lowland Scots and English sensibilities. Rum has changed its name three times over the last century. Originally it was Rum, then, when the Bullough family bought it in the late 19th century, they changed it to

View Towards Mull from Iona

Rhum in deference to their teetotal beliefs. In 1957 the island was bought by Scottish Natural Heritage and the name changed back to Rum.

Places like Mull and Skye are proving to be popular retirement spots, with the local people having a name for the Lowland Scots and English who settle there - "white settlers". Though there has been some grumbling in the past about incomers seeking to impose English values on what is essentially a Gaelic culture, they are generally welcomed.

The Inner Hebrides can also claim to have the most sacred place in Scotland, if not Britain. Iona, off the west coast of Mull, was where St Columba established his great monastery, and from where missionaries set out to convert the northern lands. St Columba wasn't the first man to bring Christianity to Scotland - that honour goes to St Ninian - but he was the most influential, and we know a lot about his life, thanks to a biography written by St Adamnan, ninth abbot of Iona, almost a 100 years after he died. Though some of it is uncritical hagiography, there is enough to see the man behind the venerated saint that is

Uig, Skye

Columba. He tells of a man who was all too human - vengeful yet forgiving, impetuous yet thoughtful, arrogant yet unassuming and boastful yet modest. Today Iona is still a place of pilgrimage, though most people now come as tourists to see and admire the later abbey buildings and experience that feeling of calm for which the island is famous.

There are other sacred sights in the Inner Hebrides, such as the ruins of Oronsay Priory and the Columban remains on Eileach an Naoimh, part of the Garvelloch group of islands.

GIGHA

17 miles NW of Campbeltown off the west coast of Kintyre

This small island, no more than six miles long by two miles wide at its widest is reached by ferry from Tayinloan. It is best to see the island on foot, and the **Gigha Path Network** makes this easy. The name Gigha (pronounced gee-yah, with a hard "g") was given to the island by the Norse king Hakon, and means "God's island". It seems to have a climate of its own, and while the rest of Argyll is enveloped in cloud, Gigha is sometimes bathed in sunshine due to the Gulf Stream washing its shores. Its highest peak, at 330 feet, is **Creag Bhan**, where you can see a 4th century inscribed stone.

Cottage, Islay

The scanty ruins of **Kilchattan Church**, behind the hotel, date from medieval times. In the kirkyard are some old grave slabs showing knights in armour. One is possibly of Malcolm MacNeill, Laird of Gigha, who died in 1493.

And behind the church, atop the Cnoc A'Charraidh (Hill of the Pillar) is the **Ogham Stone** dating from the time the island formed part of the kingdom of Dalriada. It carries a carving that reads *Fiacal son of Coemgen*, and probably marks a burial.

The 50-acre **Achamore Gardens**, near the ferry port at Ardminish, are open to the public. They were founded by Sir James Horlick, of bedtime drink fame, after he bought the island in 1944. They are famous for their rhododendrons and camellias. In 2001 the inhabitants of Gigha bought the island, and it is now managed by a trust.

ISLAY

35 miles SW of Inveraray in the Atlantic Ocean

Islay's relatively mild, wet climate has meant that the island has been inhabited for thousands of years. Clan Donald, which claims descent from Somerled, made the island the centre of their vast Lordship of the Isles, which at one time was almost a separate kingdom beyond the reach of Scottish monarchs. It is a truly beautiful island, with a range of hills to the east rising to 1,500 feet, and low, fertile farmland. It is famous for its distilleries, with over four million gallons of whisky being produced each year. Most of them have tours explaining the distilling process, and offer a dram at the end of it. An Islay malt has a peaty taste all of its own, due to the grain being dried over peat fires.

On islands in **Loch Finlaggan**, west of **Port Askaig** (where there is a ferry to Feolin Ferry on Jura and West Loch Tarbert on the Mull of Kintyre) you will find the ruins of the medieval centre of the Lordship of the Isles, with a visitor centre close by. The important remains are to be found on two of the islands in the loch, Eilean Mor (the Great Island)

The Mull of Oa, Isle of Islay

Distance:	1.9 miles (3.0 kilometres)
Typical time:	60 mins
Height gain:	60 metres
Map:	Explorer 352
Walk:	www.walkingworld.com ID:1837
Contributor:	Colin & Joanne Simpson

Access Information:

From Port Ellen an unclassified road leads west past the old distillery and is signposted to the Mull of Oa. Follow this with a final left turn along a track signposted to the American monument to reach the parking area.

Additonal Information:

The American monument atop the cliffs commemorates two troopships from the First World War which sank in these waters. HMS Tuscania was torpedoed by a German submarine on 5th Feb 1918 and sank off the Mull of Oa. HMS Otranto was involved in a collision with HMS Kashmir on 6th Oct 1918 and sank off Machir Bay.

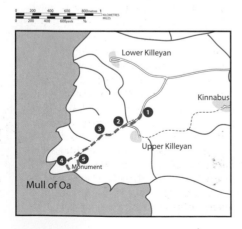

Description:

Much of the coastline of the Isle of Islay is low-lying, with rocky shores interspersed with beaches and only in the south-west are there cliffs of any note. This walk crosses the moors to the most dramatic section of cliffs, from where there are views over much of the island and across the North Channel to Northern Ireland.

Features:

Sea, Wildlife, Birds, Great Views, Moor, Ancient Monument

Walk Directions:

1 From the parking area, go through the gate and follow the track. A short distance down the track a signpost points to the right, to a recently built path that runs up the side of the field.

2 The path is obvious here, following the fence uphill.

3 At the top of the field the new path traverses rightwards and crosses a stile onto the open moorland. From here the route follows the old unmade path which can be indistinct at times, but the American monument on the skyline means there is always something to aim for. Another fence is crossed by a stile immediately before the first cliffs are reached. From here it is only a couple of hundred metres to the monument.

4 From the monument there are some views along the coast in both directions to the adjacent cliffs. It is possible to follow a faint track beyond the monument towards the headland, allowing you to look back at the nearest cliffs. In good conditions this is quite straightforward but could be quite dangerous if the grass is wet. To the south are more dramatic cliffs, including the highest on Islay at almost 200 metres. On a good day Northern Ireland can be clearly seen across the North Channel about 30km away.

5 The return can be made by the same route, passing a trig point just below the monument, but a longer alternative heads towards the bay at Port nan Gallan before returning past Upper Killeyan Farm.

and Eilean na Comhairle (the Council Island) Ancient burial slabs are thought to mark the graves of important women and children, as the chiefs themselves would have been buried on Iona. Close to Port Askaig itself are the **Bunnahabhain** and the **Caol Ila** distilleries. To the east of **Port Ellen** (which also has a ferry to Tarbert) are the distilleries of **Lagavulin**, **Laphroaig** and **Ardbeg**.

The ruins of **Dunyveg Castle**, a MacDonald stronghold, sit near Lagavulin. At one time it

Rubha a Mhail Lighthouse, Islay

was owned by a man called Coll Ciotach, or "left handed Coll". While he was away on business, the castle was captured by his enemies the Campbells, and his men taken prisoner. They then waited for Coll to return so that they could overpower him. But one of the prisoners was Coll's personal piper, and when he saw his master approach the castle, he alerted him by playing a warning tune. Coll escaped, but the piper had his right hand cut off, and never again could play the pipes. It's a wonderful story, though whether it is true or not is another matter, as the legend is also associated with other castles in Argyll, notably Duntroon.

At Ardbeg is the **Kildalton Cross and Chapel**. The incised cross dates from the 9th century, and is one of the finest in Scotland. Keeping on a religious theme, **Bowmore**, on the A874 beside the shores of Loch Indaal, has one of only two round churches in Scotland. It was built in 1767 by Daniel Campbell, who reckoned that, having no corners, the devil could not hide anywhere within it. **Bowmore Distillery** - the oldest (founded in 1779) and one of the most famous on the island - can be visited.

North of Bowmore, near Bridgend, is an Iron Age fort with the wonderful name of **Dun Nosebridge** (Landrover trips can be arranged to visit and view it), and to the southwest of the village, at the tip of the Mull of Oa (pronounced "oh"), is the **American Monument**, which commemorates the 266 American sailors lost when Tuscania sank after being torpedoed in 1918 and the Otranto was wrecked. Many of the bodies were washed up at the foot of the cliff here.

On the opposite side of the loch is a peninsula called the Rhinns of Islay, and it is here that you will find the **Bruichladdich Distillery**, which, in 2003, found itself under surveillance by American intelligence agents as the whisky distilling process is similar to the one used in making certain kinds of chemical weapons. At **Port Charlotte** is the **Islay Natural History Trust**, housed in a former whisky bond. It has a wildlife information centre, and provides information on the natural history and wildlife of Islay. Also in the village is the **Museum of Islay Life**, which tells of everyday life on the island through the ages, and has a special display on the many shipwrecks that have taken place of Islay's rugged coastline. Continue past Port Charlotte on the A874 and you will come to **Portnahaven**. About four miles from the village, and situated on the west side of the Portnahaven to Kilchiaran road, is the **Cultoon Stone Circle**. Not all the stones have survived, but three are still standing and 12 have fallen over at the point where they once stood. The ruins of **Kilchiaran Chapel**, on the west coast of the Rhinns can be reached by car via a narrow track. Though its fabric is basically medieval, its origins go right back to the time of St Columba, who founded it in honour of his friend St Ciaran. There is an old baptismal font and some carved gravestones. The nearby beach is favourite place for seals to sun themselves. Further north is the **Kilchoman Church and Cross**, accessed by another narrow track, which leaves the B8018 and goes past Loch Gorm. The cross dates from the 15th century, and was erected by "Thomas, son of Patrick". The church replaces a medieval building which once stood here, but has been boarded up, and is in a bad state of repair.

JURA

24 miles W of Inveraray in the Atlantic Ocean

Jura is an island of peat bogs, mists and mountains, notably the **Paps of Jura**, to the south. The highest mountain in the range, at over 2,500 feet, is **Ben an Oir**. The island's only road, the A846, takes you from **Feolin Ferry**, where there is a ferry to Islay, north along the east coast, where most of the island's population lives. You will pass **Jura House Garden** at Cabrach, with its collection of Australian and New Zealand plants. They thrive in this mild and virtually frost and snow free environment. **Craighouse**, with its distillery, is the island's capital. Behind the parish church of 1776 is a room with

some old photographs and artefacts of life on Jura through the ages. On the small island of Am Fraoch Eilean, south of the village, are the ruins of **Claig Castle**, reputed to be an old MacDonald prison.

A mile or so north of Craighouse is the ruined **Chapel of St Earnadail**. St Earnadail was St Columba's uncle, and the story goes that he wanted to be buried on Jura when he died. When asked where on the island, he replied that a cloud of mist would guide the mourners to the right spot. On his death, a cloud of mist duly appeared and settled where the ruins now stand.

The road then takes you north to **Ardlussa**, where it peters out. Within the old burial ground is the tombstone of **Mary MacCrain**, who died in 1856, aged 128. They seem to have been long-lived on Jura, for the stone goes on to say that she was a descendant of Gillouir MacCrain, *"who kept one hundred and eighty Christmases in his own house, and died during the reign of Charles I"*.

Just under a mile off Jura's north cost is the small island of **Scarba**. It has been uninhabited since the 1960s, though in the late 18th century it managed to support 50 people. It rises to a height of 1,473 feet, and has many Iron Age sites on its west coast. On the east coast are the ruins of **Cille Mhoire an Caibel**, surrounded by an old graveyard. Many miracles were supposed to have taken place within the kirk in early medieval times.

Between Jura and Scarba, in the Gulf of Corryvreckan, is the notorious **Corryvreckan** whirlpool. The name comes from the Gaelic Coire Bhreacain, meaning "speckled cauldron", and it is best viewed from the safety of the cliff tops on Jura (even though you have to walk about five miles from just beyond

Ardlussa to get there) as it has sent many boats to the bottom. It is caused by the combination of an immense pillar of rock rising from the seabed and a tidal race, and the best time to see it is when a spring tide is running westward against a west wind. The sound of it can sometimes be heard at Ardfern on the mainland, over seven miles away.

Legend tells us that the whirlpool's name has a different derivation. A Norwegian prince called Breachkan was visiting the Scottish islands, and fell in love with a beautiful princess, a daughter of the Lord of the Isles. Her father disapproved of the young man, but declared that he could marry his daughter providing he could moor his galley in the whirlpool for three days.

Breachkan agreed to the challenge, and had three cables made - one of hemp, one of wool and one from the hair of virgins. He then sailed into the Gulf of Corryvreckan, and while there was a slack tide, moored his boat in the whirlpool. The tides changed, and the whirlpool became a raging monster. The hemp cable snapped on the first day and the wool one snapped on the second. But Breachkan wasn't worried, for he knew that the one made from virgins' hair would keep him safe.

But on the third day it too snapped, sending the prince to his death. It seems that some of the virgins from whom the hair had come were not as innocent as they had made out.

COLONSAY AND ORONSAY

40 miles W of Inveraray in the Atlantic Ocean

The twin islands of Colonsay and Oronsay are separated by an expanse of sand called **The Strand** which can be walked across at low tide. Half way across the strand are the remains of the **Sanctuary Cross**. Any law-breaker from

Colonsay who passed beyond it and stayed on Oronsay for a year and a day could escape punishment. Colonsay is the bigger of the two islands, and has a ferry service connecting its main village of **Scalasaig** to Oban.

It is a beautiful place, full of rocky or sandy coves and areas of fertile ground. Perhaps the most beautiful part is **Kiloran Valley**, which is sheltered and warm. So warm that palm trees and bamboo grow quite happily here. It is where **Colonsay House**, stands. It is said that the builder, Malcolm MacNeil, used stones from an old chapel which stood close by when building it in 1722. Its gardens are open to the public.

Oronsay is famous for the substantial ruins of **Oronsay Priory**, perhaps the most important monastic ruins in the west of Scotland after Iona. Tradition gives us two founders. The first is St Oran, companion to St Columba, who is said to have founded it in AD 563. The second is St Columba himself. When he left Ireland, the story goes, he alighted first on Colonsay, and then crossed over to Oronsay, where he established a small monastery. However, he had made a vow that he would never settle where he could still see the coastline of Ireland. He could from Oronsay, so eventually moved on to Iona.

John, Lord of the Isles, founded the present priory in the early 14th century, inviting Augustinian canons from Holyrood Abbey in Edinburgh to live within it. The church is 15th century, and the well-preserved cloisters date from the 16th century. A series of large carved grave slabs can be seen within the Prior's House, and in the graveyard is the early 16th century **Oronsay Cross**, intricately carved, and carrying the words *Colinus, son of Christinus MacDuffie*. Another cross can be found east of the Prior's Chapel, with a carving of St John the Evangelist at its head.

EILEACH AN NAOIMH

29 miles W of Inveraray in the Atlantic Ocean

This small island is part of the Garvellochs, and is famous for its ancient ecclesiastical remains dating from the Dark Ages, which include chapels, beehive cells and an ancient graveyard. A monastery was founded here in about AD542 by St Brendan, better known as Brendan The Navigator. This was before St Columba founded the monastery on Iona. In the 10th century the monastery was destroyed by Norsemen, and the island had remained unihabited since then. It is reputed to be the burial place of both Brendan and Columba's mother, **Eithne**. There is no ferry service to Eileach an Naoimh.

SEIL AND LUING

9 miles S of Oban on the B844

These two islands are known as the "slate isles" due to the amount of slate that was quarried here at one time. Seil is a genuine island, but is connected to the mainland by the **Bridge Across the Atlantic**, designed by Thomas Telford

Clachan Bridge, Seil

and built in 1792. It is more properly called the Clachan Bridge, with the channel below being no more than a few yards wide. It is a high, hump-back bridge to allow fishing boats to pass beneath.

It got its nickname because at one time it was the only bridge in Scotland to connect an island with the mainland. Now the more recent Skye Bridge dwarfs it. On the west side of the bridge, on the island itself, is a late-17th century inn called the Tigh na Truish, or "House of Trousers". This recalls the aftermath of the Jacobite Uprising, when the wearing of the kilt was forbidden. The islanders, before crossing onto the mainland by a ferry which preceded the bridge, would

change out of their kilts here and into trousers.

On the west coast of the island is the village of **Ellenabeich**, with, facing it, the small island of Easdale. Ellenabeich was itself an island at one time, but the narrow channel separating it from the mainland was gradually filled up with waste from the local slate quarries. One of the biggest quarries was right on the shoreline, with its floor 80 feet below the water line. It was separated from the sea by a wall of rock, and during a great

Seil Island

storm, the wall was breached, and the quarry filled with water. Now it is used as a harbour for small craft.

An Cala Garden dates from the 1930s, and is behind a row of cottages that was turned into one home. There are meandering streams, terracing built from the local slate, and wide lawns. A 15-feet high wall of grey brick protects the garden from the worst of the gales that occasionally blow in from the Atlantic.

One of the former quarries' cottages in the village has been turned into the **Ellenabeich Heritage Centre** with a number of displays connected with the slate industry.

Offshore lies the small island of **Easdale**, connected to Ellenabeich by a small passenger ferry. This too was a centre of slate quarrying, and in the **Easdale Island Folk Museum** you can see what life was like when the industry flourished. It was founded in 1980 by the then owner of the island, Christopher Nicolson.

On Seil's southern tip is the small ferry port of Cuan, where a ferry plies backwards and forwards to **Luing**, to the south. This is a larger island than Seil,

though is more sparsely populated. Here too slate quarrying was the main industry. It is a quiet, restful place where seals can be seen basking on the rocks, as well as eagles and otters. Above the clachan of Toberonochy are the ruins of Kilchattan Chapel, with slate gravestones. One commemorates a Covenanter called Alex Campbell.

KERRERA

1 mile W of Oban, in Loch Linnhe

Offshore from Oban is the small rocky island of Kerrera, which can be reached by passenger ferry from a point about two miles south of the town. At the south end of the island are the ruins of 16th century **Gylen Castle**, another former MacDougall stronghold. It was built by Duncan MacDougall, brother (or son) of the clan chief, Dougal McDougall. It was sacked by a Covenanting army under General Leslie in 1647 which slaughtered all the inhabitants.

LISMORE

7 miles N of Oban, in Loch Linnhe

Lismore is a small island, no more than a

mile-and-a-half wide at its widest and ten miles long. It's name means "great garden", and it is a low-lying, fertile island connected to Oban by a daily ferry. The main village and ferry terminal is **Achnacroish**, though a smaller pedestrian ferry plies between Port Appin on the mainland and the north of the island in summer. In the village is the **Commann Eachdraidh Lios Mor** (Lismore Historical Society), situated in an old cottage that re-creates the living conditions in the Lismore of yesteryear.

Lismore, before the Reformation, was the centre of the diocese of Argyll. **Lismore Cathedral** stood at **Kilmoluaig**, near the small village of Clachan. It was destroyed just after the Reformation, but the choir walls were lowered and incorporated into the present church in 1749. The site had been a Christian one for centuries, and was where St Moluag set up a small monastery in AD 564.

Lismore was a prized island even in those days, and it seems that St Moluag and another Celtic saint, St Mulhac, had a quarrel about who should found a monastery there. They finally agreed to a race across from the mainland in separate boats, with the first one touching the soil of Lismore being allowed to establish a monastery. As the boats were approaching the shore Moluag realised that he was going to lose, so took a dagger, cut off one of his fingers and threw it onto the beach. As he was the first to touch the soil of the island, he was allowed to build his monastery. This was supposed to have taken place at Tirefour, where there are the remains of a broch now called **Tirefour Castle**, whose walls still stand to a height of 16 feet.

On the west coast of the island, facing the tiny Bernera Island, are the ruins of the 13th century **Achadun Castle**, where the Bishops of Argyll lived up until the 16th century, and further up the coast are the ruins of **Coeffin Castle**, built by the MacDougalls in the 13th century.

The highest point on the island, at a mere 412 feet, is **Barr Morr** (meaning "big tip"), but from the top there is a wonderful panoramic view in all directions.

MULL

8 miles W of Oban, in the Atlantic Ocean

The island of Mull, with over 300 miles of coastline and 120 miles of roads, is the third largest island in Scotland (only Lewis/Harris and Skye are bigger). Within its 87,535 hectares is a wild divergence of scenery, from rugged coastline to pasture and high mountains. Ths soils are, unlike some other rugged islands off Scotland's west coast, very fertile, so there is very little heather in the late summer and early autumn. However, it is still one of the most beautiful islands in the country, and it has the added advantage of being easy to reach, as a car ferry plies all day between the pier at **Craignure** and Oban.

Mull Lighthouse

Torosay Castle & Gardens

Craignure, Isle of Mull PA65 6AY
Tel: 01680 812421 Fax: 01680 812470
e-mail: torosay@aol.com website: www.torosay.com

Torosay Castle, completed in 1858 in the Scottish Baronial style by the eminent architect David Bryce, is one of the finer examples of his work, and one of the few still used as a family home while open to the public. Bryce's clever architecture results in a combination of elegance and informality, grandeur and homliness.

A unique combination of formal terraces and dramatic West Highland scenery makes Torosay a spectacular setting, which, together with a mild climate results in superb specimens of rare, unusual and beautiful plants. A large collection of statuary and many niche gardens makes Torosay a joy to explore and provides many peaceful corners in which to relax.

Tearoom Shop Free Parking Groups Welcome Holiday Cottages
Open: Daily April - end October 10.30am - 5pm Gardens all year.

On its north east side Mull is separated from Morvern on the mainland by the Sound of Mull, a deep sea trench that offers some of the best diving in Scotland. So much so that sometimes the wrecks can get very crowded with divers! One of the favourite dives is to the Hispania, sunk in 1954 and now sitting at a depth of 30 metres. She was sailing to Sweden from Liverpool with a cargo of steel and asbestos when she hit Sgeir Mor reef. A story is told that the captain refused to leave the sinking ship, thinking that he might be blamed for the accident. As the crew were rowing to safety in high seas, the last they saw of him was a figure standing on the ship saluting as it slowly submerged.

Another, unusual, wreck is of the Rondo. It sits vertically beneath the water, and though it is in two parts, it's bow is 50 metres below the surface, embedded in the sea bed, and its stern six metres below the surface.

The island's name comes from the Gaelic *Meall*, meaning a rounded hill. It is steeped in history, and was known to the Romans and Greeks. Even Ptolemy wrote about it, calling it *Maleus*. The highest peak, at 3,140 feet, is **Ben More**, the island's only Munro (a Scottish mountain above 3,000 feet).

It is home to 816 species of plants and trees, including 56 varieties of ferns, 247 varieties of seaweed, 22 species of orchid and 1,787 species of fungi. This diversity has made it popular with botanists, who visit the island throughout the year. In April many parts of Mull are carpeted with bluebells (known as harebells in England), with Grasspoint, a few miles south of Craignure, being a favourite place to see them.

The geology is every bit as diverse as its flora. It is also famous for its primroses.

And its wildlife is just as diverse. You can see birds of prey such as golden eagles, sea eagles and buzzards (UK's commonest bird of pray), as well as polecats, mountain hares, badgers, pine martens, adders, slow worms, otters, mink (which escaped from captivity) and red squirrels. And the lonely coastal cliffs are home to wild goats. Take a sea trip and you can see bottlenose dolphins, porpoises, seals and even Minke whales.

Close to Craignure is **Torosay Castle** (see panel on page 295), with its fine gardens. The castle sits in 12 acres of grounds, and is a fine Victorian mansion built in 1858 to the designs of David Bryce in the Scottish Baronial style. It was a favourite place of Winston Churchill in his younger years, and on

SEILIDEIL

Loch Don, Isle of Mull PA64 6AP
Tel/Fax: 01680 812465

Libby Fisher has plenty of experience in running and managing B&B accommodation and she knows that people want comfort, convenience, friendly atmosphere and great value for money - and the three-star **Seilideil** has it all. Its name derives from the Gaelic meaning "yellow iris", and sits by lovely Loch Don a couple of miles south from the Craignure ferry terminal.

A huge en suite family room sleeps five, with hearty Scottish breakfasts served in the newly refurbished conservatory. The produce is all fresh and local wherever possible, with lighter options available if required. Just right to set you up for a hard day's sight-seeing or indulging in one of he many sporting activities the island has to offer. There is also a self-catering unit that sleeps up to five, and with a ramp for disabled access. It too has recently been refurbished, and comes complete with new conservatory and fully fitted kitchen.

There are wonderful sea views, and it is an ideal base for exploring the island of Mull. There is so much to see and do. Climbing, golf, fishing, sailing and walking - not to mention the island's marvellous history and heritage. Tobermory and Iona are no more than an hour away by car, and both Torosay, with it's narrow gauge railway, and Duart Castle, are on Seiladeil's doorstep.

display are photographs of him in the grounds. It is open to the public from April to October, while the gardens are open all year round. The walls of the front hall are crowded with red deer antlers. Though it is open to the public, it is still the family home of the Guthrie Jones family, who live on the upper floors. **Wings Over Mull** is at Auchnacroish House, close to the castle, and brooded over by the island's second highest mountain, Dun da Ghaoithe. It is a conservation centre for birds of prey, with owls being especially well represented, though you can also see hawks, kites, eagles and even vultures. There are flying displays every day during the season, and a display on the history of falconry.

Duart Castle

The **Mull and West Higland Railway**, a one-and-a-quarter mile long narrow gauge line, connects the castle with the pier. It has a gauge of 26 cm, and was opened in 1984 specifically to link the pier at Craignure with Torosay Castle. It passes therough woodland and coastal scenery, and at one point it even crosses over a peat bog, which brought special problems when it was being built. The tiny engines that pull the carriages are a mixture of steam and diesel, with possibly the Lady of the Isles being the prettiest of the lot. It was the first engine on the line, though there are now six operating.

To the east of Torosay Castle, on a small promontory, is **Duart Castle**, perched on the cliffs above Duart Point. It is the ancestral home of the Macleans, and still houses the clan chief. Parts of it go back to the 13th century, though it is such a well defended position that there was certainly a fort here long before that. The

keep was dates from the 14th century, and was built by Lachlan Lubanach Maclean. The buildings in the courtyard were added in the 16th century by Lachlan Mor ("Great Lachlan"). In 1688 the castle was sacked by the Campbells.

It was confiscated after Culloden, as the Macleans had fought alongside Charles Edward Stuart, but in 1911 the 26th MacLean chief, Sir Fitzroy MacLean, bought it back and restored it. "Maclean" means "son of Gillean", who is better remembered as "Gillean of the Battleaxe". The name means "follower, or servant, of John", and he was said to have descended from the ancient kings of Dalriada. The Macleans of Duart had the world's first recorded tartan - the Hunting Duart.

Some Maclean chieftains were unsavoury characters. The 11th chief was one such man. He detested his wife, as she could not provide him with an heir. Unfortunately for Maclean, she was a sister of the Earl of Argyll, the most powerful man in the Western Highlands.

Maclean hatched a plot. In 1497, he had her tied up and marooned on a rocky island below the castle that flooded at each high tide. He left her there for a whole night, and next morning noted that she had gone. Seemingly distraught, he later reported her sad death to the Earl, saying that she had been washed out to sea and drowned.

Salen

The Earl was sympathetic and overcome with emotion. He immediately invited him to his castle in Inveraray, and when the chief got there, he discovered his wife alive and well and seated at the top of the table beside her brother. A passing fisherman had rescued her. Nothing was said during the chief's visit, and the meal passed pleasantly, with much small talk and smiles all round. Maclean and his wife eventually went home together, and still nothing was said. By this time the chief was terrified, as he knew that retribution would eventually come. However. the event was never mentioned again, even by Maclean's wife, and when she eventually died of natural causes, and the chief heaved a great sigh of relief. He married again, and his second wife died also of natural causes, again without bearing him an heir. So he married a third time, his new wife eventually giving birth to a son. After the birth, in 1527,Maclean had to go to Edinburgh on business. While there, he was murdered in mysterious circumstances and for no apparent reason. Retribution had come 30 years after the event.

Near Duart Point is the **William Black Memorial**, erected in memory of the 19th century writer William Black, who died in 1898. He wrote such books as *Macleod of Dare, A Princess of Thule* and *Prince Fortunatus*. They were extremely popular in their day, though they are hardly ever read now. However a new version of *Macleod of Dare* was recently published.

A single track road leaves the A849 at Strathcoil, and heads south and then east towards Lochbuie. **Moy Castle** sits on the shores of Loch Buie, ten miles south west of Craignure, at the head of a small track leaving the A849 at Strathcoil. This was the family seat of the Macleans of Lochbuie, and was built in the 15th century. Inside is a dungeon that floods twice a day with the incoming tide. In the middle of the dungeon is a stone platform where the prisoners had to huddle to keep dry. A small island a few miles south off the coast has possibly the most unusual name of any island in the Western Isles - **Frank Lockwood's Island**. It was named after the brother-in-law of a Maclean of Duart in the 19th century.

During the Jacobite Uprising in 1745 it was garrisoned by a troop of Campbells. In 1752 it was finally abandoned, and though it is still in a fine state of preservation, it is not open to the public. Close to the castle is one of the very few stone circles on Mull. There are nine stones, with the circle having a diameter of 35 feet.

To the west of Craignure, on the A849, is **Fishnish Pier**, where a ferry connects the island to Lochaline on the mainland, across the Sound of Mull. At **Salen** the road becomes the A848, and if you turn southwest along the B8035 you can visit **Macquarie's Mausoleum** at Gruline, where lies Major General Lachlan Macquarie, Governor General of New South Wales between 1809 and 1820, and sometimes called the "Father of Australia". It is a square, cottage-like building of local stone surrounded by a high wall. Also buried there is his wife Elizabeth and their son, also called Lachlan. Born on the island of Ulva in 1762, he was related to the 16th and last Macquarie clan chief, and his mother was the sister of Murdoch Maclaine, chief of Lochbuie. He joined the army at he age of 14, and quickly rose through the ranks, serving in America, Egypt, Nova Scotia and India. In April 1809 he was appointed Governor of New South Wales. However, he suffered frequent bouts of ill health, and in 1820 he resigned, having turned New South Wales from a penal colony into a prosperous state.

He died in London in 1824, and his wife built the memorial above his grave in 1834. Now it is owned and maintained by the National Trust of Australia. In the year 2000 the Australian government spent $A70,000 on its refurbishment. So famous was he in Australia that there are many towns, schools, universities, streets and even teashops named after him

At this point Mull is no more that three miles wide, thanks to **Loch na Keal**, which drives deep into the island

MULL POTTERY

Baliscate Estate, Salen, Tobermory, Isle of Mull
Tel: 01688 302057
e-mail: info@mullpottery.fsnet.co.uk
website: www.mullpottery.com

Close to the picturesque town of Tobermory you will find the **Mull Pottery**. It makes high fired, hand-thrown ceramics the designs of which are inspired by the landscapes and seascapes of Scotland's rugged west coast.

All the pottery is made by skilled craftspeople who are dedicated to producing pieces that are beautiful and unique. The pottery makes all its own glazes, and refines its own clay to a secret recipe that was first used in 1982. The white stoneware porcelain is fired to a high temperature of 1290 degrees Celsius in a carefully controlled kiln atmosphere which eliminates porosity and ensure that you get a pot that is not only beautiful, but practical as well.

If you visit the well-stocked gallery, you can see the pots being made in the workshop before choosing a pot from the complete range of products on display. Seconds at bargain prices, and the work of other craftspeople can also be purchased. The *Seashore* and *Iona* ranges of hand-thrown domestic wear are very popular, with *Seashore* reflecting the blues, greens and browns of the beach, while *Iona* captures the turquoise and blue of the waters surrounding the island.

After you've made your purchase, you can relax in the Mull Pottery's licensed Café/Bistro which serves great snacks, meals and drinks on the pottery's own table wear. There is local seafood, game and farm produce, as well as great coffee, tea and home baking.

TORLOCHAN FARM

Gruline, Isle of Mull PA71 6HR
Tel:01680 300380
(3 Star STB Rating)
e-mail: torlochan@btopenworld.com
website: www.torlochan.com
Proprietors: Emily and Andre van Rhyn

Torlochan Farm is a 40 acre croft situated in the centre of Mull. The farm, surrounded by tree covered hillsides overlooks Loch na Keal and Staffa. They offer two comfortable and spacious log cabins suitable to sleep four people, each with a modern well-fitted kitchen, dining room and sitting areas, a double room and a twin room and shower/bathroom. All bed linen, towels etc. are provided with the beds made up for your arrival. Cots and highchairs are available on request. A smaller log cabin is also available for bed and breakfast. These are available for lets all year round, with off season mini breaks also available. Torlochan Farm is ideal for children with plenty of friendly animals to play with. Well behaved pets are also welcome. Under two miles away is a large shingle beach, with other sandy beaches along the coast of Ulva ferry. Torlochan Farm is also only 15 minutes drive from Tobermory, Mull's largest village, with plenty of shops, pubs and restaurants to suit all tastes and budgets.

PTARMIGAN HOUSE

The Fairways, Tobermory Isle of Mull PA75 6PS
Tel: 01688 302863 Fax: 01688 302913
e-mail: sue.fink@btopenworld.com
website: www.bed-and-breakfast-tobermory.com

Set in an acre of landscaped grounds overlooking Tobermory Bay, the five star **Ptarmigan House** is one of the best B&Bs, not only on Mull, but in Scotland as well. It is owned and personally managed by Sue and Michael Fink, who bring with them the experience of owning and running a top class hotel on the island. The newly built house offers the very best in accommodation, and has four superb en suite rooms that are furnished and decorated to an exceptionally high standard. The furniture and fabrics have been carefully chosen to offer comfort, light and space while still retaining an informal, friendly atmosphere. All four rooms have stunning

views towards the blue waters of the bay, and come with large double beds, hospitality trays and colour TVs. One room has its own balcony, with chairs and coffee table for warm evenings. Ptarmigan House also has a heated, 30-feet indoor swimming pool.

Hearty and filling Scottish breakfasts are served in the dining room overlooking the garden and superb gourmet dinners are available each evening, with all the produce used in the kitchen sourced locally wherever possible to ensure freshness and flavour. A typical menu could include local steamed mussels, salmon, fillet mignon, Tobermory smoked haddock, scallops, roast duckling and a host of other dishes, all at reasonable prices. To finish off you could have fresh strawberries and cream in season, followed by coffee.

in a north easterly direction. Its shores are famous for their birdlife, which includes wigeon, Slavonian grebe, teal, golden eye, mallard, black-throated diver and shelduck. At the entrance to the sea loch is the 130-acre island of **Inch Kenneth**. Curiously enough, its geology is unlike that of Mull, and it is flat and fertile. The "Kenneth" in question is supposed to be St Cannoch, a contemporary of St Columba. The ruins of **St Kenneth's Chapel** date from the 13th century, and in the kirkyard are many wonderfully carved grave slabs. A tradition says that ancient Scottish kings were buried here if the weather was too rough for the royal barges to travel to Iona. One of the best grave slabs is that of an armed man lying with his head on a cushion and his feet on an unnamed animal of some kind. In one hand is a cannonball and in then other is a shield. The shield once had a coat of arms on it,

but it has long since been weathered away.

Inch Kenneth was a favourite haunt of Diana Mitford, whose father Lord Redesdale owned the island. She married the infamous Oswald Mosley, the British Nazi. When her sister Unity was recovering from a suicide bid (she had tried to shoot herself in the head), she stayed on the island until she died of meningitis brought on by the shooting in 1948.

Another owner at one time was Sir Harold Boulton, who wrote perhaps the most famous Jacobite song ever- *The Skye Boat Song*. Many people believe it is a traditional song, but in fact it was written in 1884.

When Johnson and Boswell were making their Highland tour in the 18th century, they were entertained on the island by Sir Alan Maclean, chief of the Macleans of Duart. Johnson described it

THE ANCHORAGE ON TOBERMORY BAY

28 Main Street, Tobermory, Isle of Mull PA 75
Tel/Fax. 01688 302313

As you might expect, seafood is a speciality at **The Anchorage on Tobermory Bay**. It sits right on the waterfront, close to what is undoubtedly one of the richest areas in the world for high quality shellfish and other fruits of the sea. Owned and run by Jason and Sarah Cloete, it has earned a great reputation for its fine cuisine and outstanding value for money. Jason just has to cross the road to the harbour to buy produce straight from the boats, ensuring that everything is as fresh as possible. For this reason, the menu is likely to include

langoustines, lobster, crab, oysters, mussels, lemon sole, red snapper and monkfish.

As well as seafood the restaurant also features quality assured Highland venison, beef and chicken, all sourced locally wherever possible and vegetarian dishes are also available. The Anchorage has a small but select wine list, so you are sure to find something to complement your meal.

The restaurant is open from 10am - noon for teas, coffees and delicious home baking. From noon - 3.30 lunches are served, while from 6pm - 9pm there is a full à la carte menu. It overlooks the blue waters of Tobermory harbour, where boats bob on fine summer evenings, and it has a friendly, informal atmosphere where enjoyment of the food, the wine and the company is the order of the day.

as a "pretty little island" - praise indeed from a man who disliked most things Scottish.

Mull only has two large fresh water lochs. One is the wonderfully named **Loch Ba**, close to Gruline, which has the remains of a crannog. The other, **Loch Frisa**, sits in inaccessible country in the north west of the island, and is famous for its bird life. Like Loch Ba, it has some good fishing.

Mackinnon's Cave, on the Ardmeanach Peninsula near Balnahard, can only be reached at low tide, and great care should be taken if you visit. The cave goes hundreds of feet into the cliff face, and you'll need a torch if you want to explore it. It was visited by Dr Johnson, and is said to be

Tobermory

the largest cave in the Hebrides, being over 90 feet high. A legend tells of a

---

HIGHLAND COTTAGE

Breadalbane Street, Tobermory, Isle of Mull PA75 6PD
Tel: 01688 302030
e-mail:davidandjo@highlandcottage.co.uk
website: www.highlandcottage.co.uk

Highland Cottage sits above the town of Tobermory amidst its conservation area and only a few minutes walk from the bustle of Main Street and the Fisherman's Pier. Owned and run by Josephine and David Currie, this small, award-winning hotel offers all that is best in Scottish hospitality. Its warm, friendly and informal atmosphere means you can unwind and be pampered in a real home from home atmosphere while still enjoying high standards of service and great value for money. The fully en suite rooms all reflect Jo and David's dedication to the hotel. Each one is individually furnished and decorated round an "island theme", most having antique four poster beds.

After a hard day's sight-seeing, you can relax in the hotel's lounge, where you can read one of the hotel's many books and enjoy a cup of freshly made coffee or a glass of Tobermory malt whisky. As you would expect, the hotel's cuisine is outstanding. Top quality, fresh local produce is used wherever possible, and the dishes are all prepared and presented with imagination and flare. The comprehensive wine list is sure to contain something that will complement the food. Jo and David have been in the hospitality business all of their lives, and bring a wealth of experience to running Highland Cottage. Their staff are all friendly, efficient and have a wealth of knowledge about what guests can do and see on Mull.

piper and his dog entering the cave in days gone by. The piper was killed by a witch who lived there, while his dog escaped. At the back of the cave is **Fingal's Table**, a flat rock used as an altar by early Celtic saints. Also on the Ardmeanach Peninsula is **McCulloch's Tree**, a huge fossil over 36 feet high and three feet in diameter. It is reckoned to be over 50 million years old. There is another fossil in a nearby cave. Part of the land here, including the fossils, is owned by the National Trust for Scotland. The cave can be reached by a track which branches off the A849. To the south of the Ardmeanach Peninsula is **Loch Scridain**, the largest of the island's sea lochs. Like other locations on Mull, it is famous for its bird life.

Tobermory, Mull's capital, sits on the A848 to the north west of the island. Its name means "Mary's Well", and it is an attractive small burgh with many brightly painted houses and buildings fronting Tobermory Bay. Up until 1788 it was a small village, but in that year a small fishing station was established which changed its fortunes forever. The brightly painted houses date from that time, though they were not painted until many years later. **St Mary's Well**, which gave its name to the town, can be found in Dervaig Road. At one time its waters were thought to have healing qualities.

Tobermory is the setting for the popular children's TV programme **Balamory**, though the houses you see on the programme are even more brightly painted than the real ones thanks to the magic of television. **Mull Museum** is situated in the Columba building in Main Street, and has displays explaining the history of the island. There is also a small exhibition explaining Boswell and Dr Johnson's visit in 1773. Also in Main Street is the headquarters of the

DRUIMARD COUNTRY HOUSE AND RESTAURANT

Dervaig, near Tobermory,
Isle of Mull PA75 6QW
Tel/Fax: 01688 400345
e-mail: druimard.hotel@virgin.net

Set in two acres of woodland and garden, the four **Druimard Country House and Restaurant** is a beautifully restored Victorian country manse on a hillside overlooking the Glen and River Bellart. Dervaig is said to be the prettiest village on the island, and in the grounds of the hotel is the Mull Little Theatre, Britain's smallest professional theatre. The hotel can book seats on your behalf, and a visit to one of the performances is not to be missed.

The hotel can accommodate 14 guests in its seven spacious and comfortable bedrooms, each one having remote control TV, video, tea/coffee making facilities, direct dial phones and central heating. There is a real home from home feeling here, plus a relaxed, informal atmosphere that adds to your enjoyment of your holiday on Mull. The rooms are elegant and comfortable, with the furniture and decoration being of an extremely high standard.

The residents' lounge and the conservatory have glorious views out over the Glen, and here you will find plenty of comfortable armchairs and sofas to relax in over a pre dinner drink. There are videos, books and magazines aplenty to keep you occupied as well.

Druimard House is both child and pet friendly, and high tea can be served for kids in the conservatory at 5.30pm each afternoon, the children eating from a specially prepared menu that contains many favourites. Half portions can also be provided in the restaurant. Pets can stay in the guest rooms, though it is recommended that they are kept on leads while in the grounds.

The hotel restaurant is spacious and inviting. It is open to non-residents, and takes its food seriously. Fresh local produce is used wherever possible, and the chef has been awarded a coveted AA rosette for his dishes, which are prepared with flair and imagination while still letting all the flavours of the local produce speak for themselves. Why not try the locally smoked venison with poached leeks, balsamic syrup and Parmesan wafers? Or the local king scallops with smoked bacon? A great Aberdeen Angus steak cooked to perfection? Dining here is an experience not to be missed. There is a cellar of fine wines, and to complete the meal you can enjoy one of the single malt whiskies from the hotel bar.

The hotel is ideally placed to use as a base for exploring Mull's many attractions. You can arrange sea cruises, or go on bird watching safaris. There's golf, fishing, nature study and walking. Or you can just explore the many historical sites on the island. Staying at the Druimard Country House and Restaurant is an experience not to be missed.

Hebridean Whale and Dolphin Trust, a research, education and conservation charity. There is a small visitors centre with displays on whales and dolphins. Here you can watch videos of whales and dolphins in the Hebrides, as well as, in some cases, listening to their "songs. The **Tobermory Distillery** is the only distillery on the island, and is one of the oldest in Scotland. It dates from 1798, when a local merchant called John Sinclair was granted a license to distil spirit from the local grain. It now makes five distinct single malts, and there is a visitor centre and shop.

At the bottom of Tobermory Bay lies the famous wreck of the 800-ton **San Juan de Sicilia**, (though some say it was the Florida) part of the Spanish Armada fleet. Fleeing in September 1588 from the English ships, she anchored in the bay to repair her hull and take on provisions. Being part of the Spanish fleet which had tried to attack Scotland's old enemy England, the local people made her welcome. Donald Maclean of Duart Castle agreed to supply the ship with provisions if its captain agreed to pay for them and give him 100 soldiers to attack his enemies on Coll. The Spanish captain agreed, and provisions were taken on board while repairs were carried out. However, Maclean suspected that the captain would try to sail from the harbour without honouring his part of the bargain. He therefore boarded the ship and blew it up, making good his own escape. She sank in 60 feet of water, taking 350 Spaniards with her. Stories started circulating that she had 30 million gold ducats aboard her, and though some items were recovered (which can now be seen in the local museum), successive dives to locate the ducats failed. The first dive was in the early 17th century, when the Earl of Argyll sent men down to the wreck.

Successive dives, including one by the Royal Navy, have recovered small items such as a skull, cannon shot, pieces of wood and even a gold coin. A rumour started circulating that the ducats had actually been recovered in secret, and lay hidden at Aros Castle. Sir Walter Scott owned a writing case made of wood from the wreck, and it is said that the Queen owns a snuff box made from the wood, The ship now lies completely covered in silt, and it is unlikely that anything will ever be recovered from her again (see also Fort William). Protecting Tobermory Bay is **Calve Island,** close to which there is plenty of good diving. Tobermory has one of the island's three ferry links with the mainland, this one plying to Kilchoan on the Ardnamurchan Peninsula.

Glengorm Castle lies a few miles west of Tobermory, at the end of a single track road. It was built in 1860 for local landowner James Forsyth, who instigated the Clearances in the area, removing crofters from their land and replacing them with the more profitable sheep. It is not open to the public, though there is both a flower garden and a market garden here where you can buy plants and vegetables. There is also a coffee shop. At **Bloody Bay** about a mile east of the castle a battle was fought in 1480 between the last Lord of the Isles and the mighty Crawford and Huntly families, aided by the Lord of the Isle's son Angus.

The ruins of **Aros Castle** lie a mile or so north west of the village of Salen, south east of Tobermory. They date mainly from the 13th and 14th centuries. Originally built by the MacDougalls, it later became the Mull base for the Lords of the Isles, and was the most important place on the island up until the mid-18th century. In 1608 clan chiefs were invited

TIRORAN HOUSE

Tiroran, Isle of Mull PA69 6ES
Tel: 01681 705232 Fax: 01681 705240
e-mail: info@tiroran.com
website: www.tiroran.com

Tiroran House offers a unique and delightful combination of private family home and small country house hotel. Set in its own micro-climate on the banks of Loch Scridain, this spectacular location provides a haven for nature- and food-lovers alike. The drive to Tiroran takes you through some of the most spectacular scenery in Scotland, single track roads connecting the Island through a magical landscape of rugged mountains and stepped silhouettes.

Enter Tiroran by the south drive arched by an avenue of mature Limes and bordered by spectacular displays of rhododendrons or Hydrangeas. Feel the tension release as you approach the house framed by its palms and shrubs. An oasis of tranquillity set in a natural amphitheatre of mature Larch. A

stirring burn tumbles past the house through an enchanting and serene garden down to the sea.

Here on the south side of Mull, Laurence and Katie have created an enchanting experience. Guests are treated to exquisite cordon bleu food and an elegant, relaxing home from home. The seven en suite rooms are all individually named and decorated, complete with beautiful furniture, luxurious toiletries, fresh flowers and most with stunning views, - not to mention the fabled Tiroran water, reputed to have its own healing properties. Binoculars are provided to spot grazing deer. As for wildlife, sea eagles and golden eagles circle overhead, and otters and dolphins bask and leap in the loch beyond.

Start the day with a hearty Scottish breakfast in the vine-covered conservatory, complete with panoramic views over the Loch. Then begin your exploration of the Island. Tiroran is a perfect base from which to visit the nearby islands of Iona and Staffa (home to Fingals Cave) or, for the more adventurous, to climb nearby Ben More, Mull's only Munro or take a drive round the west side via the spectacular Griban rocks, one of the best views in Scotland. Visit Ulva or one of the many places of geological or historical interest before returning to Tiroran for pre-dinner drinks followed by Katie's

excellent dinners in the intimate dining room or conservatory. After dinner retire to one of the sitting rooms and enjoy an after dinner malt in front of the log fire where the conversation flows and the day's experiences are recounted and the next days are planned.

A self-catering cottage is also available, complete with all the trimmings available in the House. Cottage guests may eat with other guests by prior arrangement and, for those with small children; the House and dining room are within baby monitor range.

Guests will leave Tiroran feeling very rested and relaxed, and undoubtedly planning their return visit. A truly special haven.

to the castle by Lord Ochiltree, lieutenant to James VI. The chiefs, suspecting nothing, boarded Ochiltree's ship, The Moon, and sat down to dine.

However, Ochiltree had an ulterior motive. He calmly stood up and announced that they were all prisoners of the king, as they had plotted against James VI and were rebellious and disloyal. The chiefs tried to leave the ship, but it was too late. It had weighed anchor and was now sailing south. The chiefs were later imprisoned in Blackness, Stirling and Dumbarton castles until they agreed to swear undying loyalty to their king.

The narrow B8073 rises up from Tobermory and passes through **Dervaig**, reckoned to be the loveliest village on the island. It is home to the 38-seat **Mull Little Theatre**. According to the Guinness Book of Records, it is the smallest professional working theatre in

the world, and puts on a season of plays every year to packed audiences. It was founded in 1966, in the converted coach house of a Free Church manse by Barrie and Marianne Hesketh, professional actors who had settled on Mull to bring up their children. Now it not only presents plays within the tiny theatre, it tours the Highlands and Islands as well. At the end of 2006 it may have to relocate, and plans are being made to build an entirely new theatre two miles outside Tobermory at Aros Park.

The B8073 continues on to the small village of **Calgary**, on Calgary Bay. The name in Gaelic means the "harbour by the dyke", the dyke being a natural basalt formation which can still be seen. Here you will find what is possibly the best beach on the island, with vast stretches of white sand. In 1883 Colonel J.F. Macleod of the Royal North West Mounted Police holidayed in Calgary,

CALGARY HOTEL

Calgary, near Dervaig, Isle of Mull PA75 6QW
Tel. 01688 400256
website: www.calgary.co.uk

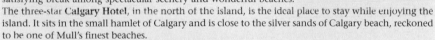

Time moves at a slower pace on the beautiful Isle of Mull. Here you can relax away from the stress and strain of modern life, and enjoy a satisfying break among spectacular scenery and wonderful beaches.

The three-star **Calgary Hotel**, in the north of the island, is the ideal place to stay while enjoying the island. It sits in the small hamlet of Calgary and is close to the silver sands of Calgary beach, reckoned to be one of Mull's finest beaches.

Recently converted from farm steadings, the hotel is full of character, and has an informal atmosphere where comfortable accommodation, good food and drink and efficient, friendly service is all. The nine rooms are spacious and welcoming, and two on the ground floor are family suites with a double room and adjoining bunkroom and bathroom. There is also a hydro-spa suite in one of the bedrooms with a spa bath. Most of the rooms have views out over woodland towards the beach, as does the lounge terrace and restaurant. The lounge is cosy and warm, with a wood burning stove and separate TV room. The Dovecote Restaurant is set within what was a

barn with a dovecot, and serves delicious food. It uses local produce wherever possible, such as beef, lamb, pork, venison, salmon and white fish, with its speciality being local shellfish.

Opposite the hotel is the Carthouse Gallery, which showcases the work of local artists - paintings, etchings, pottery, wood and ironwork. In the Calgary Chair Company you will find hand crafted chairs and carvings, made by Matthew Read, proprietor of the hotel.

ARGYLL ARMS

Bunessan, Isle of Mull PA67 6DP
Tel: 01681 700240 Fax: 01681 700717
website: www.isleofmull.co.uk

The Argyll Arms is recognised as one of the best hotels on Mull. It is situated right on the harbour front in Bunessan, where you can enjoy "dining with a view". It has recently been taken over by Margaret

Campbell, who intends to refurbish it to the highest standards. A new pub area - new restaurant - refurbished rooms - all the hotel will benefit, making it even more popular than it is at present.

ARDACHY HOUSE HOTEL

Uisken, By Bunessan, Isle of Mull, Argyll PA67 6DS
Tel: 01681 700505 Fax: 01681 700797
e-mail: cathy@ardachy.co.uk
website: www.ardachy.co.uk

The three-star **Ardachy House Hotel** is tucked away in the rugged farmlands of a typical Mull croft, seven miles east of Fionnphort, the ferry terminal for Iona. It is a three-star establishment that offers comfortable accommodation in eight bedrooms - single, double, twin or family. Seven of the rooms are fully en suite, and all have hair dryers, radios, tea and coffee making facilities. As you would expect, the food is outstanding, with all the imaginatively prepared dishes on the table d'hote menu using only fresh local produce wherever possible to allow natural flavours to predominate. Breakfasts include the hearty and filling full Scottish, though lighter options are also available if required, and the hotel is always happy to

discuss particular dietary requirements in advance. After dinner, why not enjoy a single malt whisky in the south-facing lounge? The view from the window is spectacular, featuring one of the best land and seascapes on the island. It's a panorama you will never tire of.

The west wing of the hotel has been converted into a self-catering apartment with one en suite bedroom, a delightfully furnished lounge/dining room with extra double sofa/bed and great views, and a modern, fitted kitchen. All bed linen is supplied, as is one set of towels per person. Prices include hot water and heating.

and was so impressed by the scenery that he named the Canadian city after it.

At the **Old Byre Heritage Centre**, which is about a mile from the village, Mull's visitors can learn about the island's history and heritage. There are also displays on natural history, and a half hour video.

The road continues in a south easterly direction along the shores of **Loch Tuath**, giving views across to the islands of **Ulva**, visited by Boswell and Johnson in 1773, and **Gometra**. The ancestors of David Livingstone, the African explorer and missionary, came from Ulva (see also Blantyre). From the 10th century until the 19th century, when it was sold to pay off debts, the island was owned by the MacQuarries. In 1773 Boswell and Johnson visited Ulva, and was entertained by the then MacQuarrie chief. Though they found their host to be a charming, intelligent man, Boswell wrote that the house was "mean", and that the chief was burdened with debts. At one time there was a great piping school on the island.

To summon the privately-owned ferry to Ulva, visitors slide back a small white panel to uncover a red panel which can be seen from the island. At the ferry point on the island is the small **Ulva Heritage Centre**, housed in a restored thatched cottage, with attached tearoom.

To the west of Ulva is the smaller island of Gometra, connected to Ulva by a causeway. It has been uninhabited since 1983, though Gometra House can still be seen. Since early times, Gometra was owned by the monastery of Iona, and indeed was known as "Iona's granary" on account of the crops grown there. Later it was acquired by the Campbells when James VI abolished the title of Lord of the Isles.

The B8073 then swings northeast along the northern shores of Loch na Keal before joining the B8035, which, if you turn right, takes you along the southern shore of Loch na Keal and on to the A849.

The **Treshnish Islands** is a small chain of islands well to the west of Gometra. The main islands are Lunga, Fladda, Bac Mor, Cairn na Burgh Mor and Cairn na Burgh Beg. Now uninhabited, they are a haven for wildlife, with Lunga especially being a favourite nesting site for puffins, shags, guillemots, razorbills and kittiwakes. On Cairn na Burgh are early Viking and Iron Age fortifications. Autumn is the breeding season for grey Atlantic seals, and many can be seen on all the islands' beaches at that time. Boat trips to the Treshnish Islands leave from various ports on Mull and from Iona.

Pennyghael, gateway to the Ross of Mull, sits just off the A849, on the way to

Fionnphort and the ferry for Iona. Nearby is the **Beaton Cairn**, which commemorates the hereditary doctors of the Lord of the Isles. A narrow road branches south at Pennyghael, taking you to the southern shore of the Ross of Mull at Carsaig. If you walk westwards along the beach you will reach the **Nun's Cave**, which has Celtic Christian carvings. The cave got its name because the nuns of Iona Nunnery are

Ffionnphort

supposed to have hidden here during the Reformation. The spectacular **Carsaig Arches** is further on, at Malcolm's Point. They were once caves, but the sea has eroded the 600-feet high cliffs behind them and left the arches standing.

Bunessan, nine miles west of Pennyghael, sits on the small Loch na

Lathaich, which is a faviourite anchorage for small boats and yachts. Next to the village hall, in a Portacabin, is the **Ross of Mull Historical Centre**, which gives information about the history, wildlife and people of the area. At the end of the A849 is **Fionnphort** (pronounced "Finnafort", meaning "fair port"), the

---

ELEANOR MACDOUGALL

Aridhglas, Fionnphort, Isle of Mull PA66 6BW
Tel: 01681 700780
e-mail: Eleanor@nicdhughaill.fsnet.co.uk

Eleanor MacDougall is one of Scotland's best silversmiths, making a fine range of Celtic silverware, bowls, goblets and jewellery that would make the ideal gift or souvenir of your stay in Mull or Iona. She also does commission work at very competitive prices. Eleanor studied at Glasgow School of Art, and her designs and craftsmanship are superb. She specialise in hand-raised work, which entails beating flat discs of silver over steel formers to produce objects of stunning beauty. During your stay on Mull, pay her a visit. You won't be disappointed.

RED BAY COTTAGE

Deargphort, Fionnphort, Isle of Mull PA66 6BP
Tel: 01681 700396

When John Wagstaff built **Red Bay Cottage** at Fionnphort 25 years ago as a holiday retreat, little did he realise that he would turn it into one of the best restaurants on Mull. Here the quality and freshness of the produce used is very important, with most of it being sourced locally. It's popular with both locals and tourists alike, and the sizzling, juicy steaks have become justly famous. The dining room overlooks the Sound of Iona, and you are sure to love sitting enjoying a superb meal while watching the stunning sunsets.

ferry terminal for Iona. Before crossing, a visit to the four-star **Columba Centre** should prepare you for what you'll find on the island. On the shore stands **Fingal's Rock**, supposedly thrown by the giant Fingal while in a bad temper.

IONA

36 miles W of Oban off the coast of Mull

Iona Abbey

No tourists' cars are allowed on Iona (National Trust for Scotland), though it is so small (no more than three miles long by a mile and a half wide) that everything on it can easily be visited on foot. It is one of the most sacred spots in Europe (and unfortunately, during the summer months, one of the busiest), and was where **St Columba** set up his monastery in AD 563. From here, he evangelised the Highlands, converting the Picts to Christianity using a mixture

SHORE COTTAGE B&B

Isle of Iona Argyll PA76 6SP
Tel: 01681 700744
e-mail: enquiries@shorecottage.co.uk
website: www.shorecottage.co.uk

Shore Cottage is a beautiful, modern house set, as you would expect, right on the shores of the magical Isle of Iona, off the west coast of Mull. It is only three minutes walk from the island's pier, and offers superb B&B accommodation to the discerning tourist. Owned and managed by Sarah MacDonald, it boasts three en suite bedrooms that are comfortable and spacious, each one furnished and decorated to a high standard. Value for money and great standards of service are the watchwords here, with each room having a colour TV, tea/coffee making facilities and hair dryer. Shore Cottage is noted for its breakfasts, and you can choose from a full Scottish, which is always hearty and filling, or lighter options if preferred.

Breakfast is served in the sunroom where guests can enjoy the stunning views across the Sound of Iona to Mull and Erraid. There is also a guest lounge where guests can relax and look across to Mull, admiring the scenery and the many birds that swoop above the water and the garden.

Iona is a wonderful island full of history and deserves to be visited. It is forever associated with St Columba, and you can visit the beautiful Iona Abbey, the ruins of the Nunnery, St Oran's Chapel and the graveyard - the final resting place of many early Scottish Kings. Shore Cottage is a magical B&B on a truly magical island.

AOSDANA GALLERY & STUDIO

The Columba Steadings, Isle of Iona, PA76 6SW
Tel/Fax:01681 700121
e-mail: mhairi@aosdanaiona.com website: www.aosdanaiona.com

From the Gaelic, meaning people of the art, craft or gift, Aosdana is a beautiful gallery and working studio selling contemporary artwork alongside modern and traditional Iona jewellery. Housed in an old farm steading which has been lovingly restored by Iona stone mason, Colin MacDougall with interior features by Scottish artisans, the building alone is worth a visit. Aosdana is owned and run by local artist Mhairi Killin, whose aim is to combine the historical creativity of Iona with its contemporary equivalent. Aosdana continues the traditional work of Iona silversmiths Alex Ritchie (1856-1941) and Iain MacCormick (1917-1998) represented by the extensive range of reproduction

designs on display. Each piece of jewellery is cast in sterling silver, hallmarked in Edinburgh and hand finished at the studio by local silversmiths. Inspired by Iona and using local stones, a modern range of jewellery is also on display. The jewellery is complemented by unique artwork; finely woven sculptures and wall pieces influenced by Scottish archaeology and created using delicately treated metals, wire and paper.

Aosdana offers a truly unique experience on Iona as it combines the historical work of the Island's past with the present and gives its vistors the chance to enjoy and support the creative energy of the Island. Open daily from Easter to November, 10am – 5pm or by appointment.

of saintliness, righteous anger and perseverance.

Columba's monastery would have been built of wood and wattle, and little now survives of it apart from some of the cashel, or surrounding wall. The present **Iona Abbey**, on the site of the original monastery, was founded in 1203 by Reginald, son of Somerled, Lord of the Isles, though the present building is early 16th century. It was a Benedictine foundation, and later became a cathedral. By the 18th century it was roofless, and the cloisters and other buildings were in ruins. In the 20th century they were restored by the Rev George MacLeod, a Church of Scotland minister who went on to found the **Iona Community**.

Beside the cathedral is the **Reilig Odhrain**, or St Oran's Cemetery. Within it is the **Ridge of the Chiefs**, which is supposed to contain the bodies of many West Highland chiefs who were buried here in medieval times. Close by is the **Ridge of the Kings**, where, it is claimed, no less than 48 Scottish, eight Norwegian and four Irish kings lie buried, including Macbeth. However, modern historians now doubt if any kings are buried there at all apart from some from ancient Dalriada. They say that the claims were a "marketing exercise" by the monks to enhance their abbey.

One man who does lie within the cemetery is **John Smith** the politician, who was buried there in 1994. **St Oran's Chapel**, near the cemetery, was built as a funeral chapel in the 12th century by one of the Lords of the Isles. The ruins of **St Mary's Nunnery** are near the jetty, and date from the 13th century. It too was founded by Reginald, and he placed

St Columba Hotel

Iona, Argyll PA76 6SL
Tel: 01681 700304
Email: info@stcolumba-hotel.co.uk
Website: www.stcolumba-hotel.co.uk

Iona is the island of st Columba. And if you ever visit as a tourist or
pilgrim, you should stay at the **St Columba Hotel**, where you will
find a friendly welcome and great value for money. All of the en
suite rooms are spacious and comfortable to make your stay a memorable one. The food is superb -
with only the best of local produce being used to create the imaginative dishes on the menu. If it's a
spiritual experience you are after, or just a holiday away from the stresses of modern life, then Iona is
for you, as is the St Columba Hotel.

Argyll Hotel

Iona, Argyll PA76 6SJ
Tel: 01681 700334 Fax: 01681 700510
Website: www.argyllhoteliona.co.uk

The **Argyll Hotel** is one of Scotland's most cherished hotels, situated
on the island of Iona, where once St Columba walked and preached.
It has 16 rooms, all but one of which are en suite, and each one is
cosy and comfortable, with tea/coffee making facilities. In the colder months, you'll find log fires
burning, and in the summer months you'll be entranced by the sheer beauty of this special island. The
food is great, the wine and the single malts will relieve you of the stress of modern living, and you'll be
cosseted from the moment you arrive until the moment you leave.

his sister Beatrice in charge as prioress. A
small museum has been established in
the **Chapel of St Ronan** close to the
ruins.

Just west of the cathedral is the **Tor
Ab**, a low mound on which St Columba's
cell may have been situated. Of the many
crosses on the island, the best are the
10th century **St Martin's Cross**, outside
the main abbey door, and the 16th
century **MacLean's Cross**.

In the former parish church manse
(designed by Telford) is the **Iona
Heritage Centre**, which traces the
history of the people who have lived on
the island throughout the years.

Staffa

34 miles W of Oban in the Atlantic Ocean

The most remarkable feature of this small
uninhabited island is **Fingal's Cave**,

which was visited in August 1829 by the
composer Felix Mendelssohn. Though he
found Edinburgh delightful, he was less
enamoured of the Highlands, which he
declared to be full of "fog and foul
weather". When he made the boat trip to
see the cave, he was violently seasick and
called the cave "odious". However, it
later inspired one of his most famous
works, the **Hebrides Overture**. The cliffs
are formed from hexagonal columns of
basalt that look like wooden staves, some
over 50 feet high. The Vikings therefore
named the island *Stafi Øy* (Stave Island)
from which it got its modern name.

Boat trips to the island are available
from Mull and Iona.

Coll and Tiree

50 miles W of Oban in the Atlantic Ocean

These two islands, lying beyond Mull,

can be reached by ferry from Oban. They are generally low lying, and can be explored by car in a few hours. The ferry first stops at **Arinagiour**, Coll's main village before going on to **Scarinish** on Tiree.

Robert the Bruce granted Coll to Angus Og of Islay, and it was Angus who was responsible for building **Breachacha Castle** (not open to the public) to the south of the island. Later it was owned by the MacLeans, the MacNeils and the MacDonalds. The present castle, which is largely 15th century, was restored in1965.

It was in Coll that an incident called the **Great Exodus** took place. In 1856 the southern part of the island, which was the most fertile, was sold to one John Lorne Stewart. In spite of protests from the crofters who farmed there, he raised their rents to a level they could not afford. So the tenants took matters into their own hands. Overnight, they all left their crofts and moved north to the less hospitable lands owned by the Campbells, where the rents were reasonable. Lorne Stewart was powerless to stop them leaving, and was left with no rent income whatsoever.

Tiree means the "land of corn", as it is one of the most fertile of the Inner Hebridean islands. It is sometimes called Tir fo Thuinn, meaning the "land beneath the waves", because of its relative flatness. Its highest peaks are **Ben Hynish** (460 feet) and **Ben Hough** (387 feet). In the south eastern corner of the island is the spectacular headland of **Ceann a'Marra**, with its massive sea cliffs. They are home to thousands of sea birds, and on the shoreline you can see seals basking in the sun.

Tiree has the reputation of being the sunniest place in Britain, though this is tempered by the fact that it is also the windiest. This has made the island the windsurfing capital of Scotland. Near Vaul to the north east of the island is a curious marked stone called the **Ringing Stone**, which, when struck, makes a clanging noise. Legend says if it is ever broken the island will disappear beneath the Atlantic. At Sandaig is the tiny **Sandaig Island Life Museum**, housed in a restored thatched cottage.

The **Skerryvore Lighthouse Museum** at Hynish tells the story of the Skerryvore lighthouse, ten miles to the south on rocks surrounded by open sea. It was designed by Alan Stevenson, uncle of Robert Louis Stevenson, and completed in 1842. The museum is within houses built for the Skerryvore workers.

SKYE

50 miles NW of Oban in the Atlantic Ocean

The new **Skye Road Bridge** opened in 1995 amid controversy about its tolls, although it is now free. Skye is one of the most beautiful and haunting of the Inner Hebrides, and the place has beauty and history aplenty.

Its name may come from the Norse word *skuy* meaning misty, and it is an apt description of an island that seems to get more beautiful the cloudier and mistier it becomes. Another possible derivation of the name is from the Gaelic *sgiath*, meaning "winged", and a glance at a map will show you that the island does indeed look as if it has wings. Nowadays Gaelic speakers know it as *Eileen à Cheo*, meaning the "Misty Isle". It is one of the few Inner Hebridean islands that has seen an increase in population over the last few years, due to people from the mainland settling there to find a better quality of life.

The island has been inhabited for thousands of years, and has many

Castle Moil Restaurant, Giftshop & King Haakon Bar

Kyleakin, Isle of Skye IV41 8PL
Tel/Fax: 01599 534164   e-mail: castlemoil@ukonline.co.uk

Castle Moil Restaurant & Giftshop and the adjoined **King Haakon Bar**, are situated on the seafront in the picturesque fishing village of Kyleakin, gateway to the Isle of Skye. The village sits immediately over the infamous Skye Bridge, and is a favourite stop for travellers and tourists arriving on the island. The village serves as an excellent base from which to explore the rest of the island. The family-run fully licensed **Castle Moil Restaurant** offers excellent value home-cooked dishes in a relaxed and informal environment. The menu caters for a wide range of appetites, tastes and budgets, including children, and always features fresh local fish and shellfish as well as traditional favourites such as steak pie, roast chicken and, of course,"haggis, neeps and tatties". Lighter snacks and salads are also always available, and the experience can be greatly enhanced with a bottle of wine, local malt whisky or a pint of the house real ale. Between Easter and October, the restaurant is open from 10am till 9pm.

The **Gift shop** can be accessed by its own entrance or via the restaurant, and carries a wide range of gifts and souvenirs, many produced on the island or the wider local area, including jewellery, ceramics, books, postcards and textiles.

The lively **King Haakon Bar** is very popular with locals and tourists alike, combining the authentic feel of an island pub with a mixed local and international clientele. The bar offers the full restaurant menu, as well as lighter bar snacks, and has a pool table and other bar games. It is renowned as a local entertainment hot-spot, hosting regular lively traditional and contemporary music sessions that invariably get everyone on the floor.

HEAVEN'S OCEAN artstudio

Barabhaig, Cruard, Camus Croise, Isle Ornsay, Isle of Skye, IV43 8QT
Tel: 01471 833475
e-mail: studio@heavens-ocean.co.uk
web: www.heavens-ocean.co.uk

Heaven's Ocean is the working studio/gallery of David Collins and Emma Siedle-Collins in Sleat, the southern peninsula of the Isle of Skye, also known as the Garden of Skye.

A self-taught artist and former London lawyer, David Collins works mainly in watercolour - his principal subjects being the landscapes of the West Coast and the Hebrides, in particular the mountains and coastline of Skye and the Small Isles of Eigg, Muck, Rum and Canna.

Emma Siedle-Collins works with driftwood and embroidered textiles to create unique mirrors and collage using found objects and organic and reclaimed materials. Emma's range of handmade cards are small collage in themselves, using painted background papers, wires, stamps, feathers, pressed flowers from her garden and pendants which can be worn as jewellery.

The studio, which is open at any reasonable time everyday from April to October (please call or e-mail in winter), is on the shore of Camus Croise Bay with stunning views across the Sound of Sleat to the mainland. There are easy walks around the bay and, for the more energetic, the wild unpopulated coastline beyond the studio offers wonderful views of Knoydart.

**VISIT THE ONLINE GALLERIES AT
WWW.HEAVENS-OCEAN.CO.UK TO SEE
CURRENT EXAMPLES OF OUR WORK
AND HOW TO FIND US.**

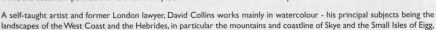

ancient cairns, standing stones, stone circles and burial mounds. St Columba is said to have visited, and baptised a Pict there by the name of Artbranan. He was an old man - a chieftain of a Geona tribe - and Columba had to talk to him through an interpreter. Later the Vikings raided the island, and then settled, bringing many Norse place names with them.

At Kyleakin, near the bridge, is the **Bright Water Visitor Centre**, with tours to the island nature reserve of *Eilean Ban* ("White Island") beneath the bridge. This was where Gavin Maxwell, author of *Ring of Bright Water*, once lived. Nearby are the ruins of **Castle Moil** , which was a stronghold of Clan Mackinnon. Legend says it was built by a princess called "Saucy Mary" who had married a Mackinnon chief, and who laid a chain from the castle to the mainland,

demanding payment from passing ships. It is totally untrue, as the Mackinnons only settled there in the 15th century. In the 17th century they abandoned the castle, and it gradually fell into disrepair.

Perhaps the most famous features on the island are the **Cuillin**, a range of mountains in the south east of the island. They are divided into the Black Cuillin and the Red Cuillin. The former are made from hard rock that has been shaped into jagged peaks and ridges by the last Ice Age, while the latter are of soft granite which has been weathered by wind and rain into softer, more rounded peaks. Though not the highest, they are perhaps the most spectacular mountains in Scotland, and present a challenge to any climber. The highest peak is **Sgurr Alasdair**, at 3,257 feet.

The A87 leaves the Skye Bridge and heads to the west of the island, passing

SKYE JEWELLERY

Main Street, Broadford, Isle of Skye IV49 9AE
Tel: 01471 820027 e-mail: info@skyejewllery.co.uk
Fax: 01471 822100 website: www.skyejewellery.co.uk
Antony Shepherd and his wife Cheryl set up Skye Jewellery 12 years go, making Celtic wedding rings. They draw their inspiration for each unique jewellery collection from the landscapes and rich cultural heritage of Skye. Each one is named after a landmark such as the mountains of Blaven, Marsco and Glamaig, and incorporates traditional Celtic knot work. All the rings are hand-crafted and have a unique sizing area which allows the ring to be enlarged or made smaller in the future without distorting or breaking the continuous knot work design.

Later they decided to set stones and pieces of Skye marbles into the rings, creating objects of great beauty. When satisfied customers requested matching earrings, the jewellery collections were born. Now the original rings are complemented by a matching range of jewellery - everything from pendants to cufflinks and earrings to tie tacks. All are available in silver, nine and 18 carat white, yellow or rose gold, or platinum. Antony and Cheryl's jewellery, for all its craftsmanship and superb design, represents outstanding value for money, and any piece would make the ideal gift or souvenir. Skye Jewellery has

gone form strength to strength, and their stunning new showroom - opened four years ago - has ensured that more and more people are becoming acquainted with their work. Their website and mail order catalogue (which can be ordered by phoning the above number) has resulted in orders from all over the world. Skye Jewellery staff are friendly and knowledgeable, and are keen to offer advice should you visit. The shop is open Monday - Saturday 8.45am - 5.30 pm, with late opening at the height of the season and Sundays 11 am - 4.30 pm.

THE HANDSPINNER HAVING FUN

The Old Pier Road, Broadford, Isle of Skye IV49 9AE
Tel: 01471 822876
e-mail: teoshandspun@yahoo.co.uk website: www.teoshandspun.co.uk

People tell us this is the woollens shop for which they have spent days looking. We spin our yarns and dye them. We design & make our own sweaters. Over 60 people make us as we are.

The "Handspinner Having Fun" was conceived in the South American hills, 25 years ago and ripened to become the best wee shop in the Highlands, quoted in *Vogue Knitting*, *Knitting*

mag and other publications on textiles.

Teo and Antonia's welcome guarantees the best little shop experience, We are by the sea, close to the Wee Pier, overlooking Broadford Bay.

Sweaters, unique hand spun and mill spun yarns, hand dyes and accessories.

SCONSER LODGE

Sconser, Isle of Skye IV48 8TD
Tel: 01478 650333 Fax: 01478 650386
e-mail: skye@sconserlodge.co.uk
website: www.sconserlodge.co.uk

The **Sconser Lodge Hotel** sits in the picturesque hamlet of Sconser, close to Skye terminal of the Raasay ferry. It is owned and managed by Debra and Philip Grice, who have worked hard to create a hotel that combines comfort, elegance and good, old fashioned value for money. Its warmth and friendliness mean that guests return again and again.

It has eight spacious bedrooms, all fully en-suite and immaculately furnished and decorated. Each one also has a colour TV, hair dryer and tea/coffee making facilities. Full Scottish breakfasts are served each morning in the dining room, with lighter options available if required. The hotel sits right on the shore, with its own jetty, and its Waterside Bar and restaurant has views out towards Raasay. You can relax with a quiet drink and admire it all in peaceful surroundings that call up the magic of Skye, or

use it as the "19th hole", as the Isle of Skye Golf Club is nearby. The cuisine is outstanding, with the menus containing dishes that combine flair and imagination with good, fresh produce that is sourced locally wherever possible, such as salmon, Aberdeen Angus beef, venison and local vegetables. A select wine list ensures you will find a wine to complement your food.

This part of Skye is rich in history and heritage, and the Sconser lodge Hotel makes the ideal base from which to explore it and the rest of the island as well.

WHITE HEATHER HOTEL

The Harbour, Kyleakin, Isle of Skye, Inverness-shire IV41 8PL
Tel: 01599 534 577 e-mail: info@whiteheatherhotel.co.uk
Fax: 01599 534 427 website: www.whiteheatherhotel.co.uk

A warm welcome awaits you at the **White Heather Hotel**. The hotel
has a genuine home from home atmosphere where you will find
friendly service, value for money and that personal touch that makes
this hotel so special. All nine rooms are en suite and have a TV, hair
drier and tea/coffee making facilities. There are also two comfortable
guest lounges where you can read a book, play a game or simply enjoy the fabulous view. You will find
that Fairtrade produce is used wherever possible both at the breakfast table and in the bedrooms.

through **Broadford**, one of its main
settlements. At Harrapool is the **Skye
Serpentarium Reptile World**, an award
winning reptile exhibition. The road
then passes through Sconser, the
southern terminus of a ferry linking
Skye to the smaller island of **Raasay**
(once visited by Boswell and Johnson),
before reaching the island's main
settlement of **Portree**.

Its name (*port an righ*, meaning
"king's harbour") comes from a visit
made to the place in 1540 by James V.
Before that it was called Kiltaragleann,
which in Gaelic means the "Church of
St Talicarin in the Glen". Across the bay
is **Ben Tianavaig**, which gives good
views out towards the island of Raasay.
The **Aros Experience** is on Viewfield
Road on the south side of the town, and
it incorporates a theatre, cinema, shops
and exhibition area.. An Tuireann Art
Centre, on Struan Road off the A87 to

Uig, is a gallery that presents
exhibitions of contemporary art and
crafts

The town is the gateway to the
Trotternish Peninsula, which juts out
for 20 miles into the Minch, that sea
channel separating the Outer Hebrides
from the mainland. A road from
Portree follows its coastline right
round until it arrives back at the town.
Dun Gerashader, a prehistoric hill
fort, lies about a mile north of Portree
just off the A855. The fort still has
some of its stone ramparts intact. Also
off the A855, about seven miles north
of Portree is the 160 feet high pinnacle
of rock known as the **Old Man of
Storr**.

To the north, the **Lealt Falls** are
possibly the most spectacular on the
island. Though not visible from the road,
there is a lay-by where you can park your
car then walk the hundred yards or so to

SPICE ISLAND

The Lane, Portree, Isle of Skye IV51 9EL
Tel: 01478 612936 e-mail: info@spice-island.co.uk

A stroll down The Lane in Portree will take you to
Spice Island, an Aladdin's cave of modern and retro
home and kitchen ware. It also stocks the famous
Therssy's Village curry mixes and spices, enabling
you to create authentic Sri Lankan meals in your
own kitchen. The service is friendly, the prices are
reasonable and there is sure to be something different
to take home among the extensive range.

VANILLA SKYE

Bayfield Road, Portree, Isle of Skye IV51 9EL
Tel: 01478 611295
e-mail:info@vanillaskye.co.uk website: www.vanillaskye.co.uk

Skye is one of the most beautiful Scottish islands, full of dramatic scenery and stirring history. It is also the home to **Vanilla Skye**, who specialise in exclusive hand-made chocolates. It can be found in Portree and you only have to ask a native of the place for the "chocolate shop", and you'll be directed straight away.

Absolutely no artificial preservatives, colourings or flavourings are used in making the chocolates and only high percentage cocoa solids are used in the manufacture of the centres and coverings, making them rich and flavoursome.

The products are all hand-made, with no machinery being used. In this way you are assured of the very best quality, as every stage in the process is carefully watched. Why not try the juicy liqueur

cherry in rich dark chocolate, sharp lemon sorbet or deep roast coffee? Whichever you choose all are coated with rich chocolate to give a luxurious texture and taste. You can also select from the range of truffles, such as apricot puree and Isle of Skye liqueur combined with white chocolate and rolled in white chocolate flakes. Or heather honey combined with chocolate and rolled in chocolate flakes and toasted oatmeal.

All the products will make your mouth water. So when you're in Portree you can't afford to miss Vanilla Skye.

CAFÉ ARRIBA

Quay Brae, Portree, Isle of Skye IV51 9DP
Tel:01478 611830
e-mail: cafearriba@btconnect.co.uk

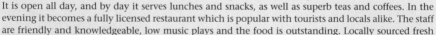

Sitting on Quayside Brae in the Isle of Skye's capital, Portree, **Café Arriba** is a lively bistro/café bar that has an intimate yet friendly atmosphere. You just can't miss it, with its whitewashed walls and bright blue and orange signing, bringing a taste of the exotic to Skye. The interior walls have warm pine, giving it a warm, informal atmosphere.

It is owned and managed by Jenny, Linda and Annie, who are determined to keep up the high standards they have set here. The service is friendly and informal, the food is great and the atmosphere is welcoming. It is open all day, and by day it serves lunches and snacks, as well as superb teas and coffees. In the evening it becomes a fully licensed restaurant which is popular with tourists and locals alike. The staff are friendly and knowledgeable, low music plays and the food is outstanding. Locally sourced fresh

produce is used wherever possible, and the menu has many dishes that show off the imagination and flare of the cooking. Some of the dishes bring the warmth and atmosphere of Mexico to Skye, so be sure to try one of them. You can order from the main menu, or from the daily changing chalked menu board.

It is spotlessly clean, and you are always sure of a warm, friendly welcome. Portree makes the perfect base from which to explore and the Café Arriba will surely become one of your main ports of call when you holiday here.

the gorge and the falls themselves. A few miles away is **Kilt Rock**, a formation of basalt rocks above the shore that resembles the folds of a kilt. **Kilt Rock Waterfall**, which plunges down some cliffs into the sea, can also be seen. The village of Staffin has the **Staffin Museum**, famous for its collection of dinosaur bones, the first ever discovered in Scotland. At **An Corran**, close to Staffin Bay, is a prehistoric rock shelter dating from 8,000 years ago.

North of Staffin, within the grounds of the Flodigarry Country House Hotel, is **Flodigarry House**, where Flora MacDonald and

Loch Portree, Skye

Isles Inn

The Square, Portree, Isle of Skye IV51 9EH
Tel: 01478 612129 Fax: 01478 612528

The family run **Isles Inn** near the harbour has eight letting rooms, six are en suite and two have private facilities. Four of the extremely comfortable rooms are tastefully decorated in a particular tartan - Gunn, Macleod, MacDonald or Nicolson with four poster beds making a stay here a memorable experience. The inn has a public bar, where a range of real ales are served, as well as single malts in front of the open fire. Lunches and dinners are also available in their restaurant, with the cuisine being truly superb. While on Skye, why not make this your base while exploring the island?

Mara

The Pier, Portree, Isle of Skye IV51 9DE
Tel:01478 612429 Fax: 01478 612541
e-mail: info@mara-direct.co.uk
website: www.mara-direct.com

Situated on the harbour at Portree, **Mara** (Gaelic for "sea") is a special shop that is just waiting for you to browse through it. Here you will find unique and thoughtful gifts based on Mairi Kennedy's own in-house designs and sourced from all over Scotland. Items for interiors; accessories; jewellery; scented products - you'll find them here, and all at prices that won't break the bank. The service is friendly and knowledgeable, and there's no obligation to buy. This is the perfect place for that gift or souvenir.

UIG HOTEL

Uig, Isle of Skye IV51 9YE
Tel: 01470 542205 Fax: 01470 542308
e-mail:manager@uighotel.com
website: www.uighotel.com

When on the magical Isle of Skye, there is no better place
to stay that the **Uig Hotel** on the Trotternish Peninsula. It
is a family-run hotel, owned and managed by Wendy and
Bill Pierce, where you can relax among some stunning
scenery and sample the best in Scottish hospitality. The
hotel has 18 fully en suite rooms (most with sea views) that are charming, comfortable and furnished
and decorated to an extremely high standard. All have tea/coffee making facilities, colour TV and
phones.

The cuisine is excellent, and uses only fresh local produce wherever possible, and this, coupled

with a great selection of wines, makes for a memorable
dining experience. Bar lunches are also available, as is
morning coffee and afternoon tea. In the lounge bar, with
its sun lounge, you can relax over a single malt or a beer
from the local Isle of Skye brewery while contemplating
your next sight seeing trip. The hotel makes the ideal base
form which to explore Skye - one you'll look forward to
returning to after a hard day in such wonderful
surroundings. In the winter months, coal and log fires
add to the ambience. The Uig Hotel remains open all day,
and has ample parking.

WOODBINE HOUSE

Uig, Isle of Skye IV51 9XP
Tel/Fax: 01470 542243
e-mail: shona_McClure@hotmail.com
website: www.smoothhound.co.uk/hotels/woodbine

The three star **Woodbine House** was built in the 1800s, and has a lovely
elevated position overlooking Uig Bay and the surrounding countryside. It
is an informal, friendly place, owned and managed by Shona McClure and
her partner Tim Rust, who moved here from the Glasgow area.

It is an elegant, whitewashed building with lots of character, and offers
peace, tranquillity and that sense of "getting away from it all". It is ideally
positioned to use as a base to explore this part of the magical Isle of Skye,
and is only a short distance from the ferry terminal for the Western Isles.

Woodbine House has four fully en suite guest rooms (one a family room), each one boasting a

colour TV and tea/coffee making facilities. The downstairs
lounge is comfortable and spacious, with spectacular
views. The dining room also has wonderful views, and it
is here that you can enjoy a traditional Scottish breakfast
or something lighter if required. Evening meals are also
served here, and they are all home-cooked to perfection
using fresh, local produce wherever possible.

Both Shona and Tim are knowledgeable about the
attractions of the area, and they are determined to
maintain the high standards they have set.

her husband Allan MacDonald settled in 1751. Some people imagine Flora was a simple, Highland lass who helped Charles Edward Stuart, disguised as her Irish maid Betty Burke, cross from the Western Isles to Skye by boat. She came, in fact, from a wealthy family who were tenant farmers on South Uist, though she herself was brought up on Skye and went to school in Edinburgh. Her husband, Allan MacDonald of Kingsburgh, was an officer in the Hanovarian army who later fought on the British side in the American War of Independence.

The sea crossing from Benbecula to Skye is remembered in the famous **Skye Boat Song**. However, it is not, as some people imagine, a traditional Jacobite song. It was written by Englishman Sir Harold Boulton in 1884.

The **Skye Museum of Island Life** at Kilmuir is near the northern tip of the Trotternish Peninsula, and is a group of seven thatched cottages furnished very much as they would have been in times long past. Here you can also learn about the crofter rebellions of the 19th century, plus exhibits connected with Charles Edward Stuart and Flora MacDonald.

Loch Chaluim Chille was at one time one of Skye's largest lochs, being over two miles long. It was drained in the early 19th century to create grazing land, and now you can walk across the old loch bed to what used to be islands to see the remains of an old Celtic monastery.

Fifteen miles west of Portree along the A850 is Dunvegan, famous for **Dunvegan Castle**, perched above the waters of Loch Dunvegan. It has been the home of Clan MacLeod for eight hundred years, and though much of it is Victorian, parts date back to the 13th century. In the drawing room is the famous Fairy Flag, revered by members of

THE LOWER DECK

The Pier, Portree, Isle of Skye IV51 9DD
Tel: 01478 613611
website: www.thelowerdeck.co.uk

The Lower Deck is undoubtedly Portree's best seafood restaurant, and is the ideal place for a great lunch or dinner. It overlooks the harbour, and its menu contains many great seafood dishes, though it changes daily with the "catch of the day". The décor has a warm, nautical theme, and you'll find that the service is always friendly and prompt. The restaurant's many dishes represent great value for money, with, in the evening, beef and chicken being added to the seafood dishes. You will be given a warm Scottish welcome if you come to The Lower Deck.

OVER THE RAINBOW

Quay Brae, Portree, Isle of Skye IV51 9DB
Tel/Fax: 01478 612555

Over the Rainbow is at the top of the Brae leading down to Portree Harbour and this year celebrates its 30th season. A family-run business specialising in the best of scottish knitwear and textiles from Shetland and The Borders, including own label designs. This shop also offers an individual range of fashion clothing and accessories alongside a choice array of jewellery, from designer hand-made to the very affordable as well as a wide selection of desirable home décor items.

FLODIGARRY COUNTRY HOUSE HOTEL

Staffin, Isle of Skye IV51 9HZ
Tel: 01470 552203 Fax: 01470 552301
e-mail: info@flodigarry.co.uk
website: www.flodigarry.co.uk

The award-winning **Flodigarry Country House Hotel** is special. It sits in the north east corner of the magical Isle of Skye near Staffin, against a stunning backdrop of the Quiraig Mountains, and has a view out over Staffin Bay that exactly sums up this part of Scotland - beautiful and romantic. It was built as a private house in 1895, and is a modern, family-run hotel that still manages to retain its period features. One of these is the billiard room, with its Eastern character, which has now been converted into an attractive bar. Another is the conservatory, with its original cast iron pillars.

All the guest rooms are fully en suite, and are cosily and comfortably furnished and decorated. They have lovely views over the mountains and sea, which adds to their considerable charm. Seven of the bedrooms are extra special - they are located in an 18th century cottage in the hotel grounds that

was the home of Flora MacDonald and her husband Alan MacDonald of Kingsburgh between 1751 and 1759, and where seven of her children were born.

The cottage guest rooms are decorated in period style, reflecting the romantic story of Flora and Bonnie Prince Charlie. There is a lovely, secluded garden and private parking while only being a few paces from the main hotel building. One of the rooms has been specially adapted for disabled guests.

The food at Flodigarry is outstanding. Residents and non-residents can enjoy traditional Scottish cuisine, served with imagination, flair and skill. And complementing the four course table d'hote menu in the dining room are excellent bar lunches served all day in the bar and conservatory. The kitchens only use good, fresh local produce in season wherever possible, ensuring that your dining experience is one you will never forget.

Why not enjoy a relaxing drink in the billiard room? There is a well-stocked bar (and this being Scotland, it has a wide range of single malts) as well as a convivial ambience. Here you can relax in absolute comfort after a hard day's sight-seeing, or walking the hills viewing the wildlife that abounds in this part of the island.

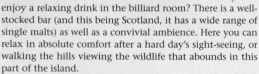

The Flodigarry Country House Hotel has a timeless feel about it. Things move at a slower pace here, and this, combined with the modern concept of high standards of service, makes it a place you'll come back to again and again. And it's the perfect place to hold a romantic wedding reception. Full details of the wedding planning service are available on request.

So come capture the magic of Skye at the Flodigarry Country House Hotel.

Clan MacLeod, which was supposed to bring success in battle. It is one of Clan MacLeod's most important possessions, and legends abound about its origins. Experts have examined the flag and say that the cloth is Middle East silk from either Rhodes or Syria. For this reason, some people have connected it to the Crusades. But the fabric dates from about 400AD to 800AD, many years before the Crusades took place. Another theory says it was the battle flag of King Harold Hardrada of Norway, who was killed in 1066. But how did he get hold of a flag from the Mediterranean? Others are content to put a fairy origin on it, citing the old legend about a MacLeod who fell in love with a fairy princess.

He asked the fairy king for his daughter's hand in marriage, but the king refused, declaring that he would eventually bring her great sorrow through his death, as he was mortal and fairies lived forever. His daughter openly wept, and the father relented, saying that they could be married, but only for a year and a day. Nine months after the marriage, a son was born to the couple, and there was great rejoicing.

However, a year and a day after the marriage, the fairy princess returned to her people, leaving behind her husband and son. Their farewells took place on the Fairy Bridge near Dunvegan, and the princess made the heartbroken chief promise that he would never give their son cause to cry, as she could hear him from Fairyland and would grieve.

After she had gone, the chief was inconsolable, and his clansmen decided to organise a great party to cheer him up. The chief took part, leaving his son in the care of a nurse. However, when she heard the laughter and music, she

GRESHORNISH HOUSE

Edinbane, By Portree, Isle of Skye IV51 9PN
Tel: 01470 582266 e-mail: info@greshornishhouse.com
Fax: 01470 582345 website: www.greshornishhouse.com

On the shores of Loch Greshornish, between Portree and Dunvegan, you will find one of Skye's best hotels - **Greshornish House**. This friendly, family-run hotel sits in ten acres of beautiful grounds, and has nine fully en suite rooms (some of them boasting four posters) that combine elegance and comfort. Superb food is served in the spacious dining room, with the cuisine using fresh local produce in its many dishes. There is also an excellent wine list, so dining here is a wonderful experience. Non residents may also eat if a table is booked well in advance.

SKYE RIDING CENTRE

Suladale, By Portree, Isle of Skye IV51 9PA
Tel: 01470 582419 e-mail: info@skyeridingcentre.co.uk
Fax: 01470 582420 website: www.skyeridingcentre.co.uk

Just 15 minutes from Portree, you will find the best riding centre on the beautiful Isle of Skye - the **Skye Riding Centre**. It provides horse riding, pony trekking and riding lessons for people of all ages and abilities, and here you can appreciate the beauty of Skye from horseback - one of the best ways of doing so. All ages and abilities - including disabled - can be catered for, and you can learn to ride at your own pace in a relaxed and friendly atmosphere. There is a horse to suit everyone, and you're assured of a warm welcome.

SHILASDAIR

The Skye Yarn Company, Waternish, Isle of Skye IV55 8GL
Tel: 01470 592297
website: www.shilasdair-yarns.co.uk

For the Skye visitor SHILASDAIR offers a peep into the misty past, when natural dying of plaids and tartans was the only way of dying. Local plants - heathers, litchens etc. - were gathered, macerated then boiled with the wool when they released their colours into the fibre.

SHILASDAIR still utilise these ancient dyeplants, complimenting them with imported natural dyestuffs like indigo and madder to produce a vibrant range of 'living' colour in their locally produced croft wools and cashmere/angora/silk blend luxury yarns, and the designer sweaters and accessories produced from them. See the croft production complex including dyehouse and showroom by following the roadsigns.

Pieces Of Ate

Brogaig, Staffin, Isle of Skye IV51 9JY
Tel: 01470 562787
e-mail: anne@piecesofate.freeserve.co.uk

For that tasty treat while you're exploring the magical Isle of Skye, head for **Pieces of Ate** near Staffin. It is owned and managed by Anne Haynes, ably assisted by her friend Catriona Purll, two English women who so fell in love with Skye that they moved here permanently. The shop is an extremely popular takeaway sandwich bar selling freshly made sandwiches, filled rolls, home-made soups, pies, pastries and hot and cold drinks. Ideal for that quick snack as you explore the island.

Beside it is Hidden Treasures, a delicatessen selling a wide range of Scottish and global produce. There is a great selection of wines as well as cold meats, muesli, cheeses, chutneys, preserves, pastas, soups and sauces. Plus you can choose from prime smoked salmon, trout, venison, cakes, and a host of

other items that should tickle your taste buds. Gift hampers are also available for special occasions, such as Christmas.

The shop is spotlessly clean and the service is friendly and knowledgeable. Have a chat with Anne or Catriona, and while you're about it ask about the establishment's Recipe of the Month, which is proving very popular in the area and beyond.

They are open seven days a week throughout the summer, and offer not only nourishing and filling snacks, but a wide range of speciality foods that are sure to please. And all in one of the most spectacular islands in the world - the magical Isle of Skye.

GLENVIEW HOTEL

Culnacnoc, by Staffin, Isle of Skye, Inverness-shire IV51 9JH
Tel: 01470 562248 Fax: 01470 562211
e-mail: enquiries@glenviewskye.co.uk
website: www.glenviewskye.co.uk

Set on the Trotternish Peninsula on the lovely Isle of Skye, the pet-friendly **Glenview Hotel** offers five extremely comfortable bedrooms - two doubles with four poster bed, one double and two twin/doubles. Four are fully en suite, while the fifth has its own private bathroom. The building was constructed in 1903, and was once a local merchant's house, and it has lost none of it's Edwardian charm. It has lovely views over the Old Man of Storr, and there is nothing better than sitting at a table or bench in the garden in the still of the evening with a quiet drink as you relax after a hard day's sightseeing.

The spacious and welcoming guest lounge has a log burner, TV, video and DVD, and in the dining room the very best of gourmet food is served. Doreen Harben and Ian Stratton have owned and run the hotel since 2002, and since then have earned a wonderful reputation for its cuisine. They are extremely proud of the food they serve, and use only the freshest local produce wherever possible.

They even boast that their seafood is "fresh from the boat to the table". The restaurant is open to non residents, and if you dine here you are in for a treat. The ambience is informal and friendly, and the prices very reasonable. The whole area surrounding the hotel is rich in history, and river and loch fishing are available. Charter boats can also be hired for sea fishing excursions into the Minch. This is a warm, inviting establishment, and should you visit, Doreen and Ian will go out of their way to make your stay both pleasurable and rewarding.

stole out of the nursery to take part, leaving the child alone. He began to cry, and no one could hear him apart from the fairy princess. She came back to the castle and lifted the child from his cradle, soothing him and singing fairy songs. When the nurse returned to the nursery, she heard the magical singing, and knew at once who it was. She burst into the room and found the child wrapped in a silk shawl.

She told the chief about the shawl, and he placed it in a locked case, vowing to take it with him wherever he went. Years later the son told his father that he miraculously remembered his mother returning. He told him that if Clan MacLeod ever needed help, he was to wave the shawl three times and a fairy army would rush to its aid.

Across the loch, and reached by the B884, is the **Colbost Croft Museum**,

KILMUIR PARK

Dunvegan, Isle of Skye, Inverness-shire IV 55 8GU
Tel/Fax: 01470 521586
e-mail: info@kilmuirpark.co.uk website: milford.co.uk/go/kilmuir.html

Kilmuir Park is the home of Gordon and Agnes Bessant, and is a modern bungalow that offers four star B&B accommodation in three fully en suite bedrooms. The rooms have TV/radios, hair dryers and tea/coffee making facilities. The furnishings are comfortable and colour coordinated to make your stay restful and relaxing. The hearty, beautifully cooked breakfasts are full Scottish, though something lighter is also available. Mairi will also cook delicious evening meals by prior arrangement, using local produce wherever possible. There is plenty of parking space, and the guest lounge has a TV, video, small library and a selection of games.

TABLES HOTEL

Dunvegan, Isle of Skye IV55 8WA
Tel: 01470 521404
e-mail: bookings@tables-hotel.co.uk
website: www.tables-hotel.co.uk

"Come as a guest and leave as a friend" - that's the proud boast of the **Tables Hotel** on the beautiful island of Skye. It sits in the centre of Dunvegan, near famous Dunvegan Castle and has wonderful views across Loch Dunvegan towards MacLeod's Table Mountains.

There are five extremely comfortable and tastefully furnished rooms, four of which are completely en suite and the other with private facilities. All have tea/coffee making facilities, hair dryer, shaver socket and radio alarm. Guests have use of the resident's lounge, with cosy, welcoming armchairs and its roaring peat fire when it's cold. Here you can watch TV or choose from the wide selection of books, magazines and board games. Or why not head for the conservatory? The views are splendid as you sip a refreshing cup of tea or coffee and contemplate your next sightseeing tour of the island or bracing walk among the magnificent countryside.

The chef uses fresh, local produce whenever possible, with the menus being imaginative and full of flair. Vegetarian dishes can also be ordered. A good selection of wines and malt whiskies are available.

The hotel is an attractive, white-washed building and the owners, Nicky and Ian Henderson, will always offer you a warm welcome. Children and well behaved dogs are welcome. They have loads of guidebooks, maps and ideas to help make your stay on the island an enjoyable one.

THREE CHIMNEYS

Colbost, Dunvegan, Isle of Skye IV55 8ZT
Tel: 01470 511258 Fax: 01470 511358
e-mail: eatandstay@threechimneys.co.uk
website: www.threechimneys.co.uk

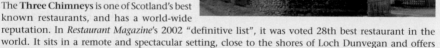

The **Three Chimneys** is one of Scotland's best known restaurants, and has a world-wide reputation. In *Restaurant Magazine*'s 2002 "definitive list", it was voted 28th best restaurant in the world. It sits in a remote and spectacular setting, close to the shores of Loch Dunvegan and offers some of the finest food available anywhere.

Housed in an old, picturesque crofter's cottage, it is owned and managed by Eddie and Shirley Spear, who will warmly welcome you to their five star establishment. Shirley is a superb cook, and has won many awards including, in 1999, a "Special Award" from the Scottish Chef Association for her outstanding contribution to cuisine in Scotland. Working with her new Head Chef Michael Smith she uses only fresh, local produce such as fabulous fresh seafood from Skye, Highland lamb, game and beef, and brings flair and imagination to the dishes. The Three Chimneys is equally famous for soups, puddings and home-baked breads.

The establishment now boasts six sumptuous rooms within The House Over-By, next door to the restaurant. The same high standards of service found in the restaurant apply here. Each stylish five star room enjoys great views out over the sea, with the décor matching the colours and contrasts seen from the windows. Breakfast is served in the Morning Room, which again overlooks the loch, where you can sometimes see seals basking on the rocks.

Dunorin House Hotel

Herebost, Dunvegan, Isle of Skye IV55 8GZ
Tel: 01470 521488
e-mail:stay@dunorin.freeserve.co.uk
website: www.dunorinhousehotel-skye.com

Situated three miles south of Dunvegan Castle, the **Dunorin House Hotel** is the perfect base from which to explore the magical island of Skye. This friendly, welcoming establishment has ten attractive and comfortable en suite rooms, all with colour TV and tea/coffee making facilities. Why not relax in the lounge with a single malt? There's a wide selection, including Skye's own malt, Talisker. The dining room has views of the Cuillins, and serves imaginative Scottish fayre, using fresh local produce in season wherever possible.

based on a "black house" (a small traditional cottage of turf or stone, topped with a thatched roof). It shows the living conditions of islanders in the past, and features an illicit still. Black houses got their name, not because they were blackened inside by the peat fire, but to differentiate them from the "white houses" which were built in Victorian and later times, and which were more modern and usually painted white.

To the southeast of the island, on the Sleat (pronounced "Slate") Peninsula at Armadale, is the **Armadale Castle Gardens and Museum of the Isles**. It sits within a 20,000 acre

Dunvegan Castle, Skye

Armadale Pottery

Armadale, Sleat, Isle of Skye IV45 8RS
Tel: 01471 844439   website: www.armadale-pottery.co.uk

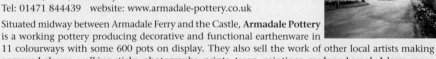

Situated midway between Armadale Ferry and the Castle, **Armadale Pottery** is a working pottery producing decorative and functional earthenware in 11 colourways with some 600 pots on display. They also sell the work of other local artists making engraved glasses, walking sticks, photographs, prints, treen, paintings, cards and wool. A large range of gemset sterling silver jewellery is on display, necklaces, bracelets, pendants and earrings in unusual gemstones from around the world, plus a host of gemstone gifts, paperweights, agate clocks, bookends, agate slices and huge amethyst geodes. If you like fossils they have fossil fish, sharks' teeth, ammonites including large fossil slabs and gemstone tables. Ample parking in a garden setting. Open every day 9.30am to 5.30pm Easter until the end of October.

Highland estate, once owned by the MacDonalds of Sleat, and was purchased by the Clan Donald Land Trust in 1971. The earliest parts of the castle date from the 1790s, when it was built by the first Lord MacDonald on the site of a farm and gardens where Flora MacDonald married in 1750. North of Armadale,

Eigg and Rum

is **Sabhal Mór Ostaig**, where short courses in Gaelic are offered. It is also the only college in Scotland where other degree courses are taught purely in Gaelic.

Dunscaith Castle, the ruins of which lie on the western side of the peninsula near Tokavaig, was abandoned by the MacDonalds in the 18th century. Legend says that the castle was built by fairies in one night, and subsequently protected by a pit full of snakes. It was the home, the legend continues, of the Queen of Skye, who taught the arts of war.

EIGG

42 miles NW of Oban in the Atlantic Ocean

In 1997 the island of Eigg was bought on behalf of its inhabitants by the Isle of Eigg Heritage Trust from the German artists who called himself "Maruma". Its most famous feature is the 1,277 feet high **An Sgurr**, which slopes gently up to a peak on one side, and dramatically plunges on the other.

Southwest of the main pier is St Francis's Cave, also known as the **Massacre Cave**. It got its name from a

gruesome event in 1577, when nearly 400 MacDonalds took refuge there when pursued by a force of MacLeods. The MacLeods lit fires at the entrance, and every one of the MacDonalds was suffocated to death. The story was given some credence when human bones were removed from the cave in the 19th century and buried. A nearby cave, MacDonald's Cave, is also known as the **Cathedral Cave**, as it was used for secret Catholic church services following 1745.

At **Kildonnan**, on the west coast, are the ruins of a 14th century church, built on the site of an ancient Celtic monastery founded by St Donan. The saint and his 52 monks were massacred in AD 617 by a band of pirates.

MUCK

39 miles NW of Oban in the Atlantic Ocean

The tiny island of Muck's improbable name comes from "eilean nam muc", meaning "island of pigs", though in this case the pigs may be porpoises, which are called "sea pigs" in Gaelic. It is reached by ferry from Mallaig, and is a low-lying island with good beaches. **Port Mor** is the main settlement and harbour, with, above it, an ancient graveyard and ruined church. On the south side of the Port Mor inlet are the scant remains of **Dun Ban**, a prehistoric fort. The highest point at 445 feet, is **Beinn Airein**, and from the top there is a good view of the whole of the island.

RUM

47 miles W of Fort William

When Sir John Bullough bought the island of Rum in 1888 he arrogantly changed its name to "Rhum", as he disliked the associations it had with alcoholic drinks. However, when the Nature Conservancy Council took over the island in 1957 they changed the name back to the more correct "Rum", meaning "wide island", and it has been that ever since. Nowadays it is a Special Site of Scientific Interest and a Specially Protected Area, as its plant life has remained almost unchanged since the Ice Age.

The main settlement is Kinloch, on the east coast. **Kinloch Castle**, overlooking Loch Scresort, was built by Sir George Bullough, John's son, as his main home on the island between 1901 and 1902. The **Bullough Mausoleum** in Glen Harris, to the south of the island, was built to take the bodies of Sir George, his father John and his wife Monica.

Kilmory, on the north coast of the island, has a fine beach and an old burial ground.

CANNA

60 miles NW of Oban in the Atlantic Ocean

Canna means the "porpoise island", and has been owned by the National Trust for Scotland since 1981, when it was given to them by Gaelic scholar John Lorne Campbell. It is about five miles long by just over a mile wide at its widest, and is usually sunny and mild. The remains of **St Columba's Chapel**, dating from the 7th or 8th centuries, with an accompanying Celtic cross, stand opposite the small island of Sanday, and have been excavated. **An Corghan**, on the east coast, is all that is left of a small tower house where a Clanranald chief imprisoned his wife, who was having an affair with a MacLeod clansman. At **Uaigh Righ Lochlain** can be seen remnants of Viking occupation, and at **Camas Tairbearnais**, a bay on the western side of the island, a Viking ship burial was uncovered. **Sanday** is a small island which lies off the south east coast, and is joined to it by a bridge, and, at low tide, a sand bar.

Canna is reached by ferry from Mallaig.

CANNA

Inner Hebrides
Tel: 01687 462466
website: www.nts.org.uk

The most westerly of the Small Isles, **Canna** is five miles long and one-and-a-quarter miles wide. Its cultural background, archaeology and ornithology make it one of the most interesting islands in the Hebrides. Sustainable farming and crofting systems are carried out on the island, which is a Special Protection Area for its large population of seabirds, especially shags, which nest in the cliffs of its dramatic shoreline. Canna is also a Special Area of Conservation. Pony trekking is available.

LOCATOR MAP

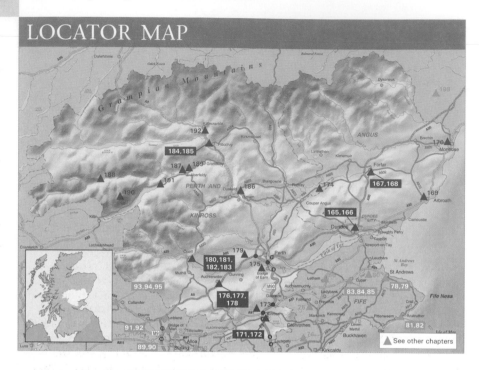

ADVERTISERS AND PLACES OF INTEREST

PERTHSHIRE, ANGUS & KINROSS 10

The two counties of Perthshire and Angus straddle the Highland Boundary Fault, which separates the Highlands from the Lowlands, while Kinross, once Scotland's second smallest county, is wholly Lowland in character. So there is a wide variety of scenery within this area, from mountains, glens and lochs to quiet, intensely cultivated fields and picturesque villages.

Perthshire is a wholly inland county, a place of agriculture, high hills and Highland lochs. It is the county of Loch Rannoch and Loch Tummel, and of possibly the loneliest railway station in Britain, Rannoch, deep within the bleak expanse of Rannoch Moor. It is also the county of the Gleneagles Hotel, one of Britain's most luxurious, and of rich farmland surrounding Perth itself. Blairgowrie is the centre of Scotland's fruit growing industry - fruit that once fed the Dundee jam makers.

The A9 from Perth heads north towards the Drumochter Pass, which reaches its highest point of 1,505 feet at the Perthshire - Inverness-shire border, overlooked by four Munros. On the way, it passes deeply wooded glens, and skirts such historic towns and villages as Dunkeld, Pitlochry and Blair Atholl. In fact, Perthshire likes to call itself the "Big Tree Country", as it has some of the most remarkable woodlands anywhere in Europe.

Perth is a city, and before local government reorganisation in the '70s, had a lord provost, one of only six places in Scotland that could claim that distinction, the others being Edinburgh, Glasgow, Dundee, Aberdeen and Elgin. No legal document has ever specifically taken that honour away from it, so it remains a city still. It is often referred to as the "Fair City of Perth", and this is no idle description. It may be in the Lowlands, but it was never scarred by the industrial developments of the 19th century, as other places in Scotland were. It remains a confident, attractive place with many fine buildings and a good quality of life.

ADVERTISERS AND PLACES OF INTEREST

Angus has a coastline that takes in high cliffs and sandy beaches. The coastal towns are famous. Carnoustie, where the British Open is sometimes held; Montrose and its almost land-locked basin where wildfowl can be seen; and of course Arbroath, with the ruins of an abbey where one of the momentous documents in Scottish history was signed - the Declaration of Arbroath. Inland, the countryside is gentle and pastoral, with the glens of Angus, such as Glen Prosen, Glen Clova and Glen Doll, being particularly beautiful as they wind their way into the foothills of the Cairngorms.

Dundee is the area's largest settlement, and the fourth largest city in Scotland. It is a place of industry, and sits on the north bank of the Firth of Tay. At one time it was one of the powerhouses of Scotland, relying on its three traditional industries of jute, jam and journalism. But it is an ancient place as well, and its roots go deep into Scottish history. One of Scotland's famous historical characters, John Graham of Claverhouse, adopted its name when he became 1st Viscount Dundee.

He was a man whose reputation is ambiguous, being loved by some and loathed by others. To admirers of the Covenanters he is Bloody Clavers, a ruthless and cruel persecutor of those opposed to the introduction of bishops into the Church of Scotland. To admirers of the Jacobites he is Bonnie Dundee, a dashing and gallant supporter of the Stuarts who was killed fighting for his king at Killiecrankie in 1689.

Kinross sits to the south east of Perthshire. It sits in a great saucer shaped depression with, at its heart, Loch Leven. The main industry is farming, and the gentle countryside, ringed by hills, is well worth exploring if only for the sense of "getting away from it all". Loch Leven is famous for its fishing, and Vane Farm Nature Reserve was the first educational nature reserve in Europe.

Bauchaille Etive Mor, Rannoch Moor

Everywhere in Perthshire, Angus and Kinross there is history. The medieval cathedrals at Dunkeld and Brechin are well worth exploring. In AD 685, at Nechtansmere, a Pictish army under King Nechtan defeated the Northumbrians and secured independence from Anglian rule. The Battle of Killiecrankie in 1689 was the first of the Jacobite battles in Scotland.

Scone, outside Perth, was where the medieval Scottish

kings were crowned as they sat on the Stone of Destiny; at Blair Atholl the Duke of Atholl keeps the only private army in Britain; Glamis Castle was the childhood home of the late Queen Mother; and Mary Stuart was held captive in a castle on an island in Loch Leven, later making a daring escape from it.

At Crook of Devon in Kinross a coven was discovered in 1662, with the witches being put on trial and subsequently executed. At Scotlandwell we have yet another place of pilgrimage. A friary once stood here, along with a holy well, and people came from all over Scotland seeking cures for their ailments. The well is still there, and the waters may still be drunk.

Then there are the literary associations. J.M. Barrie was born at Kirriemuir, and Violet Jacob was born near Montrose. The Dundee publisher D.C. Thomson has given us a host of comic characters that have delighted children (and adults) for years, such as Desperate Dan, Korky the Cat, Biffo the Bear, Beryl the Peril, Denis the Menace, Lord Snooty, The Bash Street Kids and Oor Wullie.

DUNDEE

Dundee is Scotland's fourth largest city, and sits on the banks of the Firth of Tay. It is a manufacturing town, at one time famous for the "three Js" of jam, jute and journalism. It also brims with history and heritage, and was granted royal burgh status in the 12th century, when it was one of the largest and wealthiest towns in Scotland. Dundee Law (571 feet) looms over the city, and from its summit there is a superb view south towards the Tay Bridges and Fife. A road and separate footpath (with a series of steps) take you to the summit, where there is a war memorial, an observation point and "fact panels". At one time a tunnel was bored through the flank of the hill to take a railway.

Dundee is joined to Fife by two bridges across the Tay, the **Tay Road Bridge**, opened in 1966, and the **Tay Rail Bridge**, opened in 1887. The road bridge (which replaced a ferry) opened up a huge area of north Fife to commuters wishing to work in Dundee, and also making it the main shopping centre for the area . The rail bridge replaced an earlier bridge, built in 1878. On the evening of December 28th 1879, during a violent westerly gale, the bridge collapsed while a train was crossing it. The 75 train passengers perished.

One of Dundee's best-known sons, **William Topaz McGonagall**, later wrote a poem to commemorate the disaster, which has become almost as famous as the disaster itself:

Beautiful Railway Bridge of the Silv'ry Tay!
Alas! I am very sorry to say
That ninety lives have been taken away
On the last Sabbath day of 1879,
Which will be remember'd for a very long time.

It has been called, rather unfairly perhaps, "the worst poem ever written". However, perhaps we should not judge it so harshly. McGonagall was a simple handloom weaver whose formal education stopped when he was seven years old, and he was trying to put into words the horror he felt at the tragedy. He was born in Edinburgh in 1830, the son of Irish immigrants, and came to Dundee with his parents after having lived in Paisley and Glasgow. In 1877, he

UNIVERSITY OF DUNDEE BOTANIC GARDEN

Riverside Drive, Dundee DD2 1QH
Tel: 01382 647190   Fax: 01382 640574
e-mail: botanicgardens@dundee.ac.uk
website: www.dundeebotanicgarden.co.uk

Described as the jewel in the crown of the University, the Garden is open for
public enjoyment as well as its principal function of education, conservation
and supplying plant material for teaching and research within the University of
Dundee. The Garden, set on south facing land near the banks of the River Tay,
has a wide range of trees and shrubs, tropical and temperate glasshouses, water-
garden and herb garden, as well as collections of indigenous British plants and
others from all over the world. Guided tours are available by arrangement and
to round off, why not enjoy refreshments in the coffee shop or a browse in the
gift shop. Free parking. Disabled amenities.

took to writing poetry, having felt "a
strange kind of feeling stealing over me",
and then wrote until he died in
September 1902.

The **Old Steeple** of St Mary's Church,
in the heart of the city, dates from the
15th century, and is reckoned to be one
of the finest in the country. The rest of
the building dates from the 18th and
19th centuries, and was once divided
into four separate churches. Until the
1980s, when they finally amalgamated,
there were still three churches within the
building - the Steeple Church, Old St
Paul's and St David's.

Another reminder of Dundee's past is
the **Wishart Arch** in the Cowgate. It is
one of the city's old gateways, and from
its top, George Wishart the religious
reformer, is said to have preached to
plague victims during the plague of 1544

(see also Montrose and St Andrews). Near
the arch is the Wishart Church, where
Mary Slessor used to worhip. She was
born in Aberdeen in 1848, and moved to
Dundee when she was ten. Inspired by
David Livingstone, she went to Africa as
a missionary, and died at Calabar in
1915.

RSS Discovery, Captain Scott's ship,
was built in Dundee and launched in
1901. It now forms the centrepiece of the
five-star **Discovery Point**, at Discovery
Quay. It was one of the last wooden
three-masted ships to be built in Britain,
and the first to be built solely for
scientific research. You can explore the
ship, "travel" to Antarctica in the
Polarama Gallery and find out about one
of the greatest stories of exploration and
courage ever told.

At Victoria Dock you'll find **HM**

MILLS OBSERVATORY

Glamis Road, Balgay Park, Dundee DD2 2UB
Tel: 01382 435967 Fax: 01382 435962
e-mail: mills.observatory@dundeecity.gov.uk
website: www.dundeecity.gov.uk

Mills Observatory, housed in a classically styled sandstone building, is the UK's
only full-time public observatory. Here you can see the stars and planets for
yourself through an impressive Victorian telescope and look at safe projected
images of the sun. The planetarium has an artificial night sky giving you the
chance to view constellations and planets. More can be learnt through the
changing displays, audio and visual presentations and an interactive computer.

Frigate Unicorn, the oldest British-built wooden frigate still afloat. It was built at Chatham in 1824 for the Royal Navy at a time when iron was beginning to replace wood in ship building, and carried 46 guns. The ship re-creates the conditions on board a wooden sailing ship during Nelson's time, with officers' quarters, cannons, and the cramped conditions within which the crew lived.

In 1999, **The Verdant Works**, in West Henderson's Wynd, was voted Europe's top industrial museum. Jute was once a staple industry in Dundee, employing over 40,000 people. Here, in a former jute mill, you are taken on a tour of the industry, from its beginnings in India to the end product in all its forms. You will see the processes involved in jute manufacture, you'll see the original machinery, and you'll see the living conditions of people both rich and poor who earned their living from the trade. There are interactive displays, film shows, and a guided tour.

Sensation is Dundee's science centre. Located in the Greenmarket, it is a place where "science is brought to life" using specially designed interactive and hands-on exhibits. Here you can find out how a dog sees the world, how to use your senses to discover where you are, and why things taste good or bad. The latest exhibition is Roborealm, the only one of its kind in the world. It will give visitors a chance to interact with a team of robots. The **Mills Observatory** (see panel opposite) in Balgay Park a mile west of the city centre and accessed from Glamis Road, also deals with matters scientific. It is Britain's only full time public observatory, and houses a 25mm Cooke telescope. It also has a small planetarium and display area.

The **McManus Galleries** are housed within a Gothic building in Albert Square, and contain many 18th and 19th century Scottish paintings. Within it there is also a museum of more than local interest, with a particularly fine collection of artefacts from Ancient Egypt. The **Dundee Contemporary Arts Centre** in the Nethergate specialises in contemporary art and film, and has galleries, cinemas and workshops.

Dudhope Castle, at Dudhope Park in Dundee, dates originally from the 13th century, and was once the home of the Scrymageour family, hereditary constables of Dundee. The present building dates from the late 16th century. In its time it has also been a woollen mill and a barracks. It now forms part of the University of Abertay and is not open to the public, though it can be viewed from the outside. And at the junction of Claypotts Road and Arbroath Road is the wonderfully named **Claypotts Castle** (Historic Scotland), built between 1569 and 1588 by John Strachan. It can be viewed by prior appointment with Historic Scotland.

On the Coupar Angus Road is the **Camperdown Wildlife Centre**, with a fine collection of Scottish and European wildlife, including brown bears, Scottish wildcats, wolves and bats. **Clatto Country Park** is to the north of the city, and is centred on a 24-acre former reservoir. It has facilities for water sports and fishing. The ruins of **Mains Castle**, sometimes called Mains of Fintry, is in Cairds Park, and was once owned by John Graham, a cousin of Viscount Dundee.

To the east of the city is **Broughty Ferry**, once called the "richest square mile in Europe" because of the many fine mansions built there by the jute barons. The **Broughty Ferry Museum** is at Castle Green, and housed within a castle built by the Earl of Angus in 1496 as a defence against marauding English ships. It has displays on local history, and tells the story of Dundee's former whaling fleet, at one time Britain's largest. If you visit Broughty Ferry at New Year, you can see the annual **N'erday Dook** ("New Year's Day Dip") held on January 1st, when swimmers enter the waters of the Firth of Tay. It is organised by Ye Amphibious Ancients Bathing Association, one of the country's oldest swimming clubs, and is done for charity. It attracts about 100 - 150 bathers a year, and it is not unknown for the crowd of spectators, which can be over 2,000 strong, to be wrapped up in warm woollens, scarves and gloves as the swimmers enter the water dressed only in swimsuits.

To the west of the city, on the north bank of the Tay, is the **Carse of Gowrie**, one of the most fertile areas of Scotland.

AROUND DUNDEE

MONIFIETH
6 miles E of Dundee on the A930

This little holiday resort sits at the entrance to the Firth of Tay, and has some good sandy beaches. Its golf courses were used in the qualifying rounds of the British Open. At one time it was an important Pictish settlement, and some Pictish stones were discovered at **St Rule's Church** that are now in The National Museum of Scotland in Edinburgh.

CARNOUSTIE
11 miles E of Dundee on the A930

Golf is king in Carnoustie. This small holiday resort on the North Sea coast hosted the British Open Championships in 1931 and 1999, and is a favourite destination for golfing holidays.

But it has other attractions. **Barry Mill** (National Trust for Scotland) is a 19th century working corn mill, though a mill

has stood here since at least the middle of the 16th century. You can see the large water wheel turning, and also find out how corn is ground. There is an exhibition explaining the historical role of the mill, as well as a walkway along the mill lade. Three miles north west of the town are the **Carlungie and Ardestie Souterrains** (Historic Scotland), underground earth houses dating from the 1st century AD.

BALGRAY
4 miles N of Dundee off the A90

Four miles north of the city centre, near Balgray, is the **Tealing Souterrain** (Historic Scotland), an underground dwelling dating from about AD100. It was accidentally discovered in 1871, and consists of a curved passage about 78 feet long and seven feet wide with a stone floor.

FOWLIS EASTER
6 miles W of Dundee on a minor road off the A923

This small village has one of the finest small churches in Scotland. The **Parish Church of St Marnan** dates from about 1453, and still has part of its rood screen, as well as medieval paintings dating to about 1541 and a sacrament house that is reckoned to be the finest in Scotland. Lord Gray built it in 1453 on the site of an earlier church, built in about 1242 by a member of the local Mortimer family whose husband was in the Holy Land fighting in the Crusades see also Fowlis Wester).

GLAMIS
10 miles N of Dundee on the A94

Glamis Castle is famous as being the childhood home of the late Queen Mother and the birthplace of her daughter, the late Princess Margaret. The lands of Glamis (pronounced "Glams") were given to Sir John Lyon in 1372 by Robert II, the first Stewart king and grandson of Robert the Bruce, and still belongs to the family, who are now the Earls of Strathmore and Kinghorne. In 1376 Sir John married Robert's daughter, Princess Joanna, and the castle has had royal connections ever since. The present castle was built in the 17th century to resemble a French château, though fragments of an earlier 14th century castle still survive in the tower.

Glamis Castle

Shakespeare's *Macbeth*, which he wrote in 1606, is set in Glamis, and Duncan's Hall, the oldest part of the castle, is said to have been built on the spot where Macbeth murdered Duncan. Shakespeare, like most playwrights, was more interested in drama than historical fact, and history tells us that Duncan most probably died in battle near Elgin. It may even be that Shakespeare visited Glamis, as he and his troupe of actors were sent to Aberdeen in 1599 by Elizabeth I to perform before James VI.

Tragedy seems to stalk Glamis Castle. In 1537 Lady Glamis, Janet Douglas, was burnt as a witch in Edinburgh for plotting to murder James V, and the crown seized the lands. It was a trumped up charge, as James V hated the Douglas family, and she was later declared innocent of all the charges, with the lands being restored to her son. It has the reputation of being one of the most haunted castles in Scotland. There is a Grey Lady who haunts the chapel, a Black Page, and a window which looks out from a room that doesn't appear to exist. Legend has it that in the room, which might be within the thickness of the walls of the castle, one of the Lords of Glamis and the Earl of Crawford played cards with the devil, and were sealed up because of it.

The castle is also noted for its gardens, and in springtime the mile-long driveway is lined with daffodils. In summer there are displays of rhododendrons and azaleas.

Within the village of Glamis, at Kirkwynd, is the **Angus Folk Museum** (National Trust for Scotland), housed in a row of 18th century stone cottages. It contains one of the finest folk collections in Scotland, including a "Life on the Land" exhibition baesd in an old courtyard, and a restored 19th century hearse.

A few miles north of the village is Pictish **St Orland's Stone**, with, on one side, the carving of a cross and on the other a carving of a boat containing several men.

FORFAR

13 miles N of Dundee on the A932

Once the county town of Angus, Forfar is now a small royal burgh and market town. It gives its name to one of Scotland's culinary delights - the **Forfar Bridie**. It has meat and vegetables within a pastry crust, and used to be popular with the farm workers of Angus, as it was a self-contained and easily portable meal.

The **Meffan Museum and Art Gallery** in West High Street gives you an insight

LOCHLANDS HRB LTD

Dundee Road, Forfar, Angus DD8 1XF
Tel: 01307 463621
e-mail: vandelft@btinternet.com website: www.lochlands.co.uk

Lochlands HRB Ltd comprises a caravan park, garden centre and restaurant called the Coffee Mill. The caravan park has a range of touring pitches, each with electricity, and hard standing pitches with all services. The garden centre is a riot of colour, and sells a wide range of quality items, including gardening equipment, bedding plants, seeds, shrubs, fertilisers and pots. For a refreshing cup of coffee, snack, or full lunch, you can't beat the Coffee Mill, which is housed in what was once the driving mill for the farm.

into the town's history and industries. It was built in 1898 after a daughter of a former provost left a sum of money to the town. During the Dark Ages this part of Scotland was inhabited by the Picts, who, as far as we know, had no alphabet. However, they were expert carvers, and in the museum is a superb display of carved stones. You can also walk down an old cobbled street and peer into shops and workshops. A more unusual display is one about witchcraft in Angus.

Five miles east of Forfar is **Balgavies Loch**, a Scottish Wildlife Trust reserve, where you can see great crested grebe, whooping swans, cormorant and other birds. Keys to the hide are available from the ranger at the Montrose Basin Wildlife Centre. There is a hide which is open on

the first Sunday of each month. **Forfar Loch Country Park**, to the west of the town, has viewing platforms where wildfowl can be observed feeding.

The ruins of **Restenneth Priory** (Historic Scotland) sit about a mile-and-a-half from the town, on the B9113. It once stood on an island in Restenneth Loch, but this was drained in the 18th century. It was founded by David I for Augustinian canons on the site of a much earlier church no doubt founded by the Picts, and its square tower, which is surmounted by a later spire, has some of the earliest Norman - and possibly Saxon - work in Scotland. It was sacked by Edward I, but under the patronage of Robert the Bruce it soon regained its importance. Prince

GOW ANTIQUES, RESTORATION & COURSES

Made by Jeremy Gow

Pitscandly Farmhouse, Forfar, Angus DD8 3NZ
Tel: 01307 465342 e-mail: jeremy@knowyourantiques.com
Fax : 01307 468973 website: www.knowyourantiques.com

• Three day course on antique furniture recognition, dating furniture and learning styles, recognising fakes and understanding different woods. Courses are light hearted, interactive catering for enthusiastic amateurs, collectors and professionals.

• Gow Antiques and Restoration has an extensive range of fine antique furniture for sale which can be viewed on the website or in the showroom outside Forfar.

• Jeremy also restores antique furniture specialising in veneer work, marquetry, French polishing and any cabinet making. One of three BAFRA members in Scotland.

John, one of Bruce's sons, is buried here.

A few miles north of Forfar, near Tannadice, is the **Mountains Animal Sanctuary**, for rescued ponies, horses and donkeys.

KIRRIEMUIR
15 miles N of Dundee on the A926

At 9 Brechin Road is **JM Barrie's Birthplace** (National Trust for Scotland). The creator of *Peter Pan* (first performed in 1904) was born here in 1860, the son of a handloom weaver, and the building's outside washhouse was his first theatre. The house next door has an exhibition about Barrie's life. He was a bright child, attending both Glasgow Academy and Dumfries Academy (see also Dumfries) before going on to Edinburgh University. He wrote many stories and novels, setting them in a small town called "Thrums", which is a thinly disguised Kirriemuir.

In 1930, when he was given the freedom of the town, Barrie donated a **Camera Obscura** (National Trust for Scotland) to the town, one of only three such cameras in the country. It is situated within the cricket pavilion on top of Kirriemuir Hill, and is open to the public. The **Kirriemuir Aviation Museum**, at Bellie's Brae, has a private collection of World War II memorabilia. It was established in 1987, and largely confines itself to British aviation history.

Kirriemuir is the gateway to many of the beautiful Angus glens, and in the **Gateway to the Glens Museum** in the former town hall in the High Street you can find out about life in the glens and in Kirriemuir itself. The glens lie north of the town, and go deep into the Cairngorms (see also Brechin). They are extremely beautiful, and well worth a visit. The B955 takes you into **Glen Clova**, then, at its head, forms a loop, so you can travel along one side of the glen and return along the other for part of the way. A minor road at the Clova Hotel takes you up onto lonely **Glen Doll** before it peters out. At Dykehead you can turn off the B955 onto a minor road for **Glen Prosen** and follow it as it winds deep into the mountains. A cairn close to Dykehead commemorates the Antarctic explorers Robert Falcon Scott and Edward Adrian Wilson. Wilson was born in Cheltenham, the son of a doctor, but lived in Glen Prosen, and it was here that some of the Antarctic expedition was planned. He died along with Scott in Antarctica in March 1912.

Glen Isla is the southernmost of the Angus glens, and you can follow it for all of its length along the B951, which eventually takes you onto the A93 at Glenshee and up to Braemar if you wish. You will pass the **Lintrathen Loch**, which is noted for its bird life. A couple of miles further up the glen a minor road takes you to lonely **Backwater Reservoir** and its dam.

DUNNICHEN
13 miles NE of Dundee on minor road off the B9128

Close to the village was fought, in AD 685, the **Battle of Nechtansmere** between the Picts, under King Nechtan, and the Northumbrians. It was a turning point in early Scottish history, as it was decisive in establishing what was to become Scotland as an independent nation, and not part of an enlarged Northumbria and later England (see also Brechin).

Northumbria was aggressively trying to extend its boundaries, and had already taken the Lothians and Fife, when they came north. The Northumbrians, under King Ecgfrith, were roundly beaten, and Ecgfrith himself and most of the royal court were killed. The Pictish battle plan, according to Bede, was to lure the

Northumbrians into a piece of land between Dun Nechtan, a hill fort, and an area of swamp close to the loch, where they were trapped. At the crossroads in the village is a cairn, which commemorates the battle, and a newer one was erected in 1998 close to the actual battlefield. Some people claim to have seen a ghostly re-enactment of the fighting take place in modern times. The "mere", or loch, which gave its name to the battle, was drained many years ago.

The picturesque village of **Letham**, which is close by, was founded in 1788 by George Dempster, the local landowner, as a settlement for farm workers who had been forced to leave the land because of farming reforms. It became a centre of weaving and spinning, though the introduction of power looms in nearby towns killed it off.

ARBROATH

15 miles NE of Dundee on the A92

The ancient town of Arbroath is special to all Scots. It was here, in 1320, that the nobles of Scotland met and signed the **Declaration of Arbroath**, which stated that the country was an independent kingdom, and not beholden to England. It was sent to a sceptical Pope John XXII in Rome (Bruce had previously been excommunicated), and in it, they claimed that they were not fighting for glory, riches or honour, but for freedom. They also, in no uncertain terms, claimed that they would remain loyal to their king, Robert the Bruce, only as long as he defended Scotland against the English. It was a momentous declaration to make in those days, when unswerving loyalty to a sovereign was expected at all times.

The Declaration was drawn up in **Arbroath Abbey** (Historic Scotland), with Bernard de Linton, the abbot of the abbey, being the writer. The ruins of the abbey still stand within the town, and sometimes a re-enactment of the signing is held there. A Visitor Centre tells the story of the abbey and the Declaration.

The abbey ruins date from the 12th century and later, and are of warm red sandstone. It was founded in 1176 by William the Lion for the Tironensian monks of Kelso, and dedicated to St Thomas of Canterbury. Portions of the great abbey church remain, including the south transept, with its great rose window. In 1951 the abbey was the temporary home of the Stone of Destiny after it was removed from Westminster Abbey by students with Scottish Nationalist sympathies.

In 1446 the **Battle of Arbroath** took place around the abbey. It had been the custom for the abbot to nominate a baillie to look after the peacekeeping and business side of Arbroath. He appointed Alexander Lindsay to the lucrative post, but later dismissed him for "lewd bahaviour", appointing John Ogilvie in his place. Lindsay took exception to this and arrived at the abbey with an army of 1,000 men. The ensuing battle, fought in the streets of the town, killed over 600 people, with Lindsay's army emerging triumphant. However, it was a hollow victory, as Lindsay himself was killed.

The award-winning **Arbroath Museum**, at Ladyloan, is housed in the elegant signal tower for the Bellrock

Arbroath

Lighthouse, and brings Arbroath's maritime and social history alive through a series of models, sounds and even smells.

Arbroath has had a harbour at the "Fit o' the Toon" (Foot of the Town) since at least the 14th century, and it supported a great fishing fleet. The town gave its name to that delicacy called the **Arbroath Smokie** (a smoked haddock) though the supposed origins of the delicacy are to be found not in the town, but in **Auchmithie**, a fishing village four miles to the north. The story goes that long ago it was the practice to store fish in the lofts of the fishermen's cottages. One day, a cottage burned down, and the resultant smoked fish was found to be delicious. Not only that - it preserved them.

The **Cliffs Nature Trail** winds for one and a half miles along the red sandstone cliffs towards Carlinheugh Bay. There is plenty of birdlife to see, as well as fascinating rock formations. The town is

also a holiday resort, and at West Link Parks is the 10¼ inch gauge **Kerr's Miniature Railway**, always a favourite with holidaymakers. It is open during the summer months, and is Scotland's oldest miniature railway, having been built in 1935. It runs for over 400 yards alongside the main Aberdeen to Edinburgh line.

St Vigeans

17 miles NE of Dundee on minor road off the A92

When the 12th century **Parish Church of St Vigeans** was being refurbished in the 19th century, 32 sculptured Pictish stones were discovered. They are now housed in the **St Vigeans Museum**, converted cottages close to the small knoll where the church stands. The most important stone is the St Dristan Stone, dating from the 9th century.

St Fechan, or St Vigean, was an Irish saint who died in about AD 664. The village of Ecclefechan in Dumfriesshire is also named after him.

ABERLEMNO

18 miles NE of Dundee on a minor road off the B9134

Within the village are the Pictish **Aberlemno Sculptured Stones** (Historic Scotland). One is situated in the kirkyard of the parish church, and the others are within a stone enclosure near the roadside north of the church. The one in the kirkyard shows a fine cross on one side surrounded by intertwining serpents and water horses, and a typical Pictish hunting scene on the other. It dates from the 8th or 9th century. The other two have crosses, angels, and battle or hunting scenes. Because of possible frost damage, the stones are boxed in between October and May.

BRECHIN

22 miles NE of Dundee off the A90

If the possession of a cathedral makes a town a city, then Brechin is indeed a city, even though it has a population of only 6,000. **Brechin Cathedral** dates from the 12th century, though most of what we see today is 13th century and later. It was the successor to a Celtic church which stood on the site, and which had been endowed by the Irish queen of Kenneth II, king of Scots between AD 971 and AD 995. It soon became the premier church for Angus, though by the 11th century Roman Catholic clergy had succeeded the Culdee priests.

In 1806 the nave, aisles and west front were remodelled, and between 1901 and 1902 were restored to their original design. Adjacent to the cathedral, and now forming part of its fabric, is an 11th century **Round Tower**, which rises to a height of 106 feet. These towers are common in Ireland, though this is the only one of two to have survived in Scotland (see also Abernethy). From the top a monk rang a bell at certain times during the day, calling the monks to prayer. It was also used as a place of refuge for the monks during troubled times. In Maison Dieu lane is the south wall of the chapel of the **Maison Dieu** almshouses founded in 1267 by Lord William de Brechin.

Brechin Museum has exhibits and displays about the cathedral, the ancient city crafts and local archaeology. **Brechin Castle** (not open to the public) is the seat of the Earls of Dalhousie, and within the **Brechin Castle Centre** are a garden centre, walks and a model farm. There is also **Pictavia**, an exhibition that explains about the enigmatic Picts, who occupied this part of Scotland for centuries. One of the displays explains the Battle of Nechansmere (see also Dunnichen). Their name means the "painted people", and they fought the Romans, the Vikings and the Angles. The various tribes eventually amalgamated, forming a powerful kingdom, which ultimately united with the kingdom of the Scots of Dalriada in AD 843 to form an embryonic Scotland.

At Menmuir, near the town, are the White and Brown **Caterthuns**, on which are the well-preserved remains of Iron Age forts. The hills also give good views across the surrounding countryside.

The **Caledonian Railway** runs on Sundays during summer and on Saturdays also during the peak season, when passengers can travel between the Victorian Brechin Station on Park Road and the nearby Bridge of Dun. The railway has ten steam engines and 12 diesels, and is run by the Brechin Railway Preservation Society. The Brechin branch line, on which the trains run, was closed in 1952.

To the north west of Brechin is **Glen Lethnot**, one of the beautiful Angus glens (see also Kirriemuir). Flowing through it is the West Water, and near the head of the glen is an old trail that takes you over the Clash of Wirren into Glen Esk. Illicit distillers used this as a route in days gone by, and hid their casks in the corries among the hills. For this reason it became known as the Whisky Trail.

MONTROSE

27 miles NE of Dundee on the A92

Montrose is an ancient royal burgh, which received its charter in the early 12th century. It sits on a small spit of land between the North Sea and a shallow tidal inlet called the Montrose Basin, which is a local nature reserve founded in 1981 famous for its bird life. The **Montrose Basin Wildlife Centre** (see panel below) is visited by thousands of bird watchers every year who come to see the many migrant birds.

At the old Montrose Air Station, where some of the Battle of Britain pilots trained, is the **Montrose Air Station**

Heritage Centre. In 1912, the government planned 12 such air stations, to be operated by the Royal Flying Corps, later called the Royal Air Force. Montrose was the first, and became operational in 1913. Now it houses a small collection of aircraft, plus mementoes, documents and photographs related to flying. It also houses a ghost.

The **William Lamb Studio** is in a close off Market Street, and is open to the public during the summer It celebrates the life of local artist who died in 1951. He was wounded twice in World War I, yet in 1932 was commissioned by the Duchess of York to make busts of her daughters, Princess Elizabeth and Princess Margaret. So impressed was she that she then commissioned a bust of herself.

To the west of the town, beyond the Basin, is the **House of Dun** (National Trust for Scotland). From 1375 until 1980 the estate was home to the Erskine

MONTROSE BASIN WILDLIFE CENTRE

Rossie Braes, Montrose, Angus DD10 9TJ
Tel: 01674 676336 Fax: 01674 678773

Montrose Basin is the 750-hectare enclosed estuary of the South Esk river. Virtually untouched by industrial development and pollution, the Basin provides a rich feeding ground for thousands of resident and migrant birds. The daily tidal cycle and passing seasons, each with its own characteristic pattern of birds - winter and summer visitors and passage migrants - ensure something new and different every month of the year. From here you might see eider ducks, pink footed and greylag geese, otters and much more.

Magnificent views of the wildlife can be seen through high powered telescopes and binoculars, whilst TV cameras bring the wildlife right into the centre. Unique displays show

how a tidal basin works and the routes taken by the migrating birds. There are lots of buttons to press, boxes to open, touch tables and microscopes - ideal for children - and there is a fully equipped classroom for children to enjoy a range of educational activities. A nearby hide provides a closer view of the wildlife and the shop is stocked with a range of unusual and exciting gifts. Open 15th March to 15th November, daily 10.30am-5pm and 16th November to 14th March, Friday, Saturday and Sunday 10.30am-4pm.

family, with the presnt house being designed by William Adam in 1730 for David Erskine, 13th Laird of Dun, and contains good plasterwork, sumptuous furnishings and a collection of embroidery carried out by Lady Augusta Kennedy-Erskine, natural daughter of William IV by his mistress Mrs Jordan. There are also formal gardens and woodland walks.

Montrose was adopted as the title of the Graham family when it was ennobled, and the most famous member was James Graham, 5th Earl and 1st Marquis of Montrose. He was born in 1612, and succeeded to the earldom in 1625. At first he was a Covenanter, then changed sides. He was made Lieutenant-General of Scotland by the king, and unsuccessfully tried to invade the country with an army. He later went to the Highlands in disguise to raise a Royalist army. During a succession of skirmishes, he defeated Covenanting forces due to his brilliant leadership and almost reckless courage. Charles's defeat at Naseby, however, left him powerless, and his forces were eventually soundly beaten at Philiphaugh in 1645. Afterwards he fled to the Continent but returned in 1650 in support of Charles II. Charles, however, disowned him and he was hanged.

Though not born in Montrose, George Wishart the religious reformer has close associations with the town. He attended the grammar school here in the 1520s, and went on to Aberdeen University. He later returned and taught at the grammar school, where he used the Greek translation of the Bible while teaching his pupils. For this he was accused of heresy, and he had to flee to England. In 1546 he was burnt at the stake in St Andrews on the orders of Cardinal Beaton (see also Dundee and St Andrews).

EDZELL
27 miles NE of Dundee on the B966

There has been a castle at Edzell since at least the 12th century, when one was built by the Abbot family. The present ruins of **Edzell Castle** (Historic Scotland) date from the early 16th century. It was a seat of the Lindsays, and reckoned to be the finest castle in Angus. It clearly shows that life in a Scottish castle was not the cold, draughty experience that people imagine from seeing bare, ruined walls. They could be places of refinement and comfort, and at Edzell we have evidence of this.

The gardens were especially tasteful and elegant, and were laid out in 1604 by Sir David Lindsay, though he died in 1610 before they could be completed. The walled garden has been described as an "Italian Renaissance garden in Scotland", and featured heraldic imagery and an array of carved panels representing deities, the liberal arts and the cardinal virtues.

The castle was added to in 1553 when David Lindsay, 9th Earl of Crawford and a high court judge, built the west range.

Edzell Castle

In 1562 Mary Stuart spent two nights here, and held a meeting of her Privy Council.

In 1715 the Jacobite Lindsays sold the castle to the Earl of Panmure, who were also Jacobite sympathisers, so that they could raise a Jacobite regiment. After the rebellion the castle and lands were forfeited to the crown and sold to an English company called the York Building Company, which went bankrupt in 1732. The castle gradually became ruinous, and in the 1930s the gardens were restored to their former glory. The summerhouse contains examples of the carved panelling that was in the castle in its heyday.

Kinross House

One of the delights of Edzell village is the **Dalhousie Arch**, erected in 1887 over a road into the village as a memorial to 13th Earl of Dalhousie and his wife, who died within a few hours of each other.

Edzell is the gateway to **Glen Esk**. It is the longest and most northerly of the glens, and you can drive the 19 miles to Invermark Lodge, close to Loch Lee, where the road peters out. Along the way you can stop at the Retreat, where you will find the **Glen Esk Folk Museum**, which traces the life of the people of the glen from about 1800 to the present day.

KINROSS

Once the main town in the tiny county of Kinross, which measures no more than 15 miles by nine, this small burgh now sits quietly on the shores of Loch Leven. The opening of the M90 motorway has put it within half an hour of Edinburgh, and over the last 15 years it has expanded to become a peaceful haven for commuters.

The town's **Tolbooth** dates from the 17th century, and was restored by Robert Adam in 1771. On the **Mercat Cross** are the "jougs", an iron collar placed round the neck of wrongdoers. **Kinross House** dates from the late 17th century, and was built for Sir William Bruce, Charles II's surveyor and master of works, who was responsible for the fabric of the Palace of

Holyrood in Edinburgh. It is an elegant Palladian mansion with wonderful formal gardens that are open to the public from April to September. The story goes that it was intended as a home for the ill-fated James VII, then Duke of York, in anticipation of the fact that he might not succeed to the throne, though this is unlikely.

Loch Leven is one of Scotland's most famous lochs, not because of its size (it covers 3,500 acres) or its spectacular beauty, but because of its wonderful trout fishing. Though this has gone into decline in recent years, the trout are still highly prized for their delicate pink flesh, caused by the small fresh water shellfish on which they feed. The whole loch is a National Nature Reserve, and on the south shore of the loch, close to the B9097, is the **Vane Farm Nature Reserve**, administered by the Royal Society for the Protection of Birds and part of the Loch Leven National Nature Reserve. It hosts a programme of events throughout the year, and was the first educational nature reserve in Europe.

The loch has seven islands. On **St Serf's Island**, the largest, a small Augustinian priory once stood, though all that remains are the scant walls of the chapel and the remains of a small priory and chapel. It replaced a Celtic monastery founded by Brude, the last Pictish king, in the 9th century. In 1150 an Augustinian priory was founded on the site, and staffed by monks from St Andrews. One of the priors was Andrew of Wynton, author of the *Orygynale Cronykil* ("Original Chronicle"), which was a history of Scotland.

On another island are the ruins of **Lochleven Castle** (Historic Scotland). It was a Douglas stronghold, the surrounding lands and the loch having been gifted to the family by Robert III in

Loch Leven

1390. From June 1567 until May 1568 Mary Stuart was held prisoner here, having been seized in Edinburgh for her supposed part in the murder of her husband Lord Darnley. She was 25 years old at the time, and married to Bothwell, who was also implicated in Darnley's murder. While kept prisoner in the castle, she was constantly being asked to abdicate and divorce Bothwell, but this she refused to do, as she was already pregnant by him. Shortly after she arrived on the island, she gave birth to stillborn twins, and eventually signed the deeds. But it was not her stay on the island that made the castle famous; rather it was the way she escaped.

The castle was owned by the Dowager Lady Douglas, mother of Mary's half brother the Earl of Moray, who became regent when Mary abdicated. Both she and her other sons Sir William and George Douglas looked after Mary during her imprisonment. But George gradually fell under Mary's spell, and hatched various plans for her to escape. All failed, and he was eventually banished from the island.

But someone else had also fallen under Mary's spell - 16-year-old Willie Douglas, who was thought to be the illegitimate son of Sir William, and who was kept as a page. After the various attempts at escape, Mary was being held in the third storey of the main tower, above the Great Hall where the Douglas family dined. One evening young Willie "accidentally" dropped a napkin over the castle keys, which his father had placed on the table while dining. On picking up the napkin, he picked up the keys as well.

As the meal progressed, Mary and one of her attendants crept out of her room and made for the main doorway, where Willie met them. He unlocked the door, and they both slipped out. He then locked the door behind him and threw the keys into the water before rowing the two women ashore. There they were met by George Douglas, Lord Seton and a troop of loyal soldiers, and taken to the safety of Niddrie Castle.

In those days, the loch was much bigger and deeper than it is now, and the water came right up to the doors of the castle. Between 1826 and 1836 it was partially drained, reducing its size by a quarter, and the keys were recovered from the mud. Nowadays, trips to the island leave from the pier at Kinross.

Within the town are the premises of Todd and Duncan, where a small exhibition called **Cashmere at Lochleven** traces the history of this luxury cloth. The **Scottish Raptor Centre** at Turfhills has falconry courses and flying displays. Close to Kinross every year in July is held Scotland's biggest outdoor rock festival, **T in the Park**. And every Sunday the **Kinross Market** is held, the largest indoor market in Scotland. The **Heart of Scotland Visitor Centre** gives you a general introduction to the area, and is to be found near Junction 6 of the M90 motorway.

AROUND KINROSS

MILNATHORT
2 miles N of Kinross off the M90

Milnathort is a small, former wool-manufacturing town. To the east are the ruins of 15th century **Burleigh Castle**, built of warm red stone, which was a stronghold of the Balfour family. All that remains nowadays is a curtain wall and a four-storey tower, and is said to be haunted by the ghost of a woman called Grey Maggie.

There is an interesting story attached to the castle. In 1707 the heir to the castle fell in love with a servant girl, which so displeased his father that he sent him abroad. However, he declared his undying love for her, and swore that if she married someone else while he was away, he would kill him when he returned.

After a year or so he returned, only to find that she had married a schoolmaster. True to his word, he shot him dead. He then fled, but was captured and sentenced to death. However, he escaped the gallows by changing places with his sister and donning her clothes. He later fought in the Jacobite army during the 1715 Uprising. For this, his castle and lands were taken from the family and given to the Irwins.

The **Orwell Standing Stones** are just off the A911. Two huge stones, dating to about 2000BC, stand on a slight rise. One of them fell down in 1972, and during restoration work cremated bones were discovered buried at its foot.

SCOTLANDWELL
5 miles E of Kinross, on the A911

Scotlandwell takes its name from the springs that bubble up to the surface in this part of the county, which is on the western slopes of the Lomond Hills. In the early 13th century the Bishop of St Andrews set up a hospice here, and his successor gave it to the "Red Friars", or "Trinitarians", a monastic order that had originally been founded to raise money for the release of captives in the Holy Land during the Crusades. They exploited the springs, and established a **Holy Well**. Soon it became a place of pilgrimage, bringing huge revenue to the monks. Robert the Bruce came here to find a cure for his leprosy, and held a parliament. On the slopes above the village are the **Crooked Rigs**, remnants of a medieval runrig field system

The local landowners, the Arnots of **Arnot Tower**, the ruins of which can still be seen, gazed enviously at the wealth of the Trinitarians, and decided to "muscle in" on the venture. They placed younger sons of the family within the order as fifth columnists, and when enough of them were in place, they occupied the friary and ejected those friars who weren't Arnots. They established Archibald Arnot, the Laird of Arnot's second son, as minister (the name given to the head of the friary), and began creaming off the vast wealth. At the Reformation, the lands and income of the friary were given to them, and the takeover was complete.

Today, the holy well still exists. In 1858 the Laird of Arnot commissioned David Bryce to turn it into a memorial to his wife Henrietta, and this is what can be seen today. The friary has completely disappeared, though a small plaque in the graveyard marks the spot where it once stood.

At Portmoak near Scotlandwell there's the **Scottish Gliding Centre**, where the adventurous can try an "air experience flight".

CROOK OF DEVON
5 miles W of Kinross on the A977

This small village has twice won an award for being the "best kept village in Kinross". It seems quiet enough now, but in the 1660s it achieved notoriety as a centre of witchcraft. A coven of witches had been "discovered" in the area, and in 1662 three women were tried and sentenced to be strangled to death and their bodies burnt at a "place called Lamblaires". A few weeks later four women and one man were executed in the same manner, and not long after two women were tried, one of them escaping death because of her age. The other was burnt at the stake.

By this time the other members of the "coven" had fled from the area. But in July two further women were put on trial, one of whom was executed and the other, called Christian Grieve, acquitted. The acquittal was looked upon as an affront by the local people - especially the clergy - and she was retried and eventually executed.

There is no doubt that the trials were a travesty, and that many old scores were settled by naming people - especially old women - as witches. It was also not unknown in Scotland at that time for the accused, knowing their fate was sealed, to get their own back on the accusers by naming them as witches and warlocks as well. Thus Scotland seemed to be awash with devil worship, when in fact it was very rare.

Today Lamblaires is a small grassy knoll in a field adjoining the village. It looks peaceful enough, and nothing reminds you of the horrible stranglings and burnings that took place there.

PERTH

The "Fair City" of Perth sits on the Tay, and in medieval times was the meeting place of Scottish kings and parliaments. Though a large place by Scottish

Tay Street, Perth

standards, having a population of about 43,000, its location away from the Central Belt ensured that it never succumbed to the intense industrialisation that many other towns experienced. But it did succumb to the ravages of modernisation, and many of the ancient buildings that played a part in Scotland's story have been swept away.

The city centre lies between two large open spaces, the **North Inch** and the **South Inch**, and is filled with elegant 18th and 19th century buildings. Up until the local government reorganisations of the mid '70s, it had a lord provost, and was truly a city. It even has **St Ninian's Cathedral**, which dates from the 19th century and was designed by Wiliam Butterfield. It was the first cathedral to be built in Britain since the Reformation, having been consecrated in 1850.

Perth has played a large part in the history of Scotland. James I chose it as his capital, and if he had not been murdered in the city in 1437, it might have been Scotland's capital to this day. The story of James's murder has been embellished over the years, but the facts are simple. He was an unpopular monarch, and when he was staying in the city's Dominican Friary (now gone), he was attacked by a group of nobles under the Earl of Atholl, who hoped to claim the crown. James tried to make his escape through a sewer which ran beneath his room, but was caught and stabbed to death. An embellishment to the story is that one of his Queen's ladies-in-waiting stuck her arm through the bolt holes of the door as a bar to prevent the entry of the assassins. However, it is probably a later invention.

In the centre of the city is **St John's Kirk**, one of the finest medieval kirks in Scotland. From this church, the city took its earlier name of St Johnstoune, which is remembered in the name of the local football team. It was consecrated in 1243, though the earliest part of what you see nowadays, the choir, dates from the 15th century, with the tower being added in 1511. It has some Renaissance glass, and it was here, in May 1559, that John Knox first preached after his exile in Europe. It more or less launched the Reformation in Scotland.

After the Reformation of 1560, the building was divided into three churches, with three distinct congregations. It was not until the early 20th century that the church housed one congregation again. The architect for the scheme was Sir Robert Lorimer, and the furnishings in the nave are mostly his work.

In Balhousie Castle in Hay Street near the North Inch you'll find the **Black Watch Regimental Museum**. Raised in 1725 from the ranks of clans generally hostile to the Jacobites, such as the Campbells, Frasers and Grants, its purpose was to patrol or "watch" the Highlands after the first Jacobite Uprising, the Black Watch is now the senior Highland regiment (see also Aberfeldy).

The **Perth Museum and Art Gallery** is in George Street, and is one of the oldest in Britain. It houses material whose scope goes beyond the city and its immediate area, as well as a collection of fine paintings, sculpture, glass and silver. The **Fergusson Gallery** in Marshall Place is dedicated to the painter John Duncan Fergusson (1874-1961), who, along with Peploe, Cadell and Hunter formed a group called the Scottish Colourists. The gallery, which opened in 1992, is housed in a former waterworks dating from 1832.

In 1928 Sir Walter Scott's novel *The Fair Maid of Perth* was published, the heroine of which was Catherine Glover, daughter of Simon Glover, who lived in Curfew Row. It was set in the 14th century, and tells of how Catherine, a woman noted for her piety and beauty, was sought after by all the young men of the city. David Stewart, Duke of Rothesay and son of Robert III, also admired her, though his intentions were not honourable. He was thwarted by Hal Gow, who came upon the Duke and his men trying to enter Catherine's house in the dead of night.

The ensuing skirmish resulted in one of the Duke's retainers having his hand hacked off by Hal before they fled in disarray. Catherine slept through it all, though Hal wakened her father and showed him the severed hand. The story ends happily when Hal subsequently marries Catherine. The present **Fair Maid's House** (not open to the public) does not go back as far as the 14th century. However, it is over 300 years old, and incorporates some medieval walls, which may have belonged to the original house that stood on the site. In 1867 Bizet wrote his opera *The Fair Maid of Perth* based on Scott's book, and the story became even more popular.

The **Caithness Glass Visitor Centre** at Inveralmond has viewing galleries from which you can see glass being blown into beautiful glass ornaments and vases. There is also a shop. **Bell's Cherrybank Gardens** is an 18-acre garden on the western edge of the city. It incorporates the National Heather Collection, which has over 900 varieties of heather. On Dundee road is the **Branklyn Garden** (NTS), developed by John and Dorothy Renton since 1922. One of its more unusual plants is the rare blue Himalayan poppy. **Kinnoull Hill**, to the east of Perth, rises to a height of 729 feet above the Tay. If you are reasonably fit, you can walk to the summit, where there is a folly, and get some wonderful views across the Tay to

Fife, over to Perth and beyond, and down over the Carse of Gowrie.

AROUND PERTH

SCONE PALACE
2 miles N of Perth off the A93

Historically and culturally, Scone (pronounced "Scoon") is one of the most important places in Scotland. When Kenneth MacAlpin, king of Dalriada, also became king of the Picts in AD 843, he quit his capital at Dunadd and moved to Scone. He made the move to be nearer the centre of his new kingdom and to escape from the constant Norse raids on the western seaboard. This was the beginning of the kingdom of Scotland as we know it, though it would be another 170 years before the Lowland kingdoms of Strathclyde and the Lothians were absorbed.

Scone Abbey, (now gone) was built by Alexander I in 1114 for the Augustinians,

Scone Palace

and was totally destroyed after the Reformation. Outside of it, on the **Moot Hill** (which can still be seen) the Scottish kings were crowned sitting on the Stone of Destiny (see also Dunadd and Edinburgh). It was here that Robert the Bruce was crowned king of Scotland in 1306, in defiance of Edward I of England. Traditionally, the Earl of Fife placed the crown on the monarch's head, but as he was being held in England, he could not perform the duty. Therefore his sister, Isobel MacDuff, Countess of Buchan, took his place, incurring the wrath of both Edward I and her own husband, who supported Edward's claim to the throne.

A replica of the Stone of Destiny is to be found at the summit of Moot Hill, along with a small chapel. The last king to be crowned at Scone was Charles II in 1651. This stone is also called Jacob's Pillow, and is supposed to have been the pillow on which the Biblical Jacob slept, though the present one, housed in Edinburgh, was almost certainly quarried in Perthshire. However, there are those who say that when Edward I seized the stone in 1296, he was given a worthless copy by the monks of the abbey.

Scone Palace itself is the home of the Earls of Mansfield, and dates from the early 19th century. It has collections of fine furniture, porcelain and needlework.

STANLEY
6 miles N of Perth on the B9099

The picturesque small village of Stanley sits on the River Tay, and is a former mill village. Sir Richard Arkwright had an interest in the mills here, the first of which was founded in 1786. Three large mills were built in the 1820s, powered by seven waterwheels. Four miles away are the ruins of 13th century **Kinclaven Castle**, once a favourite residence of Alexander II, who had built it. William

Wallace ambushed a small force of English troops near here in 1297, and when they took refuge in the castle Wallace besieged it, causing it to surrender.

BANKFOOT
7 miles N of Perth on A9

This small village sits just off the A9. The **Macbeth Experience** is a multi-media show that explains all about one of Scotland's most famous kings. It debunks the Macbeth of Shakespeare's play and instead concentrates on the actual man and his achievements.

MEIKLEOUR
10 miles N of Perth on A984

The **Meikleour Hedge**, just outside the village on the A93, is the world's largest. It borders the road for over 600 yards, and is now over 85 feet high. It is of pure beech, and was supposed to have been planted in 1745 by Jean Mercer and her husband Robert Murray Nairne, who was later killed at the Battle of Culloden. Jean immediately left the area, and the hedge was allowed to grow unattended for many years.

BLAIRGOWRIE
14 miles N of Perth on the A93

This trim town, along with its sister town of **Rattray**, became one burgh in 1928 by an Act of Parliament. It is noted as the centre of a raspberry and strawberry growing area. It sits on the Ericht, a tributary of the Tay, and the riverside is very attractive. **Cargill's Visitor Centre**, housed in a former corn mill, sits on its banks, and has Scotland's largest water wheel. Within the library in Leslie Street is the **Blairgowrie Genealogy Centre** where you can carry out research on the old families of the area.

The **Cateran Trail** is named after

BELMONT HOTEL

Meigle, Perthsire PH12 8TJ
Tel·01828 640232 Fax: 01828 640726
website: www.belmontarms.co.uk

Situated on the A954 half a mile south of Meigle, the **Belmont Hotel** is a substantial, stone built hostelry offering superb accommodation, food and drink for the discerning tourist. There are double, twin, single and family rooms available (one with a four poster bed), and lunches, high teas and dinners are served. This is traditional Scottish hospitality at its best, with the hotel's chef, Andrew May, being one of the ten finalists in the Scothot Chef of the Year Award 2005. There is a garden where you can relax over a drink and where there is a children's play area.

medieval brigands from beyond Braemar who used to descend on Perthshire to wreak havoc and steal cattle. It is a 60-mile long circular route centred on Blairgowrie, and uses existing footpaths and minor roads to take you on a tour of the area. It has been designed to take about five or six days to complete, with stops every 12 or 13 miles, and takes in parts of Angus as well as Perthshire.

Craighall Castle, the earliest parts of which date from the 16th century, are perched on a cliff above the Elricht. Sir Walter Scott visited it, and he used it as a model for Tullyveolan in his book *Waverley*. It now offers B&B accommodation.

COUPAR ANGUS
12 miles NE of Perth on the A94

Situated in Strathmore, Coupar Angus is a small town which was given its burgh charter in 1607. The scant remains of the gatehouse of **Coupar Angus Abbey**, founded by Malcolm IV for the Cistercians in the mid 12th century, stand in the kirkyard. At one time it was the wealthiest Cistercian abbey in Scotland. The town's **Tolbooth** dates from 1702, and was used as a courthouse and prison.

MEIGLE
16 miles NE of Perth on the b954

The finest collection of Pictish stones in Scotland was found in and around

Meigle, and they are now on display at **Meigle Museum** (Historic Scotland), in a converted schoolhouse. The largest stone, at eight feet tall, is Meigle 2, and shows a fine carved cross on side and mounted horsemen and mythical animals at the bottom. The central panel shows what appears to be Daniel surrounded by four lions, but some people have put another intrepretation on it. They say it depicts the execution of Queen Guinevere. It seems that she was captured by Mordred, king of the Picts, and that when she was released Arthur ordered her execution by being pulled apart by wild animals. The museum is open from April to September.

ERROL
8 miles E of Perth on a minor road off the A90

Set in the Carse of Gowrie, a narrow stretch of fertile land bordering the northern shore of the Firth of Tay, Errol is a peaceful village with a large **Parish Church** of 1831 designed by James Gillespie Graham which is sometimes called the "cathedral of the Carse". It gives its name to an earldom, which means that there is an "Earl of Errol" (see Slains Castle). A leaflet is available which gives details of most of the old kirkyards and kirks in the Carse. The **Tayreed Company**, based in an industrial estate, harvests reeds for thatching from reedbeds on the nearby Tay. In 1990s the

Errol Station Trust opened the former railway station as a heritage centre.

ELCHO

3 miles SE of Perth on a minor road

Elcho Castle (Historic Scotland) was the ancient seat of the Earls of Wemyss. The present castle was built by Sir John Wemyss, who died in 1572, in the 16th century on the site of an earlier fort-ification dating from the 13th century.

By about 1780, the castle had been abandoned, and it gradually became ruinous. It was re-roofed in 1830.

ABERNETHY

6 miles SE of Perth on the A913

The 75-feet high **Abernethy Round Tower** (Historic Scotland) is one of only two round towers in Scotland (see also Brechin). It dates from the end of the 11th century, and was used as a place of refuge for priests during times of trouble.

At the foot of the tower is a carved Pictish stone.

In 1072 Malcolm III met William the Conquerer here and knelt in submission, acknowledging him as his overlord. This was an act which had repercussions down through the ages, as Edward I used it to justify his claim that Scottish kings owed allegiance to him. The **Abernethy Museum**, founded in the year 2000, explains the village's history, and is housed in an 18th century building.

FORTEVIOT

6 miles SW of Perth on the B935

This little village was at one time the capital of a Pictish kingdom. In a field to the north of the River Earn stood the **Dupplin Cross**, erected, it is thought, in the 9th century by King Constantine I, who died in 877. It was taken to the National Museum of Scotland in 1998

BATTLEDOWN B&B

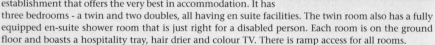

Battledown, Forgandenny, Perthshire PH2 9EL
Tel & Fax: 01738 812471
e-mail: i.dunsire@btconnect.com
website: www.battledownbb.co.uk

In the small, attractive rural village of Forgandenny, seven miles from the city of Perth, is **Battledown B&B**, a four star establishment that offers the very best in accommodation. It has three bedrooms - a twin and two doubles, all having en suite facilities. The twin room also has a fully equipped en-suite shower room that is just right for a disabled person. Each room is on the ground floor and boasts a hospitality tray, hair drier and colour TV. There is ramp access for all rooms.

The cottage is surrounded by attractive, mature gardens where guests can relax after a hard day's sightseeing in the beautiful county of Perthshire, or shopping in the small, attractive city of Perth, which sits on the River Tay. There is also a comfortable, welcoming guest lounge where guests can sit back and kick off their shoes as they plan their next day's activities - be they fishing on the Tay,

visiting the many historic houses and attractions in the area, or just motoring around admiring the marvellous scenery, beautiful villages and small market towns.

Breakfast is served between 8am and 9am on weekdays and 8.30am and 9.30am at weekends. You can choose from a delicious full Scottish breakfast or a lighter alternative, with all the produce used in the cooking being as fresh as possible. You can't go wrong if you stay at Battledown B&B. The owners, Ruth and Ian Dunsire, will offer you a warm Scottish welcome.

for restoration, after which it was housed in St Serf's Church in Dunning.

DUNNING

8 miles SW of Perth on the B934

This quiet village is mainly visited because of **St Serf's Parish Church**, with its fine early 13th century tower. The original church was probably built by Gilbert, Earl of Strathearn, in about 1200. It now houses the Dupplin Cross. A couple of miles outside the village, near the road, is a monument topped with a cross which marks the spot where, according to its inscription, **Maggie Wall**, a witch, was burned in 1657. It is the only memorial to a witch in Scotland, though no record has ever been found about the trial or execution of someone called Maggie Wall. The whole thing - including who actually built the cairn - remains a mystery.

AUCHTERARDER

12 miles SW of Perth on the A824

Situated a couple of miles north of the Gleneagles Hotel, Auchterarder is a small royal burgh with a long main street. It has been bypassed by the busy A9, and retains a quiet charm. At **Auchterarder Heritage**, within the local tourist office in the High Street, there are displays about local history. It was in Auchterarder in 1559 that Mary of Guise, Mary Stuart's mother, signed the Treaty of Perth acknowledging that Scotland was a Protestant country.

About three miles west of the town, near the A823, is the cruciform **Tullibardine Chapel** (Historic Scotland), one of the few finished collegiate chapels in Scotland that have remained unaltered over the years. It was founded by Sir David Murray of Tullibardine, ancestor of the Dukes of Atholl, in 1446.

ORTEGAS

183 High Street, Auchterarder, Perthshire PH3 1AF
Tel: 01764 664755

Having previously run a deli-sandwich bar and a restaurant in
Edinburgh, partners Chris Young and Fiona Wimpenny decided
to sell up and move to the beautiful Perthshire countryside. With
over 35 years of catering experience between them, they wanted
to escape the long hours of restaurant life, but still be involved
in quality food service. And so Ortegas deli was born. Their tiny
shop at the top of Auchterarder's High Street is an absolute tardis
of goodies for any self-respecting food-lover.

With an extensive range of over 40 Scottish and continental cheeses, charcuterie, fresh olives,
antipasti and pâtes, complemented by a fantastic array of olive oils, herbs and spices and traditional
deli food, and a small but carefully selected range of red, white and dessert wines. Every day Chris is in

the kitchen baking deli-quiche, cakes, flapjacks and of course
his famous muffins. And he now also bakes his own-recipe
handmade oatcakes, which he supplies to other Scottish delis,
the perfect companion to all those lovely cheeses.

If it's just a quick lunch on the run you're after, they also do
an excellent range of sandwiches, toasted panini and coffees to
take out. For easy entertaining, they will make up mouth watering
trays of tapas, cheeseboards or sandwich platters. Chris and
Fiona's love of good food is obvious throughout the shop, and
they will always be on hand for any advice or recipe tips, or just
a good old chat.

APPAREL

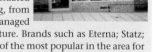

107 High street, Auchterarder, Perthshire PH3 1BJ
Tel & Fax: 01764 664985
e-mail: info@apparelmenswear.co.uk
website: www.apparelmenswear.co.uk

Apparel is a menswear shop that is really creating a name for itself. Situated
on Auchterarder's main street, it offers a range of exclusive clothing, from
smart to casual and from business to holiday wear. It is owned and managed
by Bill Robertson, who brings over 45 year's experience to the venture. Brands such as Eterna; Statz;
Odermark and Douglas& Grahame have meant that the shop is one of the most popular in the area for
men's clothing. There is also a formal hire service (including kilts).

The **Tullibardine Distillery** is built on
the site of Scotland's first public
brewery,. At James IV's coronation in
1488 beer from the brewery was drunk.
The visitors centre is open from May to
September each year.

MUTHILL

15 miles SW of Perth on the A822

Within Muthill (pronounced "Mew-
thill") are the ruins of the former

Muthill Parish Church (Historic
Scotland), which date mainly from the
early 15th century, though the tower was
probably built four centuries earlier. A
Celtic monastery was founded here in
about AD700, and before the medieval
church was built it was served by Culdee
priests and monks. The **Muthill Village
Museum** is housed in a cottage built
about 1760. It is open on Wednesdays,
Saturdays and Sundays from June to

September each year.

Three miles east of Muthill, at Innerpeffray, is **Innerpeffray Library**, one of the oldest libraries in Scotland. It was founded in 1680 by David Drummond, 3rd Lord Maddertie and brother-in-law of the Marquis of Montrose, and is housed in a building specially built for it in 1750. It contains many rare books, such as a copy of the 16th century Treacle Bible, so called because the translation of Jeremiah chapter 8 verse 22 reads, "Is there not triacle (treacle) at Gilead". There is also a 1508 *Ship of Fools*, a medieval satire written by a German writer called Simon Brant. Before moving to its present building it was housed in **Innerpeffray Chapel**, (Historic Scotland), built in 1508. The ruins of **Innerpeffray Castle** are nearby. It is a simple tower house dating from the 15th century which was heightened in 1610 for the 1st Lord Maddertie.

Drummond Castle Gardens are well worth visiting. They were first laid out in the 17th century, improved and terraced in the 19th, and replanted in the middle of the 20th. In 1842, Queen Victoria visited, and planted some copper beech trees, which can still be seen.

To the east of the village are the sites of two Roman signal stations - the **Ardunie Signal Station** and the **Muir O'Fauld Signal Station**. They were two of a series of such stations running between Ardoch and the Tay, and date to the 1st century AD.

BRACO

19 miles SW of Perth on the A822

Half a mile north of the village are the Blackhall Camps, two Roman marching camps which date to the 3rd century AD.

HUNTINGTOWER

2 miles W of Perth on the A85

Huntingtower (Historic Scotland) is a restored 15th century tower house once owned by the Ruthvens, Earls of Gowrie, and then the Murrays. Mary Stuart visited the castle twice, and in 1582 the famous "Raid of Ruthven" took place here, when the Earl of Gowrie and his friend the Earl of Mar tried to kidnap the young King James VI. Justice in those days was sometimes

Drummond Castle

GLOAGBURN FARMSHOP

Gloagburn Farm, Tibbermore,
Perth PH1 1QL.
Tel: 01738 840864
e-mail: ian_niven@btconnect.com

Gloagburn farm shop is sited on a 950-acre mixed arable farm run by Ian and Alison Niven. Ian, a third generation farmer, is best known for his free range eggs laid by the 2,000 hens, the extra large size being the most popular.

As you drive in, the ducks on the pond will greet you, especially 'Peeps' the hand reared duck. The beautiful open fronted conservatory displays a wide variety of fruit, our own farm produce and locally grown vegetables, unusual perennial plants, and great gift ideas for the garden. Inside the shop you will find one of the best selections of local and speciality foods in Perthshire.

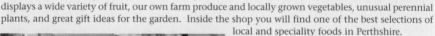

Gloagburn farm has its own range of homemade jams, marmalades, chutneys, and oatcakes tasting just like Grandma's did in the olden days. The homemade ratatouille chutney and oatcakes were awarded Gold and Silver in the Great Taste Awards. Also produced are a range of freezer meals, soups, and delicious cakes.

As you enter the shop, the aroma of fresh coffee and baking hits your nose and if you follow it you will find your self sitting down at a table and perusing the licensed café menu.

Choose to sit inside or outside in our new conservatory eating area. Breakfasts are served from 9am to 11.30am, morning coffee, cakes and freshly baked scones served all day, lunch, choice from homemade soup, sandwiches, baked potatoes, and daily specials served from 11.30 to 4.30pm. Mustn't forget the puddings with custard. Spoil yourselves and enjoy a glass of delicious organic wine.

After your wonderful freshly prepared food,

take time to explore the shop. Not only will you find great food, organic and traditional, but also beautiful gifts from the pottery ranges of Susie Watson, Bridgewater and Nicolas Mosse. Ranges of unusual greeting cards to bottles of organic wines and champagnes.

Gloagburn Farm Shop is a real day out in the beautiful Perthshire countryside. It is where traditional values still count.

swift, as the perpetrators were first executed, and then tried for treason. The castle has no connection with the John Buchan spy yarn, also called Huntingtower, which was set in Ayrshire.

FOWLIS WESTER

12 miles W of Perth on a minor road off the A85

The first name of this small village (pronounced "fowls") comes from the Gaelic "foghlais", meaning "stream" or burn. However, there is another, more intriguing derivation. It seems that long ago three French brothers settled in Scotland - one at Fowlis Wester, one at Fowlis Easter near Dundee and one at Fowlis in Ross-shire, and they each named their village after the French word for leaves, "feuilles". Above an archway in the **Parish Church of St Bean** in Fowlis Wester is a carving showing three leaves.

The church sits on a spot where a place of worship has stood since at least the eighth century. The present one dates from the 15th century, and is dedicated to an 8th century Irish saint, grandson of the King of Leinster, who preached in the area. The church has a leper's squint, a small window which allowed lepers to see the chancel area without coming into contact with the congregation. Two Pictish cross slabs from the 8th or 9th centuries are housed within the church - a ten-foot high cross slab and a smaller

one. The larger one shows two horsemen and some animals on one side and a man leading a cow and six men on the other. The smaller slab shows two men - possibly priests - seated on chairs. A replica of the larger one stands on the village green. Also in the church is a fragment of the McBean tartan, taken to the moon by American astronaut Alan Bean, who was the lunar module pilot on Apollo 12 during the second mission to the moon in November 1969, and the fourth man to walk on its surface.

CRIEFF

15 miles W of Perth on the A85

This inland holiday resort is the "capital" of that area of Scotland known as Strathearn. It sits at the beginning of Glen Turret, within which are the picturesque **Falls Of Turret**. At the **Crieff Visitor Centre** on Muthill Road you can see paperweights, pottery and miniature animal sculptures. The **Glenturret Distillery** at the Hosh, home of the famous "Grouse Experience", is Scotland's oldest, and tours (with a dram at the end) are available. . **Lady Mary's Walk**, beside the River Earn, was gifted to the town in 1815 by Sir Patrick Murray of Ochtertyre in memory of his daughter Mary.

The 3,480 feet high **Ben Chonzie**, eight miles north west of Crieff, has been described as the "most boring Munro in

HOME AND HOUND INCORPORATING DGN INTERIOR DESIGN LTD

25 Comrie Street, Crieff, Perthshire PH7 4AX
Tel:01764 654784
e-mail: sunnylawfarm@aol.com

Crieff is an historic and picturesque town in the heart of the Perthshire countryside. Here you will find one of the most unusual shops in the area – **Home & Hound**. It is an interior design company

with showroom. This retail outlet sells a wide range of design-led hand crafted home and gift items along with accessories from around the world, lighting from Italy, tableware from South Africa and baby gifts from Peru. The interior design section carries all the latest fabrics and wallpapers.

This is the place to come if you want to furnish a cottage in the country or a sophisticated flat in the city. The shop is open from Monday to Saturday with private viewings on Sunday by appointment.

But there is so much more to **Home & Hound** than furniture and fittings. This delightful shop also sells designer hound accessories not found in normal pet shops. There are sweetheart feeding bowls, Mulberry "at Home" dog beds, hand stitched Harris tweed collars, leads and coats as well as real crystal encrusted "special occasion" collars.

The staff are friendly and knowledgeable about everything they sell, and you are sure to be delighted.

COMPLIMENTS

22 West High Street, Crieff, Perthshire PH7 4DL
Tel: 01764 654017

If it's unusual gifts and up to the minute fashions you're after, then **Compliments** in the quiet, picturesque town of Crieff is just for you. It is owned and managed by Linda McLaren, who has been here 15 years, so she has a wealth of experience in both the gift and fashion trades. There's everything here from evening wear to smart casual clothing and from wedding outfit to day wear. In fact, the range of

ladies fashions at Compliments must be seen to be believed. Such prestigious names as Olsen, Tina Taylor, Marcona, Chianti and Max Pierre are represented here, and each item has been hand picked by Linda to represent the very best in fashionable elegance. Not only that - every item has been keenly priced so that you, the customer, can enjoy great value for money.

There is also a wide range of jewellery and fashion accessories that are just right for any fashion ensemble. The jewellery range includes such famous names as Gaby's, Chartage, Kit Heath Silver and Watch this Space, while there is a highly sought after range of purses, bags, scarves, soft toys, gifts and ornaments, including perfumed items. Linda and her staff are friendly and approachable, and have an in depth knowledge of the fashion items they sell. You are free to browse, with someone always there to answer any questions you may have. The interior of the shop is light and airy, and shopping here is a genuine pleasure.

AT HOME

Comrie Road, Crieff, Perthshire PH7 4BP
Tel & Fax: 01764 656515

Set in a delightful little cottage in the picturesque town of Crieff, At Home sells a wide range of gifts and home accessories that are beautiful, practical, of a very high standard and represents great value for money. The gift items, such as home fragrances, candles, ceramics and picture frames, are just that little bit special and different, and are sourced from Scandinavia, America, Scotland and so on. At Home is ideal for buying that special gift or a souvenir of your visit to Scotland. Even if you're just browsing, you'll receive a warm welcome and plenty of advice!

Scotland", though this is doing it an injustice. It can be climbed via a route leaving the car park at Loch Turret dam.

The **Baird Monument** stands on a hill to the west of the town, and was erected in memory of Sir David Baird (1757-1829) by his widow.

MADDERTY

10 miles W of Perth off the A85

To the north east of this village is the site of **Inchaffray Abbey**, of which nothing now remains apart from a low mound. The name means "island of the smooth waters", as at one time the mound was

an island within a small loch.

Maurice, Abbot of Inchaffray was Robert the Bruce's chaplain, and the keeper of a holy relic called the Arm of St Fillan. At the Battle of Bannockburn he paraded it before the Scottish troops to bring good fortune (see also St Fillans, Tyndrum and Pittenweem). A later abbot was killed at the Battle of Flodden in 1513.

COMRIE

21 miles W of Perth on the A85

This village is often called the "earthquake capital of Scotland" and the "shaky toun" as it sits right on the Highland Boundary Fault. James Melville, writing in his diary in July 1597, mentions an earth tremor, though the first fully recorded one was in 1788. A 72-feet high monument to him - the **Melville Monument** - stands on Dunmore Hill. In 1874 it was struck by lightning, and the man who climbed to its top to repair it swore he could see Edinburgh Castle.

In 1839 a major earthquake took place, causing the world's first seismometers to be set up in the village. The recently refurbished **Earthquake House**, built in 1874, now houses an array of instruments to measure the tremors. North of

The Church at Comrie

the village, in Glen Lednock, is the **De'ils Cauldron Waterfall**, overlooked by a monument to Henry Dundas, 1st Viscount Melville (1742-1811). To the south of the village, off the B827, is the Auchingarrich Wildlife Centre, with animals, a wild bird hatchery, woodland walks and an adventure playground.

Comrie was the "Best Large Village" in the 2001 Britain in Bloom contest.

St Fillans

26 miles W of Perth on the A85

St Fillans stands at the eastern end of Loch Earn, where the River Earn exits on its way to join the Firth of Tay, and is a gateway to the new Loch Lomond and Trossachs National Park. It is named after the Irish missionary St Fillan (see also Pittenweem, Tyndrum and Madderty). Two relics of the saint - his bell and his pastoral staff - are now housed within the National Museum of Scotland. On an island in Loch Earn stand the scant ruins of **Loch Earn Castle**, which belonged to

Clan MacNeish. From here they plundered the surrounding countryside before retreating to the safety of their castle. The McNabs, whom they attacked in 1612, gained their revenge by carrying a boat over the mountains, unseen by the MacNeishes, and mounting a surprise attack. The MacNeish clan chief was killed, as was most of his followers. Since then, the McNab crest has featured the head of the chief of Clan McNeish.

At the top of **Dunfillan Hill** (600 feet) is a rock known as **St Fillan's Chair**. To the southwest, overlooking Loch Earn, is **Ben Vorlich** (3,224 feet).

PITLOCHRY

This well-known Scottish town is one of the best touring bases in Scotland. It is said to be at the geographical heart of the country, and as such, it is as far from the sea as it is possible to be in Scotland. It was the 2003 winner as the "best small country town" in the Britain in Bloom contest.

Though not a large town, it relies heavily on tourism, and is full of hotels and guesthouses, making it a good stopping off point for those travelling further north. But it has its own attractions, not least of which is the marvellous scenery surrounding it. The B8019, the famous **Road to the Isles**, goes west towards beautiful Loch Tummel, whose waters have been harnessed for electricity. It passes the **Forestry Commission Visitor Centre**, which interprets the wildlife of the area. From the **Queen's View** there is a magnificent view west towards Loch Tummel and beyond. Queen Victoria stopped at this

St Fillans

point during her Highland tour in 1866 and praised the scenery, though it is said that it was Mary Stuart who originally gave the place its name when she visited in 1564.

Loch Faskally is close to Pitlochry, and is a man-made loch. It is still a lovely stretch of water, and forms part of the Tummel hydroelectric scheme. At the **Pitlochry Visitor Centre**, near the dam, there is the famous **Salmon Ladder**, which allows salmon to enter the loch from the River Tummel below. There is a viewing gallery, which allows you to watch the salmon, and displays about how electricity is produced from flowing water. Beside the loch is a picnic area, with an archway called the **Clunie Arch**. It is the exact dimensions of the tunnel that brings the waters from Loch

Loch Tummel

Tummel to the Clunie Power Station.

The **Edradour Distillery**, situated among the hills to the east of Pitlochry, is Scotland's smallest, and possibly its most picturesque distillery. It was established in 1837 and produces handcrafted malt using only local barley. Conducted tours, finished off with a

EASTER DUNFALLANDY COUNTRY HOUSE B&B

Pitlochry, Perthshire PH16 5NA
Tel: 01796 474128 Fax: 01796 474446
e-mail: sue@dunfallandy.co.uk website: www.dunfallandy.co.uk

The **Easter Dunfallandy Country House B&B** puts comfort and service first. It has three guest rooms, each one having an en suite bathroom or shower room, complete with complimentary toiletries. All are tastefully decorated to reflect the unique character of the house. Gourmet breakfasts - either traditional Scottish or something lighter if required - are served in the dining room, which retains its mellow pitch pine woodwork from the late 19th century. It makes an excellent base from which to explore the area, or as a stoping off point as you travel north or south.

THE OLD MILL INN

Mill Lane, Pitlochry, Perthshire PH16 5BH
Tel: 01796 474020
e-mail: enquiries@ highlandperthshire .com website: www.old-mill-inn.com

The **Old Mill Inn** is situated right in the centre of Pitlochry. People flock to this excellent gastropub on the weekends, enjoying the terrace and beer gardens. They come for the food and the excellent cask conditioned beers. The cooking is simple but elegant using fresh and locally sourced ingredients when ever possible. This is a great spot for a tasty, filling lunch. The interior is pleasantly comfortable and the staff friendly. There is an adventure playground and parking to the rear of the pub. Spacious accommodation is available. *Les Routiers*, *Good Pub Guide* and *AA Pub Guide* recommended. Food served all day until 10pm.

Pitlochry - Edradour - Moulin

Distance:	3.6 miles (5.8 kilometres)
Typical time:	110 mins
Height gain:	110 metres
Map:	Explorer 386
Walk:	www.walkingworld.com ID:1113
Contributor:	Ian Cordiner

Access Information:

By car or by foot from the centre of Pitlochry. Pitlochry is well served by trains and coaches on the Perth - Inverness routes and also by a number of local bus services.

Description:

This walk starts in an oak-wood and rises to a viewpoint overlooking an impressive waterfall. It then continues to rise and after leaving the wood, passes along the side of fields to reach Edradour Distillery. This is the smallest distillery in Scotland and is open most of the year to visitors.

On leaving the distillery the walk returns via a path between fields, before branching out northwards. It passes through open fields near the ruins of The Black Castle, on the way to Moulin. Next it continues through the streets of Pitlochry, passing a small wildlife garden and another distillery before returning to the start.

PLEASE NOTE At Waymark 9 the bridge over the stream has been washed away. If the water level is high or fast-flowing the route may be impassable at this point.

Features:

Hills or Fells, River, Toilets, Wildlife, Great Views, Gift Shop, Public Transport, Waterfall, Woodland, Ancient Monument

Walk Directions:

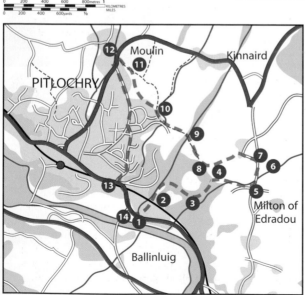

1 To start the walk, turn left as you leave Pitlochry (going east along the A924 Perth road). If you are leaving Pitlochry on foot, start the walk at Waymark 13. The narrow road to the left here passes underneath the railway line, then leads to a car park.

2 This is the real start to the walk. As you leave the car park, turn right up the hill. Keep to the right and then again go right.

3 Continue up the hill following the signs to Black Spout. When you reach the waterfall continue along the same path. Take the right fork here and continue towards the field.

4 There is a fenced-off path which separates you from the field. Continue onwards.

5 The path eventually leads to a tarred road, which you will follow to the left.

6 This is Edradour Distillery. It offers free tours from March to mid-December (although opening hours are more restricted in November and December). You may wish to break your walk and enjoy a tour which takes about 40 minutes. There is also a shop which is open all year. Toilets are located here.

7 After the distillery, continue up the narrow tarred road until you come to a passing place. Look out for the path between the road and the field and follow it.

8 When you reach a junction, turn right. Cross a small bridge and take a short cut across the field (or follow the path to the left, round the field). Rejoin the path at the other side of the field.

9 At the other side of the stream, continue up to the gate and into the next field. The path continues on through this field where animals may be present. Leave the field and move straight on along the tarred road. At the end turn right, then at the end of the wooden fence turn left and walk alongside a small stream.

10 Go through the gate and follow the path as best you can. It is not very well-marked here, but you are heading in the general direction across the diagonal of the field towards the church spire which is visible in the distance. On the way you will pass the ruins of Black Castle (marked "Caisteal Dubh" on the map). This was originally built on a crannog (man-made island) at the time of Robert the Bruce, but became uninhabited in the 15th Century when the inhabitants were killed by the plague.

11 Cross this stile in the north-west corner of the field and head for the building in the distance (which has a shored-up gable wall). It is here that you exit the field into a short narrow lane.

12 At the end of the lane turn left. Turn left again into East Moulin Road. Follow this road all the way down to Waymark 13.

13 At the bottom of the road, turn left along the main road (the A924 towards Perth). Continue on under the railway bridge.

14 Just opposite the grounds of the next distillery, there is a small wildlife garden on the south side of the road. As you continue on the north side of the road you pass the Blair Athol Distillery gates. The visitor centre entrance is a little farther on. Again tours are available but this time there is a small charge, which contains a discount voucher redeemable towards a purchase of a bottle of whisky. The distillery is open all year and toilets are also here. Continue eastwards until you again reach Waymark 1.

tasting, are available. Bell's **Blair Atholl Distillery** is the oldest working distillery in Scotland, and is also in Pitlochry.

Another place not to be missed is the **Pitlochry Festival Theatre**. It was founded in 1951, and presented its first plays in a tent. It continued like this until 1981, when a purpose-built theatre was opened at Port-na-Craig on the banks of the Tummel. It presents a varied programme of professional plays every summer, and is one of Scotland's most popular venues.

The A924 going east from Pitlochry takes you up into some marvellous scenery. It reaches a height of 1,260 feet before dropping down into Kirkmichael and then on to Bridge of Cally. On the way, at Enochdhu, you will pass **Kindrogan**, a Victorian country house where the Scottish Field Studies Association offer residential courses on Scotland's natural history. The **Dunfallandy Standing Stone** lies south of the town near Dunfallandy House, and west of the A9. It dates from Pictish times, and has a curious legend attached to it. A nun called Triduana was being forced into marriage with the son of a Scottish king, but escaped to a small chapel at Dunfallady, where she erected the "praying stone" in gratitude.

There are many fine guided walks in the area, some organised by such bodies as National Trust for Scotland, the Scottish Wildlife Trust and the Forestry Commission. A small booklet about them is available.

AROUND PITLOCHRY

SPITTAL OF GLENSHEE
13 miles NE of Pitlochry on the A93

As the name suggests, a small medieval hospital, or "spittal", once stood close to this village, which lies in the heart of the Grampian Mountains at a height of 1,125 feet. It sits on the main road north from Perth to Braemar, and surrounding it is some marvellous scenery. The Glenshee skiing area (Britain's largest) lies six miles north of the village, and is dealt with in the North East Scotland section of this guidebook.

The **Devil's Elbow** on the A93 lies about five miles north. A combination of steep inclines and double bends made it a notorious place for accidents in days gone by, though it has been much improved. At **Cairnwell** the road reaches a height of 2,199 feet, making it the highest public road in Britain. During the winter months the road can be blocked by snow for weeks on end. The **Four Poster Stone Circle** at Bad an Loin is unusual in that it only has four stones. From it there are fine views of Glen Shee.

DUNKELD
11 miles S of Pitlochry off the A9

Though it has all the appearance of an attractive town, Dunkeld is in fact a small cathedral city. **Dunkeld Cathedral** sits on the banks of the Tay, and consists of a ruined nave and a restored chancel, which is now used as the parish church.

For a short period Dunkeld was the ecclesiastical capital of Scotland. Kenneth I, when he ascended the throne as the first king of Scots in AD 843, established his capital at Scone, near Perth, and brought relics of St Columba with him, no doubt because Iona was too vulnerable to Viking attack. He placed them in the church of a Celtic monastery set up at Dunkeld, which in AD 865 was the seat of the chief Scottish bishop.

The cathedral as we see it nowadays dates from many periods. The choir (the present parish church) was built mainly in the early 14th century, while the nave (now ruined) was built in the early 15th century. Within the church is the tomb of Alexander Stewart, son of Robert II and known as the Wolf of Badenoch, the man who sacked Elgin Cathedral in the 14th century after a disagreement with

---

THE TAYBANK

Tay Terrace, Dunkeld, Perthshire PH8 0AQ
Tel:01350 727340 Fax: 01350 727979
e-mail: admin@thetaybank.com website: www.thetaybank.com.

The Taybank and its large beer garden is situated on the edge of Dunkeld with wonderful views overlooking the River Tay. With five comfortable guest rooms at remarkably reasonable prices, this is the ideal base from which to explore the area, or stay overnight as you pass north or south along the A9. Relax and sit by the river, or their cosy open fire and enjoy a meal with a beer or two. Go to the Taybank to experience their special musical atmosphere; live music and workshops occur most evenings. Join in with their Friday night Folk club, or why not start a session yourself.

the Bishop of Moray (see also Elgin, Grantown-on-Spey and Fortrose). After the Reformation the cathedral fell into disrepair, and it was not until 1600 that the choir was re-roofed and used as the parish church.

In 1689 the town was the scene of the **Battle of Dunkeld**, when Jacobite forces were defeated by a force of Cameronians under **William Cleland**. This was an unusual battle, as the fighting and gunfire took place among the streets and buildings of the town, and not in open countryside. William Cleland was fatally wounded during the encounter, and now lies in the ruined nave of the cathedral.

Dunkeld

Another, but not so famous, man lies in the nave of the cathedral. Curiously enough he lies beside William Cleland, and yet he was the grandson of the greatest Jacobite of them all, Charles Edward Stuart. The Prince's illegitimate daughter Charlotte had an affair with the Archbishop of Rouen, the result being two daughters and a son - Charles Edward Maximilien de Roehenstart, better known as **Count Roehenstart** (a name made up from "Rouen" and "Stuart"). On a trip to Scotland in 1854 he was killed in a carriage accident.

Most of the "little houses" in Dunkeld date from the early 18th century, as they were built to replace those that had been destroyed in the battle. Now the National Trust for Scotland looks after most of them. On the wall of one house in the square, the **Ell Shop**, is portrayed an old Scottish length of measurement called the "ell", which corresponds to 37 inches. Also in the square is the **Atholl Memorial Fountain**, erected in 1866 in memory of the 6th Duke of Atholl.

At the Birnam Institute is the **Beatrix Potter Gardens**, and within the Institute itself there is a small exhibition, which tells the story of the young Beatrix. She used to holiday in the area, and gained some of her inspiration from the surrounding countryside.

This is the heartland of the "big tree country", and it was in Dunkeld, in 1738, that the first larches were planted in Scotland.

GRANDTULLY
7 miles SW of Pitlochry on the A827

Grandtully is pronounced "Grantly". **Grandtully Castle**, to the west of the village, dates from the 15th century, and was a Stewart stronghold. **St Mary's Church** (Historic Scotland) was built by Sir Alexander Stewart in 1533, and was remodelled in 1633 when a painted ceiling was added that shows heraldic motifs and coats-of-arms of families connected with the Stewarts.

ABERFELDY

8 miles SW of Pitlochry on the A827

In 1787 Robert Burns wrote a song called *The Birks of Aberfeldy*, and made famous this small town and its surrounding area. "Birks" are birch trees, and the ones in question can still be seen to the south of the village, as well as the **Falls of Moness**. Some people claim, however, that Burns was actually writing about Abergeldie near Crathie in Aberdeenshire, though this is doubtful.

General Wade's Bridge, Aberfeldy

The village sits on the River Tay, and crossing it is **General Wade's Bridge**, built in 1733 by Major-General George Wade, Commander-in-Chief of North Britain from 1724 until 1740 ("Scotland" was not a name that was liked by the English establishment at the time). It is 400 feet in length, with a middle arch that spans 60 feet, and was part of a road network used to police the Highlands during the Jacobite unrest. It was formally opened in 1735, and cost £3,596, which

---

WEEM HOTEL

Weem, By Aberfeldy, Perthshire PH15 2LD
Tel: 01887 820381
e-mail: enquiries@weemhotel.com
website: www.weemhotel.com

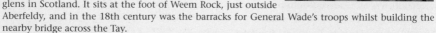

The family-owned **Weem Hotel** is the perfect place to stay while exploring Perthshire and Glen Lyon - surely one of the loveliest glens in Scotland. It sits at the foot of Weem Rock, just outside Aberfeldy, and in the 18th century was the barracks for General Wade's troops whilst building the nearby bridge across the Tay.

The hotel's ambience is relaxed and informal, with the emphasis on first class, friendly service, fresh food and comfort. The rooms are all en suite, with power showers, colour TVs, clock radios, hair driers and tea/coffee making facilities. In addition, they are individually decorated and furnished, ensuring that comfortable and stylish ambience that today's guests demand. Each room has a view of either Weem Rock or the scenery of Perthshire. The dining room serves meals that are prepared using

only fresh, local produce wherever possible, and there is a small but comprehensive selection of wines or real ales to accompany the food. Breakfasts are served in the Breakfast Room and the full Scottish breakfast is hearty and filling, and will set you up for a day exploring the many historical attractions of the area. Lighter options are also available if you prefer. You can also relax over the morning paper in the wood-panelled lounge, or enjoy a quiet drink in the evening.

The hotel is also the perfect venue for private functions and catering can be arranged.

INNERWICK ESTATE

Glen Lyon, Aberfeldy, Perthshire PH15 2PP
Tel: 01887 866222 Fax: 01887 866301
e-mail:enquiries@innerwick.com website: www.innerwick.com

If you are looking for self catering accommodation in beautiful Glen Lyon, look no further than **Innerwick Estate**. It has a range of stone built cottages and houses set in the idyllic, rural surroundings of a highland estate. Ballinloan cottage sleeps four people, the Farm House sleeps six and Innerwick Cottage sleeps four to six. All are superbly appointed, with TVs, well equipped kitchens, pillows and duvets, central heating, open fires and pay phones. If you're looking for a property that is larger, then Ballinloan House offers five star accommodation for eight in a substantial stone built house that is comfortable and cosy.

in today's terms in close to £1m.

At about the same time, six independent regiments were raised to "watch" the Highlands for signs of this unrest. These six regiments later amalgamated to form the 43rd Highland Regiment of Foot under the Earl of Crawford, and it paraded for the first time at Aberfeldy in May 1740. The regiment later became the Black Watch, and the **Black Watch Memorial**, built in 1887,

near the bridge commemorates the event.

Right on the A827 is **Dewar's World of Whisky**. Here you will find out about one of Scotland's most famous whisky firms, located in the distillery where Aberfeldy Single Malt is made.

A mile or so north west of the village, near Weem is **Castle Menzies**, home to Clan Menzies (pronounced Ming -iz in Scotland). The clan is not Scottish in origin, but Norman, with the name

GLENLYON GALLERY

Boltachan, By Aberfeldy, Perthshire PH15 2LB
Tel: 01887 820820
e-mail: glenlyon.gallery@virgin.net
website: www.glenlyongallery.com

Alan Hayman paints the birds, animals and landscapes of Scotland, but his fame goes beyond his native country, and works by him can be seen in Europe, America, Africa and Britain. Even

best selling author Wilbur Smith owns a couple of his paintings. He has exhibited at numerous exhibitions, and has held many of his own. Although galleries still pursue him, he now sells his works exclusively through his own gallery, **Glenlyon Gallery**, just outside Aberfeldy.

Here you can buy not just his paintings in oils and acrylics, but superb full-sized limited edition prints of his works as well, either framed or unframed. They illustrate his mastery of the brush and his great love of nature in all its forms and in a corner of the gallery is a small exhibition of his early work when he lived in Montrose. The gallery has been called one of the best private galleries in the country, and is in itself a four-star tourist attraction. It is open and spacious, giving people every opportunity to view and admire Alan's work.

Alan Hayman's work is much sought after, so if you buy a painting or one of his sculptures, you're not just buying a beautiful object, you're buying something that could turn into a very safe investment.

coming from Mesnieres near Rouen. James Menzies of Menzies, son-in-law of the then Earl of Atholl, built the castle in the 16th century. In 1665 the clan chief was created a baron of Nova Scotia. The last member of the main line died in 1918, and the clan was left without a chief. In 1957 the descendants of a cousin of the first baron were recognised as clan chiefs, and the present one is David Steuart Menzies of Menzies.

The castle is now owned by the Menzies Charitable Trust. Parts of it are open to the public, and it houses a Clan Menzies museum. Charles Edward Stuart spent two nights within its walls in 1746 on his way to Culloden.

KENMORE

13 miles SW of Pitlochry on the A827

Kenmore sits at the eastern end of **Loch Tay**, and was founded in about 1540 by the Earls of Breadalbane. The loch is the source of the River Tay, one of the most picturesque in Scotland. It is 14-and-a-half miles long, less than a mile wide, and plunges to a maximum depth of over 500 feet. Overlooking it, on the northern shore, is **Ben Lawers** (4,033 feet), with the **Ben Lawers Mountain Visitor Centre** (National Trust for Scotland - see panel below) on a minor

Kenmore

road off the A827. There is a nature trail, and a booklet is available at the centre.

The Scottish Crannog Centre (see panel opposite), run by the Scottish Trust for Underwater Archaeology, explains how people in the past lived in crannogs, which were dwelling houses situated in the shallow waters of a loch that offered defence against attack. They were either built on artificial islands or raised on

BEN LAWERS NATIONAL NATURE RESERVE

Lynedoch, Main Street, Killin FK21 8UW
Tel: 01567 820397 (Information Centre)
or Tel/Fax: 01567 820988 (office; Mon - Fri, 9 - 3)

The central Highlands' highest mountain, **Ben Lawers** is 1,214 m (3,984 ft), with views from the Atlantic to the North Sea. In the Trust's care are 3,374 ha (8,339 a) of the southern slopes of the Lawers range and 1,348 ha (3,33 1a) of the Tarmachan range, noted for a rich variety of mountain plants and including Meall nan Tarmachan (1,044 m, 3,425 ft). Birds include raven, ring ouzel, red

grouse, ptarmigan, dipper and curlew. Nature trail and other areas are fenced to exclude sheep and deer and to allow the restoration of trees, shrubs and herbaceous plants; projects include pioneering work to restore treeline woodland habitats. Audio visual programmes with special version for children.

THE SCOTTISH CRANNOG CENTRE

Kenmore, Loch Tay, Perthshire PH15 2HY
Tel. 01887 830583
e-mail: info@crannog.co.uk   website: www.crannog.co.uk

The Scottish Crannog Centre features a unique reconstruction of an early Iron Age loch-dwelling, built by underwater archaeologists based on more than 20 years of research and their excavation evidence from the 2,600-year-old site of 'Oakbank Crannog', one of the 18 crannogs preserved in Loch Tay, Perthshire. A crannog is a type of ancient loch-dwelling found throughout Scotland and Ireland dating from 5,000 years ago.

Visit the Centre to discover how and why these ancient people built their homes in the water, and experience first-hand how they lived. Be inspired by the pride and passion behind a living archaeological experiment. Take a look at some of our underwater discoveries; walk over water into the Iron Age on your crannog tour; and test your skills at 'hands-on' ancient crafts and technology. There is also a themed giftshop in which to browse. Special events run regularly featuring artists, musicians, skilled craft workers and other specialists who, together with our own team of Iron Age Guides, actively bring the past to life.

This is a four-star attraction with a Gold Award in Green Tourism, dedicated to operating and educating in an environmentally responsible manner. The centre aims to be informed about local amenities and sites of cultural and environmental interest so that useful advice or recommendations can be given. The Centre is open daily from **15th March to 31st October**, and on weekends throughout **November**. Opening times: March to October from 10am to 5:30pm, November from 10am to 4pm. In all cases, last full tours are one hour before closing. Groups and Schools are welcome by advance booking.

stilts above the water, and were in use from about 2500 BC right up until the 17th century. Off the north shore of the loch is **Eilean nan Bannoamh** ("Isle of the Holy Women") where once stood a small Celtic nunnery. Alexander I's wife Queen Sybilla, died here in 1122, and Alexander founded a priory in her memory.

FORTINGALL

15 miles SW of Pitlochry on a minor road off the B846

This little village has a unique claim to fame. It is said to be the birthplace of **Pontius Pilate**, the governor of Judea at the time of Christ's execution. It is said that his father, a Roman officer, was sent to Scotland by Augustus Caesar to command a unit, which kept the local Pictish clans in check. Whether Pontius

was born of a union between his father and a local woman, or whether his father had brought a wife with him, is not recorded. There is no proof that the story is true, but there was certainly a Roman camp nearby.

Sir Donald Currie laid out Fortingall as a model village in the 19th century, and it has some picturesque thatched cottages that would not look out of place in a South of England village. In the kirkyard of the early 20th century parish church is the **Fortingall Yew**, said to be the oldest living thing in Europe. The tree looks rather the worse for wear nowadays, but as it may be as much as 3,000 years old (a plaque next to it says 5,000 years, but this is doubtful), perhaps this is not surprising.

In a field next to the village is the **Cairn of the Dead**, which marks the mass grave of plague victims during the *galar mhor*, or great plague. It is said that one old woman, who was still sufficiently healthy, carried the bodies to the field on a horse-drawn sledge.

The village sits at the entrance to **Glen Lyon**, at 25 miles long, Scotland's longest, and perhaps loveliest, glen. Tumbling through it is the River Lyon, which rises at Loch Lyon, part of a massive hydroelectric scheme. At Bridge of Balgie a minor road strikes south, rising into some wild scenery and passing **Meall Luaidhe** (2,535 feet) before dropping down towards the Ben Lawers Mountain Visitor Centre (see Kenmore) and the shores of Loch Tay. Bridge of Balgie is also home to a gallery that houses prints and original paintings by renowned artist Alan Hayman.

On the B846 four miles north of Fortingall is the **Glengoulandie Deer Park**, with its herd of red deer, Highland cattle, goats and rare breeds of sheep.

KINLOCH RANNOCH
17 miles W of Pitlochry on the B846

This small village, laid out in the 18th century by James Small, a government factor, sits at the eastern end of **Loch Rannoch**, which has roads on both the northern and southern sides. It is overlooked by the conically shaped **Schiehallion** (3,547 feet), from the summit of which there is a wonderful view as far south as the Lowlands.

An obelisk in the centre of the village commemorates **Dugald Buchanan**, who died here in 1786. He was one of the Highland's greatest religious poets, and was buried at Balquidder. The **Parish Church** is one of Telford's parliamentarian churches, and was built in 1829. Usually a parliamentarian church was nothing but a plain, T-shaped

Loch Ba, Rannoch Moor

preaching box, but Kinloch Rannoch is more like a conventional church, with the Holy Table at the east end.

The B846 carries on westward past Kinloch Rannoch, and skirts the northern shores of Loch Rannoch. It eventually comes to an end at **Rannoch Station**. This station, on the Glasgow/Fort William line, is the loneliest railway station in Britain. Beyond it is **Rannoch Moor**, said to be the most desolate spot in Scotland, and "Europe's last great wilderness". In the winter, when snow covers it, it is treacherous, and no one should venture out onto it unless they're experienced. Even in summer, when it is hauntingly beautiful, it should still be treated with respect.

But the moor's landscape isn't a natural one. Even here, man has made his mark. The whole of the moor was once covered in the trees of the old Caledonian Forest, but man gradually cleared them to use as fuel and for building. The whole of the moor is littered with large boulders, debris carried by the glaciers that once covered this area.

KILLIECRANKIE
3 miles N of Pitlochry off the A9

The rather unusual name comes from the

KILLIECRANKIE

Pitlochry, Perthshire PH16 5LG
Tel/fax: 01796 473233 (Visitor Centre)
e-mail killiecrankie@nts.org.uk
website: www.nts.org.uk

On 27th July 1689, the Pass of Killiecrankie echoed with the sound of battle cries and gunfire when, nearby, a Jacobite army led by 'Bonnie Dundee' defeated the government forces. One soldier evaded capture by making a spectacular jump across the River Garry at Soldier's Leap. The magnificent wooded gorge, much admired by Queen Victoria in 1844, is tranquil now, and is designated a Site of Special Scientific Interest because it is a fine example of an oak and mixed deciduous woodland. The Visitor Centre exhibition features the battle, natural history and ranger services. In the Centre, visitors can now watch birds nesting, via a remote camera in the woodlands.

Gaelic Coille "Creitheannich", meaning the aspen wood. It was here, in 1689, that the **Battle of Killiecrankie** took place. The Pass of Killiecrankie is a narrow defile, and as government troops under General Mackay passed gingerly through it, they were attacked from above by Jacobite forces under Bonnie Dundee (see also Blair Atholl). The government troops had the River Garry behind them, so escape was impossible, and it ended in a victory for the Jacobites. Bonnie Dundee himself was killed, however. The **Killiecrankie Visitors Centre** (National Trust for Scotland – see panel above) has displays explaining the battle.

At the north end of the pass is a spot known as the **Soldier's Leap**, high above the River Garry. It is said that, after the battle, a government trooper called Donald McBean leapt across the 18-foot wide gap to escape from some Jacobites who were chasing him.

BLAIR ATHOLL
6 miles NW of Pitlochry off the A9

Blair Castle is one of the most famous castles in Scotland. It sits above the village, and with its whitewashed walls looks more like a great fortified mansion house than a castle. It is the ancestral home of the Murrays, Dukes of Atholl,

and originally dates from 1269, though what you see nowadays is mainly from the 18th and 19th century refurbishments. About 30 furnished rooms are open to the public, with fine furniture, paintings, china and armour on display. The Duke of Atholl is the only person in Britain who is allowed to have a private army, the **Atholl Highlanders**, and a small museum has displays of uniforms, weapons and musical instruments. It was raised in 1778 by the 4th Duke of Atholl to fight the colonists in the American War of Independence. However, after a posting to Ireland they were disbanded. The regiment as we know it today dates from 1839. In 1844 Queen Victoria stayed at Blair Atholl and a year later presented the regiment with two sets of colours

In the kirkyard of **St Bride's Kirk** is the grave of John Graham, 1st Viscount Dundee, known as "Bonnie Dundee", who was killed at the Battle of Killiecrankie in 1689 (see also Killiecrankie). At Bruar, four miles north of Blair Atholl, is the **Clan Donnachaidh Museum**. Though the name translates into English as Donnachie, it traces the history of the Clan Robertson, and shows their place in local and Scottish history. **The Falls of Bruar** are close by, and fall through a picturesque ravine with footbridges over them.

LOCATOR MAP

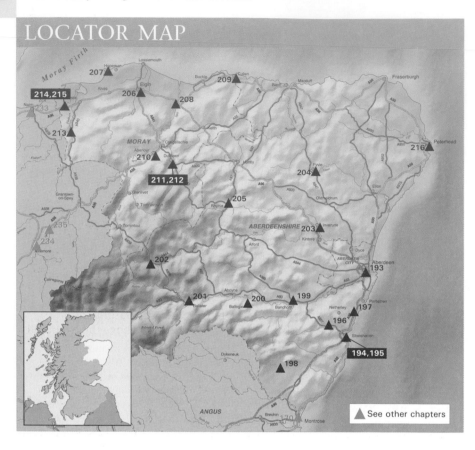

See other chapters

ADVERTISERS AND PLACES OF INTEREST

NORTH EAST SCOTLAND 11

North East Scotland is centred on Aberdeen, and consists of the counties of Aberdeenshire, Kincardineshire, Banffshire and Morayshire. The area abounds in scenery of all kinds. High mountains, wooded glens, cityscapes, beaches, rich farmland, towering cliffs and moorland - it's got the lot. And yet it is relatively unknown by those outside Scotland, apart from the city of Aberdeen and along Deeside. The beaches are quiet and uncrowded, the country lanes are a joy to drive in, and there is history and heritage aplenty.

And always in the background are the Grampians, which reach their highest peaks here. Queen Victoria popularised Deeside, a glen which goes deep into the heart of the mountains, and it has remained firmly on the tourist trail ever since. But as with many parts of Scotland, the tourist traps swarm with people, while other places, equally as interesting and picturesque, are bypassed.

To go off the beaten track in the North East is to be rewarded with some wonderful discoveries. Who, for instance, has explored the farmlands of Buchan, with their rich soil, which, even though they are above the Highland line, have more of a Lowland feel about them? How many people stop in Kincardineshire, with its fishing villages and its literary connections? It was here that Robert Burns's father was born. It was here that Lewis Grassic Gibbon, a local man, set his dark novels of country life - ones that had little to do with the quaint images of happy, rustic people that had prevailed up until then. And who, except those in the know, visit Elgin, a charming small city with the ruins of what was one of the largest and grandest cathedrals in Scotland?

ADVERTISERS AND PLACES OF INTEREST

Nowhere else in Europe is there such a concentration of historic castles - around 1,000 at the last count. The local tourist board has organised a Castle Trail, with a leaflet that explains their history and how you get to them. And then there are the distilleries. The industry is centred mainly on Banffshire and Moray, where the streams are swift flowing and the water pure. It's amazing that two distilleries a mile or so apart can make whiskies that are totally different in character. The local tourist board has laid out a Whisky Trail, and like the Castle Trail there's a leaflet to guide you as you explore it.

The inland villages are quiet and peaceful, and the market towns, such as Inverurie, Forres and Huntly, are packed with history and charm. The coastline is as dramatic as anywhere in Britain. Yet another trail, the Coastal Trail, takes you on a tour from St Cyrus in the south to Findhorn in the west. The ruins of Dunnottar Castle are perched dramatically above the sea, while the Ythan Estuary (pronounced "eye-than") is a Site of Scientific Interest, rich in aquatic and bird life as well as having archaeological sites dating back to Neolithic times. Slains Castle, south of Peterhead, was one of the inspirations for Bram Stoker's *Dracula*, and the fishing port of Fraserburgh was, for a very short time, a university town.

For all its crowds (especially in late summer when the Queen is there), Deeside cannot be missed. This long glen follows the Dee up into the heart of the Grampians with Braemar, at its heart, being officially Britain's coldest place (though summer days can be balmy and long). But don't let the seeming remoteness put you off - the glen is green and wooded for most of its length. Balmoral - Crathie - Aboyne - the names are familiar to us all through news programmes, and yet the reality of seeing them makes you realise why Queen Victoria, and subsequent monarchs, fell in love with Royal Deeside in the first place.

Aberdeen is Scotland's third largest city and Europe's oil capital. The name, which means "at the mouth of the Dee and the Don", sums up its location exactly, as the two rivers enter the North Sea here. The oil industry has brought money to the city, and it has also brought a cosmopolitan lifestyle that includes smart restaurants, boutiques, nightclubs and stylish pubs. But even here history is never far away. It was granted a royal charter by King William the Lion in 1175, and Old Aberdeen, which used to be a proud separate burgh, was granted its charter in 1489.

The other city in the region is Elgin, at one time one of the most important places in Scotland. It has lost some of that importance now, but has not lost any of its charm. It is still a busy place, and is the shopping and administrative centre for a large fertile area called the Laigh of Moray. Here too there are quiet country lanes and small villages to explore, while at Findhorn there is the Findhorn Foundation, where the emphasis is on spiritual living and alternative lifestyles. And south of the city is the only medieval abbey in Britain that still houses monks.

ABERDEEN

With a population of about 220,000, Aberdeen is Scotland's third largest city. Its nickname is the "Granite City" because of the predominant building material - one which has created a stylish and attractive place that seems to glisten in the sun. It prides itself on being Scotland's most prosperous city, due to the oil fields that lie beneath the North Sea. For this reason it is also known as the "Oil Capital of Europe", and the docks and harbours, which were once full of fishing boats, now pulse with supply ships ferrying men and machines out to the oil rigs. It also has the ferry terminal for the Shetland ferry.

But Aberdeen has two more nicknames "Scotland's Garden City" and the "Flower of Scotland". Both derive from the many gardens and colourful open spaces that can be visited. It has won awards for its floral displays (including many "Britain in Bloom" awards), with **Johnston Gardens, Hazelhead Park, Union Terrace Gardens, Duthie Park** and the **Cruickshank Botanic Gardens** offering particularly fine examples. In 2003 Aberdeen took silver in the "Nations in Bloom" competition, beaten only by Seattle, USA, and Quanzhou, China.

It is also a centre of learning, administration, shopping and business. But it has never been scarred by industry in the way that some Scottish central belt towns have. It has managed to remain above such things, and its quality of life is among the best in Britain.

And for all its bustle and modern office blocks, it is an ancient city, having been granted a charter as a royal burgh in 1175. Even then it was an important and busy port, trading with the Baltic States as well as the Netherlands and France. During the Wars of Independence it was sacked three times by the English, and finally razed to the ground by Edward III in 1337. One unexpected visitor to Aberdeen was William Shakespeare, who, with his troupe of actors, was sent by Elizabeth I to appear before the court of James VI in 1601.

There are two Aberdeens - the original one, and Old Aberdeen, which was at one time a separate burgh. Perversely Old Aberdeen was only granted its charter in 1489, and is a captivating area of old, elegant buildings and quiet cobbled streets.

The buildings you see throughout the city nowadays however, are mainly Georgian, Victorian and later, with some older buildings among them to add historical depth. The **Cathedral Church of St Machar's** in Old Aberdeen was founded in about 1131, and is dedicated to a saint who was son of Fiachna, an Irish prince. He was also a companion of St Columba, and came over from Ireland with him to found the monastery on Iona. Legend states that Columba sent him to convert the Picts in the area, and had a vision from God to build a church at a point where a river bends in the shape of a bishop's crosier just before it enters the sea. As the Don bends in this way, he established his church here in about AD 580. It's a fascinating tale, but probably untrue, as a bishop's crosier in those days was not curved, but straight.

St Machar's as we see it today dates from the 14th century and later. The choir has completely disappeared, and what you see now was the nave of the original cathedral with the ruins of the two transepts, which are in the care of Historic Scotland. In 1688 the central tower collapsed, leaving a rather truncated building with a beautiful west front with two towers. Perhaps its most famous bishop was **William Elphinstone**, Chancellor of Scotland

and producer of the first book of liturgy in the country, the *Aberdeen Breviary*. Its heraldic ceiling is magnificent, the work of Bishop Gavin Dunbar, who succeeded Elphinstone in 1518. Dunbar also erected the two west towers.

The **Brig o' Balgownie** over the Don, near the cathedral, dates from the early 14th century, and has a single, pointed arch. It is said to have been built using money given by Robert the Bruce, and is reckoned to be the finest single arch structure in Scotland. Aberdeen's other old bridge, to the south of the city, is the **Bridge of Dee**, built by Bishop Dunbar in the early 1500s.

Old Bridge of Dee

At Bridge of Don is **Glover House**, the family home of Thomas Blake Glover, the Scotsman who, it is said, inspired Puccini's opera *Madame Butterfly*. Born in Fraserburgh in 1838, his family moved to Bridge of Don in 1851, when he was 13 years old. When he left school, he began working for a trading company, and got a taste for overseas travel.

When he first went to Japan at 21, he was entering a feudal society that had been closed to the west for over 300 years. However, within one year he was selling Scottish-built warships and arms to Japanese rebels during the country's civil war. At the same time he sent young Japanese men to Britain to be educated.

He was called the "Scottish Samurai", and helped found the Mitsubishi shipyards, the first step Japan took to becoming a great manufacturing power. He also helped found the famous Kirin Brewery, and his picture still appears on Kirin labels to this day. He was later presented with the Order of the Rising Sun, Japan's greatest honour. He later built himself a house at Nagasaki, and

married a Japanese woman called Tsura, who invariably wore kimonos decorated with butterfly motifs. When Puccini came across a short story and subsequent play based on this relationship, it sowed the seeds for Madame Butterfly.

The **Church of St Nicholas** stands in St Nicholas Street. The first mention of a church on the site is a Papal Bull dated 1157, though there may have been a previous building, which was burned down during a great fire that swept through the city in 1153. At the Reformation it was divided into two churches, the East and the West. These were later united once more when the church was largely rebuilt in the 18th and 19th centuries. Of the original church only the transepts and the crypt survive. Its carillon of 48 bells is the largest of any church in Britain. There are six entrances to the kirkyard, the grandest being the granite colonnade in Union Street, designed in 1830 by John Smith, Aberdeen's city architect. Beneath what was the East Kirk is St Mary's Chapel, built by Lady Elizabeth Gordon. When she died in 1438 she was buried within it.

Union Street, Aberdeen's main thoroughfare, is over a mile long, and thronged with shops. It was laid out in the early 1800s to celebrate the union of Britain and Ireland. At one end, in Castle Street, is the city's 17th century **Mercat Cross**, standing close to where Aberdeen's long gone medieval castle stood.

Provost Skene's House, off St Nicholas Street, dates from about 1545, and is named after a former lord provost of the city, Sir George Skene, who bought it in 1669. It is a tall, solid building of turrets and chimneys, and has wonderful painted ceilings and period furniture, as well as displays on modern history. **Provost Ross's House** is in Shiprow, said to be Aberdeen's oldest street still in use. The house was built in 1593, but is named after its most famous owner, John Ross, lord provost of Aberdeen in the 18th century. It now houses the **Aberdeen Maritime Museum**, with exhibits and displays on Aberdeen's maritime history, plus a re-created "helicopter ride" out to an offshore oilrig.

Aberdeen University was founded by Bishop Elphinstone in 1494 under a Papal Bull from Pope Alexander IV. **King's College** stands in Old Aberdeen, and its chapel, built in 1505, forms one side of a quadrangle in the middle of which is a 20th century monument to its founder. The chapel's crown steeple, built in honour of James VI, was blown down in a storm in 1633, and there were dark mutterings all over Aberdeen that witchcraft was involved. The following year work started on rebuilding it. The **King's College Centre** explains the college's history.

Marischal College, another university, was founded in 1593, 99 years after King's College, which meant that the city had two universities - exactly the same number as the whole of England at the same time, as locals gleefully point out. It was founded by George Keith, 5th

Fishermen's Cottages, Aberdeen

Earl Marischal of Scotland, as a Protestant alternative to the Catholic-leaning King's College. The present imposing granite building in Broad Street dates from the 19th century, and is the second largest granite building in the world. In 1860 the two universities united to form Aberdeen University. The **Marischal College Museum**, founded in 1786, houses a collection of classical and Egyptian objects, as well as local collections.

The **Aberdeen Art Gallery and Museums** are at Schoolhill, near Robert Gordon's College. Apart from a fine collection of paintings and sculpture by such artists as Degas, Reynolds, and Epstein, it houses displays on Aberdeen's history, including finds made at various archaeological digs throughout the city. **James Dun's House**, dating from the

18th century, forms part of the museum.

The **Planetarium** at Aberdeen College in the Gallowgate Centre is a star dome, which shows the planets and stars as they "move" through the heavens. And the **Gordon Highlanders Museum** (see panel below) on Viewfield Road tells the story of what Sir Winston Churchill called "the finest regiment in the world". There is an audiovisual theatre, gardens, a children's "handling area", a shop and a café. One of Aberdeen's newest attractions is **Stratosphere** in The Tramsheds in Constitution Street, a hands-on science centre where children can explore all aspects of science, and watch a science show that explains things like colour and bubbles.

At one time there were well over 100 quarries in the city mining granite. **Rubislaw Quarry**, near the Gordon Highlanders Museum, was one of the biggest. It was still being worked right up until 1971, when it was about 465 feet deep and 900 feet across. Now it has been filled with water to a depth of 180 feet and fenced off. However, it can still

partially be seen from Queen's Road. During 230 years of quarrying, it is said to have produced over six million tonnes of granite, not just for Aberdeen, but for places like London, Russia and Japan.

In King Street is the **Aberdeen and North East Scotland Family History Society**, which has a wide range of reference material for family and genealogical research. At Blairs, on South Deeside Road, there was once a catholic seminary, which closed in 1986. The **Blairs Museum** now holds the Scottish Catholic Heritage Collection, and is open to the public. There are objects connected with the Stuart line (including Mary Stuart and Charles Edward Stuart) on display, as well as a collection of rich vestments, church plate and paintings.

On the north bank of the Dee, where it enters the North Sea, is an area called **Footdee**, or, as it is known by Aberdonians, "Fittie". This is where Aberdeen's original fishing community lived, in rows of cottages that have now been renovated and smartened up.

GORDON HIGHLANDERS MUSEUM

St Lukes, Viewfield Road, Aberdeen AB15 7XH
Tel: 01224 311200 Fax: 01224 319323
e-mail: museum@gordonhighlanders.com
website: www.gordonhighlanders.com

The story of The Gordon Highlanders spans 200 years of world history and is packed with tales of courage and tenacity on the field of battle. At the museum you can re-live the compelling and dramatic story of one of the British Army's most famous regiments, through the lives of its outstanding personalities and of the killed soldiers of the North East of Scotland who filled its ranks.

The spectacular exhibition includes a unique collection of the finest of the regiments treasures, including a remarkable display of Victoria Crosses; strikingly detailed life size and scale reproductions of some of the Regiment's finest moments in battle; state of the art touch screens to let you explore the deeds and values that made the Regiment great and stunning film presentations which convey the story of the 'Gordons'.

A stroll in the delightful museum gardens can be rounded off with light refreshments in The Duchess Jean Tea Room. A range of souvenirs are available at The Gordon Gift Shop. Open April to October, Tuesday to Saturday 10.30am-4.30pm and Sunday 1.30pm-4.30pm.

AROUND ABERDEEN

STONEHAVEN

16 miles S of Aberdeen off the A90

Stonehaven was once the county town of Kincardineshire. It is a fishing community, though the industry has gone into decline. Near the harbour stands the 18th century **Mercat Cross**, and the **Steeple**, from where James VII was proclaimed king in 1715 after landing at the town's harbour. The Tolbooth was built in the late 16th century, and is the town's oldest building. It stands on the north aside of the harbour, and was formerly a storehouse belonging to the Earl Marischal of Scotland, who lived in nearby Dunnottar Castle. Now it is the **Tolbooth Museum**, with displays and exhibits about the town's history

Stonehaven

and its fishing fleet.

Two miles south of the town is **Dunnottar Castle**. It is magnificently

Stonehaven - Dunnottar Woods - Dunottar Castle

Distance:	4.5 miles (7.2 kilometres)
Typical time:	110 mins
Height gain:	75 metres
Map:	Explorer 396
Walk:	www.walkingworld.com ID:864
Contributor:	Ian Cordiner

Access Information:

Stonehaven, 15 miles south of Aberdeen, is served by frequent rail and bus services. It can be reached from the south by the A90 and A92.

Description:

This walk starts in the town centre where there is a car park. It soon leaves the streets and leads through the quiet deciduous Dunnottar Woods in which there is an old building known as the Shell House, because the interior is picturesquely decorated with seashells.

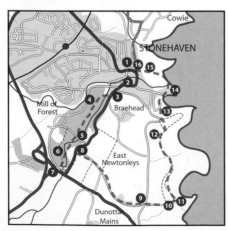

Continuing past the high walls of what is now a garden centre, it crosses a small road to proceed once more through deciduous woodland. On the way through the woods it passes the ruins of a stone structure known as Lady Kennedy's Bath.

After leaving this section, the walk follows quiet roads before reaching Dunnottar Castle. From here there is a cliff path which leads back to Stonehaven, but because of erosion this part may not be accessible and it may be necessary to follow a pavement back to the town.

The route gives spectacular views over the town and its harbour. A steep path leads down to the harbour area where hotels, shops and toilets are found. Also in this part of town is one of the oldest buildings in Stonehaven, the Tolbooth, now a museum.

Finally the walk continues along a boardwalk along the seashore and leads back to the town centre.

Features:

Sea, Pub, Toilets, Museum, Castle, Great Views, Food Shop, Public Transport, Nature Trail, Woodland, Ancient Monument

Walk Directions:

1 The walk starts at the south corner of the square in the town centre. Leave the square by going south along Barclay Street. At the end of Barclay Street turn right. Cross to the south side of the street, then cross a pedestrian bridge.

2 Immediately over the bridge, take the path to the right. Turn right at the end of the path.

3 At this junction turn left. Continue to the far corner between the houses to enter the woodland. Follow the route to the right as you pass through this gate.

4 At the steps keep left and follow the sign to Glasslaw Gate. Bear left here. You are going to take the route to the right, but first stop at a small building. It is called the Shell House and has its interior decorated with seashells. It was in fact, once an ice house. Follow the track to the right until you come to the tarred road.

5 Continue straight across the road here and continue to folllow the woodland path.

At the first Y-junction bear left. Cross the bridge then turn right. Continue past this bridge until you reach a similar one farther on.

6 From the next bridge you look down into a stone structure known as Lady Kennedy's Bath. After a short incline turn left and follow the main track until you reach the Glasslaw car park.

7 At the exit of the car park keep left. At the main road turn left.

8 Continue along the pavement until you reach a junction, where you turn right. The walk now continues along a tarred country lane and eventually reaches the coast.

9 When you reach the main road at Mains of Dunnottar Farm, turn right. Continue south for about 100m. Immediately to the south of a small lodge there is a small car park for Dunnottar Castle. Enter the castle grounds via a gate in the corner of the car park.

10 At this point the route leads to the right to the castle. If you keep left there is a path which is a cliff path back to Stonehaven. There may be a problem here. Due to costal erosion, this part may be closed as repairs to the path may be in progress.

11 There is an entrance fee to visit the castle itself. This castle was the hiding-place for the Scottish Regalia (crown jewels) in 1652. More recently the castle was used in the filming of Hamlet, starring Mel Gibson. If the coastal path is closed, retrace your steps to Waymark

9 and follow the pavement back to Stonehaven.

12 On the skyline you will see Stonehaven's war memorial. If you were able to take the cliff path, you will be able to reach the war memorial quite easily. When you leave the memorial site, turn left.

13 Across from the "Welcome to Stonehaven" sign and where the road narrows, look out for a narrow path leading to the right. Follow this steep path down towards the harbour. When you reach this narrow lane follow it to the end, where it comes out at the harbour. There are popular pubs and food sources along the seafront. Continue along the waterfront, keeping right past the white building.

14 You will pass the oldest building in Stonehaven. A former tolbooth (jail), it is now a small museum. Continue past this and take the road to the left, past a toilet block and into a car park. Continue through the car park until you come to a boardwalk, which skirts the water and leads back to the town centre.

15 When you reach the end of the boardwalk, turn left to get to the town square. On the other hand, you could continue along the path ahead which eventually leads to an open-air, heated sea water swimming pool, passing amusements and sports facilities on the way. Turning left leads up the town centre

16 Cross the main road back to the car park in the square.

sited, as it stands on a promontory 160 feet above the sea and guarded on three sides by the North Sea and on the fourth by St Ninian's Den, a steep ravine. It dates from the 13th century and later, and has seen some gruesome episodes in Scotland's history. In 1297 William Wallace torched it, burning to death every English soldier within its walls. In 1652 Cromwell's troops laid siege to it to capture Scotland's Crown Jewels. However, they were foiled by the wife of the minister of Kinneff Church, who smuggled them out (see also Inverbervie)

under the very noses of the troops.

In 1685 167 Covenanters were imprisoned in an underground cellar. Those that tried to escape were killed, while most of those that remained succumbed to disease and starvation. Those that survived were taken to the colonies.

Each year at Hogmanay the traditional **Fireball Festival** is held in Stonehaven. It takes place in the "Auld Toon" area of the town, with up to 60 men parading at midnight while swinging huge fireballs on the end of stout wires. The origins are

26a, Evan Street, Stonehaven, AB39 2EQ
Tel: 01569 760107 e-mail: woodviewcrafts@btconnect.com

Why not visit **Woodview Crafts** for a wide range of gifts that are
totally unique. Personalised embroidery on gifts, cards & clothing.
Choose what you want to say on cards, cushions, baby items, glassware or clothing, plus much more.
There is also a gorgeous range of sterling silver jewellery, hand painted silk and glasses etc, plus lots of
pocket money gifts too. So go on treat yourself or those that you love with a gift from Woodview
Crafts. Open 10am-3.45pm Mon-Sat, closed Wednesday. Telephone orders welcome.

COWTON RIDING CENTRE

Cowton Farm, Rickarton.Stonehaven,Aberdeenshire AB39 3SY
Tel & Fax: 01569 760305 e-mail: lesley@thorpel.fsnet.co.uk
website: www.cowtonridingcentre.co.uk

If you're aged four to 94, you can still learn to ride. Lesley Thorp of the
Cowton Riding Centre has been around horses all her life, and has been
teaching the skills since 1999. She also teaches trekking and hacking, and
has 18 horses at the centre. She will take individuals and groups, and even
organises treks that take in such things as local history. Pictish standing
stones and local wildlife. The centre is two-and-a-half miles from Stonehaven, and is easy to find. So
come along and treat yourself and your family to a wonderful experience.

MAIRI EWEN STAINED GLASS AND SCULPTURE

Skateraw Studio, Skateraw Road, Newtonhill, Stonehaven, Aberdeenshire AB39 3PT
Tel: 01569 731229
e-mail: mail@mairiewen.co.uk website: www.mairiewen.co.uk

Situated in Newtonhill, a picturesque fishing village nine miles south of Aberdeen,
Skateraw Studio highlights the wonderful stained glass created by Edinburgh College
of Art graduate **Mairi Ewen**. As well as undertaking commissions for domestic and
commercial glass, she also creates contemporary and traditional glass sculptures and
hanging panels. As well as treating yourself, they make ideal and thoughtful gifts,
and a visit to the studio would enhance any visit to the Northeast of Scotland.

rooted in paganism, with the light from
the balls supposedly attracting the sun,
ensuring its return after the dark days of
winter. Today the whole ceremony lasts
about half an hour, but in days gone by
it could last for up to an hour or more.

INVERBERVIE

25 miles S of Aberdeen on the A92

Though no bigger than a village,
Inverbervie is in fact a royal burgh,
having been granted its charter in 1341
by David II, who, along with his queen,
was shipwrecked off the coast as he
returned from imprisonment in France,
and was "kindly received" by the people
of the village. John Coutts, whose son
Thomas Coutts founded the famous
bank, was born here in 1699. **Hallgreen
Castle** (not open to the public) sits close
to the sea, and has associations with the
Dunnet family. The village's **Mercat**

Cross dates from 1737.

Three miles north, at Kinneff, is **Kinneff Church**, built in 1738. The previous church on the site, built in about 1242, has a unique place in Scotland's history. In 1651 the Scottish Crown Jewels were used at the coronation of Charles II at Scone, then hidden in Dunnottar Castle (see Stonehaven) so that Parliamentarian troops could not find them. But when their whereabouts became known to Cromwell, they were smuggled out by the wife of Kinneff's minister, and placed within the church. There they lay for ten years, beneath the floor. Every three months the minister and his wife dug them up, cleaned them and aired them before a fire. With the Restoration of Charles II in 1660, they were taken to Edinburgh Castle. Though no longer used for worship, the church is still open to the public and under the care of the Kinneff Old Church Preservation Trust.

ARBUTHNOTT

23 miles S of Aberdeen on the B967

The village of Arbuthnott lies in what is called The Mearns. **Arbuthnott Collegiate Church**, dedicated to St Ternan, a Pictish saint. The choir was consecrated in 1242, with the rest of the church being later. It was here that James Sibbald, priest of Arbuthnott, wrote the Arburthnott Missal in 1491. It laid out the form of service to be used at masses celebrated within the church, and can now be seen in Paisley Museum. The **Arbuthnott Aisle** contains the tomb of Hugo le Blond of Arbuthnott, whose effigy can be seen above it. Another tomb is of a later period, and is of James Arbuthnott .

The ashes of James Leslie Mitchell the author, otherwise known as **Lewis Grassic Gibbon**, lie within the kirkyard, and there is a memorial to him. He was born in the Mearns, and, when he had settled in Welwyn Garden City near London, wrote dark brooding novels about Mearns farm life, far removed from the couthy stories about simple Scottish country folk that had been published before. **The Lewis Grassic Gibbon Centre**, next to the parish hall, traces the life and works of a man who became one of the most important British writers of the 20th century.

The area has other literary associations. Robert Burn's father was born here before setting up home in Ayrshire, and in the kirkyard of the church at **Glenbervie** four miles to the northwest is the grave of Burns's great grandfather, James Burnes (the "e" in the name was dropped after Burns's father moved to Ayrshire).

Arbuthnott House, home to the Arbuthnott family, dates mainly from the 18th and 19th centuries, and is open to the public on certain days of the year. The gardens are open all year round.

MARYCULTER

6 miles SW of Aberdeen on the B9077

The land surrounding Maryculter were granted to the Knights Templar by William the Lion in the 12th century, and the order of monastic soldiers established a church and preceptory, dedicating it to St Mary. Pope Clement V suppressed the order in 1312, and at trials held at Holyrood Abbey in Edinburgh in 1319 the last Preceptor of the house at Maryculter was given as William de Middleton of the "tempill house of Culther". The lands formerly owned by the Knights Templar were then granted to the Knights of the Order of St John. On the opposite bank of the Dee a church had been established and dedicated to St Peter, and this parish became known as Peterculter. It now lies within the City of Aberdeen, while

Drum Castle

Maryculter is in Kincardineshire.

Four miles west of the village is **Drum Castle** (National Trust for Scotland), built in the late 13th century, probably by the wonderfully named Richard Cemantarius, king's master mason and provost of Aberdeen. In 1323 it was given to William de Irwyn by Robert the Bruce, and the Irvines lived in it right up until 1975. It was enlarged in 1619 by the creation of a grand Jacobean mansion.

Storybook Glen is also in Maryculter,

and is a 28-acre children's park where fairy tale and nursery rhyme characters can be found.

FETTERCAIRN

27 miles SW of Aberdeen on the B974

On the edge of the fertile Howe of the Mearns, Fettercairn is an attractive village with, at its heart, the **Mercat Cross** of 1670. In 1861 Queen Victoria and Prince Albert visited the village, and the **Fettercairn Arch** commemorates the event.

The B974 north to Strachar and Banchory on Royal Deeside has many fine views. Close to the road, about a mile north of the town, is **Fasque**, home of William Gladstone, prime minister in the late 19th century. It was built in 1829 by his father, Sir John Gladstone, son of a Leith corn merchant, and has a deer park, and is open for groups of more than 12 by prior arrangement.

Fettercairn Distillery sits to the northwest, and has guided tours (with a free dram at the end) and a visitor centre.

ALASTAIRS

The Square, Fettercairn, Aberdeenshire AB30 1XX
Tel: 01561 340610

For great food in Northeast Scotland, there is no better restaurant than **Alastairs** in the picturesque old village of Fettercairn. During the day it is a tearoom serving teas, coffee, home baking, snacks and light luncheons. In the evenings at the weekend it becomes a restaurant, serving superb cuisine that uses only the finest and freshest of local produce whoever possible, with its renowned Aberdeen Angus steaks being sourced only from certificated beef. It is spacious and elegant, with seating for 35, and has a varied and attractive wine list. So why not treat yourself to a dinner or snack in one of the most attractive restaurants in Northeast Scotland.

GARLOGIE

10 miles W of Aberdeen on the B9119

The **Garlogie Mill Power House Museum** has a rare beam engine - the only one to have survived intact in its location -, which used to power this wauk mill, which finished off woven cloth. The mill is open to the public, and there are displays about its history and machinery.

The **Cullrelie Stone Circle**, close to the village just off the B9125, dates from the Bronze Age, and consists of eight stones placed in a 33-feet diameter circle. The shallow **Loch of Skene**, to the north of the village, is a special protection area and supports an important colony of Icelandic greylag geese. Three miles to the west of the village, near Echt, is the **Barmekin of Echt**, an ancient fortified hill settlement.

BANCHORY

17 miles W of Aberdeen on the A93

This little 19th century burgh stands at the point where the River Freugh enters the Dee, and is often called the "Gateway to Royal Deeside". It once stood on the Deeside railway line that closed in 1966, and there are now plans to reopen a section between the town and Crathes, three miles to the east. In Bridge Street is the **Banchory Museum**, which has collections featuring tartans, royal commemorative china and the natural history of the area. The Scottish musician and composer **James Scott Skinner**, "the Strathspey King", was born at Arbeadie, just outside the town, in 1843, and a further display in the museum is dedicated to his life. He now lies buried in Allenvale Cemetery in Aberdeen.

Three miles east of the town is **Crathes Castle** (National Trust for Scotland - see panel on page 390). It dates from the

16th century, with some of the rooms retaining their original painted ceilings, which were only rediscovered in 1877. It was built by the Burnetts of Ley, who were granted the lands of Ley by Robert the Bruce in 1323. The ancient **Horn of Leys** hangs in the Great Hall. It is made of ivory and encrusted with jewels, and was presented to the Burnetts by Bruce at the time of the land grant. The family's coat-of-arms includes the horn. On the main stairway there is a "trip stair", which tripped up attackers who didn't know about it. Watch out also for the castle's ghost - the Green Lady. The house remained with the family until 1951, when Sir James Burnett presented it to the National Trust for Scotland. Eight themed gardens have been laid out within the old walled garden, separated by yew hedges. There is also a shop and restaurant.

KINCARDINE O'NEILL

23 miles W of Aberdeen on the A93

This little village, with its Irish sounding name, claims to be the oldest village on Deeside. It is in fact a small burgh, which was granted its charter in 1511. It was here, in 1220, that the first bridge was constructed across the Dee beyond Aberdeen, so it became an important place. The ruins of the **Kirk of St Mary** date from the 14th century. It may have been the chapel for a hospital that stood here before the Reformation. It was in use up until 1862, when a new church was built. St Mary's was thatched up until 1733, when someone shot at a pigeon perching in its roof and it caught fire.

ALFORD

26 miles W of Aberdeen on the A944

Alford (pronounced "Afford" locally, with the accent on the first syllable) is a pleasant village within a fertile area

CRATHES CASTLE AND GARDENS

Banchory, Aberdeenshire AB31 5QJ
Castle: Tel: 01330 844525 Fax: 01330 844797
Ranger service: Tel: 01330 844651
e-mail crathes@nts.org.uk website: www.nts.org.uk

King Robert the Bruce granted the lands of Leys to the Burnett family in 1323: the ancient Horn of Leys, which can be seen today in the Great Hall, marks his gift. The castle, built in the

second half of the 16th century, is a superb example of a tower house of the period. Some of the rooms retain their original painted ceilings and collections of family portraits and furniture.

A visit is enhanced by the walled garden, which incorporates herbaceous borders and many unusual plants, providing a wonderful display at all times of the year. The great yew hedges, fascinating examples of the art of topiary, date from as early as 1702. Explore the estate on the seven waymarked trails (including one suitable for wheelchairs) that lead through the mixed woodlands, along the Coy Burn and past the millpond. In the Visitor Centre a new exhibition, *A Walk on the Wild Side*, explores the wildlife on the Crathes Estate.

known as the Howe of Alford. The **Grampian Transport Museum** has displays and working exhibits about transport in the Grampian area. You can even clamber aboard some of the exhibits. Each year the Ecomarathon takes place at the museum, where vehicles have to travel as far as possibly on a set amount of fuel. The **Alford Valley Railway and Railroad Museum** is a two-mile long narrow gauge passenger railway with steam and diesel locomotives that runs between the Transport Museum and **Haughton House Country Park**, where there are woodland walks, a wildflower garden and a caravan park.

Four miles south of Alford, on the A980, is one of Aberdeenshire's finest castles, **Craigievar Castle** (National Trus tfor Scotland). With its many turrets and small windows,

Craigievar Castle

it looks like something from a fairy tale. It was built by William Forbes, who bought the land in 1610 and completed the castle in 1626. It has a fine collection of 17th and 18th century furniture, as well as family portraits. William Forbes was also known as "Danzig Willie", and was a rich Aberdeen merchant who traded with the Baltic countries. The castle is due for refurbishment between late 2005 and 2007, so people should check with the NTS before visiting.

LUMPHANAN
24 miles W of Aberdeen on the A980

Lumphanan was founded when the Deeside railway was constructed, and was the highest point on the line. The **Peel Ring of Lumphanan** (Historic Scotland) is a huge motte and bailey where a castle built by the Durward family once stood.

ABOYNE
27 miles W of Aberdeen off the A93

This small Royal Deeside town is famous for the **Aboyne Highland Games**, held in August each year. The village prospered with the coming of the railway in the 19th century, and is now a quiet settlement, popular with tourists. It is also the home of the **Aboyne and Deeside Festival**, held in July and August, which features music, drama and art. There is a lovely, but in places difficult, walk up **Glen Tanar**, two miles

west of Aboyne.

Five miles north of the town, and two miles north east of Tarland is the **Culsh Earth House**, a souterrain, or underground chamber, which is over 2,000 years old. It is a long, doglegged tunnel, which was probably not used as a house, but as a store for foodstuffs. A torch is needed to explore it. The **Tomnaverie Stone Circle** (Historic Scotland) is a mile to the south west, and dates to about 1600BC.

BALLATER
34 miles W of Aberdeen on the A93

Set among the spectacular scenery of Royal Deeside, Ballater is surrounded by wooded hills of birch and pine, and makes an excellent base for exploring an area of outstanding beauty. It is a comparatively modern settlement, and, like Aboyne, owes its growth to the coming of the railways in the 19th century. In fact, this was as far as the Deeside line came, as Prince Albert stopped a proposed extension as far as Braemar. **The Old Royal Station** has been restored, and shows what it would have looked like in Victorian times, when the Royal Family used it. The **Muir of Dinnet Nature Reserve** lies between Ballater and Aboyne, and covers 2,000 acres around Lochs Kinord and Davan.

There is plenty of good walking country around the village, and **Glen**

Sarah's Speciality Showcase,
Ballogie Shop, Ballogie,
Aboyne, Aberdeenshire AB34 5DP
Tel/Fax: 01339 886104
e-mail: sarah@butterworthpaintings.co.uk
website: www.butterworthpaintings.co.uk

The Speciality Showcase near Aboyne is managed by Sarah Harker, eldest daughter of renowned artist **Howard Butterworth**, who paints the exquisite landscapes of the area in all their moods. Here, in this converted post office and village shop you will find his lovely paintings on sale, plus cards and prints based on them. New to the range are Wentworth Collectors wooden jigsaws, as well as placemats and coasters.

NUMBER FORTY SIX

46 Bridge Street, Ballater, Aberdeenshire AB35 5QD
Tel & Fax: 01339 755515

For the best of gifts and souvenirs while exploring Deeside, head for
Number Forty Six in the picturesque town of Ballater. Here you will
find an Aladdin's cave of pottery, Scottish silverware, paintings by local
artists, prints, wood and glass. Strongly featured are the wonderful
animal sculptures -especially dogs - by the renowned English sculptor
Rosemary Cook. The interior of the shop is light and airy, and the service is friendly and knowledgeable.
Much of the giftware cannot be found anywhere else in the locality, which is yet another reason to pay
it a visit.

Muick, to the south of Ballater, has a
narrow road that takes you up towards
Loch Muick (the road ends before the
loch is reached, so you have to walk part
of the way), in the shadow of **Lochnagar**,
which, notwithstanding its name, is a
mountain rising to a height of 3,786 feet.
It gave its name to Prince Charles's book,
The *Old Man of Lochnagar*. The drive is a
particularly fine one, and takes you past
Birkhall (not open to the public) which
was bought by Edward VII before he

Crathes Church

became king. It was the Deeside home of
the late Queen Mother.

BALMORAL
42 miles W of Aberdeen off the A93

The Queen's private home in Scotland
was purchased by Prince Albert in 1852.
Four years previously, Queen Victoria
had visited and fallen in love with the
area. Though the castle as you see it
today only dates from that time, a castle
has stood here for centuries. The first
recorded reference we have is in 1484,
when it was called "Bouchmorale". The
grounds are closed when the Royal
Family is in residence. The present castle
is in Scots Baronial style, and built from
local granite.

A quarter of a mile east of the castle is
the small **Crathie Kirk**, where the Royal
Family worships while at Balmoral. It
dates from 1895, and overlooks the
remains of the original 14th century
kirk. Many of the fittings and
furnishings have been donated over the
years by members of the Royal Family.
John Brown, Queen Victoria's
controversial ghillie, lies in the
adjoining cemetery. The **Royal
Lochnagar Distillery**, established in
1845, is near the kirk, and has a visitors
centre. It was given a Royal Warrant by
Queen Victoria in 1864.

A **Victorian Heritage Trail** has been
laid out (with distinctive brown signs)

which traces the footsteps of Queen Victoria not just on Deeside, but throughout the area, and a leaflet is available from most tourism offices.

BRAEMAR

50 miles W of Aberdeen on the A93

This little village high in the Cairngorms is officially Britain's coldest place. Between 1941 and 1970 its average temperature was only 6.4 degrees Celsius. On two occasions, in 1895 and 1982, it experienced the lowest temperature ever officially recorded in Britain - minus 28.2 degrees Celsius.

Highland Games, Braemar

It sits at an altitude of 1,100 feet, and is famous for the **Braemar Highland Games**, held every September, and visited by the Royal Family. **Braemar Castle** is the seat of the Farquharsons of Invercauld, and was built in 1628 by the Earl of Mar on the site of an older castle. It was used as a base by Hanovarian troops during the 1745 Rebellion. In the drawing room can be seen the world's largest Cairngorm (a semi-precious stone) weighing 52 pounds. And in the morning room display is a collection of Native American items from the great Lakes area of Canada. They were sent to this country by two members of the family who went there seeking their fortunes.

The 72,598 acre **Mur Lodge Estate** (National Trust for Scotland) lies five miles west of Braemar on a minor road, and is part of the **Cairngorms National Park**, which came into being in September 2003 (see Grantown-on-Spey). The estate has been described as the most important nature conservation landscape in Britain, and contains four out of its five highest mountains. In medieval times, when it was owned by the Earls of Mar, it was one of Scotland's most important hunting estates. It contains many of the features normally associated with Highland landscapes, and has a wealth of wildlife, plants, trees and archaeological sites. The estate is open daily, and the Lodge itself has special open days that are well advertised.

To the south of Braemar, on the A93, is one of Scotland's most popular winter sports areas, **Glenshee**. The snowfields stretch over three valleys and four Munros, with about 25 miles of marked pistes as well as off-piste skiing. The village of Spittal of Glenshee is dealt with in the Perthshire, Angus and Kinross section of the book.

KINTORE

10 miles NW of Aberdeen off the A96

Kintore is a small picturesque royal burgh four miles south east of Inverurie. **Kintore Tolbooth** dates from 1747, when the Earl of Kintore was the provost, and **Kintore Parish Church** was built in 1819. Incorporated into the west staircase is a piece of the sacrament house of the pre-Reformation Kirk of Kinkell.

To the west of the town stood a Roman Camp known as **Devona**. The slopes of Bennachie, to the west of the town, is one of the likely locations for the **Battle of Mons Graupius**, fought in AD 84 (see also Inverurie), and no doubt Devona played a major part. It was fought between a confederation of Caledonian tribes and the army of Agricola, with no clear victor emerging.

INVERURIE

15 miles NW of Aberdeen city centre off the A96

The royal burgh of Inverurie sits where the River Urie meets the Don. A legend tells of how a Roman soldier who came to this area exclaimed "urbi in rure!" (a city in the countryside) when he first saw the settlement. The town adopted the words as its motto, and it is on the coat of arms of the burgh. However, in reality the town's name has a more prosaic meaning - the "mouth of the Urie". Mary

DAVIDSON'S SPECIALIST BUTCHERS

1 Burn Lane, Inverurie, Aberdeenshire AB51 4UZ
Tel: 01467 621212
e-mail: shop@davidsons.plus.com

If it's good quality beef, lamb and pork you're after while in Aberdeenshire, the best place to go is **Davidson's Specialist Butchers** in the old market town of Inverurie, 16 miles northwest of Aberdeen. The shop sells only the finest quality meats at very competitive prices, from pork chops and succulent lamb to local beef , venison and poultry. All meats are hand selected and matured on the bone to give you the that extra flavour that everyone appreciates.

And, as well as local meat, the shop sells something a bit more exotic - bison, zebra, alligator and crocodile steaks, which are fast becoming very popular. There are also a fine range of quality cheeses, as well as pies and bakery products that are sure to please.

The shop is spotlessly clean, and is bright and airy, which makes shopping here a pleasure. It has soothing background music to put you at your ease, and all the staff are trained to a high standard so that you are assured of the personal attention and service, as well as all the advice you need when selecting your cuts.

So if your exploring beautiful Aberdeenshire and are in self-catering accommodation or in a caravan, call in at Davidsons for all your butchery requirements.

River Don

Stuart visited the town in 1562, and stayed in the royal castle which once stood where the mound known as the **Bass** is situated. The **Battle of Harlaw** was fought near the town in 1411, and a monument now marks the spot. A Lowland army fought a Highland army under Donald, Lord of the Isles, and while the result was an honourable draw, it did stop the Highlanders from moving into the Aberdeenshire lowlands and controlling them. It was one of the bloodiest battles ever fought on Scottish soil, which earned it the nickname of "Red Harlaw".

In 1805, the **Aberdeenshire Canal** was opened which linked Inverurie with Aberdeen. Designed by John Rennie, it was never a great success, and in 1845 it was sold to the Great North of Scotland Railway Company, who drained it and used part of its route to carry their railway line. **Port Elphinstone**, to the south east of the town, recalls the canal, and part of its channel can still be seen

there. It was the only canal in Britain to be closed down every winter in case of ice and snow. Within the **Carnegie Inverurie Museum** in the Square is a small display dedicated to the canal, as well as displays on local history.

To the west of the town is the area's best-known hill, Bennachie (see also Kintore). Though not particularly high (1,600 feet) it has a distinctive conical shape, and is sometimes called "Aberdeenshire's Mount Fuji", as it can be seen from all round the area. Near the Chapel of Garrioch is the **Bennachie Visitors Centre**, where the natural and social history of the hill is explained.

Two miles south of the town are the ruins of the 16th century **Kinkell Church**, which has a particularly fine sacrament house. The ornate grave slab of Gilbert de Greenlaw, who was killed at the Battle of Harelaw, can also be seen. **Castle Fraser** (National Trust for Scotland) lies six miles south west of the town, near the village of Craigearn. Work started on it in 1575 by Michael Fraser, the sixth laird, and was finished in 1636. It has a traditional "Z" plan, and contains many Fraser portraits, fine carpets, linen and curtains.

MONYMUSK

17 miles W of Aberdeen off the B993

Monymusk was once the site of an Augustinian priory, founded in 1170 by the Earl of Mar. The **Monymusk Reliquary**, in which was kept a bone of St Columba, was one of its treasures. It dates from the 8th century, and is a small wooden box covered in silver and bronze and decorated in semi-precious stones. It was paraded before Bruce's troops at the

Battle of Bannockburn, and is now in the Museum of Scotland.

The **Parish Church of St Mary**, which formed part of the priory, dates from the early years of the 12th century. In 1929 it was restored to its original condition, and it is now one of the finest parish churches in Scotland. Inside it is the Monymusk Stone, on which is carved Pictish symbols.

OYNE

21 miles NW of Aberdeen on the B9002

Over 7,000 ancient sites have been identified in Aberdeenshire, from Pictish carvings to stone circles, and these form the basis for the **Archaeolink Prehistory Park**, which bridges the gap between ancient history and modern times by way of exhibits and hands-on displays, both indoor and out. It has some of the finest collections of ancient remains in Europe.

FYVIE

23 miles NW of Aberdeen city centre off the A947

The oldest part of **Fyvie Castle** (National Trust for Scotland) dates from the 13th century, and was once a royal stronghold. There are 17th century panelling and plaster ceilings, as well as a portrait collection that includes works by Raeburn, Romney and Gainsborough. One of the legends attached to the castle is that its five towers were built by the five great families in the northeast who owned it - the Gordons, the Leiths, the Meldrums, the Prestons and the Setons. Both Robert the Bruce and and his descendent Charles I stayed here.

The **Parish Church** dates from the 19th century, and has a fine laird's pew and wine glass pulpit. In Fyvie Old Manse in 1864 was born **Cosmo Gordon Lang**, who became Archbishop of York in 1908 and Archbishop of Canterbury in 1928.

FYVIE CASTLE

Fyvie, Turriff, Aberdeenshire, AB53 8JS
Tel: 01651 891266 Fax: 01651 891107
Ranger service: Tel: 0 1330 844651
website: www.nts.org.uk

Fyvie was once a royal stronghold, one of a chain of fortresses throughout medieval Scotland. From 1390, following the Battle of Otterburn, five successive families created probably the finest example of Scottish Baronial architecture. An old tradition claims that these families Preston, Meldrum, Seton, Gordon and Leith each built one of Fyvie's five towers. An

air of mystery is created by the ghosts and legends associated with this castle. The oldest part dates from the 13th century, and within its ancient walls is a great wheel stair, the finest in Scotland. Contemporary panelling and plaster ceilings survive in the 17th century Morning Room and the opulence of the Edwardian era is reflected in the interiors created by the first Lord Leith of Fyvie. A rich portrait collection includes works by Batoni, Raeburn, Romney, Gainsborough, Opie and Hopprier, and there is a fine collection of arms and armour, and 17th century tapestries.

The grounds and loch were designed as landscaped parkland in the early 19th century. The 18th century walled garden, has been redeveloped as a celebration of Scottish fruits and vegetables. Visitors can also enjoy the restored racquets court, ice house, bird hide, restored earth closet and beautiful lochside walks.

HUNTLY

33 miles NW of Aberdeen on the A96

Huntly is an old burgh, which was granted its charter in 1488. It sits in an area called Strathbogie, and is famous for the ruins of **Huntly Castle** (Historic Scotland). It was originally called Strathbogie Castle, and was built by the Earl of Fife in the late 12th century. While in the area in the early 1300s, Robert the Bruce took ill, and spent some time in the castle, as the then Earl, David, was one of his supporters. However he changed sides and joined the English just before Bannockburn, and subsequently forfeited the lands of Strathbogie.

They were subsequently given to Sir Adam Gordon of Huntly, who lived in the Scottish Borders (see Gordon), and he moved north to claim them in 1376. In the 16th century the name of the castle was changed to Huntly, and in the early 1550s it was rebuilt by George, 4th Earl of Huntly.

During the Reformation, the Gordons of Huntly were one of the most important Catholic families in Scotland, and fought on the side of Mary Stuart. James VI, her son, had the castle demolished when the 6th Earl, George, was implicated in an uprising against him. George fled to France, but returned, made his peace with James, and had the castle rebuilt. During the turbulent Covenanting times, the castle changed hands many times until it finally fell into the hands of the Covenanters in the early 17th century.

From about the early 18th century the castle fell into decay. But even today you can see just how stately and comfortable the place must have been in its heyday. It entertained many famous people, including Mary of Guise, mother of Mary Stuart, and Perkin Warbeck, pretender to the English throne.

In the town square is a statue to the 4th Duke of Richmond, and beneath it are the **Standing Stones of Strathbogie**, or as they are known in Huntly, the "Stannin Steens o Strahbogie". At one time they formed part of a stone circle.

The Brander Museum in the Square has collections dealing with local history, arms and armour and the works of local author **George MacDonald**, who died in 1905. His most popular stories were of fantasy and fairies, with a strong religious message. He rejected the Calvinist view, still held by some people in the Church of Scotland at the time, that art was self-indulgent and iconoclastic. Instead he argued that God could be understood through art and imagination.

Six miles south of Huntly, on the B9002 near Kennethmont, is **Leith Hall**

FUNCY PIECES

14 The Square, Rhynie, Near Huntly, Aberdeenshire AB54 4HD
Tel: 01464 861456

Funcy Pieces, right at the heart of the village of Rhynie, is the place to go for teas, coffees, home baking and traditional snacks when touring Aberdeenshire. Not only that - it sells a wide range of craft items that would make that perfect gift or souvenir of your visit. Collectibles - textiles - patchwork fabrics - paintings by local artists - photos - and a whole lot more. You can also buy literature on genealogy and family history - especially the history of local Aberdeenshire families. It's a great place to eat, drink and browse.

(National Trust for Scotland). It was the home of the Leith (later Leith-Hay) family from 1650 onwards, and contains many of their possessions. The family had a tradition of military service, and its most famous member, Andrew Hay, fought for Charles Edward Stuart.

Not far from here is Rhynie, known for its Celtic sites, Pictish stone circles, vitrified forts and castles. The village is situated on crossroads from which there is easy access to the distilleries, Deeside, Aberdeen and the coast. The local hill, Tap O'Noth is a favourite spot for hang-gliders, while mountain bikers and anglers are also well catered for.

ELLON

15 miles N of Aberdeen on the A920

Situated within an area known as the Formartine, Ellon is a small burgh or barony, which was granted its charter in 1707. It was one of the places burned down during what became known as the "Harrying of Buchan" in 1308 soon after Robert the Bruce defeated John Comyn, Earl of Buchan at Old Meldrum.

The town sits on the River Ythan, with a **Parish Church** that dates from 1777. It's hard to imagine nowadays that this little town, five miles from the coast, was once a port with a small steamer that took goods up and down the river. It is also one of the stops on the **Formartine Buchan Way**, based on disused railway tracks from Dyce, just outside of Aberdeen, to Fraserburgh. The **Moot Hill Monument** sits on Moot hill, from where justice was dispensed by the Earls of Buchan in the 13th and early 14th centuries.

Five miles west of the town, on the A920 is the **Pitmedden Garden** (National Trust for Scotland). The centrepiece is the Great Garden, laid out by Sir Alexander Seton, 1st Baronet of

Pitmedden, in 1675. In the 1950s the rest of the garden was re-created using elaborate floral designs. Four parterres were created, three of them being inspired by designs possibly used at the Palace of Holyrood in Edinburgh, and the fourth based on Sir Alexander's coat-of-arms. There is also a visitor centre and a Museum of Farming Life, which has a collection of old farming implements once used in this largely farming area.

Near the gardens are the substantial ruins of **Tolquhon Castle**, built by William Forbes, 7th Lord of Tolquhon in the 1580s. In 1589 James VI visited the house, and both his and the Forbes' coats-of-arms were carved over the doorway. William Forbes and his wife Elizabeth were buried in an elaborately carved tomb in the south aisle of the parish church at Tarves. The church has since been demolished, but the **Forbes Tomb** survives to this day.

Haddo House (National Trust for Scotland), one of the grandest stately homes in Aberdeenshire, lies six miles northwest of Ellon. It was designed by William Adam for the 2nd Earl of Aberdeen in the early 1730s, and restored in the 1880s. It is noted for its Victorian interiors within an elegant Georgian shell, and features furniture, paintings and objets d'arts. It also has a terraced garden with rose beds and a fountain. In the grounds is **Kelly Lake**, one of the few natural (as opposed to man made) sheets of water called "lake" rather than "loch" in Scotland (see Lake of Menteith, Kirkcudbright and Stenton).

ELGIN

Situated in the fertile Laigh of Moray, Elgin is a charming city with the ruins of what was one of the finest cathedrals in Scotland. Before the local government reforms in the mid-70s, there were only six towns - or cities - in Scotland that were allowed to have lord provosts, and Elgin was one of them.

The city's layout is still essentially that of the medieval burgh, with a High Street that goes from where the royal castle once stood on Lady Hill to the cathedral. It widens in the middle into a market place called the **Plainstanes**, and close to it stands **St Giles Church**. It is in neoclassical style, and was built in 1828 to replace a medieval building. In the square at its east end is the **Muckle Cross**, a Victorian rebuilding of a medieval one. On **Lady Hill** is a monument to the 5th Duke of Richmond, dating from 1839, with the statue being added 16 years later. At the far east end of the High Street is another cross. It marks the spot where Alaxander MacDonald of the Isles did penance for despoiling the cathedral. It also marks the western limit of the "sanctuary area" of the cathedral.

Just off the High Street is the **Thunderton Hotel**, housed in what was a grand medieval town house. It was once the royal residence of the town, and was where the monarch stayed when he visited. It was surrounded by orchards, gardens and a bowling green. In 1746 Charles Edward Stuart stayed here while on his way to Culloden.

Three 17th century arcaded merchants' houses are to be found in the High Street, one of which at one time housed the bank of William Duff, a member of the family which went on to become substantial landowners in the area. The award-winning **Elgin Museum** is also in the High Street, and has many important collections, including natural history, archaeology and the social history of the area. Another museum worth visiting is the **Moray Motor Museum** in Bridge Street, with its collection of old cars and motorcycles.

Work was started on **Elgin Cathedral**, or to give it its proper name, the Cathedral of the Holy Trinity, in about 1224. It was one of Scotland's grandest churches, and could compare to the great cathedrals of Europe. There had been three cathedrals in the dioceses before this one, at Birnie, Spynie and Kinneder, but the locations had all been unsuitable. By the end of the 13th century, building work was complete, though in 1390 the Wolf of Badenoch (see also Dunkeld, Grantown-on-Spey and Fortrose), set fire to it after a violent quarrel with the Bishop of Moray, who had ordered him to give up his mistress and return to his wife, Euphemia Ross.

He did a lot of damage, and work on repairing it continued right up until the Reformation in 1560. After the Reformation,

Biblical Garden, Elgin

CAPERS BISTRO

55 High Street, Elgin, Moray IV30 1EF
Tel: 01343 551273

You'll find modern and innovative food at the best café/bistro in Elgin - **Capers Bistro**, just off the main shopping street. It's the place to go for dinner in the evening, a leisurely lunch, or even just a refreshing cup of coffee as you explore this historic small city. The interior is light and airy, and the food is out of this world. It is fully licensed, and the menu contains many dishes that are presented with flair and imagination. There is car parking access right beside the restaurant, and the place has a friendly, informal atmosphere. Eating here is a memorable experience for all the right reasons.

the cathedral became a quarry for the people of the town. In 1807 a keeper of the ruins was appointed, and from then on what was left was cared for and preserved. The east gate to the cathedral precincts, known as the **Panns Port**, still stands.

To the north west of the cathedral are the ruins of the so-called **Bishop's Palace**. It had nothing to do with the bishop, and was instead the manse of the cathedral's preceptor, who looked after the sacred music. It was one of about 20 such manses around the cathedral which housed the cathedral staff. And to the north east of the cathedral is the Brewery Bridge, built in 1798 and so called becaaus a brewery stood close by until 1913.

Off Greyfriars Street stands the restored **Greyfriars Monastery**, now reckoned to give the best idea of what a

COMMERCIAL HOTEL

4-8 Young Street, Burghead, Elgin, Moray IV31 5UB
Tel: 01343 835628
e-mail: enquiries@commercialhotel.com
website: www.commercial-hotel.com

At the **Commercial Hotel** in Burghead, a small fishing village on the Moray Firth coast, can be found all that is best in Scottish hospitality. You can enjoy a relaxing and peaceful holiday among some of the best coastal scenery in the country, as well as great historical sites and sports facilities.

The hotel has recently had extensive work carried out on it, and is now one of the best small hotels in the area, boasting six extremely comfortable rooms each one fully en suite and decorated and furnished to an very high standard. TVs and tea/coffee making facilities come as standard. The hotel is friendly, informal and always welcoming, with attentive staff that is knowledgeable about what to do and see in the area. It sits at the top end of the village, a short walk from the shops and a minute's walk from the picturesque harbour, and makes the ideal base from which to explore an area that takes

in Elgin, Inverness, the Spey Whisky Trail and many more attractions.

The dining room serves delicious meals between 5pm and 8pm, the cuisine being Scottish with various influences. All the produce used in the kitchen is fresh and local wherever possible, and good use is made of the local larder - salmon, venison, beef, lamb, pork and of course, seafood. There is a full children's menu available. The lounge bar is a great place to relax after a hard day holidaying, and here you can enjoy a coffee, a beer of one of the local single malts.

medieval Scottish friary looked like. It was built n 1479, then, in the late-19th century, was restored by John Kinross, who built new walls on the foundations of the old ones.

At ther west end of the high street is the imposing façade of Dr Gray's Hospital, the town's main infirmary. It was founded by Dr Alexander Gray, who amassed a fortune in India, and built between 1816 and 1819.

Johnston's Cashmere Visitor Centre is at Newmill. There are tours round the mill, an exhibition and audiovisual that explains the making of the luxury material. There is also a shop where Johnston products can be bought, and a coffee shop.

Elgin Cathedral

The **Old Mills** is the last remaining meal mill on the River Lossie. Its history goes back to the 13th century, when it was owned by Pluscarden Abbey.

North of the city are the impressive ruins of **Spynie Palace** (Historic Scotland), the home of the bishops of Moray. The palace sits on the shores of tiny Loch Spynie, and dates from the 14th century and later. David's Tower, the main part of the building, dates from the 16th century. Spynie Church, which stood nearby until 1736, was at one time the cathedral of the diocese.

AROUND ELGIN

DUFFUS

5 miles NW of Elgin on the B9012

The ruins of the **Church of St Peter** (Historic Scotland) stand near the village. Though mainly 18th century, it incorporates work that is much older. Opposite the porch is the medieval **Parish Cross**.

Close by are the ruins of **Duffus Castle**, founded in the 12th century by Freskin, Lord of Strabrock, who later took the title and name of Lord of Duffus and Freskin or Moravia. He is the ancestor of the great Moravia, (later Moray, or Murray), family, which has played such a prominent part in Scotland's history. It would originally have been a wooden tower surrounded by a wooden palisade which not only encompassed the castle on top of its motte, or hill, but a bailey as well, where a small settlement would have flourished. The castle as we see it today dates from the 14th century onwards, and still has the finest motte and bailey of any castle in the north of Scotland. **Gordonstoun School**, attended by both

Prince Philip and Prince Charles is close to Duffus, and is housed in an 18th century mansion. It was founded by the German educationalist Dr Kurt Hahn in 1934.

Lossiemouth

LOSSIEMOUTH

5 miles N of Elgin on the A941

This holiday resort sits at the mouth of the River Lossie, and was established as a small port for the city of Elgin in the 18th century after Elgin's original port at Spynie was cut off from the sea as the River Lossie silted up. There are fine sandy beaches, and the **Lossiemouth Fisheries and Community Museum**, in a former net mending loft at Pitgaveny Quay, traces the history of the town and its fishing industry. There is also a reconstruction of the study used by **James Ramsay Macdonald**, Britain's first Labour prime minister, who was born illegitimate in a small cottage in the town in 1866.

FOCHABERS

8 miles E of Elgin on the A96

Fochabers dates from 1776, when the then Duke of Gordon decided that he didn't like the dilapidated huddle of cottages that was old Fochabers within his parkland. He therefore built a new village further north with a large spacious square, and the present day Fochabers was the result. The architect was John Baxter, an Edinburgh man who had already worked on Gordon Castle. Within the former Pringle Church in the High Street is the **Fochabers Folk Museum**, and in the square is the elegant, porticoed **Bellie Church**. Its rather quaint name comes from the Gaelic "beul-aith", meaning "the mouth of the ford".

The imposing **Milne's High School** dates from 1844, and was built using

Victorian Shop at Baxters Highland Village, Fochabers

money gifted by a native of the town who made his fortune in New Orleans.

West of the village centre and overlooking the Spey is **Baxter's Highland Village**, home to one of the best-known food firms in Scotland. It all started in 1868, when George Baxter, who worked for the Duke of Gordon, opened a small grocery shop in Fochabers. This is one of the most fertile areas in Britain, famed for its fruit, vegetables and cattle, and soon George's wife was making jams and conserves in the back shop. Now the factory and associated shops, restaurants and kids' play areas are tourist attractions in their own right.

BUCKIE

13 miles E of Elgin on the A990

Buckie is a major fishing port, based in Cluny Harbour. In the **Buckie District Fishing Heritage Museum** in Clunie Place and the **Buckie Drifter** in Freuchny Road are displays that tell the story of the fishing industry on the Morayshire coast. The **Peter Anson Gallery** is within the town's library, and

has a collection of paintings by the maritime artist Peter Anson.

Four miles west of the town is the mouth of the River Spey. It is half a mile wide, though no great port sits here. The village of **Kingston** dates from 1784, and was founded by Ralph Dodworth and William Osbourne. They came from Kingston-upon-Hull in Yorkshire, and named their village after it. It was near here that Charles II alighted after a trip from Holland on 23rd June 1650. His ship grounded in shallow water, and he had to be taken ashore "piggyback" style on the back of a villager.

The small fishing communities round about, such as **Findochty** and **Portnockie** are very attractive, and well worth visiting. Five miles southwest of

Bow Fiddle Rock, Portnockie

PUDDLEDUCK PATCH

31-33 Seafield Street, Cullen, Banffshire AB56 4SU
Tel: 01542 841888
e-mail: anne.geddes@tiscali.co.uk
website: www.puddleduckpatch.com

Puddleduck Patch, owned and managed by Anne Geddes, is in the old fishing port of Cullen on the Moray Firth coast. Here you will find everything you need for the fascinating hobby of quilting. In fact, it is a paradise for quilters and patch workers, with an extensive range of cotton fabrics. Not only that - Anne runs quilting classes and workshops from September to April each year, which are friendly, fun and informative. For dates please phone or consult the website.

The gift shop carries a fine range of items that are just right for that special gift or souvenir. There's china from Bridgewater, Burleigh and Portmeirion, Paula Bolton jewellery, Kaloo toys as well as candles, napkins and cards.

There is also a coffee shop that sells a range of teas and coffees, as well as bowls of soup, pannini, baguettes and delicious home baking. Why not try the banoffee pie? It's fabulous! Puddleduck Patch also has a refreshment licence, so you can also enjoy a glass (or two) of wine.

And if you're looking for B&B accommodation, then look no further. Puddleduck Patch offers three cottage-style rooms - a single and two twins. All the rooms are comfortable, affordable and beautifully decorated and furnished throughout. The breakfast menu is extensive, with everything served in the coffee shop itself.

So when in Cullen, make for Puddleduck Patch.

KNOCKANDHU RIDING SCHOOL

Craigellachie, Aberlour, Banffshire AB38 9RP
Tel:01542 860302 Fax: 01340 881319

A warm and friendly welcome is assured at **Knockandhu Riding School**, right in the heart of Strathspey and the Speyside Whisky Trail. There are good-natured horses for riders of all standards, from beginners to the more advanced, and here you can learn to ride, as well as learn about caring for an animal, from grooming through mucking out and feeding. Why not spend a full working day here? The day starts at 9.30am and finishes at 4.30pm, and you can spend the whole time caring for a horse, learning how to groom, muck out, tack and untack, and the basics of feeding it. You can then have two one hour lessons on riding the horse, and finally a quiz to test your knowledge.

Take a trek through Strathspey, which is full of beautiful scenery, and learn about the area's spectacular wildlife as you go. It is a truly enjoyable experience, and brings you so much closer to nature and all its wonders. Or why not go on one of Knockandhu's picnic rides? Spend half an hour riding to a secluded, beautiful spot, have a picnic lunch, then spend half an hour riding back to the riding school once more. You see more of the countryside this way.

The prices at Knockandhu Riding School represent amazing value for money, and the proprietor, Pearl Cranna, is always on hand to offer advice and help. The school sits beyond the quaintly named village of Maggieknockatur just off he A95, and is easy to find.

the town are the ruins of **Deskford Church**, within the village of the same name. It is noted for its ornately carved sacrament house. The 16th century **St Mary's Church** sits in the small fishing village of **Cullen**, to the north of Deskford, and was formerly collegiate. Cullen, a former fishing village, gives its name to one of Scotland's best known dishes - Cullen skink, a fish soup enriched with potatoes, onion and cream. The word "skink" comes from the Gaelic word for "essence".

One of the most dramatically situated castles in the area is **Findlater Castle**, which sits on a small promontory jutting into the sea. The ruins you see now date from the 15th century, and were built by the Ogilvie family, though a castle may have stood here since at least the 13th century. Care should be taken when approaching or exploring it. The name comes from the Norse "fyn", meaning "white" and "leitr" meaning "cliff", as the cliffs in this part of the country are studded with quartz.

In the village of **Fordyce**, south east of Cullen, is the **Fordyce Joiner's Workshop and Visitor Centre** in Church Street, dedicated to the skills and tools of carpentry in northeast Scotland. **Fordyce Castle** was built in 1592 by Sir Thomas Menzies of Durn, a provost of Aberdeen. It is an L-plan tower, and is not open to the public.

CRAIGELLACHIE

12 miles S of Elgin off the A95

The **Craigellachie Bridge** dates from 1814, and is Scotland's oldest iron bridge. It was designed by Thomas Telford, and has one single graceful arch spanning the Spey. The village sits in the heart of the **Malt Whisky Trail**, and most of the distilleries organise tours round the premises, with a tasting at the end. The **Speyside Cooperage**, on the Dufftown

River Spey, Criagellachie

road, has a visitor centre where you can learn about the skills involved in making and repairing whisky casks.

Craigellachie Distillery lies within the village, as does the **Macallan Distillery**, and four miles north is the **Glen Grant Distillery**. The **Glenfarclas Distillery** is seven miles southwest, near **Ballindalloch Castle**. The castle dates from the 16th century, and is the home of the McPherson-Grant family, who have lived there continuously since it was built. It is open to the public during the summer months. About four miles south of Ballindalloch is the **Glenlivit Distillery**, which again has organised tours.

A couple of miles south west is the village of Aberlour, where there is there **Aberlour Distillery**, which has a visitor centre.

DUFFTOWN

16 miles S of Elgin on the A941

Dufftown is the world capital of malt whisky and was founded in 1817 by James Duff, the 4th Earl of Fife. Built to provide employment after the Napoleonic wars, it is based around a number of distilleries, including the world famous **Glenfiddich Distillery**. The most prominent feature is the **Clock Tower**, originally built in 1839 as the town jail. The clock itself came from Banff, where it was known as the "Clock That Hanged MacPherson". McPherson of Kingussie had been sentenced to death in 1700, but was later pardoned. While the pardon was on its way to Banff, Lord Braco put the clock forward to ensure that MacPherson would hang.

Mortlach Church, which is a Scottish Heritage site, was founded on a much earlier church, thought to have stood here since the community began in AD566 and to have been in regular use as a place of worship ever since. Although much of the church was reconstructed in the 19th century, parts of the original building still survive. In the graveyard is an old Pictish cross, and inside the church is the **Elephant Stone**, again with Pictish associations. An old story tells of how Malcolm II extended the church in thanks for his victory over the Vikings in 1010.

Balvenie Castle (Historic Scotland), lies a mile north, and was once home to the Comyns and later the Stewarts and the Douglases. In the 13th century it was visited by Edward I of England, and Mary Stuart spend two nights here in 1562.

The **Keith and Dufftown Railway** connects Dufftown to the market town of Keith, 11 miles away. It was reopened

FLORAL OCCASIONS

15 Fife Street, Dufftown, Moray AB55 4AL
Tel: 01340 820567

For everything to do with flowers and floral displays, you should head for **Floral Occasions** in the whisky town of Dufftown. The shop is owned and personally managed by Margaret Brown, and is situated next to the town square, so you can't miss it. There are flowers, flowering plants, baskets, vases and a host of products to do with floral displays, so the place is colourful and bright. If you're in Morayshire, make sure you call in.

RESTAURANT LA FAISANDERIE

2 Balvenie Street, Dufftown, Banffshire AB55 4AD
Tel: 01340 821273
e-mail: chtiroastbeef@aol.com website: www.dufftown.co.uk/eats.htm

For the perfect marriage of finest Scottish produce with French style and finesse, there is nowhere better than **Restaurant La Faisanderie** in Dufftown. It is run and owned by Eric and Mandy, who have extensive experience in Michelin starred and AA rosette hotels. The menu is constantly changing to take advantage of the fine, fresh local produce that is available, such as fish from the Moray Firth, game and lamb from the moorlands and fine Aberdeen Angus beef. For that special dinner, or a lunch to remember, make La Faisanderie your first stop.

in 2000/2001 by a group of enthusiasts, and runs services between the two towns.

The 18-hole Dufftown Golf Club boasts the highest hole in the UK. Besides golf, the town caters for all types of outdoor activities including walking, fishing, shooting and cycling.

KEITH

15 miles SE of Elgin on the A96

Keith is divided into two communities, divide by the River Isla. The old Keith was founded in the 12th century on the west bank of the river as a market centre for the selling of cattle. The newer, and larger, Keith was laid out in 1755 by the Earl of Finladter on the east bank.

The town is home to the **Glenisla Distillery**, which is open to the public. The old **Packhorse Bridge** dates from 1609, though the town's oldest building is **Milton Tower**, dating from 1480. It was a stronghold of the Ogilvie family, whose most famous member was John Ogilvie. Raised a Protestant, he later converted to Roman Catholicism on the Continent and was sent back to Scotland to promote the faith, posing as a horse dealer and soldier called John Watson. He was eventually hanged in Glasgow in 1615, and was made a saint in 1976. There is a **Scottish Tartans Museum** in Keith's Institute Hall. The town is the eastern terminus of the Keith and Dufftown Railway (see Dufftown).

TOMINTOUL

27 miles S of Elgin on the A939

Tomintoul dates from 1775, when the 4th Duke of Gordon decided to lay out a new village in the aftermath of the Jacobite Uprising. It is situated at a height of 1,160 feet and is said to be the highest village in the Highlands (but not in Scotland). The A939 southwest to Cockbridge is called "**The Lecht**", and is notorious for being blocked by snow in winter. The ski area of the same name lies six miles from Tomintoul. The small **Tomintoul Museum**, in the village square, has displays on local history and wildlife.

At Cockbridge is **Corgarff Castle** (Historic Scotland), a tower house set within a curious star-shaped walled enclosure. It was built in about 1550 by John Forbes of Towie. There was a long running feud between the Forbes and the Gordons, and during a siege of the castle in 1571, John Forbes's wife Margaret held out against a force led by Adam Gordon. Eventually the castle was burned down, killing everyone within it, including Margaret.

PLUSCARDEN

6 miles SW of Elgin on a minor road

Pluscarden Priory was founded in 1230 by Alexander II and settled firstly by the Valliscaulian and then the Benedictine monks. In the 19th century the Bute family acquired the ruined buildings, and in 1943 presented them to the monks of Prinknash in England, who took up residence in 1948. This means that it is the only medieval abbey in Britain still used for its original purpose. At first it was a priory, but became an abbey in its own right in 1974. It is open to the public, and has a small gift shop.

FORRES

12 miles W of Elgin on the A96

This small royal burgh, which was granted its charter in the 13th century, was once one of the most important places in Scotland, and is mentioned in Shakespeare's Macbeth. The ground plan of the medieval settlement still forms the basis of the town today, though it is much more open and green than it was

LOGIE STEADING

Dunphail, Forres, Moray IV36 2QN
Tel: 01309 611733

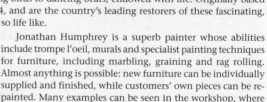

Logie Steading is a collection of small art, craft and food businesses in one location, meaning that you, the customer, can have a shopping and eating experience in a restored steading (farm courtyard) close to the historic town of Forres.

Treats at Logie is a small café selling good food at affordable prices. Since it was established in spring of 2003, it has attracted an ever-growing clientele who appreciate the quality home made soups (vegetarian and vegan), steak sandwiches, bruschettas, filled ciabattas, delicious cakes and many other tempting items. Wherever possible, the produce is organic and sourced locally. The café is licenced and sells wines and Scottish beers.

The Farm and Garden Shop sells locally produced food and hardy plants, all grown in Scotland. Many of the varieties offered can be seen growing in the mature Logie House walled garden, set above the dramatic River Findhorn which has a breathtaking walk along the river path to Randolph's Leap.

The Logie Steading Art Gallery (open from February to Christmas) exhibits for sale contemporary art - paintings, original prints, ceramics, bronzes, wood, textiles and cards. Glass is engraved on site where a local artist is able to translate customers' idea/drawings/photographs into an image possible for engraving. This is the ideal place to buy a gift or souvenir of your holiday. Prices are reasonable, and there is always someone to offer advice about your purchase.

Giles and Margaret Pearson offer a range of superb antique country furniture, folk art pieces and general high quality objets d'art. They specialise in the restoration of cane and rush seated chairs, and customers can view demonstrations of work in progress in the shop. Established in 1981, the business came to Logie Steading in 1999. The shop is naturally lit, with a high ceiling, and has ample wheelchair access. For interesting pieces of furniture, Logie Steading has the best in the area.

Michael and Maria Start have possibly the most unusual shop in Logie Steading. They repair and sell automata - beautifully crafted objects, from singing birds to dancing bears, endowed with life. Originally based in London, they moved north in 2004, and are the country's leading restorers of these fascinating, mechanical moving objects that seem so life like.

Jonathan Humphrey is a superb painter whose abilities include trompe l'oeil, murals and specialist painting techniques for furniture, including marbling, graining and rag rolling. Almost anything is possible: new furniture can be individually supplied and finished, while customers' own pieces can be re-painted. Many examples can be seen in the workshop, where there is also a selection of beautiful middle eastern rugs.

Logie Steading is a unique place, bringing together so many art, craft and food specialists in the one beautiful setting. It makes a great stop-off as you tour round Moray and the then, thanks to some large areas of parkland.

The 20-feet high **Sueno's Stone** (Historic Scotland) dates from the 9th or 10th century, and is the largest known stone with Pictish carvings in Scotland. One side shows a cross, while the other shows scenes of battle. One of the scenes might be the battle fought at Forres in 966 where the Scottish king, Dubh, was killed. It is now floodlit, and under glass to protect it from the weather. **The Falconer Museum** in Tolbooth Street was founded in 1871, and highlights the history and heritage of the town and its surroundings. It was founded using money from a bequest left by two brothers who left Forres for India. One was Alexander Falconer, a merchant in Calcutta, and the other was Hugh Falconer, a botanist and zoologist.

Dominating the town is the **Nelson Tower**, opened in 1812 in Grant Park to commemorate Nelson's victory at Trafalgar seven years before, the first such building to do so in Britain. If you're fit enough to climb its 96 steps, you'll get spectacular views over the surrounding countryside and the Moray Firth.

Brodie Castle (National Trust for Scotland - see panel on page 410) lies four miles west of the town. It is a 16th century tower house with later additions, which give it the look of a comfortable mansion. In about 1160 Malcolm IV gave the surrounding lands to the Brodies, and it was their family home until the late 20th century, and contains major collections of paintings, furniture and ceramics, and sits in 175 acres of ground. Within the grounds is Rodney's Stone, with Pictish carvings.

A couple of miles northeast of Forres is **Kinloss**, with an RAF base and the scant remains of an old abbey. It was founded

---

BRODIE COUNTRYFARE

Brodie, By Forres, Moray IV36 2TD
Tel: 01309 641555
e-mail: enquiries@brodiecountryfare.com
website: www.brodiecountryfare.com

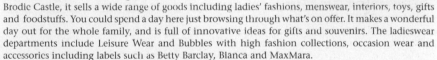

Brodie Countryfare is one of the best shops of its kind in Scotland. Situated in the village of Brodie, near the marvellous Brodie Castle, it sells a wide range of goods including ladies' fashions, menswear, interiors, toys, gifts and foodstuffs. You could spend a day here just browsing through what's on offer. It makes a wonderful day out for the whole family, and is full of innovative ideas for gifts and souvenirs. The ladieswear departments include Leisure Wear and Bubbles with high fashion collections, occasion wear and accessories including labels such as Betty Barclay, Bianca and MaxMara.

The menswear department reflects the very best in gents' fashion, with names such as Mark O'Polo, McGregor, Marlboro Classics and Sand predominating. Plus there is a huge gift department that

features traditional Scottish gifts, contemporary and design led gifts, soft furnishings, candles, toy department, table wear and books. In the food hall there are marvellous Scottish cheeses, hand-made chocolates, drinks, honey, meats and a host of other items that are sure to set your mouth watering. And once you've made your purchases, you can relax in the spacious restaurant, enjoying good food at reasonable prices, with the produce all being sourced from Northeast Scotland wherever possible.

BRODIE CASTLE

Brodie, Forres, Moray IV36 2TE
Tel: 01309 641371 Fax: 0 1309 641600
e-mail brodiecastle@nts.org.uk

Brodie Castle is a fine 16th century Z plan tower house with 17th and 19th century additions, set in peaceful parkland. The family association with the area pre-dates the castle, going back at least to Malcolm, Thane of Brodie, who died in 1285, and possibly to 1160, when it is believed Malcolm IV endowed the Brodies with their lands. The castle was damaged in an attack in 1645 by Montrose's army, but survived. It contains fine French furniture, English, Continental and Chinese porcelain, and a major collection of paintings, including 17th century Dutch art, 19th century English watercolours, Scottish Colourists and early 20th century works. The magnificent library contains some 6,000 volumes.

The grounds are famous for their unique daffodil collection in spring. Explore them along the woodland walks, one by the edge of a pond with access to wildlife observation hides.

in about 1150 by David I, and colonised by Cistercian monks from Melrose. It is said that in 1150 David founded it in thanks after getting lost in a dense forest. Two doves led him to an open space where shepherds were looking after their sheep. They gave him food and shelter, and as he slept he had a dream in which he was told to found an abbey on the spot. Before the Reformation, it was one of the wealthiest and most powerful abbeys in Scotland.

On the coast north of Forres is perhaps Scotland's most unusual landscape, the **Culbin Sands**. In 1694 a storm blew great drifts of sand - some as high as 100 feet - over an area that had once been green and fertile, causing people to flee their homes. The drifts covered cottages, fields, even a mansion house and orchard, and eventually created eight square miles of what became known as "Scotland's Sahara". Occasionally, further storms would uncover the foundations of old cottages, which were then covered back up again by succeeding storms. The sands continued to shift and expand until the 1920s, when trees were planted to stabilise the area. Now it is a nature reserve.

At **Findhorn**, on the Moray Firth coast, is the **Findhorn Foundation**, one of the most successful centres in Britain

Findhorn

for exploring alternative lifestyles and spiritual living. It was founded by Dorothy Maclean and Peter and Eileen Caddy in 1962 in a caravan park. The **Findhorn Heritage Centre and Museum** has displays on the history and heritage of the place. The village of Findhorn itself was once a busy port, trading with the Low countres and Scandinavia. Now it is a sailing and wildlife centre.

Dallas Dhu Distillery (Historic Scotland) sits to the south of Forres, and explains the making of whisky. It was built between 1898 and 1899 to produce a single malt for a firm of Glasgow blenders called Wright and Greig.

FRASERBURGH

Fraserburgh sits on the coastline just at that point where the Moray Firth becomes the North Sea. It is one of the main fishing ports in northeast Scotland, and the largest shellfish port in Europe. It was founded in the 16th century by Alexander Fraser, eighth laird of Philorth, who built the first harbour in 1546. Between 1570 and 1571 he also built **Fraserburgh Castle**. A powerful lantern was built on top of it in 1787, and it became a lighthouse, now known as **Kinnaird Lighthouse**, owned by Historic Scotland. It is a museum dedicated to Scotland's lighthouses.

The **Old Kirk** in Saltoun Square isn't as old as its name would suggest. It was built in 1803 to replace the original church built by Alexander between 1570 and 1571. Beside it is the **Fraser Burial Aisle**.

One of Alexander's grander schemes was the founding of a university in the town, and he even went so far as to obtain James VI's permission to do so. The Scots Parliament gave it a grant, and the Rev'd Charles Ferme became its first principal. Unfortunately, the Rev'd Ferme was later arrested for attending a general assembly of the Church of Scotland in defiance of the king. The embryonic university subsequently collapsed, though one street in the town, College Bounds, still commemorates the scheme.

In Quarry Road is the **Fraserburgh Heritage Centre**, which has exhibits about the history of the town, including some haute couture dresses designed by the late fashion designer **Bill Gibb**, who hailed from Fraserburgh. The most unusual building in Fraserburgh is the **Wine Tower**, next to the lighthouse. It too was built by Alexander Fraser, possibly as a chapel. It has three floors, but no connecting stairways.

At Sandhead, to the west of the town, is the **Sandhaven Meal Mill**, dating from the 19th century. Guided tours and models show how oatmeal used to be ground in Scotland. At Memsie, three miles south of Fraserburgh on the B9032, is the **Memsie Burial Cairn**, dating from about 1500 BC. At one time three stood here, but only one is now left.

AROUND FRASERBURGH

Old Deer

12 miles S of Fraserburgh on the B9030

In a beautiful position on the banks of the River South Ugie are the ruins of **Deer Abbey** (Historic Scotland), founded in 1219 by William Comyn, Earl of Buchan, for the Cistercian order of monks. Little remains of the abbey church, but the walls of some of the other buildings are fairly well preserved. It is said that it was built on the site of a Celtic monastery founded by St Columba and his companion St Drostan in the 6th century.

MINTLAW

11 miles S of Fraserburgh on the B9030

In the village you'll find the 230-acre **Aden Farming Museum**, which sits within a country park. It traces the history of farming in this rich area of Aberdeenshire through three separate themes - the Aden Estate Story, the "Weel Vrocht Grun" ("well worked ground") and the country park itself. Hareshowe Farm has been restored to what it would have been like in the 1950s.

MAUD

12 miles S of Fraserburgh on the B9029

Maud grew up around a junction in the railway line that once connected Aberdeen to Fraserburgh and Peterhead. In the **Maud Railway Museum**, housed in the village's former station, you can relive the days of the Great North of Scotland Railway through exhibits, photographs, artefacts and displays.

TURRIFF

20 miles SW of Fraserburgh on the A947

Set on the River Deveron in the heart of the Buchan farmlands, Turriff is an ancient burgh that was given its charter in 1512 by James IV. The Knights Templar once owned land in the area, and a Templar chapel stood here. **Turriff Parish Church** was built in 1794, and there are some good carvings on its belfry and walls from the previous kirk that stood on the site. In 1693 a Covenanting army controlled Turiff, but in May of the same year a force led by the Marquis of Huntly put them to flight, an event which became known as the "Turiff Trot".

Delgatie Castle, close to the town, was founded in about 1050, though the castle as you see it today dates from the 16th century. It is the ancestral home of Clan Hay, and has been in the Hay family for just under 700 years. It belonged to the Earls of Buchan until after the battle of Bannockburn in 1314, when Robert the Bruce gave it to the Hays. In 1562 Mary Stuart stayed in the castle for three days after the Battle of Corrichie, which took place to the west of Aberdeen. The Queen's troops easily defeated a force of men led by the 4th Earl of Huntly, who was killed in the battle.

Turriff was the scene of a famous incident concerning the **Turra Coo** ("Turriff Cow"), which received widespread publicity throughout Britain. New National Insurance Acts were passed in 1911 and 1913 which required employers to pay 3d per week for each of their employees. The farmers of Aberdeenshire, in common with others all over Britain, did not want to pay, as they reckoned that farm workers had a healthy lifestyle, and would not need much medical treatment. Curiously enough, the farm workers themselves supported the farmers on this issue.

One Turriff farmer in particular, Robert Paterson, refused to comply with the new regulations, so one of his cows was taken to be sold at auction to pay off his arrears. However the auction, held in Turriff, turned into a fiasco, as the cow, which had slogans painted all over its body, took fright and bolted through the streets of the town. Meanwhile, the auctioneer was pelted with raw eggs and bags of soot. Three days later the cow was taken to Aberdeen, where it was sold for £7.

It was a hollow victory for the authorities, which had spent nearly £12 in recovering the sum. And they were further annoyed to hear that Paterson's neighbours had clubbed together and bought the cow so that it could be returned to him. So, while the authorities were out of pocket over the whole affair, it had not cost Robert Paterson a penny. There are now plans to erect a statue of the "Turra Coo" to commemorate the event.

Seven miles south west of Turriff along the B9024 is the **Glendronach Distillery**, situated on the banks of the Dronach Burn. Tours are available, and there is a visitor centre and shop.

PENNAN

9 miles W of Fraserburgh on the B9031

Pennan is possibly the most spectacular of the little fishing villages on the northern coast of Aberdeenshire. It is strung out along the base of a high cliff, with many of the cottages having their gable ends to the sea for protection. It is a conservation village, and is famous as being the setting, in 1983, for the film *Local Hero*. The red telephone box, famously used in the film, was a prop. However, Pennan's real telephone box, about 15 yards away from where the prop stood, is still a favourite place for photographs.

Pennan

BANFF

20 miles W of Fraserburgh on the A98

Banff was once the county town of Banffshire, and is a small fishing port close to the mouth of the River Deveron. It is an ancient royal burgh, having been granted its charter in 1163 by Malcolm IV. The **Banff Museum** in the High Street is one of Scotland's oldest, having been founded in 1828. It has a nationally important collection of Banff silver.

Duff House is a unique country house art gallery run by a unique partnership between Historic Scotland, the National Galleries of Scotland and Aberdeenshire Council, with a fine collections of paintings by such artists as Raeburn and El Greco, as well as tapestries and Chippendale furniture. It was designed by William Adam and built between 1735 and 1740 for William Duff of Braco, who later became Earl of Fife. After a bitter wrangle with Adam, William Duff abandoned it, and it was left to James, the 2nd Earl Fife, to complete the grand plan, including the grounds. Over the years it has had a chequered career, having been a hotel, a sanatorium, a prisoner-of war camp and the scene of an attempted murder, when a Countess of Fife tried to do away with her husband.

The small town of **Macduff** sits on the opposite shores of the small bay where the Deveron enters the Moray Firth. The lands were bought by the 1st Earl of Fife in 1733, and in 1783 the 2nd Earl founded the town as a burgh of barony. It contains the **Macduff Marine Aquarium** at High Shore, which has a central tank open to the sky surrounded by viewing areas so that you get a good view of fish and marine

THE GIFT COMPANY

32 Marischal Street, Peterhead, Aberdeenshire AB42 1HS
Tel: 01779 478434
e-mail: thegiftshop@tiscali.co.uk   website: www.thegiftcompany.biz

Set in the heart of Peterhead, **The Gift Company** is not your ordinary gift shop. It offers something different - a stunning range of gifts and home accessories that make the ideal gift or souvenir. As many of the items as possible are made in Scotland, though items from around the world - if they are of a high enough quality - are also featured. The shop also features occasional furniture, such as Thakat coffee tables, and sells the exquisite pewter panels by craftswoman Linda Kerr, inspired by the work of Charles Rennie Mackintosh. You are welcome to browse.

mammals from all angles. The aquarium has a wave-making machine which adds to the experience of seeing underwater life in its true condition.

Six miles west of Banff, on the A98, is the attractive little fishing port of **Portsoy**, which is well worth visiting if only to soak in the atmosphere. Though its burgh charter dates from 1550, it was Patrick Ogilvie, Lord Boyne, who realised its potential and developed it as a port to export marble from the nearby quarries. Louis XIV used Portsoy marble on his palace at Versailles.

PETERHEAD

16 miles SE of Fraserburgh on the A982

Peterhead is the largest town (as opposed to city) in Aberdeenshire, and one of the chief fishing ports in the northeast. It was founded by George Keith, the 5th Earl Marischal of Scotland in 1587, and is Scotland's most easterly burgh. In the mid-'80s it was Europe's largest white fish port, landing 120,000 tonnes of fish in 1987 alone. Now that fishing has declined, it benefits from being one of the ports that services the offshore gas industry. The **Arbuthnot Museum** in St Peter Street tells the story of the town and its industries, and has a large collection of Inuit artefacts. It was given to the town of Peterhead in 1850 by Adam

Arbuthnot, a local man who had acquired a huge collection of antiquities.

In South Road, in a purpose-built building, is **Peterhead Maritime Heritage Museum**. This tells of the town's connections with the sea over the years, from its fishing fleet (which went as far as the Arctic in search of fish) to its whaling fleet (in its day, the second largest in Britain) and finally to the modern offshore gas and oil industries. The building was shaped to resemble a "scaffy", a kind of fishing boat once used in the area.

A few miles south of the town, at Cruden Bay, are the ruins of **Slains Castle**, built by the 9th Earl of Errol in 1597 to replace an earlier castle. It has been rebuilt and refurbished several times since then, and the ruins you see now date from the early 19th century. Now there are plans to restore it yet again, this time as holiday flats. It has literary associations of an unusual kind. While staying at the nearby village of Cruden Bay in 1895, Bram Stoker began writing Dracula, and based the vampire's Transylvanian castle on Slains. In an early draft of the novel he even has the Count coming ashore at Slains rather than Whitby.

If you want to explore the area round Slains, great care must be taken, as it sits close to a cliff top above the sea.

THE HIGHLANDS 12

When people talk of Scottish scenery, they inevitably mean the scenery of the Highlands - mountains, deep glens and dark, brooding lochs. And though other areas can also claim their fair share of such features, this is the one that has them in abundance.

Highland Cattle, River Nevis

The Highlands area has no set boundaries, and some places described in earlier chapters, such as Aberdeen and Grampian, Argyllshire and parts of Perthshire, can lay claim to being in the Highlands as well. But the area described in this chapter has the same boundaries as the local government area, and can legitimately be called the true heart of the Highlands. It stretches from the northernmost coast of the mainland down to Perthshire, and from the borders of Aberdeenshire and Moray to the rugged west coast, to taking in one or two of the Inner Hebridean islands on the way.

It is mostly wild country, with fewer roads than other parts of Scotland. Some areas are totally inaccessible unless you go by foot over difficult terrain, and if you do decide to take to the hills or moors, remember that Highland weather can be unpredictable, even in the height of summer. Take the correct clothing, and always tell someone about your intended route and your estimated times of arrival at various stages.

The capital of the Highlands is Inverness. It is a thriving city with an enviable quality of life, and its environs are reckoned to be the most rapidly growing areas in Britain, if not Europe. Seen from the A9 as you head over the Kessock Bridge, it has all the appearance of a large metropolis, with suburbs that sprawl along the Moray and Beauly Firths. But in fact its population is no more than 50,000, though this is almost growing daily, with plans just announced for the building of a huge new suburb to the west of the city. And some of the countryside surrounding it looks more like the Lowlands than the Highlands, though this notion is soon dispelled if you head southwest along the A82 towards Loch Ness.

Within the Highlands you'll find Scotland's most famous features. Ben Nevis, Scotland's highest mountain, is here, as is Loch Morar, the country's deepest loch. Loch Ness, undoubtedly the most famous stretch of water in Europe, is a few miles from Inverness, and the last full battle on British soil was fought at Culloden. Here too is Glencoe, scene of the famous massacre, as well as John O' Groats, Aviemore, Skye, Fort William, Cape Wrath and Plockton, the setting for the books and TV series *Hamish Macbeth*.

LOCATOR MAP

ADVERTISERS AND PLACES OF INTEREST

The west coast is rugged, with sea lochs that penetrate deep into the mountains. Settlements are few and far between, and most of them are to be found on the coast. Some visitors to the west coast of the Highlands are amazed at the sub-tropical plants, such as palm trees, that seem to thrive here. It's all down to the Gulf Stream, which warms the shores and makes sure that snow is not as common as you would imagine.

The east coast, from Nairn to Inverness then north to John O' Groats, is gentler, with many more settlements. Dornoch, though small, has a medieval

▲ See other chapters

cathedral, so is more of a city than a town, and at Fortrose there are the remains of another cathedral. Strathpeffer was once a thriving spa town, with regular trains connecting it to Edinburgh and London.

And between the east and west coasts are the mountains, the lochs, the tumbling streams and the deep glens. The scenery can be austere and gaunt, but never anything less than beautiful. No Gulf Stream here, and in some sheltered corners, snow lies well into the year. Glencoe/Nevis and Aviemore take advantage of this by being skiing centres, though of late snow has been in short supply.

In Caithness and Sutherland - Scotland's two northernmost counties - you'll find the Flow Country, mile upon mile of low peaks, high moorland and small lochans. This is not the dramatic scenery of the West Highlands where mountain seems to pile on mountain, but it has a ruggedness and grandeur of its own.

The Highlands is an area that takes the breath away at every turn. There are areas that are all mountains, lochs and glens, and there are areas that are as intensely cultivated as the Lowlands. There are lonely places, where another human being is likely to be miles away, and there are crowded holiday towns such as Fort William and crowded cities such as Inverness, which have a cosmopolitan air. All these qualities ensure that the Highlands is one of the most rewarding places in Britain to visit.

FORT WILLIAM

The small town of Fort William lies at the western end of Glen Mor (meaning "the Great Glen"), in an area known as Lochaber. Though it is small, in the summer months it can paradoxically get crowded with visitors all seeking the genuine, uncrowded Highlands. It is the northern "terminus" of the 95-mile long West Highland Way, which snakes through Western Scotland from Milngavie on the outskirts of Glasgow. The fort referred to in the town's name was built by General Monk in the 1650s, then rebuilt during the reign of William III to house a garrison of 600 troops to keep the Highland clans in order, and renamed Maryburgh, after William's queen. Only parts of the wall survive, as the rest was dismantled in the 19th century to make way for the West Highland Railway.

Ben Nevis

It was from Fort William that thousands of Scots sailed for the New World during that time known as the Clearances. In the early 19th century, landowners could squeeze more profit from their estates if it had sheep on it instead of people, so Highlanders were evicted from their cottages and small parcels of land. Some settled on the coast, and some emigrated.

It was the coming of the railway in 1866 that established Fort William as one of the Highland's main centres for tourism, and it has remained so to this day. A few miles east of the town is **Ben Nevis**, at 4,406 feet, Britain's highest mountain. The five-mile climb to the top, along a well-trodden path, is fairly easy if you're reasonably fit. It can also get crowded at times. The summit is reached by way of **Glen Nevis**, often called Scotland's most beautiful glen,

though there are other contenders for the title. If you do decide to climb Ben Nevis, let people know, and dress appropriately. While it may be warm and sunny at sea level, the weather on the mountain's slopes can be changeable. The rewards of the climb are immense. The Cairngorms can be seen, as can the Cuillin range on Skye and the peaks of Argyllshire. On an exceptionally clear day even the coast of Northern Ireland can be glimpsed through binoculars. At the **Glen Nevis Visitors Centre** there are exhibits about local heritage and wildlife, and, importantly, information about the weather on the mountain.

Aonach Beag (4,058 feet) and **Aonach Mor** (3,999 feet) are Ben Nevis's little brothers, lying just over a mile to the east. In the winter this is a skiing area, but it is equally popular in the summer. Britain's only mountain gondola takes you half way up the range to a restaurant and bar, and there are several walks to enjoy when you reach them.

Within the town, in Cameron Square, is the **West Highland Museum**, with exhibits and displays about the area. The most famous exhibit is the 18th century "Secret Portrait of Prince Charles Edward Stuart". It is a meaningless swirl of colours which, when reflected onto a polished cylinder, gives a likeness of the Prince. There are also some pieces of eight brought up from the Spanish galleon which sank in Tobermory Bay (see also Tobermory). On the A830 at Corpach, northwest of the town, is the award-winning **Treasures of the Earth**, one of Europe's finest collections of crystals and gemstones.

Fort William

The **Underwater Centre**, on the banks of Loch Linnhe, was opened in 2003, and cost £2.3m. It features marine life (including over 42 species of fish) and

TORLINNHE

Achintore Road, Fort William Inverness-shire PH33 6RW
Tel: 01397 702583

If it's a great bed and breakfast establishment close to Fort William you are looking for, then the three-star **Torlinnhe** fits the bill admirabl.! It has been owned and run by Tina and John Morrison for the last 15 years, and during that time they have had many satisfied customers - some of who come back again and again. The modern, detached house sits on an elevated site overlooking Loch Linnhe, on the Achintore Road (the main A82) a mile south of Fort William, with lovely views out over the loch towards the hills of Sunart.

Tina and John are proud of the high standards they have set here. The place is clean, attractive, and is well furnished and decorated throughout. There are six guest bedrooms in all - two doubles, two twins, a family room and a single. All are spacious and well maintained, and you are sure to get a great sleep here. All are fully en suite, and come with colour TV and tea/coffee making facilities as standard. There is plenty of parking space, and the mature, well-tended garden has seating where guests can relax on warm evenings and enjoy the magnificent Highland scenery. For breakfast, you can choose from a hearty Scottish, which is always filling, or a lighter option. Whatever you choose, you can be sure that the produce is sourced locally, and is as fresh as possible. Torlinnhe makes the ideal base from which to explore the Fort William area. There is just so much to see and do - climbing, walking, sailing, golf, fishing and a host of other activities. Plus there are plenty of historical sites for you to visit, and lots of majestic, Highland scenery to take your breath away.

diving shows in a large aquarium. You can even take dives yourself and get guided tours round the adjacent diver training centre.

The impressive ruins of 13th century **Inverlochy Castle** (Historic Scotland) sit one-and-a-half miles north east of Fort William. It was built by the Comyn family in the 13th century on the site of an even earlier fort, though the ruins you see now date from much later. It was here that Montrose had an important victory over the Campbells, who were Covenanters, in 1645.

Not far away, on the A82, is the 174-year-old **Ben Nevis Distillery and Whisky Centre**, which has conducted tours. One of its products is a blend of whiskies called The Dew of Ben Nevis.

Fort William is the northern terminus of the West Highland Way, a long distance footpath that starts at Milngavie just outside Glasgow. It is also the western terminus for the **Great Glen Way**, which opened in 2002. It is another long distance footpath that follows the Great Glen and Loch Ness, ending at Inverness, 73 miles away.

Fort William is also where the **Caledonian Canal** begins (see also Inverness). It is not one uninterrupted canal, but a series of canals connecting Loch Lochy, Loch Oich and Loch Ness (see Drumnadrochit for details of Loch Ness). **Neptune's Staircase** at Banavie,

Donald Cameron Statue, Fort William

near Fort William, was designed and built by Thomas Telford in the early 1800s, and takes the canal through a series of eight locks while raising it over 60 feet.

In the summer months, the **Jacobite Steam Train** travels the famous Fort William to Mallaig line. It passes along the northern shores of Loch Eil - a continuation of Loch Linnhe after it turns westward - on a 45-mile journey that has some of the most beautiful scenery in Britain.

Spean Bridge sits eight miles north east of Fort William. It was around here that commandos trained during World War II, and they are remembered by the **Commando Memorial**. It was designed by the sculptor Scott Sutherland, and depicts three commando soldiers. It was unveiled by the late Queen Mother (at that time consort of King George) in 1952 (see also Achnacarry). **The Spean Bridge Mill**, which is nearby, has demonstrations of tartan weaving as well as a clan tartan centre. At Roy Bridge was fought the **Battle of Mulroy** in 1688 between the MacDonnells and the Macintoshes, with the MacDonnells being the victors. It was the last great inter-clan battle fought in the Highlands, and the last one on British soil where

bows and arrows were used. A cairn marks the spot. The **Parallel Roads** in Glen Roy are a series of liens running parallel to each other on glen hillside. They mark the shorelines of a great loch that once filled the glen thousands of years ago, and which drained away when a great dam of ice at the beginning of the glen melted after the last Ice Age.

AROUND FORT WILLIAM

ACHNACARRY
9 miles NE of Fort William on a minor road off the B8005

Since 1665 **Achnacarry Castle** had been the home of Cameron of Locheil, known as "Gentle Locheil", one of Charles Edward Stuart's most ardent supporters. After 1745 it was burned down by Hanoverian troops. Locheil's family was banished from the country, but they

Laggan Locks, Caledonian Canal

were allowed to return in 1784, when they built a new home nearby. In 1942 the Cameron chief had to leave his home once again, when it was taken over by the British army as a training centre for commandos (see also Fort William).

A 17th century croft house close to where Achnacarry once stood now houses the **Clan Cameron Museum**, which has displays, charts and exhibits relating to the history of the clan and to the commandos who trained here during the Second World War. A minor road takes you past the museum and along the lovely banks of **Loch Arkaig**, finally petering out near its western end.

Laggan

19 miles NE of Fort William on the A82

Laggan sits between Loch Lochy and Loch Oich, two of the lochs that make up the Caledonian Canal. It was here, in 1544, that the **Battle of the Shirts** took place, fought between Clan Fraser and the combined forces of Clan Ranald and Cameron. It was fought on a hot summer's day, and the clansmen removed their plaids and fought in their shirts. There were many casualties, including the chief of Clan Fraser and his son.

Fort Augustus

28 miles NE of Fort William on the A82

Fort Augustus Abbey, on the shores of Loch Ness, was founded for Benedictine monks. It was established in 1876 on the site of a fort (named after George II's son, the Duke of Cumberland) built on the orders of General Wade between 1729 and 1742 to keep Jacobite sympathisers in check. However, this it failed to do, and was actually taken by the Jacobite army in

Fort Augustus

ICEBERG

Glass Blowing Studio, Main Road, Fort Augustus,
Inverness-shire PH33 4BD
Tel/Fax: 01456 450601 website: www.iceberg-glass.co.uk

For the perfect gift or souvenir of your visit to Scotland, head to the **Iceberg Studio** in Fort Augustus, where craftsman Dougie Wilson and his staff use their skills in glass blowing to create wonderful jewellery, hanging decorations, pendants and a variety of other items in glass. Dougie has been glass blowing since 1976 and has since built up a range of superb designs that show off both his skills and the overall beauty of glass as a medium for creating beautiful and intricate objects. Using what is called "borosilicate glass", which is strong, resistant to thermal shock, and comes in a range of beautiful colours, Dougie crafts each item, some in a single colour and some with bubbles of air or coloured inks trapped within them.

Dougie's jewellery is especially popular, and have sterling silver findings. The teardrop design comes in two sizes and many colours, and are smart and sophisticated. Also popular are the "Nessie" designs which, as the name implies, are based on the Loch Ness Monster. Spirals and dolphins also feature in the range of pendants Dougie produces and there is also a range of birthstone pendants, based on Celtic symbols.

The hanging decorations are clear glass which can be used as Christmas decorations, or to just hang anywhere in the house. The showroom also features glassware from other Scottish craft workers, and some exceptional imported glass.

1745. The abbey eventually closed in 1998, due to a decline in the number of monks. Many of the valuable books and manuscripts that were in the abbey library are now owned by the National Library of Scotland

The **Caledonian Canal Heritage Centre** is located in a converted lock keeper's cottage near the locks that take boats into Loch Ness, and explains the history and uses of the canal.

The **Highland and Rare Breeds Croft** is on Auchterawe Road, and you can see Highland cattle, red deer and rare breeds of sheep, and at the **Clansman Centre**, housed in an old school, there are presentations on ancient Highland life.

KINLOCHLEVEN

10 miles SE of Fort William on the B863

This little town sits at the head of Loch Leven, and is on the West Highland Way.

It was developed as an industrial village in the early 20th century when the North British Aluminium Company built the Blackwater reservoir and a hydro electric scheme to power an aluminium smelter which was the largest in the world at the time. Before that, it had been two small villages called Kinlochmore and Killochbeag. The **Aluminium Story Visitor Centre** on Linnhe Road at the library tells the story of the smelting works right up until the year 2000. Outside the centre is a giant sundial designed by blacksmith Robert Hutcheson that takes its inspiration from the area's history and scenery.

The **Ice Factor** on Leven Road is Britain's premier indoor mountaineering centre, and features the world's largest indoor ice climbing wall as well as Britain's largest articulated rock climbing wall. There is also a children's activity zone, audiovisual lecture theatre, steam room, plunge pool and hot tub and a cafeteria and restaurant.

BALLACHULISH
10 miles S of Fort William on the A82

The area surrounding Ballachulish ("settlement near the narrows") was once famous for its slate quarries. There are actually two villages separated by the waters of Loch Leven - North Ballachulish and Ballachulish itself, and they were once connected by ferry, which stopped running in 1975 when a bridge was built.

Ballachulish straggles along the southern shore of Loch Leven. To the west of the village a cairn marks the spot where Jacobite sympathiser **James of the Glen** was hanged for a crime he did not commit. He was found guilty of the murder of **Colin Campbell**, known as the "Red Fox", a government agent, by a Campbell judge and jury. Robert Louis Stevenson used the incident in his book *Kidnapped*. Another cairn marks the site of the murder.

To the east of Ballachulish, on the A82, is one of the most evocative places in Scotland - **Glencoe**. It was here, in 1691,

that the infamous Massacre of Glencoe took place. Because of bad weather, McIan of Clan MacDonald had failed to take the oath of allegiance to William III before the deadline, and a party of Campbell troops were sent to Glencoe to massacre his people. They pretended at first to come in peace, and were offered hospitality. But in the early hours of February 13th they set about systematically killing McIan's people - men, women and children - with few escaping. A monument in the shape of a tall Celtic cross commemorates the event.

Glencoe, further east than the village, is a wild, beautiful place, though it does get crowded in summer months with hikers and climbers. On the north side is **Aonach Eagach**, a long ridge, and on the south side three peaks of Beinn Fhada, Gearr Aonach and Aonach Dhu, known as the **Three Sisters**. About 14,000 acres within Glencoe are now owned by the National Trust for Scotland, and it has set up the **Glencoe Visitor Centre**, which tells the story of the massacre. In Glencoe village itself is the **Glencoe and North Lorn Folk Museum**, which has exhibits about the history of the area and its people.

About nine miles east of Glencoe, on a minor road off the A82, is the Glencoe skiing area with a chair lift that is open in the summer months, and gives wonderful views over Glencoe and Rannoch Moor.

ARDNAMURCHAN
30 miles W of Fort William

The B8007 leaves the A861 at **Salen** (where a small inlet of Loch Sunart is usually crowded with picturesque yachts) and takes you westwards onto the

Glencoe

Ardnamurchan Peninsula. It is single track all the way, so great care should be taken. It heads for Ardnamurchan Point and its lighthouse, the most westerly point of the British mainland, and in doing so passes some wonderful scenery.

At Glenborrodale you can glimpse the late Victorian **Glenborrodale Castle**, the home from 1933 to 1949 of Jesse Boot, founder of the chain of chemists. The castle was built in the early 20th century by C.D. Rudd, who made his fortune in South Africa. The red sandstone was quarried at Annan on the Solway firth and brought to Ardnamurchan by boat.

At Kilchoan there are the ruins of **Mingary Castle**, a stronghold of Clan MacIan before passing to the Campbells. It was visited by James IV in 1493 on one of his expeditions to subdue the Western Isles. It was briefly used in the 2002 movie *Highlander: Endgame*. Kilchoan is Britain's most westerly mainland village,

and up until 1900, when the B8007 was constructed, it was also Britain's most inaccessible, as it could only be reached by boat. Nowadays, in summer, a ferry connects it to Tobermory on Mull.

A few miles North of Salen, on the edge of the area known as Moidart, are the ruins of **Castle Tioram** (pronounced "Chirrum"). The castle sits on a small island and was originally built in the 14th century by Lady Anne MacRuari, whose son Ranald gave his name to Clan Ranald. It was burnt by the Jacobites in 1715 to prevent it being used by Hanovarian forces, and has been a ruin ever since.

At the head of Loch Moidart is a line of five beech trees. Originally there were seven, and were known as the **Seven Men of Moidart**. They commemorate the seven men who landed with Charles Edward Stuart and sailed with him up Loch Shiel, and were originally planted in the early 19th century (see Glenfinnan).

STRONTIAN

20 miles SW of Fort William on the A861

Strontian (pronounced "Stron - teeh - an", and meaning "point of the fairies") sits in an area known as Sunart, which lies to the south of Loch Shiel. The village gave its name to the metal strontium, which was discovered in 1791 in the local lead mines by a chemist called Adair Crawford. A few years later Sir Humphrey Davie gave it its name.

To the north of the village are the **Ariundle Oakwoods**, a national nature reserve.

Strontian

MORVERN

24 miles SW of Fort William

Glenfinnan Monument

Morvern is that area of the mainland that sits immediately north of the island of Mull. The A884 leaves the A861 east of Strontian and travels down through it as far as Lochaline, on the Sound of Mull the restored **Kinlochaline Castle** sits at the head of Loch Aline, and was once the ancestral home of Clan MacInnes. The clan takes a special pride in being one of the few clans in Scotland without a chief. The last one, and all his family, was butchered by John, Lord of the Isles, in 1354 at **Ardtornish Castle**, the ruins of which can still be seen a few miles from Lochaline.

The narrow B849 from Lochaline (with passing places) follows the shores of the Sound of Mull as far as Drimmin, and makes a wonderful drive.

SALEN

27 miles W of Fort William on the A861

Salen sits on the shores of Loch Sunart. There miles east (not accessible by road) is **Claish Moss**, a good example of a Scottish raised bog. Water is held in the peat, and the landscape is dotted with lochans. The peat has preserved seeds and pollen for thousands of years, so it is of interest to biologists researching the flora of the Western Highlands.

GLENFINNAN

13 miles W of Fort William on the A830

It was here, at the northern tip of **Loch Shiel**, Scotland's fourth longest freshwater loch, that Charles Edward Stuart raised his standard in 1745, watched by 1,200 Highland followers, after having been rowed a short distance up the loch from the house of MacDonald of Glenaladale on the western shores. The **Charles Edward Stuart Monument** (National Trust for Scotland) was erected in 1815 by Alexander MacDonald of Glenaladale to commemorate the event, and a small visitors centre nearby tells the story.

The **Glenfinnan Station Museum**, which lies on the Fort William - Mallaig line, and tells of the building of the line by Robert McAlpine (known as "Concrete Bob") in the late 19th and early 20th centuries. The museum's restaurant and tearoom is a restored 1950s railway carriage.

ROSHVEN CHALETS

Lochailort, Inverness-shire PH38 4NB
Tel/Fax: 01687 470221
website: www.roshven.com

Think of soaring mountains. Think of dark, brooding glens. Think of deep lochs, fiery sunsets and the romance of the highlands. The area around Lochailort has them in abundance. The village sits at the head of Loch Ailort itself, on the edge of that area known as Moidart, which has so many connections with Bonnie Prince Charlie and the Jacobites,

It is here that you will find the **Roshven Chalets**, built on Roshven Farm, and offering superior self-catering accommodation. It is a quiet location, just right for a peaceful, get away from it all holiday where you can recharge your batteries. There are five comfortable chalets, and all are just a field away from the waters of the loch, which are safe

for bathing and boats. They are of A-frame construction, with a double bedroom and twin bedroom. The lounge/dining/kitchen area is open plan, with a well appointed kitchen that has electric hob, oven, microwave, fridge and built in washer-dryer. All pots and pans, cutlery and crockery is provided. There are electric blankets on the beds, and all linen, towels and duvets are supplied. Central heating comes as standard, and the chalet is newly carpeted throughout.

ARISAIG

29 miles W of Fort William on the A830

The tiny village of Arisaig has wonderful views across to the islands of Rum and Eigg. Southeast of the village is **Loch nan Uamh**, where, on July 25th 1745, Charles Edward Stuart first set foot on the Scottish mainland. After his campaign to restore the Stuart dynasty failed, he left for France from the same shore. A cairn now marks the spot. The **Land, Sea and Islands Centre** in a derelict smithy in the village has exhibits and displays about the history and wildlife of the area.

MALLAIG

31 miles NW of Fort William on the A830

Mallaig, Britain's most westerly mainland port, is a busy fishing port and the

Mallaig Harbour

terminal of a ferry connecting the mainland to Armadale on Skye. It is also the end of the "Road to the Isles" and the western terminus for the Jacobite Steam Train (see Fort William). The **Mallaig Heritage Centre** on Station Road has displays and exhibits that tell the story of the districts of Morar, Knoydart and Arisaig. The **Mallaig Marine World Aquarium and Fishing Exhibition** sits beside the harbour, and tells the story of Mallaig's fishing industry and the marine life found in the waters of Western Scotland. Most of the live exhibits were caught by local fishermen.

Southeast of the town is water of another sort - **Loch Morar**, which is Britain's deepest fresh water loch. It plunges to a depth of 1,077 feet, and if you were to stand the Eiffel Tower on the bottom, its top would still be 90 feet below the surface. A minor road near

Morar village, south of Mallaig, takes you to its shores. Like Loch Ness, it has a monster, nicknamed Morag, which, judging by people who have claimed to see it, looks remarkably like Nessie.

KYLE OF LOCHALSH
40 miles NW of Fort William on the A87

Kyle of Lochalsh was once the mainland terminus of a ferry that made a short crossing across Loch Alsh to Skye. Now the graceful Skye Bridge has superseded it (for Skye see the Inner Hebrides chapter). Three miles east of the village on the A87 is the **Balmacara Estate and Lochalsh Woodland Garden** at Lochalsh House, with sheltered walks beside the shores of Loch Alsh, as well as mature woodlands and a variety of shrubs, such as rhododendrons, bamboo, ferns, fuchsias and hydrangeas. There is a small visitors centre at the square in Balmacara, just off the A87. Also centred on Kyle of

Kyle of Lochalsh

island as a hermit. He was killed during a Viking raid on the island of Eigg in 617. Parts of the castle date back to 1220, when it was built by Alexander II and given to an ancestor of the Mackenzies who fought beside him at the Battle of Largs. It is now the ancestral home of Clan MacRae, and has a small clan museum. It has also featured in many films, most notably *The World is Not Enough* and *Highlander*.

If you continue eastwards along the A87 you will eventually arrive at **Shiel Bridge**, at the head of Loch Duich. To the southeast is Glen Shiel, where five peaks, called the **Five Sisters of Kintail** (National Trust for Scotland) overlook the picturesque glen. Close by is the site of the **Battle of Glen Shiel**, fought in 1719 between a Hanovarian Army and a force of

Lochalsh is **Seaprobe Atlantis**, a glass-bottomed boat that takes you out into the Marine Special Area of Conservation and shows you the rich diversity of marine life in the waters surrounding Scotland.

Six miles east of the village is one of the most photographed castles in Scotland, **Eilean Donan Castle**, which sits on a small island connected to the mainland by a bridge. It's name ("Donan's Island") comes from the legend that St Donan lived lived on the

Eilean Donan Castle

THE PLOCKTON HOTEL

Harbour Street, Plockton, Ross-shire IV52 8TN
Tel: 01599 544274 Fax: 01599 544475
e-mail: info@plocktonhotel.co.uk
website: www.plocktonhotel.co.uk

Right in the heart of Hamish Macbeth country you'll find the **Plockton Hotel**, surrounded on all sides by the glorious and magnificent scenery of Western Scotland. This is the perfect base if you plan a holiday here, where sea meets land and where high mountains overlook lochs and brooding glens. But be prepared also for palm trees, for Plockton enjoys the warmth of the Gulf Stream.

In a changing world, some things remain the same, and one of them is good, traditional Scottish hospitality. You'll find it here, at the Plockton Hotel. All the bedrooms are extremely comfortable, and have en suite facilities. Many look out over Loch Carron to the hills beyond, and bring a feeling of relaxation and "getting away from it all". There are also two family suites and a cosy cottage. You'll be pampered here, as the hotel believes in high standards of service as well as value for money. The

dining room and hotel bar serves wonderful food, including local seafood caught in the clear, cold waters off Western Scotland. Plus there are succulent Highland steaks, local lamb, venison and game, washed down with a wine from the hotel's extensive cellar.

The bar serves a wide range of drinks, including, of course, single malts, and it makes the perfect place to unwind. It is a favourite with the locals, and you can join in the friendly banter and enjoy a joke or two.

ASGARD CRAFTS

The Smithy Heritage Centre, Strathcarron, Ross-shire IV54 8YS
Tel: 01520 722722
website: www.asgardcrafts.uklinex.net

Asgard Crafts specialises in wonderful reproductions of ancient Viking artefacts. Owned and managed by Catriona and Jim Glazzard, the goods are historically accurate, being manufactured using tools and techniques researched from archaeological evidence. Jim has a degree in archaeology, and is a Viking specialist, so all the objects manufactured by him are completely authentic and in keeping with Viking craftsmanship. So much so that some of the artefacts made by him are on display at the Jorvik Viking Centre in York. Jim has been making Viking objects since 2000, and now he has opened up a shop and workshop, not only to sell what he makes, but to spread a greater understanding of Viking culture and life, which has been such a strong influence on Scotland.

The shop is a pleasant, timber built building (designed to be in keeping with Viking architecture)

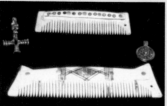

situated within the Smithy Heritage Centre, which is dedicated to local history. Here you can see some exquisite objects, from combs made of antler to Viking jewellery.

Behind the shop is the workshop, where the objects are made. Here Jim can demonstrate the many skills used by the Vikings in the making of such objects, and can tell you something of the Vikings and their culture. It's a fascinating place, and is sure to be one of the highlights of your visit to the area.

Jacobites (which included 300 Spaniards). It was the last battle fought on British soil between British and foreign soldiers, and it had no clear victor. There is a **Countryside Centre** (National Trust for Scotland) at Morvich Farm, off the A87, and it makes a good starting point for walking on some of the surrounding hills and mountains.

Northeast of Kyle of Lochalsh is the conservation village of **Plockton**, with its palm trees and idyllic location. This was the Lochdubh of *Hamish Macbeth* fame, as it was here that the TV series was filmed. It sits on Loch Carron, and on the opposite bank, opposite Strome Ferry and a few miles inland off a minor road, are the ruins of **Strome Castle** (National Trust for Scotland). It was built in the 15th century, and was a stronghold of the MacDonalds, Lords of the Isles. On **Craig Highland Farm**, near

STRATHCARRON HOTEL

Strathcarron, Wester Ross IV54 8YR
Tel: 01520 722227 Fax: 01520 722990

At the head of beautiful Loch Carron you will find the Strathcarron Hotel, owned and managed by Julie Wilkinson and her partner Martin. It boasts eight comfortable rooms, all of which are fully en suite, with tea and coffee making facilities and colour TVs. The spacious restaurant has seating for 34, and only fresh local produce is used wherever possible in the dishes. This, coupled with the wine list, ensures that every meal is a gastronomic experience. The bar area is comfortable, informal and cosy, with real ales available plus, of course, a fine selection of single malts. It is a favourite with visitors and tourists alike, and live music is sometimes featured.

CARRON POTTERY, CRAFT SHOP & ART GALLERY

Cam-Allt, Strathcarron, Ross-shire IV54 8YX
Tel:01520 722321
e-mail: robteague@ukonline.co.uk
website: www.carronpottery.co.uk

For that perfect gift or souvenir when visiting beautiful Strathcarron in Ross-shire, why not visit the **Carron Pottery Craft Shop & Art Gallery**? Situated on the shores of Loch Carron, it is a working pottery that specialises in hand thrown table wear and commissioned pieces. The craft shop also sells a wide range of Scottish crafts, including woodwork, jewellery, silver, ceramics and knitwear. Upstairs is a gallery where you can see and buy Scottish paintings in a wide mix of styles and media. There's something for everyone at the Carron Pottery, Craft Shop and Art Gallery.

CARRON RESTAURANT

Cam-Allt, Strathcarron, Ross-shire IV54 8YX
Tel:01520 722488
e-mail: carronrestaurant@supanet.com
website: www.carronrestaurant.co.uk

The family-run Carron Restaurant enjoys great views over Loch Carron, and specialises in home-cooked food such as tasty soups, bread and a very special sweet trolley. All the produce used in the kitchen is fresh, with vegetables being grown locally, so you know you will not only be getting high quality food, but great value for money as well. The speciality is steak cooked the way you like it. Of course, fresh seafood is also available in this non smoking establishment.

ROCKVILLA HOTEL

Lochcarron, Ross-shire IV54 8YB
Tel: 01520 722379 Fax: 01520 722844
website: www.rockvilla-hotel.co.uk

There is nothing like the beautiful scenery and the wide open spaces of the western Highlands of Scotland for a holiday that can be as invigorating or as relaxing as you want. In the small, picturesque village of Lochcarron, on the shores of Loch Carron itself, is the three-star **Rockvilla Hotel**, surely one of the best family-run hotels in the area. It is the ideal base from which to explore the area, with Skye, Plockton, Eileen Donan castle and so many other attractions only a short car journey away. Even Inverness and Fort William is within striking distance. But if you don't want to go that far, there is always the history and heritage of the area to explore, as well as the many opportunities for walking, climbing, fishing, golf, water sports and observing wildlife that the area affords, including dolphins, porpoise and golden eagles to name but a few.

The hotel is owned and personally managed by Wendy and Peter Bartlett, who recently took over, and have lots of plans to improve the place even further. The bedrooms - the restaurant - the bar - all will be refurbished to a much higher standard, and will reflect Wendy and Peter's commitment to quality and great value for money.

All the rooms have en suite facilities or private bathrooms and showers, as well as TV sets and tea/coffee making facilities. Most enjoy sea views out over the loch, and all are decorated to a high standard - a standard that will soon be surpassed as refurbishment work gets under way. One of the rooms is a family room, with sofa-bed, so will sleep two children and two adults. And in the lounge bar, which is cosy and welcoming, you can relax over a drink as you contemplate your next trip to explore an aspect of the area. There is a fine selection of malt whiskies, as well as real ales, wines, spirits and liqueurs. The bar is popular with both visitors and locals (always a good sign), so you'll get plenty of opportunity to mingle and enjoy the craich.

Both Wendy and Peter come from a catering background, so food is important to them. This is reflected in the hotel's restaurant, which is Taste of Scotland recommended. Local, fresh produce is used wherever possible, whether it be Aberdeen Angus beef, local lamb and pork, venison, game and seafood. In fact, most of the seafood comes from the cold, clear waters around the west of Scotland. Dietary needs are also catered for.

Being parents themselves, Wendy and Peter welcome children to the hotel, and there is plenty of parking space.

Inverness

the village, you can view rare breeds, as well as feed the farmyard animals

Kyle of Lochalsh is the western terminus for the famous Dingwall - Kyle of Lochalsh railway line (see Dingwall).

INVERNESS

Inverness is the capital of the Highlands. It is said to be the most rapidly expanding city in Britain, if not Europe, and though it only has a population of about 50,000, its hinterland supports a further 20,000. But for all its size, it still has all the feel and bustle of a much larger place, and its shopping - especially in the pedestrianised High Street, where the Eastgate Shopping Centre is located - is superb.

The city sits at the northeast end of the Great Glen, at a point where the River Ness enters the Moray Firth. It was once the capital of the Northern Picts, and it was to Inverness that St Columba came in the 6th century to confront King Brude MacMaelcon and convert him and his kingdom to Christianity. The doors of Brude's fort were firmly closed, but Columba marked them with the sign of the cross and they flew open of their own accord.

No one knows where this stronghold stood, though some people have suggested **Craig Phadraig**, a hill that overlooks the town, and on which there are the remains of a Pictish fort, and others have suggested Torvean.

The present **Inverness Castle** dates from 1835, and houses the local courthouse. Castles have stood on the site since at least the 12th century. However, Macbeth's castle, where Shakespeare set the murder of Duncan, stood some distance away, where people have claimed to have seen the ghost of Duncan in full kingly attire close to the River Ness. General Wade enlarged Inverness Castle after the uprising of

Inverness Castle

1715, and its garrison surrendered to Charles Edward Stuart when he occupied the town in 1745. He then ordered the castle to be blown up. Close to the present castle is a statue of **Flora MacDonald**, who helped Charles Edward Stuart evade capture.

Near the castle, in Bridge Street, is the **Town House**, which was completed in 1882. It was in the council chamber here, in 1921, that the only cabinet meeting ever held outside London took place when Lloyd George, the Prime Minister, wanted to discuss the worsening Ireland situation. Across from it is the **Tolbooth Steeple**, dating from the late 18th century. It was once part of a complex of buildings that contained a courthouse and jail. In Castle Wynd, in a modern building, is **Inverness Museum and Art Gallery**, which has a large collection relating to the history of the Highlands and the town in particular. Within the library, behind the bus station, is the **Highland Archives and Genealogy Centre**, where you can research your forebears.

The oldest secular building in the city is **Abertarff House** in Church Street (National Trust for Scotland), which dates from 1593. It was built as a town house for the Frasers of Lovat, and is now the local headquarters for the National Trust for Scotland. **Dunbar's Hospital** is also on Church Street, and dates from 1668. It was founded by Provost Alexander Dunbar as a hospital for the poor. It has now been divided into flats.

Balnain House (National Trust for Scotland), on Huntly Street on the opposite bank of the River Ness, was built in 1726 and for a time was a music heritage centre. Also on the opposite bank is **Inverness Cathedral,** dedicated to St Andrew, a gem of a building designed by Alexander Ross and consecrated in 1874. It was supposed to have had two large spires, but these were never built. The Eden Court Theatre, next to the cathedral, incorporates parts of the old Bishop's Palace.

The Old High Church in Church Street, dedicated to St Mary, is Inverness's parish church and was built in 1770, though parts of the tower may date from medieval times. After the battle of Culloden, the church was used as a jail for Jacobite soldiers, some of whom were executed in the kirkyard. It is said to be built on a site where St Columba once preached. The **Old Gaelic Church** was originally built in 1649, though the present building dates from a rebuilding of 1792.

Inverness is one of the few Scottish towns to have retained its traditional market, and the indoor **Victorian Market** in the Academy Street building dates from 1890, when it was rebuilt after a disastrous fire.

The magnificent **Kessock Bridge**, opened in 1982, carries the A9 over the narrows between the Moray and Beauly

TRAFFORD BANK GUEST HOUSE

96 Fairfield Road, Inverness IV3 5LL
Tel: 01463 241414
e-mail: info@traffordbankguesthouse.co.uk
website: www.traffordbankguesthouse.co.uk

Lorraine Freel and Koshal Pun welcome you to the **Trafford Bank Guest House**, where unrivalled comfort and hospitality meet high standards and a commitment to excellence. It has been awarded the much coveted five red diamond award from the AA. The interior is sumptuous yet informal, with an elegant mix of antiques and modern furniture, some of it designed by Lorraine herself,

who is an accomplished interior designer. The house is full of original paintings by Scottish artists Dorothy Stirling, Jonathon Shearer, Michael Ross and Katty McMurray from Brighton.

The guest house is non-smoking, and has two fabulous lounges. It boasts two exquisite suites with 32 inch wall hung flat screen digital TV's and silent fridges. There are an additional three stunning rooms all with TVs, DVD and CD players, hospitality trays, hairdryers and a host of other features that make all the rooms a bit special.

The Floral Suite boasts a six foot wrought iron tester bed and is a favourite with honeymoon couples. The Trafford Suite is the largest room and is ideal for families, as is the smaller Green room. The Blue Room with views to Inverness Castle contains a 6 foot double bed that can be split into single

beds. Finally the Tartan room has a 5 foot double bed and a stunning bathroom with a Victorian style rolled top bath. All the rooms are ensuite and Arran aromatic products and Skye soap are provided in all rooms so you can luxuriate in the bathtubs and let your cares slip away! A breakfast of your choice is served on Anta pottery in the unusual conservatory overlooking the stunning gardens. All the produce used in the kitchen being fresh and local. Trafford Bank is ideal for business and tourists alike. Wireless Internet connection is available throughout the house via your own laptop

Firths and connects Inverness to the Black Isle. At North Kessock is the **Dolphins and Seals of the Moray Firth Visitor and Research Centre**. The Moray Firth is famous for its bottlenose dolphins, and boats leave from many small ports so that you can observe them. This visitor centre gives you one of the best opportunities in Europe to learn about the creatures, and to listen to them through underwater microphones.

A few miles west of the town at Kirkhill is the **Highland Wineries**, based around Moniack Castle, an old Fraser stronghold dating from 1580. There are country wines, liqueurs, preserves and sauces.

AROUND INVERNESS

CROMARTY
16 miles NE of Inverness on the A832

This picturesque small royal burgh, which received its charter in the 13th century, sits on a small headland near the mouth of the Cromarty Firth. It is

Gaelic Church, Cromarty

probably the best-preserved 18th century town in Scotland, and was where many Highlanders embarked for Canada during the clearances of the early 19th century.

It was the birthplace, in 1802, of Hugh Miller, writer and the father of geology. **Hugh Miller's Cottage** (National Trust for Scotland), where he was born, is open to the public. It has a collection of fossils and rock specimens, as well as some of his personal possessions such as his geological hammer and microscope.

The **Cromarty Courthouse Museum**, as its name suggests, is housed within the old courthouse. There is a reconstruction of an 18th century trial in the courtroom itself, plus you can see the old cells, children's costumes, a video presentation giving 800 years of Cromarty history and an audio tape tour of the old part of the town.

The Cromarty Firth has always been a safe anchorage for British ships. On 30th December 1915 *H.M.S. Natal* mysteriously blew up here, with the loss of 421 lives. Many of those killed lie in the kirkyard of the **Gaelic Chapel**.

Ross and Cromarty was one of the counties of Scotland lost in the local government reforms of 1975. Originally it was two counties, amalgamated in 1889.

FORTROSE
8 miles NE of Inverness on the A832

Fortrose Cathedral (Historic Scotland) was founded by David I as the mother church of the diocese of Ross. Building began in the 1200s, though the scant remains you see nowadays date from the 14th century. One of the three fine canopied tombs is of Euphemia Ross, wife of the Wolf of Badenoch (see also Dunkeld, Grantown-on-Spey and

Elgin). The other two are of bishops, possibly Robert Cairncross and John Fraser.

Nearby **Chanonry Point** is one of the best places to observe the Moray Firth dolphins. Here, where the Firth is at its narrowest, you can sometimes see up to 40 of these graceful creatures glide through the waters or put on a fine display of jumping and diving. It was at Chanonry Point that Kenneth Mackenzie, better known as the **Brahan Seer**, was executed in 1660 (see also Strathpeffer). He had the gift of second sight, and when he was asked by the 3rd Countess of Seaforth why her husband was late returning home from Paris, he said that he was with a lady. She was so enraged that she had Kenneth executed. A cairn marks the spot.

In nearby **Rosemarkie** is the **Groam House Museum**, with exhibits and displays that explain the culture of the Picts, those mysterious people who inhabited this part of Scotland in the Dark Ages. The cathedral for the diocese of Ross was established here before moving to Fortrose, the site now being occupied by the parish church of 1819.

TAIN
23 miles N of Inverness on the A9

In medieval times, Tain was a great Christian centre, drawing pilgrims from all over Europe to the shrine of St Duthus within **St Duthus Collegiate Church**. Now an exhibition and visitors centre called **Tain Through Time** explains about St Duthus himself, the pilgrimage, and the people who made it. The museum, which is part of the centre, also has displays about Clan Ross. A church near the mouth of the river and now in ruins was built, it is said, on the site of St Duthac's birthplace.

Tain Tolbooth was built in 1707, replacing an earlier building. Half a mile north of the town is the **Glenmorangie Distillery**, which has guided tours and a museum, with a tasting at the end of the tour.

DORNOCH
30 miles N of Inverness on the A949

Dornoch Cathedral dates originally from the early 13th century. However, the church as we see it today is largely a rebuilding of the early 19th century, though there are some old features still to be seen, mostly in the chancel and crossing. Sixteen Earls of Sutherland are said to be buried within it. It was also where, in December 2000, the son of pop star Madonna and her husband Guy Ritchie was baptised. **Dornoch Castle** sits opposite the cathedral, and was built in the 15th century with later additions. It is now an hotel.

TARBAT DISCOVERY CENTRE

Tarbatness Road, Portmahomack, Tain, Ross-shire IV20 1YA
Tel: 01862 871351   Fax: 01862 871361
e-mail: info@tarbat-discovery.co.uk   website: www.tarbat-discovery.co.uk

Tarbat Discovery Centre, housed in a beautifully restored 18th century church, is a major attraction in the Highlands of Scotland. Archaeology has revealed the first Pictish monastery from the early days of Scotland's conversion to Christianity in the 6th - 9th centuries AD and the finds from the important excavations are exhibited here. Visitors can discover the workings of the archaeologists and the unfolding story of the Picts. Some wonderful carved Pictish sculpture is displayed and a gallery is devoted to Tarbat through the centuries. A gift shop offers a unique range of souvenirs.

Dornoch was the scene, in 1727 (though the stone says 1722), of Scotland's last execution for witchcraft, when an old woman called Janet Horne was burned for supposedly turning her daughter into a pony. The judge at the trial was later reprimanded for his handling of the case. The **Witch's Stone**, within a garden in Littletown, marks the spot where Janet was executed.

BRORA

45 miles NE of Inverness on the A9

Brora is a picturesque coastal village at the mouth of the River Brora. The **Brora Heritage Centre** on Coal pit Road has a hands-on guide to the history and wildlife of the area. At one time it was the location of the Highland's only coal mine, with the coal being shipped out from the local harbour until the railways took over. The **Clynelish Distillery** has a visitors centre and shop.

GOLSPIE

40 miles NE of Inverness on the A9

A steep hill path takes you to the summit of **Ben Bhraggie**, on which there is a statute by Chantry of the first Duke of Sutherland, who died in 1833. Locally, it is known as the "Mannie", and was erected in 1834 by "a mourning and grateful tenantry to a judicious, kind and liberal landlord". The words ring hollow, however, as the Duke, owner of the biggest private estate in Europe at the time, was one of the instigators of the hated Clearances of the early 19th century, and there have been continued calls to have the statue removed, and in some cases blown up. Others have argued that the statue should stay as a reminder of those terrible times.

Dunrobin Castle, the seat of the

Dunrobin Castle

Dukes of Sutherland, is the most northerly of Scotland's stately homes and one of the largest in the Highlands. Though the core is 14th century, it resembles a huge French chateau, thanks to a remodelling in 1840 by Sir Charles Barry, designer of the Houses of Parliament. Some of the castle's 189 rooms are open to the public, and there is a museum in the summerhouse.

North of Golspie, on the road to Brora, is **Carn Liath** ("the Grey Cairn"). It overlooks the sea, and is all that is left of a once mighty broch. The walls are still 12 feet high in places.

LAIRG

40 miles N of Inverness on the A836

Lairg is an old village that sits at the southeastern tip of **Loch Shin**, which, since the 1950s, has been harnessed for hydroelectricity. The loch, which is famous for its fishing, is over 18 miles long by no more than a mile at its widest, with the A838 following its northern shoreline for part of the way. Due to the hydro electric scheme, it is 30 feet deeper than it used to be.

The village became important because it sits at the meeting point of various Highland roads that head off in all directions. Five miles south are the picturesque **Falls of Shin**, which has a visitor centre and a Harrod's shop. **Ord Hill**, west of the town, has an archaeological trail, which takes you round a landscape rich in ancient sites. **Ferrycroft Countryside Centre** explains land use in this part of Sutherland since the end of the last Ice Age.

Fort George

10 miles NE of Inverness on the B9006

Fort George (Historic Scotland) was designed by the Major General William Skinner, the King's Military Engineer for North Britain (the name given to Scotland after the Jacobite Uprising). He originally wanted to build it at Inverness,

but the councillors of the town objected, saying it would take away part of the harbour. The fort was named after George II, and sits on a headland that guards the inner waters of the Moray Firth near Ardersier. Work started on building it in 1748 as a direct result of the Jacobite Uprising of 1745, and it was subsequently manned by government troops. It covers 42 acres, has walls a mile long, and the whole thing cost over £1bn to build at today's prices. It has been called the finest 18th century fortification in Europe, and has survived almost intact from that time. The **Queen's Own Highlanders Museum** is within the fort.

Nairn

16 miles NE of Inverness on the A96

Nairn is a small, picturesque holiday and golfing resort on the Moray Firth. Local

---

Milton Bank Cottages

St Callan Old Manse, Rogart, Sutherland IV28 3XE
Tel/Fax: 01408 641313
e-mail: info@miltonbankcottages.co.uk
website: www.miltonbankcottages.co.uk

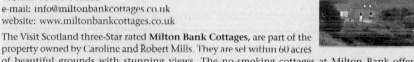

The Visit Scotland three-Star rated **Milton Bank Cottages**, are part of the property owned by Caroline and Robert Mills. They are set within 60 acres of beautiful grounds with stunning views. The no-smoking cottages at Milton Bank offer the opportunity to enjoy many activities, such as walking, golfing, fishing on river, loch and sea, cycling, and horse riding. In addition there is plenty of scope for studying wildlife such as seals and dolphins a few miles away on the Sutherland shores and watching the many birds that live in the area. Glebe Cottage sits in its own garden, and has three twin bedrooms, two bathrooms, a snug sitting room and a well equipped kitchen with dishwasher. Milton Bank Stable has a twin room facing west, and has a cosy sitting room, terrace, kitchen and shower room/toilet. Milton bank Cottage is an attractively restored two-storey cottage sitting in its own garden which has beautiful views in all directions. It has a sitting room, study, well-equipped farm-style kitchen, utility room with freezer, two twin bedded rooms and large bathroom with double-ended bath and hot tank airing cupboard. Unfortunately, only Milton Bank Stable offers wheelchair access.

In addition, Caroline offers B&B accommodation within St Callans Manse. It is comfortable and spacious, with a beautifully cooked full Scottish breakfast or a lighter option if required. Caroline is a cordon bleu cook, and offers, for an extra charge, a relaxed supper in the evening. She specialises in regional and international cuisine. Caroline and Robert can arrange informal "away day" tours, guided or otherwise, as well as extended and escorted trips. Children and well mannered dogs are most welcome.

people there will tell you that the name is a shortened version of "nae rain" ("no rain"), and indeed this area is one of the driest in Britain. It has a fine, clean beach and a large caravan park. The River Nairn, which flows through the town, is supposed to mark the boundary between the English speaking areas to the east and the Gaelic speaking areas to the west. A great royal castle stood here, built by William the Lion in 1179, but it is long gone. The **Nairn Museum** on Viewfield Drive has collections on local history, archaeology and wildlife. There is also the **Fishertown Museum**, in the heart of the fisher town area. As its name implies, this is where the fishermen that manned the town's former fishing fleet lived. There are displays and artefacts highlighting the industry.

At Auldearn, two miles east of the town (now bypassed), is the **Boath Doocot** (National Trust for Scotland),

which sits within what was a small medieval castle built in the late 12th century by William the Lion. The **Battle of Auldearn** was fought here in 1645 between 1500 Royalist troops of the Marquis of Montrose and a 4,000-strong Covenanting army under Sir John Hurry. The Covenanters, even though they outnumbered the Royalist troops, were routed, and some of the dead were buried in the kirkyard of **Auldearn Parish Church**, built in 1757.

Eight miles south of the town, at Ferness, is the **Ardclach Bell Tower**, dating from 1655. It sits above the parish church.

CAWDOR
12 miles NE of Inverness on the A96

Cawdor Castle was made famous by Shakespeare in his play *Macbeth*, though the core of the present castle was built in the 14th century by the then Thane of

GREENLAWNS

13 Seafield Street, Nairn IV12 4HG
Tel:01667 452738
e-mail: greenlawns@cali.co.uk
website: www.greenlawns.uk.com

Greenlawns is an elegant Victorian house, lovingly restored to its original splendour with seven en-suite rooms all comfortably decorated and furnished to a high standard. Three rooms are on the ground floor, and have been awarded category three disabled status. Some rooms have a bath and a shower, others have shower only. All have colour TV, tea/coffee making facilities and some rooms have safes, hair dryers and DVD players.

There is an attractive, spacious dining room and residents' lounge with a small private bar and real fire - just the place to relax after exploring the lovely seaside town of Nairn, with its historical associations and clean beach. The city of Inverness is half an hour away, as is the small city of Elgin, with the ruins of a medieval cathedral. Cawdor Castle - featured in Shakespeare's Macbeth - is only

four miles away, and is open to the public from May until the end of September from 10am-5.30pm. There are also many golf courses in the area and opportunities for fishing and other sports

Greenlawns is owned and personally run by Sheelagh and Dave Southwell, who take a great pride in the high standards they have set. They like to use fresh, local produce wherever possible in the kitchen for both breakfasts and dinners, and people return here year after year. Sheelagh's passion is genealogy, and a wide range of books and magazines is always available on the subject.

Cawdor, who was sheriff and hereditary constable of the royal castle at Nairn. He built the core - essentially the central tower - round a thorn tree which can still be seen today. The story goes that the thane loaded a donkey with gold, and let it wander round the district. The thane vowed to built the castle where it finally rested. This it did beside a thorn tree, which was incorporated into the building. Recent carbon dating suggests the tree was planted in about 1372. With its fairy tale looks and its turrets, it is said to be one of the most romantic castles in Scotland.

CULLODEN
5 miles E of Inverness on the B9006

The Battle of Culloden was fought in 1746, and was the last major battle to take place on British soil. The hopes of the Jacobites to return a Stuart king to the British throne were dashed on that cold, April day, and the clan system was smashed forever. The battlefield is on Drumossie Moor, which, in the 18th century, was a lonely, wild place.

Now it has been drained and cultivated, though the battlefield itself has been returned to the way it was. There is still a sadness about the place, and it was once said that no birds ever sang here. That's not quite true, but no one who visits can fail to be moved. You can still see the stones that mark the graves of various clans, and there is a huge memorial cairn at the centre of the battlefield. **Leanach Cottage**, which survived the battle, has been restored, and the **Culloden Visitors Centre** (National Trust for Scotland) has displays and exhibits which explain the battle. The **Cumberland Stone** is where the 25-year-old Duke of Cumberland, third son of George II and commander of the Royalist troops, watched the battle. He earned the nickname "Butcher Cumberland" for his unspeakable acts of cruelty after the battle.

Not far from the battlefield are the **Clava Cairns** (Historic Scotland), a fascinating group of three burial cairns of the early Bronze Age.

TOMATIN
13 miles SE of Inverness off the A9

Tomatin sits on the River Findhorn, just off the A9. The **Tomatin Distillery**, north of the village, is one of the highest in Scotland, and was founded in 1897. Now owned by a Japanese company, it has 23 stills, and draws its water from the Alt-na-Frithe burn. It has tours, a visitor centre and tastings.

Cawdor Castle

NETHY BRIDGE

24 miles SE of Inverness on the B970

Dell Wood National Nature Reserve is in Abernethy Forest. It is famous for its rare bog woodland, which has largely disappeared from the area because of drainage and agricultural improvements.

GRANTOWN-ON-SPEY

26 miles SE of Inverness off the A939

This beautiful and elegant tourist centre is situated in the heart of Strathspey (never, ever the "Spey Valley"), and sits at a height of 700 feet above sea level. It was built by James Grant of Grantcastle in the late 18th century and laid out in a grid plan. The **Inverallan Parish Church** in Mossie Road was completed in 1856, and commemorates the 7th and 8th Earls of Seaforth.

The 15,000-acre **Revack Country Estate** is to the south of the town, on the B970 to Nethy Bridge. It has gardens, woodland trails and an adventure playground. Revack Lodge was built as a shooting lodge in 1860.

Six miles north west of the town are the ruins of **Lochindorb Castle**, built on an island in Lochindorb, on bleak Dava Moor. This was the home of the infamous Alexander Stewart, son of Robert II, and known as the Wolf of Badenoch.

CARRBRIDGE

21 miles SE of Inverness on the A938

The arch of the original packhorse bridge still stands, and dates from 1717, when it was built by Brigadier-General Sir Alexander Grant of Grant. It also carried funeral processions to Duthil Church, and for this reason was given the

---

CAIRNGORM MOUNTAIN RAILWAY

Aviemore, Inverness-shire PH22 1RB
Tel: 01479 861261 Fax: 01479 861207
website: www.cairngormmountain.com

Almost 2km long, CairnGorm's funicular railway is the highest railway in the United Kingdom and takes you up the slopes of CairnGorm, the UK's fifth highest mountain at 1245metres and one of Scotland's most extreme arctic wilderness environments, valued for its landscape and rare habitats. Travelling up the wind scoured slopes gives a close up view of the northern Cairngorms, created and moulded by over 400 million years of geological drama while, rising above, CairnGorm itself provides a majestic backdrop. Down in the valley below, in Glen More, the panorama is no less dramatic with the ancient Caledonian pine forest and Loch Mortich creating a gentler landscape setting. The CairnGorm Mountain Experience provides an unrivalled opportunity for visitors of all ages and physical ability to relax and enjoy one of Britain's most spectacular mountain areas in safety and comfort.

Nestled just below the summit of CairnGorm the brand new Ptarmigan Station offers spectacular views and is home to the Mountain Exhibition.The story of how the mountains have evolved and how wildlife has adapted to survive in such extreme conditions, climate change, folklore and the human impact on the mountain landscape are all explored. Visitors who want to explore the mountain on foot are encouraged to make use of two, specially created, clearly marked footpaths within the ski area boundary. Both paths start from the railway Base Station. Along each route you'll find information points highlighting topics of interest.

The highest shop in the land features an interesting range of gifts to buy and the highest restaurant, with its viewing terrace, offers a menu of wholesome traditional local ingredients. The railway and restaurant are available for private functions - phone for details.

nickname of the "Coffin Bridge".

South of the village is the **Landmark Forest Heritage Park**. It is carved out of woodland, and has such attractions as a Red Squirrel Trail, Microworld (where you can explore the world of tiny insects) and the Tree Top Trail, where you take a walk through the high branches of the trees. The Timber Tower gives amazing views over the surrounding countryside. At Dulnain Bridge, six miles east of the village on the A95 is the **Speyside Heather Centre**, with over 300 species of a plant that has become synonymous with Scotland.

Glenmore Forest Park, Cairngorms

AVIEMORE

24 miles SE of Inverness off the A9

Once a quiet Inverness-shire village, Aviemore has now expanded into one of the main winter sports centres in the Highlands. The skiing area and chair lifts lie about seven miles east of the village, high in the Cairngorms. This is also the starting point of **Cairngorm Mountain Railway** (see panel opposite), which carries passengers all year round to the Ptarmigan Station, within 400 feet of the summit of the 4,084 feet high Cairngorm

itself. On the road to the skiing area is the **Cairngorm Reindeer Centre**, where Britain's only permanent herd of reindeer can be seen.

The **Rothiemurchus Highland Estate** is a magnificent area with spectacular views, deep forests and woodland trails. You can try hill walking and mountain biking, and there are guided walks and safari tours in Land Rovers. The estate contains some of the last remnants of the great, natural **Caledonian Pine Forest**, which once covered all of the

---

STRATHSPEY MOUNTAIN LODGES

Mains of Garten Farmhouse, Boat of Garten,
Inverness-shire PH24 3BY
Tel: 01479 831551 Fax: 01479 831445
website: www.strrathspeymountainlodges.co.uk

Mains of Garten Farm sits in beautiful Strathspey, and has five high quality lodges for discerning holidaymakers who want a quiet, country-based holiday. The lodges are double-glazed, and built to a high standard, with three bedrooms, spacious lounge with dinette, a well-appointed kitchen, colour TV and a patio with views over the River Spey. Pets are welcome by prior arrangement, and there is parking space beside each lodge. Angling is available on the Spey, and close by there is golf, pony trekking, canoeing and sailing.

Aviemore - Boat of Garten

Distance:	5.6 miles (9.0 kilometres)
Typical time:	150 mins
Height gain:	100 metres
Map:	Explorer 403
Walk:	www.walkingworld.com ID:1009
Contributor:	D B Grant

Access Information:

1. If using two cars you can park at Boat of Garten station or, to shorten the walk, at Waymark 9.
2. In Aviemore parking can be difficult in the holiday season, so no set car park is given here. If you intend to use the railway you might want to park somewhere near the station. You then must walk north on the A95(T) (the main street in the village). Keep to the right-hand pavement and you will come to the start of the walk path at the "end of 30mph limit" sign, at the end of the village (0.75mile from the station).

Description:

On the map this looks like a boring straight line; but in fact nowhere is it straight for more than 100 metres. Part of the Speyside Way, it has been well planned and laid out. It's wide and well surfaced (but good shoes, or boots, recommended). It's full of variety and offers good views to the northern Cairngorms. The walk is 5.5 miles from one railway station to the other, to take advantage of a return journey on the steam train; it can be shortened to four miles if you use two cars. Food, drink etc are available in the two villages and there is a licensed diner on the train (timetables available at the Tourist Information Centre, any hotel, guesthouse etc).

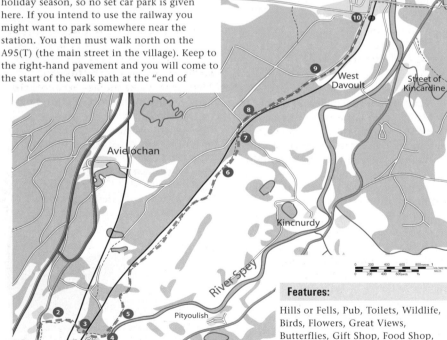

Features:

Hills or Fells, Pub, Toilets, Wildlife, Birds, Flowers, Great Views, Butterflies, Gift Shop, Food Shop, Good for Kids, Moor, Mostly Flat, Public Transport, Restaurant, Tea Shop, Woodland

Walk Directions:

1 The path starts, on the northern edge of Aviemore, at the "30mph"sign. After following the A95(T) for a short distance the track turns right , to reach double gates.

2 Through the gates, to go under the Perth—Inverness railway. Under the railway, across three wooden bridges, to go under the Strathspey Railway.

3 After going under the Strathspey Railway you soon come to a fork. Here keep left, soon to reach another fork.

4 At this fork keep left and go on, through open birch woods and old Scots pines. Where you emerge from the woodland there is another fork.

5 Keep left here, on open moorland. Continue, alternating between open woodland and moor, with views behind to the Cairngorms.

6 Continue on to reach a gate.

7 Immediately through the gate turn left on to a farm road (waymarked Speyside Way). The route soon goes under the Speyside Railway again, and a few metres on there is a junction.

8 Straight on here.You soon pass a cottage which used to have a garden display of large models, now sadly gone. Stay on this farm road; it becomes tarred on the outskirts of Boat of Garten.

9 Here, where the road becomes tarred, is where you can park your car if not using the train. Continue into Boat of Garten; on reaching the main road turn right for a few metres to arrive at the station.

10 Railway station and parking.

Highlands. Parts of *Monarch of the Glen* are filmed here (see also Kingussie). Details of all the activities are available from the Visitor Centre on the B970 south east of the village.

Aviemore is one of the termini of the **Strathspey Steam Railway**, which runs to **Boat of Garten**, five miles away. It was once part of the Aviemore to Forres line, which was closed, in the early 1960s.

KINGUSSIE

28 miles S of Inverness off the A9

Kingussie (pronounced "King - yoosy") sits in Strathspey, with good views of the Cairngorms to the east, while to the west lie the **Monadhliath Mountains**, rising to over 3,000 feet. In Duke Street sits the **Highland Folk Museum**, which gives an insight into the history and lifestyle of the ordinary people of the Highlands over the years. There is a reconstruction of a Black House (a Highland cottage) and a smoke house.

At **Newtonmore**, four miles south of the village, is another **Highland Folk Museum**, where there is a reconstruction of an 18th century Highland township. Also in the village is the **Clan MacPherson House and Museum**, which, as its name implies, recounts the history of the MacPhersons. The whole museum covers 79 acres.

The ruins of **Ruthven Barracks** (Historic Scotland) lie to the west of

Ruthven Barracks

EAGLE VIEW GUEST HOUSE

Perth Road, Newtonmore,
Inverness-shire PH20 1AP
Tel: 01540 673675
e-mail: john@eagleviewguesthouse.co.uk
website: www.eagleviewguesthouse.co.uk

Newtonmore is a bustling Highland village set in Strathspey, within the beautiful Cairngorm National Park, Britain's largest. It's here that you will find **Eagle View Guest House**, a new venture which opened in the year 2005. It offers the very best in hospitality, and is at the southern end of the village, set within half an acre of grounds that have been extensively restored by the owners, Moira and John Hewer. Guests are free to explore the gardens and sit outside in warm summer evenings.

The house itself is a warm, Victorian stone building, and it too has been extensively renovated.

The interior has been designed with the emphasis on comfort. The guest lounge has a wood burning fire, and has soft leather couches where you can contemplate your next trip out into the beautiful Highlands of Scotland. There is no TV, but a large library of books is on hand so that you can relax completely away from the cares of modern life.

There are three fully en suite guest rooms available, two doubles and a twin. The en suite facilities are sumptuous and well-appointed, with thermostatically-controlled, pressurised, non-electric showers within double-sized cubicles that give that authentic "power shower" feel. The floors and walls are fully tiled for cleanliness, and all the fittings and brasswares have a Victorian theme. In addition there is a family room and a single room with a shared bathroom. There is a flat-screen TV in each room, and these will be upgraded to digital when the area is covered, plus tea/coffee making facilities and hair dryers. The bed linen is cool yet comfortable Egyptian cotton throughout, with the doubles having wooden sleigh beds. The large driveway can accommodate up to 11 vehicles, with plenty of space for manoeuvring and turning. The breakfasts are outstanding, using only fresh local produce. You can choose from a hearty full Scottish to something a bit lighter.

Moira is a qualified driving instructor, and runs her own school. She offers residential driving courses in this beautiful part of Scotland, using Eagle View as a base, and if you are interested in this, she can supply all the details.

Newtonmore lies just off the A9, and has many amenities. It makes the perfect base from which to explore Strathspey and the Cairngorms, and it is an ideal stopping off place as you travel north or south between central Scotland and Inverness or, indeed, the Western Highlands and Skye. *Monarch of the Glen* country is also close by, as is the Speyside Whisky Trail and the skiing at the Cairngorms near Aviemore. So call in on the village, and spend some time at Eagle View!

HIGHLAND WILDLIFE PARK

Kincraig, Kingussie, Inverness-shire PH21 1NL
Tel: 01540 651270
website: www.highlandwildlifepark.org

Discover the amazing variety of wildlife found in present day
Scotland. Then step back in time and meet the creatures that roamed
the earth hundreds, even thousands of years ago - the animals of
your ancestors. Get closer than you ever thought possible as past
meets present in the spectacular setting of the **Highland Wildlife
Park**. Be amazed as you enter the world of the 'big bad wolf' which has long been part of myth,
fairytale and legend. Find out the truth about these fascinating creatures when you visit the exciting
Wolf Territory, where a raised walkway takes you right into the heart of the enclosure. Marvel at the
large reserve from the new viewpoint shelter and see herds of beautiful red deer and magnificent
Highland cattle, as well as species now extinct in the wild - enormous bison, ancient breeds of sheep
and the wild Pzrewalski's horses.

You can explore the rest of the Park on foot and wander around the themed habitats of the
capercaillie, polecat, otter, owl, red fox and many more. To make your day complete there is a coffee
shop, gift shop, children's trail and play area, free guidebooks and binocular hire. The Park opens
daily from 10am (weather permitting in winter) and closes at 4pm November to March.

Kingussie, on the other side of the A9.
They were built in 1719 on the site of a
Stewart castle dating from the 14th
century to house government troops

when Jacobite sympathies were strong in
the area. Charles Edward Stuart's army
captured them in 1746 and burnt them.
After the Jacobite defeat at Culloden,

NEWTONMORE CRAFT CENTRE

Main street, Newtonmore, Inverness-shire PH20 1DA
Tel: 01540 673026
website: www.highland-crafts-co.uk

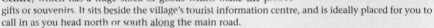

Newtonmore is a small, picturesque village situated just off the A9
Glasgow to Inverness road. It is home to the **Newtonmore Craft
Centre**, which has a huge stock of goods which make the perfect
gifts or souvenirs. It sits beside the village's tourist information centre, and is ideally placed for you to
call in as you head north or south along the main road.

There are small leather goods such as purses, wallets and handbags, as well as a great range of
knitwear with imaginative designs. There are bird and animal sculptures by such companies as Small
World and Wildtrack, or how about sheepskin rugs, mitts and slippers? Genuine Shetland hats, gloves
and scarves? Candlelights, mugs, porcelain by Highbank and Fear an Eich? You'll find them all here,
and a whole lot more besides.

There is wonderful jewellery in Celtic and Mackintosh designs, bookmarks, postcards, fudge and
tablet (a tasty Scottish sweet), tee-shirts, pens, thimbles, stickers, tea towels, oven gloves, stampers
and stamp pads, tot glasses, crystal, cross stitch and tapestry kits and much more. The Centre even has

its own resident artist, and many of his paintings and limited edition
prints are for sale. Everything in the Newtonmore Craft Centre is
realistically priced, and members of the knowledgeable, friendly staff
are always on hand to offer information and advice.

Come in and look around and while you're visiting, why not enjoy
a full lunch or a cup of coffee at the Garden Café, which forms part of
the centre? It is open from early morning to 5.30pm Monday to
Saturday.

CRAIGERNE HOUSE HOTEL

Golf Course Road, Newtonmore, Inverness-shire PH20 1AT
Tel/Fax: 01540 673281
e-mail: craigerne.hotel@virgin.net
website: www.craigernehotel.com

Situated close to the heart of the village of Newtonmore, the
Craigerne Hotel is a delightful, family-owned hotel with an
informal, friendly atmosphere and a reputation for great value
for money. The first tee of the Newtonmore Golf Club course is
only 20 yards from the hotel, so it makes an ideal base for golfing
parties. It is also ideally placed to explore Speyside, the Cairngorm and Monadhliath Mountains,
Aviemore, Inverness and *Monarch of the Glen* country.

The hotel has twelve spacious and comfortable bedrooms, including twins, doubles, singles and a
family room. Most are fully en-suite, and the furniture and decoration are of the highest order. One
room boasts a four-poster bed and most have lovely views of Speyside and the surrounding hills.

The Hotel's Restaurant serves superb food prepared from local
fresh produce when ever possible. It is spacious yet cosy and serves
a four course, table d'hote menu in the evening with a wine list
containing a good selection of modestly priced wines. After dinner,
why not enjoy a relaxing drink in one of the hotel's lounges? There
is a wide selection of single malt whiskies, as well as beer from the
local Cairngorm Brewery in Aviemore. Full Scottish breakfasts are
served each morning in the separate breakfast room, lighter options
are also available.

over 3,000 Jacobite troops mustered here
to continue the fight. However, Charles
Edward Stuart saw that further fighting
was useless, and sent a message saying
that each man should return home. Four
miles north of Kingussie is the **Highland
Wildlife Park** (see panel on page 447),
which has an array of Scottish wildlife,
plus some animals that used to roam the
Highlands but have now died out.

A few miles south west of Kingussie,
along the A86, is **Loch Laggan**, where
the BBC series *Monarch of the Glen* was
filmed. The Adverikie Estate, with its
large house, played the part of Glenbogle
(see also Aviemore).

DRUMNADROCHIT
16 miles SW of Inverness on the A82

Drumnadrochit sits on the shores of **Loch
Ness**, at Drumnadrochit Bay. It is a quaint
place, though it can get overcrowded in
the summer, due tourists flocking here to

catch a glimpse of the Loch Ness Monster,
nicknamed "Nessie". Whether a monster
actually exists or not has never been
proved, but that has never detered the
crowds. The loch measures just less than

Drumnadrochit

Loch Ness

- though in this case it was in the River Ness and not in the loch - occurs in Adamnan's *Life of St Columba*, written in the 7th century. In the year AD 565 St Columba was heading up the Great Glen towards Inverness, when he encountered a monster attacking a man in the River Ness at the point where it enters the loch. He drove it back by prayer, and the man's companions fell on their knees and were converted to Christianity.

Nowadays the monster is a bit more timid. Most sightings have been made at **Urquhart Castle** (Historic Scotland), about a mile from Drumnadrochit, and curiously enough, this is where the loch is at its deepest at 754 feet. The castle is one of the largest in Scotland, and sits on a

23 miles long by a mile wide at its widest, and contains more water than any other loch in Britain.

The first mention we have of a monster

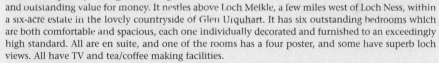

GLENURQUHART HOUSE HOTEL

Balnain, Drumnadrochit, Inverness-shire IV63 6TJ
Tel: 01456 476234
e-mail: carol@glenurquhartlodges.co.uk
website: www.glenurquhart-house-hotel.co.uk

The **Glenurquhart House Hotel** combines the very best of Scottish hospitality with good food, great standards of service, and outstanding value for money. It nestles above Loch Meikle, a few miles west of Loch Ness, within a six-acre estate in the lovely countryside of Glen Urquhart. It has six outstanding bedrooms which are both comfortable and spacious, each one individually decorated and furnished to an exceedingly high standard. All are en suite, and one of the rooms has a four poster, and some have superb loch views. All have TV and tea/coffee making facilities.

Breakfast, lunch and dinner are served in the bright, airy restaurant, which has stunning views out over Loch Meikle. The ambience here is modern yet informal, with stripped pine floors , rugs and huge windows. The menu is wide and varied, with only the freshest and finest of local produce going into the dishes. The restaurant is open to non-residents, and special diets can be catered for by prior notice. Before or after dinner, you can relax in the comfortable lounge bar while enjoying a quiet drink. There is a wide selection of ales, wines and spirits, including single malt whiskies.

The hotel also offer opulent self-catering timber lodges, which, like the hotel itself, give views of the magnificent Glenurquhart Forest. Each one sleeps up to six, and has a double, twin and bunk bedroom (cot available), cosy lounge area with TV, well-equipped kitchen and a bathroom.

promontory that juts out into the water. A fortification has stood here for centuries, but the present ruins date from the 16th century, when the Grants occupied it. Urquhart Castle has nothing to do with Clan Urquhart, whose homeland was on the Black Isle, north of Inverness, though there may have been early links. After the Jacobite Uprising of 1689 the castle was blown up and never rebuilt. A visitor centre contains a model of the castle, which shows what it was like in its heyday.

Two exhibitions vie for attention in the village, the **Loch Ness 2000 Exhibition Centre** and the **Original Loch Ness Exhibition.** They each have displays about the Loch Ness Monster.

BEAULY

7 miles W of Inverness on the A862

Within this picturesque village are the ruins of **Beauly Priory** (Historic Scotland), founded by the Bisset family in 1230 for monks of the Valliscaulian order, though what can be seen nowadays dates from between the 14th and 16th centuries, when the Frasers of Lovat were the dominant family. The north transept, which is more or less complete, is the burial place of the MacKenzies of Kintail.

It is said that the village got its name when Mary Stuart stayed in the priory in 1564 on her way to Dingwall and declared it to be a "beau lieu", or beautiful place. However, it was called Beauly long before she arrived, though the name may indeed come from the Latin for "beautiful place".

The **Beauly Centre**, next to the priory, has displays about the history of the area. There is also a reconstructed village store, a weaving centre and a Clan Fraser exhibition.

To the southwest is **Strathglass**, one of

CULLIGRAN COTTAGES

Glen Strathfarrar, Struy, near Beauly, Inverness-shire IV4 7JX
Tel/Fax: 01463 761285
e-mail: juliet@culligran.demon.co.uk

Culligran Cottages are situated west of Beauly at Struy, where beautiful Glen Strathfarrar strikes off westwards from the equally beautiful Strathglass. The scenery round here is among the most majestic and beautiful in Scotland, and one of the cottages makes the ideal base from which to explore the area. They are owned and managed by Juliet and Frank Spencer-Nairn, and sit snugly amid some stunning scenery protected under a National Nature Reserve agreement close to the waters of the River Farrar and within the Culligran Estate. The accommodation comprises a traditional stone-built cottage and four Norwegian style chalets within a naturally wooded area, and all are comfortable and extremely well appointed. The cottage sleeps up to seven people, and has three double bedrooms, a spacious sitting room, a large kitchen, bathroom and shower room.

The chalets boast an open plan living room with kitchen/dining area, a bathroom and either two

or three bedrooms. A sofa bed in the living area means that they can sleep either five or seven depending on size. All are furnished to an extremely high standard, and all have double glazing, electric heaters, cooker and fridge. Frank offers regular guided tours by Landrover of culligran Deer Farm, where you can watch and even feed the deer. A daily permit allows you to fly fish on the Rivers Farrar and Glass. If you prefer something more energetic, you can hire a Culligran bicycle and explore 15 miles of private roads in the glen. The cottages are open between March and mid-November each year, and are keenly priced.

the most beautiful glens in the area. It was here, in the early 19th century, that the Sobieski Stuarts lived in some style, claiming to be the legitimate grandsons of Charles Edward Stuart. Their claims were believed by many people, notably the Earl of Moray, Lord Lovat and the Earl of Dumfries. There is no doubt, however, that they were charlatans.

The **Wardlaw Mausoleum**, built on to the east end of Kirkhill Parish Church, is one of the burial places of Clan Fraser. It was built in 1634, and in 1998 was restored by Historic Scotland.

DINGWALL
11 miles NW of Inverness on the A862

Dingwall's name derives from the Norse "thing vollr", meaning "the place of the parliament", which shows that even in ancient times it was an important settlement. It is a royal burgh, and received its charter from Alexander II in 1227. Its castle, now long gone, was the birthplace of Macbeth in 1010. Another famous son is **Sir Hector MacDonald**, a crofter's son who was born in 1853 and joined the army as a private, rising through the ranks to become a major general and national hero. He was known as "Fighting Mac", and eventually commanded the British Army in Ceylon. In 1903, on his was back to Ceylon after a trip to London, he committed suicide in Paris after unproved accusations of homosexuality from those who objected to his lowly birth. After his death, his accusers were stunned to discover that he had a secret wife and child. A monument to him, known as the **Mitchell Tower**, stands on a hill to the south of the town on Mitchell Hill.

Within the old Tolbooth of 1730 is the award-winning **Dingwall Museum**, where the town's history is explained by way of displays and exhibits. Dingwall is the eastern terminus for the famous Dingwall - Kyle of Lochalsh railway line, which runs through some of the most beautiful scenery in Scotland as it crosses the country. The **Dingwall Canal** (now closed) is Britain's most northerly canal, and was designed by Thomas Telford in 1817, though by 1890 it had closed. It is just over a mile in length. At the end of the canal is the **Ferry Point**, which has a picnic area.

Eight miles west of the town, off the A835, are the **Rogie Falls** on the Blackwater, reached by a footpath from a car park on the main road. A fish ladder has been built to assist salmon to swim upriver. There are also woodland walks in the surrounding area.

STRATHPEFFER
14 miles NW of Inverness on the A834

At one time, this small village was one of the most famous spa resorts in Britain, and trains used to leave London regularly carrying people who wanted to "take its waters". For

Rogie Falls, near Dingwall

Silverbridge - Little Garve

Distance:	3.2 miles (5.1 kilometres)
Typical time:	90 mins
Height gain:	5 metres
Map:	Explorer 437
Walk:	www.walkingworld.com ID:847
Contributor:	D B Grant

Access Information:

About three miles north of Garve, on the A835, there are two bridges side by side across the River Blackwater. The car park is at the south end of the new bridge.

Description:

The walk begins at the old bridge over the Blackwater. The car park is large (needs to be;

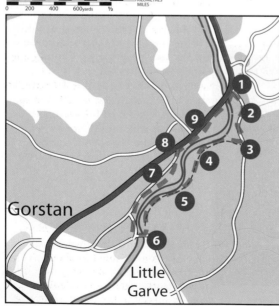

very popular stop), has toilets, and there is a picnic area overlooking the river. Paths are good and there are many view points, swimming pools and picnic sites.

At the Little Garve end you cross a long hump-backed bridge dating from mid-18th century, built as part of a road network designed. to help subdue the clans after the Jacobite rebellion.

If taking photographs and you don't have many exposures left, I suggest you keep the bulk of them for the second half of the walk.

Features:

Hills or Fells, River, Toilets, Wildlife, Flowers, Great Views, Butterflies, Good for Kids, Waterfall, Woodland, Ancient Monument

Walk Directions:

1 Cross the Old Bridge; the walk starts at its northern end. At blue marker post go down steps and take the path; it climbs above the river to join a wider path.

2 Turn right on the new path and after 200m you come to a fork.

3 At this fork go right. You descend to a viewpoint.

4 Viewpoint. Continue on the same path, which gradually descends through open pinewoods to the riverside and a viewpoint overlooking a gorge.

5 Viewpoint at gorge. Continue to hump-backed bridge.

6 The old bridge. On the other side turn right immediately. Don't go up to the wooded car park, where there is a broad landrover track. Stay on the narrower path by the riverside; you'll soon pick up a blue marker post. The path stays close to the river all the way now, with many rocky viewpoints.

7 Viewpoint. Continue...

8 Viewpoint. Continue...

9 Viewpoint. From here you soon reach the New Bridge. Pass under it and climb the steps into the car park.

this reason, it is full of hotels, B&Bs and genteel guesthouses. So fashionable was it that the local paper used to publish a weekly list of the crowned heads and aristocratic families who were "in town".

The spa days are over now, though the **Spa Pump Room** has been refurbished and re-creates the halcyon days of the village when the cream of society flocked here. You can even sample the curative waters yourself. The adjacent Victorian gardens, where Victorian society used to promenade and play croquet, have also been restored.

Ullapool

Within the disused railway station is the **Highland Museum of Childhood**, with photographs, toys, games and videos. The Angela Kellie Doll Collection is particularly fine. On the eastern outskirts of the village is the **Eagle Stone**, with Pictish symbols. Scotland's own Nostradamus, the Brahan Seer (Kenneth Mackenzie, born in the early 17th century) predicted that if the stone fell over three times, the waters of the Cromarty Firth, five miles to the east, would rise so that ships could drop anchor near where the stone stood. The stone has fallen over twice so far, and as some of the Seer's other predictions have come true, it is now embedded in concrete to be on the safe side.

ULLAPOOL

This fishing port and ferry terminal on Loch Broom was founded by the British Fisheries Society in 1788 and laid out in a grid plan to designs by Thomas Telford. By 1792 much of the work on the port buildings and some houses was completed, settlers having been given a plot of land, free stone to build a home, and land for a garden. Over the years the fortunes of the village fluctuated as the fishing industry prospered or went into recession, though it has always managed to survive.

Now the town is a tourist resort, and a centre for hill walking, sightseeing, wildlife study and fishing. It is also the mainland terminus for the Stornoway ferry, and can be a busy place during the summer months. The award-winning **Ullapool Museum and Visitor Centre** is housed in a former church designed by Thomas Telford - one of the so-called "parliamentary churches". In 1773, before the town was established, the very first settlers bound for Nova Scotia left Loch Broom in the *Hector*, and there is a scale model of the ship within the museum.

One of the hidden jewels of the West Highlands are the **Leckmelm Gardens**, three miles south of the town just off the A835. They were planted in about 1870, but by 1985 had become overgrown. In that year work began in re-establishing them and revealing the beauty that had

LECKMELM HOLIDAY COTTAGES

Leckmelm, Loch broom, Ullapool,
Ross-shire IV23 2RN
Tel: 01854 612471
e-mail: lucy@leckmelmholidays.co.uk
website: www.leckmelmholidays.co.uk

Set on the Leckmelm Estate, on the rugged west coast of Ross and Cromarty, are the **Leckmelm Cottages**, a range of self-catering accommodation. They are all beautifully equipped, and represent amazing value for money. Leckmelm House is built of traditional stone, and sits in landscaped grounds, with a paved terrace suitable for outdoor eating in summer. It has two spacious bedrooms, a double and a twin, each with pine furniture and a TV. The drawing room is sumptuous, with its central log burning fire and sofas, stereo and satellite TV. The kitchen comes fully equipped, and has a breakfast bar for quick meals and a dining table that seats up to eight. The adjacent utility room, which houses the boiler, can be used for storage and drying.

The Farm Cottage dates back to 1880, and provides accommodation for six guests. It is located on the Farm, and you may find friendly chickens and sheep visiting from time to time. There are three bedrooms - two doubles and a twin, each one being well furnished and clean. The kitchen comes fully equipped with all the basic equipment, and the bathroom has a bath, Mira shower and WC . The cottage is surrounded by a semi-enclosed garden, and is suitable for children and pets.

Campbeltown Cottages were also built in 1880, and offer warmth and comfort whatever the weather. Each cottage is individually decorated, and in total, can sleep up to 32 people, making them ideal for groups. Downstairs is a sitting room with open fire, TV, armchairs and a dining table and chairs, while upstairs, via the traditional wooden staircase, there are two bedrooms. Nos 2, 5 and 6 there is a double bed within the main bedroom, while the rest have twin beds, the second bedroom is a small bunkroom. The bathrooms have good, old-fashioned type baths, with shower above. The kitchens are well equipped. The three terraced, single-storey Lochside Cottages are situated on the edge of Loch Broom, adjacent to the farm. They were completely rebuilt in 2004, to provide the ultimate in comfort. They each have a secluded entrance, a ramp for those with limited mobility and superb views out over the surrounding countryside and loch. Each has two comfortable and well furnished bedrooms, a double and a twin, apart from no. 2, which has an extra twin room and an en-suite shower in the double room. They all have solid chestnut wooden flooring. The kitchen contains all basic equipment as well as a dishwasher, and there is an open plan kitchen/dining/living area. There is an open fire, sofas, TV and books. The Estate also has a weekly sale of home-produced meat and veg and a pool table for guest's use.

been lost for so long. The area surrounding Ullapool is famous for its golden beaches, the best ones being at **Achnahaird**, **Gruinard Bay** and **Achmelvich**.

AROUND ULLAPOOL

GAIRLOCH
22 miles SW of Ullapool on the A832

This little village, on the shores of Loch Gairloch, has one of the loveliest settings in Scotland. The **Gairloch Heritage Museum**, housed in old farm buildings, has an "illicit" still, village shop, lighthouse interior and other displays that explain how life was lived in northwest Scotland in the past.

A passenger ferry service runs two return crossings daily to Portree on the Isle of Skye.

Gairloch Harbour

Five miles northeast, on the banks of Loch Ewe are the famous **Inverewe Gardens** (National Trust for Scotland -

INVEREWE GARDENS

Poolewe, Ross shire IV22 2LG
Tel: 01445 781200 Fax: 01445 781497
e-mail inverewe@nts.org.uk
website: www.nts.org.uk

The sheer audacity of Osgood Mackenzie's vision in creating
this outstanding 50-acre garden, impressively set on a peninsula

on the shore of Loch Ewe,
is still astonishing today.
The warm currents of the
North Atlantic Drift or
Gulf Stream help nurture
an oasis of colour and
fertility, where exotic plants from many countries flourish on a
latitude more northerly than Moscow's. Himalayan
rhododendrons, Tasmanian eucalyptus, a large collection of New
Zealand plants (including the National Collection of Oleciria),
diverse Chilean and South African introductions combine to give
a colourful display throughout the year. Marked footpaths. Visitor
Centre.

HYDROPONICUM GARDEN OF THE FUTURE

Achiltibuie, Ullapool, Ross-shire IV26 2YG
Tel: 01854 622202 Fax: 01854 622201
e-mail: info@thehydroponicum.com
website: www.thehydroponicum.com

You will be amazed if you visit **The Hydroponicum
Garden of the Future**. Set in the heart of the rugged
west coast of Ross-shire, among some of the best scenery
in Scotland, you'll discover the secrets of growing
plants in pots that don't contain a scrap of soil. They'll show you that, with some crushed up rock, a
trickle of water and a bit of know-how, you can grow absolutely anything. Hydroponics is the science
of growing plants without soil. It's the water that supplies all the nutrients to make the plants grow
and thrive. Each growing house features plants and produce from different climatic zones. There is a
cottage garden full of herbs and salads, an orchard and flower border, a South of France zone growing
tomatoes, citrus fruits and olives, and a Canary Islands zone, full of fat grapes, figs, exotic tamarillos
and even bananas.

Tours round the Hydroponicum are suitable or all ages. Children can join in the Fun Trail, seeking
out gnomes in the cottage garden, butterflies in the South of France or lizards and frogs in the Canary

Islands. A new feature is the Sunshine Room, where there
are hands on exhibits. Find out about the power of the sun
and how nature can harness it to produce energy in a
sustainable way.

And, of course, you can eat in the Lily Pond Café, where,
amid beautiful flowers, you can sample home-made food
at its best, such as delicious salads made from edible flowers
and unusual leaves. During the summer months the evening
menu offers international cuisine using only the finest and
freshest of local produce. It's a great day out for everyone at
the Hydroponicum.

see panel opposite). They have plant collections from all over the world, which thrive in these northern latitudes due to the Gulf Stream. The gardens were founded by Sir Osgood Mackenzie, third son of the Laird of Gareloch. He had bought the Inverewe and Kernsary estate in 1862 and there built Inverewe House and surrounded it with gardens. The most amazing thing about Inverewe is that it is further north than some parts of Greenland, yet still manages to grow some exotic species.

Sixteen miles south east of Gairloch, and beyond beautiful Loch Maree, is the quiet village of **Kinlochewe**. It is in the heart of what is recognised to be some of the finest mountain scenery in Scotland. The **Beinn Eighe Nature Reserve**, Britain's first, has a visitor centre and nature reserve. It sits just west of Kinlochewe, along the A832.

LOCHINVER
17 miles N of Ullapool on the A837

This small fishing port sits on Loch Inver, at the end of the A837. A few miles east is Loch Assynt, on whose shores you will find the ruins of **Ardvreck Castle**, built in the 16th century by the MacLeods of Assynt. It was here, in 1650, that Montrose was kept prisoner before being taken to Edinburgh for execution. The **Assynt Visitor Centre** has small displays and exhibits about local history.

Four miles south east of the village is what has been called "the most beautiful mountain in Scotland" - **Suilven**. At a mere 2,389 feet, it is not even a Munro, nor is it the highest in the area. Seen from Lochinver, it appears to be a solitary mountain that rises sheer on all sides. It's name comes from the Norse, and means the "Mountain Pillar". However, it is the western end of a high ridge, and makes for some superb walking and climbing country.

At Achiltibuie, 10 miles south of Lochinver, and reached by a narrow road, is the **Hydroponicum** (see panel opposite), a "garden" where plants grow without soil. It calls itself the "garden of the future" and kits are available so that you too can start growing plants without soil. It was set up in the mid-1980s to show that some of the problems found in this part of Scotland -- poor soil, a short growing season and high winds - could be overcome. It now provides high quality produce (from lettuces to bananas) for homes and businesses in the area. It also now features renewable sources of energy and green technologies.

DURNESS
50 miles N of Ullapool on the A838

Durness, in Sutherland, is one of the most northerly villages in Scotland, and sits close to **Cape Wrath** - one of only two "capes" in Great Britain, the other being Cape Cornwall. To reach it,

Scourie Bay, Durness

you have to cross the Kyle of Durness from Durness itself on a small ferry and walk or take a minibus to the cape itself, ten miles away. The peculiarly named **Smoo Cave** is in the cliffs a mile-and-a-half west of the village. It consists of three chambers, and goes underneath the coast road. The name may come from the Old Norse smjugga, meaning "rock". A walkway with railings takes you down to the cave, which has had lights fitted.

There are many clean, golden beaches in the area, most of them uncrowded.

The best ones are **Balnakeil**, **Ceann na Beinne**, **Sango Beag** and **Sango Mor**.

The village has associations with John Lennon of the *Beatles*, who used to spend holidays here with his family when he was young. The **John Lennon Memorial Garden** commemorates his stays, and there is a small display of Lennon letters in the village hall.

The **Choraidh Croft Farm Park** is on the shores of Loch Eriboll, off the A838 a few miles south west of Durness.

EDDRACHILLES HOTEL

Badcall Bay, Scourie, Sutherland IV27 4TH
Tel: 01971 502080 Fax: 01971 502477
e-mail: enq@eddrachilles.com
website: www.eddrachilles.com

Escape to the peace and tranquillity of the two-star **Eddrachilles Hotel**, magnificently situated at the island-studded Badcall Bay, two miles south of Scourie. A former 18th century manse, it stands in three acres of garden, and has been completely refurbished while still retaining all of its old world charm and features. It is open from March to October each year, with all bedrooms being fully en suite, and boasting direct dial telephones, radio, TV, coffee/tea making facilities, hair dryer, trouser press and ironing facilities. The hotel is fully licensed, with the spacious and elegant restaurant serving cuisine of the highest quality. Only the freshest of local produce is used in the kitchens - seafood from Kinlochbervie and Lochinver - locally caught prawns, crabs, lobsters and mussels - salmon from Loch Duart - and organic salmon from the Orkneys. The Scottish-reared meat is sourced from the best butcher in the Highlands, and all the puddings, desserts, jams, chutneys and tablet are home-made to give you, the customer, a unique Scottish dining experience.

But for all its high standards of service, the Eddrachilles Hotel is an informal, friendly place where

you can relax and unwind in absolute comfort. The staff are friendly and knowledgeable, and staying here represents amazing value for money. It sits on the rugged west coast of Sutherland, and is the ideal base from which to explore the area. The scenery, as you would imagine, is outstanding (the waterfalls of Eas-coul-aluin, close by, are the highest in Britain ant 658 feet), and there are historic sites aplenty to visit. Plus there is bird watching, nature study, climbing, walking, golf, sailing and a host of other activities you can take part in. Though not a fishing hotel, the Eddrachilles has free access to two local lochs, and membership of the local fishing club, with access to over 30 lochs, can be arranged.

LOCH CROISPOL BOOKSHOP AND RESTAURANT

17c Balnakeil craft Village, Durness, Sutherland IV27 4PT
Tel: 01971 511777
e-mail: lochcroispol@btopenworld.com
website: www.scottish-books.net

The most north-westerly bookshop and restaurant on the British mainland is the **Loch Croisol Bookshop and Restaurant**. Here you will find an amazing range of titles, ranging from fiction, poetry, music, biography, Scottish history, politics and culture, religion, children's books, natural history and the environment, humour, food and drink and a whole lot more. It is owned and managed by Kevin Crowe and Simon Long, and they invite you to visit and browse to your heart's content. The shop is light and airy. Book tokens can be sold or exchanged, and titles not in stock can be ordered quickly and simply, and Kevin offers a search facility for out of print books. There are also regular events at the shop, such as book signings and poetry readings. It can be contacted by post, telephone or email for orders and enquiries, and books can now be purchased online at their redesigned website.

While you're browsing for books, why not treat yourself to a light snack or a coffee, as the Loch Croisal Bookshop is also a restaurant, selling a wide range of lunches, dinners, snacks, high teas and teas/coffees? All the food is freshly prepared to order using local produce wherever possible, and the prices are surprisingly reasonable. It is also tasty and filling, and many people come back again and again, not just for books, but for the excellent food.

WICK

Wick is a an ancient royal burgh on the North Sea coast, and was once the leading herring port in Europe. Up until 1975, it was also the administrative capital of Caithness, Scotland's most northerly mainland county. The name comes from the Old Norse word vik meaning "bay", and this whole area owes more to Norse culture than it does to the culture of the Gaels. **Parliament Square** near the Market place recalls the fact that James V held a parliament at Wick as he made a royal progress through Scotland in 1540.

The award-winning **Wick Heritage Centre** in Bank Row has exhibits and displays about life in Wick and Caithness. In Huddart Street in Pulteneytown on the south bank of the River Wick is the **Pulteney Distillery**, which makes the world-famous "Old Pulteney" single malt whisky. It has a visitor centre and shop, and there is a tour of the distillery plus tastings.

The **Old Parish Kirk**, dedicated to St Fergus, dates from 1830, though a church has stood here since medieval times. In the kirkyard is the **Sinclair Aisle**, burial place of the old Earls of Caithness.

An old story featuring George Sinclair, the 4th Earl, explains just how bloodthirsty times were in the 16th century. He was suspected of murdering the Earl and Countess of Sutherland so that he could marry off his daughter to their heir, and thus claim the Sutherland lands. However, in 1576, the heir left the country, and Sinclair's plans were thwarted. In revenge, he ordered his son John to lay waste to the Sutherland lands, but when he refused Sinclair had him thrown into a dungeon.

With the help of his jailer, John hatched a plot to escape. John's brother William found out about this and told his father, who executed the jailer. When William went down to the dungeon to goad his brother, John killed him with his chains. For this, his father punished him by denying him food for five days, then feeding him salt beef without giving him anything to drink. John died in agony, his tongue swollen through lack of water. His father had him buried in the Sinclair Aisle, and years later, just before he too died, full of remorse for what he had done, he asked that his heart be buried beside his son.

One mile south of the town, on a cliff top, are the ruins of the **Castle of Old Wick** (Historic Scotland), built by Harald Maddadson, Earl of Caithness, in the 12th century. It was later held by Sir Reginald de Cheyne, and then the Sinclairs, Oliphants, Campbells and Dunbars. Care should be taken when exploring the ruins.

On a hill to the south of Wick Bay is a memorial to the engineer **James Bremner**, who was born in Wick and who died in 1856. He collaborated with Brunel, and salvaged the SS Great Britain when it ran aground off Ireland.

North of Wick, the two castles of **Girnigoe** and **Sinclair** stand above Sinclair Bay. They were strongholds of the Earls of Caithness. Girnigoe is the older of the two, dating from the end of the 15th century, and it was in its dungeons that George Sinclair had his son incarcerated. Sinclair Castle dates from about 1606.

NORTH SHORE POTTERY
AND PATRICIA NIEMANN JEWELLERY

Mill of Forse, Latheron, Caithness KW5 6DG
Tel/Fax: 01593741777
e-mail: patbat@btinternet.com
website: www.northshorepottery.co.uk

Situated in Mill of Forse, where the rugged cliffs of south east Caithness sweep northwards, **North Shore Pottery and Patricia Niemann Jewellery** offer everyone the chance to purchase a gift or commission a piece, which will remind them of their stay in Caithness.

The potter, Jenny Mackenzie Ross, uses the landscapes of the countryside and rugged coast around the far north as inspiration for her delicate yet sturdy pots. She loves texture and form, and the "journey" of the pot from the soft clay on the wheel to the kiln and on to the shelf.

She also uses salt-glazes on her pots and her source for the salt is invariably kelp (a form of seaweed) found on the local shoreline. In this way, she imbues the pot with salty qualities of the sea.

Jenny shares the studio with Patricia, the goldsmith. Patricia makes unusual pieces of fine jewellery,

using gemstones, pearls and other often unorthodox materials, like limpet sea shells or found objects from the local beaches. Many of her unique pieces have to do with the inspiring quality of the environment in Caithness and often display a spark of humour. She also offers to redesign and remake her customers' loved old jewellery. Some blown glass pieces are shown as well in the studio, along with other changing exhibitions. You can watch Jenny work as she delicately throws a pot and Patricia when she makes jewellery on her workbench.

On the northern edge of the town is **Wick Airport**, Scotland's most northerly mainland commercial airport. It has flights to and from Teesside, Norwich, Aberdeen and Kirkwall.

AROUND WICK

LATHERON
15 miles S of Wick on the A9

Latheron, unlike other villages in the area, has a name derived from Gaelic "làthair roin", meaning "resort of seals". Within the old church, which dates from 1735, is the **Clan Gunn Heritage Centre**. It traces the history of the clan from its Norse origins right through to the present day. At Dunbeath, three miles south of Latheron, is the thatched **Laidhay Croft Museum**, which shows a typical Highland house, with living quarters, byre and stable all under the one roof. And in an old schoolhouse at Dunbeath is the **Dunbeath Heritage Centre**, managed by the Dunbeath Preservation Trust. It has displays, photographs and documents about the village.

Neil Gunn, one of Scotland's finest writers (author of *The Silver Darlings*), was born in Dunbeath and attended the very school in which the Heritage Centre is located.

HELMSDALE
30 miles SW of Wick on the A9

The name Helmsdale comes from the Norse *Hjalmundal*, meaning "dale of the helmet". A great battle is supposed to have been fought here between two Norse chiefs, Swein and Olvir. Swein was victorious, and Olvir fled and was never heard from again.

Within this little fishing port is **Timespan**, a visitor centre that tells the story of Helmsdale and its surrounding communities. There are exhibits about the Clearances, Picts, Norse raids, witches and so much more. **Helmsdale Castle** once stood in Couper Park, but the last vestiges of it were demolished in the 1970s due to the unstable state of the ruins. In 1567 a famous tragedy - said to inspired Shakespeare to write Hamlet - was enacted here. Isobel Sinclair had hopes that her son would claim the earldom of Sutherland. She therefore invited the then earl and countess and their heir to dinner one evening. And poured them poisoned wine. The earl and countess died, but the heir survived. Unfortunately, Isobel's own son drank the wine and died also.

The **Strath of Kildonan**, through which flows the River Helmsdale, was the scene of a famous gold rush in 1868. A local man called Robert

Gilchrist, who had been a prospector in Australia, began searching for gold in the river. He eventually found some, and once his secret was out, the Duke of Sutherland began parcelling off small plots of land to speculators. At its height, over 500 men were prospecting in the area, and a shantytown soon sprung up. But in 1870, when sportsmen complained that the prospectors were interfering with their fishing and hunting, the Duke put a stop to it all, and the gold rush was over. There is still gold there today, and it is a favourite spot for amateur gold panners.

Kyle of Tongue

Helmsdale is an excellent place for fishing and is within a short drive of championship golf courses. Both geology and archiology are prevalent in the area.

TONGUE
50 miles W of Wick off the A838

Tongue is a small village situated near the shallow Kyle of Tongue. It's name means exactly what it says, as it comes from the Norse *tunga*, meaning a tongue, in this case a tongue of land. In 1972 a causeway was built across it to take the A838 westwards towards Loch Eribol and Durness. On a promontory to the west of the village are the ruins of the small **Castle Varrich** ("Caisteal Bharraigh in Gaelic), which once belonged to Clan Mackay.

The 16th century **House of Tongue**, overlooking the Kyle of Tongue, was also a Mackay stronghold. It was destroyed in the 17th century, with the Mackays building a new house sometime in the 18th century. The gardens are open to the public.

In 1746 a ship - the Hazard - carrying gold coinage for Charles Edward Stuart's Jacobite army tried to take shelter in the Kyle of Tongue to escape HMS Sheerness, a government frigate. The crew took the coinage ashore for safekeeping, but were followed and captured by some Mackay clansmen, who were supporters of the government. The crewmen threw the coins into a loch, but most were later recovered.

Nine miles northeast of the village, within the old St Columba's Church at Bettyhill, is the **Strathnaver Museum**, with exhibits about local history, most notably the Clearances and Clan Mackay. Strathnaver was probably the most notorious area in the Highlands for the eviction of tenants so that they could be replaced with the more profitable sheep. The whole area abounds with prehistoric archaeological sites, and within the kirkyard of the museum is a burial stone dating to the 8th or 9th century. The £190,000 **Strathnaver Trail** to the east of the village opened in May 2003 and takes you round 16 sites, which date from 5000BC to the 20th century.

The A836 south from Tongue to Lairg passes alongside beautiful **Loch Loyal** for part of the way, and has some beautiful views. The ruins of **Varrich Castle** (Caisteal Bharraich in Gaelic) sit

Halladale Inn

Melvich, By Thurso, Caithness KW14 7YJ
Tel & Fax: 01641 531282
e-mail: mazfling@tinyworld.co.uk

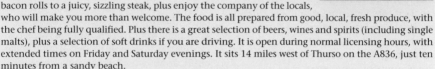

With a friendly atmosphere, you can't beat the **Halladale Inn** for hospitality, good food and great drink. Here you can get everything from bacon rolls to a juicy, sizzling steak, plus enjoy the company of the locals, who will make you more than welcome. The food is all prepared from good, local, fresh produce, with the chef being fully qualified. Plus there is a great selection of beers, wines and spirits (including single malts), plus a selection of soft drinks if you are driving. It is open during normal licensing hours, with extended times on Friday and Saturday evenings. It sits 14 miles west of Thurso on the A836, just ten minutes from a sandy beach.

Attached to the inn is a superb four-star chalet and caravan park with 14 pitches, six for caravans or motor homes with optional electric hook-up, and eight tent pitches. The chalets sleep up to four people in absolute comfort in a double and two single beds, and are all well furnished and decorated, with many facilities in the living/dining area to make your holiday a memorable one. Bed linen is provided, though guests should bring their own towels etc. There is private parking within a fenced garden, and an outside drying area. There is a £1-coin meter in each chalet for electricity.

The surrounding countryside is beautiful and tranquil, with stunning views - just right for that get-away-from-it-all holiday. Reay Golf Course is only five miles away, and there is plenty of opportunities locally for walking, bird-watching, fishing and sailing. The clean, safe beach is a favourite venue for surfing or just for relaxing on a summer's afternoon.

on a rise above the loch, with a footpath taking you to them. It dates from the 14th century, and was once a Mackay stronghold. It is said to be built on the foundations of a Norse fort.

ALTNAHARRA
51 miles W of Wick on the A836

Sitting close to the western tip of **Loch Naver**, Altnaharra is a small village famous as a centre for game fishing. Loch Naver is the source of the River Naver, one of the best salmon rivers in Sutherland, which flows northwards through Strathnaver to the sea (see also Tongue).

On a narrow, unclassified road from Altnaharra to **Strath More** and **Loch Hope** are the remains of the **Dun Dornaigil Broch**. Some of its walls rise to 22 feet, and over the entrance is a strange triangular lintel. A few miles beyond the broch is **Ben Hope**, at 3,041 feet Scotland's most northerly Munro.

The B873 strikes east from Altnaharra along Strathnaver, following the loch and then the river, until it joins the B871, which joins the A836 south of Bettyhill. It is a superb run, with magnificent scenery.

THURSO
19 miles NW of Wick on the A9

Thurso is a former fishing port on Caithness's northern coast, and is the most northerly town on mainland Britain. It was once a Norse settlement, with its name meaning "river of the god Thor". The ruins of **St Peter's Church** sit in the old part of the town, and date from the 16th century, though a church has stood here since at least the 13th century. It was once the private chapel of the Bishop of Caithness, whose summer retreat was **Scrabster Castle**, of which only scant ruins survive. In the early 17th century a witch called Graycoat was held in the church's tower. The story goes that a man was having difficulty getting his whisky to ferment properly, and blamed a stray cat that had dipped its paw in it. He attacked the cat and cut off its paw, which fell into the whisky. When he drained the barrel, he found, not a paw, but a human hand. Graycoat was then seen nursing a bandaged hand, and people quickly put two and two together, getting five. She was summoned before the kirk elders and convicted of being a witch.

The **Thurso Heritage Museum** is located within an old cottage in Lyn Street, and has displays and mementos relating to the town's past. It is open during the summer. At the mouth of the river are the ruins of the mock-Gothic **Thurso Castle**, built in 1878 by Sir Tollemarche Sinclair on the site of a much older castle. At Crosskirk, a few miles west of the town, are the ruins of **St Mary's Chapel**, dating from the 12th century. All that remains is the nave. At Holborn Head is the **Clett Rock**, a huge natural pillar, or stack, situated just offshore.

Eight miles west of the town, on the A836, is Dounreay, where Scotland's first operational nuclear reactor was built. The **Dounreay Visitor Centre** explains about nuclear power and the history of the site.

JOHN O'GROATS
13 miles N of Wick on the A99

John O' Groats is 873 miles by road from Land's End in Cornwall, and 290 miles from Kirkmaiden in Wigtownshire, Scotland's most southerly parish. It is supposed to be named after a Dutchman called Jan de Groot, who, to settle an argument about precedence within his family, built an eight sided house with eight doors which gave onto an eight-sided table. This house has now gone, though a mound marks its site. The **Last House in Scotland Museum** contains displays and artefacts about the area.

To the west is **Dunnet Head**, the most northerly point on the British mainland. Between the two is the **Castle of Mey**, the late Queen Mother's Scottish home. It is an ancient castle of the Earls of Caithness, and was built in the 16th century by the 4th Earl. **Mary-Ann's Cottage** at Westside shows how successive generations of one crofting family lived and worked over the last 150 years.

The **Northlands Viking Centre** in the Old School House at Auckengill, five miles south of the village, tells the story of the Vikings and Norsemen in the area, as well as recounting the life of John Nicolson, a local artist and mason. Ten minutes away are the remains of the **Nybster Broch**, built about 200BC to AD200

The Western Isles look like a huge kite with a long tail streaming out behind it. The body of the kite is the island of Lewis and Harris, and the tail consists mainly of the smaller islands of North Uist, Benbecula, South Uist and Barra. The whole length between Barra in the south and the Butt of Lewis in the north is about 130 miles, and they are separated from the mainland by a stretch of water called The Minch.

These islands are the last bastion of true Gaeldom in Scotland, and in some places English, though spoken and understood perfectly, is still a second language. Some are also bastions of Free Presbyterianism, where the Sabbath is strictly observed, and work or leisure activities of any kind on a Sunday is frowned upon. Visitors should, of course, respect these Sabbath customs. Unfortunately, they have given the islanders the reputation of being dour and strict, frowning on anything that smacks of pleasure. Nothing could be further from the truth. They are fun loving, friendly and always helpful. Plus there are some islands that are almost wholly Roman Catholic, never having been influenced by the Scottish Reformation in 1560.

The Western Isles are full of such contradictions. They may be where Gaelic culture is cherished and preserved, but there are more Norse influences here than Celtic, and many of the place names (especially in the north) have Norse origins. Up until the Treaty of Perth in 1266 the Western Isles were ruled by Norway, but in that year Magnus IV surrendered all of his Scottish possessions, with the exception of Orkney and Shetland, to Alexander III of Scotland.

The weather in the Western Isles, especially in winter, can be harsh, though there are occasions where it can be astonishingly mild and sunny. Snow is rare because of the Gulf Stream, but there are between 45 and 50 inches of rain a year, and the winds blowing in from the Atlantic are invariably strong. The compensations, however, are enormous. The long summer evenings can be still and warm, and at midnight in the north of Lewis it is still possible to read a newspaper out of doors.

Timsgarry, Lewis

LOCATOR MAP

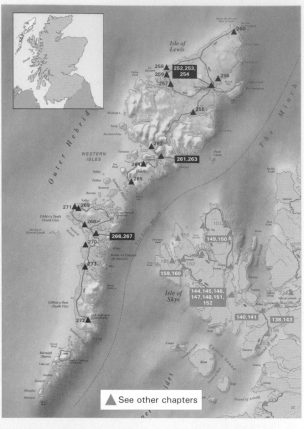

See other chapters

And the wildlife is astounding. Deer and otters abound, and the machair (the meadows bordering the sandy beaches) brim with flowers in summer. The seas are home to dolphins, basking sharks, whales and seals. In fact, some people claim that the waters surrounding the Western Isles are the most populated in Britain.

The main island is divided into two parts, Lewis and Harris, an ancient arrangement going back as far as the 13th century. Though joined geographically, they are usually considered to be two separate islands, and indeed the differences between them are marked. A natural boundary of mountains and high moorland runs between Loch Resort on the west and Loch Seaforth on the east, explaining the differences.

Lewis is the northern, and larger part, and up until the mid 1970s was within the county of Ross and Cromarty. Harris (and the smaller islands to the south) came under Inverness-shire. Now they all form one administrative area, with the capital being at Stornoway.

The underlying rock of Lewis is gneiss, one of the oldest in the world. It is largely impermeable, so does not absorb water. For this reason the interior of the island is a large, empty peat moorland dotted with shallow lochs, while most of the settlements are on the coast. Harris is more mountainous, and has peaks reaching 2,500 feet. It is also an area where the underlying rocks

ADVERTISERS AND PLACES OF INTEREST

break through to the surface like bones, giving an essentially bleak but never the less than attractive landscape. It in turn is divided into two parts, North and South Harris, with the narrow ithsmus between West Loch Tarbert and East Loch Tarbert being the boundary.

Of the main southern islands, Berneray, North Uist, Benbecula, South Uist and Eriskay are joined by causeways. North Uist connects to Harris by a ferry between An t-Obbe and Berneray, and Barra has a ferry connection with Eriskay. Each island in the chain has its own flavour, and all are noted for their quality of light, especially in summer.

The Western Isles sit on the farthest edge of Europe, with North America being the next stop. But for all their seeming isolation, they have a long history. The standing stones at Callanish - the second largest stone circle in Britain - are over 4,000 years old, and were built for pagan ritual and to record the passing of the seasons so that crops could be sown and harvested. And there are individual standing stones, duns, brochs and old forts dotted all over the landscape. The local people are proud of their history, and have established small, village-based museums everywhere.

During the Dark Ages the Western Isles were at the crossroads of trade. To the south were the Lowlands of Scotland, as well as England, Ireland and the Isle of Man. To the east, beyond Scotland, were the Norse countries. This made for a mixture of cultural influences that enriched the islands - influences that can still be seen today.

Tolsta, Lewis

Norse invasions began in earnest in the 8th century, and by about AD 850 Norsemen ruled all of the Outer Hebrides. In 1266 the islands came into Scottish hands through the Treaty of Perth. However, this did not stop the Lords of the Isles from acting almost independently of the crown. For this reason there was much friction between them and the Scottish kings, though the kings gradually imposed their authority. The islands eventually accepted this and became fully integrated into Scotland. Some historians claim, however, that the Norse language did not fully die out until the late 16th century.

Various attempts have been made over the years to encourage industry, most notably when Lord Leverhulme bought both Lewis and Harris in 1918 and tried to promote fishing. Today the islands rely on fishing, crofting and tourism, with the weaving of Harris Tweed being an important industry on Lewis and Harris. Weaving is a cottage industry, with the weavers working at home or in sheds at the back of the house. Some will welcome you into their weaving rooms and explain the processes involved in turning wool into fine cloth.

Ferries for Stornoway leave from Ullapool, and there is also a ferry connection between Oban, South Uist and Barra, as well as one from Uig on Skye to Lochmaddy and Tarbert.

STORNOWAY

With a population of about 6,000, Stornoway (from the Old Norse stjorna, meaning "anchor bay") is the only town of any size in the Western Isles. It is the administrative, educational and shopping centre, and is a surprisingly cosmopolitan place, with a sizable Asian population.

It was founded in the middle ages round an old MacLeod castle, built by the MacNicols and later taken by Leod, son of Olaf the Black, a Viking. The town has a fine natural harbour and an airport. On Lewis Street is **The Parish Church of St Columba**, dating from 1794, and in **St Peter's Episcopal Church** (1039) is David Livingstone's Bible and an old font from a chapel on the Flannan Isles, about 33 miles west of Lewis in the Atlantic. Its bell, which was made in 1631, was once the town bell

that summoned townspeople to important meetings. The **Free Church** in Kenneth Street has the distinction of being the best attended church in all of Britain, with the Sunday evening congregation regularly exceeding 1,500.

Lews Castle, now a college surrounded by public gardens, was built in the 1840s and 50s by James Matheson, a businessman who earned a fortune in the Far East trading in tea and opium. In 1843 he bought Lewis, and began a series of improvements in what was then an isolated and inward looking island. He built new roads, improved the housing and brought running water and gas to the town.

One of his pet projects was a plant to extract oil from the peat that blanketed the island, and in 1861 the Lewis Chemical Works began production. But problems beset the plant, and it actually blew up, putting the citizens of

HEATHER BUTTERWORTH

34-36 Riggs Road, Stornoway, Western Isles HS1 2RC
Tel/Fax: 01851 705351
e-mail: heatherbutte@aol.com website: www.orbdesigns.co.uk

For delightful and unique accessories made of locally woven Harris tweed there's only one place to look - Orb Designs by **Heather Butterworth**. Situated in Stornoway, it is a one-stop shop for a wide range of goods that would make the perfect gift or souvenir. Born and bred on Lewis, Heather graduated from Gray's School of Art in Aberdeen in 1990 and returned home to set up a workshop developing, designing and manufacturing a range of colourful bags, cushions, tea cosies and accessories with appliqué features. She draws her inspiration from the friendly people and wonderful landscapes and colours of the Western Isles, and can design and make items to customers' specifications.

Harris tweed is one of the most desirable and hard wearing cloths in the world, combining superb

durability, warmth, style and fashion. It conjures up images of a traditional Scottish way of life - one that is being kept alive in the Western Isles - the only place in the world where genuine Harris tweed can be woven. The wools from local, sturdy sheep are blended together before being dyed using local plants and lichens, The resultant yarn is woven into Harris tweed by craftspeople working on their own looms. Only then can the world-famous Orb trademark be bestowed on it, certifying its authenticity. Helen uses this cloth to make her great range of quality items. She has an eye for colour and texture, and this is evident in her products. All are superbly made, some having amusing, jaunty designs and others having a touch of fashion and style about them

HEBRIDEAN BREWING COMPANY

18a Bells Road/corner of Rigs Road, Stornoway,
Isle of Lewis, HS1 2RA Tel: 01851 700123 Fax: 01851 700234
website: www.hebridean-brewery.co.uk

A short distance from the centre of town, and two minutes walk from the ferry terminal you will find the premises of the **Hebridean Brewing Company**, the only alcohol producer in the Western Isles. It is owned and managed by Andrew Ribbens, who hails from South East England, but whos family originate from Lewis , so he set up the company here in 2001. There is small retail outlet on the brewery premises, and tours round the brewery are available by appointment.

Andrew claims that his company uses only the finest brewing ingredients. His brands include Islander Strong, Celtic Black Ale, Clansman, Seaforth Ale and Berserker Export Pale Ale 7.5%, each having its own, unique characteristics. The Islander is brewed using special Scots malt, and has a deep ruby colour, and a wonderful flavour that that is predominantly malty. In 2003 it won the bronze medal from the Society of Independent Brewers 'Beer of Scotland Premium Cask Category'. Celtic Black Ale is a dark porter style ale which is full of flavour, balancing an aromatic hop combined with a subtle bite and a pleasantly smooth, caramel aftertaste. Clansman is a light, Hebridean beer brewed

with Scottish malts and lightly hopped to give a subtle bittering. It makes an ideal all-day beer for general consumption. Seaforth is a Blonde Ale with bite but balanced by a citrus after taste. Berserker is based on original India Pale Ale recipies from the 19th century.They are available in bottles or as draught ales and are sold in Scotland and throughout the United Kingdom. So while exploring Stornoway, pay a visit to the micro brewery of the Hebridean Brewing Company, and buy some of their ales to take home as a gift, or as a souvenir of your holiday.

HANDA

18 Keose Glebe, Lochs, Isle of Lewis,
Western Isles HS2 9JX
Tel: 01851 830334
e-mail: handakeose@supanet.com
website: www.westernisleswelcome.com

Holiday at **Handa**, and fall in love with the Western
Isles! So says the brochure for this wonderful, modern
bed and breakfast and self-catering establishment
which takes its name from the island of Handa, a bird
sanctuary off the north west coast of Sutherland. Handa is for the exclusive use of one couple and
boasts an extremely comfortable suite with a double bedroom and wash hand basin, shaving socket,
toilet with shower, a large lounge with TV, a well stocked library and tea/coffee making facilities. The
furniture and décor are of the highest standard, and well maintained.

Behind the main building is The Stac, which was once home to the owner, Christine Morrison's
mother. It has three bedrooms - a double with en suite facilities on the ground floor, and an upstairs
double and a single, both with wash hand basins and shaving points. There is also a bathroom with
bath/shower, utility area, lounge and a modern, well equipped kitchen. It also has a colour TV, video,

radio/tape/CD players, electric blankets and hair dryer. All bed
linen is supplied, as are towels if required. There is a support
rail for the two front steps on the ground floor, making it
disabled friendly.

Dinner, if required, is served every evening at Handa at
6.30 pm. The produce is local and fresh, and you can bring
your own wine if you wish. For those staying in The Stac, there
are supermarkets, shops and restaurants in Stornoway.

Stornoway into a state of fear and alarm.
The venture finally folded in 1874.

The **Museum nan Eilean** was opened
in 1984 by the then local authority, and
is located in Francis Street. It has
artefacts and exhibits highlighting the
history and archaeology of both the
island of Lewis and Stornoway itself, and
makes a good starting point if you want
to explore the area. The **An Lanntair
Arts Centre** sits across from the ferry
terminal, and has contemporary and
traditional exhibitions, as well as varied
programmes of music and drama
highlighting the Gaelic culture.

One of Stornoway's most famous sons
was the 18th century explorer and fur
trader Sir Alexander Mackenzie, who
gave his name to the Mackenzie River in
Canada. In Francis Street, on the site of
his house, is **Martins Memorial**, built in

1885. Over 1,150 men of Lewis died in
the two world wars, and the **Stornoway
War Memorial** must be the most
imposing in Britain. It stands on the 300-
feet high Cnoc nan Uan, and itself rises
to a height of 85 feet.

The Western Isles are synonymous
with Harris tweed, and at the **Loom
Centre** on Bayhead you can find out
about its history and about how it is
woven. To attain the "orb" symbol of
genuine Harris tweed, the cloth needs to
be woven from "virgin wool produced in
Scotland", then spun, dyed and hand
woven in the Outer Hebrides.

West of Stornoway, on the Eye
Peninsula, are the ruins of **St Columba's
Church**, built in the 14th century on the
site of a small monastic cell founded by
St Catan in the 6th century. It is said
that 19 MacLeod chiefs are buried here.

COLL POTTERY

Coll, Lewis, Western Isles HS2 0JP
Tel: 01851 820219 e-mail: admin@broadbayceramics.co.uk
Fax: 01851 820565 website: www.broadbayceramics.co.uk

Situated six miles north of Lewis's capital of Stornoway, **Coll Pottery** offers the largest range of hand-made pottery in Scotland. There is truly something for everyone here, with a shop, a viewing gallery and demonstrations. The Hebridean range of bowls, aromatherapy evaporators, mugs and coasters is lively and colourful. Plus there is the Highbank range of delightful figurines of animals and birds, the Thistleware range and a host of other items that would make the perfect souvenir or a gift for a loved one. The pottery also boasts a café where you can enjoy a tea or coffee and a bite to eat after browsing.

AROUND STORNOWAY

CALLANISH

16 miles W of Stornoway on the A858

Dating back at least 4,000 years, the **Callanish Stone Circle** (Historic Scotland) is second only to Stonehenge in importance in Britain. It is more than just a circle of upright stones. Four great arms made up of monoliths radiate from it to the north, south east and west, with the northern arm (which veers slightly to the east) having a double row of stones as if enclosing an approach way. And in the middle of the circle is the tallest stone of them all, measuring over 15 feet in height.

It is a mysterious place, and has attracted many stories and myths over

THE HEBRIDEAN SOAP COMPANY LTD

25 Breasclete, West Side, Isle of Lewis,
Outer Hebrides HS2 9EF
Tel: 01851 621306
e-mail: HebrideanSoapCo@aol.com
website: www.HebrideanSoap.co.uk

Direct from Breasclete, by the banks of Loch Roag, is brought to you decadent and sumptuous handmade soap to waken your senses and calm your spirit.

Visit the new shop and working soapkitchen, (due for completion by the end of 2005) and watch the soap being made, using a vegetable fat base, precious oils and essential oils.

Enjoy the wonderful views from the premises out over majestic Loch Roag, the crofts of Breasclete and the distant mountains of Harris.

Take advantage of the 'Send-to-a-friend' gift service, and your choice of soap will be gift-wrapped and sent for a memorable and special present.

The staff at **The Hebridean Soap Company Ltd.** are passionate about soapmaking, and their islands, and are always available to answer questions, or just chat about the subjects. They can be found by taking the main road from Stornoway, past the Callanish Stones turn-off, then take a right-hand turn immediately before Breasclete school. Follow that road left and up to the top until you see the sign.

the years. One story tells of a race of giants who met to discuss how to defeat the new religion of Christianity that was spreading throughout the islands. This so incensed St Kieran, a Celtic monk and missionary, that he turned them all to stone. Another says that the stones were brought to Lewis by a great priest king who employed "black men" to erect them. The men who died building the circle were buried within it.

Callanish Stone Circle

Plus there are the more modern, and unfortunately predictable, theories that the stones were erected by mysterious beings from outer space as a means of guiding their spacecraft, though why people with such technology should need a guidance system made of stones seems equally as mysterious.

A visitors centre next to the stones tries to uncover the truth behind them, which may have something to do with primitive ritual and predicting the seasons for agricultural purposes.

CARLOWAY

17 miles W of Stornoway on the A858

The 2,000-year-old **Dun Carloway Broch**, overlooking Loch Roag, is one of the best-

Doune Braes Hotel

Carloway, Isle of Lewis, Western Isles HS2 9AA
Tel: 01851 643252 Fax: 01851 643435
e-mail: hebrides@doune-braes.co.uk
website: www.doune-braes.co.uk

You'll get a good Scottish welcome at the **Doune Braes Hotel** at Carloway, on the romantic Isle of Lewis. It is owned and managed by Eileen MacDonald, who takes a great pride in the high standards she has set and maintained here. She has strived to create a real home-from-home atmosphere which is informal and friendly, while still offering high standards of service and outstanding value for money.

The hotel has 15 fully en suite bedrooms, each with a colour TV and tea/coffee making facilities. They are well furnished, bright and airy and most have good views out over the breathtaking Lewis landscape. Two ground floor rooms have been ramped for disabled access.

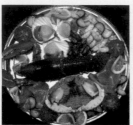

Doune Braes is renowned for its good food. It serves meals and snacks all day, seven days a week, from 12 noon to 9pm. The restaurant, which also has a ramp for disabled access, seats 36 for à la carte or bar meals. The speciality is prime, fresh, local seafood, as well as local lamb fed on heather. There is also a great range of beef, pork, poultry and vegetarian dishes.

The reception area is also disabled-friendly, and there is a lounge bar and a public bar. The public bar is popular with the locals (always a good sign) and here you can meet, enjoy a drink, a game of pool or swap yarns with the local people.

preserved brochs in Scotland. It is over 47 feet in diameter, and its walls are 22 feet high in places. Some of the galleries and internal stairways are still intact. The Doune Broch Centre has displays explaining what life must have been like

within fortifications such as this.

One-and-a-quarter miles north of Carloway is the **Gearrannan Blackhouse Village**. It faces the Atlantic, and is a huddle of traditional cottages dating from the 19th century. They have been restored by the Garenin Trust between 1991 and 2001, and were lived in up until 1974.

Shader

16 miles NW of Stornoway on the A857

The **Steinacleit Stone Circle and Standing Stones** sit on a low hill, and date from between 2000 and 3000 BC. The stones are more in the shape of an oval than a circle, and archaeologists are unsure whether it is indeed a stone circle, a burial cairn or the remains of a settlement of some kind.

Dun Carloway Broch

THE CROSS INN

Pot of Ness, Isle of Lewis, Western Isles HS2 0SN
Tel/Fax: 01851 810152
e-mail: info@crossinn.com website: www.crossinn.com

Maureen and Allan Forsyth invite you to experience the unique atmosphere of the **Cross Inn** at Port of Ness in the beautiful Isle of Lewis. At this small country hotel you will enjoy the very best in Highland hospitality, watched over by a couple whose ancestors have lived in the area for generations.

There are six recently refurbished rooms on offer, each one supremely comfortable and each one individually furnished and decorated to an extremely high standard. They are all fully en suite, and boast tea/coffee making facilities, TV and video, and a host of other features you would expect from a hotel of such quality. There is a cosy lounge bar and a public bar which is a great favourite with tourists and locals alike. Here you can meet and chat to the people of Lewis as you relax over a beer. The hotel is renowned throughout the area for its good food. You can enjoy snacks and bar meals

throughout the day in the lounge, or experience a superb evening meal in the spacious and elegant restaurant. All the produce is sourced locally wherever possible and salmon, lobster and other shellfish are invariably on the menu, as is local beef, lamb, pork and venison.

Maureen and Allan are determined to maintain the high standards they have set, and to keep the hotel as an informal and friendly establishment which you will want to come back to.

SHAWBOST

16 miles W of Stornoway on the A858

Housed within a former church, the **Sgoil Shiaboist Museum** (Shawbost School Museum) has artefacts and objects collected by school pupils 30 years ago as part of a project that illustrates the way people used to live in Lewis. Near it is the thatched **Norse Mill and Kiln**, a restored water mill of the type used in Lewis up until the mid-20th century.

The Shawbost Stone Circle, near the shores of the small Loch Raoinavat,only has two stones left standing. They are difficult to find, and good walking gear is recommended if you want to find them.

BARVAS

13 miles NW of Stornoway on the A858

At one time, most of the population of Lewis lived in small cottages known as blackhouses. On the west coast of the

Shawbost

island, at Arnol, is the **Arnol Blackhouse** (Historic Scotland), which shows what life was like in one of them. People and animals lived under the one roof, separated by thin walls, with the roof usually being of thatch and turf. They had tiny windows because of the seasonal gales and rain and the fact that glass was very expensive. The thick, dry stone walls (with a central core of clay and earth) kept the cottage cool in summer and warm in winter.

The Arnol house has been furnished in typical fashion, and it has a clay floor. There is no fireplace, the fire being placed centrally, with no chimney. The houses got their name in the mid-19th century to distinguish them from the more modern white houses, which had mortar binding the stones.

There is also an interpretation centre in a nearby cottage, which has a model of a typical blackhouse showing how they were made.

During archaeological excavations at Barvas, a 200-year-old Iron Age cemetery was uncovered. One of the finds was a beautiful iron and copper alloy bracelet, the first of its kind to be found anywhere in Scotland.

BALLANTRUSHAL

15 miles NW of Stornoway on the B857

The **Clach an Trushal** (Historic Scotland), at 18 feet high, is the tallest standing stone in Scotland, and is said to mark the site of an ancient battle, though this is unlikely. In the 19th century several feet of peat were cut away from around its base, revealing the true height.

GREAT BERNERA

18 miles W of Stornoway off the B8059

The small island of Great Bernera measures only six miles long by three miles wide at it's widest. It is connected to the mainland by the **Great Bernera Bridge**, opened in 1953 and the first bridge in the country made from pre-stressed concrete girders. The **Community Centre and Museum** has displays about the island, and also sells tea, coffee and cakes. On the lovely beach at **Bostadh** an Iron Age village has been excavated, and a reconstruction of an Iron Age house built. A cairn commemorates those men who took part in the **Bernera Riot** of 1874, when crofters stood up for their right of tenure. Three of them eventually stood trial, though a later Act of Parliament gave them the rights they were fighting for.

TARBERT

33 miles S of Stornoway on the A859

The small village of Tarbert has a ferry connection with Uig on Skye. This is the starting point of South Harris, and an isthmus no more that half a mile wide

ARDHASAIG HOUSE

Ardhasaig, Isle of Harris HS3 3AJ
Tel: 01859 50 2066/2500 Fax: 01859 50 2077
e-mail: accommodation@ardhasaig.co.uk
website: www.ardhasaig.co.uk

Ardhasaig House was originally built in 1905, and for 100 years has been a home of the Macaskill family. Since the year 2002, it is one of the best small hotels on the beautiful island of Harris. It has six fully en suite rooms that are spacious, well furnished and beautifully decorated so that you, the guest, can experience the very best in Scottish hospitality. Each room has tea/coffee making facilities and a host of features that make a stay here one to remember for all the right reasons.

In the year 2005 it was named as runner up in two prestigious award categories, "Scottish Hotel Breakfast of the Year" and "Island Hotel of the Year", and the owner, Katie Macaskill and her team are determined to use this as a base to improve even further the standards of service offered to guests.

The atmosphere is informal and friendly, as befits a hotel of this quality. There are no TVs, and for your comfort it is a fully non smoking establishment. A new bedroom has just been added in a converted barn a short walking distance from the hotel, and this is ideal for honeymooners or those just wishing to get away from it all.

Food is important in the Ardhasaig Hotel. Katie is also the chef, and she insists on only the finest and freshest of local produce in her kitchen wherever possible. As you would imagine, seafood is a speciality, though home-reared beef and local lamb feature on the menu as well. Why not start with the cream of leek soup with seeded rolls, then sample the pan seared Strond scallops with caviar cream? Or the rack of local lamb with herb crust, fig and redcurrant gravy with an accompaniment of vegetables? For dessert you could have apricot bread and butter pudding followed by a choice of teas or fresh coffee with sweet treats. However, all dietary needs are catered for. In the morning you can enjoy a full Scottish breakfast, which is hearty and filling, or you can choose a lighter option. Just right to set you up for a day sightseeing on the lovely island of Harris.

The hotel sits three miles from the ferry port of Tarbert, and has wonderful views out over the Harris hills and the Atlantic Ocean. It is centrally positioned and makes an ideal base from which to explore the whole of the island of Lewis/Harris and even take a day trip to Uist or Kilda. There is history and heritage aplenty here, plus there is so much to do. It is a walker's paradise, and there is climbing, sailing, golf, fishing, mountain biking and a host of other activities.

Of course, if you just want to relax and take it easy, then Ardhasaig House is the perfect place for you as well. It encapsulates everything that people have come to expect from the Western Isles - friendliness, a slower pace of life and informal but efficient service.

CASTAWAY CRAFTS

Pier Road, Tarbert, Western Isles HS3 3DG
Tel: 01859 502332
e-mail: castaway_crafts@hotmail.com
website: www.castawaycrafts.co.uk

Fiona Mitchell designs and makes many items from locally woven Harris tweed, selling them from her shop, **Castaway Crafts**. There is a wide range of beautiful things. Each one is individually made, and come in a wide range of colours and patterns. Fiona also offers a **self-catering caravan at Ardhasaig**, a couple of miles west of Tarbert, which has superb views. It sleeps up to six and has heating, hot water, shower, cooking facilities and a host of other amenities.

separates East Loch Tarbert, which is an arm of the Minch, from West Loch Tarbert, which is an arm of the Atlantic. In fact, *Tairbeart* in Gaelic means "isthmus" or "place of portage", where boats were dragged across land from one stretch of water to another.

Amhuinnsuidhe Castle was built in 1868 by the Earl of Dunsmore, who owned Harris. It was the Earl's wife who introduced the weaving of Harris tweed to the island. The castle was subsequently owned by the Bulmer family, which founded the cider firm. It was here that J.M. Barrie wrote his play *Mary Rose*. It is now used as an upmarket conference centre.

SCALPAY

33 miles S of Stornoway

The tiny island of Scalpay, measuring three miles by two, lies off Harris's east coast. It is connected to the mainland by

the £7m **Scalpay Bridge**, the biggest civil engineering project ever undertaken in the Western Isles. It was opened in 1998 by Tony Blair, the first serving prime minister ever to visit the Western Isles. The visit is also remembered because of the biting criticism he received from one of the island's more militant inhabitants - *culiciodes impunctatus*, more commonly known as the midge. However, the first official crossing was made in December 1997, when the island's oldest inhabitant, 103-years-old Kirsty Morrison, was taken across it in a vintage car.

RODEL

48 miles S of Stornoway on the A859

Rodel sits near the southern tip of Harris, and is famous for **St Clement's Church**, burial place of the MacLeods. It was built in 1500 by Alasdair Crotach ("hunchback") McLeod, who lived in the

BEUL NA MARA B&B

12 Seilebost, Isle of Harris, Western Isles HS3 3HP
Tel: 01859 550205
e-mail: morrison.catherine@virgin.net
website: www.beulnamara.co.uk

Across from the island of Taransay, you'll find one of the best B&Bs on the beautiful island of Harris - Beul na Mara. Owned and managed by Catherine Morrison, it offers extremely comfortable accommodation for the discerning holiday maker. All bedrooms have spectacular views, and come with en suite shower and tee/coffee making facilities as standard. Evening meals, featuring honest Scottish fare, can be provided in the evenings. The B&B also has two self-catering-cottages with superb views towards the Seilebost estuary and Taransay.

THE ANCHORAGE

The Pier, Leverburgh, Western Isles HS5 3UB
Tel: 01859 520225
e-mail: sciao@aol.com

The Anchorage in **Leverburgh** in South Harris, or An T-ob as it is called in Gaelic, is a superb restaurant/café serves breakfasts, lunches, afternoon teas and evening meals. It is owned and managed by Sally and Maurizio Lessi, who have worked hard to create one of the best eating places in the Western Isles. They have transformed the former cafe into a place with a Continental feel, where Italian flare and imagination combines with good, local fresh produce. Local seafood is a speciality with lobster, oysters, langoustines and white fish all on the menu, as are free-range eggs, delicious local black pudding and home-baked cakes and scones. There is also a mouth watering range of Italian dishes and the table licence ensures that you can enjoy a glass of wine with your food, or a bottle of the local beer, brewed in Stornoway. Or why not enjoy a cup of freshly brewed Italian coffee? The Anchorage was the first place on the Western Isles to have authentic cappuccino/latte/espresso machine (sent directly from Milan).

Sally worked in advertising in London and moved to the Western Isles after falling in love with them during a holiday. Mauritzio is Italian and has a background in catering, having once organised celebrity parties. There are superb views out over the Sound of Harris towards North Uist, and you can see sea otters, dolphins, seals and many seabirds from the windows as you enjoy your food. The ambience is relaxed and informal, and the walls are hung with the work of local artists.

church's tower from 1540 to his death in 1547. He is still within the church, in a magnificent tomb that shows carvings of his home at Dunvegan on Skye. By 1784 the church was ruinous, but in that year Alexander MacLeod of Berneray, a captain with the East India Company, restored it.

Rodel Church

OTHER WESTERN ISLES

NORTH UIST

59 miles SW of Stornoway

Like most of the Western Isles, North Uist is low lying, with more water than land making up its total area of 74,884 acres. **Loch Scadavay** is the biggest of the lochs, and though it only has an area of eight square miles, it has a shoreline measuring 51 miles in

length. It was given to the
MacDonalds of Sleat in 1495
by James IV, who sold it in
1855, having cleared many
of the tenants to make way
for sheep. The highest point
on the island, at 1,127 feet,
is **Eaval**, near the southeast
corner. The island has a ferry
service to An t-Obbe in
Harris from Berneray, and
one to Skye from
Lochmaddy, the island's
capital, and where most of
the hotels and B&Bs are to
be found. **Taigh
Chearsabhagh**, a museum and arts
centre is housed in an old inn dating
from the early 18th century. Near the
village is **Barpa Langais** a Neolithic
burial cairn with its burial chamber
almost complete. Half a mile south east
of it is the **Pubull Phinn Stone Circle**.

Sollas, North Uist

Teampull na Trionaid ("Trinity
Temple"), on the south west shore, was
once a great place of learning in the
Western Isles. Indeed some people claim
that it was Scotland's first university,
with scholars and students making their
way here from all over the country, one

AIRDABHAIGH

Carinish, North Uist Western Isles HS6 5HL
Tel: 01876 580611
e-mail: floraidh1@aol.com

Airdabhaigh means "the house by the sea", and is a
beautifully appointed bed and breakfast establishment that
also offers courses in traditional Highlands and Islands crafts.
Owned and personally run by Flora MacDonald, it is a
traditional Hebridean croft cottage that has been restored
and renovated to offer the very best of modern conveniences
while still retaining its old-world charm. It sits beside
Teampuill na Trianaid (Trinity Temple), once a great seat of
learning and possibly Scotland's first university. There are
two rooms on offer - a twin and a double, and both are
comfortable and cosy, with good furnishings and decoration.
Guests can have a full Scottish breakfast, using local produce
where possible, though lighter options include yogurt and
fresh fruits, all with home-baked bread.

But Airdabhagh offers so much more as you can also enjoy the option of taking part in one of
Flora's indigenous craft courses. You could spend your time wandering the fields and beaches collecting
dye stuffs, turning them into dyes and weaving them into small tapestries. You could learn about
Gaelic culture, its language, its poetry and its music. Other courses and workshops include paper-
making, calligraphy, creative Gaelic writing, history and historical walks and traditional Hebridean
cookery, including butter making. Flora would be more than pleased to discuss your own pastimes
and hobbies before you arrive so that she can offer something that will please and interest you.

being Duns Scotus (see also Duns).

It was founded in the early 13th century by one Beathag, a prioress from the priory on Iona and daughter of Somerled, Lord of the Isles. By the end of the 15th century, however, its influence began to wane, and during the Reformation it was attacked. Valuable books, manuscripts and works of art were tossed into the sea, and so much of the island's heritage was lost. The other building on the site is **Teampull MacBhiocair**, (MacVicar's Temple), where the teachers were buried.

It was in this area, in 1601, that the **Battle of Carinish** took place, the last battle on British soil not to have involved firearms. A troop of MacLeods from Harris was raiding the island, and took shelter in the Trinity Temple

TEMPLE VIEW

Carinish, North Uist, Western Isles HS6 5EJ
Tel: 01876 580676 e-mail: templeviewhotel@aol.com
Fax: 01876 580682 website: www.templeviewhotel.co.uk

Temple View is the only four star hotel in the whole of the Western Isles, and has ten en suite rooms that are both comfortable and furnished to an exceptionally high standard. Each one has tea/coffee making facilities, direct dial phone, colour TV and hair dryer. In addition, one of the rooms - a double/ twin - has disabled facilities. There is a cosy residents' lounge, plus a lounge conservatory with great views. The dining room uses the fruits of Scotland's larder, with local seafood being a speciality. Temple View is centrally situated for exploring North Uist, Benbecula and South Uist.

SEALLADH TRAIGH

Cladach Kirkibost, North Uist, Western Isles HS6 5EP
Tel: 01876 580248 Fax: 01876 580653
e-mail: annexure@tiscali.co.uk

Sealladh Traigh is a beautifully appointed, modern guest house on the west coast of the lovely island of North Uist with a home-from home atmosphere. It boasts two double rooms, one twin and two singles, each one furnished and decorated to an extremely high standard. The views form the B&B's conservatory of the islands of Kirkibost, Benbecula, South Uist and even Barra are spectacular. The grounds of Sealladh Traig go right down to the shore, and there is ample opportunity to study the wonderful birdlife and the seals. This is the perfect base from which to explore South Uist, Benbecula and North Uist itself.

NORTH UIST RIDING CENTRE

Griminish, North Uist, Western Isles HS6 5BZ
Tel: 07786 817577
e-mail: northuistrc@aol.com

The **North Uist Riding Centre** is situated on the west coast of the wonderful island of North Uist. Enjoy the coastal scenery on horseback as you explore the beauties of an island that is steeped in history and legend. It is an experience not to be missed. The Centre uses well-schooled native horses and ponies, including the rare Eriskay pony, from the small island of Eriskay. Ride across the white sandy beaches for which North Uist is so famous. Visit the now uninhabited island of Vallay, that can be reached at low tide, and see the old cottages and the many reminders of when it was a thriving community. You'll never forget the experience.

buildings when attacked by the MacDonalds. The MacDonalds ignored the status of the temple, and slaughtered every MacLeod clansman except two, who escaped.

On the island's west coast, off the A865, is the **Balranald Nature Reserve**, where you can see waders and seabirds on various habitats.

BENBECULA

80 miles SW of Stornoway

Benbecula is Beinn bheag a' bh-faodhla in Gaelic, meaning mountain of the fords. It is sandwiched between North and South Uist, with a landscape that is low and flat and dotted with shallow lochans, though **Rueval**, its highest peak, soars to all of 403 feet. The island marks the boundary between the Protestant islands to the north and the Roman Catholic islands to the south. There is no ferry terminal on the island,

as it is connected to South Uist and North Uist by causeways.

The main settlement is **Balivanich**, or Baile na Mhanaich, meaning "Monk's Town". It sits on the west coast, and beside it is a small airstrip. The scant ruins of **Teampall Chaluim Cille**, founded by St Torranan, lie close to the village.

To the south of the village, on the B892, are the ruins of **Nunton Chapel**, supposed to have been a nunnery built in the 14th century. It was Lady Clanranald from nearby Nunton House (built from the stones of Nunton Chapel) who gave Charles Edward Stuart his disguise as a serving girl when he escaped from Benbecula to Skye in 1746.

Borve Castle, about three miles south of Balivanich, was owned by Ranald, son of John of Islay, in the 14th century. The ruins show a typical tower house of the period. Within the school at **Lionacleit**,

MACLEAN'S BAKERY

Vachdar, Isle of Benbecula, Western Isles HS7 5LY
Tel: 01870 602659 Fax: 01870 603121
e-mail: macleansbakery@tiscali.co.uk

For the very best in quality oatcakes, it must be **Maclean's Bakery** on Benbecula. It is small, it is independent, and it puts quality and value for money before anything else. The canapé bases will set your imagination running, as you chose what to fill them with. Locally caught seafood? Local cheese perhaps? Strawberries and cream? There is also a great range of oatcakes that are just right for spearing with butter and eating with tea or coffee. Only the best Scottish oatmeal goes into them, and they add a touch of luxury to any event.

STEPPING STONES RESTAURANT

Balivanich, Benbecula, Western Isles HS7 5DA
Tel: 01870 603377

The **Stepping Stones** restaurant offers some of the best food in the Western Isles. Built of warm pine, it is spacious and light, with large picture windows. Here you can relax, enjoying a cuisine that is a mixture of Scottish and international, and which uses only the fines, freshest local produce wherever possible. The evening menu has such dishes as pan fried local lamb with onions, mushrooms and rosemary, king scallops on a brochette with bacon and tomatoes, and so much more. The prices are always reasonable, the atmosphere is friendly and informal, and you'll be made more than welcome.

three miles south of Balivanich, is a small museum.

SOUTH UIST

87 miles SW of Stornoway

Running down the east side of South Uist is a range of low mountains, with **Beinn Mhor** being the highest at 2,034 feet. The west side of the island is gentler, with fine white sandy beaches. **Lochboisdale**, in the southeast corner, is the largest village on the island, and has a ferry connection to Mallaig, Oban and Castlebay on Barra.

Lochboisdale, South Uist

The island is one of the few places in Scotland never to have fully embraced the Reformation, and is predominantly Roman Catholic. To the northwest of the island, at Rueval, is the famous statute of **Our Lady of the Isles**, overlooking Loch Bee. It was erected in 1957 and sculpted by Hew Lorimer of Edinburgh. It stands 30 feet high. At the **Loch Druidibeag Nature Reserve**, which is close by, many birds such as greylag geese and mute swans, can be observed.

LOCHBOISDALE HOTEL

Lochboisdale, South Uist, Western Isles HS8 5TH
Tel: 01878 700332 Fax: 01878 700324
e-mail: karen@lochboisdale.com
website: www.lochboisdale.com

The **Lochboisdale Hotel** dates back to the 1860s, and during all that time it has been offering superb Highland hospitality to many people who passed through its doors. Karen and Calum MacAuley, who recently took it over, are continuing the great tradition. It overlooks the picturesque harbour and has amazing views across the Minch to Canna and Rum.
Here you will find a relaxing, informal atmosphere, plenty of comfort, great service and outstanding value for money. Many people have commented that it has a real home from home feel about it.

It boasts 15 large rooms - ten double and five single. One of the doubles is a family room and can sleep up to five people. All are en-suite, of course. They are also decorated and furnished to an exceptional standard. Some of the best seafood on the island is available in the spacious, welcoming dining room. White fish - lobsters - crab - oysters - langoustines - mussels - they're all available here, freshly caught, and all the other produce that goes into making the hotel's superb dishes is fresh and local wherever possible. Why not enjoy a drink in the warmth of the lounge, where an open fire burns in the colder months? There are fortnightly music sessions that are always lively and fun.

HEBRIDEAN JEWELLERY

Iochdar, South Uist, Western Isles HS8 5QX
Tel: 01870 610288 Fax: 01870 610370
e-mail: hebbie@lineone.net
website: www.hebridean-jewellery.co.uk

Situated on the lovely island of South Uist, **Hebridean Jewellery** fashions and makes superb gold and silver jewellery inspired by ancient Celtic/ Pictish designs that go back centuries. It was founded by John Hart in 1974, and now his son, also called John, continues the fine tradition of artistry and craftsmanship that has gained the company a reputation that goes far beyond the shores of Scotland.

The Celtic/ Pictish range features superbly made Scottish kilt pins, thistles and Luckenbooth brooches (brooches traditionally given by a groom to his bride on their wedding day but not used until their first son's wedding, when it is again passed on). There are also chunky wrist and neck torcs that add that certain something to any fashion ensemble, necklaces, earrings, bracelets and penanular brooches, which are circular with long pins that were sometimes used as weapons in days gone by. There is also a selection of superb wildlife pieces, such as a silver seal mounted on a hand-picked pebble from Iochdar beach on South Uist.

There are also shops in Stornoway on Lewis and at Fort William on the mainland, both selling the complete range of Hebridean Jewellery, and catalogues can be ordered through the company's website at £2 including delivery anywhere in the UK. You can also order jewellery over a secure connection via the website.

South Uist is one of the most beautiful islands in the Western Isles, and is full of dramatic scenery, historical interest and wildlife. No visit is complete without calling in at the workshops and showroom of Hebridean Jewellery. Any one of their beautiful, hand-crafted pieces would make a superb gift, or a souvenir of your visit to one of the most magical places in Scotland.

It was in South Uist, near **Milton** on Loch Kildonan, that Flora MacDonald was born in 1722. Her house is now completely ruinous, though the foundations can still be seen. She was no simple Gaelic lass, but the daughter of a prosperous landowning farmer who died when she was young. Her mother then married Hugh MacDonald, a member of the great MacDonald of Sleat family. She was brought up in Skye and went to school in Sleat and Edinburgh.

Kildonan Museum, north of Lochboisdale on the A865, has displays and exhibits on local history, as well as a tearoom and shop. The basis of the museum is a collection of artefacts gathered by the island priest, Father John Morrison, in the 1950s and 60s. Further north along the A865 are the ruins of **Ormiclate Castle**, built between 1701 and 1708 as a sumptuous residence for the chief of Clanranald. Alas, the chief's stay there was short lived, as it burnt down in 1715 after a rowdy Jacobite party.

Off the south coast of South Uist is the small island of **Eriskay** (from the Norse for "Eric's Island"), which is joined to South Uist by a causeway opened in 2002 and costing £9.8m. It is noted for one of the most beautiful of Gaelic songs, the *Eriskay Love Lilt*. It was here, on 23rd July 1745, that Charles Edward Stuart first set foot on Scottish soil when he stepped off a French ship to reclaim the British throne for the Stuarts. The beach where he landed is now called Prince's Beach, and legend says that his first action was to plant the sea convolvulus, which now thrives here.

It was in February 1941 that another event took place, which was to make Eriskay famous. **The SS. Politician** was heading towards the United States from Liverpool with a cargo of 260,000 bottles of whisky when it was wrecked off Calvey Island the Sound of Eriskay. Legend has it that as soon as the seamen were removed from the ship to safety, work began on "rescuing" the cargo. Eventually Customs and Excise men appeared on the island, but by this time the bottles had been spirited away into peat bogs and other hidey-holes. Only 19 people were charged with illegal possession.

Sir Compton Mackenzie used the incident as the basis for his novel *Whisky Galore*, made into a film in 1948. The wreckage can still sometimes be seen at exceptionally low tide. In the late 1980s an attempt was made to get at the rest of the cargo, but this proved unsuccessful.

The highest point on the island is **Ben Scrien**, at 609 feet. It is an easy climb, and gives magnificent views. The island's native pony, the grey and black Eriskay pony, was at one time used to carry seaweed and peat on panniers slung across their back. In the 1950s they nearly died out, but now are on the increase again. They are the last surviving examples of the once common Hebridean ponies, which were popular all over the islands.

BARRA
105 miles S of Stornoway

Barra ("Barr's Island") is the southernmost of the Western Isles, separated from South Uist by the Sound of Barra. To the south is a string of tiny islands, including Sanday, Rosinish, Mingulay and Berneray.

The island's airstrip is to the north of the island, and is the fine sandy beach at **Cockle Bay**, a name which is richly deserved as cockles are still collected there today. The main settlement is to the south at Castlebay, the terminal for the Oban ferry.

Kisimul Castle, Barra

On an island in the bay itself is **Kisimul Castle** (Historic Scotland), the largest fortification in the Western Isles. Its name means "the place of taxes", and it was the home of the Macneils of Barra, chiefs of Clan Macneill, who were granted the island in the 15th century, first by the Lord of the Isles and then by James VI. Others say, however, that the Macneils have been associated with the island since at least the 11th century.

The castle was originally built in about 1030, though the present building dates from the 15th century. The island on which it is built has its own fresh water wells, and this, coupled with its position, makes it almost impregnable. A story is told of how the castle was once being besieged by the Vikings, who wanted to starve it into submission. However, they soon gave up when they saw the castle guards hang bloody sides of beef from the ramparts. It was, of course, a ruse. What had been hung from the ramparts were cow hides used to make leather, smeared with dog's blood.

In 1838 the island was sold to Gordon of Cluny, who proceeded to remove the islanders from the land and ship them off to the New World. In 1937 the island was bought back by the 45th Chief of Clan Macneil, an American called Robert Lister Macneil. The 15th century castle had been burnt down in the late 1700s, and he set about restoring it.

The old chiefs of Clan Macneil had the reputation of being haughty and proud. A story is told of a Macneil chief at the time of Noah, who was invited aboard the Ark to escape the flood. He is supposed to have arrogantly replied, "Macneil already has a boat." Another story is told of later times. After Macneil had dinner, one of his servants would go up to the ramparts of Kisimul Castle and announce to the world: "as the Macneil has dined, the other kings and princes of the world may now dine also."

The ruined **Cille-bharraidh** (Church of St Barr) is located at the north end of the island, and was the burial place of the Macneils. Also buried here is **Sir Compton Mackenzie**, who wrote *Whisky Galore* (see also Eriskay). The island is predominantly Catholic, and at Heaval, a mile north east of Castlebay, is a marble statue of the Madonna and Child called **Our Lady of the Sea**.

ORKNEY & SHETLAND 14

In 1469 James III married Margaret, the young daughter of Christian I of Denmark and Norway. Her father pledged Orkney and Shetland to the Scottish crown until such time as the dowry was settled in full. As he was crippled with debts, the dowry was never paid, and in 1472, the islands became part of Scotland, creating the kingdom of Scotland as we know it today.

The Norse influences are still strong. Gaelic was never spoken here, and the place names (and many family names) all have Norse derivations. Both sets of islands are nearer Oslo than they are London, and there have even been occasional calls for the islands to be independent of Scotland.

The Brough Ness on South Ronaldsay in Orkney is no more than eight miles from the Scottish mainland, while the Shetland Islands sit much further out to sea, with the distance between Sumburgh Head and the mainland being over 100 miles. Few people realise the distances involved, as maps of the British Isles invariably put the Shetlands in a convenient box off Scotland's north east coast. However, fast ferries and air services put the islands within easy reach of the mainland.

In the distant past they were at a major communications crossroads, and gained an importance that far outweighed their size. They were on the main route from Scandinavia to Scotland, England, Ireland and the Isle of Man, and seafarers invariably stopped off there, some eventually settling. They are rich in historical sites and remains (far too many to mention them all in this book), which show a continued occupation for thousands of years. Indeed, there are about 120 confirmed broch sites in the Shetland Islands alone. And because the landscape has never been intensely farmed or cultivated, many of these sites have remained relatively undisturbed.

The main difference between the two archipelagos can be summed up in the old saying

Kirbister, Orkney

LOCATOR MAP

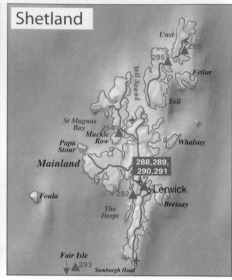

ADVERTISERS AND PLACES OF INTEREST

that an Orcadian (an inhabitant of Orkney) is a crofter with a fishing boat, whereas a Shetlander is a fisherman with a croft. Orkney is therefore the more fertile of the two, though this is relative, as the landscape is nothing like the Scottish mainland farming areas, and trees are the exception rather than the rule. One thing has brought prosperity to the islands, however, and that is North Sea oil. It has transformed their economies, but at the same time has remained remarkably unobtrusive, apart from places like Sullom Voe in Shetland, the largest oil terminal and port in Europe.

The Orkney archipelago consists of about 70 islands, only 19 of which are inhabited. The largest island is Mainland, where the islands' capital, Kirkwall, is located. It is a small city as well as a royal burgh, as it has its own medieval cathedral, the most northerly in

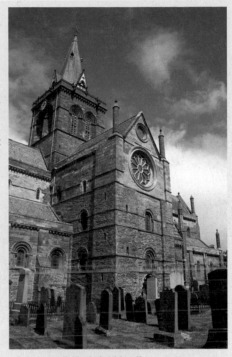

St Magnus Cathedral, Kirkwall

Britain and the most complete in Scotland. Most of the islands are connected by ferry, and the best way to explore the smaller ones is on foot rather than by car. Some of the sites, such as Skara Brae, are world famous and must not be missed.

Up until government reorganisation Shetland was a county in its own right called Zetland, with the county buildings at Lerwick. It has about 100 islands, with less than 20 being inhabited. Its largest island is again called Mainland, and it is here that Lerwick is situated. It is the island's capital, and the most northerly town in Britain. Every year in January the ancient "Up Helly Aa" festival is held, where a Viking ship is paraded through the streets of the town before being ceremonially burnt. Its origins go back to pagan times, when, in the depths of winter, people feared that the warmth of summer might not return. To attract it, they lit fires. - a case of like attracting like. The Vikings of the Shetlands went a stage further, and burnt one of the objects that were dear to their culture - a boat.

ORKNEY WINE COMPANY

Operahalla, St Ola, Kirkwall, Orkney KW15 1SX
Tel: 01856 878700   Fax: 01856 878701
e-mail: info@orkneywine.co.uk   website: www.orkneywine.co.uk

Britain's most northerly winery, the **Orkney Wine Company**, is run by Emile and Marjolein van Schayk, a Dutch couple who settled in Orkney in 1997 after living in Kirkcolm near Stranraer for two years. Emile had been making his own wines as a hobby for six years before setting up the company in 2001, his first recipe having been given to him by a shepherdess. Now the Orkney Wine Company makes quality wines in the traditional way from berries, flowers and vegetables, many of them locally grown and gathered in the clean, island air. The natural fermentation process means that the alcohol content is higher than that found in grape-based wines. Only 18 Carat, the carrot whisky wine, is fortified with an eight-year-old Orkney single malt whisky. The wines are produced within a deliberate environmentally friendly policy.

You are very welcome to visit the winery, which is just a few miles south of Kirkwall, off the A961. You will have the opportunity to sample and compare the wines before you buy. There is a varied range of seductive and exciting combinations, like Strubarb, a cunning concoction of strawberries and rhubarb. Or Blaeberry Hairst, a full bodied and smooth blueberry wine. Or how about Elderberry Borealis, named after the famous Northern Lights. This is a dark, port style wine with a spicy bite to it. Plus there's Black Portent, Cranberry, Gorse and a whole lot more.

A true taste of Orkney!

KIRKWALL

The capital of Orkney has a population of about 4,800, and was granted its charter as a royal burgh in 1486. It sits almost in the centre of Mainland, and divides the island into East Mainland and West Mainland. It is a lively, busy place of old stone buildings and streets paved in flagstones, with a shopping centre that serves all of the islands. The old name for the town was

Kirkwall

Kirkjuvagr, meaning the "church inlet", that church not being the cathedral, but the Church of St Olaf. All that is left of the early medieval building is a doorway in St Olaf's Wynd.

St Magnus Cathedral was founded in 1137 by Saint Magnus's nephew Rognvald Kolsson (who was later canonised), though the cathedral as you see it today dates from between the 12th and 16th centuries. The story goes that Magnus was the son of Erlend, one of two earls who ruled Orkney. The King of Norway deposed the earls, and appointed his own son Sigurd as Overlord. The King and his son then set out on a raiding party for Wales, taking Magnus with them. However, Magnus refused to take part in the usual rape and pillage,

deciding instead to sing psalms. The Norwegian king was displeased, and young Magnus had to flee.

After the king's death, he returned to Orkney, and in 1117 arranged to meet with Haakon, the new ruler of the islands, to claim his inheritance. However, Haakon had him murdered by an axe blow to the skull. At first, it is said that Magnus was buried in a small church on Birsay, but 20 years later his remains were taken to St Olaf's Church and finally to the new cathedral when it was consecrated. Some people regarded this story as more of a legend than historical fact, but in 1919, during some restoration work, a casket containing human bones was found embedded high up in one of the cathedral's pillars. The

skull had been split open with an axe. In the 18th century the remains of St Rognval were also discovered embedded in a pillar.

The ruined **Bishop's Palace** (Historic Scotland) dates mainly from the 12th century, when it was built for Bishop William the Old. The Round Tower (called the "Moosie Too" by locals), however, was built by Bishop Reid between 1541 and 1548. It was within the palace, in 1263, that King Haakon IV of Norway died, having just been defeated at the Battle of Largs (see also Largs). He was buried in Kirkwall Cathedral, but his body was later taken back to Bergen in Norway.

The notorious Patrick Stewart, Earl of Orkney and grandson of James V, built the adjacent **Earl's Palace** (Historic Scotland) between 1600 and 1607. The Stewart earls were hated in the islands

because they exploited the people and bled them dry. Patrick himself was arrested by James VI and executed for treason in 1615.

Within Tankerness House, built in 1574, is the **Orkney Museum**, which contains artefacts and exhibits about the island. The wooden box that contained St Magnus's bones, discovered within a pillar in the cathedral, is one of the exhibits. Tankerness House originally belonged to then cathedral, and was the home of Gilbert Foultie, the last archdeacon. It later became the property of the Baikie family, one of the islands' principle landowners. The Baikie Drawing room within the museum shows what a typical late 18th and early 19th century drawing room would have looked like. The **Orkney Wireless Museum** is at Kiln Corner, and has examples of wartime and domestic

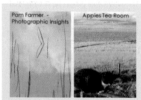

FURSBRECK POTTERY

Harray, Orkney KW17 2JR
Tel/Fax: 01856 771419
e-mail: harraypotter@applepot.co.uk
website: www.applepot.co.uk

Andrew Appleby is the original Harray potter! His workshop is in the Old Schoolhouse in Harray, a few miles west of Kirkwall on Mainland Island. However, the correct name of the pottery is **Fursbreck Pottery**, and it is here that Andrew has been throwing pots both large and small for over 30 years. He calls his work "practical pottery with style", and this is no idle boast. He is recognised as one of the most skilful and imaginative potters around, having established his craft business in the 1970s and having built a solid reputation for design, innovation, skill and practicality. Couple this with great value for money and you have the ideal place to buy a thoughtful gift for someone (or even just yourself) or a souvenir of your holiday on the magical Orkney Islands.

Andrew uses fine terracotta which fires at a high temperature, giving excellent glaze quality. Everything he throws is oven, dishwasher and microwave proof apart from his plates, which, though happy in a dishwasher, need to be warmed gently, preferring hot water to the sudden heat of an oven.

Design is everything to Andrew - and not just to make his thrown items beautiful. Practical matters have to be considered as well. For that reason his teapots and jugs pour nicely, casseroles cook stupendously well and the food cooked in them is always delicious. In addition, the mugs, beakers and goblets are fine and light, and a joy to drink from.

As Andrew hand-crafts all his pots, each one is unique, and stamped with its own individual character. There are full dinner services, wine sets, tea sets, casseroles, soup bowls, salt bowls and spoon and individual pieces that are both exciting and stylish.

The traditions of pottery are also important to Andrew. He has always been inspired by the craftsmen of old, and the influences of the past are always evident. The "Roman Black" glaze for which he is famous emulates the Terra Negra of first century Rome. Now he is recreating the famous Neolithic grooved ware found at Skara Brae, one of the most remarkable ancient sites in the world - and he invites you to come along and see his astounding results.

Andrew is also interested in good food, and sells organic smoked salmon and sea trout by mail order - the smoking is a secret recipe. Why not ask about this if you visit his workshop? You'll see him at work, and be able to buy some of his pottery and maybe some really good food as well.

SHEILA FLEET JEWELLERY

Tankerness, Orkney KW17 2QT
Tel: 01856 861203 Fax: 01856 861204
e-mail: info@sheila-fleet.co.uk
website: www.sheila-fleet.co.uk

Orkney has been the inspiration for so many artists and crafts people. Being from South Ronaldsay, one of the Orkney Islands, Sheila Fleet is no exception. After studying at Edinburgh College of Art, she worked in London and travelled extensively in Germany, Switzerland and Holland.

For eight years, she was a designer/model maker for Corocraft, one of the largest established jewellery companies in the world at that time. Eventually she came home to Orkney and joined a local company as their first professional designer and model maker. In 1993, she established her own company Sheila Fleet Jewellery, which has become very collectable with customers in Britain and around the world.

Sheila uses the Orkney landscapes as her inspiration when designing her exquisite items. The 'Rainbow' collection, for instance, captures the colours of the rainbow as seen in a wide, Orkney sky. In the execution of the designs, she uses enamels to convey the wonderful colours of red, orange, yellow, green, blue, indigo and violet. Colour and movement are very important to Sheila, and she aims to produce three different collections each year.

Take some time to view her website where you will see a superb range of silver jewellery such as 'Flight inspiration' based on bird forms. Each piece of jewellery captures the elegant movement of a bird in flight.

Her Headlands collection takes inspiration from the Orkney coastline. Reflecting the soft undulating shapes of the land then contrasted by using enamel called Shallows which represents the colour of the sea coming in over the shoreline.

Within every collection she designs pendants, earrings, brooches, bracelets, cufflinks and rings. Her ring collection is very extensive and can be made in silver, enamel, gold, platinum and set with diamonds. Each piece of jewellery comes beautifully boxed with a design origination card.

Sheila's fascinating and newly expanded workshop is in Tankerness, a few miles west of Kirkwall, the islands capital. Visitors are welcome to come and see her workshop, you can even have rings made to measure whilst you watch. Her work can also be seen at her Gallery on Bridge Street in Kirkwall, the prestigious Jenners department store in Edinburgh and Jenners at Loch Lomond Shores, Balloch.

Sheila Fleet Jewellery welcomes visitors and is open all year round Monday – Saturday 9am – 5pm, Sunday openings in summer from 10am – 4pm (June – August).

ORKNEY STAINED GLASS

Monquhanny, Shapinsay, Orkney KW17 2DZ
Tel: 01856 711276
e-mail: enquiries@orkneystainedglass.com
website: www.orkneystainedglass.com

Set in a former church built in 1856, **Orkney Stained Glass** is the perfect place to go for that special gift or a souvenir of your holiday on Orkney. It is situated on the island of Shapinsay, which is just a short ferry crossing from Kirkwall. The craftspeople working there combine traditional and modern glass techniques with contemporary design to produce a distinctive range of jewellery, light catchers, mirrors, lamps and jewellery boxes. Commissions in copper foil or for leaded windows and mosaic panels are also undertaken. The light, landscapes and wildlife of the Orkneys appear frequently on Orkney Stained Glass's work. Fish - whales - pebbles on a beach - sunsets over a jade green sea - all are captured on glass so that when the objects are held up to the light they shimmer and sparkle. Ancient people of Orkney provide inspiration as well. Some of Orkney stained Glass's jewellery is based on old Celtic and bronze age designs.

The company is owned and run by Judi and Stu Wellden, who offer day, or residential two-day courses in stained glass design and production, from the basics to advanced, with personal tuition throughout. They run from March through to November, with students receiving full board, either in en suite rooms or rooms with private bathrooms. The food on the courses is excellent, using local Orkney produce. The workshop gallery has extensive views of the surrounding islands, and you are free to browse with absolutely no obligation to buy.

wireless sets used on the islands. It was founded by local man Jim MacDonald, who had a lifetime's fascination with wireless and radio sets, and amassed a huge collection.

On a building in Castle Street is a plaque commemorating **Kirkwall Castle**, which was dismantled in 1615 and finally demolished in 1865. It had been built in the 14th century by Henry Sinclair, first Earl of Orkney. He had been given the title by Haakon of Norway in 1379, long before the islands became part of Scotland. His descendent William, the third earl, built Rosslyn Chapel in Midlothian, and his name has been linked to a pre-Columbus transatlantic crossing, the holy grail and the Knights Templar (see also Rosslyn).

GALLEY INN & SHORE RESTAURANT

Front Road, St Margaret's Hope, Orkney KW17 2SL
Tel: 01856 831526
e-mail: thegalleyinn@hotmail.com
website: www.galleyinn.co.uk

You should never visit the Orkneys without visiting the **Galley Inn & Shore Restaurant** in St Margaret's Hope. It is the perfect place to relax over a quiet drink as you take in the slower pace of life on these lovely islands. The place has a relaxed atmosphere, and is a popular place for visitors and locals to meet and chat. The Shore Restaurant serves food that is prepared from fresh, local ingredients. Everything from a simple bar meal to a lunch or dinner is available, and for your comfort, the restaurant is non-smoking. The service in the recently refurbished bar and restaurant is quick, efficient and friendly.

STANDING STONES HOTEL

Stenness, Orkney KW16 3JX
Tel: 01856 850449
e-mail: standingstones@sol.co.uk
website: www.standingstoneshotel.com

The three star **Standing Stones Hotel** takes its name from the many ancient monuments found on Orkney - monuments that remind us of the history of the islands, and which goes back thousands of years. The hotel sits close to possibly the most mysterious of the stones - the Stenness Standing Stones on Mainland Island, a few miles west of Kirkwall, the island's capital. Stand in the garden of the hotel and look across the Loch of Stenness, and you will see one of the world's unique landscapes - a landscape that takes in neolithic Orkney in all its mystery and splendour.

And yet the hotel itself was only built in 1981, combining tradition and friendliness with high standards of service and outstanding value for money. It sits back off the main Kirkwall-Stromness Road, and is so easy to get to from ferry terminals and the islands' airport. It has an informal atmosphere, and makes a great base from which to explore the islands. It boasts 17 rooms, 12 twin, two double and three single, all with en suite facilities and all with telephone, colour TV,, tea/coffee making facilities and hair dryer. They are all extremely comfortable, with décor and furnishings of the highest standard. Here you can have as relaxed or as energetic holiday as you like while savouring all the modern amenities the hotel has to offer. You know that you are being well looked after here.

The hotel's spacious restaurant, the Brodgar Restaurant, named after the Ring of Brodgar, another of Orkney's neolithic sites, serves memorable food within an ambience that lends itself to enjoyment and relaxation. Only fresh local produce in season is used to create the many imaginative dishes that combine traditional Scottish cooking with many subtle influences from Europe and beyond. And the wine list is comprehensive, so there's sure to be a wine that suits your palate.

Why not enjoy a quiet drink in one of the two lounge bars, or the Stenness Lounge Bar, where tasty and excellent bar meals are served at lunchtime and in the evenings? The well-stocked bar offers wines, spirits (including single malts), ales and locally brewed beer, liqueurs and soft drinks. The place is popular with the local people (always a good sign) and here you can meet and talk to them.

There is so much to do and see on Orkney. Bird watching - golf - walking - rock climbing - nature study - fishing - diving in the clear northern waters - cycling - and so much more. Plus, of course, the islands are alive with history. Mysterious, ancient monuments are all around to be explored and appreciated. If you come to Orkney, you must stay at the Standing Stones Hotel.

AROUND KIRKWALL

Lamb Holm

7 miles S of Kirkwall on the A961

Lamb Holm Italian Chapel

After the sinking of the Royal Oak by a U-boat in 1939 a string of islands to the south of Mainland were joined by causeways called the **Churchill Barriers**, which would prevent submarines from slipping through again. On the 99-acre Lamb Holm, one of the islands, is the ornate **Italian Chapel**. It was built by Italian prisoners-of-war who were working on the causeways and who had been captured in North Africa in 1942. The work is remarkable considering its basis is two Nissen huts and various pieces of cast-off metal and wood. In 1960 some of the ex-POWs were invited to return to the island to restore it. Mass is still said here every day during the summer months.

Maes Howe

8 miles W of Kirkwall off the A965

Maeshowe (Historic Scotland), on Mainland, is Britain's largest chambered cairn, and was excavated in 1861. In 1910 it was taken into state care, at which time the mound was "rounded off" to give it the appearance we see today. When archaeologists reached the main chamber, they discovered that the Vikings had beaten them to it, as there was Norse graffiti on the walls. The name "Maes Howe" comes from the Old Norse and means "great mound". It is a great, grassy hill, 36 feet high and 300 feet in circumference, and was built about 2,700 BC. A long, narrow passage leads into a central chamber with smaller side chambers, which are roofed and floored with massive slabs.

Also looked after by Historic Scotland are the four **Stenness Standing Stones**, the largest such stones in Orkney. Originally, it is thought, there were 12, and they formed a circle 104 feet in diameter, and date from about the same time as Maes Howe. The tallest stone is 16 feet tall. Not far away is an even taller stone, the **Watch Stone**, which is 18-and-a-half feet tall. To the north of the Stenness Stones, and near the shore of Harray Loch, is the **Barnhouse Settlement**, a neolithic village discovered in 1984. Agricultural activity over the years has destroyed much of it, though it is reckoned there were 15 dwellings on the site.

The **Ring of Brodgar**, also dating from about 2700 BC, still has 27 of its original 67 stones. They are smaller than the Stenness Stones, and stand on a strip of land between two small lochs. Legend says that long ago a group of giants came to this spot during the night, and that one of their number began playing the fiddle. The giants began to dance in a circle, and so carried away were they that they never noticed the sun starting to rise. When the light struck them, they were turned to stone.

ORPHIR

9 miles W of Kirkwall off the A964

During early Norse rule, Orphir was one of the main Orcadian settlements. **Orphir Church** was built in the 11th or 12 century and dedicated to St Nicholas, some say by Haakon, who murdered St Magnus, possibly as an act or penance after a pilgrimage to Jerusalem. It was a circular church about 18 feet in diameter, with a small apse at its eastern end, and was the only such medieval church in Scotland. Nothing now remains apart from the apse and some of the east wall. Bu Interpretation Centre, next to the church, explains the ruins.

HOUTON BAY LODGE

Houton Bay, Orphir, Scapa Flow, Orkney KW17 2RD
Tel & Fax: 0044 (0)1856 811320   Mob: 07909952344
e-mail: sales1esp@aol.com
website: www.houtonbaylodge.com

On the edge of beautiful Scapa Flow sits the four star **Houton Bay Lodge,** offering comfort, a friendly, informal atmosphere and outstanding value for money. It has access for wheelchairs and fully en suite double, family, twin and single rooms. Houton Bay Lodge has a luxurious honeymoon suite for couples wanting a romantic weekend. All rooms have writing desk, trouser press, iron and ironing board, hairdryer, tea/coffee making facilities, safe, fridge, CD radio alarm, remote control colour TV and leather reclining seats with leather footstools. There is a cosy lounge bar, billiard/games room, conservatory, internet, candlelit restaurant and the food, which is outstanding and has a mention in the *Good Food Guide to Scotland*. Make this your base when you explore the wonderful Orkney Isles.

PETER ROWLAND - DESIGNER SILVERSMITH

Crumbreck, Orphir, Orkney KW17 2RF
Tel/Fax: 01856 811347

Peter Rowland is a family-run business that was set up in 1995. The gallery and workshop is in a picturesque location that looks out to the dramatic scenery of the island of Hoy, off the west coast of Orkney's main island. Here Peter designs and creates superb items made from silver, helped by his wife Jane, who attends to the business side of things. Born and trained in Cheshire, he draws his inspiration from the many landscapes, changing skies and wildlife of the Orkney Islands.

His workshop was once a typical crofter's cottage, but in 1994, when he decided to set up his business, it was in need of renovation, which he did all by himself over the next two years. Most of it was totally rebuilt of local stone, providing a family home with attached workshop. Peter's work is all hand-made, using skills that have been passed down for generations of silversmiths. He specialises in the design and manufacture of limited editions, and undertakes many individual commissions. In 2002 he won the joint top award in the Scottish Select competition for a silver jug, ladle and two spoons.

A commission will start with Peter preparing designs which are shown to the client, and gradually

an exquisite object will emerge as the designs are talked over, amended and finally approved. And his limited editions soon become collectors' items, so well designed and crafted are they.

For all of this, Peter's prices are still remarkably reasonable, and a piece of silverware or jewellery from his workshop would make a welcome gift for a loved one or a special souvenir of a visit to the Orkneys.

STROMNESS

15 miles W of Kirkwall on the A965

This little burgh faces Orkney's second largest island, Hoy. Though it looks old and quaint, it only received its burgh charter in 1817, and was founded in the 17th century. The **Stromness Museum** in Alfred Street has displays on **Scapa Flow**, whaling, lighthouses and the Hudson's Bay Company (which had a base here, and

Stromness

employed many Orcadians). Scapa Flow, between Hoy and Mainland, is one of the best natural harbours in the world. After World War I the German fleet was brought to Scapa Flow while a decision was made about its future. However, the German officers decided the fleet's future themselves - they scuttled the ships, and most still lie at the bottom of the sea, a constant attraction for divers.

THE QUERNSTONE

38 Victoria Street, Stromness, Orkney KW16 3AA
Tel/Fax: 01856 851010
e-mail: elaine@quernstoneknits.com
website: www.quernstoneknits.com

The Quernstone is situated in the centre of the quaint old town of Stromness, and sells an amazing range of quality gifts at affordable prices. It has been trading for over 20 years, and its windows are packed with great ideas, and you are sure to be impressed by the quality and price of the items on offer. This is the place to go if you're looking for gifts or souvenirs that are just that little bit different. Come in and browse around - there is absolutely no obligation to buy. If you are looking for locally crafted jewellery, for instance, then this is the place for you. There is also a wide range of yarns, handbags, toiletries, toys and stationery. You might prefer instead to look at the bright, well-designed soft furnishings on the upper floor, or the ceramics, glassware, lampshades and furniture. This is also the place to buy your cards, as it carries a huge stock. Everything, in fact, to brighten and smarten up both you and the home. The shop is an Aladdin's cave of good design. You could almost spend a day here just admiring everything on offer.

At 2 Dundas Street, also in Stromness, is Quernstone's knitwear shop, another fascinating place that is full of colour and good design. Here the Quernstone's own knitwear designs are on show, specialising in hand-framed and hand-knitted garments in quality yarns. The range includes easy-to-wear shapes of universal appeal, from casual cropped jerseys to elegant long coats. Other knitwear brands are also stocked, including a selection of menswear, ensuring that you have a wide range to choose from. There is also a complimentary range of accessories, jewellery and gifts - in fact, something for everyone.

HOY

17 miles W of Kirkwall

Hoy is Orkney's second largest island, and sits off the west coast of Mainland. The **Old Man of Hoy** is Great Britain's tallest and most famous sea stack. Made of sandstone, it is over 445 feet high, and sits off the island's north west coast, a constant challenge to climbers. The first successful climb was in 1966, and TV cameras were there to record it. At the southwest end of the island is a **Martello Tower**, erected between 1813 and 1815 to protect the island from the French.

Ferry Terminal to Hoy

The **Dwarfie Stone** is unique in the United Kingdom - a burial chamber dating from at least 3000 BC cut into a great block of sandstone. Some people claim, however, that it was not a tomb, but an ancient dwelling. The most amazing thing about it is that it was hollowed out using nothing but horn tools, antlers and pieces of rock.

CLICK MILL

13 miles NW of Kirkwall on the B9057

Click Mill (Historic Scotland), with its turf covered roof, is the islands' last surviving example of a horizontal watermill, and got its name from the clicking sound it made when turning. They were once common throughout Scandinavia.

At Harray, a couple of miles south of the mill, is the **Corrigall Farm Museum**, housed in a 19th century farmhouse. Exhibits include a working barn with grain kiln and a loom.

SKARA BRAE

17 miles NW of Kirkwall on the B9056

In 1850, at the Bay of Skaill, a storm uncovered the remains of a village which was at least 5,000 years old - older even than the Pyramids. It is the oldest known

Old Man of Hoy

Skara Brae

prehistoric village in Europe, and the remains are now looked after by Historic Scotland. They show that the people who built it from stone were sophisticated and ingenious, and that the houses were comfortable and well appointed, with beds, dressers and cupboards made of stone, as wood was hard to come by. Archaeological evidence tells us that it was built by neolithic people who farmed, hunted and fished. When it was built, it stood some distance from the sea, but due to erosion over the years the sea is now on its doorstep.

Close by is **Skaill House**, the finest mansion in Orkney. The main part of the house was originally built in 1620 for George Graham, Bishop of Orkney, though it has been extended over the years. It houses a fine collection of furniture, including Bishop Graham's bed, on which are carved the words *GEO. GRAHAM ME FIERI FECIT* ("George Graham caused me to be made").

When the Skaill was being built, 15 skeletons were uncovered to the south of the

South Wing. In the 1930s skeletons were also uncovered under the house itself. It is now thought that the house was built on the site of a Christian Pictish cemetery. It is no wonder that Skaill is said to be haunted.

Brough of Birsay
21 miles NW of Kirkwall off the A966

This little island, which is connected to the mainland at low tide by a narrow causeway, has the remains of a Norse settlement and an early medieval chapel dedicated to St Peter (once the cathedral of the diocese of Orkney), built on the foundations of a chapel that may date back to the 7th or 8th centuries. After he was killed, St Magnus was possibly buried here until such time as his body could be taken to the newly built St Magnus Cathedral in Kirkwall. When visiting the island, the times of tides must be taken into account. The tourism office at Kirkwall can advise.

The area on Mainland opposite the island is also called Birsay, and here you

Earls Palace, Birsay

Birsay to Marwick via Marwick Head

Distance:	2.8 miles (4.5 kilometres)
Typical time:	120 mins
Height gain:	100 metres
Map:	Explorer 463
Walk:	www.walkingworld.com ID:1528
Contributor:	Colin and Joanne Simpson

Access Information:

The route as described starts from the right-angled bend on the B9056 where it overlooks Birsay Bay and finishes on the shores of Mar Wick - another bay to the south of Marwick Head. If you don't have the benefit of transport back to your start point you can backtrack from the Kitchener Memorial and follow a path to the minor road, which can be followed back to the start.

Additional Information:

The Kitchener Memorial which stands on the highest cliffs was erected in memory of all those on board HMS Hampshire (including Lord Kitchener, minister for war) which sank off these shores in 1916.

Description:

This walk traverses the top of what are possibly the best sea cliffs on Orkney. There are excellent views north to Westray and south to Hoy and the more distant Scottish mainland - the peaks of Morven and Ben Loyal being particularly prominent. Of particular interest are the seabird colonies on the cliffs which include puffins, guillemots and fulmars.

Features:

Sea, Wildlife, Birds, Flowers, Great Views, Moor

Walk Directions:

1 Start by following the track that heads straight on (approaching from the A967) between the field gate and a standing stone that forms the corner of a fence. This is the track heading due west from the corner, not the one heading north.

2 After 300 metres and after an open area (sometimes used for parking), the track bends to the south and starts to follow the coast. From the bend in the track there are good views back over the bay to the Brough of Birsay.

3 Continue parallel to the cliff edge and now rising gently, the path fairly indistinct at times.

4 As you continue, the cliffs to your side become larger. After around a kilometre of gentle uphill, a path comes in from the left (this is the direct route to the headland from a car park) and the path becomes much more distinct, running between a fence and the cliff. There are excellent views back along the cliffs.

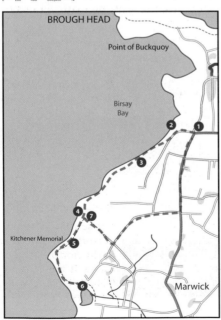

5 When you reach the highest point, topped by the Kitchener Memorial, there are superb views south to the island of Hoy (with the famous Old Man of Hoy visible right of the cliffs) and beyond, to the Scottish mainland. A path continues past the memorial to rejoin the fence and then follows the fence south-westwards, before turning the headland and dropping downhill to the bay of Marwick.

6 At the foot of the slope the path follows the water's edge to reach the road and the end of the walk. A sign facing the way back welcomes those walking in the opposite direction.

7 As an alternative to the end of the walk (if transport cannot be arranged), you can turn back from the memorial and retrace your steps to this gate. Go through the gate and follow a path to a car park from where you can follow the road back to your start point - giving a total distance of 7km for the walk.

can see the ruins of **Earl Stewart's Palace**. It was built about 1574 by Robert, Earl of Orkney, a cruel, unpopular man and father of Patrick, who was even more cruel and unpopular. The **Kirbuster Farm Museum**, also on Mainland, has examples of farm implements used on Orkney over the years, and a Victorian garden.

South of the island, at Marwick Head, is a squat tower - the **Kitchener Memorial**. It was erected in memory of Kitchener of Khartoum, who was killed when HMS Hampshire, on which he was travelling to Russia to discuss the progress of the war, struck a German mine near here in June 1916. Only 12 people survived the sinking of the ship.

ROUSAY

14 miles N of Kirkwall

This island is sometimes known as the "Egypt of the North", as it brims with archaeological sites. The **Taversoe Tuick Chambered Cairn** has two chambers, one above the other. The **Blackhammer Cairn**, the **Knowe of Yarso Cairn** and the **Midhowe Cairn** can also be seen. The **Broch of Midhowe** has walls that still stand 13 feet high.

On **Egilsay**, a small island to the east, are the superb ruins of the 12th century **St Magnus's Church**, with its round tower. It was on Egilsay in 1115 that Magnus was killed. A cairn marks the spot of the martyrdom.

WESTRAY

27 miles N of Kirkwall

The substantial ruins of **Noltland Castle** lie to the north of the island. It was built by Gilbert Balfour, who was Master of the

Rousay

WEST-RAY JEWELLERY

Mid Ouseness, Westray, Orkney KW17 2DN
Tel/Fax: 01857 677400
e-mail: Geordie@westrayjewellery.com
website: www.westrayjewellery.com

George Thomson of **West-Ray Jewellery** is a craftsman of the highest standard. He learned his trade with a local jeweller in Kirkwall, but after his marriage decided to return to his native island of Westray to become a fisherman and crofter while still repairing jewellery and producing private commissions.

In the year 2000 he realised a life long ambition when he set up his own jewellery business, finding his inspiration in the landscapes, history and wildlife of the Orkneys. In his workshop he produces exquisite jewellery items in gold and silver from the designs of talented designers on Westray. The Skaill collection is based on the shell designs of Julie Hagan, who is a local woman inspired by the things of nature on her native island. Or there's the St Boniface range, the design taken from an incised cross on a stone slab found in 1920 among the ruins of the Church of St Boniface on Papa Westray.

Items in many ranges on offer include earrings, pendants, chokers, bracelets, rings and bangles, and all are made to exacting standards. Call in at George's workshop and browse round and see the many fine items on sale. Choose something as a gift for a loved on or as a souvenir of your visit to the island.

HUME SWEET HUME

Pierowall Village, Westray Orkney KW17 2DH
Tel/Fax: 01857 677259
e-mail: info@humesweethume.com
website: www.humesweethume.com

Owned and personally run by sisters Lizza and Jenna Hume, Hume Sweet Hume is situated on the lovely island of Westray, north of mainland Orkney. Life moves at a more leisurely pace here, and it makes the perfect place for a quiet, relaxing holiday away from the stresses and strains of modern life. Having completed art school courses and obtained degrees, Lizza and Jenna decided to return to their home island to set up their business within the landscape that has always inspired them.

The shop creates and sells a great range of interior accessories such as cushions and throws, as well as innovative and functional fashion accessories. Largely designed by Lizza and Jenna, items are

made using a combination of textile techniques including textured knitting, weaving, embroidery, layering and felting. All items look to the Orkney land and seascape for their inspiration, with local beach pebbles often incorporated in designs. To increase the range of products available in the shop quality items by other designers are also on display. The shop is licensed, so you can buy a wide range of spirits, fine wines, and local wines made by the Orkney Wine Company.

All products are available to purchase at the shop on Westray or in other outlets throughout the UK. You can also order online via the Hume Sweet Hume website. Prices are reasonable and you can be assured that design and quality are always of the highest.

Household to Mary Stuart and Sheriff of Orkney. At Pierowall, the island's main settlement, are the ruins of the **Ladykirk**. To the east of Westray is the smaller island of **Papa Westray**. It connected to Westray by air, the flight (which lasts two minutes) being the shortest scheduled air flight in the world.

LERWICK

Lace Knitting, Lerwick

The name "Lerwick" comes from the Norse for "muddy bay", and up until the 17th century that's all it was - a muddy bay surrounded by a handful of crude dwellings. It is capital of Shetland and was granted its burgh charter in 1818. It was originally developed by the Dutch in the early 17th century to service their herring fleet, and from there gradually grew into a small town. It is the most northerly town in Britain, and, with a population of about 7,000, sits on the island of Mainland. It is so far north that during June you could read a newspaper at midnight out of doors without any artificial light.

Every year, on the last Tuesday in January, the festival of **Up Helly Aa** is held. After being hauled through the streets of the town accompanied by men carrying torches and dressed as Vikings, a Viking longboat is set on fire. Though an enjoyable and spectacular sight, it is a ritual which is thought to date back to pagan times, when darkest days of winter were feared. It was thought that the light from celebrations of this kind attracted the light of the sun, which would then gradually return, lengthening the days. The introduction of a Viking ship, however, was a Victorian idea. Before

SHETLAND SOAP COMPANY

11 Commercial Street, Lerwick, Shetland ZE1 0DL
Tel/Fax: 01595 690096
e-mail: susanne@shetlandsoap.co.uk
website: www.shetlandsoapcompany.com

Shetland is a special place - remote, windy and with dramatic scenery that haunts the mind. It is as close to Bergen in Norway as it is to Aberdeen, and has long been influenced by its Norse heritage. It's in Lerwick, Shetland's capital, that you'll find one of its hidden treasures - the **Shetland Soap Company**. It sits at the heart of the town, and manufactures and sells a wide range of soap products that are shipped to all corners of the United Kingdom. The company uses the smells, sights and landscapes of the islands to create products whose fragrances echo the smell of the sea, the warmth of the sun and the clean, crisp air that makes the islands so unique. It also uses traditional and contemporary methods to produce a superb range of soaps, creams, gentle shampoos,

bubble baths and shower gels. They make fantastic gifts or souvenirs, and they are all reasonably priced so that you can stock up with some of the purest products available.

All the Shetland Soap Company's soaps are completely ethical, with none of the ingredients or finished products having been tested on animals. The soap is 98 - 100 per cent natural, and produces a creamy, non drying lather that is kind to even the most delicate of skins. It is made to the company's own special recipe, as are the creams, which are rich and moisturising. They are great for baby-soft hands knees, feet and elbows. Try the Shetland Rescue cream, whose healing formula works wonders on badly chapped skin, and other irritations. And the shampoos, bubble baths and gels are just as pure. They are generously fragranced, with a variety of exciting aromas that are sure to please. If you want to be really adventurous, why not try the "bath bombs" - they are fun, fizzy and fragrant, making a bath a luxury experience not to be missed. The company thinks of itself as a community business, as it works closely with local people and those with disabilities so that they can gain skills and experience in a commercial environment.

The shop and workshops are situated next to the local tourist office, so you can't miss them. Here you can see the soaps and other products actually being made, and also browse the shop, which stocks all the exciting range of products. There is a range of special gift items, or you can buy individual items to create your own unique selection. These can then be gift wrapped for you to present to loved ones. Or you can have wedding favours created to your own specification.

The shop is open Monday - Saturday from 9.30am to 5pm, with occasional Sunday openings during cruise ship visits. You are free to visit and browse. You'll surely find something that will take your fancy and want to buy.

that tar barrels were used.

Like Orkney, all the islands are rich in ancient remains. There are also many small interpretation centres and museums - too many for all of them to be mentioned in this book.

The number of days in the year when the temperatures rise above 75 degrees are few in Shetland, but there are compensations, not least of which is the quality of light and the almost 24 hours of daylight at the height of summer. And there is less rain here than in Fort William or even North Devon.

Fort Charlotte, named after George III's wife, was built in the 1780s on the site of 17th century fortifications to protect the town from the Dutch, whom, the British government felt, had too much power in the area due to its large herring fleet which was based here. **Shetland Museum** gives an insight into the history of the islands and its people, and has some marvellous displays on archaeology. There is also an excellent photograph archive and occasional art exhibitions. It will be closed until 2006, when new premises at Hays Dock will be completed.

The wonderfully named **Böd of Gremista** is located north of the town,

Shetland Pony

and was the birthplace in 1792 of **Arthur Anderson**, co-founder of the P&O line. He joined the Royal Navy, and subsequently fought in the Napoleonic wars. In 1833 he co-founded the

ANDERSON & CO

60-62 Commercial Street, Lerwick,
Shetland ZE1 0BD
Tel: 01595 693714 Fax: 01595 694811
e-mail: pottingers@aol.com
website: www.shetlandknitwear.com

Part of the fun of a holiday is shopping. And if you're holidaying on Shetland, then that means shopping for Shetland knitwear. For hundreds of years Shetlanders have been making some of the best knitwear to be found anywhere, and in **Anderson & Co** you will find one of the biggest collections on the islands. In fact, its sole purpose is to bring genuine Shetland knitwear to a discerning public who know about design, quality and great value for money. The shop can be found in the heart of Lerwick, the island's capital, and was established as long ago as 1872. It specialises in Fair Isle hand-knitted sweaters, button-up garments and vests, as well as hand and hand frame knit openwork lace jumpers and cardigans. Where the design allows, all garments are made in the traditional, seamless circular knit fashion that is unique to the islands.

Being so close to Scandinavia (Bergen in Norway is no more than 187 miles away) the garments are strongly influenced by the designs found there. But though it is so far north, Shetland still benefits from the warm waters of the Gulf Stream, which has meant that the hardy local sheep thrive, giving a top quality fleece that is soft yet durable. All the products on display in the shop are produced the old fashioned way - in the knitters' own homes, using hand and machine techniques. The quality control and finishing is of the highest standard imaginable, and yet the prices represent remarkable value for money.

Ladies, gentlemen and children can choose from jumpers, cardigans, tank tops, gloves, scarves and hats that are all lovingly designed and crafted to be hard wearing and warm. Get your beautifully crafted Shetland shawl which will become a treasured heirloom. There are also Shetland rugs and sheepskins as well as a selection of souvenirs many of which are unique to Anderson & Co.

Whilst in Shetland why not see the countryside and stay at Snarraness House, West Burrafirth, Bridge of Walls where you're sure of a warm welcome. This is a tranquil, idyllic, paradise nestled just beyond an isthmus. Wild life is abundant and with the sea visible from all the rooms you can relax and enjoy the beautiful views or walk through the hills and listen to the silence while you watch for otters, seals or dolphins. Accommodation comprises two double, one twin - two en-suite - one Private. Dinner avaialable on request. Evelyn can be contacted at Anderson & Co or at home.on 01595 809375.

Peninsular Steam Navigation Company, which, in 1937, became the Peninsular and Oriental Steam Navigation Company. The 18th century building has been restored as a small museum and interpretation centre highlighting the island's maritime history.

AROUND LERWICK

BRESSAY

1 mile E of Lerwick

The island of Bressay sits opposite Lerwick, and shelters its harbour. The **Bressay Heritage Centre**, close to the ferry terminal, illustrates through displays and exhibits what life was like on the island in former times. The tiny island of **Noss**, off its west coast, is a nature reserve, one of the oldest on the Shetlands. Boat trips to the island are available. Bressay has some fine walks, notably on its east coast. Its highest point is **Ward Hill**, at 742 feet.

The ruined **St Mary's Chapel** is at Cullingsbrough Voe, on the island's east coast. It may date back to Viking times, and is the only cruciform church on the Shetland Islands.

MOUSA

13 miles S of Lerwick

There are about 70 confirmed broch (a round, fortified tower) sites in Shetland, and the best preserved is at Sandwick on this tiny uninhabited island off the east coast of Mainland. The **Broch of Mousa** (Historic Scotland) was built sometime during the Iron Age from local stone, and is over 40 feet high and 49 feet in diameter. It has lost its uppermost courses, but is still in a remarkable state of preservation, and shows the typical layout of these curious buildings, which are found nowhere else but in Scotland.

The double walls slope inwards as they get higher, and embedded in them are staircases (which you can use to climb to the top) and defensive galleries. Like other brochs, no mortar was used in its construction.

JARLSHOF

25 miles S of Lerwick on the A970

Lying close to Sumburgh Airport on Mainland, Jarlshof is one of the most important historical sites in Europe, and has been continuously occupied from the Bronze Age right up until the 17th century. There are Bronze Age huts, Iron Age earth houses, brochs, wheelhouses from the Dark Ages, Norse longhouses and medieval dwellings. It is managed by Historic Scotland, and there is a small museum and interpretation centre.

At **Old Scatness**, close to Jarlshof, is an archaeological site centred on a number of ancient brochs, wheelhouses and medieval dwellings. There is a living history area with demonstrations that reproduce ancient technologies using authentic materials. It was discovered in 1975 when a road was cut through what was thought to be a natural mound. Old walls were discovered, and work began on excavating the site in 1995.

The **Ness of Burgi**, a small promontory jutting out into the sea, lies to the west of Jarlshof, and has an Iron Age fort.

FAIR ISLE

46 miles S of Lerwick

The most southerly of the Shetland Islands lies almost half way between Shetland and Orkney. It is owned by the National Trust for Scotland, and is one of the remotest inhabited islands in the country, with a population of about 65. It was originally called Fridarey, meaning "island of peace", by Norse settlers. In

1558 one of the Spanish Armada vessels, the *El Gran Grifon*, was shipwrecked here. About 200 men managed to struggle ashore, and theye were looked after by the islanders as best they could. However, the sailors, hungry and exhausted, began killing of the ilanders' animals for food, and they were eventually shipped off to Shetland from where they were sent home. In 1948 a Spanish delegation dedicated a cross on the island to those Spaniards who had died.

The island was once owned by George Waterston, who was the Scottish Director of the Royal Society for the Protection of Birds, and who founded a bird observatory in 1948. **The George Waterston Memorial Centre and Museum** has displays about the history and wildlife of the island. The **Feely Dyke**, a turf wall separating common land from modern crofting land, may date from prehistoric times.

Fair Isle knitting is famous the world over, and it is a craft that is still carried out to this day, using traditional patterns.

SCALLOWAY
6 miles W of Lerwick on the A970

Though only six miles from Lerwick, this small village sits on the Atlantic coast while its larger neighbour sits on the coast of the North Sea. Its name comes from the Norse "Scola Voe", which means the "Huts by the Bay".

Up until 1708 it was once Shetland's capital, but as Lerwick expanded so the centre of power shifted eastwards. **Scalloway Castle** dates from around 1600, and was built by Patrick Stewart, who was executed 15 years later in Edinburgh for treason (see also Kirkwall).

During World War II the village was a secret Norwegian base, and from here

KILN BAR/CAFÉ

Main Street, Scalloway, Shetland ZE1 0TR
Tel: 01595 693150 Fax: 01595 695320

Set in the village of Scalloway, a few miles south west of Lerwick, the islands' capital, the **Kiln Bar/Café** was built originally as a fishing station where fish were cured before being shipped to the markets. Hence its name - the KilnBar/Café. It sits right on the waterfront, and is a cosy, welcoming place, built of old, local stone, with open beamed roofs. Here you can relax over a drink or two while chatting to the friendly locals, who will make you more than welcome.

The café seats up to 30 in absolute comfort, and features traditional cooking, with a mixture of up to six main meals on the specials board, including, of course, local fish. All the produce is fresh and local wherever possible. The meals are all reasonably priced, and are served between 9am and 2pm from Monday to Saturday. The service is quick and friendly, and there is plenty of space so that you can sit in comfort while eating. The bar area is tiled, and you can order and eat food here as well. On the overhead beams are many shields from the unique Shetlands festival of "Up-Helly-Aa", held annually at New Year. There is also a wide-screen TV, a pool table and two darts areas. The bar serves a

wide range of drinks, including McEwan, John Smith and Belhaven beers, Guinness stout, spirits, wines, liqueurs and a fine range of soft drinks. You can also order Shetland's own vodka drink - Jago, a delightful mixture of vodka and Scottish cream.

The Kiln Bar/Café is the ideal place to relax after sampling all the wonders that Shetland has to offer, It is centrally located, and always offers a warm, Shetland welcome to those people in search of good food and great drink.

FAIR ISLE

Shetland ZE2 9JU
website: www.fairisle.org.uk

One of the most isolated inhabited islands in Britain. In a successful effort to stem depopulation, the Trust has encouraged and initiated various improvements, including a renewable energy project using wind power. The intricate, colourful knitted patterns, which take their name from the island, are famous and the Fair Isle Knitting Co operative sells island knitwear world wide. Additional crafts now include traditional wooden boat building, spinning, weaving, dyeing, felting, locker hooking, wood-turning and fiddle making, and the manufacture of straw backed chairs, spinning wheels and stained glass windows.

Fair Isle is a bird-watcher's paradise, A warm welcome awaits visitors, with opportunities to observe exceptional flora, fauna, archaeology, spectacular cliff scenery and traditional crofting pr actices. The Trust, in partnership with the islanders and the Bird Observatory, is currently working on marine protection.

Norwegians used to be ferried across to their country in fishing boats (nicknamed "Shetland buses") to mount sabotage operations and bring back resistance fighters who were on the run from German troops. The small **Scalloway Museum** in Main Street tells the story of these men, as well as the story of Scalloway itself.

TINGWALL

6 miles NW of Lerwick on the A970

Law Ting Holm near Tingwall was

BUSTA HOUSE HOTEL

Busta, Brae, Shetland ZE2 9QN
Tel: 01806 522506 Fax: 01806 522588
e-mail: reservations@bustahouse.com
website: www.bustahouse.com

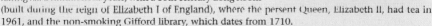

With 22 fully en suite rooms, the **Busta House Hotel** is one of the leading hotels on Shetland. The building is a historic place, dating back hundreds of years, with a 16th century Long Room (built during the reign of Elizabeth I of England), where the persent Queen, Elizabeth II, had tea in 1961, and the non-smoking Gifford library, which dates from 1710.

But for all its age, the hotel is firmly in the 21st century where high standards of service, great cuisine, comfort and value of money are concerned. All the rooms are named after Shetland islands, and all have direct-dial telephone, modem port, tea/coffee making facilities, TV and hair dryer. They are well furnished and decorated, and have a comfortable, welcoming feel to them. Regrettably, none are on the ground floor, and lifts or elevators were not invented in the 16th, 17th or 18th centuries!

Food is important at the Busta House Hotel. The Pitcairn Restaurant serves only the finest dishes, all prepared from fresh local produce wherever possible, and bar meals are also available. The menu

has been put together with imagination and flair, and this, along with a fine wine and malt whisky list, means that you will have a dinner to remember. You can relax in the lounge or bar area and Busta House has something which is a rarity on Shetland - a garden, where you can relax or stroll on a summer's evening. The hotel makes a perfect base and the staff are knowledgeable about what to do and see. There's even a ghost in the hotel - but don't worry - it's a warm, friendly one, and it will leave you alone to enjoy your stay.

where the ancient Shetland Islands parliament, or Althing, used to meet. It sits on a small promontory (which in Norse times was an island) jutting out into the Loch of Tingwall.

Just off the Scalloway - Tingwall Road is the **Murder Stone**, a prehistoric standing stone. It got its name from a local legend, which states that murderers were made to run between Law Ting Holm and the stone pursued by relatives of the murdered person. If the murderer made it to the stone unscathed, he wasn't executed, if he didn't, his pursuers killed him. The **Tingwall Agricultural Museum** has a collection of old crofting tools.

TANGWICK
33 miles NW of Lerwick on the B9078

The **Tangwick Haa Museum**, based in Tangwick Haa, has displays and artefacts about the local history of the northern part of Mainland. The haa ("hall") itself dates from the 17th century, and was built by the Cheyne family, the local landowners. It was restored by the Shetland Amenity Trust and opened as a museum in 1988.

BODDAM
20 miles S of Lerwick on the A970

The **Crofthouse Museum** comprises a thatched house, steading and water mill, and illustrates what life was like in a 19th century Shetland Island croft. Furnished in home-made furniture of the type used on the Shetland Islands. It would have housed an extended family of children, parents and grandparents, and the men would have earned their living from the sea while the women worked the land. In the summer months it hosts a programme of traditional music and stories.

WHALSAY
18 miles NE of Lerwick

This small island, no more than six miles long by two miles wide, is connected to Mainland by a ferry from Dury Voe. There are superb coastal walks and many ancient remains. The 393-feet high **Ward of Clett** is its highest point, and from here a good view of the east coast of Mainland can be enjoyed. The granite **Symbister House**, in the island's ferry port, is the finest Georgian house in Shetland. It was built by the Bruce family, who nearly bankrupted themselves in doing so, something that did not trouble the people of the island, as the family had oppressed them for years. It now forms part of the local school. The grounds are said to be haunted by the ghost of a sailor.

FETLAR
40 miles NE of Lerwick

The small island of Fetlar is no more than seven miles long by five miles wide at its widest, and sits off the east coast of Yell, to which it is connected by ferry. **The Fetlar Interpretive Centre** at Beach of Houbie has displays on the island's history, wildlife, history and folklore, as well as genealogical archives. There is also an archive of over 3,000 photographs.

In the middle of the island are three mysterious stone circles known as **Fiddler's Crus**, which almost touch each other. Close by is the **Haltadans**, another stone circle, where 38 stones enclose two stones at its centre. The story goes that the two inner stones are a fiddler and his wife who were dancing with 38 trolls in the middle of the night. As the sun rose in the morning, its light turned them all to stone.

GUTCHER B&B & WIND DOG CAFÉ

Gutcher, Yell, Shetland ZE2 9DF
Tel: 01957 744201 Fax: 01957 744366
e-mail: margaret.tulloch@btopenworld.com

Yell is an island that sits to the north of Shetland's main island, Mainland. It is a beautiful place of wide open spaces, clean air and wonderful seascapes. And it is here, at Gutcher, where the ferry leaves for Unst, Britain's most northerly island, that you'll find the three-star **Gutcher B&B** and **Wind Dog Café**. The B&B was originally built as a shop but now offers first class accommodation that is both comfortable and spacious. It is owned and personally managed by Margaret and Lawrence Tulloch. It has four bedrooms - two single, a twin and a double, with the double and twin having a view of the Bluemull Sound separating Yell from Unst. It makes the perfect base from which to explore Shetland's northerly islands, which are rich in history and wonderful landscapes. This part of Shetland is possibly the best place to see otters, plus there is an abundance of birdlife, such as curlews, whimbrels, plovers and red-throated divers.

The Wind Dog Café takes its name from a "wind dog", which is how an incomplete rainbow is described in Ireland. It sits opposite the B&B, and serves wonderful food prepared only from the finest and freshest of local produce wherever possible. There is a strong emphasis on fresh fish such as haddock, lemon sole, catfish and salmon, as well as shellfish such as scallops and mussels from the clear, cold waters off Yell. The café is spacious and welcoming, and the prices are always reasonable. For a great, friendly welcome and outstanding value for money stay at the Gutcher B&B and eat at the Wind Dog Café.

The island is a bird sanctuary, with the highest density of breeding waders in Britain.

YELL

30 miles N of Lerwick

The second largest island in Shetland is about 20 miles long by seven miles wide at its widest, and is connected to Mainland. Though its population is close to 1,000, it still has lonely moorland and a varied coast that lend themselves to hill walking and bird watching.

The whitewashed **Old Haa of Burravoe** ("Old Hall of Burravoe"), at the island's south east corner, is the oldest complete building on the island, and dates from 1637. It now houses a small museum and interpretation centre, and has a digital recording studio. A tapestry commemorates the crashing of a Catalina aircraft in 1941 close to Burravoe, with only three out of the crew of ten surviving. The **Lumbister RSPB Reserve** sits almost in the middle of the island, between Whale Firth (said to be the smallest "firth" in Scotland) and the A968, the island's main road. Here you can see the red-throated diver, eider, dunlin, great and Arctic skua, dunlin, wheatear, curlew, merlin and snipe.

UNST

46 miles N of Lerwick

Unst is the most northerly of the Shetland Isles, and at **Hermaness**, where there is a nature reserve, is the most northerly point in the United Kingdom that can be reached on foot. Offshore is **Muckle Flugga**, with its Out Stack, ot

ORDALE HOUSE

Balta Sound, Unst, Shetland ZE2 9DT
Tel: 01957 711867
e-mail: pandebyrne@tesco.net
website: http//homepages.tesco.net/pandebyrne

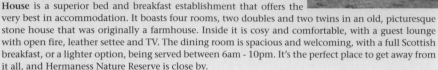

Set on the east coast of Britain's most northerly island of Unst, **Ordale House** is a superior bed and breakfast establishment that offers the very best in accommodation. It boasts four rooms, two doubles and two twins in an old, picturesque stone house that was originally a farmhouse. Inside it is cosy and comfortable, with a guest lounge with open fire, leather settee and TV. The dining room is spacious and welcoming, with a full Scottish breakfast, or a lighter option, being served between 6am - 10pm. It's the perfect place to get away from it all, and Hermaness Nature Reserve is close by.

"Oosta", being the most northerly point in the United Kingdom. At the southeast corner of the island are the gaunt ruins of **Muness Castle**, the most northerly castle in Britain. The castle dates from 1598, and was built by Lawrence Bruce of Cultmalindie, a relative of the wayward Stewart dynasty that ruled the islands, and a man every bit as cruel and despotic as they were. He was appointed sheriff of Shetland, and when Patrick Stewart succeeded his father Robert as the Earl of Orkney, Lawrence felt so threatened that he built the castle as a place of safety. In 1608 Patrick came to Unst with 36 men to destroy it, but retreated before he had a chance to do so . In about 1627 a party of French raiders attacked and burnt the castle, and it was never rebuilt.

At **Harnoldswick**, in the north of the island, is **Harald's Grave**, an ancient burial cairn that is supposed to mark the grave of Harold the Fair of Norway. **Burra Firth**, on the northern coast, is one of Britain's tiniest firths, and certainly its most northern. Everything here is Britain's "most northern" something or other. The Post Office is Britain's most northerly post office, and **Wick of Shaw** is the most northerly dwelling house. The village's Methodist church is the county's most northerly church, and was built between 1990 and 1993, with a simple layout based on a traditional Norwegian design.

TOURIST INFORMATION CENTRES

ABERDEEN
23 Union Street
Aberdeen
AB11 5BP
Tel : 01224 288828
Fax : 01224 252219
Jan – Dec

ABERFELDY
The Square
Aberfeldy PH15 2DD
Tel : 01887 820276
Jan – Dec

ABERFOYLE
Trossachs Discovery Centre
Main Street
Aberfoyle FK8 3UQ
Tel . 00707 200604
April – Oct weekends Nov – Mar

ABINGTON
Welcome Break
Motorway Service Area
Junction 13, M74
ML12 6RG
Tel : 01864 502436
Fax : 01864 502571
Jan – Dec

ALFORD
Railway Museum
Station Yard
Alford AB33 8AD
Tel : 019755 62052
Easter – Oct

ALVA
Mill Trail Visitor Centre
Alva FK12 5EN
Tel : 08707 200605
Jan – Dec

ANSTRUTHER
Scottish Fisheries Museum
Harbourhead
Anstruther KY10 3AB
Tel : 01333 311073
April – Oct

ARBROATH
Market Place
Arbroath DD11 1HR
Tel : 01241 872609
Jan – Dec

ARDGARTAN
By Arrochar G83 7AR
Tel : 08707 200606
Fax : 01301 702432
April – Oct

AUCHTERARDER
90 High Street
Auchterarder PH3 1BJ
Tel : 01764 663450
Fax : 01764 664235
Jan - Dec

AVIEMORE
Grampian Road
Aviemore PH22 1PP
Tel : 0845 22 55 121
Jan – Dec

AYR
22 Sandgate
Ayr KA7 1BW
Tel : 0845 22 55 121
Jan - Dec

BALLATER
The Old Royal Station
Station Square
Ballater AB35 5QB
Tel : 013397 55306
Jan - Dec

BALLOCH
The Old Station Building
Balloch G83 8LQ
Tel : 08707 200607
April - Oct

BANCHORY
Bridge Street
Banchory AB31 3SX
Tel : 01330 822000
Easter – Oct

BANFF
Collie Lodge
Banff AB45 1AU
Tel : 01261 812419
Easter – Oct

BIGGAR
155 High Street
Biggar ML12 6DL
Tel : 01899 221066
Easter – Sep

BLAIRGOWRIE
26 Wellmeadow
Blairgowrie PH10 6AS
Tel : 01250 872960
Jan – Dec

BO'NESS
Seaview Car Park
Bo'ness EH51 0AJ
Tel : 08707 200608
Fax : 08707 200608
April – Sep

BOWMORE
The Square
Isle of Islay PA43 7JP
Tel : 08707 200617
Jan - Dec

BRAEMAR
The Mews
Mar Road
Braemar AB35 5YP
Tel : 013397 41600
Fax : 013397 41643
Jan – Dec

BRECHIN
Pictavia Centre
Haughmuir
Brechin
Tel : 01356 623050
Easter – Sep

BRODICK
The Pier
Brodick, Isle of Arran
KA27 8AU
Tel : 0845 22 55 121
Jan – Dec

CALLANDER
Rob Roy Centre
Ancaster Square
Callander FK17 8ED
Tel : 08707 200628
Fax : 01877 330784
*March – Dec &
    Weekends Jan – Feb*

CAMPBELTOWN
Mackinnon House
The Pier
Campbeltown PA28 6EF
Tel : 08707 200609
Jan – Dec

CARNOUSTIE
1B High Street
Carnoustie DD7 6AN
Tel : 01241 852258
Easter – Sep

CASTLEBAY
Main Street
Castlebay, Isle of Barra
HS9 5XD
Tel : 01871 810336
Easter – Oct

CASTLE DOUGLAS
Market Hill Car Park
Castle Douglas DG7 1AE
Tel : 01556 502611
Easter – end Oct

CRAIGNURE
The Pier
Craignure, Isle of Mull
PA65 6AY
Tel : 08707 200610
Fax : 01680 812497
Jan – Dec

CRAIL
Museum & Heritage Centre
Marketgate
Crail KY10 3TL
Tel : 01333 450859
April – Oct

CRATHIE
The Car Park
Crathie AB35
Tel : 013397 42414
Easter – Nov

CRIEFF
High Street
Crieff PH7 3HU
Tel : 01764 652578
Jan – Dec

DAVIOT WOOD
Picnic Area, A9
Daviot Wood by Inverness IV1
    2ER
Tel : 0845 22 55 121
April – Oct

DORNOCH
The Square
Dornoch IV25 3SD
Tel : 0845 22 55 121
Jan – Dec

DRUMNADROCHIT
The Car Park
Drumnadrochit
IV63 6TX
Tel : 0845 22 55 121
Jan - Dec

DRYMEN
The Library
The Square
Drymen G63 0BL
Tel : 08707 200611
Fax : 01360 660751
May – Sep

DUFFTOWN
Clock Tower
The Square
Dufftown AB55 4AD
Tel : 01340 820501
Easter – Oct

DUMBARTON
Milton
A82 Northbound
G82 2TZ
Tel : 08707 200612
Fax : 08707 200612
Jan – Dec

DUMFRIES
64 Whitesands
Dumfries DG1 2RS
Tel : 01387 253862
Fax : 01387 245555
Jan – Dec

DUNBAR
143A High Street
Dunbar EH42 1ES
Tel : 0845 22 55 121
April - Oct

DUNBLANE
Stirling Road
Dunblane FK15 9EP
Tel : 08707 200613
Fax : 08707 200613
May – Sep

DUNDEE
21 Castle Street
Dundee DD1 3AA
Tel : 01382 527527
Jan – Dec

DUNFERMLINE
1 High Street
Dunfermline KY12 7DL
Tel : 01383 720999
Fax : 01383 730187
Jan - Dec

DUNKELD
The Cross
Dunkeld PH8 0AN
Tel : 01350 727688
Jan – Dec

DUNOON
7 Alexandra Parade
Dunoon PA23 8AB
Tel : 08707 200629
Fax : 01369 706085
Jan – Dec

DUNVEGAN
2 Lochside
Dunvegan, Isle of Skye IV55
    8WB
Tel : 0845 22 55 121
April – Oct

DURNESS
Durine
Durness IV27 4PN
Tel : 0845 22 55 121
April – Oct

EDINBURGH
Edinburgh & Scotland
  Information Centre
3 Princes Street
Edinburgh EH2 2QP
Tel : 0845 22 55 121
Jan – Dec

EDINBURGH AIRPORT
Main Concourse
Edinburgh International Airport
Edinburgh EH12 9DN
Tel : 0845 22 55 121
Jan – Dec

ELGIN
17 High Street
Elgin IV30 1EG
Tel : 01343 542666
Jan – Dec

EYEMOUTH
Auld Kirk
Market Square
Eyemouth TD14 5HE
Tel : 0870 608 0404
Easter – Oct

FALKIRK
2-4 Glebe Street
Falkirk FK1 1HU
Tel : 08707 200614
Jan – Dec

FORFAR
45 East High Street
Forfar DD8 2EG
Tel : 01307 467876
Easter – Sep

FORRES
116 High Street
Forres IV36 0NP
Tel : 01309 672938
Easter – Oct

FORT AUGUSTUS
Car Park
Fort Augustus PH32 4DD
Tel : 0845 22 55 121
April – Oct

FORT WILLIAM
Cameron Centre
Cameron Square
Fort William PH33 6AJ
Tel : 0845 22 55 121
Jan – Dec

FORTH BRIDGES
Queensferry Lodge Hotel
St Margaret's Head
North Queensferry KY11 1HP
Tel : 01383 417759
Jan – Dec

FRASERBURGH
3 Saltoun Square
Fraserburgh AB43 5DA
Tel : 01346 518315
Easter – Oct

GATEHOUSE OF FLEET
Car Park
Gatehouse of Fleet DG7 5EA
Tel : 01557 814212
Easter – end Oct

GLASGOW
11 George Square
Glasgow G2 1DY
Tel : 0141 204 4400
Fax : 0141 221 3524
Jan – Dec

GLASGOW AIRPORT
International Arrivals Hall
Glasgow International Airport
PA3 2ST
Tel : 0141 848 4440
Fax : 0141 849 1444
Jan – Dec

GRANTOWN ON SPEY
54 High Street
Grantown on Spey PH26 3AS
Tel : 0845 22 55 121
Mar – Oct, Dec

GRETNA
Unit 10
Gretna Gateway Outlet Village
Glasgow Road
Gretna DG16 5GG
Tel : 01461 337834
Jan - Dec

HAMILTON
Road Chef Services
M74 Northbound
ML3 6JW
Tel : 01698 285590
Fax : 01698 891494
Jan – Dec

HAWICK
Drumlanrig's Tower
Tower Knowe
Hawick TD9 9EN
Tel : 0870 608 0404
Easter – Oct

HELENSBURGH
The Clock Tower
Helensburgh G84 7PA
Tel : 08707 200615
April – Oct

HUNTLY
9a The Square
Huntly AB54 5AE
Tel : 01466 792255
Easter – Oct

INVERARAY
Front Street
Inveraray PA32 8UY
Tel : 08707 200616
Fax : 01499 302269
Jan – Dec

INVERNESS
Castle Wynd
Inverness IV2 3BJ
Tel : 0845 22 55 121
Jan – Dec

INVERURIE
18 High Street
Inverurie AB51 3XQ
Tel : 01467 625800
Jan – Dec

ISLAY *SEE* BOWMORE

JEDBURGH
Murrays Green
Jedburgh TD8 6BE
Tel : 0870 608 0404
Jan – Dec

JOHN O'GROATS
County Road
John o'Groats KW1 4YR
Tel : 0845 22 55 121
April – Oct

KELSO
Town House
The Square
Kelso TD5 7HF
Tel : 0870 608 0404
Jan - Dec

KILCHOAN

Pier Road
Kilchoan PH36 4LH
Tel : 0845 22 55 121
April – Oct

KILLIN

Breadalbane Folklore Centre
Main Street
Killin FK21 8XE
Tel : 08707 200627
March – end Oct

KINROSS

Heart of Scotland Visitor Centre
Junction 6, M90
KY13 7NQ
Tel : 01577 863680
Jan – Dec

KIRKCALDY

The Merchant's House
339 High Street
Kirkcaldy KY1 1JL
Tel : 01592 267775
Jan – Dec

KIRKCUDBRIGHT

Harbour Square
Kirkcudbright DG6 5HY
Tel : 01557 330494
Jan - Dec

KIRKWALL

6 Broad Street
Kirkwall, Orkney
KW15 1DH
Tel : 01856 872856
Fax : 01856 875056
Jan – Dec

KIRRIEMUIR

Cumberland Close
Kirriemuir DD8 4EF
Tel : 01575 574097
Easter – Sep

LANARK

Horsemarket
Ladyacre Road
Lanark ML11 7LQ
Tel : 01555 661661
Fax : 01555 666143
Jan – Dec

LARGS

The Railway Station
Main Street, Largs
KA30 8AN
Tel : 0845 22 55 121
Apr - Oct

LERWICK

The Market Cross
Lerwick, Shetland
ZE1 0LU
Tel : 08701 999440
Jan – Dec

LINLITHGOW

Burgh Halls
The Cross
Linlithgow EH49 7AH
Tel : 0845 22 55 121
April – October

LOCH LOMOND

Gateway Centre
Loch Lomond Shores
Balloch G83 8QL
Tel : 08707 200631
Fax : 01389 722177
Jan – Dec

LOCHBOISDALE

Pier Road
Lochboisdale, Isle of South Uist
HS8 5TH
Tel : 01878 700286
Easter – Oct

LOCHGILPHEAD

Lochnell Street
Lochgilphead PA31 8JL
Tel : 08707 200618
April – Oct

LOCHINVER

Kirk Lane
Lochinver IV27 4LT
Tel : 0845 22 55 121
April – Oct

LOCHMADDY

Pier Road
Lochmaddy, Isle of North Uist
HS6 5AA
Tel : 01876 500321
Easter – Oct

MELROSE

Abbey House
Abbey Street
Melrose TD6 9LG
Tel : 0870 608 0404
Jan - Dec

MOFFAT

Churchgate
Moffat DG16 9EG
Tel : 01683 220620
Easter – end Oct

MONTROSE

Bridge Street
Montrose   DD10 8AB
Tel : 01674 672000
Easter – Sep

NEWTONGRANGE

Scottish Mining Museum
Newtongrange EH22 4QN
Tel : 0845 22 55 121
Easter – Oct

NEWTON STEWART

Dashwood Square
Newton Stewart DG8 6EQ
Tel : 01671 402431
Easter – end Oct

NORTH BERWICK

Quality Street
North Berwick EH39 4HJ
Tel : 0845 22 55 121
Jan – Dec

NORTH KESSOCK

Picnic Site
North Kessock IV1 1XB
Tel : 0845 22 55 121
April – Oct

OBAN

Argyll Square
Oban PA34 4AR
Tel : 08707 200630
Jan – Dec

OLD CRAIGHALL

Old Craighall Service Area A1
by Musselburgh EH21 8RE
Tel : 0845 22 55 121
April - Oct

PAISLEY

9A Gilmour Street
Paisley PA1 1DD
Tel : 0141 889 0711
Fax : 0141 848 1363
Jan - Dec

PEEBLES

High Street
Peebles EH45 8AG
Tel : 0870 608 0404
Jan – Dec

PERTH

Lower City Mills
West Mill Street
Perth PH1 5QP
Tel : 01738 450600
Fax : 01738 444863
Jan – Dec

PITLOCHRY

22 Atholl Road
Pitlochry PH16 5BX
Tel : 01796 472215/472751
Fax : 01796 474046
Jan – Dec

PORTREE

Bayfield House
Portree, Isle of Skye IV51 9EL
Tel : 0845 22 55 121
Jan – Dec

ROTHESAY

Winter Gardens
Rothesay, Isle of Bute
PA20 0AJ
Tel : 08707 200619
Jan – Dec

ST ANDREWS

70 Market Street
St Andrews KY16 9NU
Tel : 01334 472021
Fax : 01334 478422
Jan – Dec

SELKIRK

Halliwells House
Selkirk TD7 4BL
Tel : 0870 608 0404
Easter – Oct

STIRLING DUMBARTON ROAD

41 Dumbarton Road
Stirling FK8 2LQ
Tel : 08707 200620
Jan – Dec

STIRLING PIRNHALL

Motorway Service Area
Junction 9, M9
Tel : 08707 200621
Jan - Dec

STIRLING ROYAL BURGH

Royal Burgh of Stirling Visitor
 Centre
The Esplanade
Stirling FK8 1EH
Tel : 08707 200622
Jan – Dec

STONEHAVEN

66 Allardice Street
Stonehaven AB39 9ET
Tel : 01569 762806
Easter – October

STORNOWAY

26 Cromwell Street
Stornoway, Isle of Lewis HS1
 2DD
Tel : 01851 703088
Fax : 01851 705244
Jan – Dec

STRANRAER

28 Harbour Street
Stranraer DG9 7RA
Tel : 01776 702595
Fax : 01776 889156
Jan – Dec

STROMNESS

Ferry Terminal Building
Stromness, Pier Head
Orkney KW16 3AA
Tel : 01856 850716
Fax : 01856 850777
Jan – Dec

STRONTIAN

Acharacle
PH36 4HZ
Tel : 0845 22 55 121
April – Oct

TARBERT HARRIS

Pier Road
Tarbert, Isle of Harris
HS3 3DG
Tel : 01859 502011
Jan - Dec

TARBERT LOCH FYNE

Harbour Street
Tarbert PA29 6UD
Tel : 08707 200624
April – Oct weekends Nov – Mar

TARBET LOCH LOMOND

Main Street
Tarbet G83 7DE
Tel : 08707 200623
April – Oct

THURSO

Riverside
Thurso KW14 8BU
Tel : 0845 22 55 121
April – Oct

TOBERMORY

The Pier
Tobermory
Isle of Mull PA75 6NU
Tel : 08707 200625
Fax : 01688 302145
April - Oct

TOMINTOUL

The Square
Tomintoul AB37 9ET
Tel : 01807 580285
Fax : 01807 580285
Easter - Oct

TYNDRUM

Main Street
Tyndrum FK20 8RY
Tel : 08707 200626
April – Oct

ULLAPOOL

Argyle Street
Ullapool IV26 2UB
Tel : 0845 22 55 121
Jan - Dec

INDEX OF ADVERTISERS

ACTIVITIES

ANTIQUES AND RESTORATION

ARTS AND CRAFTS

FASHIONS

GIFTWARE

HOME AND GARDEN

JEWELLERY

PLACES OF INTEREST

SPECIALIST FOOD AND DRINK

Looking for more walks?

The walks in this book have been gleaned from Britain's largest online walking guide, to be found at *www.walkingworld.com*.

The site contains over 2000 walks from all over England, Scotland and Wales so there are plenty more to choose from in this book's region as well as further afield - ideal if you are taking a short break as you can plan your walks in advance. There are walks of every length and type to suit all tastes.

Want more detail for the walks in this book? Next to every walk in this book you will see a Walk ID. You can enter this ID number on Walkingworld's 'Find a Walk' page and you will be taken straight to the details of that walk.

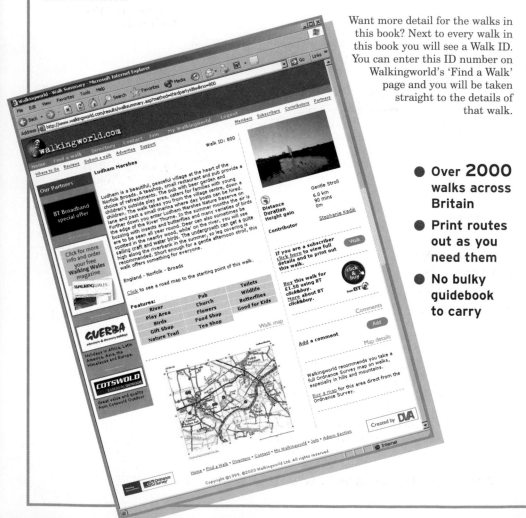

- Over **2000** walks across Britain

- Print routes out as you need them

- No bulky guidebook to carry

Walkingworld routes contain much more detailed instructions and mapping than can be given in a printed book. The walk descriptions have photographs at every major decision point to help you to navigate and each comes with an Ordnance Survey 1:50,000 scale map. Once you have found a walk you like, simply print it out on standard A4 paper and you are ready to go!

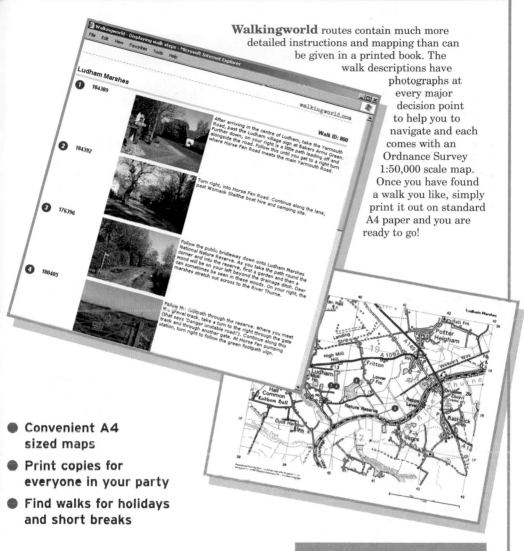

- ● **Convenient A4 sized maps**
- ● **Print copies for everyone in your party**
- ● **Find walks for holidays and short breaks**

A modest annual subscription gives you access to over 2000 walks, all in Walkingworld's easy to follow format. The database of walks is growing all the time and as a subscriber you gain access to new routes as soon as they are published.

Visit the Walkingworld website at *www.walkingworld.com*

INDEX OF WALKS

ORDER FORM

To order any of our publications just fill in the payment details below and complete the order form. For orders of less than 4 copies please add £1 per book for postage and packing. Orders over 4 copies are P & P free.

Please Complete Either:

I enclose a cheque for £ [   ] made payable to Travel Publishing Ltd

Or:

Card No: [   ]   Expiry Date: [   ]

Signature: [   ]

NAME: [   ]

ADDRESS: [   ]

TEL NO: [   ]

Please either send, telephone, fax or e-mail your order to:

Travel Publishing Ltd, 7a Apollo House, Calleva Park, Aldermaston, Berkshire RG7 8TN
Tel: 0118 981 7777   Fax: 0118 982 0077   e-mail: info@travelpublishing.co.uk

	PRICE	QUANTITY		PRICE	QUANTITY
HIDDEN PLACES REGIONAL TITLES			*COUNTRY PUBS AND INNS*		
Cornwall	£8.99	....	Cornwall	£8.99	....
Devon	£8.99	....	Devon	£8.99	....
Dorset, Hants & Isle of Wight	£8.99	....	Sussex	£8.99	....
East Anglia	£8.99	....	Wales	£8.99	....
Gloucs, Wiltshire & Somerset	£8.99	....	*COUNTRY LIVING RURAL GUIDES*		
Heart of England	£8.99	....	East Anglia	£10.99	....
Hereford, Worcs & Shropshire	£8.99	....	Heart of England	£10.99	....
Lake District & Cumbria	£8.99	....	Ireland	£11.99	....
Lancashire & Cheshire	£8.99	....	North East	£10.99	....
Northumberland & Durham	£8.99	....	North West	£10.99	....
Peak District	£8.99	....	Scotland	£11.99	....
Sussex	£8.99	....	South of England	£10.99	....
Yorkshire	£8.99	....	South East of England	£10.99	....
HIDDEN PLACES NATIONAL TITLES			Wales	£11.99	....
England	£11.99	....	West Country	£10.99	....
Ireland	£11.99	....			
Scotland	£11.99	....			
Wales	£11.99	....			
HIDDEN INNS TITLES					
East Anglia	£7.99	....			
Heart of England	£7.99	....			
North of England	£7.99	....			
South	£7.99	....			
South East	£7.99	....			
Wales	£7.99	....			
West Country	£7.99	....			
Yorkshire	£7.99	....			

Value [   ]

Postage and Packing [   ]

Total Value [   ]

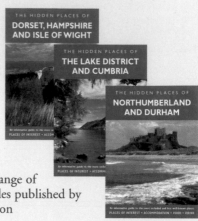

READER REACTION FORM

The *Travel Publishing* research team would like to receive reader's comments on any visitor attractions or places reviewed in the book and also recommendations for suitable entries to be included in the next edition. This will help ensure that the *Country Living series of Guides* continues to provide its readers with useful information on the more interesting, unusual or unique features of each attraction or place ensuring that their visit to the local area is an enjoyable and stimulating experience. To provide your comments or recommendations would you please complete the forms below and overleaf as indicated and send to:

**The Research Department, Travel Publishing Ltd,
7a Apollo House, Calleva Park, Aldermaston, Reading, RG7 8TN.**

Your Name:

Your Address:

Your Telephone Number:

Please tick as appropriate:

Comments ☐   Recommendation ☐

Name of Establishment:

Address:

Telephone Number:

Name of Contact:

READER REACTION FORM

COMMENT OR REASON FOR RECOMMENDATION:

READER REACTION FORM

The *Travel Publishing* research team would like to receive reader's comments on any visitor attractions or places reviewed in the book and also recommendations for suitable entries to be included in the next edition. This will help ensure that the *Country Living series of Guides* continues to provide its readers with useful information on the more interesting, unusual or unique features of each attraction or place ensuring that their visit to the local area is an enjoyable and stimulating experience. To provide your comments or recommendations would you please complete the forms below and overleaf as indicated and send to:

**The Research Department, Travel Publishing Ltd,
7a Apollo House, Calleva Park, Aldermaston, Reading, RG7 8TN.**

Your Name:

Your Address:

Your Telephone Number:

Please tick as appropriate:

Comments ☐   Recommendation ☐

Name of Establishment:

Address:

Telephone Number:

Name of Contact:

READER REACTION FORM

COMMENT OR REASON FOR RECOMMENDATION:

READER REACTION FORM

The *Travel Publishing* research team would like to receive reader's comments on any visitor attractions or places reviewed in the book and also recommendations for suitable entries to be included in the next edition. This will help ensure that the *Country Living series of Guides* continues to provide its readers with useful information on the more interesting, unusual or unique features of each attraction or place ensuring that their visit to the local area is an enjoyable and stimulating experience. To provide your comments or recommendations would you please complete the forms below and overleaf as indicated and send to:

The Research Department, Travel Publishing Ltd,
7a Apollo House, Calleva Park, Aldermaston, Reading, RG7 8TN.

Your Name:

Your Address:

Your Telephone Number:

Please tick as appropriate:

Comments ☐   Recommendation ☐

Name of Establishment:

Address:

Telephone Number:

Name of Contact:

READER REACTION FORM

COMMENT OR REASON FOR RECOMMENDATION:

READER REACTION FORM

The *Travel Publishing* research team would like to receive reader's comments on any visitor attractions or places reviewed in the book and also recommendations for suitable entries to be included in the next edition. This will help ensure that the *Country Living series of Guides* continues to provide its readers with useful information on the more interesting, unusual or unique features of each attraction or place ensuring that their visit to the local area is an enjoyable and stimulating experience. To provide your comments or recommendations would you please complete the forms below and overleaf as indicated and send to:

**The Research Department, Travel Publishing Ltd,
7a Apollo House, Calleva Park, Aldermaston, Reading, RG7 8TN.**

Your Name:

Your Address:

Your Telephone Number:

Please tick as appropriate:

Comments ☐   Recommendation ☐

Name of Establishment:

Address:

Telephone Number:

Name of Contact:

READER REACTION FORM

COMMENT OR REASON FOR RECOMMENDATION:

INDEX TO TOWNS & PLACES OF INTEREST